The Computational Brain

Computational Neuroscience
Terrence J. Sejnowski and Tomaso A. Poggio, editors

The Computational Brain

Patricia S. Churchland and Terrence J. Sejnowski

A Bradford Book
The MIT Press
Cambridge, Massachusetts
London, England

Second printing, 1993
© 1992 Massachusetts Institute of Technology

This book was set in Palatino by Asco Trade Typesetting Ltd., Hong Kong and was printed and bound in the United States of America.

Library of Congress Cataloging-in-Publication Data

Churchland, Patricia Smith.
  The computational brain / Patricia S. Churchland and Terrence J. Sejnowski.
    p.   cm.
  "A Bradford book."
  Includes bibliographical references and index.
  ISBN 0-262-03188-4
  1. Brain—Computer simulation. 2. Neural networks (Computer science) 3. Neural circuitry.
I. Sejnowski, Terrence J. (Terrence Joseph) II. Title.
  [DNLM: 1. Brain—physiology. 2. Computer Simulation. 3. Models, Neurological.
4. Neurosciences—methods. WL 26.5 C563c]
QP356.C48   1992
612.8′2′0113—dc20
DNLM/DLC
for Library of Congress   91-28056
                                                                              CIP

Contents

Series Foreword

Computational neuroscience is an approach to understanding the information content of neural signals by modeling the nervous system at many different structural scales, including the biophysical, the circuit, and the systems levels. Computer simulations of neurons and neural networks are complementary to traditional techniques in neuroscience. This book series welcomes contributions that link theoretical studies with experimental approaches to understanding information processing in the nervous system. Areas and topics of particular interest include biophysical mechanisms for computation in neurons, computer simulations of neural circuits, models of learning, representation of sensory information in neural networks, systems models of sensory-motor integration, and computational analysis of problems in biological sensing, motor control, and perception.

Terrence J. Sejnowski
Tomaso Poggio

Preface

To understand how neurons give rise to a mental life, we must know what they do, both individually as single cells and collectively as coherent systems of cells. The idea that brains are computational in nature has spawned a range of explanatory hypotheses in theoretical neurobiology. This book represents one slant on current computational research relevant to neurobiology, a slant both on the conceptual foundations and the benchmark studies. We mustered our plans for this book against the backdrop of several earlier projects: *Parallel Distributed Processing*, edited by Dave Rumelhart and Jay McClelland (1986), and *Neurophilosophy* (P. S. Churchland, 1986). Since those books went to press, much has changed. Powerful new tools for modeling neurons and circuits of neurons have become available, and a conceptual framework for neuro-computational projects has been steadily greening out. Puzzling questions abound on every side, however, concerning such matters as algorithms for weight-setting in neural nets and the extent to which they can be valuable in neuromodeling; concerning biological realism in neural net models and what degree of realism is necessary to make a model useful; and highly focused questions such as what exactly is "Hebbian learning" and what are "grand-mother" cells.

The questions that became pivotal in *The Computational Brain* were questions that have been biting our heels more or less incessantly. The book is thus shaped by what has bothered or beguiled us, individually and jointly. We learned a great deal from the conversations in the laboratory, some of which extended over many months. Francis Crick launched the institution of after-noon tea in the Computational Neurobiology Laboratory at the Salk, and teatime quickly became the daily occasion for close discussion of ideas and data, flying untried balloons, and giving the broad questions a hearing. It was a time for emerging from the comfortable burrows of safe detail into the wide-open prairie of no-holds-barred. Crick characteristically pushed the questions about how the brain works further and more relentlessly. Moreover, it was typically his hunches, breadth, and steel-edged skepticism that supplied a sense of balance both when we thought we knew what we were doing and when we were pretty sure we didn't. Virtually everyone who visited the Computational Neurobiology Lab was coaxed or bullied into dilating on the philosophical (grand-scale, background, or fuzzy) questions facing computational neuroscience. From these "confessions," we drew ideas and inspiration, and garnered the pluck to stick our necks out a bit.

Several explanations-cum-apologies are in order. The first is for our decision to facilitate easy reading by including only the unavoidable minimum of references in the text itself. We found that long lists of authors in the text make the reader stumble, and hence we elected to use notes for many references rather than follow standard practice in technical writing. Despite our best efforts to refer as fully as possible in the notes, we undoubtedly have missed some essential references, and we apologize in advance for unwitting omissions. The next apology is owed because in choosing instances of research to exemplify a point, we inevitably found ourselves drawing on the research that was most familiar to us, and that often meant research based in California, especially in San Diego. Important and interesting work in computational neuroscience is going on all over the globe, and to have done an exhaustive survey before beginning to write would have meant a deadline receding faster than the progress line. We therefore apologize if we seem rather provincial in our selection preferences. The third apology is for the length. We began the project with the strict understanding that primers are best if brief. In the execution, alas, it became impossible to live within the bounds. As it is, a number of additional topics might well have been included but for permitting the book an embarrassing girth. We therefore apologize—both because the book is too long and because it is too short. Fourth, we decided in the interests of smooth reading to abide by the practice of using "he" as the third-person pronoun referring indifferently to males and females. This reflects nothing ideological. If anything, it is a concession to Mrs. Lundy, whose unflinching dictum in grammar school was that ideological shoe-horning frustrates readability.

Many people helped enormously in writing the book; it simply could not have been done by just the two of us. Most particularly, Paul Churchland gave unstintingly of his imagination and ideas; the daily ritual was to think through everything, page by page, model by model, over capuccino at Il Fornaio. Antonio and Hanna Damasio talked through every major issue with us; they broadened and deepened our perspective in all dimensions, but especially in thinking about what neuropsychological results could tell us about micro-organization. Beatrice Golomb, V. S. Ramachandran, Diane Rogers-Ramachandran, Alexandre Pouget, Karen Dobkins, and Tom Albright helped with representation in general and visual representations in particular; Rodolfo Llinás helped with many issues, but especially in thinking about time; Gyori Buzsáki, Larry Squire, David Amaral, Wendy Suzuki, and Chuck Stevens with plasticity; Carver Mead with thinking about the nature of computation, time, and representation. Shawn Lockery, Steve Lisberger, Tom Anastasio, Al Selverston, Thelma Williams, Larry Jordan, Susan Shefchyk, and James Buchanan gave us much useful advice on sensorimotor coordination. Mark Konishi and Roderick Corriveau gave us invaluable criticism and advice on many chapters and saved us from several embarrassments. Many thanks are also owed to Paul Bush for preparing the glossary, Shona Chatterji for drawing and cheerfully redrawing many figures, Mark Churchland for the cover and for useful criticism, Georg

Schwarz for manuscript preparation, and David Lawrence for rescues from macfrazzles. A special debt is owed to Rosemary Miller, whose wit and wisdom kept the boat afloat. Others who helped in indispensable ways include: Richard Adams, Dana Ballard, Tony Bell, Anne Churchland, Hillary Chase Benedetti, Richard Gregory, Geoff Hinton, Harvey Karten, Christof Koch, Bill Lytton, Steve Nowlan, Leslie Orgel, Hal Pashler, Steve Quartz, Paul Rhodes, Paul Viola, Ning Qian, and Jack Wathey.

P.S.C. was supported by a University of California President's Humanities Fellowship, a grant from the National Science Foundation (87-06757), and the James S. McDonnell Foundation. T.J.S. was supported by the Howard Hughes Medical Institute and grants from the Drown Foundation, the Mathers Foundation, the National Science Foundation, and the Office of Naval Research.

The Computational Brain

1 Introduction

Major advances in science often consist in discovering how macroscale phenomena reduce to their microscale constituents. These latter are often counterintuitive conceptually, invisible observationally, and troublesome experimentally. Thus, for example, temperature in a gas turned out to be mean kinetic energy of the constituent molecules; the varied properties displayed by matter turned out to be a function of the component atoms and their arcane properties such as electron shells; bacteria—not Divine vengeance—were found to be the proximal cause of smallpox and bubonic plague; and the reproduction of organisms, we now know, depends on the arrangement of four bases in the molecule DNA.

Our psychological life, too, is a natural phenomenon to be understood. Here as well, the explanations will draw on properties of the infrastructure that are certainly veiled and probably arcane, an infrastructure whose *modus operandi* may seem alien to our customary self-conception. Perhaps this is inevitable, since the very brain we wish to understand is also the brain whose unaided observation is focused at the macrolevel and whose design seems to favor large-scale concepts for the explanation of its own behavior; for example, superstructure concepts such as "is hungry," "wants food," "believes honey is in the hole up the oak tree," and "sees the grizzly bear approaching."

Neurons are the basic structural components of the brain. A neuron is an individual cell, specialized by architectural features that enable fast changes of voltage across its membrane as well as voltage changes in neighboring neurons. Brains are assemblies of just such cells, and while an individual neuron does not see or reason or remember, brains regularly do. How do you get from ion movement across cell membranes to memory or perception in brains? What is the nature of neuron-neuron connectivity and interactivity? What makes a clump of neurons a nervous *system*?

At this stage in the evolution of science, it appears highly probable that psychological processes are in fact processes of the physical brain, not, as Descartes concluded, processes of a nonphysical soul or mind. Since this issue has been discussed at length elsewhere (for example, P. M. Churchland 1984, P. S. Churchland 1986), and since Cartesian dualism is not taken very seriously either in mainstream philosophy or mainstream neuroscience, it is not necessary to repeat the details of the arguments here. Suffice it to say that the

Cartesian hypothesis fails to cohere with current physics, chemistry, evolutionary biology, molecular biology, embryology, immunology, and neuroscience. To be sure, materialism is not an established fact, in the way that the four-base helical structure of DNA, for example, is an established fact. It is possible, therefore, that current evidence notwithstanding, dualism might actually be true. Despite the rather remote possibility that new discoveries will vindicate Descartes, materialism, like Darwinian evolution, is the more probable working hypothesis. That being so, it does not seem worthwhile to modify the basic neuroscience research program and its scaffolding of physicalistic presuppositions to accommodate the Cartesian hypothesis, though scientific tolerance counsels that the door not be closed until the facts themselves well and truly close it. Whether modifications to micro/nano/pico level sciences such as quantum physics will be called for as a result of advances in neuropsychology is likewise conceivable (Penrose 1989), but so far there is no moderately convincing reason to expect that they will.

Arguments from ignorance are to be especially guarded against in this context. Their canonical form is this: neuroscience is ignorant of how to explain X (consciousness, for instance) in terms of the nervous system; therefore it cannot be so explained. Rather, it can eventually be explained in terms of Y (pick your favorite thing, for example, quantum wave packets, psychons, ectoplasmic retrovibrations, etc.). The canonical form lends itself to endless seductive variations, particularly ones in which failures of imagination massage intuition: "We cannot *imagine* how to explain consciousness in terms of neuronal activity ...; how could physical processes like ions crossing membranes explain the awfulness of pain?" In its denuded rendition, the argument from ignorance is not mildly tempting, but in full regalia, it may seem beguiling and exactly what reharmonizes such "intuition dissonance" as is provoked by reflecting on the physical basis of the mental. A version of the argument convinced the German mathematician and philosopher, Leibniz (1714), and in the past two decades, variations on Leibniz' basic theme have surfaced as the single most popular and appealing justification for concluding that neurobiological explanations of psychological phenomena are impossible. (For instances of the argument in many different and alluring guises, see Thomas Nagel 1974, J. C. Eccles 1977, John Searle 1980, 1990, and Roger Penrose 1989.) From the revolutions wrought by Copernicus, Galileo, Darwin, and Einstein, it is all too apparent that "intuition dissonance" is a poor indicator of truth; it is a good indicator only of how one idea sits with well-favored others. Establishing truth or probability requires rather more.

The working hypothesis underlying this book is that emergent properties are high-level effects that depend on lower-level phenomena in some systematic way. Turning the hypothesis around to its negative version, it is highly improbable that emergent properties are properties that cannot be explained by low-level properties (Popper 1959), or that they are in some sense irreducible, causally *sui generis*, or as philosophers are wont to say, "nomologically autonomous," meaning, roughly, "not part of the rest of science" (Fodor 1974, Pylyshyn 1984). The trouble with characterizing certain properties as irreducibly emergent is that it assumes we can tell in advance whether something can be explained—*ever* explained. Obviously such a claim embodies a prediction, and as the history of science shows all too clearly, predictions grounded in ignorance rather than knowledge often go awry. In advance of a much more highly developed neurobiology than currently exists, it is much too soon to be sure that psychological phenomena cannot be explained in terms of neurobiological phenomena. Although a given phenomenon such as protein folding or awareness of visual motion cannot *now* be explained, it might yield to explanation as time and science go on. Whether it does or not is a matter of empirical fact, not a matter of *a priori* divination. Searching for reductive explanations of emergent properties does not entail that we should expect the explanations to be simpleminded or breezily cobbled up or straightforwardly readable off the data points; it means only that the betting man keeps going.

Two groundbreaking discoveries in the nineteenth century established the foundations for a science of nervous systems: (1) macro effects displayed by nervous systems depend on individual cells, whose paradigm anatomical structures include both long tails (axons) for sending signals and treelike proliferations (dendrites) for receiving signals (figure 1.1); (2) these cells are essentially electrical devices; their basic business is to receive and transmit signals by causing and responding to electric current. Within this elegantly simple framework, truly spectacular progress has been made in unravelling the intricate story of exactly how neurons work. In this century, and especially within the

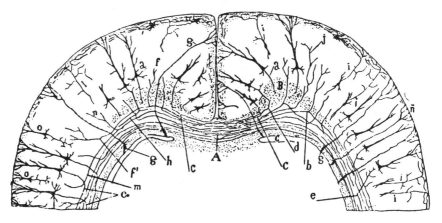

Figure 1.1 Drawing by Cajal based on his Golgi-stained sections of the superior part of the cerebral hemispheres and corpus callosum of a mouse of 20 days. A, corpus callosum; B, antero-posterior fibers; C, lateral ventricle; *a*, large pyramidal cell; *b*, callosal fiber bifurcating into a branch that is arborized in the gray matter and another that continues in the corpus callosum; *c*, callosal fiber that comes from an axon of the white matter; *d*, callosal fiber the originates in a pyramidal cell; *e*, axons of lateral pyramidal cells which follow a descending course in the corpus callosum without forming part of the commissure; *f*, *f'*, the two final branches coming from a fiber of the corpus callosum and arborizing in the gray matter; *g*, epithelial cells; *h*, fiber from a large pyramid, giving off a fine collateral to the corpus callosum; *i*, fusiform cells whose axons ascend to the molecular layer; *j*, terminal arborization of a callosal fiber originating on the opposite side. (With permission. Santiago Ramón y Cajal, 1890. Reprinted in DeFelipe and Jones, eds., 1988, *Cajal on the Cerebral Cortex.* Oxford: Oxford University Press.)

last three decades, an enormous amount has been learned about neurons: about their electrophysiology, microanatomy, connectivity, and development; about the large assortment of neurochemicals that mediate signaling from one neuron to the next; inside a neuron, about the cell's membrane, its roster of channel types, and their specific roles in receiving, integrating, and sending signals; about transmitter release, and about the range, structure, and mechanisms of receptors. Even the genetics of the proteins that constitute the various receptors is now steadily coming into view. (Nathans 1987, 1989, Gasic and Heinemann, 1991, Heinemann et al. 1990).

Recent progress in neuroscience is genuinely breathtaking and deservedly captivating. But, the naif might wonder why, if we know so much about neurons, do we not yet understand how the brain works—or at least how, say, the visual system or the motor system works? Assuming that detailed knowledge of the parts automatically confers (or nearly so) knowledge of the whole, then we ought to understand—more or less, at least in silhouette—how animals see, learn, and take action. In fact, however, we do not. Perhaps the hitch is that microlevel progress notwithstanding, we still do not know nearly enough about the fine-grained neural facts. All that is needed, runs this argument, is more of the same—indeed, much, much more of the same. This strategy is sometimes referred to as the pure bottom-up approach. It counsels that if brains are, after all, just assemblies of cells, then once we truly understand every facet of cell function, the principles of brain function will be evident, by and large. Perhaps. But perhaps not.

The overarching contention of this book is that knowledge of the molecular and cellular levels is essential, but on its own it is not enough, rich and thorough though it be. Complex effects, such as representing visual motion, are the outcome of the dynamics of neural networks. This means that while network properties are dependent on the properties of the neurons in the network, they are nevertheless not identical to cellular properties, nor to *simple* combinations of cellular properties. Interaction of neurons in networks is required for complex effects, but it is dynamical, not a simple wind-up doll affair.

A telling illustration derives from research by Allen Selverston (1988) on the stomatogastric ganglion of the spiny lobster (figure 1.2).[1] The network in question contains about 28 neurons and serves to drive the muscles controlling the teeth of the gastric mill so that food can be ground up for digestion. The output of the network is rhythmic, and hence the muscular action and the grinders' movements are correspondingly rhythmic.

The basic electrophysiological and anatomical features of the neurons have been catalogued, so that the microlevel vitae for each cell in the network is impressively detailed. What is not understood is how the cells interact to constitute a circuit that produces the rhythmic pattern. No one cell is responsible for the network's rhythmic output; no one cell is itself the repository of properties displayed by the network as a whole. Where then does the rhythmicity come from? Very roughly speaking, from the pattern of interactions among cells *and* the intrinsic properties of component cells. What, more precisely speaking, *is* that? How does the network create rhythm? How is it

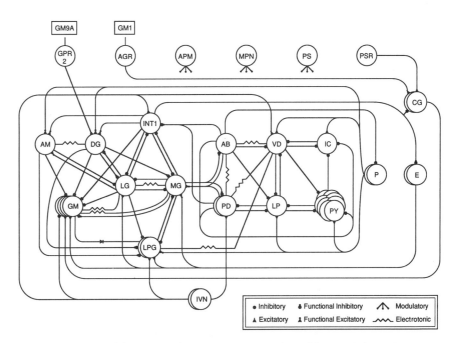

Figure 1.2 Diagram of the circuit in the stomatogastric ganglion of the spiny lobster. The circuit normally has 28 neurons, and for each, its connectivity (whom it affects and who affects it), sign of connectivity (excitatory or inhibitory), and mode of effect (chemical or electrical) have been discovered. Labels on cell bodies stand for their individual names. (Courtesy Allen Selverston.)

that the network can produce different rhythms under different biochemical conditions?

Research on the stomatogastric ganglion is legendary in neurobiology, partly because it is a fair test case for the bottom-up strategy: if the purely bottom-up approach works anywhere, it should work on the stomatogastric ganglion. If the macrolevel answers are supposed to fall out of the microlevel data, they ought to do so here. Yet we are disappointed. As Selverston ruefully points out, the purely bottom-up strategy has all the earmarks of a half-strategy. Moreover, the plea, "If only more microlevel details of the neurons were discovered, then the explanation would be evident," tends now to fall on skeptical ears. What the stomatogastric ganglion seems to be telling us is that we need to figure out the interactive principles governing the system, and that although interactive hypotheses should be constrained by microlevel data, their job is to characterize higher-level features. Boiled down, the lesson is that microlevel data are *necessary* to understand the system, but not *sufficient*. To echo a remark of Maxwell Cowan, even if we did know about all the synapses, all the transmitters, all the channels, all the response patterns for each cell, and so forth, still, we would not know how an animal sees and smells and walks.[2]

There is a broader rationale for modeling that goes beyond neuroscience in particular and applies to science generally. Why bother with models at all, one might ask? Why not just perform experiments and record the observations? Though the answers may be obvious, they are perhaps worth listing. First, models help organize the data and motivate experiments; they suggest how data might fit together to yield an explanation of a phenomenon. It is, therefore, better to have some model than none at all. In fact, of course, scientists do always have some hypothesis or other that provides the motivational and interpretive framework for their research, though background hypotheses may be neither cleanly articulated nor well-honed. A quantitative model is a step forward because it brings background assumptions to the light of day and permits a more exacting analysis of why they might or might not be true. The further philosophical point is that models increase in believability as they survive tough experimental tests (Popper 1959, P. S. Churchland 1986). Especially in the pioneering days of a discipline, when data are relatively sparse, progress is closely tied to *ruling out* a class of models and hypotheses. Indefinitely many models can be equally consistent with a set of data; to make real strides one must seek to falsify an ostensibly plausible model. Consequently, models that suggest potentially falsifying experiments are critical.[3] Should a model survive a demanding experimental test, to that degree it is more probable; saved from the scrap heap of dead hypotheses, it lives on to be tested against yet further experimental data. Should it be falsified, it then becomes a springboard for the next model.

Computational neuroscience is an evolving approach that aims to discover the properties characterizing and the principles governing neurons and networks of neurons. It draws on both neurobiological data and computational ideas to investigate how neural networks can produce complex effects such as stereo vision, learning, and auditory location of sound-emitting objects. To put it crudely, it has one foot in neuroscience and one foot in computer science. A third foot is firmly planted in experimental psychology, and at least a toe is in philosophy, so evidently the enterprise is multipedal. Of which more anon.

Probably the closest academic kin of computational neuroscience is systems neurobiology, a branch of neuroscience that traditionally has focused on much the same set of problems, but did not explicitly ally itself with computer modeling or with an avowedly information-processing framework for theories. A precocious ancestor went by the name of "cybernetics," which, inversely to systems neurobiology, generally leaned more heavily on the engineering and psychophysical sides, and more lightly on the neurobiological side. Coined more recently, "connectionism" usually refers to modeling with networks that bear only superficial similarities to real neural networks, while "neural net modeling" can cover a broad range of projects. Ironically perhaps, "neural net modeling" is usually identified with computer modeling of highly artificial nonneuronal networks, often with mainly technological significance such as medical diagnoses in emergency wards.[4] "PDP" ("parallel distributed processing") is generally the preferred label of cognitive psychologists and some computer scientists who seek to model rather high-level activity such as face recognition and language learning rather than lower-level activity such as visual motion detection or defensive bending in the leech.

As we use the term, "computational neuroscience" aims for biological realism in computational models of neural networks, though *en route*, rather simplified and artificial models may be used to help test and explore computational principles. Academic garden-plotting is a comically imprecise trade because the carrots regularly wander in with turnips and the turnips with the potatoes. Each of us (P.S.C. and T.J.S.) is cheerfully guilty of wandering into neuroscience from his mother discipline, so we emphatically do not mean to tut-tut academic "cross-fielding." On the contrary, we view the blurring of the disciplinary boundaries between neuroscience, computer science, and psychology as a healthy development to be wisely encouraged. In any case, perhaps a crude survey will help orient the greenhorn—or even the old hand—to the clustering of goals, tactics, and prejudices manifest in the "network" game.

The expression "computational" in computational neuroscience reflects the role of the computer as a research tool in modeling complex systems such as networks, ganglia, and brains. Using the word in that sense, one could have also computational astronomy or computational geology. In the present context, however, the word's primary force is its descriptive connotation, which here betokens the deep-seated conviction that what is being modeled by a computer is itself a kind of computer, albeit one quite unlike the serial, digital machines on which computer science cut its teeth. That is, nervous systems and probably parts of nervous systems are themselves naturally evolved computers—organically constituted, analog in representation, and parallel in their processing architecture. They represent features and relations in the world and they enable an animal to adapt to its circumstances. They are a breed of computer whose *modus operandi* still elude us but are the mother lode, so to speak, of computational neuroscience.

A number of broad clues about computation in nervous systems are available. First, unlike a digital computer which is general purpose and can be programmed to run any algorithm, the brain appears to be an interconnected collection of special-purpose systems that are very efficient at performing their tasks but limited in their flexibility. Visual cortex, for example, does not appear able to assume the functions of the cerebellum or the hippocampus. Presumably this is not because visual cortex contains cells that are essentially and intrinsically visual in what they do (or contain "visons" instead of "auditons"), but rather it is mainly because of their morphological specialization and of their place in the system of cells in visual cortex, i.e., relative to their input cells, their intracortical and subcortical connections, their output cells, and so on. Put another way, a neuron's specialization is a function of the neuron's computational roles in the system, and evolution has refined the cells better to perform those roles.

Second, the clues about the brain's computational principles that can be gleaned from studying its microstructure and organization are indispensable to figuring out its computational organization because the nervous system is a product of evolution, not engineering design. Evolutionary modifications are always made within the context of an organization and architecture that are already in place. Quite simply, Nature is not an intelligent engineer. It cannot dismantle the existing configuration and start from scratch with a preferred design or preferred materials. It cannot mull the environmental conditions and construct an optimal device. Consequently, the computational solutions evolved by Nature may be quite unlike those that an intelligent human would invent, and they may well be neither optimal nor predictable from orthodox engineering assumptions.

Third, human nervous systems are by no means exclusively cognitive devices, though the infatuation with cognition fosters a tacit tendency to assume so. Nervous systems must also manage such matters as thermoregulation—a very complex function for mammals—growth, aspects of reproduction, respiration, regulation of hunger, thirst, and motor control, and maintenance of behavioral state, such as sleeping, dreaming, being awake, and so forth. Thus an evolutionary modification that results in a computational improvement in vision, say, might seem to have the earmarks of an engineering prizewinner. But if it cannot mesh with the rest of the brain's organization, or if it marginalizes critical functions such as thermoregulation, the animal and its "prizewinning" vision genes will die. Given these reasons, *reverse* engineering, where the device is taken apart to see how it works, is a profitable strategy with respect to the brain. By contrast, a purely *a priori* approach, based entirely on reasonable principles of engineering design, may lead us down a blind alley.

Fourth, it is prudent to be aware that our favorite intuitions about these matters may be misleading, however "self-evident" and compelling they be. More specifically, neither the nature of the computational problems the nervous system is solving nor the difficulty of the problems confronting the nervous system can be judged merely by introspection. Consider, for example, a natural human activity such as walking—a skill that is typically mastered in the first year or so of life. One might doubt whether this is a computational problem at all, or if it is, whether it is a problem of sufficient complexity to be worth one's reflection. Since walking is virtually effortless, unlike, say, doing algebra, which many people do find a strain, one might conclude from casual observation that walking is a computationally easy task—easier, at least, than doing algebra. The preconception that walking is computationally rather trivial is, however, merely an illusion. It is easy enough for toy manufacturers to make a doll that puts one foot in front of the other as long as she is held by the child. But for the doll to walk as we do, maintaining balance as we do, is a completely different task. Locomotion turns out to be a complicated matter, the ease implied by introspection notwithstanding.

Another computational issue of critical importance in generating hypotheses in computational neuroscience concerns the time available for performing the computation. From the point of view of the nervous system, it is not enough to come up with solutions that merely give the correct output for a given input. The solutions must also be available within milliseconds of the problem's presentation, and applications must be forthcoming within a few hundred milliseconds. It is important that nervous systems can routinely detect signals, recognize patterns, and assemble responses within one second. The ability of nervous systems to move their encasing bodies appropriately and swiftly was typically selected at every stage of evolution, since by and large natural selection would favor those organisms that could flee or fight predators, and catch and cache prey. *Ceteris paribus*, slow nervous systems become dinner for faster nervous systems. Even if the computational strategies used by the brain should turn out not to be elegant or beautiful but to have a sort of evolutionary do-it-yourself quality, they are demonstrably very fast. This tiny response-time rules out as just too slow many kinds of ostensibly elegant computational architectures and clever computational principles. This point is all the more significant when it is considered that events in an electronic computer happen in the nanosecond (10^{-9}) range, whereas events in neurons happen in the millisecond (10^{-3}) range.

A related consideration is that organic computers such as brains are constrained in the amount of space available for the essential elements—cell bodies, dendrites, axons, glial cells, and vascularization—and the cranial capacity is in turn limited by the mechanisms of reproduction. In mammals, for example, the size of the pelvic cavity of the mother constrains head size of offspring, and therefore brain size of offspring. What this all means is that the length of wiring in nervous systems must also be limited—evolution cannot just help itself to indefinite lengths of connecting wire but must make every centimeter count. In a human brain, for example, the total length of wiring is about 10^8 meters and it has to be packed into a volume of about 1.5 liters. The spatial configuration of sense organs and muscles on the body and the relative position of the afferent and efferent systems will also be relevant to the computational genre that has been selected in the evolution of nervous systems (figure 1.3). One strategy the brain uses to economize on wire is to map the processing units so that neighboring units process similar representations. Another strategy involves sharing wire, meaning that the same wire (axon) can be used in coding a large range of representations (Mead 1989). The computational genre adopted for a nervous system will, therefore, be constrained not only by temporal factors but also by spatial factors.

Computation is also limited by power consumption, and on this matter too the brain is impressively efficient. For example, a neuron uses roughly 10^{-15} joules of energy per operation (e.g., one neuron activating another at a synapse). By contrast, the most efficient silicon technology currently requires about 10^{-7} joules per operation (multiply, add, etc.) (Mead 1989). Using the criterion of joules per operation, the brain is about *7 or 8 orders of magnitude* more power efficient than the best of the silicon chips. A direct consequence of their energy efficiency is that brains can perform many more operations per second than even the newest supercomputers. The fastest digital computers are capable of around 10^9 operations per second; the brain of the common housefly, for example, performs about 10^{11} operations per second when merely resting.

Finally, there are constraints imposed by the materials of construction. That is, cells are made out of proteins and lipids, they have to rely on mitochondria for their energy supply; nervous systems must have the substances and dispositions necessary for growth and development, and they must exploit such features as the membrane properties of cells and the available chemicals in order to function as an organic computer. Additionally, the nervous system

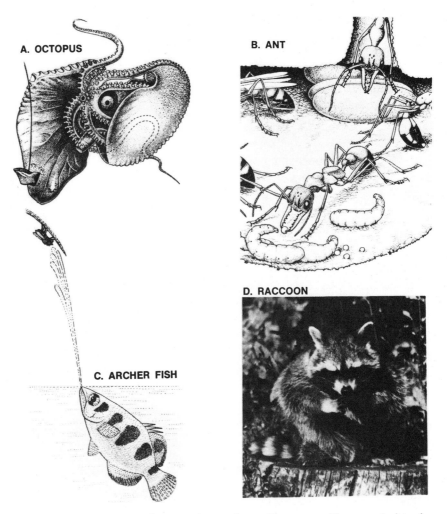

Figure 1.3 Evolutionary specializations of manipulation. The octopus (A) can manipulate objects with its tentacles, which are modified limbs; the ant (B) moves things with its pincers, which are modified jaws (mandibles). The archer fish (C) can use its mouth and pharynx to shoot droplets of water at airborne insects, an elementary form of tool use. The raccoon (D) performs dextrous manipulations of foodstuffs with its handlike paws. (From Shepherd 1987.)

needs a constant supply of oxygen and a reliable supply of nutrients. Evolution has to make what it can out of proteins, lipids, membranes, amino acids, etc. This is not altogether unlike the engineering make-do game where the given materials are limited (a finite number of popsicle sticks, rubber bands, and paper clips), and the task, for example, is to build a weight-supporting bridge. Indeed, John Allman (1990) has suggested that brain expansion in homeotherms was spurred by the need to engage in intense prey-catching in order to keep the home fires burning, as it were. In the competition for large amounts of fuel, homeotherms with sophisticated neural machinery that upgraded prey-catching and predator avoidance would have had an advantage.

Two conceptual ideas have structured much of how we tend to conceive of problems in computational neuroscience. First is the notion of *levels*, and the

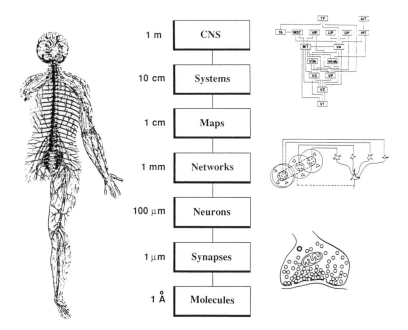

Figure 1.4 Schematic illustration of levels of organization in the nervous system. The spatial scales at which anatomical organizations can be identified varies over many orders of magnitude. Icons to the right represent structures at distinct levels: (top) a subset of visual areas in visual cortex (van Essen and Maunsell 1980); (middle) a network model of how ganglion cells could be connected to simple cells in visual cortex (Hubel and Wiesel, 1962), and (bottom) a chemical synapse (Kandel and Schwartz, 1985). (From Churchland and Sejnowski 1988.)

second concerns the *co-evolution* of research on different levels. In the brain, there is both large-scale and small-scale organization, and different functions take place on higher and lower levels (figure 1.4). One sort of account will explain how signals are integrated in dendrites; a different account will explain the interaction of neurons in a network, or the interaction of networks in a system.[5] A model that captures the salient features of learning in networks will have a different face from a model that describes the NMDA channel. Nevertheless, the theories on one level must mesh with the theories of levels both higher and lower, because an inconsistency or a lacuna somewhere in the tale means that some phenomenon has been misunderstood. After all, brains are assemblies of cells, and something would be seriously amiss if neurons under one description had properties incompatible with the same neurons under another description.

That there are levels of organization is a matter of fact; co-evolution of research, on the other hand, is a matter of research strategy in light of the presumed fact. The hallmark of co-evolution of theories is that research at one level provides correction, constraints, and inspiration for research at higher and at lower levels (figure 1.5). Computational space is undoubtedly vast, and the possible ways to perform any task are probably legion. Theorizing at a high level without benefit of lower-level constraints runs the risk of exploring a part of that space that may be interesting in its own right but remote from where

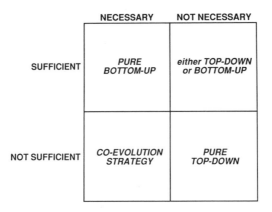

	NECESSARY	NOT NECESSARY
SUFFICIENT	*PURE BOTTOM-UP*	*either TOP-DOWN or BOTTOM-UP*
NOT SUFFICIENT	*CO-EVOLUTION STRATEGY*	*PURE TOP-DOWN*

Figure 1.5 Possible research strategies for trying to understand how the brain works as they divide on the question of the importance of cellular and molecular levels in theories of brain function. Some neuroscientists may prefer the pure bottom-up strategy; some psychologists and philosophers prefer the pure top-down strategy; probably no one falls into the upper right box, but we added it to round out the possibility-table; the co-evolutionary strategy (lower left) is the one adopted in this book.

the brain's solutions reside. Thus microlevel constraints and the testing of hypotheses against microlevel facts are of central importance.

On the other hand, research from neuropsychology neuroethology, and psychophysics, as well as experimental psychology generally, provide the detailed characterization of what needs to be explained at lower levels. Without a scientific delineation of cognitive and other psychological capacities, lower-level research has only incomplete and confused ideas about the very capacity whose mechanisms are the focus of research. Thus, for example, in studying the neuronal mechanisms of motion perception in visual areas MT and MST, it is wasteful not to have up-to-date information on the psychophysics of visual motion detection. Research on computational principles can profitably co-evolve with research in neuroscience and in psychology, for something new is to be learned from the brain about powerful computational methods, and neuroscience in return can absorb abstract discoveries in the theory of computing and practical discoveries in the construction of computing machines.

It is on the *network level* that we decided to concentrate discussion. We made this decision because network models can be more highly constrained by neurobiology than can high-level psychological models and because network models are more straightforwardly testable against the actual networks modeled. At the same time, we prefer models of capacities that are well studied in psychology and neuropsychology so that we can take advantage of economizing constraints from top-down research. This usually means that the capacities themselves will be rather low level; visual motion detection rather than planning, bending in the leech rather than chess playing in the human. For us, this is an advantage since it is discouraging to put effort into a model of some brain function if the model can be assessed only abstractly or aesthetically. Consequently, the models we select for more intensive discussion in this book will be models that generally exhibit the "accessibility" features: the bending reflex in the leech, a model of the vestibulo-ocular reflex (VOR), and models of visual capacities such as stereopsis. Our particular choices are also guided by the independent virtues of these models. There are, of course, some drawbacks to "neurally close" models. In a nutshell, how realistic should they be before useful results drown in the detail? How much of the teeming detail is needed to get a reasonably accurate model? These questions will be taken up mainly in chapters 3 and 4.

Although "neurally close" models of "psychophysically dissectable" capacities are our preference, we hasten to say that we recognize that other scientists have quite different preferences, and that ideas useful for the science of the mind-brain may come from widely diverse locations in the research spectrum. Not only are we cognizant of the value of modeling research outside the compass of our particular prejudices, we would be dismayed if everyone were to share our prejudices, for the co-evolutionary advice regarding methodological efficiency is "let many flowers bloom." And at this stage in the history of neuroscience, the advice is entirely reasonable. First, because it is far too early in the hunt to know where the Big Breakthroughs will come or what they will look like. Second, because ultimately what is wanted is a story, unified from top to bottom—from behavior, through systems to networks to neurons and molecules: a unified science of the mind-brain.

Mathematical models and computer simulations of the single neuron have a distinguished tradition, beginning with Hodgkin and Huxley in 1952 and continuing with highly detailed and revealing models of motor neurons (Rall, 1964), Purkinje cells (Bush and Sejnowski, 1991); hippocampal pyramidal cells (Traub et al., in press), and dendritic processing (Segev et al., in press, Koch et al. 1990). The single neuron is not the main focus of this book, however, since a good choice of accessible texts with that focus already exists.[6] To have put single neuron modeling on center stage would have meant not only redescribing the familiar, but also bypassing some little-known but ought-to-be-known models aimed at the network level. Our discussion by no means excludes single neuron models, however, and several detailed cellular models are introduced in the context of network models in which they might find a place (chapters 5 and 6). Moreover, we emphasize the importance of single neuron models as the bedrock and fundament into which network models must eventually fit. Network models are thus considered not in isolation from single neuron models, but as having a future wherein the two enmesh.

The rationale for a primer is threefold. First, we calculated it would be useful to present and discuss the conceptual framework of the emerging discipline of computational neuroscience, accompanied by a selection of sterling or anyhow seminal examples to flesh out the ideas. Sometimes, for both neophyte and cognoscenti, it can be worthwhile to step back from the crowd of trees and have a look at the shape of the woods.

Second, there are four broad constituencies—neuroscience, psychology, computer science, and philosophy—each voicing a specific and entirely legitimate demand with respect to neuromodeling, and each harboring a specific complaint about other constituencies. Having encountered these demand-complaint pairs on innumerable occasions and being convinced of the some-time fruitfulness of boundary-fuzzing, we wanted to have a go at satisfying the demands and addressing the complaints. Made concise for presentation and arrayed to display parallelism, the demand/complaint pairs are articulated be-low:

The neuroscientist:

1. Show me results of neuromodeling that help explain or predict experimental results.

2. They (the nonneuroscientists) do not know anything much about neuro-science even though they are doing "neural modeling."

The psychologist:

1. Show me results of neuromodeling that help explain or predict psychologi-cal functions and behavior.

2. They (the nonpsychologists) do not know anything much about the results from psychophysics and psychology even though they are modeling psycho-logical capacities and performance.

The computer scientists:

1. Show me results of neuromodeling that help understand the nature of com-putation and representation or that yield new ideas about these things.

2. They (the noncomputer scientists) do not know anything much about elec-trical circuits, mathematical analyses, or existing theory of computation.

The philosopher:

1. Show me results of neuromodeling that are relevant to philosophical prob-lems concerning the nature of knowledge, the self, and the mind.

2. They (the nonphilosophers) do not understand some of the useful, time-saving, and agony-saving contributions of philosophers in constraining ques-tions about how the mind works.

Since the demand/complaint pairs from the various constituencies are relat-ed, it seemed reasonable to try to combine our responses in an integrated text as a sort of conversation with diverse people. Moreover, since the constituen-cies are diverse, we wanted the book to be broadly accessible. New technical books and vast numbers of technical articles are appearing at a dizzying rate, and we judged that a less technical, more introductory text might be helpful in orienting in the midst of the technical literature. Where there are equations, we have given an English paraphrase, but in any event, they are skippable without substantial loss. References at the chapter ends permit the reader to follow up the discussion. To round out the presentation, we judged it necessary to in-clude a brief exposure to basic neuroscience and to the foundational issues in computational theory. Thus, chapters 2 and 3 provide some background discussion on neuroscience and the science of computation. An appendix on neuroscience techniques and a glossary are also included.

The third element in the rationale was more self-oriented. The project forced us to leave intermittently the relative solace of the technical details to see what we could discern of the broader landscape and its contours. In a sense, then, the project has been an excuse to paint in broad strokes as well as an exercise in policing our implicit convictions and our covert enthusiasms. We found ourselves constantly hectoring each other with questions of this form, for many values of X and Y: what is the point of X, what does Y really mean, is X really of any use to anybody? In forcing each other to articulate answers, we often bumped up against the illusion that one's assumptions are generally well-honed, well-grounded, and entirely coherent with the rest of one's beliefs.

In chapters 4 to 7, we assume a basic background knowledge and proceed to introduce computational models. The first ones discussed are rather abstract models of visual functions that incorporate some neuronal details, but where the neural data are still unavailable, perforce they mirror the want of data. Models introduced in later chapters are increasingly realistic neurobiologically. Plasticity, introduced in chapter 5, has been modeled at many levels, from the very spare models that are virtually innocent of physiology, to higher-fidelity models of dendritic spine behavior whose grain is so fine as to include ion concentration parameters and diffusion times. In chapter 6 on sensory-motor integration, we chart the progress in Lockery's modeling of the bending reflex in the leech from a simple static model to the next increment of complexity, a model with dynamical properties, to plans—if not the finished product—for a model that includes channel properties. Likewise, the modeling of adaptation in the vestibulo-ocular reflex, though incomplete, includes the known dynamical and physiological properties of the circuits. Incorporating more cellular detail, Grillner's model of swimming in the lamprey has many physiological properties, including time constants for cellular responses and channel properties.

Obviously one intends that a model capture the salient features of reality modeled. At the same time, however, this desideratum should not equate a high degree of realism with a high degree of scientific value. Different models are useful for different purposes. At certain levels and for certain questions, abstract, simplifying models are precisely what is needed. Such a model will be more useful than a model slavishly realistic with respect to every level, even the biochemical. Excessive realism may entail that the model is too bedizened and rich to analyze or understand or even run on the computers available. For other questions, such as dendritic spine dynamics, the more realism at the biochemical level, for example, the better. But even here, the model will probably not be improved by taking into account quantum properties at the level below, or the cell's circuit cohorts on the level above. There is, of course, no decision procedure for the problem: how realistic should my model of X be, for many values of X? Each case has to be thought out on its own, and solved with imagination and horse sense.

"Data rich, but theory poor" is a description frequently applied to neuro-science. In one obvious respect, this remains true, inasmuch as we do not yet know how to explain how brains see, learn, and take action. Nevertheless, theory in the form of computational modeling is rapidly catching up with the neurobiological data base. To be sure, there is still a great deal of experimental data that has not yet found a modeling home. Although the store is by no means exhausted, the modeling enterprise is slowed by gaps in our experimental knowledge, and these gaps need to be filled before extensive modeling can proceed. The experiments whose results are needed cannot be done by computer—they can be done only by anatomists, physiologists, biochemists, and geneticists working on real nervous tissue; by neuropsychologists studying patients with brain damage; and by psychologists studying normal humans and other animals. A lesson revealed by the modeling efforts is that there are many places where we are data poor, many questions that simply cannot be addressed in a computer model because the relevant data on which the model must rely are not yet available. Of course, assessments of wealth are essentially relative, both to where one *was*—in which case neuroscience is data rich and theory rich—and where one *wants to be*—in which case neuroscience is both data poor and theory poor.

The next few decades will be the formative years for computational neuro-science. Predicting what we shall understand of the brain by 2020 is, needless to say, a mug's game. Nevertheless, the hunch that exciting things are in store is difficult to subdue, and the thrill of discovering what we are and how we work is luring more and more students into the field. They often bring with them novel perspectives from their mother fields, as well as a bold inventiveness, a gift prized by a developing field that needs new ideas—unorthodox and otherwise. Withal, it is a remarkable time in the history of science.

2 Neuroscience Overview

1 INTRODUCTION

If we are to understand how the brain sees, learns, and is aware, we must understand the architecture of the brain itself. The brain's computational style and the principles governing its function are not manifest to a casual inspection. Nor can they be just inferred from behavior, detailed though the behavioral descriptions may be, for the behavior is compatible with a huge number of very different computational hypotheses, only one of which may be true of the brain. Moreover, trying to guess the governing principles by drawing on existing engineering ideas has resulted in surprisingly little progress in understanding the brain, and the unavoidable conclusion is that there is no substitute for conjuring the ideas in the context of observations about real nervous systems: from the properties of neurons and the way neurons are interconnected.

This chapter focuses on the "neuroscience" component of the "computational neuroscience" synergy. Ideally, computer modelers should know as much neuroscience as practising neuroscientists. In fact, however, there is too much neuroscience to be thoroughly mastered even by a single neuroscientist. An anatomist may know a lot about his designated region of the visual cortex, rather less about other cortical areas and subcortical brain structures, less again about central pattern generation in the spinal cord, and even less about plasticity of the vestibulo-ocular reflex. Our aim is to prepare the reader, from whatever constituency, for the general conceptual framework we deploy and the specific neurobiological examples discussed within that framework. Consequently, the material in this chapter is organized to cohere with a computational approach to exploring certain aspects of nervous system function. Because levels turn out to be pivotal in our grand scheme of things, characterizing levels in neurobiology is a matter of the first importance. The presentation in this chapter is therefore keyed to illustrating anatomical and physiological properties seen at different levels. Although understanding the techniques whereby neurobiological data are gathered is also essential, to keep the wagons moving we elected to provide this in the appendix at the end. Although this chapter is meant to provide some basic neuroscience background,

Substantial portions of this chapter are taken from Sejnowski and Churchland (1989).

in the context of specific neurocomputational models, relevant neuroscience will be introduced.

2 LEVELS IN NERVOUS SYSTEMS

Discussions concerning the nature of psychological phenomena and their neurobiological bases invariably make reference to the notion of "levels." In trying to be a bit more precise about what is meant by "level," we found three different ideas about levels in the literature: *levels of analysis, levels of organization, and levels of processing*. Roughly speaking, the distinctions are drawn along the following lines: levels of organization are essentially anatomical, and refer to a hierarchy of components and to structures comprising these components. Levels of processing are physiological, and refer to the location of a process relative to the transducers and muscles. Levels of analysis are conceptual, and refer to different kinds of questions asked about how the brain performs a task: into what subtasks does the brain divide the tasks, what processing steps execute a subtask, and what physical structures carry out the steps? In what follows, we elaborate on these distinctions.

Levels of Analysis

A framework for a theory of levels, articulated by Marr (1982), provided an important and influential background for thinking about levels in the context of computation by nervous structures.[1] This framework drew upon the conception of levels in computer science, and accordingly Marr characterized three levels: (1) the computational level of abstract problem analysis, decomposing the task (e.g., determining the 3-D depth of objects from the 2-D pattern on the retina) into its main constituents; (2) the level of the algorithm, specifying a formal procedure to perform the task so that for a given input, the correct output results; and (3) the level of physical implementation, constructing a working device using a particular technology. This division really corresponds to three different sorts of questions that can be raised about a phenomenon: (1) how does the problem decompose into parts?, (2) what principles govern how the parts interact to solve the problem?, and (3) what is the stuff whose causal interactions implement the principles?

An important element in Marr's view was that a higher-level question was largely independent of the levels below it, and hence computational problems of the highest level could be analyzed independently of understanding the algorithm which performs the computation. Similarly, the algorithmic problem of the second level was thought to be solvable independently of understanding its physical implementation. Thus his preferred strategy was top-down rather than bottom-up. At least this was the official doctrine though, in practice, downward glances figured significantly in Marr's attempts to find problem analyses and algorithmic solutions. Ironically, given his advocacy of the top-down strategy, Marr's work was itself highly influenced by neurobiological considerations, and implementation facts constrained his choice of problem and nurtured his computational and algorithmic insights. Publicly, the advocacy of the top-down strategy did carry the implication, dismaying for some and comforting for others, that neurobiological facts could be more or less ignored, since they were, after all, just at the implementation level.

Unfortunately, two very different issues were confused in the doctrine of independence. One concerns whether, as a *matter of discovery*, one can figure out the relevant algorithm and the problem analysis independently of facts about implementation. The other concerns whether, as a *matter of formal theory*, a given algorithm which is already known to perform a task in a given machine (e.g., the brain) can be implemented in some other machine which has a different architecture. So far as the latter is concerned, what computational theory tells us is that an algorithm can be run on different machines, and in that sense and that sense alone, the algorithm is independent of the implementation. The formal point is straightforward: since an algorithm is formal, no specific physical parameters (e.g., vacuum tubes, Ca^{2+}) are part of the algorithm.

That said, it is important to see that the purely formal point cannot speak to the issue of how best to discover the algorithm in fact used by a given machine, nor how best to arrive at the neurobiologically adequate task analysis. Certainly it cannot tell us that the discovery of the algorithms relevant to cognitive functions will be independent of a detailed understanding of the nervous system. Moreover, it does not tell us that any implementation is as good as any other. And it had better not, since different implementations display enormous differences in speed, size, efficiency, elegance, etc. The formal independence of algorithm from architecture is something we can exploit to build computationally equivalent machines once we know how the brain works, but it is no guide to discovery if we do not know how the brain works.

The issue of independence of levels marks a major conceptual difference between Marr (1982) and the current generation of researchers studying neural and connectionist models. In contrast to the doctrine of independence, current research suggests that considerations of implementation play a vital role in the kinds of algorithms that are devised and the kind of computational insights available to the scientist. Knowledge of brain architecture, far from being irrelevant to the project, can be the essential basis and invaluable catalyst for devising likely and powerful algorithms—algorithms that have a reasonable shot at explaining how in fact the neurons do the job.

Levels of Organization

Marr's three-level division treats computation monolithically, as a single kind of level of analysis. Implementation and task-description are likewise each considered as a single level of analysis. Yet when we measure Marr's three levels of analysis against levels of organization in the nervous system, the fit is poor and confusing at best.[2] To begin with, there is organized structure at different scales: molecules, synapses, neurons, networks, layers, maps, and systems (figure 2.1). At each structurally specified stratum we can raise the computational question: what does that organization of elements do? What does it contribute to the wider, computational organization of the brain? In addition, there are physiological levels: ion movement, channel configurations, EPSPs (excitatory postsynaptic potentials), IPSPs (inhibitory postsynaptic potentials), action potentials, evoked response potentials, and probably other intervening levels that we have yet to learn about and that involve effects at higher anatomical levels such as networks or systems.

The range of structural organization implies, therefore, that there are many levels of implementation and that each has its companion task description. But if there are as many types of task descriptions as there are levels of structural organization, this diversity could be reflected in a multiplicity of algorithms

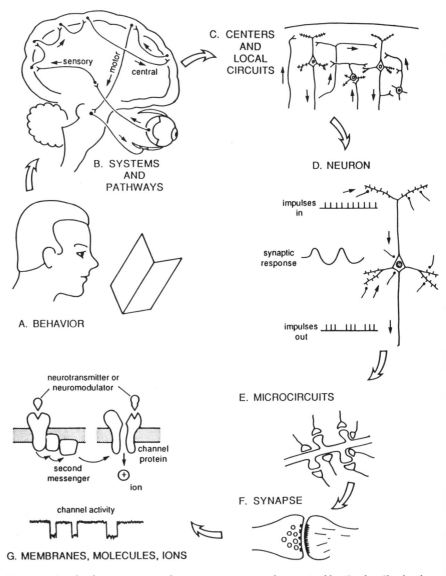

Figure 2.1 Levels of organization in the nervous system, as characterized by Gordon Shepherd (1988a).

that characterize how the tasks are accomplished. This in turn means that the notion of *the* algorithmic level is as over-simplified as the notion of *the* implementation level.

Note also that the very same level of organization can be viewed computationally (in terms of functional role) or implementationally (in terms of the substrate for the function), depending on what questions you ask. For example, the details of how an action potential is propagated might, from the point of view of communication between distant areas, be considered an implementation, since it is an all-or-none event and only its timing carries information. However, from a lower structural level—the point of view of ionic distributions—the propagating action potential is a computational construct whose regenerative and repetitive nature is a consequence of several types of non-linear voltage-dependent ionic channels spatially distributed along an axon.

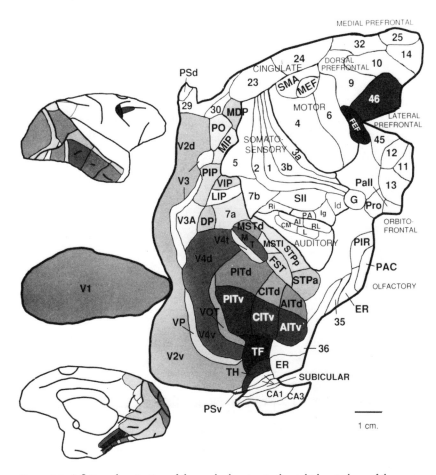

Figure 2.2 A flattened projection of the cerebral cortex in the right hemisphere of the macaque monkey. Stippling indicates cortical areas implicated in visual processing. (Upper left) Lateral view of macaque brain, showing visual areas. (Lower left) Medial view of macaque brain. (Reprinted with permission from van Essen and Anderson 1990.)

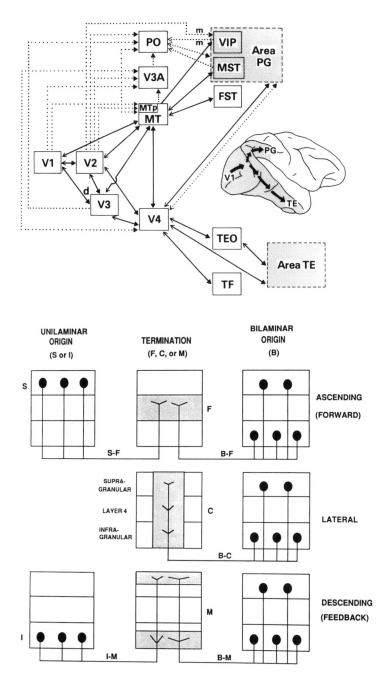

Figure 2.3 (Top) Schematic diagram of some of the cortical visual areas and their connections in the macaque monkey. Solid lines indicate projections involving all portions of the visual field representation in an area; dotted lines indicate projections limited to the representation of the peripheral visual field. Heavy arrowheads indicate forward projections; light arrowheads indicate backward projections. (From Desimone and Ungerleider 1989.) (Bottom) Laminar patterns of cortical connectivity used for making hierarchical assignments. Three characteristic patterns of termination are indicated in the central column. These include preferential termination in layer 4 (the F pattern), a columnar (C) pattern involving approximately equal density of termination in all layers, and a multilaminar (M) pattern that preferentially avoids layer 4. There are also three

Levels of Processing

The focus for this levels concept is the link between anatomy and what is represented in the anatomy. As a first pass, it assumes that the greater the distance from cells responding to sensory input, the higher is the degree of information processing. Thus the level-rank assigned is a function of synaptic distance from the periphery. On this measure, cells in the primary visual area of the neocortex that respond to oriented bars of light are at a higher level than cells in the lateral geniculate nucleus (LGN), which in turn are at a higher level than retinal ganglion cells. Because the nature of the representations and the transformations on the representations are still poorly understood, only the relative level—x is higher or lower than y—rather than the ordinal level—first, second, etc.—is referred to.

Once the sensory information reaches the cerebral cortex, it fans out through cortico-cortical projections into a multitude of parallel streams of processing. In the primate visual system, 25 areas that are predominantly or exclusively visual have been identified (van Essen et al. 1991; figure 2.2). Many (perhaps all) forward projections are matched by a backward projection, and there are even massive feedback projections from primary visual cortex to the LGN. Given these reciprocal projections, the processing hierarchy is anything but a one-way ladder. Even so, by examining the cortical layer into which fibers project, it is possible to find some order in the information flow. Forward projections generally terminate in the middle layers of cortex, and feedback projections usually terminate in the upper and lower layers.[3] So far, however, the function of these feedback pathways is not established, though the idea that they have a role in learning, attention, and perceptual recognition is not unreasonable. If higher areas can affect the flow of information through lower areas, then strictly sequential processing cannot be taken for granted (figure 2.3).

The organization typical of earlier sensory areas is only approximately, roughly, and incompletely hierarchical.[4] Beyond the sensory areas, moreover, not even that much hierarchy is manifest. The anatomy of frontal cortex and other areas beyond the primary sensory areas suggests an information organization more like an Athenian democracy than a Ford assembly line. Hierarchies typically have an apex, and following the analogy, one might expect to find a

characteristic patterns for the cells of origin of different pathways. Bilaminar (B) patterns, shown on the right, include approximately equal numbers of cells from superficial and deep layers (no more than a 70%–30% split) and are found to occur with all three types of termination pattern. Unilaminar patterns, shown on the left, include predominantly superficial-layer inputs (S pattern) which correlate with F-type terminations, and predominantly infragranular-layer (I pattern) inputs which correlate with M-type terminations. Within this general framework, a number of variations on a theme can be encountered. Some pathways terminate primarily in superficial layers, but they are grouped with the M pattern because they avoid layer 4. Other pathways are quasi-columnar, but do not include all layers; they are classified as a C pattern if the labeling in layer 4 is neither heavier nor sparser than in adjoining layers. Filled ovals, cell bodies; angles, axon terminals. (From Felleman and van Essen 1991.)

brain region where all sensory information converges and from which motor commands emerge. It is a striking fact that this is false of the brain. Although there are convergent pathways, the convergence is partial and occurs in many places many times over, and motor control appears to be distributed rather than vested in a command center (Arbib 1989, Altman and Kien 1989; figure 2.4).

The assumption that there is a sensory-processing hierarchy, if only to a first approximation, affords the possibility of probing the processing stages by linking various behavioral measures, such as task-relative reaction time (RT), to events taking place in the processing hierarchy at different times as measured by cellular response. To put it more crudely, temporal ordering helps determine what is cause and what is effect. Accuracy of response under varying conditions can be measured, and both humans and animals may be subjects. This is an important method for triangulating the brain areas involved in executing a certain task and for determining something about the processing stages of the task. For example, on the physiological side, one may measure the

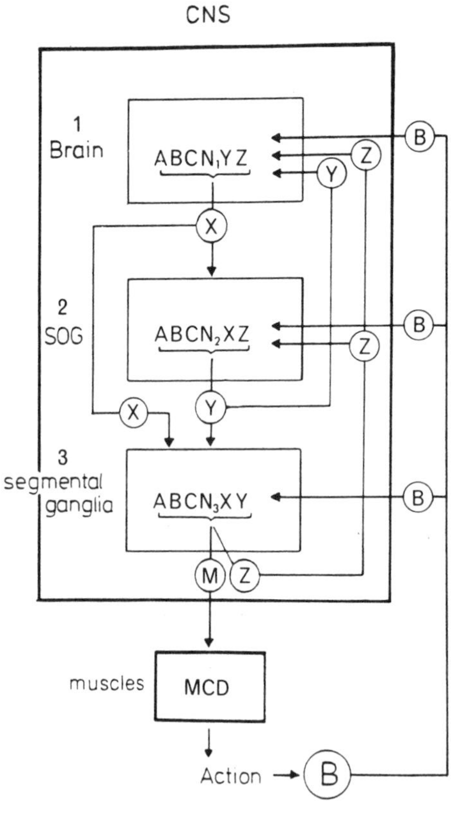

Figure 2.4 Model for decision-making in the insect nervous system. In the CNS, stations 1, 2, 3 contain local networks 1, 2, 3. These stations approximate the brain, the subesophageal (SOG), and segmental ganglia of the locust. The output of each station results from a consensus between the activity of the inputs and the local networks in that station, so the output of each station is different. The stations are thus linked in several parallel loops, and the output of the whole system is the consensus of the activity in all the loops. (From Altman and Kien 1989.)

delay between the presentation of a moving target and the first response by motion-sensitive cells in visual area MT, and on the behavioral side one may measure the response latency relative to degrees of noise in the stimulus. One surprise is that the latencies for signals reaching the visual areas in the cortex are so long, relative to the behavioral RT. The latency for MT is about 50–60 msec, and about 100 msec in inferotemporal cortex. Since human RT to a complex object is on the order of 150–200 msec including assembling the motor response, sending the signal down the spinal cord, and activating the muscles, this suggests that surprisingly few processing steps intervene between detection in MT and preparing the response in the motor cortex, striatum, cerebellum, and spinal cord. Such data help constrain theories about the nature of the processing.

By way of illustration, consider a set of experiments by William Newsome and colleagues (1989) in which they show a correlation between the accuracy of the behavioral response to motion detection and the spiking frequency of single neurons responding to motion stimuli in MT. (Newsome et al. 1989) In the task, tiny dots move randomly on a TV screen. The monkey is trained to respond as soon as it detects coherent motion, to either the right or the left. Across trials, what varies is the number of dots moving coherently and their direction of motion. The monkey detects direction of motion with as few as four dots moving coherently, and his accuracy improves as the number of dots moving together increases. What about the cells in MT? Suppose one records from a cell that prefers right-going motion. The visual display is set up so that it is matched to the cell's receptive field, with the result that the experimenter has control of the minimum stimulus needed to produce the maximum response. So long as fewer than four dots move coherently, the cell does not respond. With increasing numbers of dots moving coherently in the cell's preferred direction, the cell responds more vigorously. Indeed, the accuracy curve displayed in the monkey's behavior and the spiking-frequency curve displayed by the single cell are, to a first approximation, congruent (figure 2.5). This implies, to put it crudely, that the information contained in the cellular responses of single sensory neurons and the information contained in the behavioral response are roughly on par. It should, however, be kept in mind that the monkeys were very highly trained on this task and that the sensory stimulus was chosen to match the optimal response of each neuron. In a naive monkey, there may not be such close correspondence between the response of the single cell and the overt behavior.

The next phase of the experiment tests whether the information carried by directionally selective cells found in MT is really used in generating the response. To do this, Newsome and colleagues presented *left*-going visual stimuli, and at the proper latency they electrically stimulated the column containing cells preferring *right*-going visual stimuli. How did the animal behave? Would the electrical stimuli demonstrate its effectiveness by overriding, at least sometimes, the visual stimuli? The monkey behaved as though he saw right-going stimuli; more exactly, the electrical stimulus decreased the probability that the animal would respond to the visual stimulus and increased the

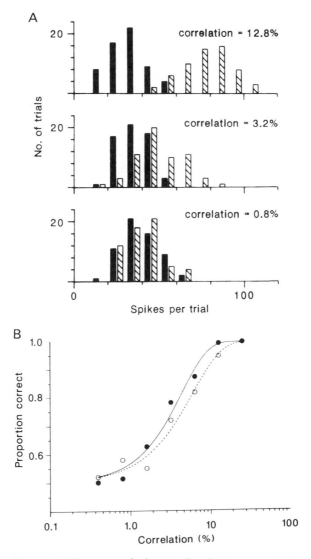

Figure 2.5 (a) Responses of a directionally selective neuron (in visual area MT) at three different motion correlations spanning physiological threshold. Hatched bars represent responses to motion in the neuron's preferred direction; solid bars indicate responses to motion 180° opposite to the preferred direction. Sixty trials were performed in each direction for each of the three correlation levels. Response distributions for a range of correlation levels were used to compute a "neurometric" function that characterized the neuron's sensitivity to the motion signal, and could be compared with the psychometric function computed from the monkey's behavioral response. (b) Comparison of simultaneously recorded psychometric and neurometric functions. Opens circles, psychophysical performance of the monkey; filled circles, performance of the neuron. Psychophysical performance at each correlation is given by the proportion of trials on which the monkey correctly identified the direction of motion. Neuronal performance is calculated from distributions of responses of the directionally sensitive MT neuron. The physiological and psychophysical data form similar curves, but the data for the neuron lie to the left of the data for the monkey, meaning that the neuron was somewhat more sensitive than the monkey. (From Newsome, Britten, and Movshon [1989]. Reprinted by permission from *Nature* 341: 52–54. Copyright © 1989 Macmillan Magazines Ltd.)

probability that it would respond as though presented with a stimulus in the opposite direction. This result implies that the cells' responses—and hence the information carried in those responses—are behaviorally significant (figure 2.6).

During the past hundred years, experimental psychologists have assembled an impressive body of RT information, and it is a valuable data base upon which neuroscientists may draw. Thus consider also a set of studies by Requin and colleagues (Requin et al. 1988, Riehle and Requin 1989). In the first stage, they measured the monkey's RT where the task was to make a wrist flexion in a certain direction and by a certain amount as indicated by a signal. There were basically three conditions: the monkeys were precued or not, and if they were precued, the cue indicated either the direction or the extent of the movement. Precuing was found to have a large effect on the RT but only a slight effect on the movement time, showing that precuing has its major effect on programming and preparing for the movement, rather than on the speed of execution of the movement. Additionally, if the advance cue specified where but not how much, the RT was shortened more than if the cue specified how much but not where. This suggests that information about extent of movement cannot be efficiently incorporated until the system knows the direction of the movement.

In the second stage, Riehle and Requin investigated the electrophysiological properties of cells in the primary motor cortex (MI) and the premotor cortex (PM). They found execution-related neurons, which were more common in MI, and preparation-related, directionally selective neurons, which were more common in PM. This coheres with other physiological data, and implies that PM probably involves an earlier stage of processing than does MI, since PM has more to do with preparing for the movement than with executing it. Moreover, within the class of preparation-related cells in PM, they found two subclasses: those related to programming the muscle movements, and those related to preprocessing the general components of the movement program. This is another instance of research that narrows down hypotheses about relative order of processing and the structures involved in a distinct aspect of processing by establishing behavioral reaction times and by correlating those data with specific responses of cells.[5]

3 STRUCTURE AT VARIOUS LEVELS OF ORGANIZATION

Identification of functionally significant structure at various spatial scales in nervous systems proceeds in partnership with hypotheses about a given structure's role in the nervous system's performance and the manner in which that structure's own subcomponents are organized to constitute the mechanisms to carry out that role. To be sure, functional architecture at various spatial scales is all part of one integrated, unified biological machine. That is, the function of a neuron depends on the synapses that bring it information, and, in turn, the neuron processes information by virtue of its interaction with other neurons in local networks, which themselves play a particular role by virtue of their place in the overall geometry of the brain.

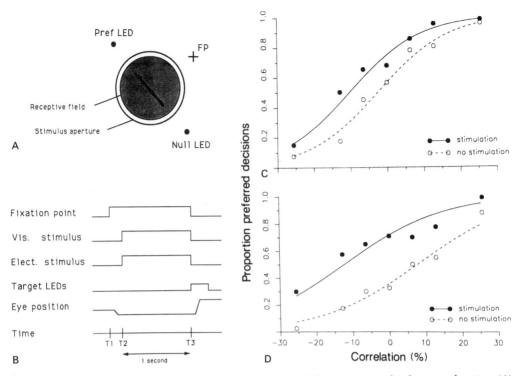

Figure 2.6 Microstimulation in cortical area MT biases perceptual judgments of motion. (A) Schematic diagram of the experimental protocol showing the spatial arrangement of the fixation point (FP), receptive field (shaded), stimulus aperture (thick circle), and response light emitting diodes (LEDs). (B) Schematic drawing illustrating the temporal sequence of events during a microstimulation trial. At time T_1 the fixation point appeared, and the monkey transferred its gaze to the fixation point, as indicated by the deflection in the eye position trace. At time T_2 the visual stimulus appeared, and the train of electrical stimulation pulses began. The monkey was required to maintain fixation for 1 sec until time T_3. The fixation point, the visual stimulus, and the microstimulation pulses were turned off at time T_3, and the target LED turned on. The monkey then indicated its judgment of motion direction by making a saccadic eye movement to one of the two response LEDs. (Right) The effect of microstimulation on performance for two stimulation sites in area MT (C and D). The proportion of decisions in the preferred direction is plotted as a function of the percent correlation in the moving dots during the stimulus presentation (positive correlation values indicate motion in the neuron's preferred direction). In half the trials (closed circles), microstimulation was applied simultaneously with the visual stimulus; the other trials (open circles) contained no microstimulation. The shift in the curves caused by the microstimulation is equivalent to adding 7.7% correlated dots (C) and 20.1% (D). (From Salzman, Britten, and Newsome 1990. Reprinted by permission from *Nature* 346: 174–177. Copyright © 1989 Macmillan Magazines Ltd.)

Accordingly, which structures really constitute a level of organization in the nervous system is an empirical, not an *a priori* matter. We cannot tell, in advance of studying the nervous system, how many levels there are, nor what is the nature of the structural and functional features of any given level. Some techniques used to study various levels will be surveyed in the appendix. In this section, seven general categories of structural organization will be discussed. In fact, however, the count is imprecise, for several reasons. Further research may lead to the subdivision of some categories, such as systems, into finer-grained categories, and some categories may be profoundly misdrawn and may need to be completely reconfigured. As we come to understand more about the brain and how it works, new levels of organization may be postulated. This is especially likely at higher levels where much less is known than at the lower levels.

Systems

To standardize references to brain locations, prominent landmarks, including major gyri, fissures, and the major lobes have been labeled (figures 2.7, 2.8). Using tract-tracing techniques, neuroanatomists have identified many systems in the brain. Some correspond to sensory modalities, such as the visual system; others, for example, the autonomic system, respect general functional characteristics. Yet others, such as the limbic system, are difficult to define, and may turn out not to be one system with an integrated or cohesive function. The components of these systems are not neatly compartmentalized but are distributed widely in the brain and are connected by long fiber tracts. For example, a particular brain system for long-term memory may involve such diverse structures as the hippocampus, the thalamus, the frontal cortex, and basal forebrain nuclei (Mishkin 1982). In this respect brain systems contrast quite vividly, and perhaps discouragingly, with systems designed by an engineer, where components are discrete and functions are compartmentalized.

One of the earliest systems concepts was that of a reflex arc, such as the monosynaptic reflex in the knee-jerk response (Sherrington 1906; figure 2.9). The pathways of some reflexes have now been traced in great detail; examples are the vestibulo-ocular reflex, which stabilizes images on the retina when the head is moving (Robinson 1981), and the gill withdrawal reflex in *Aplysia*, which has been a focus for research into the molecular mechanisms of plasticity (Kandel et al. 1987). The reflex arc is not a useful prototype for brain systems in general—or even, it appears, for most reflexes, such as the stepping reflex in the cat, or the nociceptive reflex (withdrawal of limb from a painful stimulus). Take, for example, the smooth pursuit system for visually tracking moving targets, where one pathway originates in the retina, leads to the lateral geniculate nucleus (LGN), to the cortex and through distinct visual topographic areas, down to the pons, and eventually to the oculomotor nuclei (Lisberger et al. 1987). (See chapter 6.) Despite the machine-like quality of smooth pursuit, it is to some extent under voluntary control and depends on expectation as well

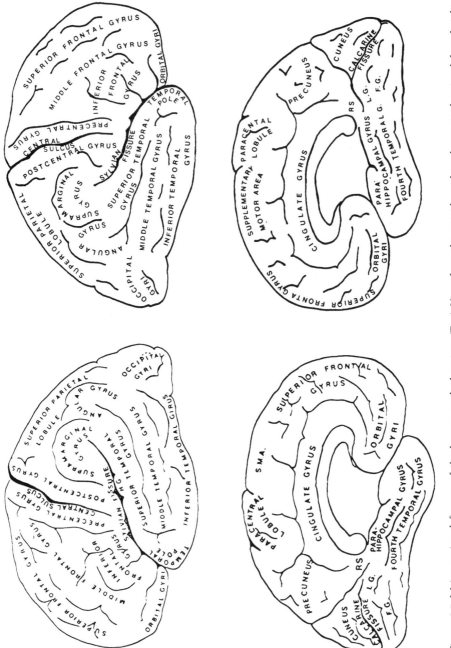

Figure 2.7 Major gyri and fissures of the human cerebral cortex. (Top) View from the outside or lateral aspect, showing left and right hemispheres. (Bottom) View of the inside, or medial, aspect of right and left hemispheres. Note that the hemispheres are not exact mirror images of each other. The precise location of gyri and fissures as well as the degree of asymmetry varies from brain to brain. (Courtesy Hanna Damasio.)

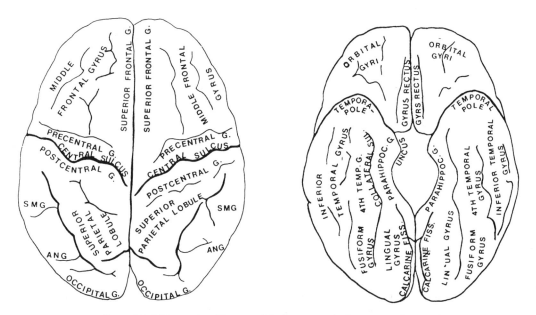

Figure 2.8 Major gyri and fissures of the human cerebral cortex. (Left) View from above (dorsal aspect). (Right) View from below (ventral, or inferior, aspect). (Courtesy Hanna Damasio.)

as the visual stimulus. Behaviors more sophisticated than simple reflexes probably exploit more complex computational principles.

In this regard, two important features of brain systems should be mentioned. First, there are almost always reciprocal (feedback) connections between brain areas, at least as rich in number as the feedforward connections. For example, the recurrent projections from the visual cortical area V1 back to the LGN are about ten times as numerous as those from the LGN to the V1. Second, although the simple models of reflex arcs suggest that a single neuron may be sufficient to activate the neuron on which it synapses, in fact a large number of neurons are almost always involved, and the effect of any single neuron on the next is typically quite small. For example, an important feature in the visual system is that input from a specific neuron in the LGN generally makes relatively weak synaptic contacts on a large population of cortical cells rather than a strong synaptic effect on just one or a few neurons (Martin 1984). This implies that cortical neurons rely on a convergence of many afferents, and correlations between pairs of neurons tends to be relatively weak.[6] There may be interesting exceptions to this; for example, chandelier cells in cortex make inhibitory connections on the axon hillocks of their targets, and they may, as single cells, have a strong, decisive effect on their target cells. Another exception is the strong influence that single climbing fibers have on single Purkinje cells in the cerebellum.

Topographic Maps

A major principle of organization within many sensory and motor systems is the topographic map. For example, neurons in visual areas of cortex, such as

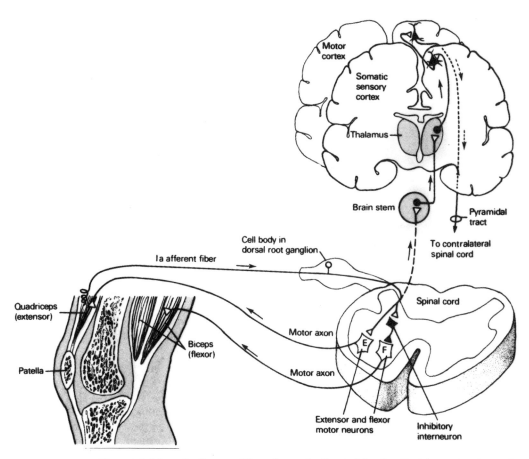

Figure 2.9 Schematic diagram of the pathways for the stretch reflex. Stretch receptors in muscle spindles react to changes in length of the muscle, and afferent fibers carry this information along the dorsal roots to the spinal cord where they synapse on extensor motoneurons, which extend the knee, and inhibitory interneurons, which reduce activity in motor neurons that produce contractions of the antagonistic flexor muscles. Both of these actions combine to produce a coordinated expression of the knee-jerk reflex. This information is also conveyed to higher brain centers, which in turn can modify the reflex behavior through descending pathways to the spinal cord. (From Kandel 1985.)

V1, are arranged topographically, in the sense that adjacent neurons have adjacent visual receptive fields and collectively they constitute a map of the retina. Because neighboring processing units (cell bodies and dendrites) are concerned with similar representations, topographic mapping is an important means whereby the brain manages to save on wire and also to share wire (Mead 1989). It is significant that the maps are distorted, in the sense that some regions of the body surface occupy larger regions of cortex than others. The fovea, for example, occupies a relatively large part of V1, and the hands occupy a relatively large area of the somatosensory cortex. In visual area MT of the macaque, which contains many neurons selective for direction of motion, the lower half of the visual field has greater representation than the

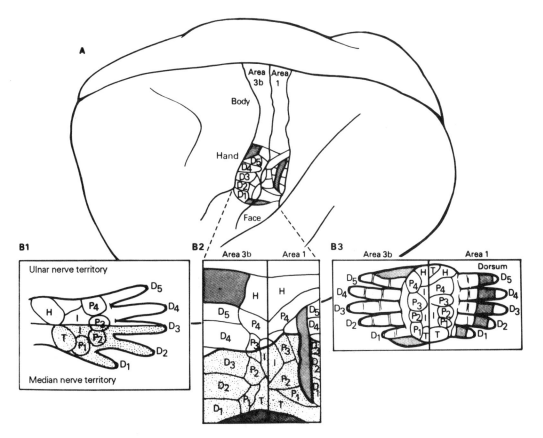

Figure 2.10 Schematic drawing of the multiple representations of the body surface in the primary somatic sensory cortex of the owl monkey. Because the cortex of the owl monkey is relatively flat, most of the body representation is located on the surface rather than in the convolutions found in the species of most other primates. (A) Two representations of the hand are shown in areas 3b and 1. (B) The hand of the owl monkey is innervated by the median and ulnar nerves, which have different territory on the ventral surface (B1) and are represented in adjacent areas of cortex in each of the two maps (B2). The topographical organization of the cortical map for the ventral surface of the hand is highly ordered (B3) in both areas. Cortex devoted to the ventral surface is indicated in white; that devoted to the dorsal surface, in dark shading. D_1 to D_5, digits; P_1 to P_4, palmar pads; I, insular pad; H, hypothenar pads; T, thenar pads. (From Kandel and Schwartz 1985).

upper half. This makes sense because it is the lower half of the visual field where hand skills—searching for termites, picking up lice, and so forth— require the greatest acuity (Maunsell and van Essen 1987.)[7]

In the visual systems of monkeys, physiologists have found about 25 distinct areas, most of which are topographically mapped.[8] A similar hierarchy of multiple topographic maps is found for body location in the somatosensory system (Kaas et al. 1979; figure 2.10), for frequency in the auditory system (Merzenich and Brugge 1973), and for muscle groups in the motor system (Ferrier 1876, Asanuma 1973). One possible exception is the olfactory system, but even odors may be spatially organized at the level of the olfactory bulb (Stewart et al. 1979). To some extent the different sensory maps can be distinguished by differences in the fine details in the laminations of neurons (see next section) and their cellular properties, but often these are so subtle that only physiological techniques can distinguish boundaries between different cortical areas.

Some brainstem structures, such as the superior colliculus, also display this organization. The cerebellum appears to have patches of partial maps, though the principles do not seem clear, and these areas may not be maps in any real sense at all. Some areas seem to lack a strong topographic organization, and for other areas the topographic organization is quite complex, for example the basal ganglia (Selemon and Goldman-Rakic 1988). Cortical areas anterior to the central sulcus seem sparser in topographic maps, but research may show that what they map are abstract, not sensory, representations, and hence such maps cannot be discovered by methods used to establish response patterns to peripheral stimuli. In bat auditory cortex there are topographic mappings of abstract properties such as frequency differences and time delays between emitted and received sounds, properties that may help the bat to echolocate prey (Suga et al. 1984), and in the barn owl internal spatial maps are synthesized from binaural auditory inputs (Konishi 1986, Knudsen et al. 1987). There are some areas of cortex, such as association areas, parietal cortex, and some parts of frontal cortex, for which it has not yet been possible to find properties that form orderly mappings. Nonetheless, projections between these areas remain topographic. For example, Goldman-Rakic (1987) has shown that in the monkey projections from parietal cortex to target areas in the prefrontal cortex, such as the principal sulcus, preserve the topographic order of the source neurons.

Maps of the surface of the body in the brain are formed during development by projections that become ordered, in part, through competitive interactions between adjacent fibers in the target maps (see chapter 5). Some of the neurons undergo cell death during this period, and with the possible exception of olfactory receptors, no new neurons are formed in the mature mammal (Cowan et al. 1984). However, competitive interactions between neurons continue, to some extent, even in adulthood, since the territory in cortex devoted to a particular part of the body surface can shift as much as 1–2 cm, but not much farther, weeks after injury to sensory nerves or after excessive sensory stimulation (Pons et al. 1991). Thus, regions in somatosensory cortex that are silenced following denervation of a sensory nerve will eventually become responsive to nearby regions of the body. It is not yet known how much of this rearrangement is due to plasticity in cerebral cortex, or perhaps in subcortical structures that project to cortical maps. Auditory maps, particularly in the superior colliculus, are also modifiable both in development, and in the adult following partial deafness (King and Moore, 1991). Nonetheless, this evidence, and further evidence for synaptic plasticity summarized below, make it difficult to think of the machinery in the adult brain as "hardwired," or static. Rather, the brain has a remarkable ability to adapt to changes in the environment, at many different structural levels and over a wide range of time scales.

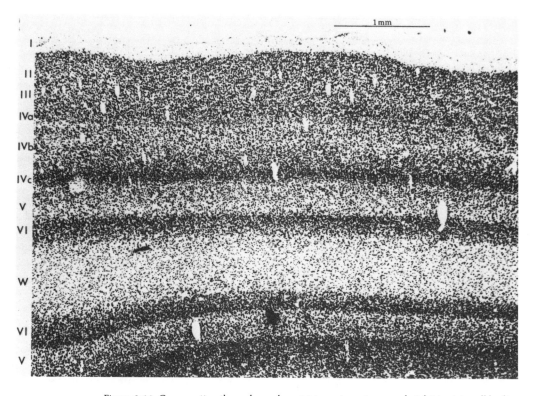

Figure 2.11 Cross-section through monkey striate cortex using cresyl violet to stain cell bodies. Laminations are clearly visible; the layers are numbered at the left. W, white matter. Deeper layers of the buried fold of cortex are shown in the lower part of the figure. (From Hubel and Wiesel 1977.)

Layers and Columns

Many brain areas display not only topographic organization, but also laminar organization (figures 2.11, 2.12). Laminae are layers (sheets) of neurons in register with other layers, and a given lamina conforms to a highly regular pattern of where it projects to and from where it receives projections. For example, the superior colliculus receives visual input in superficial layers, and in deeper layers it receives tactile and auditory input. Neurons in an intermediate layer of the superior colliculus represent information about eye movements. In the cerebral cortex, specific sensory input from the thalamus typically projects to layer 4, the middle layer, while output to subcortical motor structures issues from layer 5, and intracortical projections originate chiefly in (superficial) layers 2 and 3. Layer 6 mainly projects back to the thalamus (see figure 2.3). The basal ganglia do not have a laminar organization, but rather a patchwork of islands which can be distinguished by developmental and chemical markers (Graybiel and Hickey 1982).

As well as the horizontal organization seen in laminae, cortical structures also display vertical organization. This organization consists in a high degree of commonality between cells in vertical columns, crossing laminae, and is

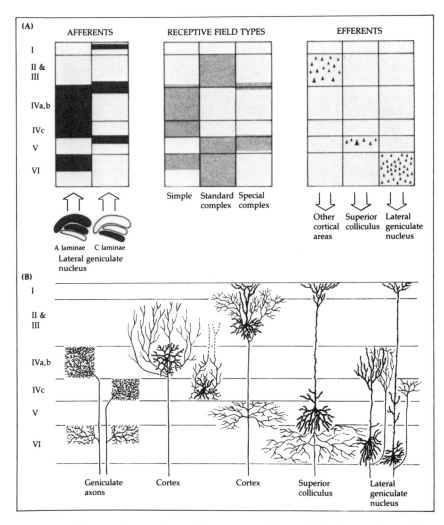

Figure 2.12 Schematic diagram of cortical connections in the cat. (A) Distribution of inputs from layers of the lateral geniculate, showing that geniculate axons project to different cortical laminae as a function of layer of origin in the geniculate. Cortical neurons with similar receptive field properties cluster together in particular lamina. The origin of fibers leaving a region of cortex varies as a function of target. (B) Schematic arborization patterns of the main cell types in laminae I–VI. (After Gilbert and Wiesel 1981.)

reflected both anatomically in terms of local connections between neurons (Martin 1984, Lund 1987) and physiologically in terms of similar response properties (Hubel and Wiesel 1962). For example, a vertical penetration of an electrode in visual cortex reveals cells which share a preference for stimuli with the same orientation (e.g., a bar of light oriented at about 20° from the horizontal). Another vertical penetration nearby will show cells which prefer a different orientation. Inputs and outputs are also organized in columns, such as the ocular dominance columns in V1, and inputs into the principal sulcus which alternate between parietal projections from the same side and projections from the principal sulcus in the opposite hemisphere (Goldman-Rakic 1987).

Typically, the vertically organized connectivity patterns do not result in columns with sharp boundaries, and the response properties tend to vary continuously across the cortex. Hence the expression "vertical column" may be slightly misleading. Thus for cells in visual area V1, orientation varies over the cortex smoothly, save for some fractures and singularities (Blasdel and Salama 1986), and a similar organization can be found in area V2 (Swindale et al. 1987), which receives a topographically mapped projection from V1. There are, however, places where vertical, cross-laminar columns with quite sharp boundaries are seen, for example the ocular dominance columns in layer 4 of area V1 and the "barrels" in the rodent somatosensory cortex, where each barrel contains cells preferentially sensitive to stimulation of a particular whisker (Woolsey and van der Loos 1970) (figure 2.13). Sharp anatomical boundaries are, however, the exception rather than the rule. Also, the spatial scale of columnar organization can vary from about 0.3 mm for ocular dominance columns to 25 μm for orientation columns in monkey visual cortex.

Topographic mapping, columnar organization, and laminae are special cases of a more general principle: the exploitation of geometric properties in information processing design. Spatial proximity may be an efficient way for biological systems to assemble in one place information needed to solve a problem. To consider a simple case, suppose it is necessary to compare differences between stimuli at neighboring locations, where comparison requires signals be brought together. Then topographic organization may achieve this efficiently while minimizing the total length of the connections. This is desirable since most of the volume of the brain is filled with axonal processes, and there are limitations on how big the brain can be as well as temporal tolerances that must be met. Lateral inhibitory interactions within the spatial maps are used to make comparisons, enhance contrast at borders, and perform automatic gain control. Mutual inhibition within a population of neurons can be used to identify the neuron with the maximum activity, a type of winner-take-all circuit (Feldman and Ballard 1982). (See also chapter 5, last section.)

Local Networks

Within a cubic millimeter of cortical tissue, there are approximately 10^5 neurons and about 10^9 synapses, with the vast majority of these synapses arising from cells located within cortex (Douglas and Martin 1991) (figure 2.14). These

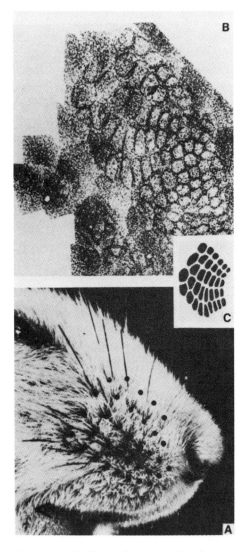

Figure 2.13 (A) Snout of a mouse; the vibrissae (whiskers) are marked by dots. (B) Sections across the somatosensory cortex that receive input from the snout. Each of the rings or "barrels" corresponds to an individual vibrissa, and are spatially organized to preserve the neighborhood relations of the vibrissae (C). (Reprinted with permission from Woolsey and van der Loos 1970.)

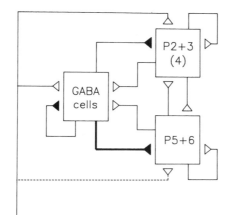

Thalamus

Figure 2.14 Schematic diagram of a microcircuit in the cerebral cortex that may be repeated again and again. Three populations of neurons interact with each other: inhibitory (GABA) cells, shown with solid synapses; and excitatory cells (open synapses) representing (i) superficial (P2 + 3) and (ii) deep (P5 + 6) layer pyramidal cells. Each population receives excitatory input from the thalamus, which is weaker (dashed line) to deep pyramidal cells. (Reprinted with permission from Douglas et al. 1989.)

local networks have been very difficult to study owing to the complexity of the tangled mass of axons, synapses, and dendrites called the neuropil. Nevertheless, some general features of local networks are beginning to emerge. For example, the orientation tuning of cells in V1 must emerge from nonoriented inputs and activity in local networks in ways that we are just beginning to understand (Ferster and Koch 1987).

Most of the data available on local networks are based on single-unit recordings, and to achieve a deeper understanding of the principles governing networks, it will be necessary to monitor a large population of neurons (see Appendix for recording techniques). Even a local network involves many cells, but only small populations can be studied by exhaustive sequential recordings from single cells. Consequently, we run the risk of generalizing from an atypical sample, and of missing circuit properties that can be inferred only from a richer profile. Therefore, to understand the principles of local networks, much more work must be done to determine the dynamical traffic within a larger population of cells over an extended period of time (figure 2.15).

Computer simulations may help to interpret single-unit data by showing how a population of cells could represent properties of objects and perform coordinate transformations. For example, network models of spatial representations have been constructed that help to explain the response properties of single cells in parietal cortex (Andersen and Mountcastle 1983, Zipser and Andersen 1988; figure 2.16). Another network model has been used to explain how the responses of single neurons in visual cortex area V4 could compute color constancy (Zeki 1983, Hurlbert and Poggio 1988). Network simulations can also suggest alternative interpretations for known response properties. For

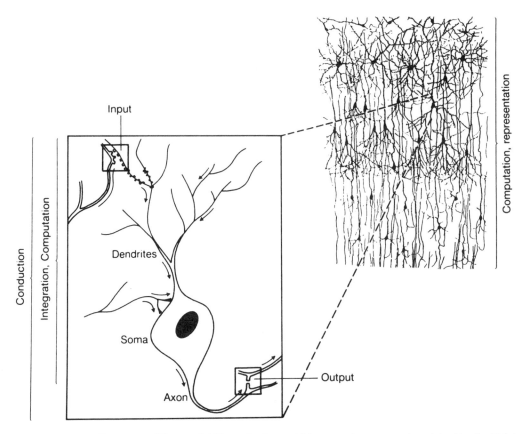

Figure 2.15 (Upper right) Network of pyramidal neurons in mouse cortex, stained by the Golgi method, which stains only about 10% of the population. (Lower left) Schematic of a generalized neuron showing one of its inputs to a dendrite, one to the cell body, and one of its axonal contacts. (Reprinted with permission from Dudai *The Neurobiology of Memory: Concepts, Findings, and Trends* [1989]. Copyright © Oxford University Press.)

example, there are certain oriented cells in V1 whose response summates with the length of the slit or edge of light up to the borders of the receptive field, but then the response diminishes as the length increases. This property, called "end-stopping," has recently been related to the extraction of the 1-D curvature of contours (Dobbins et al. 1987) and the 2-D curvature of shapes in shaded images (Lehky and Sejnowski 1988). An example of this approach is given in chapter 4 on visual processing.

Neurons

Ever since Cajal's work in the late nineteenth century, the neuron has been taken as an elementary unit of processing in the nervous system (figure 2.17). In contrast to Golgi, who believed neurons formed a continuous "reticulum," or feltwork, Cajal argued that neurons were distinct, individual cells, separated from each other by a spatial gap, and that mechanisms additional to those operating intracellularly would have to be found to explain how the signal

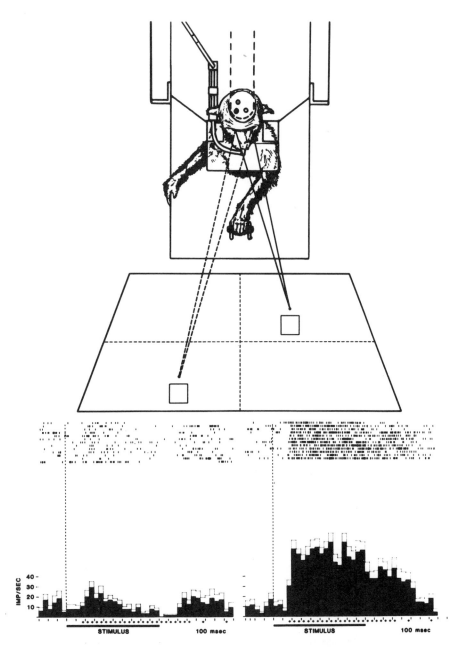

Figure 2.16 Illustration of the single-unit technique used to study the response of neurons in the parietal cortex of an awake, behaving monkey. The animal fixated a small target light placed at a series of positions on the screen, with its head fixed. The results obtained at two positions are shown here. At each fixation position a square was flashed for 1 sec at 10° above the point of fixation. Recordings from a single neuron are shown below the screen. Each line represents a single trial, and each small nick made on the line represents the discharge of an impulse by the neuron. The impulses were summed in the histograms on the bottom panel. The right side of the figure shows the responses for fixation to the left and down, and the left side shows the responses for fixation to the right and up. This and other experiments show that this class of neurons in parietal cortex has receptive fields that are specific to a retinal location, but the degree of activation of the neuron to a visual stimulus within the receptive field is modulated by the position of the eye. (See also chapter 4, section 10.) (From Andersen and Mountcastle 1983.)

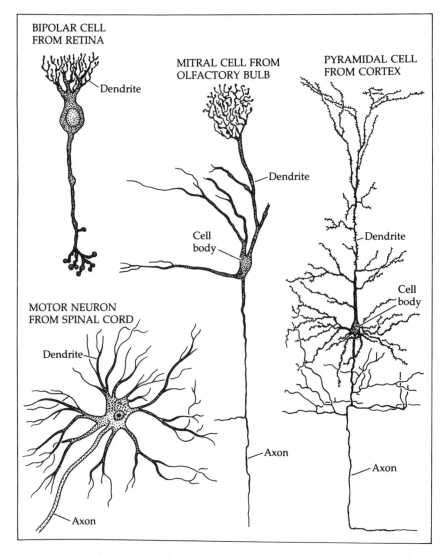

BIPOLAR CELL
FROM RETINA

Dendrite

MITRAL CELL FROM
OLFACTORY BULB

Dendrite

Cell
body

PYRAMIDAL CELL
FROM CORTEX

Dendrite

Cell
body

MOTOR NEURON
FROM SPINAL CORD

Dendrite

Axon

Axon

Axon

Figure 2.17 Examples of neurons illustrating the variety of shapes in different areas of the brain. (With permission from Kuffler, Nicholls and Martin [1984]. *From Neuron to Brain*. Sunderland MA: Sinauer Associates.)

passed from neuron to neuron. Physiological studies have borne out Cajal's judgment, though in some areas such as the retina, syncytia of cells that are electrically coupled have been found (Dowling 1987). As it turns out, these are rather more like the structures Golgi predicted because the cells are physically joined by conducting "gap junctions." These electrical synapses are faster and more reliable than chemical transmission, but are more limited in flexibility.

There are many different types of neurons, and different parts of the nervous system have evolved neurons with specialized properties. There are five general types of neurons in the retina, for example, each with a highly distinctive morphology, connectivity pattern, physiological properties, and embryological origin. In recent years, moreover, physiological and chemical differences

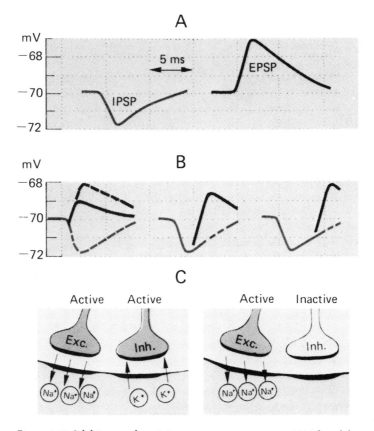

Figure 2.18 Inhibitory and excitatory synapses on a neuron. (A) The inhibitory postsynaptic potential (IPSP) means that the postsynaptic cell hyperpolarizes (dropping from −70 mV to −72 mV), and the excitatory postsynaptic potential (EPSP) means that the postsynaptic cell depolarizes (from −70 mV to −67 mV). (B) The EPSP was triggered about 1, 3, and 5 msec after the onset of the IPSP. (C) The subsynaptic conductance changes occurring when excitatory and inhibitory synapses are activated simultaneously (left) and when only the excitatory synapse is activated (right). (From Schmidt [1978]. *Fundamentals of Neurophysiology*. Berlin: Springer-Verlag.)

have been found within classes. For example, 23 different types of ganglion cells (whose axons project to the brain through the optic nerve) and 22 different types of amacrine cells (which provide lateral interactions and temporal differentiation) have been identified (Sterling et al. 1983). There are seven general types of neurons in the cerebellum and about 12 general types in the neocortex, with many subtypes distinguishable by their chemical properties such as the neurotransmitters they contain. The definition of a neuronal type is somewhat arbitrary, since judgments are often made on the basis of subtle morphological differences, which can be graded rather than categorical. As more chemical markers are found, however, it is becoming clear that the diversity of neurons within cerebral cortex has been vastly underestimated. On anatomical and immunocytochemical criteria, therefore, the number of subtypes of cortical neurons is probably between 50 and 500 (Sereno 1988).

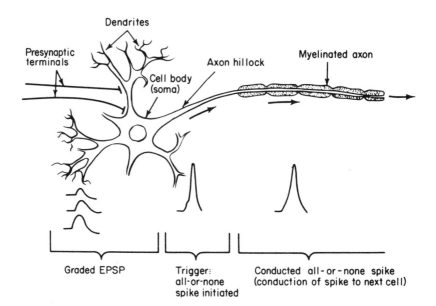

Figure 2.19 Summary diagram showing the location on a motor neuron of various electrical events. In many neurons, dendrites and cell bodies respond with graded EPSPs or IPSPs; the action potential is triggered in the axon hillock and travels undiminished down the axon. (From Thompson 1967.)

On the basis of their effects, neurons divide in two general classes: excitatory and inhibitory (figures 2.18, 2.19). The effect of an excitatory signal is to increase the probability that the postsynaptic cell fires, and the effect of an inhibitory signal is to decrease that probability (figure 2.19). Some neurons also have modulatory effects on other neurons, principally by releasing peptides or monoamines (see section 4). Another useful classification concerns projections: some cells ramify only within a confined area such as a column, for example stellate cells in cortex; other neurons, such as pyramidal cells, have long-range projections out of an area, where the route goes via the white matter rather than directly through the cortex itself. Research on the properties of neurons shows that they are much more complex processing devices than previously imagined (table 2.1). For example, dendrites of neurons are themselves highly specialized, and some parts can probably act as independent processing units (Shepherd et al. 1985, Koch and Poggio 1987).

Synapses

Chemical synapses are found in nervous systems throughout phylogeny, and they are a basic unit of structure that has been highly conserved during evolution. A synaptic bouton has a surface area of a few square micrometers and forms a highly stereotyped apposition with the postsynaptic membrane, which itself is highly specialized (figure 2.20). Synapses are the primary gateways by which neurons communicate with one another, and they consist of specialized

Table 2.1 Selected biophysical mechanisms, possible neural operations they could implement, and computations they might help perform

Biophysical Mechanism	Neural Operation	Example of Computation
Action potential initiation	Analog OR/AND one-bit analog-to-digital converter	
Repetitive spiking activity	Current-to-frequency transducer	
Action potential conduction	Impulse transmission	Long-distance communication in axons
Conduction failure at axonal branch points	Temporal/spatial filtering of impulses	Opener muscle in crayfish
Chemically mediated synaptic transduction	Nonreciprocal two-port "negative" resistance Sigmoid "threshold"	
Electrically mediated synaptic transduction	Reciprocal one-port resistance	Coupling of rod photoreceptors to enhance detection of signals
Distributed excitatory synapses in dendritic tree	Linear addition	α, β cat retinal ganglion cells Bipolar cells
Interaction between excitatory and (silent) inhibitory conductance inputs	Analog AND-NOT, veto operation	Directional-selective retinal ganglion cells Disparity-selective cortical cells
Excitatory synapse on dendritic spine with calcium channels	Postsynaptic modification in functional connectivity	Short- and long-term information storage
Excitatory and inhibitory synapses on dendritric spine	Local AND-NOT "presynaptic inhibition"	Enabling/disabling retinal input to geniculate X-cells
Quasi-active membranes	Electrical resonant filter analog Differentiation delay	Hair cells in lower vertebrates
Transmitter regulation of voltage-dependent channels (M-current inhibition)	Gain control	Midbrain sites controlling gain of retinogeniculate transmission
Calcium sensitivity of cAMP-dependent phosphorylation of potassium channel protein	Functional connectivity	Adaptation and associative storage of information in *Aplysia*
Long-distance action of neurotransmitter	Modulating and routing transmission of information	

From Koch and Poggio (1987).

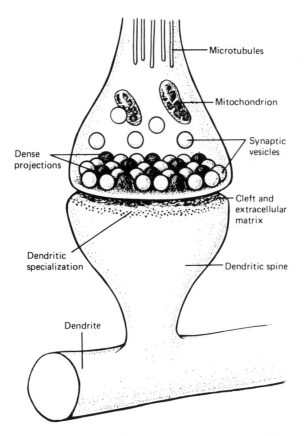

Figure 2.20 Schematic diagram of a synapse on a dendritic spine. Dense projections in the presynaptic membrane are surrounded by vesicles that presumably contain neurotransmitter molecules. This morphology characterizes a type I synapse, which is excitatory. Type II synapses (not shown) have flattened vesicles as viewed in the electron microscope following glutaraldehyde fixation, and they are often inhibitory. (From Gershon et al. 1985.)

presynaptic structures for the release of neurochemicals and postsynaptic structures for receiving and responding to those neurochemicals. Evidence is accumulating that signaling between neurons at synapses can be selectively altered by experience (Alkon 1984). Other, structural components of neurons might also be modified through experience, such as the shape and topology of dendrites as well as the spatial distribution of membrane channels (Purves and Voyvodic 1987).

Our understanding of the nervous system at the subcellular level is changing rapidly, and it is apparent that neurons are dynamic and complex entities whose computational properties cannot be approximated by memoryless response functions, a common idealization. It remains an open scientific question how the integrity of memories that span decades can remain intact if the neural substrate is as fluid as preliminary reports indicate, especially if, as it seems, networks of neurons both process and store information.

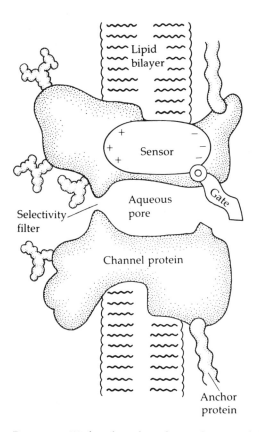

Figure 2.21 Working hypothesis for a voltage-gated channel. The transmembrane protein is shown with a pore that allows sodium ions to flow between the extracellular and intracellular sides of the membrane when the gate is open. (With permission from Hille [1984]. *Ionic Channels of Excitable Membranes.* Sunderland MA: Sinauer Associates.)

Molecules

The integrity of neurons and synapses depends on the properties of membranes and the internal cytoskeleton of the neuron. The membrane serves as a barrier a few nanometers (10^{-9}) thick separating the intracellular and extracellular aqueous compartments. The membrane itself is a two-dimensional fluid medium in which integral membrane proteins and other molecules form associations. Some integral membrane proteins have an important role in maintaining the ionic milieu inside and outside the cell. For example, membrane proteins that serve as ion channels can be voltage sensitive,[9] chemically activated, or both. They may thus permit or prevent the passage of ions across the membrane, which in turn can affect the propagation of a signal down the length of the axon or neurotransmitter release at the presynaptic terminal (figure 2.21). In a sense, the membrane allows the intracellular compartment of a neuron to respond selectively to extracellular signals, and it is this selectivity that endows different neurons with specialized information-processing capabilities. Axon membrane typically contains channels and conductances that permit it to spike when depolarization reaches a certain threshold. Exactly how dendrite membrane works is much less well understood. Dendrite spiking has been seen in the cerebellum (Llinás and Sugimori 1980), and the conventional wisdom according to which axon membrane is "active" while dendrite membrane is "passive" is undoubtedly a simplification that obscures the subtle, complex, and computationally critical respects in which dendrite membrane is active.

Electrical signaling in neurons is achieved by ionic currents which are regulated by ion channels and ion pumps in the cell membrane. Signaling between neurons is mediated by neurotransmitter receptors in the postsynaptic membrane that respond to particular neurotransmitter molecules by transiently and selectively changing the ionic conductance of the membrane. There are also receptor molecules along the membrane outside of the synaptic site that appear to be functional, but their role is not known (Somogyi et al. 1989). In addition, some receptors can activate one or more second-messenger molecules that can mediate longer-term changes (figure 2.22). Second-messengers in neurons can be activated by more than one receptor. Hence there is a network of interacting chemical systems within a neuron, which can itself be considered a chemical parallel distributed processor.

4   A SHORT LIST OF BRAIN FACTS

A central part of the basic strategy for figuring out how a novel device works is reverse engineering. That is, when a new camera or chip appears on the market, competitors will take it apart to find out how it works. Typically, of course, they already know quite a lot about devices of that general kind, so the problem can be manageable. Although we have to use reverse engineering to study the brain, our starting point is much further back, inasmuch as we know so little about devices of that general kind. From our vantage point, the brain is essentially a bit of alien technology, and hence it is especially difficult to know, among the facts available to us, which are theoretically important and which are theoretically uninteresting. We may actually misunderstand some aspects of brain organization and as a consequence be blocked from having some important insight into mechanisms crucial for cognition. For example, some distinctions made in gross anatomy may turn out to conceal close relationships between distant brain regions, or it may turn out that the functional properties of some synapses in the central nervous system are very different from peripheral synapses in autonomic ganglia and neuromuscular junctions, which have been very well studied.

Since this chapter looks at neuroscience against a background of computational aims, it seems appropriate to raise this question: what are the most basic structural features relevant to neural computation? It goes without saying that many more constraints will be relevant in the context of a specific problem, but we present these 13 as a kind of prolegomenon to problems generally. Short of having formally conducted a proper survey, we conjecture that the following baker's dozen are among those likely to find their way on to a must-know list,

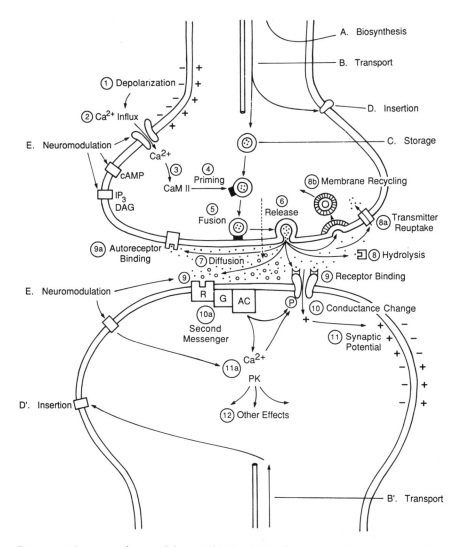

Figure 2.22 Summary of some of the main biochemical mechanisms that have been identified at chemical synapses. A–E, Long-term steps in synthesis, transport, and storage of neurotransmitters and neuromodulators; insertion of membrane channel proteins and receptors, and neuromodulatory effects. 1–12, these summarize the more rapid steps involved in immediate signaling at the synapse. IP$_3$, inositol triphosphate; CaM II, Ca^{2+}/calmodulin-dependent protein kinase II; DAG, diacylglycerol; PK, protein kinase; R, receptor; G, G protein; AC, adenylate cyclase. (Reprinted with permission from Shepherd 1988.)

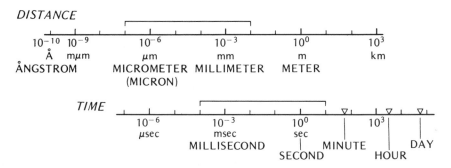

Figure 2.23 Logarithmic scales for spatial and temporal magnitudes. Brackets indicate the scales especially relevant to synaptic processing. (Reprinted with permission from Shepherd 1979.)

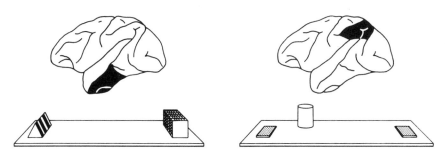

Object Discrimination   **Landmark Discrimination**

Figure 2.24 Two behavioral tasks that distinguish between the functions of the inferior temporal (IT) and posterior parietal (PP) cortex. (Left) IT lesions, in black, cause a severe impairment in learning to discriminate between two objects based on their features, but the lesions do not affect spatial capacities. (Right) PP lesions cause an impairment to spatial tasks, such as judging which of two identical plaques is closer to a visual landmark (cylinder), but do not affect object discrimination learning. (From Mishkin, Ungerleider and Macko [1983]. Object vision and spatial vision: two cortical pathways. *Trends in Neurosciences* 6: 414–417.)

although we understand very well that opinion can diverge in considerable and surprising ways, and also that a current list will undoubtedly be quickly outdated (for comparable lists, see Crick and Asanuma 1986 and Shepherd 1988). (See figure 2.23 for scales of magnitudes.)

1. *Specialization of Function* There is specialization of function in different regions of nervous systems. This is a ubiquitous and critical feature of nervous system organization, seen in animals from the lowly leech to the human. The specialization enjoyed by regions more distant from the periphery, such as orbitalfrontal cortex of humans, is difficult to determine, though by using a convergence of techniques, including lesions, staining, single-cell recording, evoked potential, and developmental data, the range of likely possibilities can be narrowed (figure 2.24). Specialization so characterized is actually a large-grain feature of an area, based on the statistical distribution of cell response properties and the major input and output pathways. Thus V1, for example, is referred to as a visual area and S1 as a somatosensory area. At a finer grain,

however, the specialization of areas is consistent with the existence of atypical cell types and connectivity. Thus while the preponderance of tested cells in V1 are indeed visually tuned, there exist some cells coding for nonvisual signals, such as eye movement.

2. *Numbers: Neurons and Synapses* The estimated number of neurons in the human nervous system is about 10^{12}; the number of synapses is about 10^{15}. The rat brain has about 10^{10} neurons, and about 10^{13} synapses. In 1 mm^3 of cortical tissue there are about 10^5 neurons and 10^9 synapses. A handy rule of thumb is 1 synapse/μm^3. A single neuron may have thousands or tens of thousands of synapses. Stevens (1989) has calculated that the number of synapses per neuron for a piece of cortex 1 mm thick from a cat or a monkey is 4.12×10^3. The main exception to this is the primary visual cortex of primates, where cells are more densely packed and the number of synapses is about 1.17×10^3 for a piece of cortex 1 mm thick.

3. *Numbers: Connectivity (Who Talks to Whom)* Not everything is connected to everything else. Each cortical neuron is connected to a roughly constant number of other neurons, irrespective of brain size, namely about 3% of the neurons underlying the surrounding square millimeter of cortex (Stevens 1989). Hence, although the absolute number of input lines to a cortical neuron may be quite large, cortical neurons are actually rather sparsely connected relative to the population of neurons in a cell's neighborhood. Most connections are between, not within, cell classes (Sereno 1988). Forward projections to one area are generally matched by recurrent projections back to the area of origin.

4. *Analog Inputs/Discrete Outputs* The input to a neuron is analog (continuous values between 0 and 1), and a neuron's output is discrete (either it spikes or it does not), though some neurons may have analog outputs. Whether a neuron has an output is governed by a threshold rule; that is, whether the cell spikes depends on whether the integration of the inputs exceeds a certain threshold. The profusion of input lines to a single neuron probably represents sensible computational and engineering design for a network of neurons with these properties (Abu-Mostafa 1989a).[10]

5. *Timing: General Considerations* Getting the timing right is an essential feature of nervous systems and, more particularly, of analog computation (Mead 1989). Whether and how dendritic signals traveling soma-wards will interact depends on the time of their arrival at the common node. The magnitude of signals eventually reaching the axon hillock depends on such interactions. In perception, the time scale of the computation must be matched to the time scale of events in the external world, and in motor control it must be matched to the time it takes for the body parts to move (Mead 1989). When outputs of different computational components need to be integrated, the time scales of the various processors contributing values must also match. In short, the system has to operate in real time. Hence nervous systems must be architecturally rigged so that when a process takes time, it takes the right amount of time.

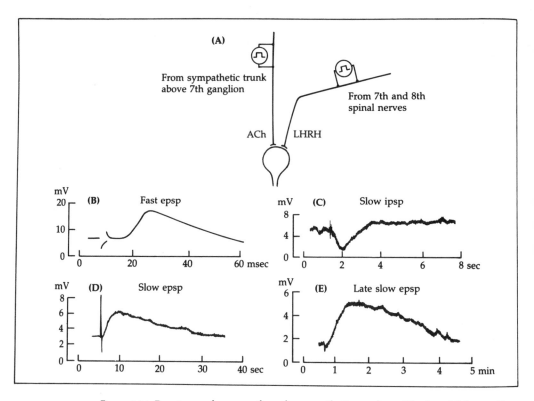

Figure 2.25 Four types of synapses from the sympathetic ganglion of the frog. (A) Innervation of a sympathetic neuron in the ninth ganglion of the paravertebral chain of the bullfrog; the diagram shows the separation of the cholinergic (ACh) and noncholinergic (LHRH) innervation. (B) A single preganglionic stimulus produces a fast EPSP. (C) Repetitive stimulation produces a slow IPSP lasting about 2 sec; the fast EPSP is blocked with a nicotinic blocking agent. (D) Repetitive stimulation also produces a slow EPSP which occurs after the first two responses and lasts about 30 sec. (E) The late slow EPSP, produced by stimulating preganglionic fibers, lasts more than 5 min after repetitive stimulation. (With permission from Kuffler, Nicholls and Martin [1984]. *From Neuron to Brain.* Sunderland MA: Sinauer Associates.)

6. *Timing: Particular Values* An action potential (spike) lasts about 1 msec. Synaptic transmission, including electrotonic conduction in dendrites, takes about 5 msec. Synaptic potentials can last from a millisecond to many minutes (Kuffler 1980) (figure 2.25). Transmission velocity in myelinated axons is about 10–100 meters/sec; in unmyelinated axons it is less than 1 meter/sec. These are general ranges, not precise values.

7. *Cell-to-cell Effects* The effect of an individual synaptic input on a post-synaptic cell is weak, amounting to 1%–5% of the firing threshold. There may be some important exceptions to this trend, such as the strong effects of an individual synapse of a chandelier cell or a basket cell in the cerebral cortex (Martin 1984).

8. *Firing Patterns* Different types of neurons have different firing patterns (figure 2.26). Some neurons in the thalamus have multiple intrinsic firing patterns, and the particular pattern displayed on a given occasion is a function of

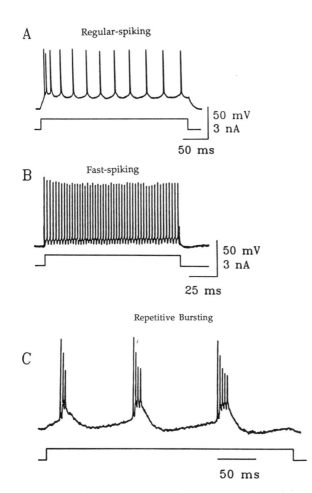

A Regular-spiking

50 mV
3 nA

50 ms

B Fast-spiking

50 mV
3 nA

25 ms

Repetitive Bursting

C

50 ms

Figure 2.26 Differences in intrinsic firing patterns of cortical neurons. (A) When stimulated with a suprathreshold step of depolarizing current, regular-spiking neurons respond with an initial high-frequency spike output that rapidly declines to much lower sustained frequencies. Intracellular voltages are displayed in the top trace, injected current steps in the bottom trace. (B) Under similar conditions, fast-spiking cells generate high frequencies that are sustained for the duration of the stimulus. (C) Repetitive intrinsic bursting to a prolonged stimulus. Mean interburst frequency was about 9 Hz. (From Connors and Gutnick [1990]. Intrinsic firing patterns of diverse neocortical neurons. *Trends in Neurosciences* 13: 98–99.)

the cell's recent depolarization or hyperpolarization history (Llinás and Jahnsen 1982). The ionic conductances of some cells, for example in the brain stem, endow those cells with oscillatory properties. Such a cell may act as a pacemaker or as a resonator (responding preferentially to certain firing frequencies) (Llinás 1988). Most neurons are spontaneously active, spiking at random intervals in the absence of input. Different neuron types have different characteristic spontaneous rates, ranging from a few spikes per second to about 50 spikes per second.

9. *Receptive Fields: Size and Center-Surround Organization* Under the classical definition, the receptive field is that region of the sensory field from which an adequate sensory stimulus will elicit a response. In the somatosensory system,

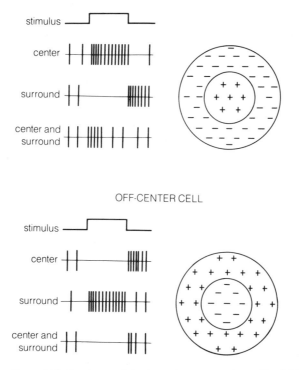

ON-CENTER CELL

OFF-CENTER CELL

Figure 2.27 Two types of circular center–surround receptive fields in the retina. When the light is shone on the center of the receptive field, the on-center cell responds vigorously, the off-center cell is silent. When the light is shone in the annular surround, the opposite effect is achieved. Under diffuse illumination of both the center and the surround, both cells respond weakly. (With permission from Coren Ward [1989]. *Sensation and Perception*, 3rd ed. Copyright © 1989 Harcourt Brace Jovanovich, Inc.)

the receptive field size varies over the body surface: those for the fingertips are smaller than those for the palm of the hand, and very much smaller than those for the arm. Receptive fields of cells in higher areas of visual cortex tend to be much larger than those in the earlier stages (one sixth of a degree in the foveal region of V1, compared to values ranging from 10 to the whole visual field in inferotemporal cortex). Retinal ganglion cells (cells carrying signals from the retina) have what is called a *center-surround organization* (figures 2.27, 2.28). This organization comes in two variations: (1) a stimulus in the center of the cell's receptive field excites it, but a stimulus in an area surrounding the receptive field inhibits it. This arrangement is known as "on-center/off-surround." (2) The opposite arrangement, namely, a central stimulus inhibits but a surround stimulus excites the cell, is known as "off-center/on-surround." Off-center cells respond maximally to dark spots, while on-center cells respond maximally to light spots. The information carried by the ganglion cells pertains to the comparison between the amount of light falling on the center of the field and the average amount of light falling on the surround, not absolute values of light intensity at the transducer. A center-surround organization is also evident in

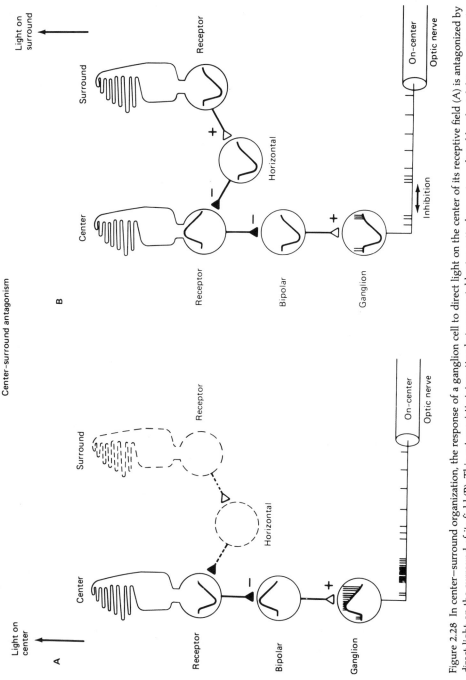

Center-surround antagonism

Figure 2.28 In center–surround organization, the response of a ganglion cell to direct light on the center of its receptive field (A) is antagonized by direct light on the surround of its field (B). This antagonistic interaction between neighboring retinal areas is mediated by the inhibitory action of a horizontal cell. (Reprinted with permission from Kandel and Schwartz 1985.)

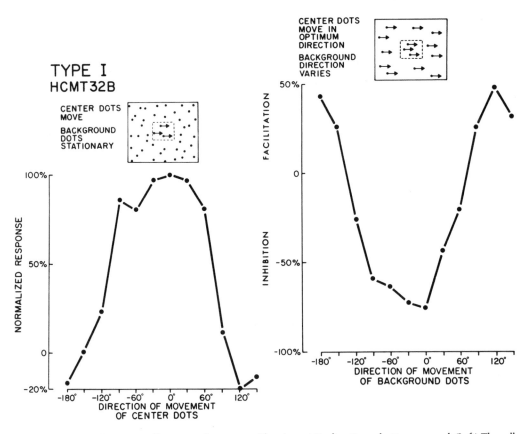

Figure 2.29 Response of a neuron with antagonistic direction-selective surround. (Left) The cell responds vigorously when the dots in the center of the stimulus move (shown above) in the preferred direction but the dots in the surround are stationary. Negative percentages in the graph indicate inhibition relative to the level of spontaneous activity. (Right) The same cell responds very differently to its preferred direction of motion in the center when the dots in the surround also move in the cell's preferred direction. (From Allman et al. 1985.)

the receptive fields of somatosensory neurons in the thalamus and cortex (Mountcastle 1957) (figures 2.27, 2.28).

10. *Receptive Fields: Nonclassical* Events outside the classical receptive field of a cell have been found to modulate selectively the responses of the cell (Nelson and Frost 1978, Allman et al. 1985) (figure 2.29). The effects are selective since they vary as a function of the type of surround stimuli. Nelson and Frost (1985) reported an inhibition as well as a highly specific form of facilitation of the responses of orientation-tuned cells in visual cortex of cats as a nonclassical field effect. Some area 17 cells that were normally responsive to a vertical bar in their receptive fields showed enhanced responses when distant[11] area 17 cells, co-oriented and co-axial to the first, were experimentally stimulated. Zeki (1983) has shown that certain wavelength-dependent neurons in V4 are influenced by the color balance in the surround. The surround effects of cells in the middle temporal (MT) area, where receptive fields are typically $5°-10°$, can extend $40°-80°$ (Allman et al. 1985). Receptive fields are almost certainly more dynamical than previously assumed. For example, repeated stimulation

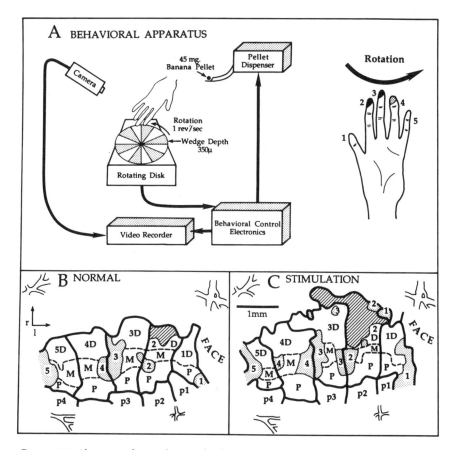

Figure 2.30 Alteration of cortical maps after habitual stimulation. (A) The experimental proto-col, showing the fingertips stimulated by the rotating disk. (B) Map in the somatosensory cortex of the left hand of the monkey before the stimulation experiment. Stippled area corresponds to fingertips 2, 3, and 4. (C) Map of the same region after the stimulation experiment. (From Merzenich et al. 1990.)

to the fingertips results in an expansion of the regions of the somatosensory cortex whose neurons have receptive fields in the fingertips (figure 2.30). Recent experiments in in V1 of visual cortex also suggests that receptive fields are labile in that a cell's receptive field may expand when its preferred area on the retina is lesioned (Gibert and Wiesel, in press).

11. *Specific and Nonspecific Systems* In addition to the specific system projecting to the neocortex via the thalamus, such as is seen in the visual, auditory, and somatosensory systems, there are five sources of widely projecting neurons each associated with a specific neurotransmitter, which may play important roles in the sleep—dreaming—waking cycle, in memory, and in awareness and attention. The five are as follows: the locus coeruleus in the brain stem (norepinephrine), the raphe nucleus in the midbrain (serotonin), the substantia nigra in the midbrain (dopamine), the nucleus basalis in the basal forebrain (acetylcholine), and special groups of cells in the mammillary region of the hypothalamus (GABA) (figure 2.31).

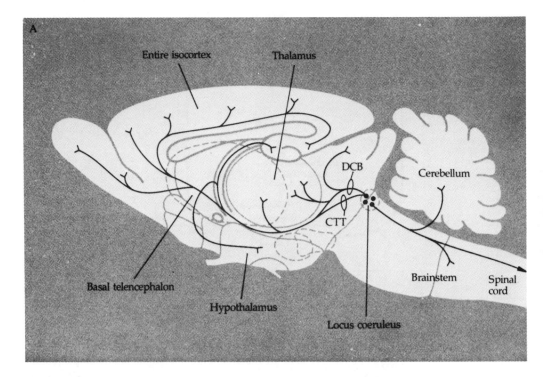

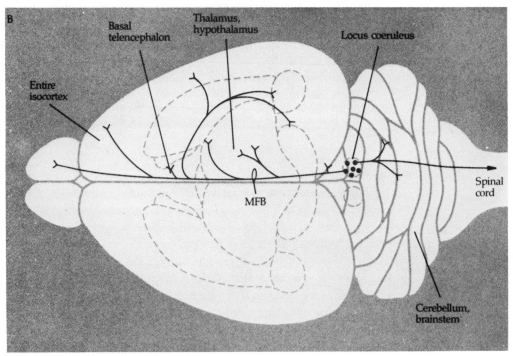

Figure 2.31 Neurons originating in the locus coeruleus project very widely all over the brain, including the cerebellum, brain stem, thalamus, and all over the cerebral cortex. The neurotransmitter they release is norepinephrine. (Reprinted with permission from Angevine and Cotman 1981.)

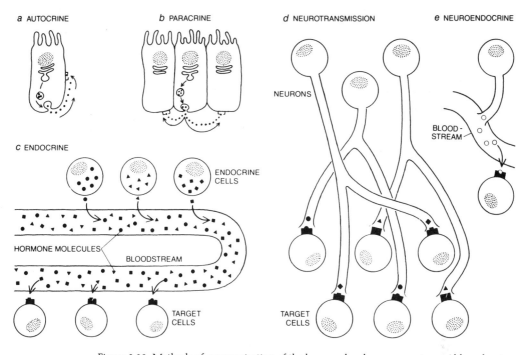

Figure 2.32 Methods of communication of the hormonal and nervous systems. Although auto-crine hormones (a) act on the cell that releases them and paracrine hormones (b) act on adjacent cells, most hormones are in the endocrine system and act on cells or organs anywhere in the body. Endocrine glands (c) release hormone molecules into the bloodstream, where they come in contact with receptors on target cells, which recognize the hormones meant to act on those cells and pull them out of the bloodstream. Neurons (d) communicate by releasing neuro-transmitters close to target cells. In neuroendocrine action (e) a neuron releases substances that act as hormones directly into the blood. (Reprinted with permission from Snyder 1985.)

12. *Action-at-a-distance* Some neurotransmitters may be released not only at a synaptic site, but may also be dumped into the extracellular space to have an action at a nonsynaptic site some distance from the point of release (Jan et al. 1978) (figure 2.32). Originating in the endocrine system, hormones, such as estradiol, can also reach neurons after traveling through the circulatory system and can alter neural activity.

13. *Parallel Architecture* The brain appears to be highly parallel in that there are many parallel streams of input for a given function. For example, in the monkey two parallel streams from the retina, starting with different types of ganglion cells, project to two distinct sets of layers of the lateral geniculate nucleus—the parvocellular and magnocellular layers, respectively—which in turn project to distinct sublaminae in layer 4 of cortical area V1 of the visual cortex (Hubel and Livingstone 1987, Livingstone and Hubel 1987). The streams are not cleanly segregated, however, and there are probably interactions at every stage (Schiller et al. 1990, Logothetis et al. 1990).

Selected Readings

Abeles, M. (1991). *Corticonics: Neural Circuits of the Cerebral Cortex.* Cambridge: Cambridge University Press.

Changeux, J.-P. (1985). *Neuronal Man*. Oxford: Oxford University Press.

Churchland, P. S. (1986). *Neurophilosophy: Toward a Unified Science of the Mind-Brain*. Cambridge, MA: MIT Press.

Dowling, J. E. (1987). *The Retina: An Approachable Part of the Brain*. Cambridge, MA: Harvard University Press.

Groves, P. M., and G. V. Rebec (1988). *Introduction to Biological Psychology*, 3rd ed. Dubuque, IA: Wm. C. Brown.

Hall, Z. W. (1991). *Molecular Neurobiology*. Sunderland MA: Sinauer.

Hubel, D. H. (1988). *Eye, Vision and Brain*. New York: Freeman.

Jeannerod, M. (1985). *The Brain Machine*. Cambridge, MA: Harvard University Press.

Kandel, E., J. Schwartz, and T. M. Jessell, eds. (1991). *Principles of Neural Science*, 3rd ed. New York: Elsevier.

Kelner, K., and D. E. Koshland, eds. (1989). *Molecules to Models: Advances in Neuroscience*. Washington, DC: American Association for the Advancement of Science.

Kuffler, S. W., J. G. Nicolls, and A. R. Martin (1984). *From Neuron to Brain: A Cellular Approach to the Function of the Nervous System*, 2nd ed. Sunderland, MA.: Sinauer.

LeVay, S., and S. B. Nelson (1991). Columnar organization of the visual cortex. In *The Neural Basis of Visual Function*, ed. J. R. Cronly-Dillon. London: Macmillan.

Levitan, I. B., and L. K. Kaczmarek (1991). *The Neuron: Cell and Molecular Biology*. Oxford: Oxford University Press.

Shepherd, G. M. (1987). *Neurobiology*, 2nd ed. Oxford: Oxford University Press.

Shepherd, G. M. (1990). *Synaptic Organization of the Brain*, 3rd ed. Oxford: Oxford University Press.

White, E. L. (1989). *Cortical Circuits*. Boston: Birkhauser.

Selected Journals and Reviews

Current Opinion in Neurobiology. (Current Biology) Review papers on subfields in neuroscience.

Journal of Cognitive Neuroscience. Quarterly journal (MIT Press). Articles on systems neuroscience with emphasis on cognitive processing.

Seminars in Neuroscience. Quarterly journal (Saunders). Each issue is on a special topic in neuroscience.

Trends in Neurosciences. Monthly journal (Elsevier). Contains brief but very useful reviews of special topics and is a good source of up-to-date references to the literature.

Concepts in Neuroscience. (World Scientific). Contains discussions of conceptual issues.

Annual Review of Neuroscience. Palo Alto, CA: (Annual Reviews). Comprehensive reviews of the literature.

3 Computational Overview

1 INTRODUCTION

What is computation? In virtue of what is something a computer? Why do we say a slide rule is a computer but an egg beater is not? These are, in a way, the philosophical questions of computer science, inasmuch as they query foundational issues that are typically glossed over as researchers get on with their projects.[1] Like the philosophical questions of other disciplines (What is the nature of life? [Biology] What is the nature of substance and change? [Physics and Chemistry]), the answers become more convincing, meaningful, and interconnected as the empirical discipline matures and gives more ballast to the theory. In advance of understanding that there are atoms, how atoms link together, and what their properties are, one simply cannot say a whole lot about the nature of substance and change. It is not, however, that one must say *nothing*—in that event, one could not get the science started. The point rather is that the theory outlining the elementary ideas of the discipline gradually bootstraps itself up, using empirical discoveries as support, and kicking away old misconceptions in the haul.

The definition of computation is no more *given* to us than were the definitions of light, temperature, or force field. While some rough-hewn things can, of course, be said, and usefully said, at this stage, precision and completeness cannot be expected. And that is essentially because there is a lot we do not yet know about computation. Notice in particular that once we understand more about what sort of computers *nervous systems* are, and how they do whatever it is they do, we shall have an enlarged and deeper understanding of what it is to compute and represent. Notice also that we are not starting from ground zero. Earlier work, especially by Turing (1937, 1950), von Neumann (1951, 1952), Rosenblatt (1961), and McCulloch and Pitts (1943), made important advances in the theory and science of computation. The technological development of serial, digital computers and clever software to run on them was accompanied by productive theoretical inquiry into what sort of business computation is.[2]

Agreeing that precise definitions are not forthcoming, can we nonetheless give rough and ready answers to the opening questions? First, although we may be guided by the example of a serial digital computer, the notion of "computer" is broader than that. Identifying computers with *serial digital* computers is neither justified nor edifying, and a more insightful strategy will be to see the conventional digital computer as only a special instance, not as the defining archetype. Second, in the most general sense, we can consider a physical system as a computational system when its physical states can be seen as representing states of some other systems, where transitions between its states can be explained as operations on the representations. The simplest way to think of this is in terms of a mapping between the system's states and the states of whatever is represented. That is, the physical system is a computational system just in case there is an appropriate (revealing) mapping between the system's physical states and the elements of the function computed. This "simple" proposal needs quite a lot of unpacking.

Functions: Computable or Noncomputable, Linear or Nonlinear

Since this hypothesis concerning what makes a physical system a computational system may not be self-evident, let us approach the issue more gradually by first introducing several key but simple mathematical concepts, including "function," and the distinction between *computable* and *noncomputable* functions. To begin, what is a function? A function in the mathematical sense is essentially just a mapping, either $1:1$ or many$:1$, between the elements of one set, called the "domain," and the elements of another, usually referred to as the "range"[3] (figure 3.1). Consequently, a function is a set of ordered pairs, where the first member of the pair is drawn from the domain, and the second element is drawn from the range. A computable function then is a mapping that can be specified in terms of some *rule* or other, and is generally characterized in terms of what you have to do to the first element to get the second. For example, multiply the first by 2, $\{(1, 2), (2, 4), (3, 6)\}$, expressible algebraically as $y = 2x$; multiply the element from the domain by itself $\{(6.2, 38.44), (9.6, 92.16)\}$, expressible algebraically as $y = x^2$, and so on.

What then is a noncomputable function? It is an infinite set of ordered pairs for which no rule can be provided, not only now, but in principle. Hence its specification consists simply and exactly in the list of ordered pairs. For example, if the elements are randomly associated, then no rule exists to specify the mapping between elements of the domain and elements of the range. Outside of mathematics, people quite reasonably tend to equate "function" with "computable function," and hence to consider a nonrule mapping to be no function at all. But this is not in fact how mathematicians use the terms, and for good reason, since it is useful to have the notion of a noncomputable function to describe certain mappings. Moreover, it is useful for the issue at hand because it is an empirical question whether brain activity can really be characterized by a computable function or only to a first approximation, or perhaps whether some of its activities cannot be characterized at all in terms of computable functions (Penrose 1989).

What is a *linear* function? Intuitively, it is one where the plot of the elements of the ordered pair yields a straight line. A *nonlinear* function is one where the plot does not yield a straight line (figure 3.2). Thus when brain function is

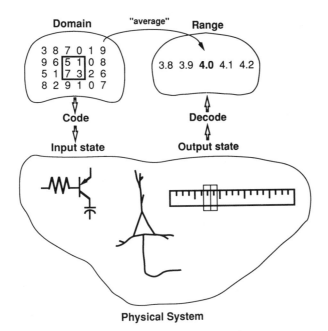

Figure 3.1 Mapping between a domain and a range can be accomplished by a variety of physical systems. There are three steps: (1) The input data is coded into a form appropriate for the physical system (electrical signal in an electrical circuit, chemical concentration in neuron, position of a slider in a slide rule). (2) The physical system shifts into a new state. (3) The output state of the physical system is decoded to produce the result of the mapping. The example shown here is the "average" map that takes four values and produces their average. Such a mapping might be useful as part of a visual system. Mappings could also be made from the domain of temporal sequences, and the range could be a sequence of output values.

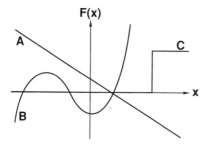

Figure 3.2 Examples of functions $F(x)$, plotted along the vertical axis, of one variable, x, plotted along the horizontal axis. Function A is a linear function. Function B is a nonlinear function. Function C is a discontinuous function.

described as "nonlinear," what this means is that (a) the activity is characterized by a computable function, and (b) that function is nonlinear. Notice also that the space in which functions are plotted may be a two-dimensional space (the x and y axes), but it may, of course, have more than two dimensions (e.g., an x axis, y axis, and also w, v, z, etc. axes).

Because the notion of a *vector* simplifies discussion enormously, we introduce it here. A vector is just an ordered set of numbers. For example, the set of incomes for 1990 of three vice-presidents in a corporation can be represented by the vector $\langle \$30, \$10, \$10 \rangle$; the eggs laid per week by five hens as $\langle 4, 6, 1, 0, 7 \rangle$; the spiking frequency of four neurons/sec as $\langle 10, 55, 44, 6 \rangle$. By contrast, a scalar is a single value rather than a many-valued set. The *order* in the set matters when we want to operate on the values in the set according to an order-sensitive rule. Systems, including the nervous system, execute functions that perform vector-to-vector mapping. For example, from the stretch receptors' values to the muscle contraction values, or from the head velocity values to eye velocity values.

A geometric articulation of these concepts compounds their value. Any coordinate system defines a state space, and the number of axes will be a function of the number of dimensions included. A state space is the set of all possible vectors. For example, a patient's body temperature and diastolic blood pressure can be represented as a position in a 2-D state space. Or, if a network has three units, each unit may be considered to define an axis in a 3-D space. The activity of a unit at a time is a point along its axis, so that the global activation of all the units in the net is specified by a point in that 3-D space (figure 3.3). More generally, if a network has n units, then it defines an n-dimensional activation space, and an activation vector can be represented as a point in that state space. A sequence of vectors can be represented as a trajectory in the state space.[4] Thus the patient's body temperature and blood pres-

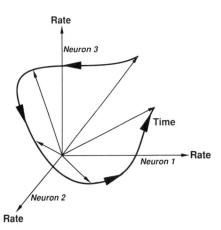

Figure 3.3 Schematic diagram of the trajectory of a three-neuron system through state space. The state of the system is a 3-D vector whose components are the firing rates of the three neurons. As the firing rates change with time, the tip of the vector traces out a trajectory (thick line). For more neurons the state space will have a higher dimension.

sure followed through time results in a trajectory in a 2-space. A function maps a point in one state space to a point in another state space—for example, from a point in stretch-receptor activation space to a point in muscle spindle activation space.

These notions—"vector" and "state space"—are part of linear algebra, and they are really the core of the mathematics needed to understand model networks. They are mercifully simple conceptually, and they are rather intuitively extendable from easily visualizable 2-D cases to very complex, n-D cases, where n may be thousands or millions. Although volumes more can be written on the topic of linear algebra, this is perhaps enough to ease the entry into the discussion of model neural networks.[5]

Computers, Pseudocomputers, and Cryptocomputers

The mathematical interlude was intended to provide a common vocabulary so that we might return to the question of characterizing, albeit roughly, what about a physical system makes it a computer. To pick up the thread left hanging during the mathematical interlude, let us hypothesize that a physical system computes some function f when (1) there is a systematic mapping from states of the system onto the arguments and values of f, and (2) the sequence of intermediate states executes an algorithm for the function.[6] Informally, an algorithm is a finite, deterministic procedure, e.g., a recipe for making gingerbread or a rule for finding the square root.

We count something as a computer because, and only when, its inputs and outputs can usefully and systematically be interpreted as representing the ordered pairs of some function that interests us. Thus there are two components to this criterion: (1) the objective matter of what function(s) describe the behavior of the system, and (2) the subjective and practical matter of whether we care what the function is. This means that delimiting the class of computers is not a sheerly empirical matter, and hence that "computer" is not a natural kind, in the way that, for example, "electron" or "protein" or "mammal" is a natural kind. For categories that do delimit natural kinds, experiments are relevant in deciding whether an item really belongs to the category. Moreover, there are generalizations and laws (natural laws) about the items in the categories and there are theories interleaving the laws. Nonnatural kinds differ in all these respects, and typically have an interest-relative dimension.

"Bee," for example, is a natural kind, but "gem" and "weed" are not. Objects are considered gems depending on whether some social group puts special value on them, typically as status symbols. Plants are considered weeds depending on whether gardeners (serious gardeners?) in the region happen to like having them in the garden. Some gardeners cultivate baby's breath as a desirable plant; other gardeners fight it as a weed. There is no experiment that will determine whether baby's breath is really a weed or not, because there is no fact of the matter—only social or idiosyncratic conventions.[7] Similarly, we suggest, there is no instrinsic property necessary and sufficient for all computers, just the interest-relative property that someone sees value in interpreting a system's states as representing states of some other system, and the properties of the system support such an interpretation. Desk-top von Neumann machines exist precisely because we are keenly interested in the functions we build and program them to execute, so the interest-relative component is dyed in the wool. For this reason, and because these machines are so common, they are the prototypical computers, just as dandelions are prototypical weeds. These prototypes should not, however, be mistaken for the category itself.

It may be suggested as a criticism of this very general characterization of computation that it is *too* general. For in this very wide sense, even a sieve or a threshing machine could be considered a computer, since they sort their inputs into types, and if one wanted to spend the time at it, one could discover a function that describes the input–output behavior. While this observation is correct, it is not so much a criticism as an apt appreciation of the breadth of the notion. It is rather like a lawn-growing perfectionist incredulously pointing out that on our understanding of "weed," even dandelions might be nonweeds relative to some clime and some tribe of growers. And so, indeed, they might be some farmer's cash crop. Nor is this idle fancy. Cultivated dandelion greens now appear as a delicacy in the specialty section of the greengrocery.

Conceivably, sieves and threshing machines could be construed as computers if anyone has reason to care about the specific function reflected in their input–output behavior, though it is hard to see what those reasons might be (figure 3.4). Unlike desktop computers that are engineered precisely for their computational prowess, sieves and threshing machines are constructed for other reasons, namely their sheerly mechanical prowess in the sorting of objects according to size and shape. Not too much emphasis should be placed on the link between purposeful design and use as a computer, however, for a fortuitously shaped rock can be used as a sundial. This is a truly simple computer-trouvé, but we do have reason to care about the temporal states that its shadow-casting states can be interpreted as representing.

There is perhaps a correct intuition behind the criticism nonetheless. Finding a device sufficiently interesting to warrant the description "computer" probably also entails that its input–output function is rather complex and inobvious, so that discovering the function reveals something important and perhaps unexpected about the real nature of the device and how it works. Thus finding out what is computed by a sieve is probably not very interesting and will not teach us much we did not already know. How a sieve works is dead simple. In contrast, finding out what is computed by the cerebellum will teach us a lot about the nature of the tissue and how it works.

A computer is a physical device with physical states and causal interactions resulting in transitions between those states. Basically, certain of its physical states are arranged such that they represent something, and its state transitions can be interpreted as computational operations on those representations. A slide rule is taken to compute—for example, (Mult 2, 7) to give 14 as the output—by dint of the fact that its physical regularities are set up in such a way as to honor the abstract regularities in the domain of numbers; the system of Aubrey holes at Stonehenge computes eclipses of the sun by dint of the fact

Figure 3.4 Garrett's improved threshing machine, 1851. The wheat was fed in from above, and the grain was removed by the rubbing action of the beater bars on the drum as it rotated inside the fixed concave. The grain fell onto a sieve below and the chaff was blown away by the fan system on the right. (From *The Illustrated Science and Invention Encyclopedia*. Westport, CT: H. S. Stuttman, 1983.)

that its physical organization and state transitions are set up so that the sun stone, moon stone, and nodal stone land in the same hole exactly when an eclipse of the sun occurs. Notice that this would be so even in the highly unlikely event that Stonehenge was the fortuitous product of landslides and flooding rather than human contrivance.

Nervous systems are also physical devices with causal interactions that constitute state transitions. Through slow evolution, rather than miraculous chance or intelligent design, they are configured so that their states *represent* —the external world, the body they inhabit, and in some instances, parts of the nervous system itself—and their physical state transitions execute computations. A circuit in mammalian brain stem evolved to compute the next position of the eyeball based on the angular velocity of the head. Briefly, the neuronal activity originating in the semicircular canals represents head velocity, and the interneurons, motor neurons and eyeball muscles are physically arranged such that for head velocity of a certain amount, the neurons causally interact so that the muscles of eyeball change tension by exactly the amount needed to compensate for the head movement. (For more on this circuit and its computation, see chapter 6). Loosely speaking, this organization evolved "for" this task; a little more strictly speaking, this circuit came to be the way it is by random mutations and natural selection; in standard epigenetic circumstances and relative to the ancestor's nervous system and to the system's other components, this organization enhances somewhat the organism's chances of surviving and reproducing.

There is a major contrast between manufactured and biological computers. Since we construct digital computers ourselves, we build the appropriate relationship into their design. Consequently, we tend to take this mapping for granted in computers generally, both manufactured and evolved. But for structures in the nervous system, these relationships have to be discovered. In the case of biological computers, discovery may turn out to be very difficult since we typically do not know what is being computed by a structure, and intuitive folk ideas may be misleading.

By contrast with systems we conventionally call computers, the *modus operandi* of some devices are such that a purely causal explanation, without reference to anything having been computed or represented, will suffice. A mouse-trap or a sieve, for example, is a simple mechanical device. Purely causal explanations will likely suffice for some aspects of brain activity too, such as the ion pump in neuronal membranes by virtue of which sodium is pumped out of the cell, or the manner in which binding of neurochemicals to receptors changes the internal chemistry of the cell. Bear in mind, however, that even at this level, an ion, such as Na^+, *could* represent a variable like velocity. At this stage, no one is really convinced that this is in fact so, but the possibility is not ruled out simply because ions are very low-level entities. Effects at higher levels of organization appear to require explanations in terms of computations and representations. Here a purely causal story, even if the line is still fairly clean, would give only a very unsatisfying explanation. For example, a purely causal or mechanical explanation of the integration of signals by dendrites is unenlightening with respect to what information the cell is getting and what it does with it. We need to know what this interaction means in terms of what the patterns of activity represent and what the system is computing.

Consider, for example, the neurons in parietal cortex whose behavior can be explained as computing head-centered coordinates, taking positions of the stimulus on the retina and position of the eyeball in the head as input (Zipser and Andersen 1988). Knowing that some neurons have a response profile that causes other neurons to respond in a certain way may be useful, especially in testing the computational hypothesis, but on its own it does not tell us anything much about the role of those neurons in the animal's visual capacity. We need additionally to know what the various states of neurons represent, and how such representations can be transformed by neural interactions into other representations. At the network level, there are examples where the details of connectivity and physiology of the neurons in the network still leave many of the whys and wherefores dangling, while a computational approach that incorporates the physiological details may make contact with the broader brainscape of tasks, solutions, environmental niche, and evolutionary history.[8]

There is a nonmathematical sense of "function," according to which the jc performed by something is said to be its function. In this sense, the heart is said to function as a pump, rather, than say as a noisemaker to soothe babies on their mother's breast. Though making a "ka-thump" sound is something the heart does, and though babies appear to be soothed by it, this surely is not the heart's *function*, meaning, roughly, its "primary job." Functional assignments can reasonably be made in the context of evolutionary development, what the animal needs to survive and reproduce, its environmental niche, and what would make sense given the assignment of function to related structures. In this "job" sense of function, the function of some part of the nervous system is to compute some function (in the mathematical sense), such as position for the eyeball given head velocity.

There is nothing mystical about characterizing a biological structure as having a specific function, even though neither god nor man designed the structure with a purpose in mind.[9] The teleological trappings are only that, and the teleology is eliminable or reducible without remainder in an evolutionary framework. To assign a computational role to a circuit is to specify a job of that circuit—detecting head velocity, for example. Consequently, the considerations that bear on determining the job of an organ such as the liver bear also on the assignment of computational role to neuronal structures. That the nervous system evolved, and that maladaptive structures tend to be weeded out in the evolutionary contest, restricts many functional hypotheses—in both senses of "functional"—that are logically possible but just not biologically reasonable. The crux of the matter is that many biologically irrelevant computational hypotheses can be culled out by a general functional truth about nervous systems, namely that *inter alia* they serve to help the animal move adaptively in the world.[10]

In this chapter we shall characterize a range of computational principles that may be useful when addressing the question of computation in nervous systems. As we shall see, moreover, the computational perspective will allow us to ask questions of biological systems that might not otherwise have been asked. The computational principles introduced here will be applied first to a number of examples chosen for their pedagogical value rather than for immediate biological salience. They allow us to introduce the basic ideas in a simple fashion, and this is their single, overriding virtue. They are not meant to be hypotheses concerning the mechanisms underlying the computational properties of real nervous systems. In chapters 4 to 6 neurobiological realism will be of paramount concern, but an understanding of the basic concepts is the entry ticket to these chapters.

2 LOOKING UP THE ANSWER

Conceptually, the simplest computational principle is "look up the answer." A look-up table is simply some physical arrangement in which answers to specific questions are stored. The engineering trick is to rig the table so that access to answers is fast and efficient, for if it is slow and clumsy, calculating the answers *de novo* might be preferable. Inasmuch as look-up tables are really repositories of precomputed answers rather than devices for working out the answer on the spot, it may be suggested that they are not genuine computers at all. For the purist, however, accepting this semantic refinement promotes confusion. A look-up table does after all effect a mapping, it instantiates a rule, and its states represent various things. That, given our groundfloor criteria, qualifies it as a computer. Call it unglamorous, call it humdrum, but a look-up table embedded in a mechanism for delivering answers can as properly be called a computer.

The easiest way to think of a look-up table is simply as an array of boxes each of which says, in effect, "if x is your problem, then y is your answer," for specific x and y. In other words, it does a matching job. For example, the truth table for exclusive "or" looks like this:

P	Q	XOR
T	T	F
T	F	T
F	T	T
F	F	F

This mode of representing the truth conditions happens to be very convenient, though many other, less convenient arrangements are easily imagined. And as students are usually told, it requires no significant intelligence to use this look-up table: just ask your question (e.g., what is the value when P is true and Q is false?), go to that row, and scan the answer.

A second but more powerful look-up table is the slide rule. Actually it is a multiplexed look-up table, since it stores answers not only for multiplication tasks, but also for finding sines, cosines and logarithms. When the task is multiplication, one enters the question (what is 3×7?) by sliding the center piece and cursor, and scanning the answer at the cursor. Moreover, while the truth table can handle only discrete functions, a slide rule can do continuous functions. To accommodate the variety of arithmetic questions and answers on two pieces of wood, the look-up table is metrically deformed (figure 3.5). As before, there are other ways of physically structuring a look-up table to perform exactly these tasks, but the flat, pocketable slide rule is in fact a wonderfully convenient and efficient way to do so.

Extending the idea a bit further, consider the Tinkertoy look-up table constructed in 1975 by a group of MIT undergraduates to play the game of tic-tac-toe[11] (figure 3.6). Making the "table" part of this device consists in storing a set of ordered pairs, where the first element is a possible game position, and the second element is the correct move, given that game position. In operating, the machine looks for a match between its current position and one of the possible positions sitting in storage. Finding the match will automatically divulge what to do next.

The first step in building the Tinkertoy look-up table was to decide on a representation for the state of the board using just the resources of Tinkertoy pieces. The second step was to use rotation and reflection symmetries to reduce the total number of game positions in the table, since the more entries

Figure 3.5 The object in the center is an oversized slide rule. The authors are on either side.

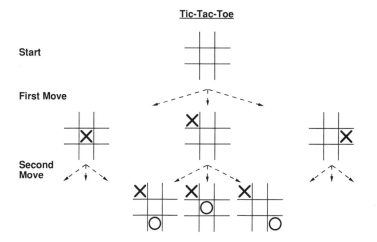

Figure 3.6 The first three levels of the game tree for tic-tac-toe. The 3 × 3 board at starting position is in the center, and the first move must be in one of three board positions (arrows) irreducible by mirror and reflection symmetries. The next level gives several possible replies by the opponent.

the larger the storage and the longer the time to search for a match. Thus a board with nothing but an X (or an O) in the upper right corner can be dealt with in the same way as a board with nothing but an X (or an O) in any of the other corners, and this consequently reduces the number of stored first positions by six, a substantial savings. These economies are important in reducing the number of entries in the look-up table to a manageable number—in this case from 300,000 to 48. The next step was to design a mechanical system that could match a position on the board with one of the 48 irreducible positions, and to retrieve the correct move (figure 3.7).

Although the tic-tac-toe example may at first seem frivolous, it cleanly illustrates a number of points relevant to computational neuroscience. First, look-up tables can be constructed from unorthodox materials but still come up with the same answer as do conventional electronic circuits. Second, the Tinkertoy computer is not a general-purpose computer; rather, it was built to solve one specific problem. So far as nervous systems are concerned, the analogy is that the genes probably wire up some neural circuits on the look-up table blueprint with the consequence that the animal is prepared at birth to do such things as snuffle around for a warm spot and then suck at whatever soft, mouth-sized thing sticks out. Circuits that yield sucking behavior in rats are probably not general-purpose devices, but are dedicated more or less exclusively to sucking.

The theoretical lesson is that if a problem is conceptually reducible to a look-up table problem, then, cost and efficiency aside, it could in principle be implemented by look-up table mechanisms. Cost is rarely irrelevant, however. It is especially pertinent here, since precomputing the answers for each problem requires a substantial, and sometimes exorbitant, investment in the construction of the machine. From an evolutionary point of view, it might be too costly or too difficult to precompute certain tasks, such as semantics or place-in-the-social-scheme or dinner-whereabouts, and hence many things must be learned by the infant organism.

How practical really is the look-up table approach? The answer depends on a number of factors, including the complexity of the problem to be solved, the architectural pliancy of the available materials, and the size limits of the look-up table. Chess, unlike tic-tac-toe, appears to be a poor candidate for the look-up table solution. There are approximately 10^{40} game positions—far more than the capacity of any existing machine.[12] The complexity factor can be reduced considerably using the economy described above; namely, take advantage of the underlying symmetries and position similarities in the problem to reduce the number of entries. Given this possibility, it remains to be seen whether the look-up strategy is indeed utterly unrealistic for chess. For many real-world problems, as in the problem of visually recognizing an object, advantage can be taken of translation, rotation, and scaling invariances, as well as smoothness and continuity constraints, to reduce the number of stored categories. The possibility to consider is that look-up craftsmanship may be seen at various stages in nervous system processing, even if it is not ubiquitous.

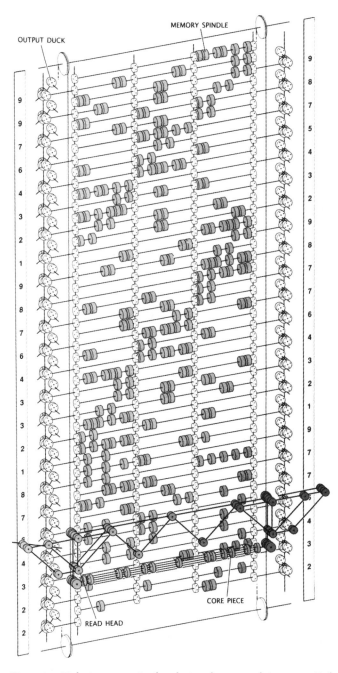

Figure 3.7 Tinkertoy computer for playing the game of tic-tac-toe. Each memory spindle encodes a possible game position, along with the optimal response. The read head, loaded with the current game position in the core piece, moves down the memory spindles, one by one, until there is a match. This activates the output duck, which drives the correct move. Compare this special-purpose computer with the general mapping scheme in figure 3.1. (From Dewdney [1989] Computer recreations: a Tinkertoy computer that plays tic-tac-toe. Copyright © 1989 *Scientific American*.)

If the number of stored question–answer pairs is large, then the search-for-a-match time may be prohibitively long. The Tinkertoy look-up machine, for example, compares the current board position to each of the stored board positions, one at a time, until the match is found. This is a rather ponderous business, especially if the search procedure is sequential. Parallel search could provide time economies, as we shall see later. Time is not the only consideration; wiring too must be kept within bounds. Consider, for example, the size of a look-up table needed to handle ordered pairs of the form ⟨edible goodie at coordinates x,y,z moving at velocity v/body position #⟩. Given the number of independently movable body parts and the number of possible locations and speeds, the look-up table would have to be massive, at a minimum. The wiring cost scotches the idea. For nervous systems, brief times and sparse wiring are generally preferable, other things being equal, so the question is whether there are any neural structures that can be usefully understood as look-up tables.

Until rather recently, the superior colliculus in cats suggested itself as a neural instantiation of a look-up table, at least to a first approximation. The simple story runs like this. The colliculus has a number of layers, or laminae. On its upper layer, the colliculus represents location of visual stimuli on a retinotopic map, while on its bottom layer is a "motor map" representing position of the eyeball muscles suitable for foveating the eye to various locations. Other layers in the structure represent whisker-stimulus location. The maps are deformed with respect to each other so that they are in register. The effect is that a line dropped from the visual map intersects the motor map in a location that causes the eyeballs to move so as to foveate the location of the visual stimulus. The anatomy itself facilitates the look-up of motor answers, just as the "anatomy" of a slide rule facilitates look-up of mathematical answers. The organization enables the system to foveate a peripheral visual stimulus quickly and accurately. It is a kind of two-dimensional slide rule, where the visual and motor surfaces are appropriately aligned so that a position of a peripheral stimulus is mapped onto a where-the-eyeballs-should-be position. According to this conjecture, the anatomy executes a kind of "visual grasp" transformation (figure 3.8).

What is wrong with the colliculus look-up story? As so often in biology, as more data come in, the whole situation begins to look much more complex than the unencumbered, unqualified hypothesis asserts. To begin with, the relation between the visual input and the motor output is not as straightforward as simple "visual grasp"; there are descending fibers from the cortex that affect collicular output, and attentional processes play an important if poorly understood role in collicular function. Although there do exist ostensible "drop line" connections between mapped layers, it is not yet known exactly what these connections do. In particular, the long time delay between the signal entering the sensory layer and a signal reaching the lower motor layer undermines the hypothesis that these connections straightforwardly execute "visual grasp." So withal, the colliculus cannot be taken as an unproblematic case of a neural look-up table.

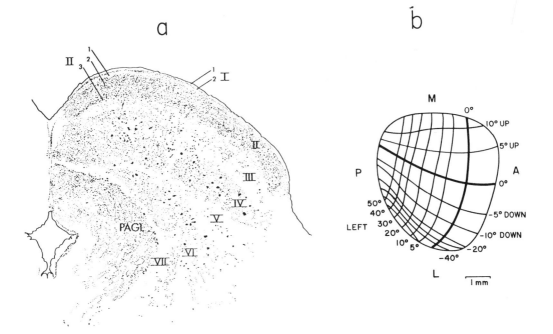

Figure 3.8 Organization of the cat superior colliculus. (a) Cross section through the colliculus showing cell bodies of neurons in each lamina (numbered). (b) Map of the eye movements produced by stimulating the deep layers of the colliculus with an electrode. The coordinates refer to the deviation of the eye from its center of gaze that is produced by electrical stimulation. M, medial; L, lateral; A, anterior; P, posterior (Adapted from Schiller 1984.)

The example is instructive nonetheless, for the discrepancies between the pure look-up configuration and the complicated anatomy and physiology of the colliculus suggest that it well behooves evolution to fancy up a true-blue look-up table into something that can do rather more complicated things. Consider first that the colliculus needs also to take head position into account, since the eyes move relative to the head, and hence relative to the ears and the whiskers. In addition to its "in register" drop lines, the system may find it can make good use of connections to other areas of the map, and to the whisker and ear-position maps interleaved in the neural stack, noting that whiskers and ears too can move relative to the head (in some mammals) but with their proprietary degrees of freedom. But if the colliculus takes these other matters into account, pure look-up conforming to the slide-rule style is not what is going on. Were the eyes stuck fast in the head, and were "foveation" to whisker and auditory stimuli absent, the colliculus might approximate more closely a look-up table. As it is, the complexities of the colliculus suggest that even if evolution had fashioned a pure look-up table, it would soon evolve to master these complex and interrelated operations. That is, neurons would have to perform additional computational steps between input and output.

To return to the matter of computer design, one means for reducing storage space consists in allowing the structures doing the transformations to adjust themselves to existing conditions. Thrift bids the system to store only vectors (game positions) it actually uses rather than all possible vectors, and this requires that the system learn which vectors these are. What is the cost of this flexibility? If the system is to adapt, the adaptation should be in the *correct* direction. Alas, we cannot very well have a look-up table for the question "is my modification in the right direction?" without going hog-wild over the space limitations. So adaptation pulls the system even further away from the slide-rule paradigm.

But if nervous systems are not using pure look-up tables, what are they doing? The fast answer, to which the rest of the book is an extended elaboration, is this: they are computing with nets. As we shall see later in this chapter, neural nets may have certain properties akin to look-up tables. Consequently, this look-up table prologue is not merely a "first-we-crawl" exercise, but a foundation that will help us understand what actual neural nets are doing. Before moving to a discussion of how nets compute, one further preliminary point must be laid on the board.

Might a close but imperfect match sometimes suffice? For many tasks, especially recognition and categorization tasks, the answer is "yes, close is close enough." Accordingly, an additional modification to the true-blue look-up table consists in storing not every possible entry, but rather storing prototypes or exemplars of the categories. With this stratagem, we trade off a degree of precision for a saving of space, but the system must now take some computational steps to determine similarity to stored vectors. Eventually we shall want a net that avails itself of both economies: it stores prototypes, and it has the plasticity to learn prototypes.

To embody prototypes in a computer, related items are clustered near or less near to an exemplar, according to their degree of similarity. Items stored in this manner define a similarity space in the machine, and distance from the prototype defines a similarity metric. This is known as a *nearest-neighbor* configuration, and there are many possible architectures for realizing it and many possible ways to style nearest-neighbor algorithms to exploit the organization for computational purposes. If a conventional digital machine is chosen for the implementation, then the machine will have to be spatially prodigal to accomplish complex tasks, for it has to store all the entries, make the distance measures, find the match, and deliver the answer. Clever ways to store data in hierarchical trees have been devised, but even these bog down when the going gets realistic. This gloomy prospectus may be sufficiently discouraging to degrade the look-up idea to nothing more than a charming curiosity, rather like an ornithopter[13]—conceivable perhaps, but practical, probably not. On the other hand, though a digital machine may be impractical in this sphere, there is an architecturally very simple organization that will do the job, and do it cheaply, efficiently, and in satisfyingly few steps. That is a net. In the next several sections, we shall look at a number of types of networks, starting with very simple examples and moving on to networks of greater power and sophistication.

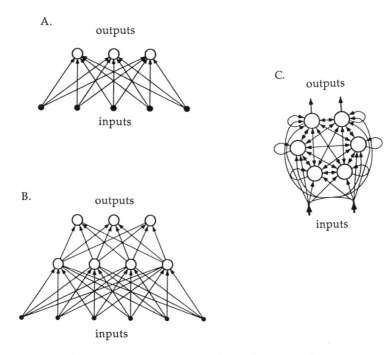

Figure 3.9 Three types of networks. (A) Feedforward network with one layer of weights connecting the input units to the output units. (B) Feedforward network with two layers of weights and one layer of hidden units between the input and the output units. (C) Recurrent network with reciprocal connections between units. (Adapted from Hertz et al. 1991.)

3 LINEAR ASSOCIATORS

What is a net? The architecture of the canonical net consists of units, loosely based on neurons, connections (generously speaking, axons) between the units, and weights (generously speaking, synapses) on the connections (figure 3.9). Some units receive external input, some deliver the output, and some may do neither. Because there is more than one input unit and more than one output unit, the ingoing and outcoming representations are vectors, meaning ordered sets of values (e.g., $\langle 3.2, 668.9, 0 \rangle$) rather than single values (scalars, e.g., 668.9). Signals with various magnitudes are passed between units. That is the nub of a net. How can a net compute anything? The abstract explanation is reassuringly simple: the weights on the units are set in such a way that when the input units are given certain values, the output units are activated appropriately. This means that a mapping is achieved and hence that a function is executed. Now to follow the recipe for making a net in a concrete case, we have to decide how to set the weights, whether they are modifiable and if so how, what range of activity values a unit may take and how they are determined, how to represent the input vectors, and the nature of the connectivity between units (network topology). Obviously this means that the canonical description carves out a vast area of computational space, within which specific nets occupy small regions. The canonical description thus stands to a running

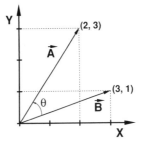

Figure 3.10 Computing the inner product between two vectors is a fundamental operation in a feedforward associative network. The example given here is for two-dimensional vectors, but the same relationships apply to vectors with more components. The inner product is defined as $\mathbf{A} \cdot \mathbf{B} = A_x B_x + A_y B_y = 2 \times 3 + 3 \times 1 = 9$, where A_x is the x component and A_y is the y component of vector $\mathbf{A}$. The angle θ between the vectors can be computed from the relationship $\cos \theta = (\mathbf{A} \cdot \mathbf{B})/(\|\mathbf{A}\| \cdot \|\mathbf{B}\|)$, where $\|\mathbf{A}\| = \sqrt{A_x^2 + A_y^2}$ is the magnitude of $\mathbf{A}$. In the network shown in figure 3.9a, vector $\mathbf{A}$ might represent the activity levels of the input units and vector $\mathbf{B}$ could be the weights from the input units to an output unit. The inner product can then be interpreted as the sum of the weighted inputs to the output unit.

neural network model like a dictionary definition of an airplane stands to a veritable machine itself.

In the 1970s, more or less independently, a number of people were developing associative nets, including Leon Cooper, James Anderson, Teuvo Kohonen, Gunther Palm, Christopher Longuet-Higgins, and David Willshaw.[14] How do associative nets work? In a nutshell, they associate an input vector with an output vector, essentially following the "parallel architecture/similarity-measure/look-up table" format outlined above. The key mathematical task that networks can perform is computing inner products; that is, taking two vectors and multiplying them component by component and then adding up the products. So if one vector represents the input from a set of units and the other vector is a stored prototype, then the inner product yields a measure of the overlap between them, and hence of their similarity. Geometrically, the inner product is proportional to the cosine of the angle between the vectors, so when there is perfect congruence of the vectors, the angle would be zero (figure 3.10). This is a readily manipulable measure of vector similarity. How are the vectors (prototypes) stored? They are stored in the weights connecting the input units to an in individual output unit. This means that each component in the prototype vector is assigned to one weight, and these weights are attached to a summing unit, which adds up all the products of these two vectors (weight vector and input vector). This summing unit is the output unit.

In the garden variety network, the output of the summing unit is proportional to the sum of the products. The output therefore is a linear transformation of the input, and the network is called a *linear associator*. For example, for a small network with three input lines and three output units, there are nine possible weights, which can be written as an array of numbers. One such 3×3 weight matrix is:

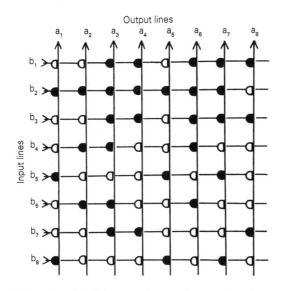

Figure 3.11 A Willshaw net showing the input lines (horizontal), the output lines (vertical), and the connections between them. The weights on the connections are binary and can be zero (open circles) or one (closed circles). Thus, the picture is a graphical representation of the weight matrix. (From Willshaw, 1989.)

$$w_{ij} = \begin{bmatrix} 0 & -1 & 2 \\ 1 & 0 & 1 \\ 2 & -1 & 0 \end{bmatrix}$$

The components of the output vector of the network are given by:

$$y_i = \sum_j w_{ij} x_j \qquad (1)$$

For the input vector $x_i = (1, 1, 1)$, the output vector is given by $y_i = (1, 2, 1)$. For the input vector $x_i = (1, 2, 3)$, the output vector is given by $y_i = (4, 4, 0)$. (Multiply the first component of the vector by the first item in the top row [1×0], the second component by the second item in the top row [2×-1], the third by the third [3×2]. Add the products [$= 4$]. Repeat for each row.)

As you would expect, there are many variations on the simple linear associator theme, and changes are rung on whether the input and output units take on continuous or binary values, and whether the weights are continuous or binary (figure 3.11). Notice that many inner products can be computed in parallel, one for each summing unit, and the more the summing units, the bigger the net. Additionally, each of the products (weights × inputs) can be computed in parallel. The result is that only one step is required to produce an output vector that is associated with the input vector. What is described here is the paradigmatic net for matching a sample to a stored prototype. This is evidently a classification task: for each category a representative example must be provided, and this is encoded as a vector. As a rule, the less overlap between the prototype vectors the better, since it is preferable that an input unambiguously match a prototype.

The explanation so far shows how to get *a* mapping from input to output, but it has not addressed how to set the values of the weights in order to get the *correct* mapping from input to output—to get the net to give the correct answer when it is asked a question. This is obviously of the essence if the net is to be of any use. The method by which the prototype vector is encoded matters enormously to the success and efficiency of the net, and different coding strategies will variously ease or gum up the operations. It is not in general known how to go about organizing the preprocessing for nervous system tasks such as vision and speech recognition, but some information is available for simpler processes such as visual tracking during head movement (chapter 6). As we discuss later, if one wants to get some insight into the characteristics of the preprocessing for good matching of input to stored vectors, then the brain will be a valuable source of ideas. The general point about preprocessing is this: at the level of sensory input, the vectors can look very different because there are many possible patterns of, say, a dog. The preprocessing has to be done in a such a way that if the many different patterns all trigger the output vector "dog," they must be mapped onto the weights so this happens. In other words, the system needs a many : 1 mapping. Exactly how to set this up varies from case to case, and more discussion of this topic follows.

A slight modification of the paradigm net yields a network that performs *autoassociative content-addressable memory*. This means that the net can produce an output that is as close as possible to a prestored vector given only part of the vector as input. This is a vector completion task, in other words. To do this, you need as many output units as input units, so that the weight matrix is square. The weights w_{ij} from unit j to unit i are constructed from an outer product of the stored vectors

$$w_{ij} = \sum_{\alpha} x_i^{\alpha} x_j^{\alpha} \qquad (2)$$

where x_i^{α} is the ith component of the α-th stored vector. For example, if one of the stored vectors is $(1, 5, 2)$, then its contribution to the square weight matrix is

$$w_{ij} = \begin{bmatrix} 1 & 5 & 2 \\ 5 & 25 & 10 \\ 2 & 10 & 4 \end{bmatrix}$$

These input vectors could be presented to the network one at a time, and the weights could be computed incrementally by adding each contribution to produce the sum. This is perhaps the simplest and best known of all learning rules, the Hebb rule, so-called because it reflects Hebb's hunch that connection weights between two units should strengthen as a function of the correlated activity of the connected units. Note that the weight is built up from the product of input activities and desired output activities.

The Hebb rule is loosely speaking a "get-similar" rule. It says, "Make the output vector the same as the one you saw before which it most closely resembles." Consider what will happen, then, when an incomplete or noisy version of an input vector x_i is presented to the network with a weight matrix configured according to eq. (2). If we substitute the weights in eq. (2) into eq. (1), then the output can be rewritten as:

$$y_i = \sum_\alpha x_i^\alpha \left[\sum_j (x_j^\alpha x_j) \right] \tag{3}$$

Roughly speaking, this means the output vector is composed from a linear combination of the stored vectors, x_i^α, where each vector is weighted by the term in the square brackets, representing the inner product, or overlap, between the input vector and the stored vector. In the *auto*associative network the desired output vector is the closest stored input vector; at best, the output vector will be identical to the stored input vector. Such a network can perform vector completion or vector correction, but it cannot associate two different vectors. The basic autoassociative net can be modified quite simply to handle *hetero*associations. Whereas the autoassociative net stored the outer product of (x_i^α, x_j^α), the heteroassociative net needs to store the outer product of two nonidentical vectors, (z_i^α, x_i^α). Once trained, the heteroassociative network will produce an output proportional to z_i^α, when x_j^α is present in the input vector.

What happens if the noisy vector matches more than one stored vector? Then the output will be a weighted sum of the stored vectors (i.e., ambiguous inputs will produce hybrids of the nearest matching vectors). As more and more vectors are stored according to the Hebb rule, there will be more and more ambiguities and the performance of the network will correspondingly degrade. Indeed, an important fact about all such matrix associators is that they work very well so long as only a small number of patterns are stored, but their capacity is limited and they do get filled up surprisingly quickly. To meet this storage room problem, modifications of the Hebb rule have been proposed that increase a little the capacity of the network.

The first strategy is to use only a small subset of units to represent any given item. This is also known as making the vectors sparse (Willshaw 1981). If there are n units, Willshaw found that optimal storage occurred when $\log n$ units are used to represent each item. The advantage of making the vectors sparse is that there is less overlap between representations, and hence a given network can store a greater number of representations.[15]

A second way to economize on space is to normalize the incoming activation by inhibitory connections, assuming that all the input connections are excitatory. In a Hebb network, the number of synapses that are most highly enhanced by an input vector is proportional to the square of the number of units that the input activates. It follows that by going to a sparse representation, the number of units activated by any given pattern is reduced. Feedforward inhibition achieves this by normalizing the total activity so that all input patterns produce, on average, equal excitation. This achieves an economy because it prevents a single, highly active input vector from hogging the synapses.

A third way to increase the capacity of the network is to introduce a nonlinear threshold for the output units. This means that should the summed inputs fail to reach a prescribed value, then there is no output. Thus only the most strongly activated units produce an output. A sort of cleaning out of marginal activity is thereby achieved, making room for business that counts. While housecleaning is not to be scoffed at, what turns out to be really progressive about adding nonlinearity is that it makes the net far more powerful, permitting it to perform computations much more complex than anything a linear net can handle. In other words, a whole panoply of computable functions hitherto impossible for the net becomes within its range. Nonlinearity in the response functions of the units is the next development in the evolution of invented nets.

4 CONSTRAINT SATISFACTION: HOPFIELD NETWORKS AND BOLTZMANN MACHINES

What sorts of problems demand a net with nonlinear properties? Consider the problem of recognizing an object in a visual image. The object may be in an unusual perspective, it may be partially occluded in a cluttered scene, lighting conditions may be poor, or the object may be an individual that has never been seen before. One of the first steps in visual processing separates the object from the surrounding clutter. This segregation of figure from ground has important consequences for the interpretation of an object in an image, as illustrated in figure 3.12 showing the classical vase/face reversal. Depending on which part of the image is considered the figure and which the ground, the silhouette can be interpreted as either as a vase or as two faces in profile. This also illustrates an important feature of how the visual system deals with ambiguity, namely that only one of the interpretations can be perceived at any given time. Furthermore, one can flip between the two interpretations by shifting attention. Note that this shift need not be an overt shift in gaze, but rather an internal attentional shift that at least sometimes is under conscious control. Could figure–ground segmentation be performed by a look-up table?

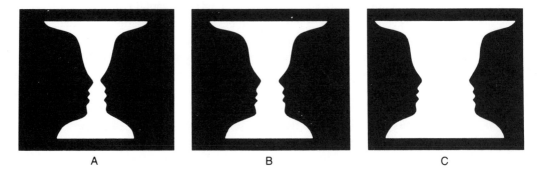

A   B   C

Figure 3.12 Figure-ground reversal. There are two perceptual interpretations of these images: a pair of black faces, or a white vase. The perceptual interpretation can be influenced by conscious attention and biased by features in the image. Thus, the faces interpretation is usually favored in A and the vase interpretation is favored in C. One interpretation appears to exclude the other (try to imagine a face "kissing" a vase). (With permission from Coren and Ward [1989]. *Sensation and Perception*, 3rd ed. Copyright © 1989 Harcourt Brace Jovanovich, Inc.)

The main reason to think it could not is that the solution requires the system to have a global perspective even though it does not have a "global unit." For example, the transitions between the face and the vase interpretations seem to occur coherently over the entire image. This evidently betokens a global computation, but the difficulty is that in the early stages of processing, single neurons respond only to local regions of the image. That is, early processing is local processing. The puzzle, therefore, is this: how are these local measurements integrated into a globally consistent interpretation? This type of computational problem involves the mutual satisfaction of many partial constraints, and they must be satisfied not serially, for that would lead to impossible "solutions," but simultaneously, so that a globally coherent solution is found. Consider, for example, a corner of the object. Local analysis may indicate two contiguous regions but the relationship between these two regions and regions in another corner of the object depend on constraints that link overlapping patches between these regions. Constraints such as continuity of objects and three-dimensional geometry of objects often must be incorporated into the computation to arrive at a consistent global interpretation (Ballard et al. 1983).

The Gestalt psychologists identified a number of the principles and constraints governing the interpretive process. "Gestalts" were taken to be global organizations that emerged from multiple interactions between features in an image. For example, in figure 3.13 lines that converge are seen as receding in depth. Despite identifying some of the constraints governing global interpretation, Gestalt psychologists were unable to produce a convincing mechanism for applying the constraints and resolving conflicts between constraints in achieving a consistent interpretation of the image. One of the factors that makes this a difficult problem is that the number of possible interpretations explodes combinatorially. Accordingly, a one-shot look-up table would have to have an impossibly large number of entries to accommodate all possible shapes. So for this kind of task, at least, the true-blue look-up strategy is inadequate.

In this section we shall describe a new type of computational principle that can accomplish the constraint satisfaction by a process of "relaxation." Rather than looking up a precomputed answer, a parallel system of processing

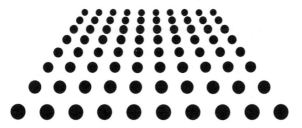

Figure 3.13 This two-dimensional array of dots evokes a strong sense of depth. Information about depth is provided by perspective (converging lines of dots) and texture (change in dot size). (From Gregory [1970]. *The Intelligent Eye*. New York: McGraw-Hill.)

units converges through local interactions to the correct global interpretation. As suggested earlier in discussion of the superior colliculus, however, this does not mean that a look-up configuration would exclude constraint satisfaction processes—there may be ways of merging the two. In addition, there is a natural way to incorporate top-down constraints from stored knowledge into the bottom-up flow of sensory data (see Chapter 5).

The linear associators described in section 3 have a feedforward topology; i.e., the information flows from input units through to output units. To do constraint satisfaction in a network, however, the topology has to be changed. In particular, it has to be changed to allow information to circulate among the output units so that the units can arrive at a mutually consistent answer. This means feedback. Feedforward nets are like a hierarchical assembly line: the basic components are made and passed on, the stage 2 components are assembled, then the stage 3 assembly is done, and the widgets pop out the delivery chute. In a feedback arrangement where there is communication between agents, there can be cross talk and plan revision, intermediate decisions can be tendered, and a mutually agreeable solution can be found. The nets featured in this section will have two new properties: feedback and nonlinearity (figure 3.14).

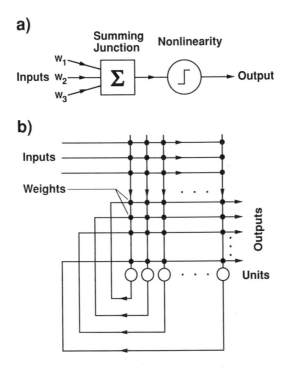

Figure 3.14 Nonlinear feedback network. (a) Each processing unit performs a nonlinear operation on the linearly weighted sum of its inputs. (b) Diagram of recurrent network. Each unit receives inputs from outside the network and feedback connections from other units in the network. Each intersection of a horizontal line with a vertical line (large filled dot) represents a weight.

Networks with feedback connections can have a wide range of dynamics, including oscillating solutions and chaotic behavior. Two difficult questions must be confronted in building nets to solve constraint satisfaction problems: (1) how can the weights be adjusted bit by bit to embody the task constraints? And (2), if the net is left to run, will it find a stable configuration that represents the desired solution? Both questions grow alarmingly complex in the case of nonlinear nets with feedback.

Nets, in contrast to digital computers running programs, are set running without any specification of intermediate steps. Rather, one relies on the dynamics of the net to take it to a stable state. Consequently, whether the net is a successful net depends on whether the dynamics of the units' interactions allow it to converge on the solution. But, and here is the kicker, how can one know whether it is a successful net—maybe its failure to converge so far just means it has a long and drawn-out "settling" schedule. The trouble is that the nature of the interactions between representations in nets displays no obvious orderliness, and in the early days of nets, a theory to explain and predict their behavior was essentially nonexistent. In 1982, John Hopfield showed, for a particular class of feedback networks, that their dynamics is such that convergence to a solution could be proved.[16] Additionally, his insights opened a line of research that eventually led to powerful solutions to the problem of how to adjust weights in a feedback net.

Hopfield's results were actually very surprising because he applied the tools and techniques of theoretical physics to the ostensibly different business of computation by nets. Hopfield's question was this: might the interactions between representations in nets that end up delivering an answer to a question be described by the same laws that describe the behavior of certain systems in physics? "Not likely" seems the first-blush answer, since there is no intuitively obvious reason to suspect that the regularities of *computational* interaction and regularities of *physical* interaction should be even formally similar. Hopfield's hunch, however, was reverse. If he was right, then network models, or at least one class of them, would be gifted with a whole parcel of powerful theory for free. Some order in the confusion might then be forthcoming.

Most physical systems do not recommend themselves as displaying behavioral regularities suitable to the computational context. To have properties analogous to computational states of a net, a system needs a richness of states comparable to that of a net. The prototypical model of a magnetic substance is a well-behaved lattice in which particles interact rather straightforwardly with their neighbors so that at a low temperature all the particles are spinning up or all are spinning down. In other words, local interactions between particles lead easily to a single global "solution." A consequence is that a given lattice can only store one bit of information, and indeed this is the principle exploited by core memories in early digital computers. The simple lattices are, however, a poor analogy for how a network might store information, precisely because they lack a rich range of stable states.

It turns out that spin glasses are an unusual kind of substance that do have a suggestive richness, and it was from spin glasses that Hopfield drew his regu-

Annealing

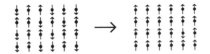

High Temp   **Low Temp**

Mean Field Approximation

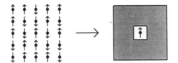

Figure 3.15 Annealing (top) and mean field approximation (bottom) in the 2-D Ising model representing states for each lattice site in a ferromagnet. The Ising model consists of a lattice of spins, each of which can be either up or down. Each spin can interact with its nearest neighbors such that the state with the lowest energy has all the spins lined up in the same direction. (Top) At a high temperature the directions of the spins are random because the thermal energy causing the fluctuations is much larger than the interaction energies, but as the temperature is reduced, the spins become aligned to the same direction. In this ground state the collection of spins behaves like a magnet. In a spin glass model the interactions can be negative as well as positive so that the ground state does not have all the spins pointing in the same direction. At intermediate temperatures the behavior of the system can be complex because of the many combinations of interactions that can occur. (Bottom) The mean field approximation replaces the sum of the local interactions with a single, average field. This approximation ignores corrections that arise from the fluctuations of the local field from its average. In a Hopfield network with binary units (only values of 0 and 1), the mean field approximation replaces the binary unit with a unit that has continuous values between 0 and 1. (Adapted from Hertz, Krogh, and Palmer [1991]. *Introduction to the Theory of Neural Computation*. Copyright © 1991 Addison-Wesley, Redwood City, CA.)

larities and equations. A spin glass is characterized by particles with spin, either up or down, in *mixtures* of attractive and repulsive interactions (figure 3.15). Suppose the spin glass starts at an excited state—at a high temperature. If the spin glass is rapidly cooled, the physics of the system are such that it "seeks" the nearest local energy minimum. Unlike a spin system in which all interactions are attractive, yielding a single energy minimum (all spins pointing in the same direction), spin glasses have many local energy minima owing to the mixture of interactions, attractive and repulsive. This property of spin glasses is called "frustration," to reflect the inability of the system to come to a unanimous decision but rather to end up in pockets of conflicting decisions. As we outline below, inherent in the dynamics of the physical system of interacting spins are the properties that enable it to represent and compute. The next step is to design nets that mimic spin glasses in the relevant dynamical respects, with their computing and representing properties more firmly in hand. As we show below, Hopfield's solution to the decision problem is to lay the grid of equations describing the cooling of spin glasses on the settling of networks into a stable configuration.

The units in the Hopfield net have two states, on (1) and off (0), just as the electrons can spin up or down (Amit 1989). Let s_i be the state of unit i. The connections between units are symmetrical, such that if unit j is connected to unit i with strength w_{ij}, then there is a reciprocal connection of equal strength connecting i to j. Thus:

$$w_{ij} = w_{ji} \tag{4}$$

The energy of the system, defined by analogy with that of spin glasses, is:

$$E = -\frac{1}{2} \sum_{ij} w_{ij} s_i s_j \tag{5}$$

Roughly, the energy E is simply the sum of all of the weights connecting units which happen to be on, scaled, and inverted in sign, so that the network has the same formal properties as those of a physical system.[17]

What does relaxation involve? The basic way to think of it is as an algorithm. "Pick any unit at random, flip it; i.e., change its 0 or 1 value. If the overall effect is to lower the energy level of the net, accept the change; otherwise refuse it. Do this again and again to arbitrarily chosen units until no single flip of a given unit will reduce the energy level of the entire net." A little more formally, suppose that the net is in some given state $\{s_i\}$, where each of the units is assigned a value of 0 or 1, and the corresponding energy of the net is given by E in eq. (5). If one of these units, s_i, has a current value 0, then it makes no contribution to the total energy level. If its value is now changed from 0 to 1, then E changes by ΔE_i, which is given by the following equation:

$$\Delta E_i = -\sum_j w_{ij} s_j \tag{6}$$

If the change to the single unit should decrease energy so that $\Delta E_i < 0$, i.e.,

$$\text{if} \sum_j w_{ij} s_j > 0 \tag{7}$$

then this change will be accepted and the system has a new global state with an overall lower energy (figure 3.16). This is precisely the *update rule for binary threshold units in a net*. It reflects the traditional view that neurons do not spike unless their total input at a given moment exceeds some threshold. The units in a Hopfield net are updated asynchronously, one at a time. This is a deterministic update rule, but choice of the next unit to update is stochastic. If an extra term is added to the energy equation to represent the threshold θ_i for each neuron, then:

$$E = -\frac{1}{2} \sum_{ij} w_{ij} s_i s_j + \sum_i \theta_i s_i \tag{8}$$

The term on the right adds a tilted plane to the energy landscape; that is, the

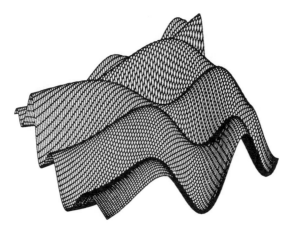

Figure 3.16 The dynamics of a Hopfield network in state space is visualized. All possible states of the network are represented by points in an x–y plane, and the height of the surface is the energy of the corresponding state of the network. At each time step the state of the network moves downhill in the energy landscape. (From Hertz et al. 1991.)

energy is incremented by the values of the thresholds of all the units that are currently active. This is analogous to adding an external magnetic field to the spin glass.[18]

With repetition of the update procedure, picking one unit after another and changing its value from 0 or 1, the global energy state of the system continues to decrease. This cannot proceed forever, of course, because the energy has a lower bound. It therefore follows that in a finite number of steps, which typically is a handful of interactions through all the units, the network converges to a stable state. The energy of the stable state is a local energy minimum, because what "energy minimum" means is that flipping any single unit would increase the energy of the system. The minima are called "attractors" because there is a basin of states around each minimum all of which will converge to the same minimum, as shown in figure 3.17.

Hopfield saw that the local energy minima in spin glasses could be a physical embodiment of prototypes in associative memory. Thus if we make a net with the formal properties of a spin glass, and we designate attractors to be the prototype vectors, then when the network is given a vector-completion job, we know from its spin glass template that the net has the dynamics to complete the input pattern. This is a bit like saying that since we know the dynamical properties of a granite ball rolling down a hill, then a rubber ball rolling down a wooden inclined plane will have relevantly similar dynamical properties.

This formal analogy between the thermodynamics of spin glasses and the dynamics of Hopfield nets has a number of important consequences. First, we get for free the powerful theoretical framework developed by physicists for analyzing such systems. Issues concerning the capacity of the network to store prototypes and the probability of correctly retrieving the desired prototype are consequently more manageable. Second, the framework invites visualiza-

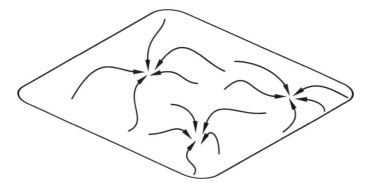

Figure 3.17 Convergence of a network to stable local minima from different starting points. Each point in the plane is a state of the network. The energy landscape has "basins" that will "attract" the state of the network, as illustrated by the trajectories. The process of reaching the stable states at the bottoms of the basins is a form of relaxation, or pattern completion through relaxation. (Adapted from Hertz et al. 1991.)

tion of the dynamics of networks as trajectories in high-dimensional land-scapes. In other words, the geometric representation of the state transitions gives the visual imagination something to feed off, and invites an exploration of extensions of the basic idea. Using the dynamical framework, we can begin to bring nonlinear networks to heel; that is, to understand their capabilities, and most important, to give us insight into how best to design networks to solve particular computational problems (figure 3.18).

In the original Hopfield nets, only transitions to states of lower energy are admissible, which guarantees convergence only to a *local* minimum. How can a net be designed to find the *global* minimum? The trick, it turns out, is to permit an increase in the energy, but only in a restricted way. The best strategy for achieving this was provided by Kirkpatrick et al. (1983), who invented the technique of simulated annealing for global optimization. Crudely speaking, annealing is the process of heating a material such as a metal or glass to a high temperature, then gradually lowering the temperature. The result is that the substance forms crystals. If the annealing process is gradual enough, the material will end up at its global energy minimum. For metals, slow annealing leaves the metal ductile. In contrast, quenching the material by sudden cooling leaves the material in a local energy minimum, perhaps far from the global minimum. Typically, fast annealing produces a brittle state (e.g., steel) that may have other properties such as taking an edge.

To design a network to find the global minimum, we want the networks to copy the dynamics of annealing. So we first do the formal analog of heating it up, and then letting it slowly cool. In the informational context the analog of annealing requires a new update rule (rule for specifying what a unit's next state is, given its current state and its input) which will prevent the network from getting stuck in a local minimum. Such a rule is:

If ΔE_i is the energy gap as expressed in eq. (6) for state s_i of a unit i, then set s_i to 1 with the probability p_i given by

Figure 3.18 Three examples of pattern completion by a Hopfield network. Seven different images were sorted in a single network, where each unit represents a pixel in a 130×180 array. Input patterns are the images shown in the left column, intermediate states in the middle column, and final states in the right column. In the top sequence, a spider emerges from a noisy image. In the middle sequence, a bottle in one half of the image is used to retrieve a paired bottle. In the bottom sequence, the complete image of a dog is retrieved from a small patch of its ear. (Adapted from Hertz et al. 1991.)

$$p_i = \frac{1}{1 + e^{-\Delta E_i/T}} \tag{9}$$

where T is the effective temperature of the system (figure 3.19). At very high temperatures, this probability approaches $1/2$, and all states in the system are equally likely. As the temperature approaches 0, the sigmoid curve for the probability gets steeper and steeper and approaches a step function which is the binary threshold rule used in the original Hopfield network. Notice, therefore, that the Hopfield network corresponds to a system that is quenched to zero temperature.

Relaxation of the net amounts to imposing a dynamics where states of the units change according to the update rule. Thus, the lower the energy of a state, the the more probable it is that the fluctuating system will be in that state. This follows as a theorem from statistical mechanics, based on the Boltzmann distribution, hence the name of the net of this configuration, the Boltzmann machine. If enough updates are performed at temperature T to reach an equilibrium (the system is fluctuating around its average energy), then the probability of a global state with energy E_i is given by:

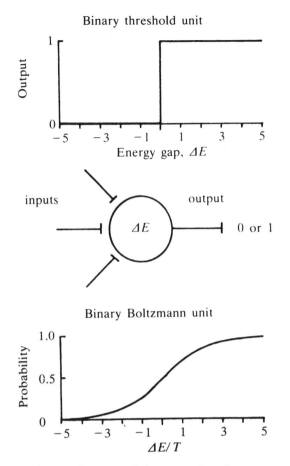

Figure 3.19 The output of a binary unit depends on its inputs and on the output rule (middle). For a unit in a Hopfield network, the output is 1 if the sum of the weights from input units that are active, ΔE, is greater than 0, and 0 otherwise (top). This is called the binary threshold rule. For a unit in the Boltzmann machine, the output value is 1 with a probability given by a sigmoid function of ΔE (bottom). The input is scaled by the temperature T. (From Kienker et al. [1986]. Separating figure from ground with a parallel network. *Perception* 15: 197–216.)

$$P_i \propto e^{-E_i/T} \tag{10}$$

It follows that the lowest energy state is the most probable, and that this state becomes increasingly probable as the temperature is lowered. Thus, at the end of the slow annealing process, with very high probability (approaching 1) the system will be at the global energy minimum.

This architecture was used by Hinton and Sejnowski (1983, Ackley et al. 1985, Kienker et al. 1986) to study problems in perception that require a global minimum. They called this the Boltzmann machine, reflecting formal equivalence between Ludwig Boltzmann's contribution to statistical mechanics and the network's dynamical properties. Independently, Hopfield and Tank (1985) developed a similar approach to optimization using continuous valued units rather than the binary units deployed in the Boltzmann machine. What is the relation between these two networks, given the choice between binary and continuous values? At equilibrium, the units of a Boltzmann machine fluctuate on and off with a probability that depends on the average of the fluctuating input values. The mean of these fluctuations during a certain time interval represents the probability that the unit will have the value 1, and this probability is a continuous valued number between 0 and 1. Hopfield and Tank used these continuous probability values as the activation values of the units. This is the heart of the connection between the two nets. Eqs. (8)–(10) can, therefore, be solved for continuous valued units, in which case the result is called "the mean field approximation" (figure 3.15). Hopfield and Tank showed that the mean field approximation could be applied successfully to a large variety of classical optimization problems, including very difficult ones such as the traveling salesman problem and finding the minimum wire lengths for creating integrated circuits and even nervous systems.[19]

Now, it has been shown mathematically that finding *the* best solution to such problems is difficult in the extreme, so the pressing question is whether nets do indeed find the best solution. The answer is generally "no" for the Hopfield and Tank network. This is not as disappointing as one might surmise, however, since these networks often find *good* solutions *very rapidly*, even if they typically do not find the uniquely best solution. A Boltzmann machine, in contrast to the Hopfield and Tank network, is guaranteed to find the global minimum, so long as it is cooled slowly enough (Geman and Geman 1984).[20] Nevertheless, depending on the situation, it may be more efficient to cool the network at a moderate rate and go with a "just-fine" solution than to wait around for the Boltzmann machine to settle into the best. The optimal rate of cooling will be different for each network.

Using statistical mechanics to analyze a network and prove that it can find solutions to global optimization problems is a beautiful mathematical result. What good is it computationally? Given that the dynamics of a Boltzmann machine conform to the dynamics of annealing, of this much we can be certain: it will search the energy landscape and find the global energy minimum. If the network is representing an instance of an optimization problem (e.g., what is the shortest line connecting all the dots with no redundancy?) and the output values are representing the solution, *then the dynamics guarantee that the answer is forthcoming*. Since optimization problems are difficult to solve, and the more variables the more horrendous they become, this is a very useful result. As we shall see below, it is the key to developing rules for automatized weight-setting in a net and it is also the key to using model nets as a tool for analyzing real neural nets. As we shall also see, there is an additional practical matter of how long the process takes.

A brief aside: notice that in the Boltzmann machine, matters of computation, of algorithm, and of implementation are not really separable. It is the very physical configuration of the input that directly encodes the computational problem, and the algorithm is nothing other than the very process whereby the physical system settles into the solution. This contrasts rather vividly with the standard separation of hardware and algorithm in digital computers.[21]

How does this framework help with the weight-adjusting question raised earlier? This needs a bit of stalking, so we shall advance by going back to the problem of separating figure from ground in a visual image. Recall that the problem is to identify which parts of an image belong to the figure and which to the background. A watered-down version of this problem, suitable for the context at hand, is this: suppose the stimulus consists only of boundary lines of an object, perhaps with gaps and noise; suppose also that there is an initial bias that latches on to either the general location of the inside of the figure or the general location of the nonfigure. This version of the problem assumes that the difficult task of deciding what in the stimulus constitutes a boundary has already been solved and the remaining problem is to decide, for any given patch, whether it is figure-inside or figure-outside (ground). This residual task—the segregation task—is by no means trivial, since a decision that a local patch is figure-inside depends on the status of patches elsewhere, even patches at considerable remove. This means that a globally consistent solution is required of the net. To display its results, the net "colors in" the pixels inside the figure, leaving the area outside the figure uncolored. How can the machine figure out what pixels to color?

This is the kind of global problem that relaxation nets should be able to solve through local interactions between neighboring units. Just such a network was constructed fitting the Boltzmann machine design. Given the simplifications to the problem, there are just two variables to represent: (a) locations of boundaries, and (b) x belongs to figure (and its negation, "x does not belong to the figure," which is equivalent to "x belongs to the ground"). The states of the machine can be displayed as a stack of two-dimensional, in-register grids, one composed of "edge" units and the other of "belongs-to-figure" units (figure 3.20). "Edge" units have a pointer to specify which direction is "in," and they have orientation, either horizontal or vertical. "Belongs-to-figure" units fill in their space. The output is essentially a topographic map of the image, in which every pixel is either filled in or not, and for each pair of pixels, either there is a boundary or not.

The weights in the network are then chosen to reflect the relationships between the "hypotheses" specifying "edge here" or "belongs to figure." Thus units representing two nearby patches of an image are connected with reciprocal excitatory connections, say of strength $+10$, thereby instantiating the property of objects to be continuous across the image. Edge units have excitatory connections with the unit it points toward ($+12$), with two flanking units ($+10$), and reciprocal inhibitory connections with the unit it points away from (-12). In addition to connections between units, there are connections from sensory inputs that bias the edge units along the boundary of the figure. There is also an attentional bias, which activates figure units near the center of the figure. This tells the net on which side of the boundary to color-fill. To switch figure–ground, the bias shifts so that the net fills the counterpart set of pixels.

The weights embody the constraints of the problem, in this case, object continuity across space, and object discontinuity at boundaries. Interactions between units are such that the final decision about whether a patch belongs to

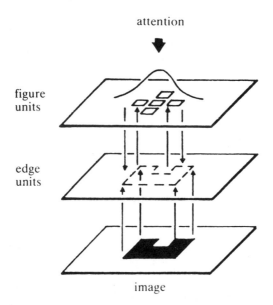

Figure 3.20 Schematic diagram of a figure–ground network using layers of binary units. Each layer is an array of units that are interconnected within and between layers. The edge units receive "bottom-up" activation at the locations of contrast boundaries in the image (shown below), and the figure units receive "top-down" activation from a Gaussian "spotlight" of attention (shown above). During the relaxation process these two inputs are maintained at constant values. (From Kienker et al. 1986.)

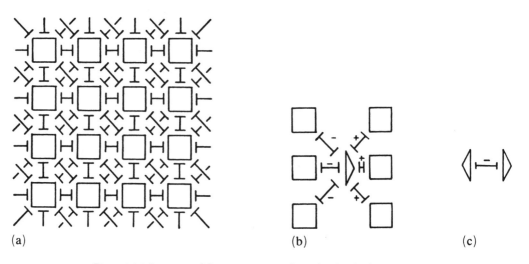

(a)   (b)   (c)

Figure 3.21 Summary of the connections and weights for the figure–ground network. (a) Each figure unit (square) is reciprocally connected to each of its eight nearest neighbors by an excitatory weight (+10). (b) Each edge unit (arrowhead) points in the direction of the figure and has excitatory connections with the figure unit it points toward (+12) and two flanking units (+10), as well as having inhibitory connections with the figure unit it points away from (−12) and the two flanking figure units (−10). (c) Two edge units that represent figures on opposite sides of the contour mutually inhibit each other (−15) to implement the constraint that the figure can be on only one side of the boundary, not both. In addition, there is excitation between adjacent edge units with the same orientation. This pattern of connectivity is repeated throughout the array. (From Kienker et al. 1986.)

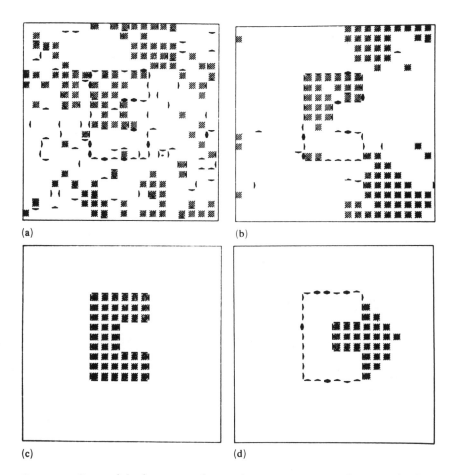

(a)

(b)

(c)

(d)

Figure 3.22 States of the figure–ground network at successive stages during simulated annealing: high temperature in (a), medium temperature in (b), and low temperatures in (c) and (d). The attention is centered on the waist of the C in (a)–(c) and is located outside the C in (d). In the final state, the figure units are uniformly filled up to the boundary, and the edge units at the boundaries are all pointing toward the figure. (From Kienker et al. 1986.)

the figure is made only after balancing all of the evidence from other units connected to it by positive and negative weights. Figure 3.21 illustrates more exactly how such a network can be constructed and the weights set.

The visual input to the network specifies the boundary of an object much as oriented cells in the cortex would be activated by luminance boundaries. The goal of the network is to decide which regions in the image should belong to the figure and which to the ground. The network starts at a high temperature, where all the figure units have a roughly equal probability of being activated. As the temperature is lowered, the figure units have a tendency to cluster together because of the excitatory weights connecting them. These clusters will dissipate unless they are stabilized by a bounding contour (figure 3.22). Whether the inside or the outside of the boundary is filled in depends on where the "spotlight of attention" biases the figure units, as shown in figure 3.22(c) and (d). This annealing procedure is successful in segmenting these simple images because the correct global configuration of figure and edge units is in

Figure 3.23 Image of a figure with an incomplete outline that may still be perceived as a familiar object. (With permission from Coren and Ward [1989]. *Sensation and Perception*, 3rd ed. Copyright © 1989 Harcourt Brace Jovanovich, Inc.)

fact the state of the network with the lowest energy. The procedure is also forgiving, in the sense that the network will fill in properly even should the input be somewhat degraded, that is, should there be a few gaps in the boundary. In this respect, it resembles human perception (figure 3.23) (Mumford et al. 1987).

This network is an instance of a more general computational approach known as "relaxation labeling" that has been applied to a variety of problems in computer vision (Waltz 1975, Hummel and Zucker 1983). In the figure-ground example of constraint satisfaction performed by a Boltzmann machine, the weights on the units were set by hand, meaning that the modeler had to figure out by rather long and laborious trial-and-error procedures what weights were needed to ensure that the global energy minimum really is the solution for any figure–ground problem. Ideally, what one would like is an automated procedure for setting weights, perhaps triggered by showing the network examples of question–answer pairs, and then letting it "figure out" what weights would do the job. How could a network do that? How could a network automatically adjust its weights appropriately?

5 LEARNING IN NEURAL NETS

Learning[22] algorithms for automated weight-setting in networks come in two basic molds: supervised and unsupervised. The basic difference concerns whether the net infers a weight modification from a report on its behavioral performance. Supervised learning relies on three things: input, the net's internal dynamics, and an evaluation of its weight-setting job. Unsupervised learning uses only two: input, and the dynamics of the net; no external report on its behavior vis-a-vis its weight-setting progress is provided. In either case, the point of the learning algorithm is to produce a weight configuration that can be said to represent something in the world, in the sense that when activated by an input vector, the correct answer is produced. Nets using unsupervised learning can be configured such that the weights embody regularities in the stimulus domain. For example, if weights are adjusted according to a Hebb rule, then gradually, without external feedback and with only input data, the net structures itself to represent whatever systematicity it can find in the input, such as continuity in boundaries. This means that unsupervised nets are useful in creating feature detectors, and consequently unsupervised nets can be the front end of a machine whose sensory input must be encoded in some perspicuous fashion before it is sent on for use in such tasks as pattern recognition and motor control.

We emphasized that unsupervised learning has no access to external feedback, and we now take up the possibility that it nevertheless allows for internal error feedback. Because there is a confusion in the literature concerning error feedback and the convention for applying the label "supervised," we propose explicit labels for the distinction between external and internal feedback. When the feedback is external to the organism, the learning is called *"supervised"*; when there is an internal measure of error, we call the learning *"monitored"* (figure 3.24). Consider, for example, a net required to learn to predict the next input. Assume it gets no external feedback, but it does use its previous inputs to make its predictions. When the next input enters, the net may be able to use the discrepancy between the predicted input and the actual input to get a measure of error, which it can then use to improve its next prediction. This is an instance of a net whose learning is unsupervised, but monitored.[23] More generally, there may be internal measures of consistency or coherence that can also be internally monitored and used in improving the internal representation. The confusion in the literature is owed in part to the fact that the very same algorithms used for supervised learning can be suitably internalized for monitoring. Clarity of the semantics is especially important in discussing feedback modes in nervous systems, where certain kinds of supervised learning may be unbiological, but error detected by a monitor in one part of the nervous system is a plausible teaching signal for another part of the nervous system.

Is there a type of system that acquires organization even though it is neither supervised nor monitored? In real nervous systems, some aspects of development, such as establishing connections between nerve cells, might be considered candidates for self-organization of this kind. In models with unsupervised learning, such as competitive learning, it initially appeared that no internal objective function served as a monitor. Subsequent analysis has shown, however, that objective functions can be found for each of these models. Optimization of these implicit functions is responsible for the ability of the network to

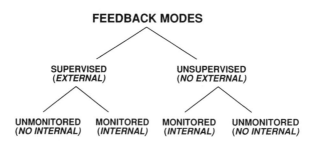

FEEDBACK MODES

SUPERVISED
(EXTERNAL)

UNSUPERVISED
(NO EXTERNAL)

UNMONITORED
(NO INTERNAL)

MONITORED
(INTERNAL)

MONITORED
(INTERNAL)

UNMONITORED
(NO INTERNAL)

Figure 3.24 Taxonomy of learning procedures. Supervised learning occurs when there is feedback on the performance of the system from the external environment. If the feedback is a scalar reward, it is called reinforcement learning. The learning is called monitored if the system has an internal measure of error. These distinctions refer to the *system* and not the algorithms used; thus backpropagation of error, which is normally used in supervised, unmonitored (S& ∼ M) systems, could also be used in an unsupervised, monitored (∼ S&M) system. For example, a feedforward net with fewer hidden units than input units can be trained to reproduce input patterns—a form of image compression (Cottrell et al. 1987). A more sophisticated example of an ∼ S&M net uses information-theoretic measures internal to the net to train the hidden units to predict the values of neighboring hidden units (Becker and Hinton 1989). An example of a supervised, monitored (S&M) system is the associative search network with internal predictors (Barto et al. 1981). In this system, the internal predictor learns to anticipate the reward; the difference between the predicted reward and the actual reward is used to adjust weights to hidden units. The internal monitor can be quite a sophisticated high-dimensional error signal, as in motor learning when a distal measure of performance (missing the basket) is used for adjusting a complex motor program (jump shot) (Jordan and Rumelhart 1990).

organize itself into a computationally successful state (Durbin and Willshaw 1987, Linsker 1990b). The conjecture, therefore, is that all successful self-organizing systems, including biological ones, have an implicit objective function that is optimized during the learning process (Sejnowski 1987). For an example, see section 5.9 on the development of ocular dominance columns.

Supervised learning comes in various grades as a function of the report card format. The report-card may (1) merely say "Good answer" or "Bad answer" (Sutton and Barto 1981, 1990), (2) specify a measure of the size of the error with some degrees of precision, or (3) give rich detail, saying, in effect, "You said the answer was abcd; the answer should be ahcp." Given the range available in (2), this allows a continuum of report-card formats. Regardless of the format of the report card, the point of feedback is to give the net opportunity to reduce the error in its output.

In the original Hopfield nets, the learning rule was an update rule in the Hebbian mold. The problems given the net were, however, carefully chosen to be solvable by it. The class of problems solvable by these nets using the Hebb rule is rather narrow, embracing only first-order statistical problems. That is, problems where the question is "do feature A and feature B correlate?," which in machine terms means "are the A-unit and the B-unit on together and off together?" Problems beyond its scope are higher-order statistical problems, e.g., "what is the correlation story for {A, B, C, D}, or for {EF, EH, GH}?" Going beyond these narrow limitations is desirable, since many problems cannot be solved using only lower-order statistics. To target high-order problems, the basic architecture of the machine must be expanded to include units that intervene between external input and behavioral output. Called "hidden units," they typically connect to the input units, to each other, and to output units when there are any. Adding one or more layers of hidden units allows the net to handle high-order statistics, for, crudely speaking, the extra set of connections and extra dimension of interactions is what permits the net a global perspective despite its local connectivity.

The ability of hidden layers to extract higher-order information is especially valuable when the number of input units is large, as it is, for example, in sensory systems. Suppose an input layer has n units in a two-dimensional array, as does the retina, or a one-dimensional array, as does the cochlea. If the units are binary, then the total number of possible input patterns is 2^n. In fact, neurons are many valued, so the problem is really somewhat worse. Suppose all patterns (state combinations) were equally likely to occur, and suppose one hidden unit represents exactly one input pattern. This would make it possible to represent any function in the output layer by suitable connections from hidden units. The trouble arises when n is very large, e.g., a million, in which case the number of possible states is so large that no physical system could contain all the hidden units. Since not all possible input patterns are equally likely, only a very small subset of all possible input patterns need be represented by the hidden units.

Accordingly, the problem for the hidden units is to discover what combinations of features are ignorable, which features systematically occur together or are otherwise "cohorted," and among *those*, which are the combinations to "care" about and represent. The information for this last task cannot be garnered from inside the net itself, but must be provided from the outside. The division of labor in a net with hidden units looks like this: unsupervised learning is very good at finding combinations but cannot know which subset to "care" about; supervised learning can be given criteria to segregate a "useful" subset of patterns, but it is less efficient in searching out the basic combinations. So by means of unsupervised learning, a basic sorting is accomplished; by means of supervised learning, a subset of basic combinations can be extracted as the "useful" ones.

As the net runs, hidden units may be assigned states according to either a linear or a nonlinear function. If the hidden units are linear, there is an optimal solution called the *principal components*[24] (figure 3.25). This procedure can be used to find the subset of vectors that is the best linear approximation to the set of input vectors. (As we shall see in chapter 5, in a model devised by Miller and Stryker (1990) for development of ocular dominance columns in visual cortex, Hebbian learning finds principal components.) Principal component analysis and its extensions are useful for lower-order statistics, but many of the interesting structures in the world—the structures brains "care" about—are characterized by high-order properties. If luminance is taken as the 0th order property, then boundaries will be an example of a first-order property, and characteristics of boundaries such as occlusion and three-dimensional shape will be higher-order properties. Nonlinear hidden units are needed to represent

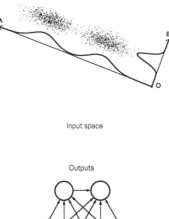

Input space

Outputs

Inputs

Figure 3.25 A feedforward, unsupervised network that performs principal component analysis. The input vectors, represented by dots in the plane, form two elongated clusters. The first principal component direction, along the line A, is the projection that maximizes the variance of the inputs. Discriminating along this direction is likely to be helpful in separating inputs into two or more classes. The direction of the second principal component, B, is the axis with maximum variance in the subspace orthogonal to A. These directions can be easily extracted from the inputs by the network below, which uses a modified form of the Hebbian learning rule on the feedward weights (Oja 1982) and an anti-Hebbian learning rule on the lateral connection between the output units (Rubner and Tavan 1989, Leen 1991). Following learning, the weights to each output unit correspond to the direction of a single principal component. Moreover, multi-layered networks with localized receptive fields can successively extract more complex features from the input space (Linsker 1986, Kammen and Yuille 1988). (From Hertz et al. 1991.)

these higher-order properties. If hidden units are to self-organize so that they can represent these properties, procedures more poweful than principal component analysis must be found.

How then should weights of hidden units be adjusted so that the net can do higher-order problems? Finding a suitable weight-change rule looks really tough, because not only are the units *hidden*, but they may be *nonlinear*, so trial and error is hopeless, and no decision procedure, apart from exhaustive search, exists for solving this problem in general. Moreover, any solution to the weight-adjustment problem depends critically on the architecture and dynamics of a given net. For most architectures and dynamics, the solution is simply not known.

In the specific case of the Boltzmann machine, however, a procedure whereby its nonlinear hidden units can learn to extract higher-order properties is known. The crux of the procedure depends on Boltzmann machines having an interesting property at equilibrium, namely their states have a Boltzmann distribution, eq. (10), which gives, for any global state of the system, the probability of that state occurring at equilibrium. This means that at equilibrium we

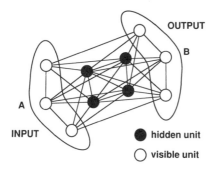

Figure 3.26 Schematic diagram of a Boltzmann machine. The units in the network have binary values and the connections between them are reciprocal. The weights on the connections can be trained by presenting patterns to the input units in the presence and the absence of output patterns and applying the Boltzmann learning rule. During the learning process, all of the weights in the network are modified, including those among the hidden units, which do not receive direct information from outside the network. The hidden units develop features that allow the network to perform complex associations between input patterns and output patterns. Hidden units give Boltzmann machines powerful internal representations not available to networks containing only visible units.

know the global consequences of any local weight change (which will change the energy). Now take the converse of this rule, and we have, for any desired global state, a simple procedure for increasing the probability of that state occurring by changing a weight locally.

It is important to emphasize that all the globally relevant information needed to update the weight is available locally. This may seem contradictory, given that units may be connected only with their immediate neighbors. It is, however, a simple consequence of the net's connectivity: a unit's neighbors are connected to its neighbors, who are in turn connected to all their neighbors, and so forth. Given the connectivity and the Boltzmann distribution at equilibrium, it is guaranteed that information from synaptically distant units is propagated throughout the net. The weight modification rule, therefore, is:

$$\Delta w_{ij} = \varepsilon[\langle s_i s_j \rangle_{\text{clamped}} - \langle s_i s_j \rangle_{\text{free}}] \tag{11}$$

where ε is the rate of learning, s_i is the binary value of the ith unit, and $\langle \ldots \rangle$ indicates that the quantity ... should be averaged over time after the network has reached equilibrium.[25] In the clamped condition, both the input and output units are fixed to their correct values, and in the free condition, only the inputs are so fixed (figure 3.26). This is in the supervised mode; in unsupervised mode, none of the units is fixed in the free condition.

Each application of the learning rule is a cycle with three steps: (1) clamp value of inputs, let machine come to equilibrium in the clamped condition, then compute co-occurrences of pairs of units; (2) compute co-occurrences of states in the absence of the inputs (unclamped condition and let the machine find equilibrium again); (3) subtract the two, and adjust the weight proportionally to the difference (the compare condition). Although the net is certain to learn correctly, the drawback is that it requires many, many three-step cycles to learn one input pattern, and it must repeat this for every input pattern it is to learn.

We have seen how a Boltzmann machine could do pattern completion, in that once trained-up, if the net were given an incomplete pattern as input, it would go into a state representing the complete pattern. Can we get it to do an input–output mapping? Yes, and here is how to move from an unsupervised Boltzmann machine to a supervised Boltzmann machine without changing architecture or algorithm but only by "externalizing" the feedback. First, arbitrarily split the array of input units into two groups, A and B. The only procedural modification consists in feeding group A the same input pattern # during *both* the clamped phase and the compare phase. The second group, B, of input units is more conventional; it is fed its pattern * only during the clamped phase. In effect, then, the hidden units are coming to associate pattern # with pattern *. This can look like pattern completion on the part of the hidden units, but because the hidden units also have reciprocal connections to the inputs, it can look like the hidden units give output * for input #. That is, think of the hidden-to-group-B input connection as a kind of output. Then we have the arrangement whereby in the trained-up net we can feed the net #, and via the hidden reciprocal connection pattern * appears in group B. This means that group B is, for all intents and purposes, an external teacher, telling the net (during group B's clamped phase) what new thing to associate with #.

It takes only one counter-example to sunder an impossibility claim. Boltzmann learning in a net with hidden units—and even with nonlinear hidden units—was a counter-example to the received wisdom according to which the learning problem for multilayered networks was intractable (Minsky and Papert 1969). With the door open, weight-adjusting rules other than that used in the Boltzmann machine were sought. It is now clear that there are many possible solutions to the weight-adjusting problem in a net with hidden (and possibly nonlinear) units, and other solutions may draw on nets with a different architecture and with different dynamics. Thus nets may have continuous valued units, the output function for a unit may have complex nonlinearities, connections between units need not be symmetric, and the network may have more interesting dynamics, such as limit cycles and constrained trajectories. Weight-adjusting problems are really solved by an ordered triple: ⟨architecture, dynamics, parameter-adjusting procedure⟩. In the final section of this chapter we shall outline a very general approach to handle all of these cases.

6 COMPETITIVE LEARNING

Because including a "teacher" as an adjunct to a network is informationally expensive, not to mention biologically unrealistic, it is important to explore the domain of unsupervised learning procedures. As a first pass, a rule of thumb for identifying those features in the sensory input stream that are likely to be useful in categorizing is this: the more frequently a feature occurs in various input vectors, the more likely it is to be salient in categorizing an input as belonging to a certain class. For example, if for a certain bottom creature the presence of predators typically co-occurs with a looming darkness, then it would make sense for units in the network to extract changes in intensity at all possible locations in the visual field and represent them in its output. Extracting what is criterial rather than performing all-feature coverage also has an obvious advantage for image compression where the goal is to represent an image with the fewest bits of information. Thus, if boundaries of objects are marked by discontinuities in luminance, then a network might most efficiently represent objects by allowing a single unit to represent a long length of luminance border. In short, it is cheaper to represent a stretch of border with a single unit rather than have many units representing small segments of a straight border. In this sense we get information compression.

In addition to the Boltzmann style of unsupervised learning, other kinds of interactions can self-organize so that the network embodies compressed representations.[26] Consider a simple two-layer network with a set of input units, and one layer of weights connecting them to a set of output units, laterally connected by mutual inhibition. This arrangement is competitive in the sense that the mutual inhibition will create a winner-take-all profile at the output level: if an input pattern happens to excite unit 1 to a greater degree than any of the other output units, then unit 1's consequent activity will tend to suppress the others to a greater degree than they are suppressing unit 1. This is an example of relaxation of a network into a stable pattern. As with the earlier examples of relaxation, this network is guaranteed to converge to a final state in which unit 1 is strongly active when input pattern A is presented, while its cohort output units are suppressed. It is assumed that the activity level of the output unit is 1 in case it is a winner, and 0 otherwise. This is what permits characterization of the output unit's representation as winner-take-all.

The description so far has been confined to the net's *activities* given an input. The next matter concerns using this base to set the weights so that when pattern A is next presented, the network will go straightaway to the correct representation. Learning in this net can be accomplished by changing the weights to the winner unit i according to this rule:

$$\Delta w_{ij} = \varepsilon x_j \tag{12}$$

where x_j is the jth component of the input vector, and the ith output unit is the winner. The rule is essentially Hebbian inasmuch as weights increase when pre- and postsynaptic units are concurrently active. As the label implies, in winner-take-all mode, only the winning output unit is active. Although this rule for weight adjustment should work in principle, in practice it is inadequate because the weights can grow without bound and eventually one unit will dominate the rest, and will be activated for any input pattern, thus losing the capacity to discriminate between patterns. How can we rig it so that the unit is excited when and *only when* particular input vectors are presented? Recall that the activity of an output unit is the inner product of the input vector and the weight vector. The strategy is to adjust the weights so that the weight vector for each unit becomes congruent with the input vector it specializes in. This can be accomplished without hand-setting by modifying eq. (12) as follows:

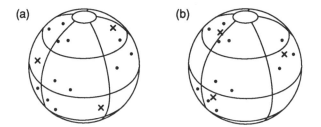

Figure 3.27 Competitive learning. The dots represent input vectors normalized to unit length, so they lie on a sphere. The weights are similarly normalized, and the input weights for the output units are indicated by crosses. (a) Organization of the network before learning. (b) After learning, each output unit has migrated to a cluster of input vectors. (From Hertz et al. 1991)

$$\Delta w_{ij} = \varepsilon(x_j - w_{ij}) \tag{13}$$

The main effect of this algorithm is to move the weight vector directly toward the input vector. Accordingly, if the weight vector and input vector are already congruent, no change will be made and the weight vector will top out.

So far we have considered the behavior of the network when it has but one pattern to represent. Suppose now that it is given many different input vectors, and hence that there are many different patterns to be represented. How will the net manage? When there are fewer output units than input vectors, each output unit will become specialized for clusters of overlapping input vectors, as illustrated in figure 3.27. In this way, the network will tend to develop output units that are sensitive to features common to its preferred input vectors, with each output specializing for a different particular feature. Consequently, what any given unit can be said to represent is a *prototype* of the range of nonidentical but overlapping vectors that turn it on.

There are three general weaknesses with networks of this type so far as adequate representation of patterns is concerned. First, sometimes critical information in a pattern may not correspond to the most frequently occurring feature, and so may fail to be represented by the net. A bottom creature who represents predators as looming shadows may thus be fooled by a predator with a thin dangling stinger, and this could be trouble if the predator is especially deadly, however rare. The second weakness is that this procedure picks out the lowest-order features, but it may be the higher-order features such as those that characterize the differences between faces that are critical for classification. Finally, relational invariances such as rotation, dilation, and translation need to be extracted before the patterns can be compared. Strategies for overcoming these drawbacks will be considered in chapter 4.

The third difficulty concerns stability of the weight configurations. The weights may shift even when the input is relatively familiar but the order of input vectors varies, and the instability problem is yet more acute should the network be given novel input vectors. In the real world, some forgetting may be advantageous, but on the other hand, it is often essential that previous learning not be wiped out by new encounters. Some provision needs to be made to retain relevant and important aspects of what has already been learned

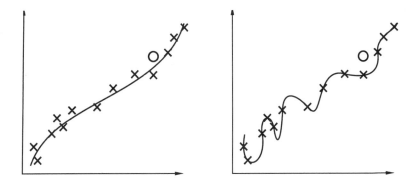

Figure 3.28 Curve fitting and overfitting. The data points are given (X) and the goal is to pass a curve through them. It is known that the data contain noise. A smooth curve (left) does a better job of predicting a new data point (O) than does a kinky curve (right). The degree of smoothing and the choice of interpolating function depend on the data and are central issues in approximation theory.

while learning new things. How nervous systems manage to do this is not understood, but one solution for artificial networks, explored by Carpenter and Grossberg (1987), is to add new units when novel inputs are encountered. There are many variations of the competitive network theme, including generalizing the basic architecture to multilayered networks (Fukushima 1975).

7 CURVE FITTING

The classic example of fitting parameters to a model is curve fitting, that is, fitting a host of noisy data points with a smooth function, using the least squares method (figure 3.28) (i.e., minimize squared error for the whole set). For a fit with a straight-line function, the squared error E is given by this equation:

$$E(m, b) = \frac{1}{2} \sum_i^N [mx_i + b - y_i]^2 \tag{14}$$

where m is the slope, b is the intercept with the y-axis, and there are N data points, (x_i, y_i). When the error is at the minimum, the gradient of E with respect to the parameters (m and b) $= 0$. That is,

for m: $\dfrac{\partial E}{\partial m} = \sum_i^N (mx_i + b - y_i)x_i = 0$

for b: $\dfrac{\partial E}{\partial b} = \sum_i^N (mx_i + b - y_i) = 0$
$\tag{15}$

These are two simultaneous equations with two unknowns. This is a relatively easy problem. Nevertheless, as the number of dimensions of the state space increases, and the number of parameters needed to fit the data increases, then the problem becomes much more difficult. Thus we may be looking for a curve, not in a 2-D space, but in a 10-D or 100-D or 10,000-D space. The traditional solution consists in solving the equations algebraically, which is quite manageable so long as the number of parameters and the number of data points are

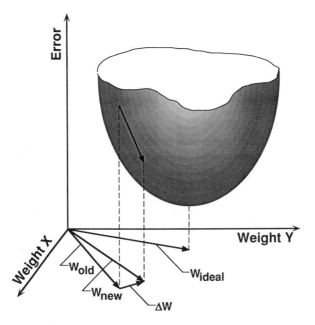

Figure 3.29 Error surface and gradient descent. The goal is to find the set of weights that gives the minimum error. For a given set of parameters (shown here for two weights plotted in the x–y plane) the gradient of the error surface is computed to find the direction of steepest descent. The weights are incrementally changed by ΔW along this direction, and the procedure is repeated until the weights reach W_{ideal}, which gives minimum error. For a nonlinear network the error surface may have many local minima.

small. As soon as either is large, then the algebraic method is nasty and unmanageable. Fortunately, there is a way, other than the traditional algebraic technique, to find the solution. This involves using knowledge of the gradients to iteratively update the estimates for the parameters.[27] This is essentially like iteratively updating weights in a net, and can be given geometric representation (figure 3.29). In iterative curve fitting we update according to this rule:

$$\Delta m = -\varepsilon \frac{\partial E}{\partial m}$$

$$\Delta b = -\varepsilon \frac{\partial E}{\partial b} \tag{16}$$

where Δm is the change in m, Δb is the change in b, and ε is the learning rate.

Instead of computing the exact gradient, the parameters can be adjusted after every sample, or after averaging a few samples. This speeds up convergence, which can be guaranteed if the learning rate, ε, approaches zero sufficiently slowly. This procedure is called gradient descent because at every step the parameters are changed to follow the gradient downhill, much as a skier might follow the fall line. We encountered gradient descent earlier in the context of Boltzmann learning procedures, where iterative application of the weight update rule gradually led us to better performance.[28]

To apply gradient descent, one must have a mathematically well-defined measure, such as mean squared error, to optimize, as well as an efficient way to calculate the gradients. Models that are dynamical and have many parameters have to be represented in a many-dimensional state space. Accordingly, the amount of computer time to perform the calculations may be astronomical, so it is essential to find efficient ways of computing. Exploring such procedures for some classes of models, such as feedforward nets and recurrent nets with linearly summing weights and nonlinear input–output functions led to important breakthroughs in the 1980s. (See section 8.)

When the curve-fitting task is fitting a *straight line*, gradient descent guarantees convergence to the global minimum of the error function. By contrast, there is no such guarantee for the general nonlinear problem, where the error surface may have many local minima, though if one is lucky, they will be close enough to the global minimum that it will not matter much if the net stops in one. For most of the problems presented in the later chapters, finding the true global minimum is unnecessary, and there are many equally good local minima. Thus if a net is started running with its initial weights randomly set to small values, it is likely to end up with one of these good solutions.

8 FEEDFORWARD NETS: TWO EXAMPLES

In feedforward networks the input leads directly to an output without feedback. Because feedforward nets have significant advantages in speed and simplicity, it is worthwhile exploring what computations a feedforward network can handle. In this section, we show that a feedforward network with one layer of weights cannot compute an extraordinarily simple function. Understanding the whys and wherefores of the limitations is instructive, and yields insights into the geometrical nature of feedforward networks. This is important, because it is the geometry of a network that determines what can be represented and how things can be represented; in appreciating that, we can see how to overcome these limitations:

Exclusive "or"

The look-up table for a function called the exclusive "or" (XOR) was introduced earlier. The question now is whether this very function can be executed by a net; more specifically, the question concerns what sort of network architecture is necessary to execute this function. Finding a suitable architecture turns out to be instructive because of the failures and what they imply for a whole range of functions. To milk the lesson from the failures, we consider first the archetypal simple net. It consists of one output unit, taking value 0 or 1 (representing "false" and "true"), and two input units that carry the values of the component propositions.[29] This simple net has three free parameters: the two weights from the input units to the output units, and a single threshold or bias on the output unit. The architecture of this net determines the function for the output:

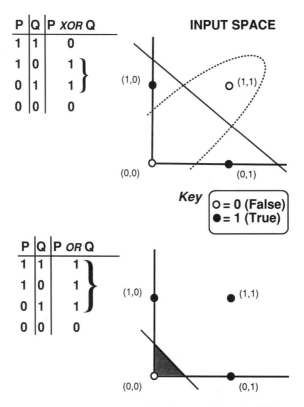

P	Q	P XOR Q
1	1	0
1	0	1
0	1	1
0	0	0

INPUT SPACE

(1,0)   (1,1)

(0,0)   (0,1)

Key O = 0 (False)
● = 1 (True)

P	Q	P OR Q
1	1	1
1	0	1
0	1	1
0	0	0

(1,0)   (1,1)

(0,0)   (0,1)

Figure 3.30 *XOR* is not a separable function. The truth table for *XOR* is shown on the upper left and is plotted on the upper right. No line in the plane can separate all of the closed dots (true, or 1) from all of the open dots (false, or 0). In contrast, the OR function, shown below, can be separated by the line shown in the bottom right. A network with one layer of weights can be found to represent a function if it is separable, but no such network can be found if the function is nonseparable, like *XOR*.

$$o = H(w_P P + w_Q Q + b) \tag{17}$$

where o is the output, H(input) is a binary threshold function (figure 3.19), w_P and w_Q are the weights for the binary inputs P and Q respectively, and b is the bias.

Does there exist any configuration of weights and the bias such that the output unit correctly assigns values to the compound? For this simple net, the answer is "no," and figure 3.30 (top) illustrates why. The input space has an axis for each of the two units, and points representing the four possible input vectors. If the output unit can solve the problem, it must be able to group together the inputs that give 1, and in another group, the inputs that give 0. Geometrically speaking, the function restricts the border between these two regions of the input space to a straight line. On one side of the decision border, all inputs drive the output over threshold, giving 1; on the other side, the inputs are below threshold, giving 0. No such straight line exists.

For contrast, the output unit of the simple net can execute the inclusive "or" (*OR*), and the input space for the same network architecture clearly does admit of a straight line appropriately dividing the inputs (figure 3.30, bottom). Why does the decision border have to be straight? Because the architecture of the net is consistent only with a linear function, and hence limits how the inputs can be segregated for training to give the correct output. In other words, the exclusive "or" is not a *linearly separable function*, and hence no learning algorithm can find a solution to the weight configuration problem in the simple net because none exists. Intuitively, this can be seen by reflecting on the logic of the *XOR*. Analyzed in English, it comes out thus: (*P XOR Q*) is true if and only if either *P* is true or *Q* is true, *but not both P and Q are true*. It is this extra twist on the back end of the basic OR function that needs to be accommodated. The point is that we need take the output of the more basic OR function, and operate on it again to get a higher-order property. Can the simple net be embellished to handle what is in effect a function on the output of a function? Yes, and the modification is both blindingly obvious in retrospect and was frustratingly opaque in prospect.

The crucial modification consists in adding an intervening unit—a hidden unit—that is interposed between the inputs and the outputs. This supplements the weights by three, and adds another bias unit. With a new total of seven parameters, the new question is this: are there weight-settings such that the net will solve the problem? This time the answer is "yes," for the role of the hidden unit is to handle the second-order operation; that is, it gets its input from *P* and *Q*, and recognizes when not both *P* and *Q* are true. In fact, more than one weight configuration will suffice to do the job. The next question, of course, concerns automated training: is there a gradient-descent procedure for adjusting the weights? Insofar as the units are binary, gradient descent cannot be used to adjust the weights between the input units and the hidden unit. The trouble is that small changes to these weights will have no effect on the output, save in the case where it is close to the threshold of the hidden unit.

In the 1960s, model net research had developed to the point where the need for hidden units to handle nonlinearly separable functions was understood, but how to automate weight-setting, especially for the hidden units, was not (Rosenblatt 1961, Minsky and Papert 1969). As we saw earlier, automated adjustment of hidden unit weights was achieved in the Boltzmann machine in the early 1980s. How to do this for a feedforward network remained baffling. In 1986, Rumelhart, Hinton, and Williams, discovered[30] that the trick is to push the output of each hidden unit through a squashing function, that is, a smoothly varying function that maps the hidden units' input onto output (figure 3.31). Hitherto, the output from the hidden units was a step function of the input. The smoothly varying function, however, means that small changes on the weights of the hidden unit's inputs allow the hidden unit to abstract the higher-order property in small error-correcting steps, and hence to learn to recognize when both *P* and *Q* are 1. The net effect of adding hidden units and putting their output through a squashing function is that the input space can now be divided by a curvy decision border.

The backpropagation algorithm starts with small, randomly chosen weights and proceeds incrementally, just as in the earlier curve-fitting example. The

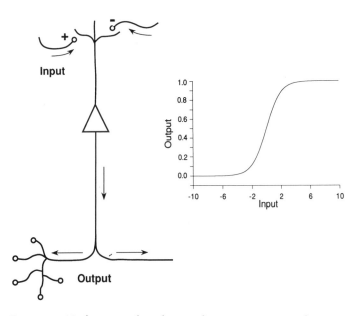

Figure 3.31 Nonlinear squashing function for a processing unit. The inputs are weighted and summed, and a bias is added (or threshold subtracted) before passing the total input through the sigmoid, shown on the right. The output of the unit is close to zero for large negative inputs, has a roughly linear region around zero input, and saturates for large positive inputs. This type of nonlinearity characterizes the firing rate of some neurons, such as motor neurons, as a function of the injected current from synaptic inputs on its dendrites, as shown on the left. Neurons also have complex temporal properties that are not captured by this static form of nonlinearity.

main difference is that the error surface for least-square curve fitting has a single minimum (figure 3.29), whereas the error surface for a network with hidden units may have many local minima. Consider a feedforward network such as the one in figure 3.32 with units having a nonlinear squashing function $\sigma(x)$ as in figure 3.31:

$$\sigma(x) = \frac{1}{1 + e^{-x}} \tag{18}$$

For an input pattern that produces an output value o_i, the error is defined as

$$\delta_i(\text{output}) = (o_i^d - o_i)\sigma_i'(\text{output}) \tag{19}$$

where o_i^d is the desired value of the output unit provided by a "teacher," and $\sigma'(\text{output})$ is the derivative of the squashing function. This error can be used to modify the weights from the hidden layer to the output layer by applying the delta rule[31]:

$$\Delta w_{ij} = \varepsilon\delta_i(\text{output})h_j \tag{20}$$

where h_j is the output from the jth hidden unit. The next problem is to update the weights between the input units and the hidden units. The first step is to compute how much each hidden unit has contributed to the output error.[32] This can be done by using the chain rule. The result is:

$$\delta_j(\text{hidden}) = \sigma_j'(\text{hidden}) \sum_i w_{ij}\delta_i(\text{output}) \tag{21}$$

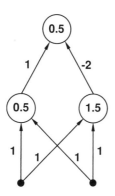

Figure 3.32 *XOR* network. The weights are shown on the connections (lines), and the thresholds are shown inside the units (circles). Thus, an input of ⟨0, 1⟩ produces a pattern of ⟨1, 0⟩ on the hidden units, which in turn activate the output unit. An input of ⟨1, 1⟩ produces ⟨1, 1⟩ on the hidden units, and the output unit will be turned off. In effect, the right hidden unit becomes a feature detector for the ⟨1, 1⟩ pattern and overrides the influence of the left hidden unit. Other solutions are possible.

Once we know the error for each hidden unit, the same delta rule used for the output units (eq. 20) can be applied to the weights from the input layer to the hidden layer. This procedure (backpropagation of error and suitable weight modification) can be applied recursively through arbitrarily many layers of hidden units. As a practical point, the gradients for the weights can be accumulated for several patterns and the weights updated according to the average gradient.[33]

Let us now shift gears and think about this in terms of an error surface. Think of the error surface as a state space where the vertical axis represents percentage of error, and each of the remaining axes represents a weight in the system (figure 3.29). As the weights change, the position in error space will change. The error surface for fitting straight lines to data by minimizing the squared error is a concave basin with a single minimum. In contrast, the error surface of the *XOR* network with hidden units has a more complex error surface, one whose topography has ravines and assorted potholes known as local minima. If, however, the net starts out with small, randomly chosen values for the seven parameters, adjusting each weight to minimize the error over the set of four input—output conditions, then the system eventually ends up at a set of parameters that truly solves the problem (figure 3.32). In fact, there are many combinations of parameters that will do equally well, and depending on the random starting place, the system will find one or the other. If the initial weight-settings are too large, then the net may land in a local minimum that is not a solution to the problem, so the lore is to start the weights low. Although the backpropagation of error can be used to create networks that can solve the *XOR* problem, that problem is sufficiently simple that many other techniques can also be used to solve the problem.

Many problems resemble XOR in the respect that they are not linearly separable; indeed, one might say that most interesting computational problems have that property. The discovery concerning the role of hidden units in extracting higher-order features and the versatility obtained by squashing functions on their outputs have therefore opened the door to network solutions to many complicated problems.[34] Even when a researcher does not have a clue what function maps input onto output, he may construct a network that does solve the input–output problem, whereupon he may then work backward to track down the function the network has learned to compute, though this may not always be a simple matter. In the next section, we illustrate an instance where a network was successfully trained even though the input–output function executed by the trained-up net was quite unknown to the modelers.

Finally, the *XOR* problem may seem pedagogically germane but biologically superfluous. Despite appearances, this turns out to be a hasty judgment, for *XOR* nets can be iterated into systems that have unexpectedly useful properties from a biological point of view. As we shall see in chapter 4, the basic *XOR* net is the electronic equivalent of a "gear" in the sense that it admits of many variations, and many *XOR* nets can be assembled into one large net that can solve very complex problems. Notice too that the negation of (*P XOR Q*) means the same as (*P* if and only if *Q*), and thus training an interconnected array of negated XOR (NXOR) units is a way of finding necessary and sufficient conditions on certain higher-order representations.

Having shown that *XOR* can be represented and learned in a feedforward network, we now consider what other functions a feedforward net might compute. The surprising answer is that a feedforward net with a sufficiently large number of hidden units can be trained to approximate with an arbitrarily small error any mathematically well-behaved function (White 1989). To be sure, this is a reassuring theoretical result, but what does it really mean in practical terms? Networks with hundreds of hidden units and hundreds of thousands of weights have been trained successfully on a wide range of problems. In the next section, we present one example to illustrate the general approach. One important practical consideration, however, concerns how much computer time and how many examples a net needs to learn a function as the number of hidden units becomes very large. This is the *scaling* problem, and we shall return to this difficulty later in the chapter.

Discriminating Sonar Echoes

Consider a feedforward net trained up by the backpropagation of error method to distinguish between sonar echoes of rocks and sonar echoes of mines (Gorman and Sejnowski 1988a, b) (figure 3.33). This is, in fact, a rather difficult problem because to the untrained ear, at least, no difference is discernible. The net has an input layer with 60 units, a hidden layer with 1–24 units, and two output units. To prepare the sonar echoes for input to the net, a given sonar echo is run through a frequency analyzer and is sampled for its relative energy level in 60 different frequency bands. These 60 values, normalized so that 1 is maximum, are then entered as activation levels in the respective input units

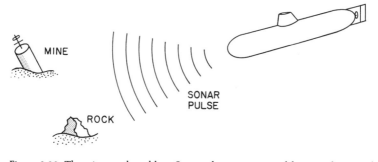

Figure 3.33 The mine–rock problem. Sonar echoes are returned from an object on the seabed. Is this a mine or a rock? There are subtle differences in the echoes that can be used to perform a pattern discrimination, but the differences between echoes from different sides of the same object are as great as the differences between echoes from different objects. Human sonar operators can be taught to make the discrimination after many training sessions. (From P. M. Churchland [1988] *Matter and Consciousness*, 2nd ed. Cambridge, MA: MIT Press.)

(figure 3.34). The activation is fed forward to the level of hidden units, there to be transformed as a function of the weights in the hidden units. The hidden units then pass activity to the two output units which may have any value between 0 and 1. Once the net is trained up, the output units signal $\langle 1, 0 \rangle$ when a mine echo is entered as input, and $\langle 0, 1 \rangle$ when a rock echo is entered as input. Initially, however, the weights are randomly set, and we cannot expect the net to give systematically correct outputs.

Training of the net correctly to categorize proceeds in the following way. We give the net examples of mine echoes and rock echoes, one by one. For each case, the actual values of the output units is measured against what the values ought to have been, given the input. This difference is a measure of error, which can then be used to compute small changes in the weights of the units in the system. This is a gradient-descent procedure, and slowly the weights of the network are adjusted so that when fed a mine echo, either a familiar old example or a brand new case, it gives a value of $\langle 1, 0 \rangle$, or close to that, and when fed a rock echo, it responds with something close to $\langle 0, 1 \rangle$. (For a more detailed but still basic account, see P. M. Churchland 1989.)

Following training, the accuracy of the classification of new echoes was very good—as good or better than trained humans and other classification methods. In a network with three hidden units, it was possible to analyze the features discovered by the training procedure (figure 3.35). The most important features of the input signals were the frequency bandwidth, the onset time, and the rate of decay of the signal. These general features, which could have been discovered by data analysis techniques, accounted for about 50% of the successfully classified echoes. The remainder of the echoes were more difficult to classify because they did not follow the general trend. To classify these exceptional cases, the hidden units developed weights that recognized clusters of echoes that shared the same spectral features. The more closely the input resembles the prototype, the more near will be the activation vector to the prototypical activation vector. The two-pronged strategy adopted by the hid-

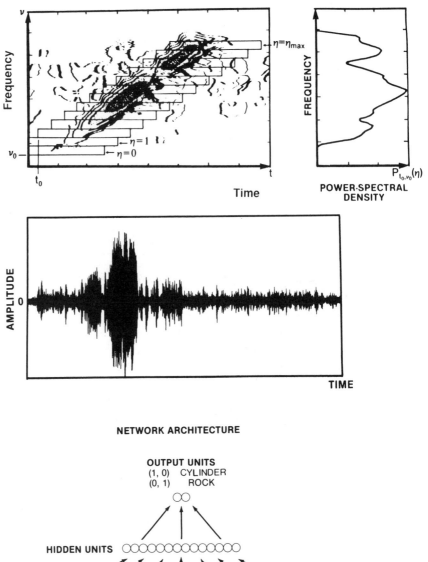

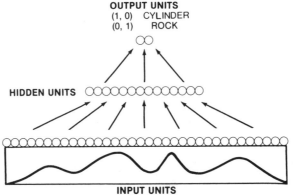

Figure 3.34 Preprocessing for sonar target recognition network. (Center) Time course of a typical sonar echo. (Top) Spectrogram of sonar echo power as a function of frequency and time showing that the frequency of the band containing the most power (black regions) increases with time. The integrated power as a function of frequency, graphed on the right, is used as the input to the network. (Bottom) Network architecture with 60 input units, 1–24 hidden units, and 2 output units. The output units are continuous-valued, and when the net is trained, the output for a metal object will be close to (1, 0) and for a rock, will be close to (0, 1). (From Gorman and Sejnowski, 1990.)

den units exploited large-scale regularities and finer scale distinctions in different ways.

NETtalk

Another example where analysis of the hidden units revealed that different strategies were discovered for different types of inputs is NETtalk, a network that was trained to pronounce English words (Sejnowski and Rosenberg 1987). The input to NETtalk was letters of the English alphabet arranged in a window of seven letters. The output layer could represent 54 different phonemes, and each output is in effect the answer to the question of how to pronounce the central letter in the input window. The words marched through the window, one letter at a time, and the output of the network provided a string of phonemes that were played through a speech synthesizer (figure 3.36). The activity patterns on the hidden units were analyzed with a clustering technique to discover how the different letter-to-sound correspondences were coded. Interestingly, the vowels were segregated from the consonants and followed a different coding scheme. For vowels, the most important partitioning factor was the letter, but for consonants, the partitioning depended more on similarity in the sounds than on letters. What may account for this difference is that any given vowel letter may have a relatively large range of phonemic possibilities, but consonants are much more limited. Contrast, for example, the range of different sounds that may be associated with the letter "e" and those with the letter "f."

Essentially the same clustering emerged in all networks trained with the same words, even though they differed in the way that the hidden units shared the patterns. As in the mine–rock network, NETtalk found general patterns that would suffice for the preponderance of cases, dealing with the remaining exceptional cases by finding some way to cluster them, and coding that clustering into the weights. The way to view this two-step strategy is that the network finds a kind of default activation pattern for the standard cases, but when it detects a special feature indicative of an exceptional case, the default response is overridden. Only about 15% of the hidden units become significantly activated by a particular input, so the coding scheme was neither local nor completely distributed.

9   RECURRENT NETS

The mine–rock network, trained by a parameter-adjusting procedure, is feedforward, in the sense that the direction of information flow is strictly from input to the first layer, passing forward through intervening layers, to the output layer. True, the error signal is passed backward to adjust the weights, but this is better thought of as external tinkering with the weights than as information downflow—as part of the *weight modification* rather than *unit activation*. More precisely, there was no flow of information *as input* from higher-level to lower-level units. Notice that a purely feedforward system is a purely

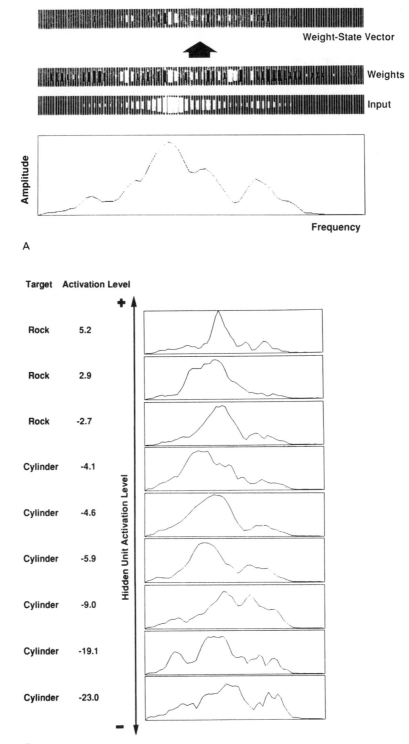

A

B

reactive system; that is, one which responds with an output only to the input, where its response is a function of the external input signals together with the existing configuration of weights. What does feedback, conceived as *internal* input, do for a network (figure 3.37)?

The general answer is that feedback endows a network with several important capacities: (a) to incorporate multiple time scales into the processing units, (b) to process temporally extended sequences of inputs, (c) to generate oscillations and modifiable rhythms of varying durations, and (d) to resolve ambiguities such as figure–ground ambiguities and segmentation ambiguities. Nets with feedback are also called *recurrent nets*.[35] In a recurrent net, the effect of an external input is not isolated from what went on in the net before, since internal inputs (feedback) also contribute to the activation of the hidden units. In recurrent nets the significance of external input varies across three general types of case: (1) the net may have output only when there is both external and internal input; (2) the net may have output even when there is no external input, but the continuous activity must be initially triggered by external input; or (3) internal input alone will suffice to activate an output, though the net's output can be modified by the addition of external input.

A theme that will be sounded and resounded throughout this book concerns time and the necessity for network models to reflect the fundamental and essential temporal nature of actual nervous systems. External processes and events are extended in time and for a nervous system successfully to recognize and respond may require temporally extended representation; movements required for behavior involve sets of bodily motions sequenced in time; short-term memory is a trick for allowing present access to the recent past, and longer-term memory to the more remote past; learning is adapting to the present on the evolutionary-tried assumption that the future resembles the past. Birds and humans recognize patterns of temporally extended song; recognizing that someone is waving or becoming angry is not recognizing merely a single input vector, it is recognizing an ordered *sequence* of vectors. We shall see in later chapters how network models of visual functions, behavior, and sensory–motor integration deal with the matter of temporal realism. The

Figure 3.35 Typical spectral envelopes of sonar signals used as inputs to a network and their categorization by a trained network. (A) Input pattern is amplitude as a function of frequency (below), which corresponds to activity levels of input units (above). The area of each white rectangle is proportional to the amplitude of the signal in each frequency band. These input values are multiplied by the weights to a hidden unit to produce a weight-state vector (top). Inhibitory weights are shown as black rectangles. The input to a hidden unit is the sum of the components in the weight-state vector. (B) Prototypical input patterns ranked according to the activity level evoked in a single hidden unit. Each input pattern, shown on the right, is the average for a cluster of similar weight-state vectors. Each average pattern activated the hidden unit according to the level shown on the left. The features that characterized the rock for these prototypes were frequency bandwidth, onset time, and decay rate. Each of three hidden units in the network preferred a different onset time but had the same preference for bandwidth and decay rate. Exceptional input patterns did not fall into any of these clusters and were discriminated with a different type of coding. (From Gorman and Sejnowski, 1988a)

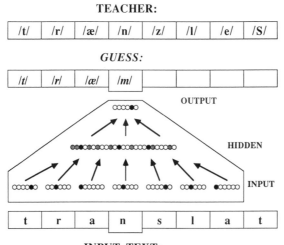

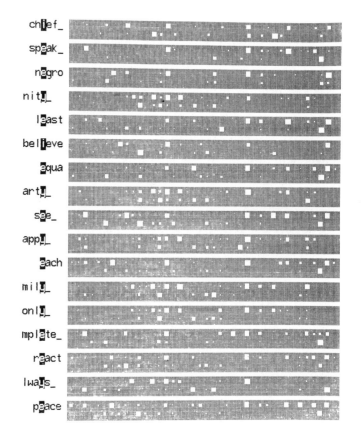

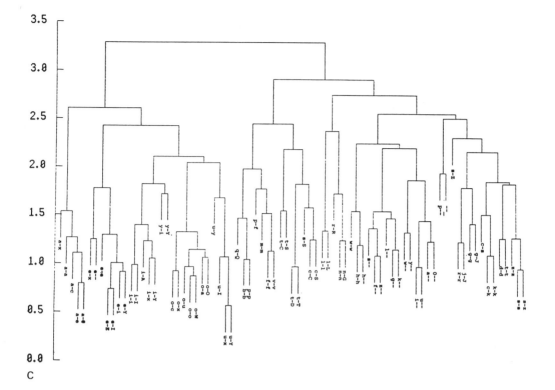

C

Figure 3.36 (A) Schematic of NETtalk architecture showing only some units and connectivity. Each group of 29 input units represents a letter. The 7 groups of input units were transformed by 80 hidden units. These hidden units then projected to 26 output units, which represented 54 phonemes. There were a total of 18,629 weights in the network. (B) Activity patterns on the 80 hidden units for the words shown on the left. The highlighted letters in the center of the window are all pronounced with the same sound. The area of each white square is proportional to the activity level of a single hidden unit. (C) Hierarchical cluster analysis of the average activity levels on the hidden units for each letter-to-sound correspondence (l-p for letter "l" and phoneme "p"). The closest branches correspond to the most nearly similar activation vectors of the hidden units. (From Sejnowski and Rosenberg 1987. Parallel networks that learn to pronounce English text. *Complex Systems* 1: 145–168.)

goal here will be only to understand the general features of recurrent nets that render them temporally responsive.

A crude but instructive first step in handling temporal structure with nets is to map a temporal sequence onto a spatial sequence, and then rely on the proven capacity of networks to do spatial recognition tasks. Vice versa, a spatially extended sequence such as the written word can be moved past a time "window." (See, for example, Sejnowski and Rosenberg's NETtalk, figure 3.36.) In this approach, a vanilla feedforward net will suffice, where temporal sequences with "before" and "after" relations are transformed into spatial sequences with "to the left of" and "to the right of" relations. In a speech recognition problem, for example, this is accomplished by pushing the train of input events through the input units from one side to the other. Each time-batch of sound hops from unit to unit until it has been through the entire set of

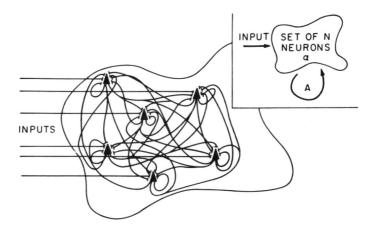

Figure 3.37 General recurrent network model. The units in the network form connections with each other, and their responses can outlast incoming inputs. (From Anderson et al. 1981.)

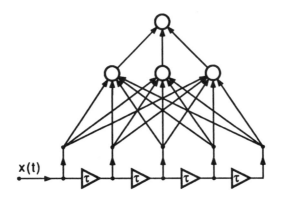

Figure 3.38 A time-delay neural network. The input $x(t)$ enters the network on the left and each input is successively delayed by τ. Thus, the input to the feedforward network at time t is $x(t)$, $x(t - \tau)$, $x(t - 2\tau)$, ..., $x(t - 4\tau)$. This type of architecture has been popular for speech recognition (Tank and Hopfield 1987, Elman and Zipser 1988, Waibel et al. 1989, Lippmann 1989). (From Hertz et al. 1991.)

inputs, the first one in being the first one out. Simplifying somewhat, a subset of hidden units thus see the phonemes in order, e.g., first "c," then "a," then "t," and its flanking hidden units respond to the peripheral phonemes as context. In engineering this arrangement for pushing through the input is known as a tapped delay line (figure 3.38). Such a net can still be purely feedforward, but it is rather limited in the temporal complexity it can accommodate. Feedback loops turn out to be a remarkably fruitful architectural modification for transforming a sheerly static, reactive net into a temporally replete, internally generative system. How can feedback connections allow for this?

The fundamental point here is disarmingly simple: for short time scales, on the order of milliseconds, let the temporal properties of representation derive from the properties of the physical interactions in the network itself. As Carver Mead (1987) is fond of putting it, "Let time be its own representation." The

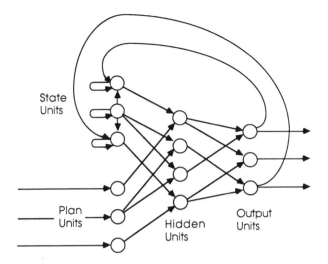

State
Units

Plan
Units

Hidden
Units

Output
Units

Figure 3.39 Recurrent Jordan network. In addition to the feedforward inputs, an additional set of inputs receives copies of the output units. These input units, through self connections, preserve a decaying copy of the last several outputs. Different sequences of outputs can be generated. (From Jordan 1989.)

point is, the network has instrinsic temporal structure: activation arrives at the hidden units before it arrives at the output units, signal summing and passing takes time, and so forth. Thus Mead's intent is that we exploit the existing temporal properties of activity in the network to do such things as represent temporal patterns of sensory stimuli. For a network to be sensitive to what happened in the immediate past, it must have a memory of what happened; this can be a spatial memory in which "to the left of" means "before," or it can be a dynamical memory in which, for example, recurrent loops keep a signal "alive" or transient changes in synapses keep the memory alive. Longer time intervals—for example, remembering that one learned to drive before Kennedy was assassinated—require a very different style of representation.

There are many ways of putting feedback into a network, including lateral interactions between units within a layer, feedback from a higher layer to lower layers, or, in the most general case, any unit may have reciprocal connections. In this event, any unit then can be an input unit, or an output unit, or both. To illustrate how feedback connections can greatly enhance the power of a feedforward net, we have chosen a recurrent net endowed with restricted feedback connections (Jordan 1989; figure 3.39). The goal of the network is to produce a sequence of actions a1, a2, a3 ... when given a single input, characterized as a command, such as "pick up an apple" or "say the word 'popsicle,'" or, for the Jordan net, "draw a rectangle." For nervous systems to execute commands such as these, a large number of muscles must each receive, over an extended time period, its appropriate sequence of activation. Additionally, since the various muscles must be coordinated for the right things to happen, the various sequences of activation must themselves be coordinated. The Jordan net tackles the basic issue of how a net might produce the appropri-

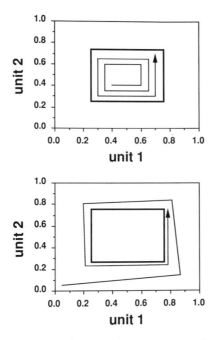

Figure 3.40 Output of a recurrent network trained to trace a rectangle. The values of two output units are plotted on the *x* and *y* axes, and successive points in time are joined by a straight line. (Top) Trajectory of a network that was started from a point inside the rectangle. (Bottom) Trajectory taken when the network was started outside the rectangle. The rectangle is called a stable limit cycle of the network because the closed repetitive trajectory can recover from small perturbations. (Based on Jordan 1989.)

ate temporally extended sequence of outputs given a command, and his architectural modification to the vanilla feedforward net consists of two types of feedback connections.

The task for the Jordan net is to draw a rectangle, as shown in figure 3.40. The Jordan net copies the values of the output units into the input layer; specifically, they are copied onto a selected set of units that serve to provide internal input. In the Jordan net, these special input units also have positive feedback connections onto themselves. The long recurrent connections provide the hidden units with information about the recent history of the output layer via the special input units. On a given pass, the hidden units will get both *brand-new* external information from the regular input units together with *recent history* information from the special input units. Notice also that the output of the network can continue to deliver and even to change its delivered messages despite freezing the external inputs. The reason is simply that the internal inputs continue to activate the hidden units, and indeed this is what endows the network with the capacity to generate temporal sequences.

What is achieved by the short recurrent connections—the self-exciting connections? Their effect is to create a short-term memory, inasmuch as a signal that produces a level of activity in the unit will decay slowly rather than cease abruptly, for the self-excitation maintains the activity. (This is equivalent to making the unit a leaky capacitor, which is analogous to the membrane time constant of a neuron.) At a given moment, therefore, a special input unit represents a weighted average of previous values of the output. Thus not only does the network have available to it information about the current output, but it has a history, albeit a temporally decaying history, of previous outputs as well. Accordingly, contraction of muscle C can be influenced by what muscle B was doing 20 msec before, and by what muscle A was doing 20 msec before that. In this way, a smooth sequence of behavior can be orchestrated.

Note that unless the Jordan net is halted externally, its output is an infinite temporal sequence (see figure 3.40). That is because it will endlessly retrace its path once it finishes the last side of the rectangle and returns to the rectangle's first side. This is an achievement denied to Hopfield nets and Boltzmann machines despite their recurrent connections. These latter networks have only stable attractors (they converge to a point, not a trajectory), owing to the symmetry of the feedback connections. In such a network, information cannot circulate repetitively.

It should be emphasized that Jordan trained his recurrent network using the same backpropagation algorithm developed for plain feedforward networks. The weights of the *feedback* connections in this instance were fixed, though in a more general reccurrent network, it may be necessary to train even these weights as well as the feedforward weights. Generalizations of the backpropagation technique have been developed for the wider range of cases, and examples will be given in chapters 4 and 5.

Not only did Jordan's network train up nicely to execute the desired trajectory, but so trained, it has a robust representation of its goal. That is, when the net starts out from some arbitrary initial state, or if it is perturbed off the trajectory, it will head to the correct output pattern. In the mathematical theory of dynamical systems, this behavior is called a *stable limit cycle*. The reason this is interesting is that the output pattern might well not have been stable, in which case any small deviation due to noise or an imperfection in the input would send the net careening off into useless behavior. This is important because for real neural nets, noise and imperfection are the order of the day. Imagine training networks, such as motor networks in the brain, to guide a hand to produce a complicated trajectory such as a signature. The signature will not be identical each time, owing to differences in the writing surface, the writing instrument, the musculature, the starting position, and so forth. A network that has the property of being stable when perturbed will compensate for those deviations, and nervous systems appear to be like that.

Although the Jordan net trains up well on the "draw-a-rectangle" task, more difficult problems demand not just a mapping of one input to an output sequence, but a variety of different inputs to their appropriate output sequences, and more difficult yet again, a range of *sequences of inputs* to suitable sequences of outputs. Here we bump up against the limitations of the Jordan net. It cannot be trained up on these more difficult tasks because the temporal memory provided by the recurrent connections decays in time. This constant decay rate means that an older input may not be able to exert a significant effect at a more distant time, even though at that time it is the needed piece of information. Such problems occur routinely in language, both spoken and written, where there may be long-range interactions between words, as when a pronoun refers back to a proper name or a verb must agree with its earlier-mentioned subject. If the sentence is long, containing many embedded clauses, as much as a minute may pass before the verb or pronoun that must agree with the subject makes its appearance. Humans typically have little problem nonetheless, in either production or comprehension. Somewhere in the system, therefore, a representation of the word is on hold for a duration longer and with an impact greater than that allowed by the brief recirculating types of memory exhibited by the Jordan network. Yet the on-hold duration is also shorter than the weight modification corresponding to long-term memory.

What can be done to accommodate this time requirement? Basically, there are three general options: (1) change the network's time constants—for example, by increasing the temporal duration of an input's influence; (2) change the architecture—for example, by trying different configurations of feedback, of hidden layers, and so forth[36]; (3) change the activation function. For brevity, we consider only the third option, and that only succinctly. Recall that the original activation function described earlier specified the output of a unit as the weighted sum of the inputs, operated on by a squashing function to get nonlinearity. One modification defines the output as the weighted *product* of the inputs:

$$y_i = \sigma \left[\sum_{jk} w_{ijk} x_j x_k \right] \tag{22}$$

where $\sigma(x)$ is the squashing function shown in figure 3.31, and w_{ijk} is a weight that represents the influence of the jth and kth input units together on the ith output unit.

This results in what are called "higher-order nets," in contrast to the first-order nets that use the traditional activation function (Giles et al. 1990). It is possible with these second-order recurrent networks to model what are called "finite state automata." These are defined as devices that take sequences of input vectors and produce sequences of output vectors, and whose state transitions may depend on an internal but finite memory. Although networks of second-order units can model finite state automata, the drawback of continuing to higher and higher orders is that the number of weights in the network increases with the power of the order of the network. This quickly constitutes a practical obstacle.

Each of these revisions to the basic net has its strengths and its limitations. What works best will depend on the problem the net is asked to solve. The point of emphasis then is that there are oodles of ways to tailor a net, and the choices are governed by the fit between problem and solution. It may not be too rash to suggest that evolution tries various wrinkles in network design and seizes upon those that solve the problems. The nervous system may not, therefore, conform throughout to a single network blueprint, but may exhibit a variety of principles in a variety of places, depending on the task and how things shook out in the evolutionary hurly-burly. The matter of problem–solution fit has become a fertile area for research by mathematicians who have been able to analyze the capacities of various network designs, and by engineers who have found networks to be an effective medium for matching problems and solutions.

10 FROM TOY WORLD TO REAL WORLD

The technical journals contain many examples of model nets that can solve dazzlingly difficult problems, but the cautious and sceptical will wonder whether the successes are marched into the limelight while the black sheep are herded backstage. In particular, it will be asked whether the model nets can solve only problems cleanly isolated from their messiness *au naturel*; whether they solve problems in the midst of their real-world welter and with their real-world complexity. Whether a solution adequate to a pasteurized fragment of a complex problem is also adequate to the problem entire and on the hoof is by no means obvious.

Real-worldliness has two principal aspects. (1) Real-world inputs generally have many more dimensions than toy-world inputs. The scaling problem concerns whether a net scaled-up to incorporate all the relevant dimensions can still perform the task in real time. If the scaling is exponential, then the net fails; if the scaling is polynomial, the net scores better but still poorly; if the scaling is linear, then the net may be acceptable. Best of all, it should have constant scaling. (2) Real-world inputs do not come to nervous systems informationally packaged into separate batches earmarked for separate problems. For example, visual information concerning motion, stereo, shape, etc. has to be separated by the nervous system, and objects do not arrive at the retina bagged and labeled. This is another instance of the segmentation problem (section 4). (See Abu-Mostafa 1989b.)

Assuming evolution availed itself of a "more is better" ploy in upgrading its neural nets, then perhaps we can follow that ploy and just make the standard design larger and larger. In fact, however, model nets of 1980s vintage do not scale very well, and the scaling gimmicks evolution lucked on to have not been fully figured out by neuromodelers. For example, a network that successfully recognizes phonemes presented in isolation typically flounders when it has to deal with phonemes ensconced in their natural habitat—continuous speech from a variety of speakers. A speech recognition system may succeed in identifying the vowels of one person's voice, or single words in isolation, but fares poorly when confronted with the natural flow of speech from a commonplace range of voices—male, female, children, whispers, gruff, squeaky, bell-like, accented, etc. Why this happens can be seen quite clearly in figure 3.41, where the sound patterns from a female speaker saying soft "a" may overlap with those of a child saying soft "e."

How might the standard model nets be modified to improve their scalability? In line with the "more is better" adage, the simplest approach is just to enlarge the network. The justification goes like this: if a net with ten input units

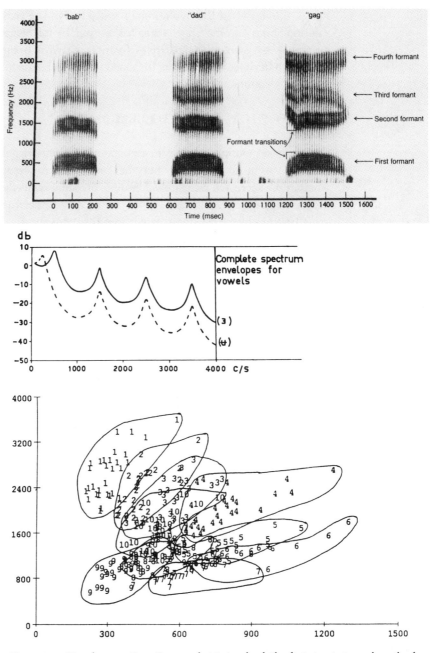

Figure 3.41 Vowel recognition. To see what is involved, the first step is to analyze the frequencies in utterances containing the vowel, for example, "bab," "dad," and "gag," as shown. The spectrogram for an utterance of each word is shown in the top panel. The areas with the highest power density are darkest, and the segment relevant to the vowel occurs about halfway through each spectrogram. The next step is to locate the formants. In the middle panel, power is plotted as a function of frequency for two vowels. The leftmost peak in a line corresponds to the bottommost dense area (around 500 Hz) of one spectrogram for the vowel segment (e.g., for "a" in "bab"), and is called the first formant; the next peak (second formant) corresponds to the second dense area (around 1500 Hz). Note the different location of the first formant for the two vowels. (From G. Fant 1973.) The third step is to assess similarity in how different speakers utter

can do speech recognition for one speaker, perhaps a network with 100 units can cope with any normal speaker. The "fatten-it-up" approach generally works up to a point, but invariably fattening-up brings its own serious difficulties. First, as the number of connections in the network increases, the amount of data required to train a network becomes very large and the amount of training time goes up enormously. The reason is that each weight in the network is a degree of freedom that needs to be constrained by data. Therefore, the more settable weights, the more data needed to constrain them, and hence the larger the training set required to do the job. A second and more serious problem concerns how information is distributed in the network.

Consider what happens when a new voice is tested on the speech recognition network. Either the network recognizes the voice's patterns or it does not. If the network succeeds, then all is well. But if the network errs on the new voice, then this failure is remedied by training the network on that voice, with concomitant adjustments to the weights. The trouble is that though these weight modifications are needed to accommodate the new voice, they may well degrade the weight configurations for the old voices. To avoid losing the previous recognition capacities, therefore, the net must be trained anew on the entire old training set *plus* the new pattern. Obviously this procedure gets increasingly cumbersome proportionally to the size of the training set. One reason the standard net scales poorly is that changing one weight in the network repartitions the hidden unit activation space, and that means it changes the hidden unit activation vector for any input, old and familiar though it may be.

The aforementioned trouble reflects the fact that in a net there is an interaction between the data and the weights, in the sense that training on new data has an impact on all the weights, not just a preselected subset of the weights. A further and deeper trouble derives from the interaction between the weights. Error information is used to compute the gradients for the weights. Error, however, is a function of all the data *and* all the weights. When the net is trained up on a new example, there is not only an interaction between data and weights, but also an interaction between the weights. For if one weight changes in response to error, so do other weights. In other words, the gradients must be recalculated when a weight changes.

What can be done to avoid retraining holus-bolus and thus to avoid the time cost of scaling-up? One answer is to allow hidden units to be sensitive only to a limited range of input patterns.[38] This can be accomplished by using radial basis functions as the activation functions of the hidden units. Formally, what this means is that given an input vector x_i, then the output of a hidden unit that receives this input is given by:

the same vowel. The analysis proceeds by taking each speaker's utterance of a particular vowel sound (coded by a number; 1 stands for ē as in "heed") and plotting the first formant (horizontal) against the second formant (vertical). The analysis of ten vowel sounds uttered by 30 speakers shows that there is considerable overlap in the regions occupied by different vowel sounds depending on which speaker utters the sound. (From Nowlan 1990.)

$$F(\mathbf{x}) = e^{-\sum_i ((x_i - k_i)/\sigma)^2} \tag{23}$$

where k_i is at the center of the radial basis function, and σ is the width of the Gaussian distribution specified by the function. Informally, this means that there is an activation function according to which a hidden unit's largest response occurs when the input vector matches k_i, and the response falls off rapidly corresponding to the degree of mismatch. Considered three-dimensionally, the radial basis function carves out a sphere in the input space. Considered two-dimensionally, the radial basis function is rather like the tuning curve of a sensory cell, where the cell's best input is the one to which it maximally responds. Analogously, a hidden unit maximally responds when the input vector matches the center of its "tuning curve."

The main advantage of the radial basis function is that during the process of training, a given input affects only a few of the hidden units at a time, so part of the network can be modified without affecting how the rest of the network responds to other inputs. It will be evident, however, that in addition to weighting the radial basis functions for the various patterns the net is to recognize, one must also specify the centers k_i for the functions and their widths, σ. If the input space is low dimensional, one trick is uniformly to cover the space with spheres of a given size, in effect hand-wiring the tuning curves of the hidden units. In a high-dimensional space, however, the number of spheres required uniformly to cover the space may be very large, for the number of spheres goes up with the power of the dimension, n^N, where n is the number of spheres for covering each dimension, and N is the number of dimensions. Fewer spheres may be required if only some portions of the input space are of interest. So although one aspect—the interaction between weights—of the scaling problem is addressed by this strategy, other problems arise.

A related answer also pursues the decoupling strategy, but this time by decoupling the network so that subnets work on independent elements of the problem and training modifies only the relevant subnet. The answer implies that one can use a solution to the segmentation problem to help solve the scaling problem. Subdividing the network might be done by hand, in effect designing individual networks for individual elements of the problem. This is a rather ad hoc remedy. Worse, it presupposes that one already knows how to sort out the elemental problems and knows to which subnet information is relevant. We stand to be cruelly disappointed if we bank on this presupposition. Additionally, the holus-bolus problem may merely have been exchanged for the new and vexing problem of how to integrate these individual nets.

A more sophisticated proposal is that the network should *learn* how to cluster related information in subnetworks, each of which disposes of the information proper to it, but interacts minimally with other subnets. On this proposal, the network finds its own problem-elements and segregates the input accordingly. As we have seen, competitive, unsupervised learning algorithms have been designed to segregate input by staging a competition between units for input patterns. The way this works is that the unit most highly activated by a particular pattern wins, in the sense that it alone has its weight modified to

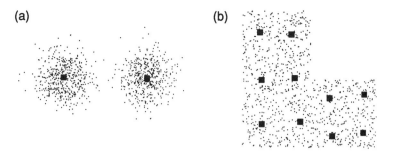

(a)   (b)

Figure 3.42 Vector quantization by competitive learning. Each input pattern is a point in the plane. Inputs that maximally stimulate an output unit are shown as black squares. During the competition for inputs, the output units station themselves strategically to cover the inputs. The output units are thus prototypes and each input is assigned to the nearest one. In (a) the inputs are from a pair of Gaussian probability distributions and in (b) the inputs are uniformly distributed over an L-shaped region. (From Hertz et al. 1991.)

become even more sensitive to that pattern, thus earning the right to represent that vector. *Ipso facto*, it will be less sensitive to very different input patterns, allowing some other unit to muscle in and win the right to represent the different pattern. This is called "vector quantization," reflecting the strategy of quantizing a group of related vectors into a single vector. By following this weight-modification principle, the net eventually fits itself out with units that are prototypes, inasmuch as each unit gathers to itself the range of input patterns that is more similar to its prototype vector than to the prototype vector of any other unit (figure 3.42). The network accordingly partitions the input space into groups of similar vectors, thus performing a preprocessing task.

Although unsupervised clustering successfully segregates the incoming information, it does not solve the problem of creating subnetworks. The idea of competition between the units can, however, be applied to whole networks with the result that independent subnets are created (Nowlan 1990, Jacobs et al. 1991). The strategy is this: appoint "mini-nets" instead of single units to compete for representation rights, where the mini-nets have their private array of hidden units, modifiable weights, and connections (figure 3.43). Mini-nets not only compete for the right to represent an input pattern, they are also trained by backpropagation of error to represent their patterns more and more correctly. Thus early in the training phase, mini-net *C* may give an output closer to the desired output than any of its competitors, *A* and *B*. The "teacher" then picks it out, and using the error measure, adjusts *C*'s weights in the correct direction using backpropagation of error. The other mini-nets are on recess for that input pattern. Each mini-net is activated by the input vector, but a winner-take-all strategy decides which mini-net is trained.

How is it decided which mini-net output is *the* answer to the input question? On the side, so to speak, there is another net that is trained up at the same time. This can be thought of as a "referee net," trained to select winning mini-nets for any given input pattern. The referee net takes the same inputs as the other

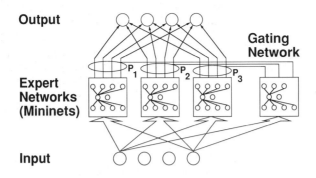

Output

Gating Network

Expert Networks (Mininets)

Input

Figure 3.43 A system of mini-nets (experts) with a gating network (referee). Each expert is a feedforward network, and all experts receive the same input and have the same number of outputs. The gating network is also feedforward, with normalized outputs (P_j), and an input which is the same as the input received by the expert networks. The referee acts like a multiple-input, single-output, stochastic switch. The probability that the switch will select the output from expert j is Prob P_j, which is the jth output of the gating network. The expected value of the output of the system is: $\sum_j p_j o_j$, where o_j is the output of the mininet j.

mini-nets, and its output is its probabilistic prediction of which mini-net has the right answer. The teacher computes the error measure here as well, and sends modification signals back to the referee net. The upshot is that once the whole slew is trained up, the teacher can retire, and the trained-up referee will correctly select which mini-net answer is the answer for any given pattern-recognition question. (This is highly simplified, but see Nowlan 1990 and Jacobs et al. 1991.) No referee was required in the simple clustering configuration because the winner is simply the most active unit. In the Jacobs et al. approach, the winner is determined by which mini-net is the expert for the particular input vector.

The Jacobs et al. configuration scores very well on the multiple-speaker vowel recognition problem, and it can efficiently process 74 different voices, correctly identifying vowels of these voices. This gets us a bit closer to real-world speech recognition. An analysis of the mini-nets reveals that they tend roughly to divide labor so that some end up an expert on children's voices, others on women's voices, and yet others on men's voices. The lesson of consequence, however, is that some measure of success in coping with the scaling problem can be achieved by configuring nets so that with experience they specialize. Specialization by substructures is a principle that fits well with neurobiology and with findings from human subjects. For example, in direct cortical stimulation of bilingual subjects, George Ojemann has observed interference with Greek only and not English, or English only and not Greek, where the intervening distance may be as small as 10 mm (Ojemann 1988, 1990).

11 WHAT GOOD ARE OPTIMIZATION PROCEDURES TO NEUROSCIENCE?

A common misconception is that an artificial net is a waste of time if the parameter-adjusting procedure component of the triple ⟨architecture, dynamics, procedure⟩ is not maximally biological; that essentially nothing can be inferred about the actual net simulated by the model net; and that the expectation that it will be useful is just wishful thinking in the worst of the tradition of black-boxology. According to this view, until we know how nervous systems parameter-adjust—and there may be many procedures that govern parameter-adjusting in nervous systems—model nets are charming demonstrations that an input–output function can be executed, and that weight-adjusting will lead a net to the correct input–output function, but nothing can be revealed about how real neural nets execute that function unless the parameter-adjusting procedures are the same, or at least similar. Why is this a misconception?

The fast answer, to be duly expanded below, is this: assuming the architecture is relevantly similar to the anatomy, and assuming the dynamics are relevantly similar to the physiology, then so long as both the actual net and the model net use some parameter-adjusting procedure to minimize error, then they will each end up at locations on the error surface that are rather close. How close the final positions are depends on how similar the architecture and dynamics are, but the critical point is that *error minimization is an optimization procedure*, so it is reasonable to expect that however a given net finds its error minimum, it will be as close to the error minimum found by another net as long as the architecture and dynamics of the two nets are closely similar.

How a physical system comes to be configured such that it computes some function may be—indeed is virtually certain to be—different from how the theorist goes about finding out what function the system is computing. As we shall see anon, modelers sometimes use optimization procedures such as backprop as a way of shaping a network model into an input–output configuration that resembles the input–output configuration of an actual neural system. One aim may be to have an accessible "preparation" to analyze in order to find out what function the neural system is computing. Another aim, as even most sceptics emphasize, is to generate ideas from the organization and behavior of the net. Although backprop is enormously helpful in smithing up a model with capacities analogous to the actual neural network, it is *not* assumed that the neural system came to be organized as *it* is by backprop. Obviously, one might say. Nevertheless, this bears noting inasmuch as criticism of computational models is often directed toward optimization techniques for getting a model into suitable neural configuration, on grounds that the technique is not very biological. Whatever other criticisms might be apt, this one is surely misdirected. Think of backprop not as aiming to mimic neurogenesis or real synaptic modification, but rather as a tool to aid discovery of what function a grown-up network is in fact computing and how in fact it manages to compute that function. These discoveries are what enables us to use the net as a source of ideas.

As a means of clarifying the argument, let us work up to the test case by first considering several easier cases. Suppose two model nets are constructed, with identical architecture and identical dynamics, but rather different procedures for parameter adjusting to find the error minimum, and suppose, to make it more relevant, that one was supervised and the other was monitored. They then learn, by the parameter-adjusting procedure, the same input–output function. What would you predict about the properties of the nets once each has found its error minimum? Well, you would expect that the free parameters at training end have the same values, or close to. One net may take a circuitous route down the error surface, the other may be more direct, but they are bound to end up in the same, or closely adjacent, places. In this game we assumed the identity of architecture and dynamics in order to make the point that each model could use a distinct route to wend down to its error minimum.

Imagine now a slightly different game where the identity of architecture is not given at the outset, but the net's function is given. Suppose that the Zygons deliver us an up-and-running model network with its input–output function pinned to its shirt, but whose architecture and dynamics we are to discover by experimental techniques that can give us mostly only local information. The game is to figure out how Zygon-net works. To this end, we construct a model net, call it Home-net, constraining its architecture and dynamics by using whatever local information we can get about Zygon-net. We then train Home-net to execute the same input–output function that we know Zygon-net executes, where Home-net uses an off-the-shelf parameter-adjusting procedure for minimizing error. The Zygons being good engineers, we reasonably expect they trained up their net using some parameter-adjusting procedure or other, though its specifics we are never told. The crucial question is this: can one infer anything about Zygon-net's global properties from the global properties of Home-net? Would it be useful to make predictions about undiscovered local properties of Zygon-net on the basis of what Home-net's properties imply about those local properties? The answers appear to be positive in both cases. To be sure, the inferences about Zygon-net's global properties—and hitherto unknown local properties—are only probabilistic. Consequently, the degree of probability the hypotheses enjoy will be a function of the similarity between the architecture and dynamics of Zygon-net and Home-net, notwithstanding whatever differences may exist in the parameter-adjusting procedures. The important point is that the learning procedures are error-minimizing procedures, so the Zygon-net and Home-net are similar in the respects that matter. This "just-so" story brings us one step closer to the neurobiological case.[37]

Now we cannot make this next step unless we have reason to think the brain is in the error-minimization business. Is it? Four basic considerations are relevant to answering this question: (1) In nervous systems generally, and most obviously in mammals, there are too many parameters (e.g., 10^{15} synapses in human brains) for them all to be set genetically, so at least some must be set by some other procedures. (2) During development there is massive synaptogenesis and also massive cell death, some of which appears to be governed by competitive principles (Rakic 1986, Constantine-Paton and Ferrari-Eastman 1987), that have the character of an optimizing process. Crudely speaking, the connections which are most robust and useful as the substrate for some functions tend to survive. (3) In both the developing and the adult animal, some of these parameters are set as the nervous system uses feedback to adapt behavior to circumstances. There are many examples of homeostatic error-correcting mechanisms, such as changing the gain of the vestibulo-ocular reflex in response to magnifying goggles (see chapter 6), calibrating motor performance in learning how to play tennis, and fine-tuning the matching of images from the two eyes. (4) Natural selection culls nervous systems that are outperformed by those of predators, prey, or conspecifics in the reproduction game. To this extent, and relativized to in-place structures, the selection pressure on nervous structures can be characterized as error-minimizing. This is just to state the familiar thesis of natural selection in a neurobiological context: the modifications to nervous systems that are preserved are by and large those modifications that contribute to (at least do not undermine) the organism's survival in its niche.

A possible misunderstanding should be forestalled here. In describing the evolutionary modification of nervous structures as error minimization (and hence as optimization), we do not assume anything Panglossian about evolution. Consequently we are not letting ourselves in for a scolding from Gould and Lewontin[39] for the sin of supposing that if natural selection slides down an error gradient, characterized relative to available structure and environmental niche, the nervous system is therefore the best of all possible systems. First, the parameter-adjusting procedures at the evolutionary level may find only a local minimum, not necessarily the global minimum. In other words, evolution may find not the best *possible* solution, but only a satisfactory solution. "Satisficing" is good enough for survival and reproduction, and apart from natural selection there is really nothing to push evolution to do better, nor, of course, is there a particular path for it to follow.

Returning now to the relevance of model nets to real neural nets, imagine that Critter-net is an up-and-running neural circuit in some living nervous system. Suppose, for example, that it is the neural circuit for visual tracking of moving objects when the head is moving. By experimentation in anatomy, physiology, and pharmacology, the values of many of the parameters in the system are known. Thus we may know the number of cell types, we may have rough estimates of the numbers of each type, what cells project to where, the receptive field properties of cells, whether certain synapses are excitatory or inhibitory, and so on. The specific weights, however, are unknown. Suppose Computer-net is constructed by fixing the known parameters. Those parameters whose values are unknown, such as the weights, will be fixed as Computer-net is trained up on the input–output function using an error-minimization procedure for adjusting the parameters. Can we infer anything about Critter-net's global properties from the global properties of Computer-net? Would it be useful to make predictions about undiscovered local and global properties of Critter-net on the basis of the local and global properties of Computer-net? Given that nervous systems are probably computing error minimization, or at least cost functions of some kind, then the answers appear to be positive. As before, however, *the probability of the inference depends on the degree of similarity between the architecture and dynamics of Critter-net and Computer-net.*

A different but related point concerns the significance of parameter asymmetries between nets with identical architecture and dynamics. Learning algorithms can be thought of as efficient devices for searching the parameter space for combinations of values that optimize some input–output function. When there are many thousands of parameters, the probability that the global minimum of the real neural net and that of the model net are precisely the same, weight for weight, is actually rather low. This may prompt the inference that the model net is next to useless in understanding the real neural net. In fact, the situation is nothing like so gloomy. To begin with, experience with parameter-adjusting procedures applied to many problems shows that networks can perform equivalently even though the specific values of the weights may be quite different.

In the simplest case, a net and its mirror image are equivalent. In a rather backhanded way, the fact that optimization procedures cannot be counted on to find the global minimum, but only local minima, helps upgrade the probability of a model net's being useful. Regardless of the starting point in parameter space, if the net keeps going downhill and improving its performance, it is likely to find a good solution at the bottom, though it may not be the very best. This means that a net trained up on many different occasions from randomly set starting weights carves out a region of parameter space of different but equivalent solutions—of different but equivalent weight-assignments. And the same is likely to be true of nervous systems. That is, even homozygotic twins' brains may be very different in their weight-by-weight (parameter-by-parameter) configuration, even if their circuits and their capacities be functionally equivalent. The idea is then that two *regions* of parameter space are, on sheerly mathematical grounds, more likely to overlap than two *points* in parameter space. So if an optimizing procedure circumscribes regions rather than localizing points, this is all to the good. Thus when a model net is highly constrained by neurobiological data, the probability is nontrivial that the region of parameter space defined by the model net and the real neural net will overlap. In either case, one can use additional neurobiological data to error-correct one's way closer to the parameter-space region of the real neural net. [For the statistical analysis of learning in artificial neural nets, see White (1989).]

The main point, therefore, is that model nets may be a valuable source of ideas relevant to real neural nets. By analyzing the features of the trained-up net, one can make predictions concerning the actual nervous system, which can then be tested neurobiologically. This is especially useful when the model's results illuminate global properties, for these are surpassingly difficult to find by neurobiological techniques but are easy to reveal in artificial nets. The useful results are by no means restricted to global properties, for model nets may also reveal important but unanticipated local properties. Consequently, surprising results can be gleaned from a model net that would not be discovered by looking only at a real neural net. Newfound neurobiological parameters can then be ploughed back into the model as added constraints. The newly parametrized model will generate new hypotheses and predictions, and the co-evolutionary gambit can be repeated. Notice that co-evolution of model net and neural knowledge is really an error-correcting process, where the goal is minimizing error in the model net by comparison with the real neural net.

The basic argument regarding the value of model nets to neuroscience has a number of important pieces, and it can be summed up as follows: (1) It is reasonable to assume that the evolution of nervous systems can be described by a cost function; development and learning in nervous systems are probably also describable by a cost function. In other words, by dint of parameter-adjusting procedures, nervous systems, ontogenetically and phylogenetically, appear to be finding local minima in their error surfaces. (2) Model nets that are highly constrained by neurobiological data concerning architecture and dynamics of the neural circuit being simulated may use backprop as a search procedure to find local minima. (3) Identical nets using the same cost function and sliding into error minima will nonetheless vary considerably in the specific values assigned to their parameters. This is because the triple ⟨architecture, dynamics, error-minimization procedure⟩ carves out a *region* of weight space, and many different weight configurations can be found in that region. (4) There is no guarantee that the local minima found by the model net will overlap the local minima found by the real neural network, but it is reasonable to assume so given points (1) and (3). That is, it is not unlikely that the region of weight space carved out by the equivalent model nets and the neural nets will at least overlap. (5) That assumption can be tested against the nervous system itself, and additional constraints derived from neurobiological data can be added to the model net to move it closer to the real neural net's region of parameter space. This is itself an error-minimization procedure at the theory-generating level. (6) Thus the model nets can be viewed as hypothesis generators.[40]

Until rather recently, setting the parameters in neurobiological models was done largely by hand. (See, for example, Hodgkin and Huxley 1952, which is discussed further in chapter 6.) But in large nets with many parameters and nonlinear hidden units, hand-setting parameters is impractical to say the least. As we have argued, model nets, in the context of the error-correcting co-evolution with neurobiology, can lead to interesting results, and in general to better results than obtained via guess-and-by-golly or hunch-driven parameter setting. The point is important, but it should not be oversold. To repeat an earlier caution, computer models of nets are a tool—but only one tool among others; they are not a replacement for the basic neurobiological techniques that have sustained neuroscience so far. The proof of the proverbial pudding is of course in the eating, and thus it is by examples of useful models that the case for network modeling as a valuable tool is most convincingly made. The remaining chapters of the book are, therefore, largely devoted to presenting examples we have found useful or at least suggestive.

In the previous section we leaned rather heavily on the desirability of constraining a model net with neurobiological data to increase the probability that the model can tell us something about the real neural net. There is an important dimension in which that must be qualified and explained. In neuroscience, as anywhere else in science, no model is 100% realistic. A good and useful model of the solar system, for example, will not necessarily have actual gas clouds drifting around Jupiter; a good and useful model of magnetism will not necessarily provide for the rusting of iron. The central point is this: what goes into the model depends on what one is trying to explain, and in the nervous system, that is intimately related to the level of organization one is targeting. (Recall levels of organization in chapter 2, and figure 2.1.) A little more exactly, if one is modeling a function or task of a given level of brain organization, the model should be sensitive to structural constraints from the level below and to input–output properties described for the level above.

Not uncommonly, a model will be criticized as unrealistic for failing to include very low-level properties. A model of a neural circuit such as the vestibulo-ocular reflex (VOR) (see chapter 6) may include only the pathways required by the model to perform equivalently to the real net, it may average over dendritic integration, and it may ignore altogether the details of membrane channel properties. Does this mean the model is too unrealistic to be useful? We shall show more directly and specifically in chapter 6 why the model can be useful nonetheless, but for the moment, suffice it to say that lower-level properties such as channel properties are not necessary to simulate a neuron's contribution to that aspect of the VOR up for explanation, namely image stabilization. The model certainly needs to incorporate constraints regarding latencies and feedback loops (level above) and constraints regarding the net effect at synapses and the firing rate of neurons in the circuits (level below), but it does not need to be sensitive to the precise mechanisms by which a neuronal membrane operates to yield these firing rates (*two* levels below). There may be other aspects of the VOR circuit where these properties will be required for the explanation sought—for example, exactly how synaptic plasticity is managed. When synaptic plasticity *is* what is being modeled, however, then these properties should be included. More generally, if one were modeling how a neuron integrates signals, then membrane properties are relevant and must be included. In that event, however, higher-level properties, such as receptive field and feedback connections (two levels up), are probably not relevant.

Some modeling discussions seem to presuppose a kind of "realism pecking order." For example, it may be argued that until the whole neuron is thoroughly and completely modeled, modeling even a small circuit such as the VOR is premature. According to this argument, a circuit model will have to idealize the neuron, leaving out such details as the membrane channel types and their physiology. This, it will be complained, makes the model "unrealistic," and hence dismissable. An even more pure realist can dismiss the whole neuron-modeling project on grounds that there is no point in modeling the neuron until one has completely modeled the dynamics of transmitter release, including such constraints as numbers of vesicles that fuse, spatial layout of receptors, and production and packaging of neurotransmitters. Undoubtedly the biophysicist can top that; he wants first a model of protein folding. But this is surely silly. Do we really need a model of protein folding in order to get a grip on the essentials of how the VOR achieves stabilization of a visual image during head movement? Part of what perpetuates the realist pecking order is this: any given modeler tends to think his favored modeling level is *the* important level, that lower levels are properly ignorable, and modeling levels higher than his favored level is premature and unrewarding.

Realist one-upmanship needs to be put in perspective. First, models that are excessively rich may mask the very principles the models were built to reveal. In the most extreme case, if a model is exactly as realistic as the human brain, then the construction and the analysis may be expensive in computational and human time and hence impractical. As noted in chapter 1; modeling may be a stultifying undertaking if one slavishly adheres to the bald rule that the more constraints put in a model, the better it is. Every level needs models that are simplified with respect to levels below it, but modeling can proceed very well in parallel, at many levels of organization at the same time, where sensible and reasonable decisions are made about what detail to include and what to ignore. There is no decision procedure for deciding what to include, though extensive knowledge of the nervous system together with patience and imagination are advantageous. The best directive we could come up with is the woefully vague rule of thumb: make the model simple enough to reveal what is important, but rich enough to include whatever is relevant to the measurements needed.

13 CONCLUDING REMARKS

The look-up table was introduced as our first and simplest parade case of computation. Because look-up tables appeared to be rather limited in their capacity to solve difficult computational problems, other computational principles were sought. It is surprising then to realize that a trained-up network model can be understood as a kind of look-up table. Once the parameters are set, the network will give the output suitable to the input, and the answer to any given question is stored in the configuration of weights. Not, to be sure, the way answers are stored on a slide rule, but in the sense that an input vector pushed through the matrix of weights (and squashing function) is transformed so that the output vector represents the answer. Not, notice, by way of many intervening computational steps, but merely by vector-matrix transformation.

By analogy with the ⟨board position/next position⟩ pairs prestored in the Tinkertoy computer, the net's weight configuration, characterized as a matrix through which the input vector is pushed, can be thought of as "storing" prototypes as ⟨input vector/hidden unit activation⟩ pairs, "storing" being in scare quote to reflect the extension of its customary sense. As we saw above, when the net has learned to distinguish rock echoes from mine echoes so no further weight-adjusting is required to deliver correct answers, the weights partition the activation space of the hidden units in such a way that activation values of the hidden units fall on one side or the other of the partition (see next chapter, figure 4.17). The key difference between the run-of-the-mill look-up table and the trained-up network is that the network can correctly classify novel signals and thus has the capacity to generalize from training cases to new cases. In this respect, trained-up networks have a flexibility denied to run-of-the-mill look-up tables. This flexibility of a net is not mysterious. It derives from the net's assorted design features; for example, the output values of its hidden units may be continuous, and working as groups the units can interpolate smoothly between samples.

These networks might be considered examples of "smart look-up tables." They operate in very high-dimensional spaces, since weight space will have as many dimensions as there are weights, and activation space for the hidden units will have as many dimensions as there are hidden units. The consequence of these design features is that though the training set is finite, the network will give good answers to inputs it has never seen before. The inputs will, however, have some resemblance to previously seen inputs, and that will be enough to ensure correct categorization. It must be emphasized that the learning process is not itself a look-up table operation—rather, parameter-adjusting is a relaxation process. Similarly, fitting the Tinkertoy pieces together is not itself a look-up table operation. In the network, it is only the *result* of parameter-adjusting procedures that produces something construable as having a look-up table configuration. Moreover, a single (smart) look-up table can be traded in for a hierarchy of (smart) mini-look-up tables, so that an approximate answer can be cranked out at one stage, then shunted to a further stage for finer tuning. In this event, speed is traded for spatial miniaturization. Some of the speed can, however, be bargained back by adopting parallel search.

The insight that trained-up nets are look-upish raises the question of whether this might be useful in understanding circuits in nervous systems. Is it possible that some parts of the brain are taking advantage of the look-up table principle in some highly evolved version of that genre? Time considerations suggest they might well be. The time delays for conduction of a signal down an axon and across a synaptic cleft, together with the time delays for signal integration in the dendrites and cell body, add up to about 5 or 10 msec per neuronal step. If a nervous system is to give a motor response to a sensory stimulus with a latency of a few hundred milliseconds or less, then for certain stages in processing, the neuronal anatomy is probably configured for look-up short-cuts. Visual pattern recognition, for example, can be done in about 200 300 msec, which means there is only time for about 20–30 neuronal steps from retinal stimulation to motor output (Thorpe and Imbert 1989, Thorpe 1990).

Evidently the response latency for many tasks, including visual recognition, shows that there is insufficient time for the brain to be engaged in following the massive set of 3000–50,000 steps (or more) found in conventional computer vision programs (Feldman and Ballard 1982). Figuring out the next move in chess or figuring out how to make a bridge with popsicle sticks is, by contrast, relatively slow, and clearly involve many steps, but whether these are steps in a long sequence of look-ups representing possible ⟨move-next move⟩ pairs, or whether some rely on different principles altogether remains to be seen. Given their finite capacity, nervous systems cannot store answers for every possible contingency. To cope with novelty, nervous systems must cycle through multiple states to search for an adequate solution. With practice, however, the new problem–solution pairs can be compiled into a look-up table.[41]

Selected Readings

Abu-Mostafa, Y. (1989a). Complexity in neural systems. Appendix D of Mead (1989), *Analog VLSI and Neural Systems*. Reading, MA: Addison-Wesley.

Arbib, M. (1987). *Brains, Machines, and Mathematics*. Berlin: Springer-Verlag.

Arbib, M. A., and J. A. Robinson, eds. (1990). *Natural and Artificial Parallel Computation*. Cambridge, MA: MIT Press.

Carbonell, J. G., ed. (1989). *Artificial Intelligence* (special volume on Machine Learning), vol. 40, nos. 1–3; see especially the chapter by Geoffrey Hinton on connectionist learning.

Durbin, R., C. Miall, and G. Mitchison (1989). *The Computing Neuron*. Reading, MA: Addison-Wesley.

Hanson, S. J., and C. R. Olson, eds. (1990). *Connectionist Modeling and Brain Function: The Developing Interface*. Cambridge, MA: MIT Press.

Haugeland, J. (1985). *Artificial Intelligence: The Very Idea*. Cambridge, MA: MIT Press.

Hertz, J., A. Krogh, and R. G. Palmer (1991). *Introduction to the Theory of Neural Computation*. Redwood City, CA: Addison-Wesley.

Johnson-Laird, P. (1988). *The Computer and the Mind*. Cambridge, MA: Harvard University Press.

Kelner, K., and D. E. Koshland, eds. (1989). *Molecules to Models: Advances in Neuroscience*. Washington, DC: American Association for the Advancement of Science. (See especially chapter V, Neural Modeling.)

Kohonen, T. (1987). *Content-Addressable Memories*, 2nd ed. Berlin: Springer-Verlag.

Lippmann, R. P., J. E. Moody, and D. S. Touretzky (1991). *Advances in Neural Information Processing Systems 3*. San Mateo, CA: Morgan Kaufmann.

McClelland, J., and D. Rumelhart (1988). *Explorations in Parallel Distributed Processing*. Cambridge, MA: MIT Press. Comes with computer programs that simulate many of the networks discussed in this chapter.

McClelland, J., D. Rumelhart, and the PDP Research Group (1986). *Parallel Distributed Processing: Explorations in the Microstructure of Cognition*, vol. 2. Cambridge, MA: MIT Press.

Mead, C. (1989). *Analog VLSI and Neural Systems*. Reading, MA: Addison-Wesley.

Miller, K. D., guest ed. (in press). *Seminars in the Neurosciences*. Vol. 4, no. 1. *Use of Models in the Neurosciences*.

Nilsson, N. J. (1990). *The Mathematical Foundations of Learning Machines*. San Mateo, CA: Morgan Kaufmann. Reprint of the first edition (1965) with a new introduction by T. J. Sejnowski and H. White.

Poggio, T. (1990). A theory of how the brain works. In *Cold Spring Harbor Symposium on Quantitative Biology: The Brain*, vol. 55, ed. E. Kandel, T. Sejnowski, C. Stevens, and J. Watson. 899–910.

Rumelhart, D., J. McClelland, and the PDP Research Group (1986). *Parallel Distributed Processing: Explorations in the Microstructure of Cognition*, vol. 1. Cambridge, MA: MIT Press.

Schwartz, E. L., ed. (1990). *Computational Neuroscience*. Cambridge, MA: MIT Press.

Touretzky, D. S., ed. (1989). *Advances in Neural Information Processing Systems*, vol. 1. San Mateo, CA: Morgan Kaufmann.

Touretzky, D. S., ed. (1990). *Advances in Neural Information Processing Systems*, vol. 2. San Mateo, CA: Morgan Kaufmann.

Wasserman, P. D., and R. M. Oetzel (1990). *NeuralSource: The Bibliographic Guide to Artificial Neural Networks*. New York: Van Nostrand Reinhold.

Widrow, B., and S. D. Stearns (1985). *Adaptive Signal Processing*. Englewood Cliffs, NJ: Prentice-Hall.

Selected Journals

Neural Computation: a bimonthly journal published by MIT Press; contains reviews, articles, views, notes, and letters on the theoretical principles of neural circuits from the biophysical level to the systems level.

Network: Computation in Neural Systems: A physics-oriented journal on biological and artificial neural networks. Bristol, UK: IOP Publishing Ltd.

IEEE Transactions on Neural Networks: Engineering-oriented journal on artificial neural networks. New York: Institute of Electrical and Electronic Engineers, Inc.

Neural Network: Official journal of The International Neural Network Society. New York: Pergamon Press.

4   Representing the World

1   INTRODUCTION

The question of how the brain represents its world, both inner and outer, has traditionally been construed as a philosophical question through and through, posed not in terms of the brain but the mind, and addressable not experimentally, but from the comfort of the proverbial armchair. Part of what is exciting about this epoch in science is that both of these assumptions have gradually lost their stuffing, and experimental science—the mix of ethology, psychology, and neuroscience—continues to press forward with empirical techniques for putting the crimp on these ancient questions. A corner that many philosophers[1] thought was utterly unturnable has in fact been turned, if not in popular philosophy, then certainly within the mind/brain sciences.

The venerable old paradigm depicted humans as blessedly perched on the apex of the Great Chain of Being, lucky to have been created in the image of God, and fitted out with a nonphysical, immortal soul housing a freely exercisable will, a consciousness that experienced feelings and sensations, and a rational faculty that mercifully could transcend the merely mundane, for example by proving mathematical theorems. The old paradigm was frankly supernaturalistic. It exhibited both species chauvinism in quite spectacular degree and a profoundly nonempirical acceptance of nonphysical forces, stuffs, and mechanisms.

The new paradigm is naturalistic, and it is shaped in the scientific image. By pulling out the linchpin assumption that humans are set apart from the natural order, it changed everything. The naturalistic approach to the mind–brain, foreshadowed by Hobbes and de La Mettrie in the seventeenth century, became a live possibility in the nineteenth, largely by dint of advances in microscope and staining technology, a nonoccult understanding of electricity, and the commanding scientific leadership exemplified in the breadth and depth of success of physics and chemistry. The pioneers were mind/brain scientists, especially du Bois-Reymond, Helmholtz, Cajal, Golgi, Jackson, and Wertheimer, and the massive backdrop against which the the naturalistic vision made sense was Darwin's perspective on the origins of biological complexity. Although essentially constant in its ultimate goal, naturalism has been redirected and revivified by recent discoveries in neuroscience and by a growing confluence with the computational and behavioral sciences.

How do neurons represent—anything? Because of their proximity to the periphery, and in view of the opportunity to correlate neuronal responses with controlled stimuli, the sensory systems are a more fruitful starting point for addressing this question than, say, the more centrally located structures such as the cerebellum or the hippocampus or prefrontal cortex. The intensive study of single cells in various sensory systems, but particularly in the visual system of cats and monkeys and the auditory system in barn owls and bats, has yielded neurobiological data that are the mother's milk for the infant science of neurocomputation.

Before proceeding to explore the neurobiology of representing, it may be useful to flag a distinction, albeit a rather obvious one. There is a difference between a *current representing*, such as perceiving or imagining grandma riding her bicycle, and an *abeyant, or stored, representation* that is part of one's background knowledge, such as the knowledge of the periodic table or where one hid the biscuits or how to change a tire. The word "representation" is ambiguous between a perception I now have of grandma, and the ability to imagine or recognize or think about grandma, though I may not be exercising this ability at this very moment. Obviously most of one's knowledge is abeyant; only a fraction is occurrent. Yet by some means, abeyant representations can become occurrent and, moreover, can contribute to the properties of occurrent representations without becoming occurrent themselves.

In this chapter, we address the broad question of how nervous systems represent in the occurrent sense; chapter 5, on memory, will consider stored representations. The logic of the problem of sensory representation requires that we begin with some general brush-clearing, and then go on to consider how neurons encode information, using as a springboard the comparison between "grandmother" coding and distributed coding. Because the visual system is the most intensely researched sensory system, both physiologically and psychophysically, and because the computer models selected for later discussion pertain to visual processing, the discussion draws most heavily from research in the visual domain. To anchor the ensuing discussion, we shall pause in section 3 for a brief introduction to the basic anatomy and physiology of the visual system.

2   CONSTRUCTING A VISUAL WORLD

Sensory transducers are the interface between the brain and the world. They are specialized cells, such as rods and cones in the retina, hair cells in the cochlea, taste buds on the tongue, stretch receptors in the muscles, and many, many more[2] (figure 4.1). Transducers have evolved to respond selectively to different external physical parameters, such as light waves, sound waves, chemicals, motion, pressure and other mechanically deforming forces, electrical fields, magnetic fields, temperature, and so forth.[3] In response to a stimulus,

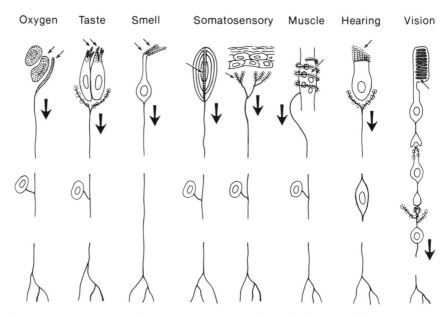

Figure 4.1 Different types of sensory receptors in vertebrates. Small arrows indicate sites where sensory stimuli act. Stippling indicates sites for transduction of the sensory stimuli and also for synaptic transmission; both of these types of site mediate graded signal transmission. Large arrows indicate sites of impulse transmission. (With permission, from Shepherd 1988.)

transducers may depolarize or hyperpolarize in graded fashion, and that exhausts their behavioral repertoire (figure 4.2).

Constrained by transducer output, the brain builds a model of the world it inhabits. That is, brains are world-modelers, and the verifying threads—the minute feed-in points for the brain's voracious intake of world-information—are the neuronal transducers in the various sensory systems. The remarkable thing is that although the input from the periphery is relatively meager—light waves impinging on the retina, for example—one's visual world nevertheless is shot through with hyperimmense richness. Note too that whereas the human visual system has some 10^8 transducers, only about 10^6 axons leave the retina for the brain. What happens to all that information? About 10^{10} neurons are engaged in visual processing beyond the periphery. What are all those neurons doing?

Signal integration and signal processing occur at every synaptic stage in a ladder of densely interactive networks. By virtue of these interactions, sensory systems somehow generate full-blown, full-dress, world-beater perceptions. Is this because at every stage new conduits from the periphery deliver freshly transduced signals? No. The analogy to avoid here is that of building a tiny model village in the rumpus room, where every addition or change to the town must be injected from the outside. It is precisely this *disanalogy* that makes sensory processing so remarkable. Somehow, out of the resources of the many cells in the system—out of their intrinsic physiological characteristics, the synaptic routes from the periphery, and their distinctive anatomical con-

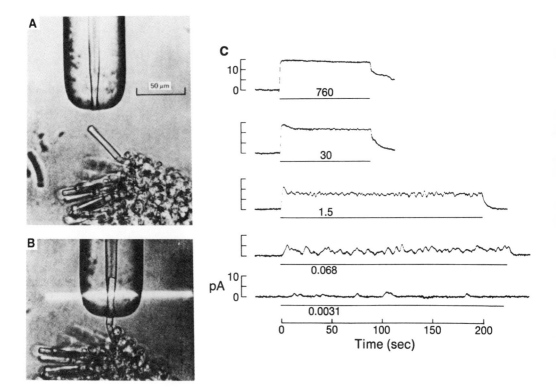

Figure 4.2 Recording the responses from single isolated rod photoreceptors of the toad. (A) Suction electrode approaching the outer segment of a receptor protruding from a piece of retina. (B) Outer segment is sucked up into the electrode. Light bar is shone on small parts of the outer segment, while membrane current, proportional to longitudinal current flowing along the outer segment, is recorded by the electrode. (C) Recordings of receptor responses, showing quantal events at low illumination (bottom), merging to a smooth, graded response at higher illumination (upper traces). Note that these are recordings of membrane current (in pA: 10^{-12} amp); the upward deflections signal the current flows associated with the membrane hyperpolarization that is characteristic of vertebrate photoreceptors. Intensity of light stimulation in photons μm^{-2} sec^{-1}. (With permission from Shepherd 1988a; adapted from Baylor et al. 1979a,b.)

nections with other cells—a visual world, full of enduring objects, locatable in space-time coordinates, replete with color, motion, and shape, is what we perceive.

The explanation cannot be remotely analogous to passive registry of light patterns on photosensitive film. In contrast to the passivity of the film, the brain's processing of transducer signals must be intensely active. Past experiences play a significant role in current perception, in what we literally see. A mature brain recognizes quickly and without effort words on a page, the trail of mice, the parched state of a plant, the embarrassment of a colleague, an eclipse of the moon. Identical stimuli can correspond to radically different perceptions. An English speaker and a German speaker perceive something entirely different in the phoneme sequence \Empedocles lēpt\. That is, in an English context, speakers hear "Empedocles leaped" (meaning he took a jump). In a German context, speakers hear "Empedocles liebt" (meaning he

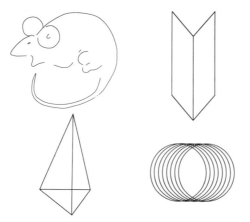

Figure 4.3 Reversible figures. The visual system sees, for example, either an old man or a rat, but not a blend of both, and the perceptions may flip back and forth. This property suggests that the computational process involves a winner-take-all mechanism to decide the perceptual output.

loved). So far as sheer phonetics of the stimulus is concerned, and hence so far as the hair cells of the ear are concerned, there is nothing to choose. Reversible figures, such as the Necker cube and old-man/rat are compelling examples in vision where one and the same stimulus may be perceived in very different ways (figure 4.3). If nothing in the *stimulus* changes, then the brain must be causing the difference. (This is not necessarily obvious. Eccles (1982) claims reversible figures are actually evidence for a nonphysical soul, on grounds that because the stimulus is the same, the brain events must be the same, so only the soul with its nonphysical flexibility could switch between radically different perceptions.)

The animal's genes carve out the general contours of a brain's capacities and, in particular, the directions and degrees in which it may be modified. Within these contours, experientially based modification has its province. Although it is the devil's own job to specify accurately what the limits are, or how the limitations shift at various developmental stages, it is evident that brains do not enjoy unbounded plasticity.[4] Not everyone can learn to read, not everyone has binocular depth perception (chickens do not have any at all), and dichromat humans cannot distinguish red from green, try as they might. Nor can processing close to the periphery of the nervous system be assumed to be passive. There are efferent connections in some birds to the retina and in reptiles, birds, and mammals to the cochlea, and there is modulation of somatosensory signals in the spinal cord.

From psychophysical research emerges a more substantial sense in which the brain contributes to perception. For example, normally the human visual system processes shading gradients consistent with the assumption that things generally are lit from above and only exceptionally from below. Hence certain shaded contours, such as moon craters, could be seen either as convex or concave, but they are automatically seen one way or the other according as the lighting assumption dictates (figure 4.4). With conscious effort (concentrat-

Representing the World

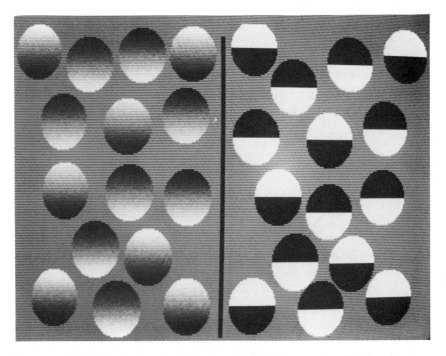

Figure 4.4 (Left) The visual system takes it as the default assumption that the objects are illuminated from above, and thus interprets the ovals with light tops as convex and those with light bottoms as concave, and the two types tend to form groups. When the book is turned upside down, the ovals take on the reverse orientation in depth. (Right) The two-tone ovals convey the same luminance polarities as those on the left, but in the absence of gradual shading, they contain no depth information. It is difficult if not impossible to see them as convex or concave, and they do not form groups as those on the left do. (Courtesy V. S. Ramachandran; based on Ramachandran 1988.)

ing on imagining a floodlight on the floor), one can make the objects' convexity flip to concavity. But it is noteworthy that the flip is not limited to the single shape foveated, but all the shapes in the set; that is, there is "capture," reflecting the brain's knowledge that if one in the set is lit from below, then probably all in the set are. (It is easier to get the flip by turning the photo upside down than by the "conscious effort" tactic.)

This exercise demonstrates several things. One is that the assumption about light sources seems to be embedded in the very manner in which the peripheral signals are processed in visual cortex. It may be that this is substantially an evolutionary bequest. That is, normally, the light source is the sun or, more rarely, the moon, but at least from the sky. Swift and accurate perceptual judgment would be aided by making that assumption the default assumption, revisable under special conditions, such as observing bottom-lighting. Indeed, that the system is "fast and dirty" is suggested by the reversal in curvature observed when the shaded images are viewed with the *head* upside down. That is, the system does not compensate (the images flip) when one turns upside down, rather as though the circuit equates "above" with "where the top of the head is." Whether an animal reared in an environment where bottom-lighting was the norm would have the corresponding assumption adopted by its brain is not known, but the possibility is testable. It is known, for example, that cats reared in strobe-light conditions never acquire proper motion detection or discrimination.[5] Thus the evolutionary contribution may be more like this: in standard (light overhead) conditions, visual cortex develops so the overhead light-source assumption is favored (Ramachandran 1988).

Results similar in their implication for the perceptual processing of motion, color constancy, size constancy, and binocular depth perception suggest that certain physical principles are, by virtue of the very wiring and neuronal physiology, part of the fabric of the nervous system. They are defeasible by competing principles on suitable occasions, where the defeasibility conditions too are embedded in the fabric of high-order networks or, alternatively part of a winner-take-all game at the same level implemented as a recurrent net. According to Ramachandran's hypothesis (1988, 1990a,b), processing in visual cortex works according to assorted rules of thumb—inchoately specified genetically, stabilized in the computational architecture of the cortex during development, and defeasible computationally, sometimes by top-down influences. None of this is evident in our experiences, however, and intuition unaided by experiment misdirects us.

Neuroethologists emphasize that in investigating how a brain represents the world, it is important to understand both the animal's behavioral repertoire and also the specific range of physical parameters a particular species uses to inform and initiate behavior (Heiligenberg 1991). Understanding how the animal conducts its business in its environmental niche will help us understand the scope and limits of the animal's capacity, and hence what its brain does with a signal from the periphery.

Two related points add depth to the neuroethologist's slant. First, what in the world is represented by a given nervous system depends on the animal's environmental niche, on how it makes its living, and thus on its evolutionary history. Bees can represent light in the ultraviolet range, and this is useful because it enables them to detect the business end of certain flowers; rattlesnakes can detect in the infrared, and this helps them prey upon rodents in the dark. Humans, like most other primates, have stereo vision, which presumably is helpful in breaking a prey's or a predator's camouflage, and generally in facilitating highly accurate localizing of objects relative to each other, especially within arm's length. Together with the advantageous opposable thumb, binocular depth perception is an enormous boon to fine sensory-motor control.

The second point, perhaps of most salience to philosophers, is this. Brains engage in world-representing not for the pure, sweet Platonic joy of it, but essentially because the animal needs to survive (Konishi 1991). An animal needs sensory information to guide behavior so that it may succeed in living another day, or at least living long enough to pass on its genes. Thus it is instructive to study a brain's sensory and cognitive computations in the light of how they connect to motor control. This is not to denigrate Platonic pleasures, but only to emphasize that cognitive styles and cognitive improvements are tightly connected to natural selection. As animals' nervous systems differ in sensory selectivity, so they may display differences in their cognitive investments (Gallistel 1990). Thus ravens may be able to "count" to seven or eight, while dogs cannot. The arithmetic capacity, albeit a humble one, may be an evolutionary consequence of the ravens' reproductive strategy, such as needing to keep track of the number of eggs in its clutch so it can ditch cowbird eggs. In other tasks—for example, herding sheep—dogs may have a far greater capacity. Methodologically, the advantage cited by neuroethologists for their strategy is exactly one touted earlier (chapter 1): namely, top-down data constrain bottom-up hypotheses, thus narrowing the search space. Quite simply, it is more efficient to have some idea of what you are looking for than not.

3 THUMBNAIL SKETCH OF THE MAMMALIAN VISUAL SYSTEM

The primate retina transforms patterns of light on the 100 million photoreceptors into electrical signals on the mere one million axons in the optic nerve, and the 100 : 1 ratio of units suggests heavy-duty signal processing and information compression. There are two types of photoreceptors: rods—low-acuity, high-sensitivity transducers that function even in dim light, and cones—high-acuity, low-sensitivity transducers that function best in daylight, enabling form and color perception. At the fovea, cones are packed densely and rods sparsely, but in the parafoveal regions, rods outnumber cones by a factor of ten. The rods and cones respond, to photons of certain wavelengths, with degrees of hyperpolarization (figure 4.5). Between the photoreceptors and the ganglion cells that carry signals to higher brain centers, there are two layers of cells that conduct the earliest stages of visual processing. The time delay between photons impinging on the cones to a signal traveling up a ganglion cell axon is about 25 msec, primarily because photoreceptors are relatively slow, but also because there are a minimum of two synaptic steps in the retina. The ganglion cell axons make up the optic nerve, and by and large they are center-surround cells, but collectively and implicitly they carry information about color, motion, contours, and location of stimulus such that the visual cortex can extract such information as shape, direction and speed of motion, surface reflectance, color constancy, shapes, and depth (figure 4.6).

The primate visual system has two main pathways: (1) the more axonally numerous pathway from the retina to the lateral geniculate nucleus (LGN) of the thalamus and then to the cortex, and (2) a pathway that projects from the retina to the superior colliculus. The retinal ganglion cell pathway bifurcates so that half the axons cross to the opposite side, and half remain on the same side as they arise. Ganglion cells fall into three main classes: (1) Parvo cells are small and their axons terminate in the upper layers of the LGN, also known as the parvocellular layer ("parvo" meaning "small"). (2) Magno cells are larger and their axons terminate in the lower layers of the LGN, also known as the magnocellular layer ('magno" meaning "large"). Some of the magno cell popu-

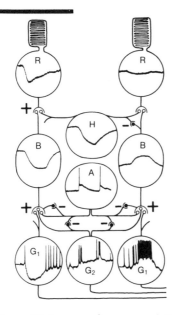

Figure 4.5 Summary diagram correlating synaptic organization of the vertebrate retina with some of the intracellularly recorded responses from the mudpuppy retina. This figures attempts to show how the receptive field organization of the hyperpolarizing bipolar cells, off-center ganglion cells, and on-center ganglion cells is established. The responses occurring in the various neurons upon illumination (bar above left receptor) are indicated. A, amacrine cells; B, bipolar cells; R, receptors; H, horizontal cell; G, ganglion cells; + with open circle, excitatory synapses; − with filled circle, inhibitory synapses. (Reprinted by permission of the publishers from *The Retina: An Approachable Part of the Brain* by John E. Dowling, Cambridge MA: Harvard University Press. Copyright © 1987 by John E. Dowling.)

lation projects not to the LGN but to the superior colliculus. (3) Remaining cells project mainly to the superior colliculus (figure 4.7).

In the LGN, cells are segregated not only according to the parvo–magno classification, but also according to eye of origin, a property known as ocularity. From the LGN, neurons project to visual cortex. In monkey, all these cells project to V1, and more specifically, mainly to layer 4C (figure 4.8). In the cat, there are also projections from the LGN to other cortical visual areas besides V1 such as V2. The segregation of classes of cells is preserved to some degree. The parvo cells project mainly to the lower stratum of layer 4C of V1, with some branches reaching the topmost stratum of 4C. The magno cells project to the upper stratum of layer 4C and into 4B. Neurons reaching middle and lower layers of 4C preserve ocularity, that is, they respond exclusively to stimuli from the right eye or the left eye. Some neurons in the upper stratum of 4C of V1, however, show binocularity, and may respond equally strongly to stimuli in their receptive field of either eye, or they may show varying degrees of preference for stimuli from one eye. Some cells here are still monocular, and cells are clumped together depending on their ocularity. Layers 2, 3, and 4 of V1 also contain cells whose axons project out of V1 to other areas of cortex,

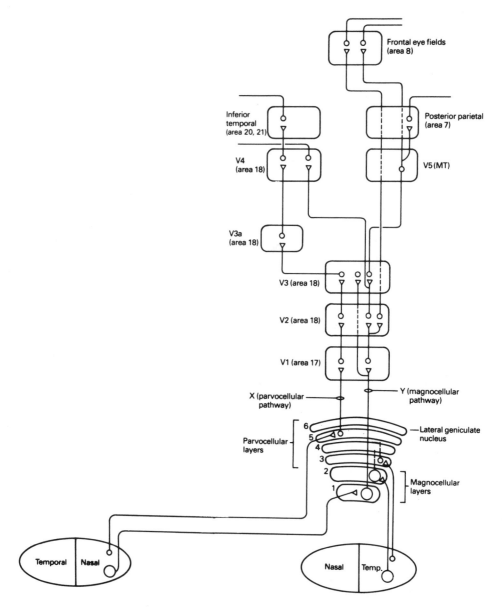

Figure 4.6 Highly schematic view of the projections from the retina to various visual areas of the cerebral cortex, with distinct synaptic stages at different structures, illustrating some degree of hierarchy in the processing of visual information. (Adapted from van Essen 1979.)

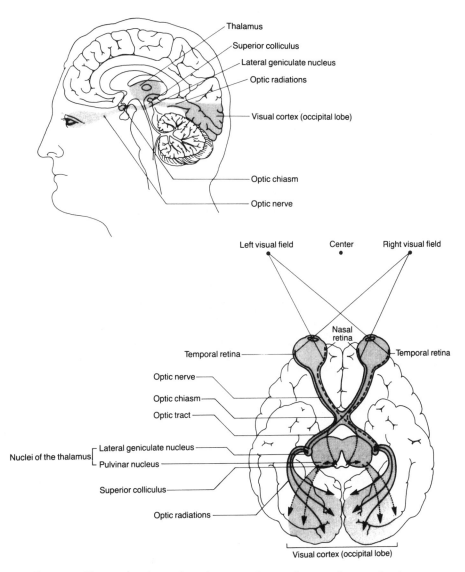

Figure 4.7 The visual pathways from the eye to the visual cortex, showing also the separate pathway of the ganglion cells to the superior colliculus. (Top) Sagittal section. (Bottom) Ventral view, without the brain stem or cerebellum.

A

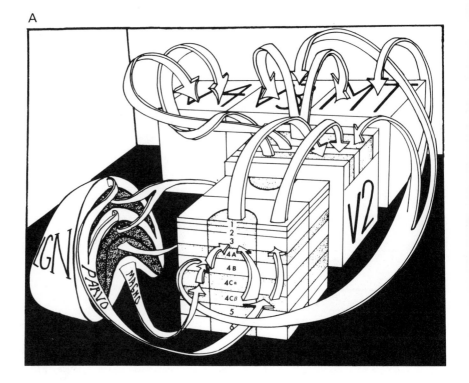

B

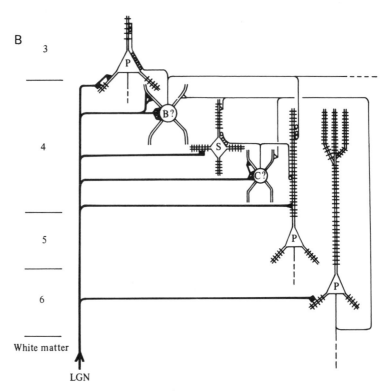

and layers 5 and 6 contain cells that project to deep brain structures, including the LGN and the superior colliculus.

The main physiological properties relevant to later discussion are as follows: cells in the LGN and many cells in layers 4C α have a simple center-surround organization (see chapter 2). Cells in 4B and in the next strata flanking 4C α have a very different response. Instead of a receptive field with circular symmetry, their excitatory and inhibitory regions are separated by straight lines (figure 4.9). For example, a cell may be tuned to respond maximally to a bar of light at 30° in the middle of its receptive field. These are known as *simple cells*, and it has been suggested that their receptive field properties may result from the convergence of a set of center-surround cells on the simple cell. Although this is very plausible, it has not yet been established[6] (figure 4.10). *Complex cells* are the most common cell type in the early visual cortex. They are found mainly in layers 2, 3 and in the 5, 6 border region. Like simple cells, they are tuned to respond to elongated stimuli, such as slits or bars, in their receptive field, and they prefer certain orientations to others. But unlike simple cells, they respond best when their favorite stimulus is moving in a particular direction across their receptive field; if the cell does respond to a stationary stimulus, the stimulus can be located anywhere in the receptive field. For example, a cell might respond best to a 30° stimulus moving in a downward direction. Some simple and complex cells show length summation, which means that the longer the line within its receptive field, the more vigorous the response. Other cells are "end-stopped," which means that their receptive field has a flanking inhibitory region such that if the stimulus length exceeds the boundaries of the excitatory field, the cell is inhibited. This inhibitory field has the same orientation selectivity as does the excitatory field (Pollen et al. 1971, 1988).[7]

The continuation of segregation of magno and parvo pathways after V1 is illustrated schematically in figure 4.11. Roughly speaking, one pathway goes from V1 through to the inferior temporal cortex and appears to be specialized for perception of form and color.[8] The second very general pathway goes from V1 to the posterior parietal cortex and appears specialized for perception of motion, location, depth, and low-contrast luminance (see figure 2.3;

Figure 4.8 (A) Illustration of the principal connections between the lateral geniculate nucleus (LGN), striate cortex, and extrastriate visual areas in the primate. Presence or absence of dark stippling in the LGN indicates eye preference of the cells. Separate connections are shown for magno- and parvocellular layers. Connections are shown for one eye only. Frontmost block is a portion of V1 containing half of a left eye column and half of the neighboring right eye column. Light stippling indicates staining for the enzyme, cytochrome oxidase. Staining is present throughout layers 4A and 4C but is localized to blobs in other layers. No staining is present in 4B. In V2, staining takes the form of alternating thick and thin dark stripes separated by unlabeled stripes. Cytochrome oxidase staining in other areas is not shown. Many connections are not shown. (From LeVay and Nelson 1991.) (B) Local circuitry of neurons that receive direct input from LGN afferent fibers. P, pyramidal cell; B?, large GABAergic cell (presumed basket cell); S, spiny stellate cell; C?, small GABAergic cell. Triangles, excitatory synapses on somata or dendritic shafts; square, excitatory contact on spines; circles, inhibitory synapses. (From Martin 1988.)

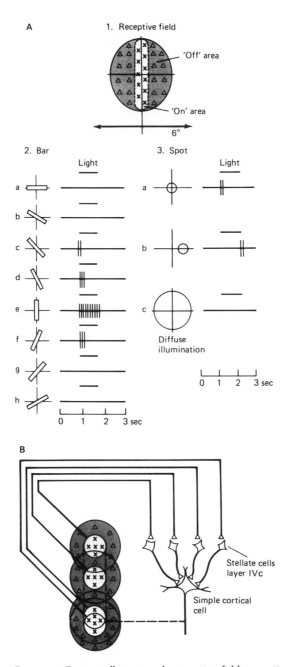

Figure 4.9 Diagram illustrating the receptive field properties of a simple cell in the primary visual cortex. (A) 1. The receptive field has a narrow central excitatory area flanked by symmetrical inhibitory areas. 2. The best stimulus for this cell is a vertically oriented light bar ($1° \times 8°$) in the center of its receptive field. Other orientations are less effective in driving the cell. 3. In contrast to a vertical bar, a small spot of light in the excitatory center of the field (a) gives only a weak excitatory response. A small spot in the inhibitory area (b) gives a weak inhibitory response. Diffuse light (c) is ineffective. (B) Hubel and Wiesel's (1962) hypothesis to explain how center-surround cells could be connected to a simple cell so that the latter responds selectively to bars of light in a particular orientation. (From Kandel 1985; adapted from Hubel and Wiesel 1962.)

(Ungerleider and Mishkin 1982). Two caveats must be mentioned: (1) The functional description is drawn from available data, but available data about pathways, cell-to-cell connectivity, area boundaries, and lesion effects are far from complete. (2) Some data show that the two major cortical pathways are not cleanly segregated, for there seem to be interconnections and hence cross talk (Schiller et al. 1990). Anatomical data support this claim, as do physiological data. For example, cells in MT are tuned to respond to movement in a certain direction and at a preferred velocity. They do not respond simply to a colored stimulus. Nevertheless, they are not entirely insensitive to color inasmuch as the cell's response to moving stimuli may be affected if the stimuli are colored. It is therefore important to understand that the basic two-pathway hypothesis is only a rough beginning, and it may undergo much revision in the next decade or so.

The cells in V1 are mapped retinotopically, in the sense that neighboring cells have neighboring receptive fields. Retinotopy—the property whereby place on the retina is directly represented by place in the brain—is both experimentally well established and theoretically seminal (figure 4.12). Topographic mapping of the transducer surface is a general property found in other sensory systems as well, including the auditory system, where the analog of spatial location is frequency, and the somatensensory system, where the surface of the body is topographically mapped. When a cell's specificity of response is determined by the spatial location of its inputs, this is known as *place-coding*.[9] More generally, evolution has found place-coding to be such a useful strategy that in some cases the brain transforms certain nonspatial properties, such as temporal relations, into place-code. More generally, it is possible that for many properties, relative position of the property in a *state space* can be coded in terms of spatial location in a two-dimensional or three-dimensional spatial region of the nervous system.

Consider an example where place-coding shows itself to be a very efficient means of handling complex information. Masakazu Konishi and colleagues[10] showed in studies of the barn owl that neurons in the nucleus laminaris compute interaural time delay, thereby locating the sound source in the horizontal plane; neurons in one of the lemniscal nuclei encode interaural amplitude differences, thereby locating the sound source in the vertical plane. The intersection of these two sets of coordinates locates the sound source very accurately in 2-D space (see figures 7.2, 7.3). Just as one might expect they should, therefore, these two classes of information are combined to give a precise location of the sound source so the owl may intercept prey in the dark. They are nonlinearly combined in the inferior colliculus. These space-specific neurons in the inferior colliculus form a map of auditory space, and they project to the optic tectum where an auditory-visual map of space is found. Although the owl can locate the source just on the basis of auditory information, any available visual information also helps. Thus the further combination of auditory and visual information also gives an exact space-specific map of cells. The owl's precise head movements would seem to be the outcome of connections between high-level place-coded sensory neurons and neurons in the motor system (Konishi 1991).

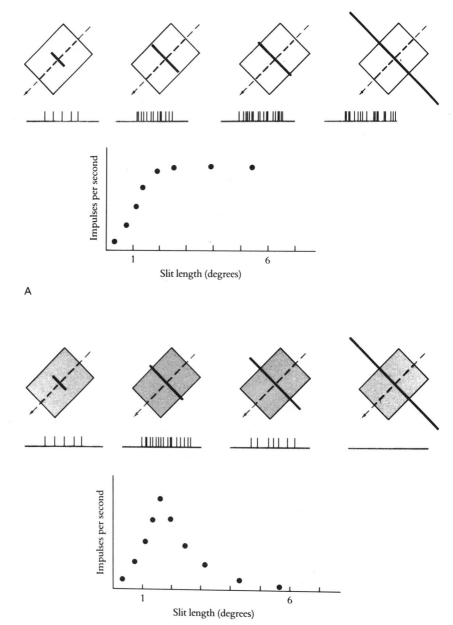

A

B

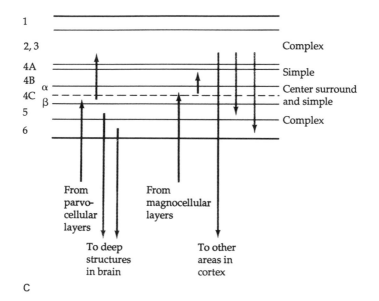

C

Figure 4.10 (A) An ordinary complex cell responds to various lengths of a slit of light. The duration of each record is 2 sec. (B) This is an end-stopped cell. It responds mildly when the slit of light covers a bit of its receptive field, most strongly at about 2°, but the response declines again as the slit lengthens. At 6° or longer the cell ceases to respond. (C) A rough indication of where simple, complex, and center-surround cell bodies are located in the cortical laminae. (From *Eye, Brain and Vision* by D. H. Hubel. Copyright © 1988 by Scientific American Books, Inc. Reprinted by permission of W. H. Freeman and Company.)

Note also that the neurons that make up the space-coded map are interconnected, and lateral inhibition appears to sharpen the location-selectivity of each cell. The place-coding of the inferior colliculus neurons, it should be emphasized, does not preclude a neural-net description of the function of the inferior colliculus.

Place-coding is a representational principle at the level of maps. The next question is: what principles do nervous systems use at the level of networks and neurons? Consider now all the neurons at a particular level of the visual system, say V1, that respond to a particular region of space. In V1, for example, there might be many thousands satisfying this description. What does any one of those single neurons contribute to the representation? The same thing? Different things? How is its contribution related to its interaction with other neurons? In other words, the question is how a neuron, given that it has a certain receptive field, response repertoire, and cortical address, codes for certain properties—motion, color, and so forth.

4   REPRESENTING IN THE BRAIN: WHAT CAN WE LEARN FROM THE VISUAL SYSTEM?

Gross recordings (EEG recordings, evoked potentials) from large populations of neurons have been used to map regions of the brain that were specialized for

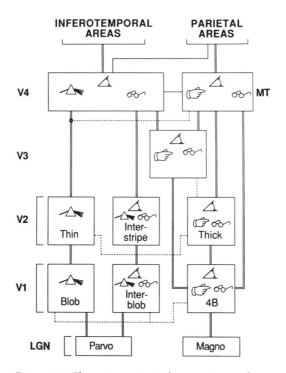

Figure 4.11 The major anatomical connections and neuronal response selectivities in early visual areas of the macaque monkey. Icons symbolize response preference of many cells in that area: prism = wavelength; angle = orientation; pointing finger = direction; spectacles = binocular disparity. (Reprinted from DeYoe and van Essen [1987]. Concurrent processing streams in monkey visual cortex. *Trends in Neurosciences* 11: 219–226.)

sensory processing and control of movements. Identification of areas specialized for visual, auditory, and somatosensory processing were made by these means. It also possible to clock the arrival of the peripheral signal in visual cortex, whether or not the person was aware of the signal, and to chart the time course of canonical wave patterns for the next second or two after stimulation presentation. Having mapped modality-specific regions in cortex, the next question was, What exactly is going on in those regions such that the animal perceives its environment? Crudely speaking, there were two strategic intuitions regarding what to do next.

According to one argument, the critical variables were at the population level, and hence that was the correct level to investigate. Research on the individual neuron, it was alleged, would not reveal the properties of the group (Fox 1970). There were two major reasons why this argument lost adherents; one concerned techniques, the other concerned concepts. Available population techniques, which had quite good temporal resolution, were used to plot out various rhythmic patterns. But they were not able to address the "what" or "how" of processing. They could not distinguish between a response to a red stimulus and a green stimulus, between a moving stimulus and a stationary stimulus, between perception of a tree and perception of a face. Conceptually, the population-level argument was soft because no one knew what was repre-

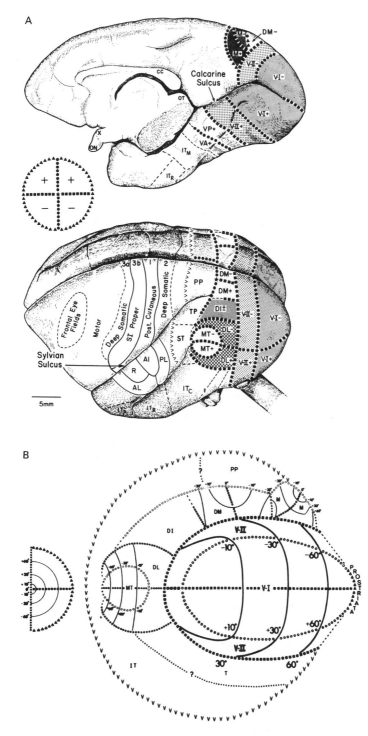

Figure 4.12 (A) Medial and dorsolateral views of the cortex of the owl monkey showing visually mapped areas. (B) Schematic unfolding of the visual cortex of the left hemisphere in the owl monkey. Icons to the left provide the key to the mapping relations between visual field and cortex: the vertical axis is represented by filled circles, the horizontal axis by filled squares, and the perimeter by arrowheads. Note the orderly mapping of the visual field in various cortical areas and the relatively large areas devoted to the fovea. (From Allman [1982]. Reconstructing the evolution of the brain in primates through the use of comparative neurophysiological and neuroanatomical data. In *Primate Brain Evolution*, ed. Armstrong and Falk. New York: Plenum.)

sented by evoked potential waveforms. Everyone knew what a neuron was and a little about what it did; nobody knew what a supraneuronal unit might be nor anything about what it might do. Although further refining of population recordings was advocated as a means of zeroing in on the relevant processing parameters, frustration with the strategy led inexorably to the study to individual neurons. The second argument thus emerged as a result of the single-cell work, pioneered by Kuffler (1953) on retinal ganglion cells and by Mountcastle (1957) on the somatosensory cortex, and then, with discipline-shifting effect, by Hubel and Wiesel (1962, 1977) on the visual cortex of cats and monkeys.

Partly by accident, Hubel and Wiesel discovered the response selectivity of neurons in visual cortex to a light-dark edge in a given orientation. Changing the edge's orientation reduced the vigor of the cell response. Other cells showed different orientation selectivity; next-neighbor cells shared orientation preference, close but not next neighbors preferred an orientation different by a few degrees of visual angle, and so on (figure 4.13). The population displayed a quite orderly preference profile across an area of cortex. The specificity and organization at the level of the single cell were stunning, and provoked an intensive physiological exploration of posterior cortex to see what else could be found, and also to understand what factors of connectivity and physiology account for the selective responses of the cells.

Following these and comparable discoveries in motor cortex (Evarts 1966, 1981), single-cell research became the center of gravity in neuroscience. Indeed, the period from 1962, the year of publication of the first Hubel and Wiesel results, until the present time may with only minor exaggeration be called "The Era of the Single Neuron" in neuroscience. Part of the single cell's popularity was owed to the fact that there were clear, if ticklish, techniques for stimulating and recording from single cells, and for varying conditions by manipulating pharmacological variables to inhibit or enhance the effects and also to lesion out select groups of neurons. The connectivity between cells was obviously critical for understanding the response selectivity of cells, and hence the rationale for detailed anatomical research was straightforward. In other words, researchers knew what to do, and they did it. Guided by top-downish results in psychophysics and clinical neurology, they began to unravel the microstructure of the sensory cortices. Techniques for accessing cell assemblies were, by contrast, less well-defined, and there was no breakthrough regarding processing specificity of assemblies comparable to that made by single cell physiology.

The heyday of the single cell was by no means merely technique driven. At the theoretical level also, the single cell seemed destined for center stage. The experimental success in discovering response patterns of neurons led to a view of the nervous system as a confederation of specialist neurons, where neurons become more highly specified the more highly placed they are in the information processing hierarchy. A theory of information processing in cortex began to condense around four points: (1) observed cellular response selectivity, (2) a processing hierarchy from less specific to more specific responses, roughly

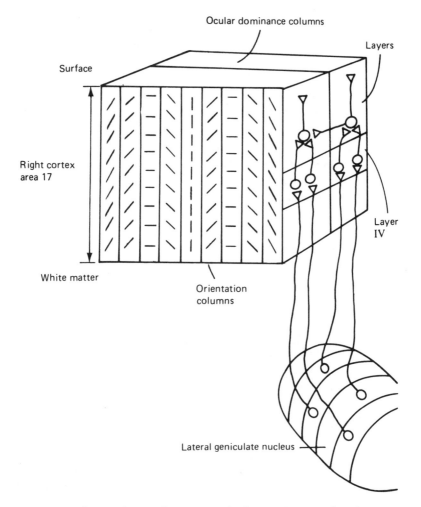

Figure 4.13 Schematic diagram showing cortical columns containing cells with a response preference for stimuli in a particular orientation. (Based on Hubel and Wiesel 1962; reprinted from Kandel and Schwartz 1985.)

corresponding to synaptic distance from the periphery, (3) with increasing specificity of cellular responses from retina to LGN to V1, there are fewer and fewer cells responding to the stimulus, and this pattern may be extrapolated beyond V1, and (4) the segregation of parallel pathways for processing distinct properties of the visual stimulus, such as motion and color (Barlow 1972, Konishi 1991). The inference drawn from these key points was that coding becomes increasingly specific up the steps of the hierarchy. On the extreme end of the local coding hierarchy, there is a convergence of signals culminating in a unique representation, whereupon the motor system uses this representation to command a suitable action. Since exactly this organization is seen in parts of some nervous systems—for example, in the electric fish, *Eigenmannia* (Heiligenberg 1991)—the question is how generally this strategy obtains.

The explanatory crux of the idea of *local coding* is that uniqueness in pattern recognition at the perceptual level derives from uniqueness in the response of a cell (or one of its clones). On Barlow's hypothesis (1972), an estimated 1000 active neurons may represent a visual scene, and any given neuron represents about as much as is represented by a single word, such as red or ball, along with positional information. Thus in recognizing and responding to a red bouncing ball, there is a small group of cells (the "red," "bouncing," and "ball" cells) at the hierarchy apex responding exactly to that state of affairs; to recognize Grandma in her Sunday best bicycling to church, one needs a set of cells (and possibly their clones) at the hierarchy apex that collectively respond exactly to that and to nothing other than that—not, for example, to Grandma in her garden clothes spreading fertilizer. Of course, the cell representing "grandmother" will also respond in the second situation, but the "bicycle" neurons will not. One could be even more extreme and require that a single cell respond to the first scene, and a different single cell respond to the second scene. This is not a widely shared view, mainly because of the number of specific neurons needed for pattern recognition would fast outstrip the number of neurons available.

The high degree of cellular selectivity, corresponding precisely to the relevant degree of perceptual discrimination, earned this theory the nickname of *"grandmother cell"* theory of neuronal representation. Although known almost universally by that name, it is also referred to as the "local-coding" or "punctate-coding" theory of neuronal representation. For brevity and clarity, one needs a canonical term; we shall use "local-coding." Using a "one-cell-for-one-word" calculation is necessarily rough, since some words are perceptually richer than others; for example, "circus" and "dying" are richer than "red" and "bouncing." Moreover, the reasons for postulating a unique cell for prototypical red would suggest unique cells for nonprototypically red things such as "red hair," which is rarely ripe-tomato red; "red face," parts of which are really only rather pink; "red onion" and "red potato," which have a burgundy-colored skin and white insides, and so on.

The main appeal of local coding is that just as there appear to be feature detectors for oriented bars or spots of light moving at a specific velocity, so also there are feature detectors for states of affairs described by a word or possibly a phrase. The local-coding theory did fit hand in glove with the experimental success of single-cell physiology. If, in contrast to the local-coding theory, perception was instead a population effect, no one had a successful technique to access such effects nor to begin to figure out how perceptual specificity was achieved.

Local-coding theory enjoys decided theoretical virtues. It recommends a means whereby very high-grade selectivity in perception might be achieved, and thus explains how we can distinguish visually, in about 200 msec or even less, between Queen Elizabeth and Princess Margaret, between Magic Johnson and Alajuwon. The "Magic Johnson" cell either responds or it doesn't, and thus we can give a very fast and decisive answer regarding whose face we glimpsed. Assuming a connection to command neurons,[11] local coding explains the high-grade specificity and speed in behavioral response. That is, there can be a very clean mapping between the local-coded cell and a complex motor act.

To many researchers in the two or three decades after the Hubel and Wiesel discoveries, the empirical data seemed smoothly to entail the local-coding theory and to more or less foreclose alternatives.[12] The theory was appealing partly by contrast to the floundering cell-population approach, and partly, we conjecture, because of its under-the-table affinity with "pictures-in-the-head" metaphors, inasmuch as a single cell's firing in response to a single entity made the matter of how a cell represented that entity seem almost self-explanatory: it was a reliable *indicator* of that entity.

In the last decade, research on the question of how neurons represent has drawn on the idea of *vector coding*. Also known as "distributed representing," "state space representing," and "multidimensional representing," the concept of vector coding has become both the stalking horse for criticism of local coding and a new framework within which to interpret the neurobiological data. Again, out of consideration for clarity and brevity and reflecting no ideological subtext, we select one label from the lot. The choice is "vector coding." Essentially, the criticism of local coding squares off in three places, and each will be discussed in the next section. (1) Local coding is underdetermined even by its best evidence; that is, the available evidence is perfectly consistent with vector coding; (2) recognizing new things and producing motor responses to new things are problematic on the local-coding theory, much less so on the vector-coding theory; (3) the patterns recognized visually by a human in a lifetime vastly outstrip the number of sensory processing neurons in the entire human nervous system. On the positive side of the ledger, vector coding appears to be more computationally pliant than local coding, though new developments could change that. Moreover, vector coding avoids the "running-out-of-neurons" problem, and it is not only consistent with the data, but predicts the increasing specificity seen in the data. Moreover, vector coding begins to pick up the loose threads from the sidelined population argument and to reconnect them to data on the single-cell level (figure 4.14).

5   WHAT IS SO SPECIAL ABOUT DISTRIBUTION?

On the face of it, the difference between local and distributed representations—between local and vector coding—falls rather short of spine-tingling, barn-burning stuff. Reduced to the barest essentials, the difference comes to this: vector coding uses many cells to code a representation; local coding uses one. Not, it would seem, a difference to die for. The rivalry lacks even more luster when it is considered that local coding may use clones if it wants safety through redundancy. Since both coding strategies use many cells in a single representation, the differences now seem at the vanishing point. Is the matter of distribution really significant, or is it just one of those academic hair-splitters on which it profiteth not to waste one's time?

First, our depiction of the local-coding hypothesis as requiring "one neuron codes one object" is a bit of a strawman, since typically no one defends a view

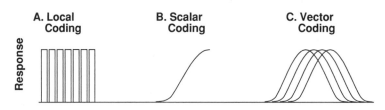

Figure 4.14 Three methods of encoding information. (A) Local coding: a separate unit is dedicated to each feature the system distinguishes. (B) Scalar encoding: features are encoded by the firing rate of a single neuron. (C) Vector coding: features are encoded in the pattern of activity in a population of units that have broad, overlapping tuning curves.

quite this pure. The strawman version of vector coding would hold that every neuron contributes to every representation. No one defends this either. It is useful nonetheless to have the pure versions on the table, if only to see by contrast what the differences are and what issues matter.

The second point to be emphasized here is that vector coding and local coding are not mutually exclusive choices for nervous systems; different nervous structures may use different strategies, and some networks may use a mixed strategy (see section below on hyperacuity.) For example, representation of scalar values can be efficiently achieved with local coding (Heiligenberg 1990), but vectorial values may be more efficiently represented using distributed coding.

Distribution, we shall argue below, is genuinely important—it is important both theoretically and experimentally. In argument, the appearance of triviality cedes to the reality of substance. In the right context and with the right backdrop, the seemingly trivial differences between local and vector coding get amplified and reconceived, so that in the end the differences are the very opposite of academic gimcrackery. Rather, they are substantial, research-directing, conceptually clarifying differences. To explain how we see this issue, we shall walk through it slowly.

What Is Vector Coding?

A vector, recall, is an ordered set of numbers. How can neurons code by vectors? Consider a population, n, of neurons. Distinct representations will be coded as the overall set of activity levels across the neurons in the relevant population. Assume for the nonce, what may not in fact be true, that the representational activity of a single cell can be identified with the average rate of firing of that cell. (Exact spike timing rather than average spike frequency may itself be important, but we shall ignore that here.) One and the same neuron may thus participate in the representation of many different items, and no one neuron represents an item all by itself. To keep it dead simple, suppose there are four neurons, each with five activity levels ranging from 0 to 4. Thus $\langle 3, 1, 0, 1 \rangle$ specifies a particular pattern of activity during a certain time interval, $\langle 4, 2, 0, 1 \rangle$ specifies another distinct pattern. In the limiting case where only one unit exists, the vector will have only one element, in which case vector coding and local coding amount to the same thing. Whether the components of a vector correspond to microfeatures in the world is a further and independent question; the answer does not follow automatically from vector coding. That is, in some instances, the vector components may correspond to features such as the color, shape, motion, etc. of an object, but in other cases there may be no identifiable microfeature corresponding to any component (figure 4.15).

Simple three-layer connectionist networks provide a useful starting place to introduce certain concepts crucial to understanding the differences between local and vector coding. Just as these models greatly oversimplify the neurobiological reality, so they simplify the conceptual lay-of-the-land. For that very reason, they are a fine kick-off point, but in order to go on, as we should like to do, to put these concepts to good biological purpose, they must be suitably reconfigured to accommodate the complexity of actual nervous systems. That will constitute the second stage of the discussion.

Several preliminary points need articulation. First, as Shastri and Feldman's (1986) work demonstrates, a connectionist model may quite well employ parallel processing without distributed representations, and in that event advertises itself as a "PP" model rather than the full-dress PDP model. Indeed, it is often convenient for PDP models to "grandmother" the output. In Feldman's model, single nodes stand for a single variable such as "bird" or "seagull." Second, distributed representations may be coded either coarsely, which permits overlap in response selectivity of the unit, or finely, which implies that the unit responds only to a very narrow range of stimuli. Different computational considerations may constrain an architecture one way or the other, as we discuss below (see section 10). Thus distributed representations are not *ipso facto* coarse-coded representations. In theory, local coding too can choose between the coarse/fine alternatives. In practice, however, it would make no evident sense for local-coded representations to be coarsely coded, since it would be like taking an in-focus image and fuzzing it. Hence coarse-coded grandmother cells probably are not much in service, though redundancy considerations might provoke this.

As a brief digression, it should be remarked that redundancy is useful for three main reasons: (1) not all membrane activity in a neuron is signal, some is noise, and hence redundancy improves the signal-to-noise ratio. (2) If more than one neuron is responding to a signal—for example, a low-intensity signal—then redundancy increases the effective rate of firing, again improving the signal. (3) If one cell should die or be otherwise impaired, its clone can continue to perform its role so that overall function is not impaired.

How does the occurrent/abeyant distinction for representations look within the vector-coding framework? Representations in the occurrent and abeyant senses involve properties of units in two very different ways: (1) occurrent representations are patterns of *activation* across set of units, and (2) stored representations are configurations of *weights* between the units (figure 4.16). Which representation is now "on the air" (occurrent) is then a function of the input vector and the extant configuration of weights. To milk the conceptual

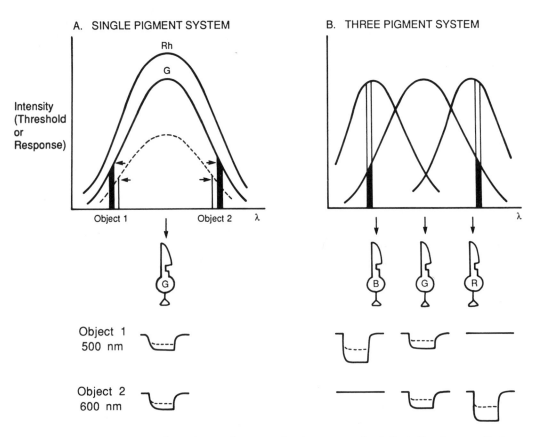

A. SINGLE PIGMENT SYSTEM

B. THREE PIGMENT SYSTEM

Intensity
(Threshold
or
Response)

Rh

G

Object 1   Object 2   λ

λ

G

B   G   R

Object 1
500 nm

Object 2
600 nm

Figure 4.15 Color coding mechanism at the photoreceptor level, illustrating the necessity for more than one visual pigment. (A) A single pigment gives a receptor different sensitivities to different wavelengths of light, responding maximally to light at about 534 nanometers (nm), so-called "green". Notice that the receptor cannot distinguish between objects reflecting at 450 nm and those reflecting at 600 nm. If the luminosity is decreased (dashed line), the receptor could not distinguish between a change in luminosity and a change in wavelength (arrows). Sample recordings of the G (green) receptor under these conditions are shown below. (B) A three-pigment system can distinguish wavelength independently of intensity. The pigments have overlapping spectra. The two objects stimulate the three photoreceptors (B, blue; R, red) but to different degrees, so that the color code for each object is unique, and maintained despite a reduction in luminosity (dashed lines in recordings). (With permission from Shepherd 1988; based on Gouras 1985a.)

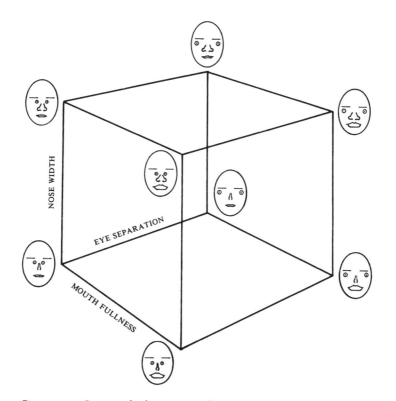

Figure 4.16   Cartoon of a face space to illustrate the idea that faces vary along a number of dimensions, represented as axes of the state space, and that a system might code for faces using vectors whose elements represent such features as distance between eyes, fullness of mouth, and width of nose. Obviously faces have many features that are coded by mammals, and even the three features included here are dubiously crude. (Courtesy P. M. Churchland.)

value out of these ideas, it is productive to view them through the notion of a state space.

The Conceptual Fecundity of "State Space"

In chapter 3 we explored the notion of a state space (also known as "co-ordinate space," "feature space," or "phase space"). Recall that any coordinate system defines a state space, and the number of axes is a function of the number of dimensions included. Each of four neurons in a network may be considered to define an axis in a 4-D space, where the activity level of a neuron at a time is a point along its axis, and the intersection of four coordinates specifies a point in the 4-D state space. If coding is distributed (vector coding), then an occurrent representation is a position in activation state space as specified by the vector whose elements are the activity values of all the partici-pating units (figure 4.16).

   A trained-up network is one in which, for appropriate input vectors, the network gives the correct response, expressed in terms of an output vector. Training up a network involves adjusting the many weights so that this end is achieved. This might be done in a number of different ways. One might hand-set the weights, or the weights might be set by back-propagation of error or by an unsupervised algorithm. Weight configurations too are characterizable in terms of vectors, and at any given time the complete set of synaptic values defines a weight state space, with points on each axis specifying the size of a particular weight. Thus training-up a network can be thought of as moving a point in the weight space, from the initial, randomly set position to the final, minimal-error position.

It is conceptually efficient to see the final resting region in weight space as embodying the total knowledge stored in the network. Notice that all incoming vectors go through the matrix of synaptic connections specified by that weight-space point. *Explicit* representations, such as recognition of an input pattern, thus depend on *implicit* representations, namely the configuration of weights, construed as a point in weight space. In the language introduced earlier, occurrent representations thus depend on stored representations.

Miraculously, it may seem at first, a huge domain of different input vectors will map onto suitably matched vectors in the output domain, as a function of a single weight configuration. It is, of course, no miracle. It is merely that weights in a network can be set to embody a function; indeed a three-layer net can embody any mathematically well-behaved function whatever (Hornik et al. 1989). More succinctly, and a touch bombastically, any representable world can be represented in a network, via configuration of the weights.[13]

It is in this sense that a configuration of weights embodies the knowledge needed to answer a variety of different questions and stored knowledge contributes to occurrent representations. To emphasize the obvious, it is not as though little pictures are stored, one on top of the other. Storage in weight configurations is a very different, if essentially simple idea. A matrix is an array of values, and the elements of an incoming vector can be operated on by some function to produce an output vector. It means, therefore, that different vectors, pushed through one and the same matrix plus squashing function, will give different answers. (The squashing function, as discussed in chapter 3, provides the essential nonlinearity, but for brevity we shall not always explicitly say "matrix *plus squashing function*," but only "*matrix*.") So, for example, NETtalk, can be asked, How do you pronounce "though," "trough," "astigmatism," etc.? Assuming the network has found a minimum-error point in weight space, it will give accurate answers most of the time. Were we to extend this idea to nervous systems, the weight configuration of synapses is a kind of living matrix, through which vectors can be pushed to give appropriate outputs destined for the next layer of processing.

What is the relation between a weight space and an activation space? Basically, a point in weight space dictates the partitioning of activation space. A learning algorithm changes the weights, and a good learning algorithm changes the weights so that the network finds a point in weight space where errors are minimized (figure 4.17). This means both that weight configurations cluster similar things, but also that weight configurations may be sensitive to very fine differences between things, consequently dividing the activation

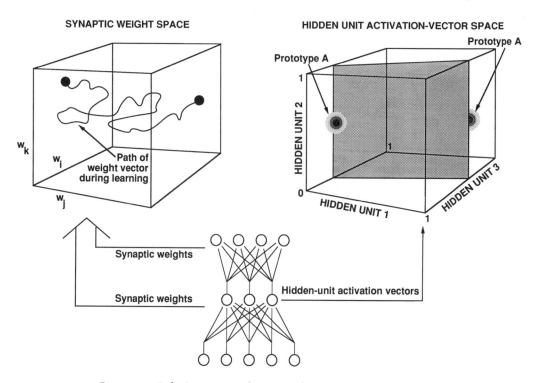

Figure 4.17 (Left) Synaptic weight space, whose axes are weights. This is the space of all possible weight combinations from the synapses in the network. (Bottom) A schematic network. (Right) Activation-vector space whose axes are hidden units. This is the space of all possible activation vectors across the population of hidden units. In this ultrasimple case, there is one partition dividing the space, with regions on each side of the partition where the prototypical examples are located. (Based on P. M. Churchland 1989.)

space between two rather similar kinds of things. At the behavioral level, the result is that humans can distinguish between apples and plums, and also between varieties of red apple: Macintosh, Jonathan, Spartan, Rob Roy, Winesap, and so on. The learning typically proceeds by example, since the differences are subtle and virtually impossible to articulate.

Additional utility can be pressed from this concept. An activation space will also be a similarity space, inasmuch as similar vectors will define adjacent regions in space. This means that similarity between objects represented can be reflected by similarity in their representations, that is, proximity of positions in activation space. Similarity in representations is thus not an accidental feature, but an intrinsic and systematic feature. It is, consequently, a feature exploitable in processing. Nearby vectors can cancel small differences and highlight similarities, thereby allowing the network to generalize as well as distinguish.

The idea expands easily to encompass more complex representations. Thus similarity in motor output defines similarity in state space trajectories; similar but not identical motor behavior will have similar but not identical trajectories. Rhythmic behavior is represented as a loop in motor state space, and similar rhythms will have similar loops (figure 4.18). To put it in economic terms,

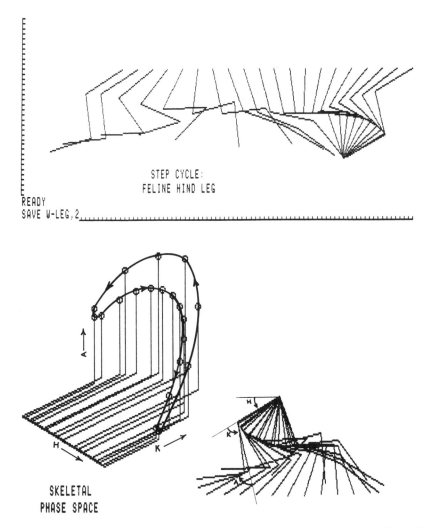

Figure 4.18 A state space characterization of rhythmic movement of a leg, as in locomotion. (From P. M. Churchland.)

coding by vectors gives us the similarity metric for free. Learning, as we saw, is a matter of reconfiguring weights, where any given configuration can also be described as a partitioning of activation space into similarity subspaces. Learning is therefore changing the similarity gradients within the partitions.

What good does this conceptual framework of activation space and weight space really do for us? Apart from putting the wheels on the conceptual notion of representation, and this is no mean thing, the concept does something comparable for processing. And the "combine," as one might say, is a very impressive thing. In brief, it delimits a general conception of processing that together with the distributed theory of representations provides a powerful tool for thinking about how a network works, and, as we shall argue anon, it provides a shoehorn into thinking about how brains represent and compute.

Encoding theories are theories of representing, but a theory of representing cannot fly without the other wing—its correlative theory of processing, i.e., a theory of computation. How is specific information extracted from transducer output? How is information integrated? What is the contribution of stored representations to perception, and how is this accomplished? How are processing and storage related? According to the very general theory at hand, processing consists in convolving representations (vectors) through a matrix of synapses. That is, in its most general aspect, processing is a matter of vector-vector transformation, where the architecture of the neural connectivity is the substrate for the transformations. To recall an earlier suggestion, in nervous systems the weight configuration is a kind of living matrix, through which vectors can be pushed to give a range of outputs. Remember though, that while we aim ultimately to see whether these ideas can apply to real nervous systems, we are still in the realm of simple computer network models.

In the domain of simple models, this hand-in-glove conception of representation and computation is powerful. In one encompassing theory, we can see, albeit roughly, how learning and representing fit together, how perceptual prototypes can be developed, how similarities in perception, cognition, and motor control reflect similarities at the network level, how a huge amount of information may be stored very efficiently in a relatively small network, how some representing effects can be slow (weight change) and some fast (vector activation), how partitioning of similarity space structures the processing and enables it to be at the same time swift, accurate, and nonmiraculous.

Distribution and redistribution of representations gives an informational fan-out, and this is relevant to the question of how precise representing is possible with rather coarse units. Coming at this problem from another angle, distribution means that subsets of information can be pulled out and relocated with relevant information from other representations, then to be further convolved. Consider, for example, that 3-D information is implicitly carried (one might say buried) in the output from the retinal ganglion cells. How can the information be extracted and made usable? An efficient and fast way to do this is to distribute and redistribute the information, to convolve the representations through the living matrix of synapses, until it shows up on our recording electrodes as a cell tuned to stimulus velocity in a specific direction, or to an illusory boundary, or to a human face. Topographic mapping then is a means whereby vector coding can bring to heel the problem of assembling relevant information. As Kohonen's 1984 model showed, in a competitive learning net, the system will self organize so that nearby vectors map onto nearby points of the net, assuming that the connections are short range. That the brain avails itself of this organization is not so much a computational necessity as a wiring economy. Far from being inconsistent with topographic mapping, vector coding exploits it.

At the level of experimental psychology, this general vector-matrix framework invites fruitful speculation concerning how certain otherwise puzzling phenomena, such as associative memory, might be explained. Before turning to the question of neurobiological realism, we shall consider the general approach that can be taken by the theory that representation is vector coding, and processing is vector-vector transformation through a matrix.

A major perceptual problem is to explain similarity relationships in perceptual recognition, and it is important to see that a general account falls quite naturally out of the vector-coding approach. Recognizing similarities and analogies in many domains, including perception, cognition, and motor control, can be seen as a matter of position (or trajectory) in similarity space, as defined by n-dimensional vectors. This also gives a perspective on the profile of perceptual misjudgments, such as mistaking poison oak for Oregon grape, or perceptual illusions, such as seeing a letter where one has been omitted (grapfruit), or omitting a word where there there is an extra. It gives a general means of understanding prototype phenomena in perception and cognition— for example, why carrots are rated as more typical vegetables than is corn, and why corn is rated as more typically a vegetable than is parsley.

This general vector-coding/vector-matrix processing framework makes roughly comprehensible the ease with which humans extend concepts to new members of the class; that is, extending "bird" from robins and crows to seagulls, flamingoes, ostriches, Big Bird on Sesame Street, cartoon birds such as Foghorn Leghorn or Donald Duck, and even to humans, such as the tall and skinny Uncle Ichabod in his loose-fitting cloak, and so on. Having seen photographs of Bertrand Russell in middle years, one can directly pick out the youthful Russell and the Russell in old age. They are more similar to each other than they are to photographs of other humans. One does not confuse the aged Russell with the aged Winston Churchill or the aged Bernard Shaw, and the recognition is fast. The various portraits of Russell occupy adjacent regions of similarity space; more correctly, their activation vectors are relevantly similar. For the same reason, a cartoon of Richard Nixon, for example, is readily identifiable as Nixon, especially when his features are heavily exaggerated to push into a region of similarity space far from the face of anyone else. It also makes comprehensible extensions of a word such as "red" from the paradigm red wagon to redhead (which is more rusty colored) or red robin (which has only a touch of red on it) to "red herring," which, literally, is smoked to a dark brown color (see especially Lakoff 1987).

Assuming vector coding, a number of curious but familiar pattern recognition phenomena are approachable quite directly. For example, how can a network generate an approximate answer when no exact answer is available? Appeal again to the idea of similarity space, as defined in terms of vectors specifying patterns of activation. How can a neural network recognize a pattern even when the stimulus is degraded or partial, as it very frequently is? By means of vector completion, achieved when the vector is quite large and the missing components are but few (figure 4.19).

Vector-coding and vector-matrix computation are robust; that is, they display functional persistence in the face of damage. Dropping a few neurons from the vector basically just leaves a minor vector-completion task. Dropping many neurons probably means that a recognition impairment can be observed in behavior, such as loss of face recognition (prosopagnosia) or loss of visual

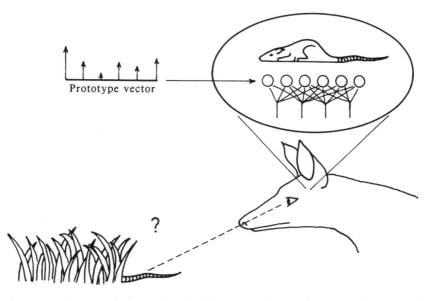

Prototype vector

Figure 4.19 A cartoon illustrating the idea of vector completion. The input to the retina with respect to the rat is limited to light reflected from only the rat's tail. But the coyote's visual system completes the vector, allowing the coyote to suspect that there is a rat in the grass. (From P. M. Churchland, 1989)

recognition of objects (visual agnosia). With relatively minor damage, a network can continue to work, albeit with some loss in accuracy, but it is not stopped dead in its tracks by tiny lesions. Major damage means one route through the matrices is closed, and hence someone might have normal visual acuity, but fail utterly to recognize visually that an object is a dog or a clock. Nonetheless, the *sound* of barking or ticking gives instant recognition, because the route for the auditory information is uninterrupted, and auditory vectors are transformed quite normally. In other words, we understand visual agnosia not as loss of highly specific cells at the hierarchical apex, the "dog" cell, for example, but as non-access to some matrix by visual vectors, with normal access of auditory or perhaps olfactory vectors (Damasio 1990).

Extending motor repertoires, like the extension of perceptual categorization, typically exploits similarities; learning to pitch a curveball is different, but not very different, from pitching a fastball; learning to swim on one's back is different, but not totally so, from swimming on one's front, which is not totally different from floating; learning to write involves slow transitions from learning to make neat lines, to connecting lines, to smooth and continuous flowing of lines. The conceptual resources inherent in this idea can stand a bit of emphasis: it gives us a way of looking at how brains might generalize to novel cases, and how such extension makes good biological sense.

Analysis of units' activity in computer models of networks make it comparatively easy to observe the nuts and bolts of vector-coding and vector-matrix transformations, and how artificial neural nets can produce highly specific representations; for example, the representation of vowels in NETtalk (see chapter

3; figure 3.36) and, as we shall see later in this chapter, the representation of binocular depth.

Since this discussion is also a comparison of the properties of local coding and vector coding, it may be useful to note that there is no comparable theoretical framework to enfold local coding; no equivalently general account of the processing of representations from simple signals to finely tuned cells is included in the picture; no account that addresses the relation between processing and learning, nor the basis for similarity relations in motor control, perception, and cognition. This is not to say that no such account could be generated or that it is somehow precluded by the logic of local coding. It is only to underscore the point that vector coding automatically brings with it a general theory of processing.

6 WORLD ENOUGH AND TIME

At the risk of tedium, we have scrupulously inserted the qualifiers "general" or "abstract" before "theory" and "framework," mainly to remind readers that the theory's stamping ground is the simple, artificial, three-layer net, not the living, breathing nervous system. Secondarily, it is to guard our several flanks from the criticism that the details are still outstanding. Indeed they are. The precise nature of the vectors and the matrices in real networks is yet to be discovered, along with the principles governing plasticity. There is, however, a deeper problem, one that concerns whether nervous systems honor *at all* the distinction between vectors of activation and matrices for processing.

The trouble is that the broad-band distinction between activation and weights—between processed and processor—is beautifully tailored for artificial neural nets but of questionable fit for real nervous systems. In the discussion so far, *dynamical* features are essentially absent, inasmuch as there is no provision for time taken. Yet in real neurons, the dynamics are everywhere critical. If there are information-bearing events, these are events with a real time duration; if there are structures that store information by changing that very structure, those changes take time and endure for a time. There are many processes, at many time scales, interacting, augmenting, and interfering. They do not, alas, come with "activation" or "weight" written on their sleeves (figure 4.20). The question is not, therefore, just one of plugging in the details as they become available. Rather, it is whether the details can be plugged into that framework at all. Can the abstract distinction between activation and weight modification be rolled over into a time-sensitive division, or is time the undoing of the whole approach?

After chewing on this question, and taking diametrically opposing views over many weeks, our brains did eventually relax into a stable configuration. Whether this position minimized error, we can only hope. In the event, we agreed that applying the distinction between processed and processor to real systems would be an approximation at best. Worse, it might require some jury-rigging, a generous dollop of rather ad hoc judgments, and occasional contrary-to-fact assumptions. Such maneuvers are, of course, not unique to

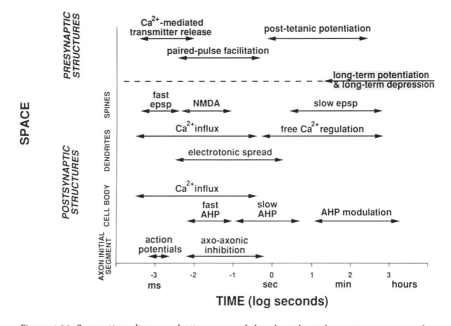

Figure 4.20 Space–time diagram plotting some of the physiological events occurring within neurons. Each process is represented by a horizontal line, arrows indicating the range of time scales over which the process takes place. The vertical scale locates the anatomical structure in which the process takes place. For example, the fast Na$^+$ spikes initiated in the axon hillock have a time scale of 1 msec. In contrast, Ca^{2+} influx through voltage-sensitive channels known to occur in both the cell bodies and the dendrites of some neurons has a much longer time scale. Some forms of after-hyperpolarization (AHP) following an action potential are activated by Ca^{2+} and have a much longer time course than the action potential itself. Changes in the synaptic efficacy, such as post-tetanic potentiation (PTP) and long-term potentiation (LTP) can last for many minutes and hours. NMDA refers to a glutamate receptor that is important in triggering LTP. A standard framework for understanding information processing in the nervous system tends to emphasize the two ends of the temporal spectrum: (1) the milliseconds range, counting such events as signals, and (2) the minutes and hours range, counting such processes as yielding changes in the weights. This figure suggests, however, that such a distinction is an idealization. Phenomena such as short-term memory and adaptation tend to fall in the middle range.

computational neuroscience; recall assuming perfect elasticity in thermo-dynamics, finessing turbulence in newtonian physics, and marginalizing jumping genes in early molecular biology. The inevitability of imperfections notwith-standing, it is probably productive to push the framework as far as is reason-able, given its utility as a conceptual tool. At the same time, other theoretical approaches should be developed to see whether they can plumb more deeply and sweep more broadly. The methodological point is a bit of scientific prag-matism: begin with the paradigmatic activations, namely action potentials, and with the paradigmatic weight modifications, namely changing synaptic weights (volume of neurotransmitter released, materializing synapses, dying synapses, resetting threshold). Then extend the categories from the home base as judicially as possible, checking all the while to see whether the approach continues to bear fruit or whether it has become barren and burdensome.

To begin to see how the conceptual investment might be rolled over, consider that neither activation nor weight modification in real neurons denotes a single, simple process, as they do in computer networks. Rather, they embrace a range of physical processes that vary in temporal schedules. Some weight changes may be transitory; post-tetanic potentiation (PTP), for example, lasts on the order of a minute. Other weight changes, such as long-term potentiation (LTP), may endure for many days, perhaps decaying according to some intrinsic timetable. In addition, there may be transitory weight changes, perhaps a few hundred milliseconds, waiting to be found (von der Malsburg 1985). Assuming so, they might involve changes at the synapse, as do PTP and LTP, but then again they might occur elsewhere. There may also be changes that are not specific to a synapse but involve the entire neuron. Extension of after-hyperpolarization (AHP) following high activity is a possible candidate for such a nonsynaptic weight change (Alkon 1984). Modifications in spine shape, both brief and long term, along with growth of new spines and new synapses may also be counted in the class of weight-modification implementations.

The activation vector can be influenced by a wide range of factors with distinct temporal schedules, including variations in the speed of electrotonic spread of signals in the dendrites, and endogenous spiking timetables that may vary as a function of neurotransmitter specificity (Marder et al. 1987) or physiological set (Llinás 1988). As remarked earlier, not every cellular process can be sorted into either the activation vector drawer or the processing matrix drawer—some processes that interact with these two may best be thought of as neither one nor the other. For example, different diffusion times of Ca^{2+} in spines and in cell bodies are a factor, but at least in the pioneering days, they can be taken into consideration without forcing a decision as to whether Ca^{2+} diffusion is really part of activation or really part weight configuration. Biology is messy, if clever, bearing the stamp of a make-do homesteader rather than an optimizing architect. Evolution, it is evident, exploits whatever odds and ends are handy in order to fit out the system to thrive, neglecting as inconsequential the scientists' penchant for clean criteria and tidy categories.

How should the middle-grounders, which are not obviously part of activation nor obviously part of weights and weight-plasticity, be treated? There is no uniform answer, and each will have to be understood for the phenomenon that it is. The important thing is that the general framework can quite well be put to good, if limited, use without making a firm decision, or even any decision, with respect to each of the middle-grounders. The temporal context does not nullify the distinction between weights and activations, therefore; it merely puts it on its biological fours. Over the long haul, with computational advancement and new neurobiological discoveries, some of the middle-grounders may fall naturally into one category or the other, while some may fit into neither. That there should be a range of time scales is in keeping with what we know of memory at the behavioral level. Some information may be used in the first second or so after presentation; other information—for example, plans and intentions—may need to be kept around for minutes and hours, and some information may need to be kept, in slimmed-down form, indefinitely. If we are lucky, some problems may be the go-away variety, but others may be so deep as to recommend a radically different approach.

In the course of trying to understand what adding the dynamics would do to the basic theoretical framework, we recognized that the time spread of informationally relevant processes in cells may presage a rather short theoretical half-life for the vector-matrix framework. Though the framework may serve well enough as a first approximation, it may stumble over its limitations when required to take the next step. Given that there are many cellular events with different time schedules interacting in complex ways, perhaps we need to contemplate a more radical line, postulating a *spectrum* instead of a sharp *division* between activation and weight modification.

On this line, prototypical activation, such as spiking, occupies one end of a spectrum, and prototypical weight modification, such as LTP, occupies the other end. Thus construed, the temporal spread of *process duration* is one with *processor-processed gradations*. The gap between the *processed* and the *processor* is sealed over, and any differences amount to differences in degree. Something can therefore be moderately weight-ish and lightly activation-ish, while some other process might be weight-ish in low degree and activation-ish in high degree. Speed of response is now the *only* thing that distinguishes activation from weight modification, and it does so relatively, not absolutely.

On this proposal, it would follow that even the trusty distinction between *information* and *channel carrying the information* is itself only approximately applicable—and strictly *inapplicable*—to the nervous system, perhaps in the way that the old thermodynamical law, P is proportional to T/V, is only approximately applicable and strictly inapplicable to the behavior of gases.[14] If such an elementary distinction collapses, we are bound to rethink matters from the ground up, including how to conceive of the very problems at hand. This is not necessarily a bad thing, and conceptual upheavals in science are nothing new. But it is not a thing to be taken on for a lark.

Synapses functioning as dynamical variables rather than as slowly changing weights could have many computational uses. For example, von der Malsburg (1985) has for many years advocated fast weight changes for computing pattern matching in vision. We expect that the next generation of models will find many other uses for changes on intermediary time scales. (See also Feldman et al. 1990.) As this goes to press, Hopfield (1991) has suggested that changes in synaptic strengths represent fluctuations in olfactory inputs, and hence, as he puts it, "...the connection strengths are not merely algorithm, they are also essential data for understanding the environment" (1991, p. 6465).

The worry that got rubbed out of the lamp in this section concerns time. Although we may have succeeded in coaxing the problem back into the lamp, the success is provisional, and the matter of time arises again and again in later chapters. Dynamics, it cannot be stressed too much, are critically important to sensorimotor integration, to perception, to generation of motor patterns, and to information storage and retrieval—our main topics in later chapters. Our brains are dynamical, not incidentally or in passing, but essentially, inevitably, and to their very core.

What Is Coarse Coding?

To maximize efficiency and achieve high-grade accuracy, vector coding almost demands that each element contributing to the vector be coarsely coded. "Coarse" and "fine" signify a contrast in tuning. In fine coding, the cell is responsive to a very narrow bandwidth of signal—for example, bars of light exactly vertical or exactly horizontal. In contrast, coarse tuning means that the neuron displays a broad tuning curve, responding maximally to a rather narrow band of signals, and with gradually decreasing vigor as a function of the stimuli's similarity distance from the "best" stimulus. Neurons in visual cortex appear to be coarsely coded; a given cell may respond maximally to a vertical bar, but still quite vigorously to bars at 15° or 20°, somewhat less vigorously to bars at 30°, even less to bars at 45°, and even somewhat to bars at 90°[15] (figure 4.21).

Coarse coding, oddly enough, turns out to provide the basis for an explanation of hyperacuity, that is, the perceptual detection of intervals smaller than

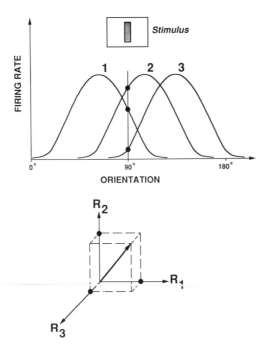

Figure 4.21 Schematic figure showing the tuning curves of three neurons in visual cortex in response to a bar of light in different orientations. For example, when the bar is at 90°, neuron 1 fires at a medium rate, neuron 2 at a high rate, and neuron 3 at a low rate. The three firing rates are elements in a vector which precisely designates the orientation of the bar in the state space. Note that the firing rate of a single neuron is not enough to determine uniquely the orientation because two different orientations can fire the cell by the same amount. For example, neuron 1 will fire at the same rate for both 90° and 10° bars.

the resolving power of any single transducer. For example, humans and monkeys can perceive binocular depth differences that are smaller than the diameter of an individual photoreceptor cell. (See section 9, Computational Models of Stereo Vision.) Hyperacuity is not as mysterious as it first seems. Assuming coarse coding, it can be explained in terms of the "group portrait" of the coarse-coded tuning curves. By contrast, explanation of hyperacuity in terms of local coding with finely tuned cells looks decidedly problematic given the number of cells required. Granted, of course, that these are really explanation sketches, rather than rounded-out explanations, but they have a coherence and interlacing nature that might help the experimental sortie.

Does Tuning Selectivity of Neurons Imply Local Coding?

At the risk of belaboring the obvious, we mention that there is a gigantic logical difference between the following: (1) A is *consistent* with B, and (2) A *entails* B. The second is much the stronger logically, and hence demands satisfaction of more stringent conditions. Thus having red spots is consistent with having measles, but it does not entail having measles. The red spots are consistent also with having poison ivy, chicken pox, or hives and hence, note, with *not* having measles at all.

Hierarchical organization, pathway segregation, and tuning selectivity in neurons are consistent with, but do not entail, local coding. They are also consistent with vector coding. Because this point may not be obvious at first, let us take a closer look. On the vector-coding scheme, processing stages are vector transformations: vector input, vector output. Not much may happen at any one stage, but a series of small changes in a long series will add up. Consider the following scenario: a single electrode finds a cell in temporal cortex responding preferentially to faces, perhaps just to an individual face, say, that of Grandma Edna (Perrett et al. 1987). In fact, however, the recording electrode has merely found one member of a larger set, a member whose particular contribution to the vector for that stage of "Edna-processing" happens to be sufficiently large to be noticed. Other cells whose responses are less dramatic make contributions that are likewise important, even, for example, by not responding at all to Edna-stimuli. The set, let us imagine, has a response pattern as follows when the stimulus is Edna's face: $\langle 0, 0, 3, 1, \ldots 9, 0, 4, 2 \rangle$. Every element in the vector is important, not just the maximally responding cell with value $= 9$ (call this cell "γ"), which is the cell our electrode poked. Indeed, that cell may be misdubbed the "Edna face-cell" should the truth of the local-coding hypothesis be taken for granted. Notice, however, that according to vector coding, higher processing levels very probably will harbor some cells that respond vigorously to complex stimuli, though not because we are finding "grandmother cells," but only because the *vectors* will represent stimuli with more and more specificity.

To exclude the vector-coding hypothesis, it would have to be shown that (1) γ does not respond with comparable vigor to any non-Edna, or any non-grandmother, and, even more stringently, (2) that γ does not have some role in

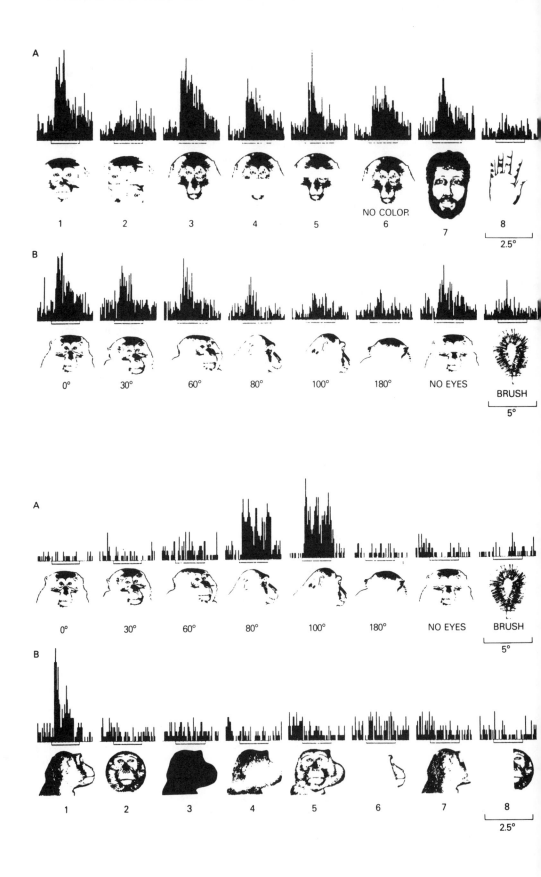

the vector (activation pattern) for any representation other than Grandma Edna. Some distance might be covered with (1), inasmuch as one could assemble a random assortment of objects and see how γ responds (Harries and Perrett 1991, Desimone 1991) (figure 4.22). From a logical point of view, however, this is much less satisfying than is often assumed. Notice that γ's failure to respond to any object in the laboratory does not mean γ would not respond to some other object drawn from the zillions we have not yet tried. The logical lesson then is that no response to # implies nothing about whether the cell might respond to %. If that is discouraging, notice that trying to drum up the conditions for (2) is actually far worse. It would have to be shown that there is no other pattern of activation in which γ has a role. Now since γ might have, say, value = 1 in some vector, value = 0 in some other vector, as well as its value = 9 in the case of Grandma, even showing that γ does not spike vigorously to a telephone does not imply that it has no role in representing a telephone. Moreover, having 0 activation is not to have no value; it is to have the value = 0, and that is perfectly consistent with having a role in vectorial representation.

Another reason for skepticism is this: to know that the cell's response is causally connected to the perceptual representation of Edna, as opposed to just correlated in some indirect way with the stimulus, more must be shown than mere correlation of response with stimulus. Establishing a causal role requires showing at a minimum (a) that the cell in question projects to the part of the brain that produces the relevant motor behavior, and (b) that under the appropriate physiological conditions, the output from the specialized cell does in fact drive the motor response. These are quite stringent conditions, and a lot must be known about the entire system to know that they are satisfied. In only a few instances has this sort of detail been discovered. Walter Heiligenberg (1990) has shown this for the system that controls the jamming avoidance response in *Eigenmannia*. Initially he found that at early stages of processing, representations were distributed, and that the neurons collectively contained enough information to account for the ability of the animal to discriminate small time differences in the arrival time of electromagnetic signals (Heiligenberg et al. 1978). In fact, however, the nervous system did not use the population directly

Figure 4.22 (Top) Responses of a neuron within the superior temporal sulcus in inferotemporal (IT) cortex that responds selectively to faces. Stimuli were colored slides; the stimulus-on period is indicated by the bar under each histogram. Each histogram is based on a minimum of 10 trials per stimulus. (A) The neuron responded well to two different monkey faces and to a human face, but not when the internal components were rearranged. Eliminating the eyes, or the nose, or the color reduced but did not eliminate the response. The neuron was also tested with a large number of additional nonface stimuli (not shown), and it responded very poorly or not at all to each of them. (B) This neuron was tuned to the frontal view of the face. (Bottom) Responses of a different IT neuron, found in the same cortical region as the cell above, but which responds best to profile views of faces. Other conditions as above. (A) Responses to one monkey face in different degrees of rotation. (B) Responses to profile of face and to profile with components removed or altered. Removing or altering any of the components of the profile eliminated the response. (From Desimone 1991.)

to drive the response. Instead, the population projects to a smaller group of cells in which individual cells code the information, and it is these "grand-mothered" cells rather than their distributed precursors that are directly involved in controlling the response. This makes sense because these neurons are coding scalars rather than high-dimensional vectors. In this example, the physiological discovery of the "grandmothering" was made possible because Heiligenberg had been able to deduce the algorithm executed by these cells in advance from the behavior together with constraints from anatomy (Konishi 1991).

What are the prospects for establishing something comparable in the visual cortex? First, unlike the case of *Eigenmannia*, we do not know what algorithms the visual cortex uses. Second, the links from visual cortex to the motor system are not direct and have not yet been fully studied. Some progress has been made (Newsome et al. 1989), however, though it is too early to know exactly what this implies regarding vector coding or local coding at this level.

Finally, what about the combinatorial virtues of vector coding or, to put it negatively, the combinatorial *failings* of local coding? Consider again the mini-net that contains four neurons, each capable of five activity levels. On the vector-coding strategy, there are 5^4 possible combinations, and hence 625 different items can be represented. By contrast, if strict local coding (one neuron for one object) is used, the representing potential is numeric: 4 units at maximal activation can represent only 4 different things. To beef up the numbers, suppose now that each neuron can be in one of five states, where each state represents a different thing. Still the local coding strategy lags far behind vector coding, for now the net can represent at most 4×5 things, 30 times fewer than the vector-coding network. In other words, the representing potential of local coding scales linearly with the number of units, whereas the representing potential of vector coding is *exponential*. This makes a big difference even with just four units; the larger the system, however, the vaster the gap between the power of the two coding strategies.[16] (Probably not all possible vectors correspond to distinctly different items. Most will never occur, and the ones that do will be partitioned into isolated similarity classes. The central point is, however, that there is much more room in a product space using vector coding than in a scheme using local coding.)

The mathematical point is sometimes downplayed, on grounds that we encounter much the same sensory world, day in and day out, so a relatively small number of "grandmother cells" might in fact suffice to recognize all the patterns that need to be recognized. Granting the supposition, nothing much is gained since the problem does not go away. Although we do see many of the same objects every day, they change over time, they appear in different guises, in different positions, engaged in different behavior, in different contexts, lighting, and circumstances, and so on and on, some of which may be handled by preprocessing, much of which not. Indeed, to recognize an object as one and the same despite changes almost certainly requires vector coding. For as we saw earlier, similarities, and hence identities through changes, can be accommodated much more easily by vector coding than by local coding. In any case, novelty in experience should probably be taken very seriously, even if we restrict ourselves to novelty in linguistic and musical patterns and leave vision aside.

7   SHAPE FROM SHADING: A NEUROCOMPUTATIONAL STUDY

We have argued that one cannot *infer* simply from the response-selectivity of a cell to its being "grandmothered" for stimuli of the kind that provokes the large response. A cell that maximally responds to a 45° moving edge may be one contributor to a many-element vector rather than a local-coded 45°-moving-edge-detector all on its own. The further question about the cell and its functional role is this: can we at least infer that it is in the business of detecting 45° moving edges, albeit as a contributor to a vector? Most people, even the typically cautious, will answer "yes" to this question. Surprisingly, perhaps, it can be shown that here too the answer is "no." It is important to be clear that the issue concerns what can and cannot be *inferred* about cell function from certain data, not what the data in fact are reported to be. What is the argument for this surprising result?

The result derives from a computational model of how a simple three-layer network might solve the perceptual problem of how we see the shape or contour of something, given information only about shading (Lehky and Sejnowski 1988). In contrast to a model that discovers something's shape from its boundaries (Kimia et al. 1989), this model focuses on within-boundary shading gradients (Horn and Brooks 1989). One of the primary properties of a surface is curvature. Some surfaces, such as a tabletop, are flat and have no intrinsic curvature. Other surfaces, such as cylinders and spheres, are curved, and around each point on a surface the degree of curvature can be characterized by the direction along the surface of maximum and minimum curvature. It can be shown that these directions are always at right angles to each other, and the values are called *principal curvatures* (Hilbert and Cohn-Vossen 1952). The principal curvatures and the orientation of the axes provide a complete description of the local curvature (figure 4.23).

One problem with extracting the principal curvatures from an image is that the gray-level shading depends on many factors, such as the direction of illumination, the reflectance of the surface, and the orientation of the surface relative to the viewer. Somehow our visual system is able to separate these variables and to extract information about the shape of an object independently of the other variables. Pentland (1984, 1989a) has shown that a significant amount of information about the curvature is available locally. Nevertheless, some information, such as direction of light source, cannot be locally extracted. A network model constructed by Lehky and Sejnowski (1988, 1990a) will extract curvature information from shaded images, where backpropagation of error was used to train up the network, and examples of shaded shapes make up the training set (figure 4.24).

Many examples of simple surfaces (elliptic paraboloids) were generated and presented to the network. A set of weights was found with this training

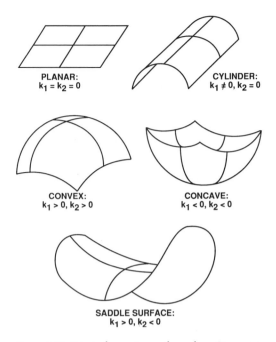

Figure 4.23 Principal curvatures of a surface. At a point on the surface the principal curvatures are the two tangent vectors along which the curvatures are maximum and minimum. The signs of the two principal curvatures k_1 and k_2 determine whether the surface is convex, concave, or saddle shaped. If a principal curvature is zero, then the surface is flat along that direction.

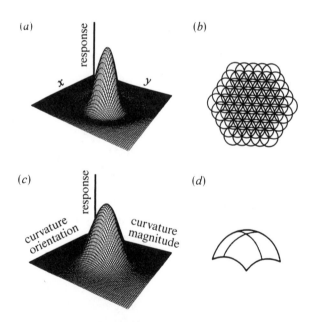

Figure 4.24 (a) Receptive field of an input unit. This is the Laplacian of a two-dimensional Gaussian function, which provides a circular center-surround organization as seen in figures 2.27 and 2.28. This figure shows an on-center unit, but the networks also contains off-center units. (b) Input units organized into hexagonal arrays. Circles represent receptive field centers, showing a high degree of overlap. The input image was sampled by on-center and off-center arrays of 61 units. (c) Output units had two-dimensional tuning curves in a parameter space defined by orientation and magnitude of the principal curvatures. (d) Schematic surface showing two principal curvatures (maximum and minimum) at the center of the surface. (From Lehky and Sejnowski 1990.)

procedure that, independent of direction of illumination, extracted the principal curvature of three-dimensional surfaces and the direction of maximum curvature from shaded images. The input to the network comes from an array of on-center and off-center receptive fields similar to those of cells in the lateral geniculate nucleus. The output layer is a population of units that conjointly represent the curvatures and the broadly tuned direction of maximum curvature. Most of the units of the intermediate layer, which are needed to perform the transformation, develop oriented receptive fields during training (figure 4.25). Their receptive fields are similar in fact to those of the simple cells in the visual cortex of cats and monkeys that respond optimally to oriented bars and edges. It is important to emphasize that these properties of the hidden units were not put into the network directly, but emerged during training on the shape-from-shading task. The system "chose" these properties because they are useful in performing the shape-from-shading task.

Recall that the hidden units were required to extract information about the principal curvatures and principal orientations of surfaces. In the trained-up network, the hidden units represent an intermediate transformation for a computational task quite different from the one that has been customarily ascribed to simple cells in visual cortex—they are used to determine the shape from the

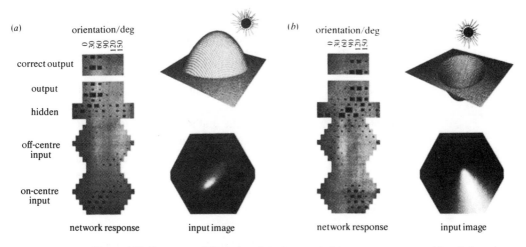

Figure 4.25 Response of the network to two typical images, one convex (a) and the other concave (b). Input icons show the responses of 61 on-center and 61 off-center input units, calculated by convolving their receptive fields with the image. The area of a black square is proportional to a unit's activity. Converging synaptic inputs from the input layer produced activity in the 27 hidden units, depicted in the 3×9 array above the input hexagons. The hidden units in turn projected to the output layer of 24 output units, shown in the 4×6 array at the top. This output should be compared with the 4×6 array at the very top (separated from the rest) showing the correct response for the image input. In the 4×6 arrays, the six columns correspond to different peaks in orientation tuning (0, 30, 60, 90, 120, and 150). Rows correspond to different curvature magnitudes. The top two rows code for positive and negative values of the smaller principal curvature (C_S); the bottom two rows code the same for the larger principal curvature (C_L). (From Lehky and Sejnowski 1990a.)

shading, not to detect boundaries. It turns out, however, that the hidden units have *receptive field properties similar to those of simple cells in the visual cortex* (Lehky and Sejnowski 1988). In other words, the receptive field properties of the model's hidden units might seem to license the inference that the cells are specialized for edge-detection or bar-detection. Yet their demonstrable and acquired function is to extract curvature from shaded images. Their inputs were exclusively smoothly varying gray levels. Therefore, bar and edge receptive-field properties do not necessarily mean that the cell's function is to detect bars and edges in objects; it might be an intermediate step to detect curvature and shape, as in the network model, or perhaps some other surface property such as texture. A further observation was that the degree of activation itself carries information, and hence one needs to get more quantitative than just "active" or "not active." The general implication is that there is no way of determining the function of each hidden unit in the network simply by "recording" the receptive-field properties of the unit. This, in turn, implies that, despite its intuitive plausibility, the receptive-field-to-function inference rule is untenable.

To continue in this vein, it was found that output cells of the net, which were trained to report principal curvature and principal orientation, could also respond like a complex cell with end-stopping in visual cortex when given a bar as stimulus. If one had "recorded" from such a unit when it was presented with the bar, one might have concluded from its response that it was an end-stopped bar detector. Yet until the test presentation, it had never been exposed to a bar at all (figure 4.26).

To determine the function of a unit, information about its output—about its "projective field"—was also essential in the network model (Lehky and Sejnowski 1988). It is the projective field of a unit that provides additional information needed to interpret the unit's computational role in the network. Although in a network model the projective field could be examined directly, in real neural networks it can only be indirectly inferred by examining the next stage of processing. Whether or not curvature is directly represented in visual cortex, for example, can be tested by designing experiments with images of curved surfaces. Consistent with the vector-coding hypothesis, it would not be surprising to find simple cells responding to a range of distinct inputs—for example, to within-boundary shading as well as to boundaries. Even if it does not respond much to a curved image, the cell may nevertheless be a component in a vector that does represent curvature.

It may be objected that this model is really irrelevant to the neurobiology of extracting shape representations from shading signals because it lacks realism in several important dimensions. For example, unlike real neurons, its units may have both excitatory and inhibitory effects. Second, it is feedforward only, and it is very well known that the brain has feedback projections. Third, the model incorporates only a small subset of a real neuron's repertoire of responses. Even if some computationally interesting results emerge, they cannot be expected to have much to do with the real nervous system.

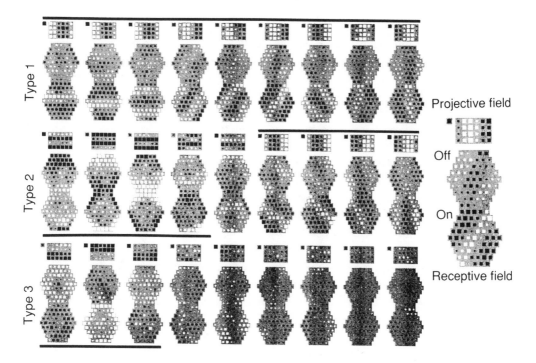

Figure 4.26 Diagram showing connection strengths in the network. Each of the 27 hidden units is represented by one hourglass-shaped icon, showing an input receptive field from on- and off-center units, and an output projective field (4 × 6 array at the top). Organization of the 4 × 6 array as in figure 4.25. Excitatory weights are white, inhibitory ones are black, and the area of a square indicates the connection strength. Isolated square at the upper left of each icon indicates the unit's bias (equivalent to a negative threshold). The units are showed grouped together by type based on the organization of the receptive and projective fields (black lines). This grouping was made by hand as part of the analysis of the model but is not a property of the model itself. (From Lehky and Sejnowski 1990a.)

Although it is true that the model lacks realism in the respects cited, it is important to be clear about what can and cannot be learned from the model. This is a model that addresses the network level, and it asks not how layer 4C neurons in V1 come to exhibit the response properties they do, and hence how the connectivity and the intrinsic electrophysiological properties result in those responses. Rather, it starts with the physiological data that 4C neurons have certain responses, and then asks whether a network of units with just such responses could solve the shape-from-shading problem. The answer that indeed they can is an answer to just *that* question, and if the model fails to do more—for example, to answer the question of how 4C cells respond the way they do—this is not a shortcoming, however much one wants an answer to that also. In other words, there is a difference between a model that mimics the response properties, and a model that mimics generation of the response properties. In any case, to have a model at this level is better than having none at all, for it helps to organize data and motivate new experiments at the appropriate levels. Since the model is at the level of response properties, one experiment concerns how real cells in visual cortex might in fact respond to images of three-dimensional objects for which shading is an important cue to shape. (For an earlier discussion on realism and models, see chapter 3, section 12.)

The shape-from-shading model has some methodological significance. It needed only enough neurobiological realism, namely geniculate-like input, vector coding, vector-matrix transformations, to show two interesting things. First, that a simple three-layer net trained by a back-propagation learning algorithm can solve, and solve very successfully, a part of shape-from-shading tasks. This is an instructive demonstration, at least because conventional AI attempts to solve this problem have not delivered a working solution. Yet for a network, learning to estimate local shape from shading by generalizing from examples was simplicity itself.[17] If nothing else, this demonstrates the computational muscle of networks. But there is something else. Namely, a portrait of how vector coding of neurons might, and we do mean *"might,"* actually go some distance in solving the actual problem in brains. At least in its broad character if not in its specific details, the model has the right sort of smell. Second, it shows that a first-blush interpretation of single-cell recordings based solely on correlations between stimulus presented and response properties of the cells could in fact be highly misleading. Receptive field information alone is not enough to interpret a cell's function. Given the favored assumptions behind "feature detector" cells and exclusively bottom-up research strategies, this is a demonstration whose ripples extend a long way.[18]

8 STEREO VISION

Vision in primates is stunningly rich and involves many factors; pattern recognition, color constancy, size constancy, motion parallax, motion capture, Mach bands, texture gradients, perspectival effects, saccades (fast and slow), foveation, and tracking—for starters. If one aims to simulate the whole kaboodle at one throw, there are far too many variables to cope with, and far too vast a data base to incorporate. On the other hand, if the problems are combed apart and addressed one by one—for example, shape-from-shading or 3-D perception—the ever-present risk is that the solution will be a toy solution because the *interaction* between mechanisms will be neglected, yet interact is precisely what the mechanisms do. Notwithstanding its shortcomings, the second alternative may still be preferred, on grounds that getting a littlewhere is usually preferable to getting nowhere. With luck, the simple models can teach us something that can then be used in the next round of simulation when another increment of realism is earmarked.

In this section, the problem of stereopsis has been combed out from the rest of the capacities tangled in the fleece. Admitting all the while that stereopsis is not an isolated module, we can nevertheless describe some of its psychophysical parameters and something of the neural anatomy believed to be relevant. With these in hand, we can begin to study the problem in computer networks, in hopes at least of understanding the questions more deeply and exactly, if not actually generating full-dress hypotheses for the mechanisms.

Psychological Parameters

As a child, one notices that one sees slightly different things with each eye. In particular, when looking at the ruler behind the inkpot, winking the right eye revealed the digits "2" and "3" that were not seen when the left eye winked; winking the left eye, one could see "5" which was not visible when winking the right eye. Things in the center of the desk, and especially in the foreground, occupy quite different relative positions. What does this mean? Are other people like that? Why, when both eyes are open, do these differences not cause problems? Why do the differences seem to vanish?

It is not introspectively obvious that the differences in what is seen by the two eyes enables stereo vision, the binocular perception of depth. After all, with only one eye open, one could still see that the ruler was behind the inkpot, but in front of the protractor. In the fields, one could still see which bales of hay were closer than others, and one could see that the mower was closer than the baler. But in these instances, as we now know, other cues to depth were at work: *occlusion* of the eraser by the inkbottle, *texture* and *size* gradients showing which bales are in front of which, motion parallax indicating that the mower was closer than the baler, as well as perspectival effects and a general knowledge of how things look. By casual introspection, it is hard to grasp exactly what is lost when binocular vision is reduced to monocular vision, other than loss of a lateral chunk of the visual field. Stereoptic vision, like motion parallax and color constancy, is something one uses routinely but in blissful unawareness of its very existence.

David Brewster and, independently, Charles Wheatstone (famed inventor of the Wheatstone bridge) figured out in the mid-nineteenth century that disparities in the two retinal images were used by the visual system to produce a perception of depth. Brewster built a stereoscope in 1849 that could present one picture to each eye. The pictures were identical save that elements of one scene are shifted slightly to the left or to the right of the other, thus producing a disparity, on the retinas, where light from those elements falls.[19] Varying the disparity between the pictures by different amounts, Brewster could alter the degree of depth seen (figure 4.27). A makeshift stereoscope consists of a long envelope separating the images at one end and the eyes at the other. One can also learn to "free fuse" images either by crossing the eyes or by relaxing vergence so the eyes diverge. Note, however, that depth reverses from one method to the other.

The normal distance between human eyes is about 6 cm, and that fixes how deep stereo vision reaches. With 6 cm of interocular distance, good 3-D perception shades off at about 100 meters because light from objects at that distance falls on the two retinas at essentially the same place. Beyond 100 meters, differences in depths of objects have to be cued by something other than retinal disparity, though there is no phenomenological signpost indicating this shift in perceptual burden as stereo shades off. In other words, retinal images at infinity (virtual infinity) are identical, and hence at long distances, relative motion, perspectival effects, and occlusion are the critical depth cues.

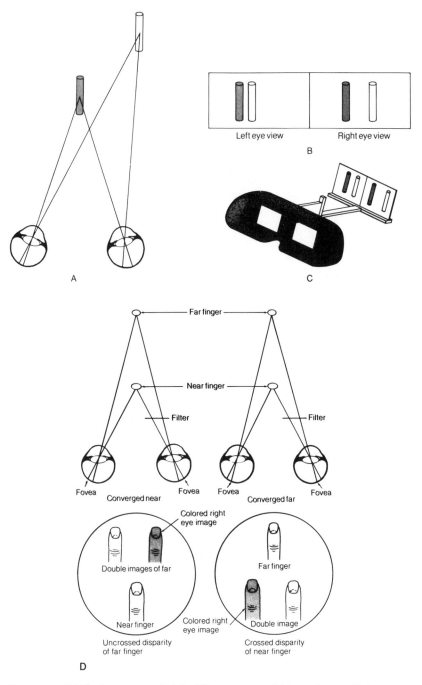

Figure 4.27 (A) The two eyes see slightly different aspects of the visual scene. (B) A stereogram is a flat representation that mimics the differences between two retinal images of an object seen in depth. (C) A stereogram is viewed in a stereoscope which allows for the separate but simultaneous stimulation of the two eyes. (D) Fixating on the near object gives double images of the far object (left). Fixating on the far object gives double images of the near object (right). (With permission from Coren and Ward [1989]. *Sensation and Perception*, 3rd ed. Copyright © 1989 Harcourt Brace Jovanovich, Inc.)

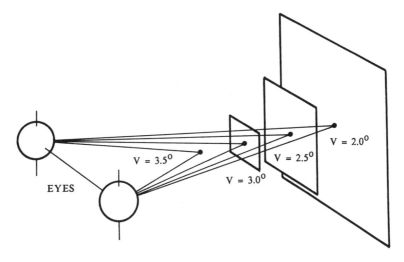

Figure 4.28 Three visible planes at distinct fixation points. Fixation is determined by rotating the eyeballs to four different vergence angles, with fixation at infinity defining vergence = 0. The three planes here portrayed correspond to the planes that are discernible in the stereo-pair shown in figure 4.38. (Courtesy of P. M. Churchland.)

If, as in a frog, the two eyes see entirely different scenes, one has double vision unless one channel is suppressed. Primate eyes see somewhat different scenes. Why do we not have double vision? The answer, roughly, is that where in space one fixates, there the brain fuses two 2-D representations into one 3-D representation. One can fixate at varying depths by changing vergence; that is, changing the position of fovea by rotating the eyeballs in their sockets (figure 4.28). Suppose the plane of fixation is 20 cm in front—roughly reading distance. Objects at that distance will have zero disparity, and the two foveated images from each eye are fused into one. Objects in front of or behind the fixation plane will fall on disparate retinal locations, and this disparity gives the brain information about the depth of the objects relative to the plane of fixation. Since fixation involves vergence, position of the eyeballs can be used by the brain in computing absolute depth of the fixated object. (See also Cumming et al. 1991.)

At the point of fixation, light from an object falls on the same location in the two retinas. A horopter is the curved surface that wraps around the viewer's visual field; it is defined as the set of points at which light falls on the same retinal location. Within a region about 10–20 min of arc (arc min) behind and in front of the horopter, mildly disparate images can be fused by the brain to yield perceptions of single, crisply defined objects. This area is known as Panum's fusional area, and its shape varies somewhat as a function of viewing distance (figure 4.29). Phenomenologically, objects in the fusion plane look crisp, boundaries are clean, and relative depth is starkly evident. Fusability of images into single perceptions shades off as object locations approach the boundary of Panum's area. At greater distances from the horopter the disparity increases, and just past the border of Panum's area images may be unfusable.

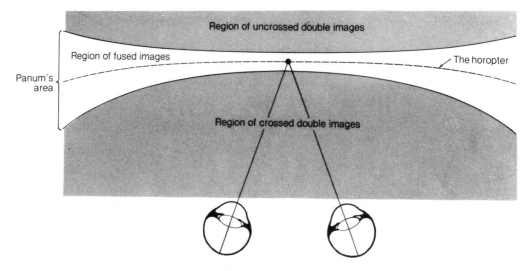

Figure 4.29 The horopter and Panum's fusional area are shown for one fixation distance. Images of objects at distances closer to the observer than the fixation distances are called "crossed" and those further are "uncrossed." (With permission from Coren and Ward [1989]. *Sensation and Perception*, 3rd ed. Copyright © 1989 Harcourt Brace Jovanovich, Inc.)

At yet further distances from the horopter, either deeper or closer, the images may be unfusable, and accuracy in depth discriminations will fall off. By attending to unfusable perceptions without changing the fusion distance, one can detect double images of single objects, especially in the foreground. The brain normally deals with unfused patches in the two images in the following way: one or the other of the discrepant patches tends to be suppressed, mainly as a function of such factors as attention and informational intensity, and the suppression may shift back and forth from one unfused patch to the other. It is only within Panum's rather slim area that images are fused and depth discrimination of objects is highly accurate. Normally the eyes make many fast vergence shifts, as fast as every 200 msec, creating the compelling illusion that the fusional area encompasses most of one's visual field. By experimenting carefully, however, Panum's area can be shown to be really a rather narrow band surrounding the plane of fixation.

Stereopsis is best within the arm's length horopter, where, of course, it is also especially useful. Here is where one threads needles, takes out splinters, draws, and carves. Using mirrors, one can effectively increase the interocular distance, thereby increasing the distance at which crisp 3-D perception is possible. The recipe is rather simple. Extend a rod on either side of a helmet, attaching angled mirrors at the end to deliver images to a centrally located V of mirrors that in turn reflect light into the eyes. This arrangement effectively mimics having eyes at the rod's ends. Although simple in conception, this is a bit tricky in execution (bashing the rod ends into trees is a hazard, for example). An easier method of achieving much the same result uses photographs, preferably slides.

Take two pictures, 6 inches apart, or a foot apart, or even several miles apart. Mount them on a sheet so they can be fused by any of the methods mentioned, and much greater depth can be seen. This is a simple way of getting retinal disparity for faraway images that otherwise are isomorphically located. Foreground objects in wide-baseline stereograms cannot be fused because the disparity is too great, but the brain conscientiously ignores that as noise. Faraway objects, such as familiar mountain ranges, can be seen in a stunning depth not seen with the unaided eyes. A side effect is that objects in wide-baseline stereograms seem miniaturized, as though one were a giant looking down on a Lilliputian scene. Actually this is not so odd. It reflects the brain's presumption that it normally sees in depth no farther than 100 meters because the interocular distance is normally only 6 cm. When a mountain, a thunderhead, and a cityscape all appear in binocular depth, the objects are assumed to be within 100 meters of the eyes. Hence, they would have to be very tiny for stereopsis to take them all in.

Is stereo perception dependent on object recognition? The surprising answer, discovered by Bela Julesz (1971), is "no." How could this question be tested experimentally? Julesz covered two pages with dots in random configuration. Any single page looked at on its own resembled merely snow. By carefully shifting specified sets of dots—for example, those within a square—to the left in one picture, and then free-fusing or viewing the pair through a stereoscope, a 3-D perception of a square of dots raised above background dots can be seen (figure 4.30). No raised square exists in either picture; a square standing well out from the dotty background is seen only because retinal disparity was artificially contrived, and, from the brain's point of view, retinal disparity means depth. Thus the brain is fooled into seeing depth where none truly exists.

Sometimes fusing the Julesz stereograms takes a minute or so, during which the brain rummages through various vergences, hunting for some match of retinal images that will permit fusion and thus resolve into a coherent scene. When it finds the only match there is, namely the square of shifted dots, it fixates at a virtual "plane," rendering all the other dots disparate on the retina and hence at a different depth from the square. This suggests that when sets of stereogram dots are matched at a fusional area, the match is imposed throughout the visual field in the sense that everything is assigned its depth relative to the plane of fixation. All the dots within the square's boundaries appear to stand out; all the dots outside appear to be behind the square. Note also that on the second exposure to a random dot stereogram following a previously successful fusing, the pair fuses dramatically faster than on the first exposure, indicating that the brain has learned where the relevant vergence lies.

How does the brain figure out what to fuse and where in depth to fixate? Because one performs no conscious calculations, it may seem that it must be just obvious to the brain. But, of course, it isn't. If two images are to be fused as a representation of a single object, they will have to be a lot alike, and especially in a random dot stereogram the brain seems to be presented with a difficult task of figuring out which pairs of dots to match. This problem is known in the

Left eye view A Right eye view

1	0	1	0	1	0	0	1	0	1
1	0	0	1	0	1	0	1	0	0
0	0	1	1	0	1	1	0	1	0
0	1	0	Y	A	A	B	B	0	1
1	1	1	X	B	A	B	A	0	1
0	0	1	X	A	A	B	A	1	0
1	1	1	Y	B	B	A	B	0	1
1	0	0	1	1	0	1	1	0	1
1	1	0	0	1	1	0	1	1	1
0	1	0	0	0	1	1	1	1	0

1	0	1	0	1	0	0	1	0	1
1	0	0	1	0	1	0	1	0	0
0	0	1	1	0	1	1	0	1	0
0	1	0	A	A	B	B	X	0	1
1	1	1	B	A	B	A	Y	0	1
0	0	1	A	A	B	A	Y	1	0
1	1	1	B	B	A	B	X	0	1
1	0	0	1	1	0	1	1	0	1
1	1	0	0	1	1	0	1	1	1
0	1	0	0	0	1	1	1	1	0

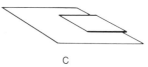

Displaced center square

B

C

Figure 4.30 (A) Random-dot stereogram. (B) How A is constructed. (C) A central square is seen floating above the background when two views are fused. (From Julesz [1971]. *Foundations of Cyclopean Perception.* Chicago: University of Chicago Press.)

literature as the correspondence problem. Normally the problem is easier than in Julesz stereograms, because normally matches are highly constrained by the uniqueness of the scene; for example, there is only one horse, a dog is to the left of the horse, and a haystack is partly occluded by the horse. A brain that has been around knows not to match up a haystack image with a horse image. Essentially what happens is that the brain does a vergence rove, searching for a fixation point where matching makes sense. Being a highly parallel processor and generally encountering unambiguous scenes, the brain fuses and fixates quickly and unproblematically. Motivational and attentional factors, of course, enter into the decision on where to fixate. A movement in an otherwise quiescent scene causes the eyes to flick to the moving object and fixate at its depth plane.

So-called "false" stereo, wherein retinal images are matched despite failure to correspond to the same external object, is rarely a hazard in everyday settings. False stereo occurs only where there are repeating objects against an undifferentiated background. Even then, inadvertent false stereo is rare, and one usually has to make an effort to produce it. For a conducive condition, find a row of knobs on a flat black panel or a recurring pattern of simple shapes on plain wallpaper. False stereo results when two images, actually corresponding to two adjacent knobs, are processed by the brain as representing just one knob, and consequently are matched and fused to appear as one knob hovering in depth behind the panel. Having achieved false stereo, the visual system makes the false knob suddenly look larger, because for its angular size *at that depth* it would have to *be* large (figure 4.31). This is size constancy[20] playing its role. But alter the uniformity of the scene, by draping an object over the panel or putting an identifying mark on a knob, and the illusion vanishes, to be maintained only with considerable conscious effort, if at all.

Eye movements—not only vergence changes, but also saccades and gaze shifts—are enormously useful to the visual system in settling on what matches with what. Trying to solve the correspondence problem in the absence of eye movement jacks up the difficulty enormously, and AI attempts to so solve the problem may have led to a misestimation of the brain's task and its degree of difficulty. This anticipates discussion of computational models of depth perception in the next section.

One additional observation concerning stereo vision should be mentioned. Apparently, about 10% of humans either are stereo deficient or have no binocular depth perception at all, and rely on nonstereo cues for depth judgments. This is not introspectively noticed by the subject and is not behaviorally detectable either, save by some task like the Julesz random-dot stereograms which cannot be processed by stereo-blind subjects. The absence of binocular depth comes as a surprise to the subject, prompting curiosity about what "true" 3-D depth perception is like. Other depth cues, especially motion parallax and occlusion, are very efficient, and stereo-blind humans manage very well without noticeable effect save when called upon to do extremely fine 3-D work such as eye surgery, watchmaking, or fielding in baseball (figures 4.32, 4.33.)

Figure 4.31 Each of the white rectangles is the same size, but in the different settings, they appear different sizes. (With permission from Coren and Ward [1989]. *Sensation and Perception*, 3rd ed. Copyright © 1989 Harcourt Brace Jovanovich, Inc.)

Figure 4.32 This figure appears to have ridges and valleys, but the undulations are owed to variations in the density of the texture of the pattern. (With permission from Coren and Ward [1989]. *Sensation and Perception*, 3rd ed. Copyright © 1989 Harcourt Brace Jovanovich, Inc.)

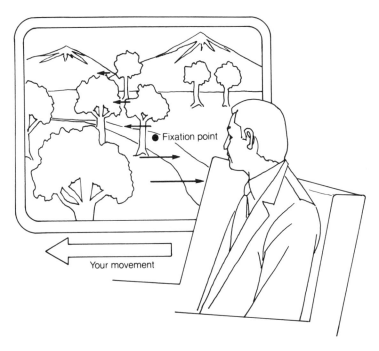

Figure 4.33 Motion parallax. When the observer is moving, objects at varying distances from the observer appear to move either in the same direction as the observer, in which case they are in depth beyond the plane of fixation, or in the opposite direction, in which case they are in depth in front of the plane of fixation. (With permission from Coren and Ward [1989]. *Sensation and Perception*, 3rd ed. Copyright © 1989 Harcourt Brace Jovanovich, Inc.)

Neurophysiology and Anatomy

For the brain to generate stereo vision, there must be the means for the brain to compare retinal images *relative to varying planes of fixation*. Hubel and Wiesel (1963) discovered that striate cortical cells were not uniform in their response to a visual stimulus, but some cells were strongly monocular, and were flanked by other cells responding somewhat to stimuli from both eyes, though preferring one or the other, flanked in turn by cells that were binocular (figure 4.34). The interleaving of ocular dominance patches in upper and lower layers and regions of binocularity in V1 and V2 of the monkey have the look of an architecture suited to process disparities and matchings in retinal images. On this proposal, the correspondence problem would be solved rather early in the processing hierarchy, and backprojections from higher areas might feed in other depth cues to play some role under certain conditions, especially when the situation is ambiguous. One important anatomical observation is that very few of the synapses in V1 and V2 originate from neurons in the LGN. Most (Douglas and Martin 1990a) of the connections are intracortical—they are cortical cells talking to other cortical cells, either within the same vicinity or from cortical areas farther afield.

Cells tuned to depth (i.e., to disparity) relative to the plane of fixation have also been found in V1 and V2 of the alert monkey[21] and in striate cortex of the

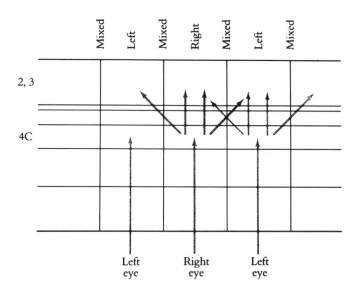

Figure 4.34 Cells in layer 4 of V1 show ocularity, but above there is overlap and blurring because of lateral and diagonal connections. (From *Eye, Brain and Vision* by D. H. Hubel. Copyright © 1988 by Scientific American Books, Inc. Reprinted by permission of W. H. Freeman and Company.)

anesthetized cat.[22] In the literature, cells that respond to stimuli at the point of fixation, and hence at zero disparity, are referred to as "tuned" cells, mainly because they have a very narrow tuning curve (figure 4.35). Since this label is rather imperspicuous, we found ourselves referring to them as fixation cells. A second class of cells respond to stimuli in their preferred 3-D volume of space in *front* of the plane of fixation; a third class responds to stimuli in their preferred 3-D volume of space *behind* the plane of fixation. In the literature (G. F. Poggio 1984) these are called "near" and "far" cells, though we note that these labels do not make the relativity to the plane of fixation evident, whereas "fore" and "aft" (or perhaps hither and yon) do. A fourth general class of cells is more eclectic: these cells respond with rather broad tuning curves to stimuli at the plane of fixation, but they also respond to stimuli in both of two preferred 3-D volumes, one fore and one aft of the plane of fixation. When the plane of fixation is marched either forward or backward, the receptive "volumes" of all four classes of cells tend to follow so that they always remain at the same relative distance to the plane of fixation and have the same retinal coordinates. The cells tested in the monkey by G. F. Poggio were predominantly within Panum's fusional area, and either moving lights or winking lights were used to drive the cells.

The cells described above seem to be representing depth-relative-to-the-fixation-plane. Are they perhaps locally coded place cells—that is, are they "grandmother" cells for relative place? The answer to the coding question goes against local coding of relative place, but the physiological data are rather subtle. First, relative depth cells are typically also directionally sensitive (they prefer their motion in a certain direction) and orientation selective (they prefer their bars to be at specific angles). Second, cells typically have a tuning curve for disparity, and the greater the distance of the receptive field from the plane of fixation, either fore or aft, the broader is the tuning curve of the cell. Put in terms of disparity, at zero disparity the tuning curves are very narrow, and they broaden as the disparity increases. Cells preferring the plane of fixation itself have an average bandwidth of 5 arc min and peaks that are almost entirely restricted to the range $\pm 0.1°$. Cells preferring depths in front of or behind the plane of fixation have their steepest slope near zero disparity and have peaks about $\pm 0.2°$ disparity. This looks like coarse coding, and if the system is to achieve its customary acuity and, indeed, its customary *hyperacuity*, vector coding is a virtual certainty. This can be seen more directly in the computer simulation discussed below.

Why would we expect to see this broadening of tuning curve corresponding to a cell's preferred distance (fore or aft) from the plane of fixation? The functional explanation that suggests itself is simply that the greatest acuity is needed close to the plane of fixation, since that is where precision in judgments about grasping, aiming, and manipulating are likely to matter most. Bearing in mind that a nervous system has limits on the number of cells it can have, this sort of organization makes sense.

9   COMPUTATIONAL MODELS OF STEREO VISION

To recapitulate the stereo problem, suppose the 3-D scene contains a dog in front of a fir tree in front of a barn. Each 2-D retina is stimulated with a pattern of light from the scene, and because the eyes are spaced apart, the elements in one image are differentially shifted laterally with respect to each other. How does the brain solve the correspondence problem—that is, the problem of what patterns in the left image correspond to patterns in the right image, as representing one and the same object? To be a bit clearer about exactly what it takes to solve it, let us look at the correspondence problem in more detail. First, as a technical term, "correspondence" hereafter refers to those pairs of points on the right and left retinas where the light reflected from a point on a given object falls. What sort of function would map the corresponding points for all scenes and how might it be computed?

Solving correspondence is tricky, for several reasons. First, the corresponding points can have discontinuities, since the boundary of an object usually signifies a discontinuity in depth (at the boundary of the dog one may see another object, a partially occluded tree, but the tree is farther from the observer than the dog.) Second, there may be stimulations on the right retina for which there are no corresponding stimulations on the left retina, and vice versa, owing to occlusion and eye separation. Third, if an object has a uniform interior expanse, devoid of distinctive featural markings, then for most of the image, there is nothing unique to match, and locating the correct correspondences for in-between points is problematic. Fourth, the information regarding correspondences is sparsely located, and so interpolation is necessary. Finally, fifth, there will be noise, both from the measurements of the gray levels by the

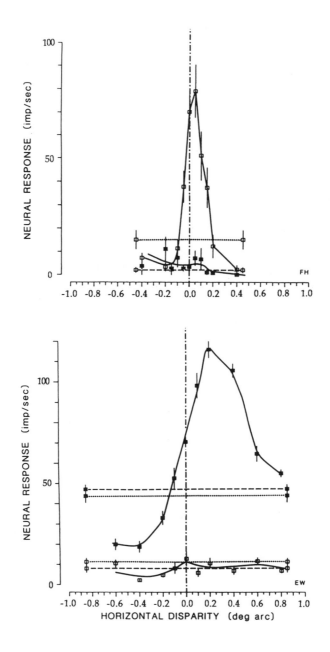

Chapter 4

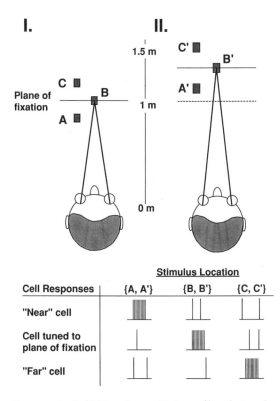

Figure 4.35 (Left) Disparity sensitivity profiles of a tuned excitatory neuron (top) and a narrow far cell (bottom) in the macaque monkey. Filled squares represent responses to one direction of stimulus motion; open squares represent responses to the diametrically opposite direction. Horizontal lines indicate the amplitudes of the monocular responses to the preferred direction. (From Poggio 1984.) (Right) Schematic diagram showing responses of three cells—near cell, tuned cell, and far cell—as the subject fixates at two different depth planes. A near cell gives its greatest response when the stimulus is in front of the plane of fixation.

transducers, and from information compression (100 million photoreceptors, 1 million ganglion cells).

Asking a device to solve the correspondence problem is asking a lot, and for the nervous system, it may have been evolutionarily manageable as well as computationally smart to solve it in stages, perhaps processing other visual information pari passu. In trying to break down the problem, the key fact is that portions of right and left retina may be highly correlated, in the sense that the pattern of gray levels over a stretch of left retina will be very similar to a pattern in right retina, but shifted by an amount determined by the relative depth of the perceived object from the plane of fixation. To get the correct conceptual bead on how this fact might be useful, envision the situation by analogy. If, god-like, we could slide the two images past each other in the horizontal plane, we could quickly find a registration between the two dog images in the foreground and, sliding a bit further, one that lines up the fir tree images but not the dog images, and finally, one that lines up the barn but not the fir tree or the dog, though, to be sure, the lining up is only approximate.

Finding registration by shifting the images motivates what is called the *compatibility function* (also called the "matching function"). In its simplest version, the compatibility function is defined for images with only two gray levels (black and white). The function represents registration of retinal points depending on position of stimulus on the retina plus some specific shift, *d*. The compatibility *C* is equal to 1 if and only if the location on the two retinas have the same value, given the shift. Otherwise it is 0.

The compatibility function is auspiciously simple, relative to the range of subtleties in correspondence listed above. Possibly the nervous system computes such compatibilities, yielding what one might call "coarse stereo," as a first step toward full-blooded depth perception. Finding compatibilities would be an incomplete solution, however, for some noise and some false matches in the images may remain. Consequently further processing, perhaps to include additional cues relevant to depth perception, would be in order. The first question, therefore, is whether it is plausible that the brain should compute compatibilities as a first step. Could it do so easily, given the physiological and anatomical resources? The first glimmer that this idea is worth pursuing devolves from proposing that the output cells of a net computing compatibility could stand as the disparity-sensitive cells—the near, far, and fixation cells.

Four basic issues arise concerning the hypothesis that image-matching yields coarse stereopsis: (1) how far can an economical but powerful feedforward net go in solving the problems of relative depth assignments by finding compatibilities; (2) how biologically plausible is such a net; (3) what sort of mechanism will clean-up noise, suppress false fusions, and disambiguate; and (4) at what stage should other depth cues, such as motion parallax, be factored in? We consider these questions in order.[23]

Finding Compatibilities: Matching and Coarse Stereopsis

How can a net compute compatibilities? Paul Churchland's (1992) compatibility model (Fusion-Net) is a solution to compatibility not for the whole depth field, but only relative to the given plane at which the eyes have verged, and compatibilities are found anew for each vergence shift; i.e., at a given vergence, Fusion-Net looks only at the cases where $d = 0$, $+1$, or -1. One rationale for narrowing the domain is that the nervous system can efficiently swallow a forkful while it might be overwhelmed by trying to stuff in a five-course dinner at one go. A further rationale derives from the psychophysical observation that accurate depth judgments are restricted to Panum's fusional area.

For the next clue, notice that when L and R in the compatibility function take on binary values, the possible values of the function can be represented on a table. So displayed, the table reveals its equivalence to the truth table for negative *XOR* (*NXOR*) (figure 4.36). Feedforward nets, as we saw in chapter 3, can solve the XOR problem. It follows, therefore, that an *NXOR* net can compute the compatibility function. In Fusion-Net, three sets of connections from the input layer compute three planes of compatibilities. Finally, any given *NXOR* net is a local operation, and to extend the field, the basic *NXOR*

A.

P	Q	XOR	Not - XOR
T	T	F	T
T	F	T	F
F	T	T	F
F	F	F	T

B. **Not-XOR-Net**

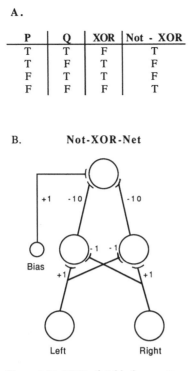

Figure 4.36 (A) Truth table for negative exclusive "or." (B) Simple net that learns the negative exclusive "or" function.

configuration can be instantiated many times. In this way, the network takes advantage of spatial invariance which, as noted in chapter 3, achieves economy, not only computationally but also in the wiring-up. Thus, by means of an array of simple *NXOR* nets, and with the task confined close to the plane of fusion, Fusion-Net will do the equivalent of image-sliding to three distinct vergences without actually sliding the images (figure 4.37).

To see it work, present the net with the random-dot stereogram in figure 4.38, where each retina sees one of the 60 × 60 pixel arrays. Humans can see three depths in this stereogram—a little square above a medium square above a background. To succeed, therefore, the net must find the raised squares in the central region and report their relative depth. We might present the stereo pairs at a vergence of 2°, at which the background plane would be fixated; or at 2.5°, at which the large raised square would be fixated; or at 3°, at which the small foreground square would be fixated. To highlight the role of the near and far cells, let us present the pairs to the net at 2.5°—at which vergence the middle square is fixated—so that all three planes might be simultaneously captured by the net. The net's output at this vergence is portrayed in the three elements of figure 4.39. The high-resolution fixation layer registers systematic correspondences within the area of the large raised square, indicating a family of adjacent co-depth elements, while the low-resolution far and near cells do the same for the background plane and for the small foreground square, respectively.

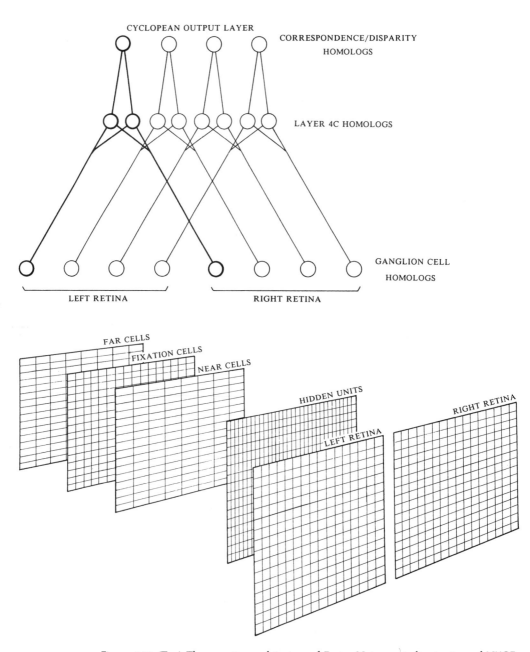

Figure 4.37 (Top) The repeating architecture of Fusion-Net: a periodic structure of NXOR subnets. Here the corresponding retinal input in each subnet is perfectly topographic, and the output layer corresponds to the "fixation cells" of mammalian visual cortex. Two additional populations of subnets are not included in this figure but are represented below. (Bottom) The units in Fusion-Net are shown simply as squares in an array to display the population. (Courtesy P. M. Churchland.)

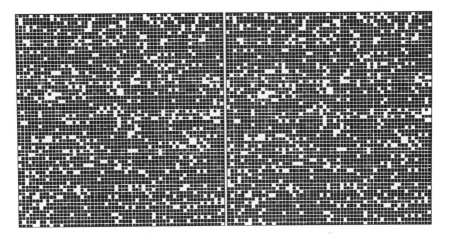

Figure 4.38 A ten-level, gray-scale, random-dot stereogram portraying three square planes of decreasing size. Although the full range of gray scales is difficult to reproduce effectively in print, Fusion-Net was presented with ten clearly distinct gray-scale levels as input. A system sensitive to ten such levels automatically confronts a low noise level of only 10% accidental correspondences outside of the fusional areas, as opposed to 50% noise in systems sensitive only to black and white inputs. (Courtesy P. M. Churchland.)

a)   **b)**   **c)**

FAR CELLS   FIXATION CELLS   NEAR CELLS
(Low Resolution)   (High Resolution)   (Low Resolution)

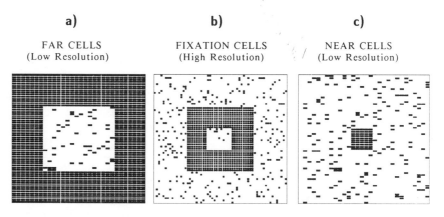

Figure 4.39 (b) Fusion-Net's output at the high-resolution "fixation" layer given the stereo pair of figure 4.38 as input, at a vergence of 2.5°. (a) Simultaneous output at the "far cell" layer. (c) Simultaneous output at the "near" cell layer. (Courtesy P. M. Churchland.)

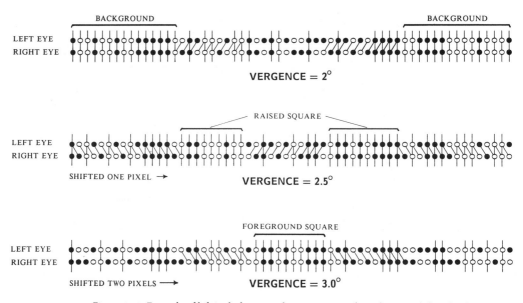

Figure 4.40 Example of left/right horizontal-row correspondence between left and right images at three difference vergences. At vergence = 2.5°, the vertical lines represent the correspondences picked up by the fixation layer. The right-diagonal lines represent the correspondences picked up by the "near cells." The left diagonal lines represent correspondences picked up by the "far cells." (Courtesy P. M. Churchland.)

So far, therefore, the net has been shown successively to verge or fixate at three different depths, and its output is an array of "tuned cells" that report the image-pair in register—zero disparity—at that depth. Indeed, this much alone is sufficient to break camouflage, and thus to find the leopard in the dappled shade. The second phase of the story involves determining the relative depths of images of objects fore and aft the plane of fixation. How can the net be sensitive to a tiny amount of disparity? The answer requires no new principles. Basically, what the net needs to know are not just the values of retinal cohorts, but also the values of *neighbors* of the cohorts, and perhaps of neighbors of the neighbors, and so forth. Figure 4.40 shows how the connections to iso-located cohorts gives image registration information, and how additional connections to the right and left neighbors of these cohorts gives slightly fore and slightly aft information. Connections to rather more distant neighbors gives information about more distant fore and aft objects. But all this still involves only that simplest of configurations, the NXOR net.

The output of Fusion-Net must now be reconsidered, for there are really three general types of output cells. The tuned units, as we saw above, code for zero disparity, but negative and positive cohort-neighbor matches are coded by near and far units, respectively. In other words, the "diagonal" connections straightaway give information about secondary correspondences, and hence about depth relative to the plane of fusion, and it does so without a supplementary vergence change. Subject to some qualifications, these three populations of output cells will simultaneously detect the angular size, shape, and

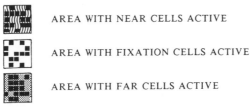

AREA WITH NEAR CELLS ACTIVE

AREA WITH FIXATION CELLS ACTIVE

AREA WITH FAR CELLS ACTIVE

Figure 4.41 Representation of the collective activity of the various units in Fusion-Net's population. The only area free of binocular rivalry is the 30 × 30-pixel square, which is also the area of uniform "fixation-cell" activity. The background and foreground squares are slightly confused by binocular rivalry, and are appropriately coded by activity in the "far cells" and "near cells," respectively. Depth of fixation varies with ocular vergence. In this way, the 3-D structure can be represented. (Courtesy P. M. Churchland.)

position of objects at three adjacent depths. The fixation (tuned) units provide a high-resolution image of affairs at precisely the current fixation depth, and near and far units provide a lower resolution image of affairs in front of and behind the plane of fixation. Figure 4.41 displays what is "seen" by the "far cells," "fixation cells," and "near cells" when the vergence = 2.5°.

Five characteristics of Fusion-Net can now be summarized: (1) The network is fast; it is a feedforward net. (2) Constructed as an array of *NXOR* mini-nets, the net learns the correct weights quickly (in only about 2000 trials). (3) At any given vergence, the low-resolution data can be used to guide the system concerning where to verge next for high-resolution perception. This contributes to vergence and fusion efficiency. (4) Fusion-Net mimics the psychophysical fact that within the narrow Panum's fusional area, resolution is excellent, but it falls off fore and aft. (5) Near and far units, like real near and far cells, are so not absolutely, but relative to the plane of fixation, and they move with vergence as it walks forward and backward. They are not entirely fixed even relative to one another, since at high vergences (when the plane of fixation is close to the eyes) "nearness" and "farness" is very close to the plane of fixation, but as the plane is more distant, "nearness" and "farness" are a little more expansive. As a corollary virtue, notice that this entails a major economy in the number of cells needed to perform the task at varying depths. That is, one and the same "aft" unit gives "aft" information relative to all planes of vergence, not just one. Our next step is to ask what the output of Fusion-Net leaves undone for the subsequent stage, and what processing that stage will involve. As a preliminary, let us delve a bit deeper into whether Fusion-Net is plausible, at least to a first approximation.

First, will it scale? As noted above, adding near and far cells to the basic *NXOR* network entails no penalty in computational time nor in training time, since the additional connections constitute simply yet more *NXOR* mini-nets, to be trained up simultaneously with all of the others.

Second, is Fusion-Net neurobiologically plausible? For starters, its topographical organization and its accommodation of tuned, near, and far units are uncontrived. Additionally, the net requires binocular cells, which exist in abundance in striate cortex (layers 2 and 3). It also requires inhibitory connections on the hidden units at layer 4c to encode mismatch information, which is at least consistent with the known anatomy and physiology, since some 20% of cortical cells are inhibitory. A prima facie implausibility is that in the model, each input unit projects both an excitatory and an inhibitory connection to the hidden layer, but in fact neurons are exclusively one or the other. By adding interneurons, however, the model can conform to this constraint.

Because the net performs interretinal stimulus comparisons that require no antecedent processing about complex shapes (tree, dog, barn), or about motion or color, it can perform its unit-unit comparisons quite early in the visual processing business. This is consistent with the occurrence of binocular cells in layers 2 and 3 of striate cortex. Pettigrew (1990) puts the point more strongly: "Perhaps the most striking feature shared in common by both avian and mammalian systems is the avoidance of abstract feature analysis until after pathways from both eyes have converged." And to be sure, this is implied by Julesz's psychophysical studies showing that color, motion, and form are not necessary for stereoptic depth perception. On the other hand, stereo is not the only depth cue, and motion parallax, shape, shading, and occlusion are very powerful depth cues with which stereo information interacts. As we shall see below, these may be presumed to be engaged after the initial feedforward pass that gives coarse stereo results.

Does Fusion-Net make evolutionary sense? First, the detection of boundaries not discernible monocularly (camouflage-breaking) can be successfully accomplished with only binocular fusion, and hence without the additional fore and aft depth judgments. This suggests that the evolutionary more basic function was binocular boundary detection, upon which stereopsis subsequently developed. In this hypothesis concerning ontogeny, we concur with Pettigrew (1990). This hypothesis predicts that some binocular animals will have only camouflage-breaking fusion, but not full-blown stereopsis. This seems to be true. Pettigrew reports that in an electrophysiological survey of 21 species in eight avian orders, disparity-sensitive neurons were found in only nine species, five of which were owls. He notes that binocular birds whose prey catching is restricted to the air tend not to have disparity-sensitive neurons, whereas birds, such as many species of owls, that also hunt while on the ground and in dim light are more likely to. This makes sense for several reasons: detection on the ground is made more difficult by prey camouflage, and at low light levels color boundaries will not be visible. The development of stereopsis from binocular range-finding seems straightforward, since it requires no new computational principles, just more *NXOR* connections, but of the slightly diagonal sort. It is not too difficult to imagine a useful bit of miscoding that might bring this about, and do so independently in a number of different species.

Does Fusion-Net square with data on phylogenetic development? Broadly speaking, yes. It is striking that coarse stereoptic discrimination in humans makes its appearance rather suddenly at about 8 weeks after birth, which is roughly when hyperacuity in detecting alignment also becomes manifest, and, most suggestively, follows closely on the heels of the infant's gaining control over eye movements in order to verge and fixate (Atkinson and Braddick 1990). The basic circuits for stereo vision are most likely genetically programmed, and once vergence is under control, depth perception could kick in straightaway. Coarse stereo competence precedes by many months facility with other depth cues such as motion parallax and occlusion, which seem to be more difficult and to involve more "training on examples." If Fusion-Net is anything to go by, the real neural network responsible for coarse stereo vision may be easy to assemble. In the model net, the connections needed for both range-finding and coarse depth judgments are entirely uniform, the weight-settings on the hidden units merely have to be uniform across the population rather than tailored to a specific value or tailored uniquely for an individual unit. Given the falling-off-a-log simplicity in design, it would easy to specify the protostructure independently of visual experience, and fast tuning according to some learning procedure would follow exposure to stimuli.

Fusion-Net turns out to be surprisingly powerful, but insofar as it lacks recurrent connections, not all noise is suppressed, some false matches persist as viable, and sometimes a patch will be fused as part of a foreground plane, and when fusion shifts, the patch will fuse again, but as part of a background plane. What sort of recurrent connections might clean up the image and achieve the higher goal? Mutually inhibitory connections between the three classes of output cells would put the net's output much closer to the goal of simulating human stereopsis.

Using a Cooperative Algorithm

The basic strategy of combining a matching function with a cooperative procedure was figured out by David Marr and Tomaso Poggio (1976). They first computed the compatibilities for all depth planes, and used that as a starting point for an iterative algorithm that then computed unique correspondences. The nub of their strategy was to recreate in a configuration of units a 3-D replica of the external 3-D world of objects, so that along a given line of sight, there is a neuron for every depth plane. In its most straightforward implementation, therefore, this is a 3-D grid of units, with spacing of units at the behest of the engineer (figure 4.42). The representational arrangement is as follows: the units in the net stand in a $1:1$ relationship with points in 3-D space, including, of course, a depth location. Activity of a unit in a given model location, x,y,d, represents the information "object at x,y,d." These representations have the same format, therefore, as the compatibilities.[24] How can such an arrangement solve the correspondence problem?

The basic constraints Marr and Poggio implemented in the cooperative algorithm were these: matched groups at the same plane of fusion probably mean "same object," whereas matched groups on the same line of sight but at different planes probably mean false fusions. The crux of the computational strategy is that units interact positively with units in the same depth plane and negatively with units in the same line of sight but at a different depth plane. The first are, as it were, friends to hold hands with, and hence there are excitatory connections between cells at the same depth plane, and the second are pariahs to be snubbed, and hence there are inhibitory connections between cells at different depth planes on the same line of sight (figure 4.43). The units thus compete to see which activated group is the strongest, the winner taking all, and hence the winning group represents the answer to the correspondence question. This global processing takes about 10 to 20 iterations of neighborhood assessments and weight updates. In the final round, assorted clusters of units at various depths will be active, corresponding to the objects of assorted sizes found at the various depths in the external 3-D scene. By this cooperative procedure, noise and false fusions can be reduced.

In their original model, Marr-Poggio used a compatibility function that found compatibilities at all depths, and, in turn, the output of the cooperative algorithm gave all winning correspondences for all depths. If the Marr-Poggio model is correct, then at a given plane of fixation, images of objects at various depths fore and aft the plane of fusion should be equally crisp and well defined. That this is false is readily determined. At arm's length, focus on your thumb. Objects, such as a coffee cup 10 inches directly behind the thumb and a rose 3 inches in front can be perceived, but they are rather fuzzy and their boundaries may be indistinct and doubled, even though the images fall within the foveation area. Next, verge most distantly and fuse the coffee cup. This time what is seen are double, fuzzy, semi-transparent thumbs, not a crisp, well-fused, and well-defined thumb in front of the crisp, well-fused, and well-defined coffee cup. Because vergence shifts are swift and perception remains smooth, and

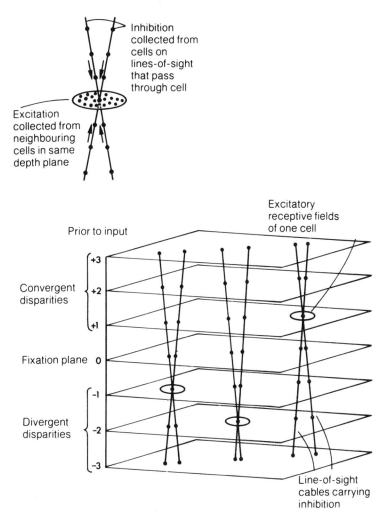

Figure 4.42 Three-dimensional schema of the Marr-Poggio cooperative network. Each of the seven layers represents one plane of depth, the central one being the one for zero disparity, the upper three for near disparities, and the lower three for far disparities. For simplicity, only three units are shown, but units in all planes have similar connectivity patterns. (From Frisby 1980; based on Marr and Poggio 1976.)

because close attention is typically paid only to what is at the plane of vergence, the illusion is created that images are fused through many depths simultaneously. This is not unlike the illusion that foveal vision covers most of the visual field, whereas in fact it covers only about 3°, which is roughly equivalent to the area covered by two thumbs at arm's length.

In humans, the fusion-latency of the first-pass at a random-dot stereogram can be rather long, perhaps reflecting iterations in a cooperative procedure, but perhaps reflecting only "vergence hunting," as the visual system tries various vergences to find one where matches are satisfying. Additionally, it should be mentioned that the very inhibitory interactions that allow the Marr-Poggio model to reduce noise also diminish its capacity in solving the screen-door

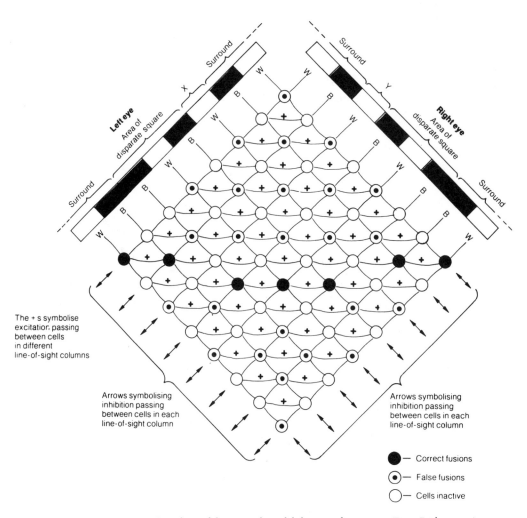

The + s symbolise excitation passing between cells in different line-of-sight columns

Arrows symbolising inhibition passing between cells in each line-of-sight column

Arrows symbolising inhibition passing between cells in each line-of-sight column

● — Correct fusions

⊙ — False fusions

○ — Cells inactive

Figure 4.43 One plane of the network model shown in figure 4.42. (From Frisby 1980.)

problem; that is, the capacity to see objects in depth behind a grid such as a screen-door or a chain-link fence.[25] That is, the Marr-Poggio net fails on the screen-door test because it represents objects as nongappy, in the sense that the holes get filled in by the units' interactions. Consequently, because a foreground object is inevitably represented by the net as nongappy, then when the net is presented with a foreground object that is in fact gappy, such as a screen door, it blissfully fills in the gaps, and nothing behind the screen door will be detected. (Fusion-Net, by contrast, fuses both planes successfully.)

Investigating the scope for improving the screen-door performance of a Marr-Poggio style net, Qian and Sejnowski (1989) motivated their modifications with the observation that when one fuses a Julesz stereogram, there appears to be two rather different components: (1) a set of dots appears to stand in front of a background, but the foreground figure still consists of dots with gaps between; it does not consist of a continuous, uninterrupted figure. (2) There does appear to be a smooth, uninterrupted depth plane in the foreground that is not straightforwardly visible but is nonetheless apprehended, as though the gaps were in some sense interpolated so that the plane is represented as continuous but without being represented as a dense, filled-in object. Qian and Sejnowski reasoned that a two-stage process—finding the matches and then interpolating without gap filling—might permit the net a more adequate response in the screen-door test. And indeed, a net that finds matches without gap filling does perform better on the screen-door test (figure 4.44). In contrast to the trial-and-error method used by Marr-Poggio to set the weights, backpropagation was used to find the weight settings for the Qian-Sejnowski net, but the second stage—interpolation to construct a nonvisible plane—was left for another net.[26]

The Marr-Poggio model is both elegant and powerful as applied to random-dot stereograms, but because it uses cooperative computation, the question that must be raised is whether it might be too slow. Making real-time comparisons between the model and the nervous system is inconclusive because the model is highly idealized in many respects. For example, the model has binary units, whereas neurons are not binary; real neurons have dendrites, and the time for dendritic signal processing will include factors such as dendrite length. Additionally, because compatibilities were found for all depths, much more work was left for the cooperative algorithm than if compatibilities were restricted to Panum's fusional area. Suffice it to say that cooperative procedures are typically time intensive, and since fusion at a new vergence appears to be accomplished in about 200 msec, an extended roster of arm-wrestling contests is almost certainly too plodding a method when answers are needed quickly.

The answer to the time question depends critically on the quality of the output from the matching function. For example, if it is Fusion-Net that supplies the output, then given the restriction to Panum's fusional area, the output may need little additional work. Moreover, for most real-world images, very little cleaning up may be required, and hence not more than a few iterations to disambiguate and bring the noise to zero might suffice. In the spirit of James Gibson, it should be observed that real-world images have nothing like the noise and ambiguity of random-dot stereograms. The visual system evolved to cope with the real world, and random-dot stereograms, though manageable, are not what the visual system normally encounters. Additionally, as we shall discuss below, Fusion-Net can be more successful if its task is to find compatibilities not in the retinal image, but in the ganglion cell's version of the image, namely *changes* in gray levels. Moreover, sometimes humans do perceive false fusions, as, for example, in the wallpaper illusion, though extra cues such as flecks of paint mean that in practice false fusions are far less frequent than might be predicted on theoretical grounds. In any case, the cleaning up by a cooperative procedure should not be so thorough as to preclude fusion through a screen door.

With these considerations in mind, it may be expected that the output of Fusion-Net should feed into a mechanism whose main task is to integrate the assortment of depth cues, and which, en passant, reduces whatever noise and ambiguity remain. That is, instead of postulating a mechanism whose sole

a)

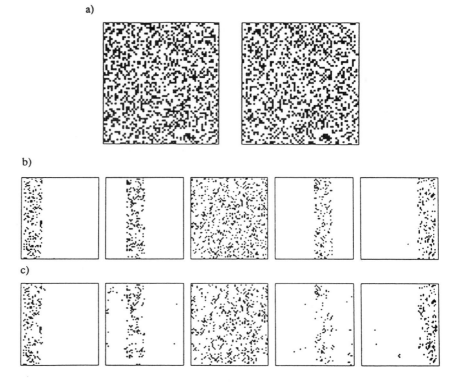

b)

c)

Figure 4.44 (a) A 68 × 68 random-dot stereogram which when fused reveals a spotty staircase going through a "dirty window," i.e., there is a foreground plane on the right, another foreground plane to its left, a "dirty window" plane behind that for the "transparency." Behind the dirty window are two more steps in depth. This is not easy to free-fuse, and may take a few minutes with a stereoscope (a long envelope should do), but when it does fuse the effect is very striking. The stereogram illustrates first that, independently of monocular cues and solely on the strength of disparity cues, the human visual system can see more than one depth plane at a given location in space. (b) This shows a distinct panel for each depth plane discernible in (a); these patterns at the depth planes are the targets for the cooperative net. Each dot represents a correct match between black dots in the right and left images corresponding to that depth. (c) These are the final matches assigned by the cooperative network. Notice that there are some false assignments that do not accord with correct matches in (b). A careful scrutiny of the stereogram in (a), however, reveals that the human visual system also produces occasional false matches. This is not surprising given that the dirty window spots are all too easily fused (and hence confused) with spots on a depth plane. (From Qian and Sejnowski 1989.)

chore is to reduce noise and ambiguity in Fusion-Net output, we suggest that noise reduction and disambiguation are achieved mainly as a by-product of the integration of the motley depth cues, including motion parallax, shape, size, occlusion, and texture gradients.

Unsupervised Learning of Stereo Invariants

Fusion-Net was trained using a supervised algorithm, namely backpropagation. Might it be possible for an *unsupervised* learning algorithm to discover disparity as an invariant if a network were simply presented with examples of stereo pairs and competitive interactions allowed to occur? (See chapter 3.) Finding invariants is unlike the extraction of lower-order features because what is relevant is the shift of dots, not the pattern of dots; that is, what matters is whether there is a significant match-up between the input vector from the left eye and that from the right. In Fusion-Net we saw that finding the match-up points is a bit like sliding the vectors back and forth. Representing disparity as an invariant means knowing where the vectors should match relative to a given plane of fusion. Whereas the values in the vectors are first-order properties, the degree of shift needed to get a match between vectors is a second-order property. To see this a bit more easily, consider some specific depth plane, say arm's length, and consider several surfaces in the same vertical plane at that depth. The surfaces might be, for example, several pages of a paint-sample book lined up vertically—each unique, but all at arm's length relative to the viewer. The point is that the input patterns entering the two eyes from the top picture will be disparate to exactly the same degree as those from the middle picture and those from the bottom picture. For the system to detect this systematicity, it is irrelevant that the top of the page has colors of blue, the middle colors of pink, and the bottom colors of green. This means that relative to a given depth, disparity is a property invariant across the range of features in the input patterns. Whereas paint colors may vary widely from page to page, the disparity in this example remains the same; it is an invariant.

It turns out that competitive, unsupervised networks are able to learn to represent disparity as an invariant (Schraudolph and Sejnowski 1991). This is somewhat surprising because the competitive nets discussed in chapter 3 had the notable weakness that so long as first-order properties (such as color) could be represented by the output units, higher-order (relational) properties (such as invariants) were not represented. The canonical competitive net discussed in chapter 3 had to be modified in two important ways for it to represent invariants. First and most importantly, the learning rule adopted for feedforward connections was *anti*-Hebbian. That is, once the competitive interactions are completed in the sense that the winner-take-all decisions regarding the output units have been made, the weights to the winner are decreased rather than increased, as specified in the following rule:

$$\Delta w_{ij} = -\varepsilon y_i x_j \tag{1}$$

where x_j is the input vector and y_i is the output vector.

The second modification prescribes that the output is not a sigmoid function of the input, but a Gaussian function of the input. The effect of this departure from canonical competitive nets is to make a large output conditional on a *balance* of inputs rather than on a maximal input.

With these modifications, the Schraudolph and Sejnowski competitive net gradually comes to represent disparity as an invariant. After being presented with Julesz random-dot pairs, one shifted by a constant amount to the left of the other, the output units developed sharply tuned disparity selectivities, as shown in figure 4.45. Broader tuning curves were developed when the input vectors were drawn not from the black-or-white arrays typical of Julesz random-dot stereograms, but from images containing many gray levels with continuous rather than discrete intensity changes. It may be that assortments of broad and narrowly tuned disparity-selective cells in the nervous system are needed to do justice to the variety of patterns of light intensity that retinas encounter.[27]

Depth Cues and the Real World

Random-dot stereograms are the favored input for computer-modeling studies of stereopsis. They are easily entered as data, they are quantifiable, and they serve as a convenient benchmark test across experiments and laboratories. They are, nevertheless, highly artificial, and in pulling us away from the typical case, they may divert us from the main principles of nervous system computation. That is, the problem of representation in the nervous system may be understood rather differently when real-world images are considered. Real-world images only rarely contain a single type of feature such as an isolated black dot against a white background. Most of the time, our visual images contain extended borders, differently shaped and differently oriented borders, many textural styles, and slowly varying gray levels as well as rapid changes, such as high-contrast borders. A real-world scene is seldom as uniform in luminance changes, type of boundary, size of object, orientation, and so on. The closest real counterpart might be perception in a blizzard or in a darkened planetarium. Even these are richer, however, since there is motion and some variation in object size. What difference does this make to how we understand the computational process?

To begin with, these considerations prompt revision of the estimate of how much might standardly be accomplished by Fusion-Net. Let us explore this in a bit more detail. Owing to information preprocessing and information compression in the retina, the input to a cortical cell typically signifies a spatial or temporal change in luminance in the cell's receptive field. Consequently, most cortical neurons in visual cortex respond best to edges, borders, motion, and disparities, and, crudely, to where things are happening. A cell tends to remain at its base firing rate unless there is a change in its receptive field. Now if the input to Fusion-Net is modeled on the input to cortical cells, then it consists of these preprocessed signals. Given the variation in types and degrees of changes in real-world images, and given that the preprocessing magnifies the

a

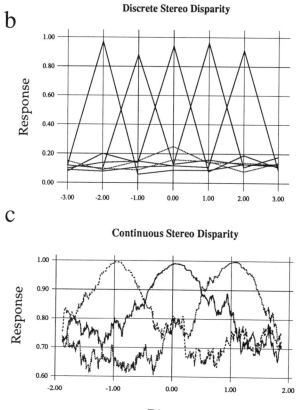

b Discrete Stereo Disparity

c Continuous Stereo Disparity

Disparity

Figure 4.45 Competitive anti-Hebbian learning of disparity invariants. A single-layer feed-forward network, with the architecture shown in figure 3.25, was used, with these differences: (1) the outputs of this net had a Gaussian input-output function instead of a sigmoid function, and (2) the learning rule was anti-Hebbian on the feedforward connections once a winner-take-all decision had been made on the output layer. In (a) the weights are shown to one output unit from the five left and five right input units. The input consisted of random-dot stereograms with shifts ranging from −3 to +3 pixels. The output units shown specialized in a shift of +1 pixel disparity. (b) This shows the disparity tuning of five different output units, each sharply tuned for a shift of a specific degree, ranging from −2 to +2 pixels. (c) Another network was trained with depth surfaces (inputs) having continuous gray levels rather than binary values, and Gaussian distributions spread over more than 1 pixel. The tuning curves for three output units are shown (solid line, dashed line, dotted line). In this net, the disparity tuning curves of the output units were much broader than those in (b). (From Schraudolph and Sejnowski 1992.)

changes it finds, there will be a far greater variety in measurements of change—and hence of input to the cortex—than there is for random-dot presentations. Just by virtue of this very fact, therefore, the number of possible matches in real-world images is enormously reduced, and therewith the number of false fusions.

We have seen that coarse stereopsis may emerge from matching rather lower-level representations such as luminance changes in a small spatial region, but there is also evidence of a contribution of higher-level representations to stereopsis. For example, Gregory and Harris (1974) have shown that subjective depth contours can be perceived using a stereogram of Kaniza shapes (figure 4.46A). This is a very striking perceptual effect, the more so because there are *no* matchable signals from the retina corresponding to the subjective contours—the contours, after all, do not exist in the stimulus. In studying this effect, Ramachandran (1986) discovered that the segmentation of the visual scene into objects and surfaces can profoundly influence the early visual processing of stereopsis. More precisely, Ramachandran found that when a stereogram with illusory contours was given a background consisting of vertical lines (square wave grating at 6 cycles/degree), the illusory square pulled the corresponding lines of the surface forward.

That the lines "filling" the illusory square should have been seen in front of the lines interpreted as the background is quite remarkable, given that all the vertical lines are in fact at zero disparity (figure 4.46B). Ramachandran suggests that in this example the visual system appears to make a stereo interpretation on the basis of the disparities in the disc shapes, and then fills in the subjective contours at the relevant depth in the 3-D image. Part of the reason this example is fascinating is that it sets up a tension between the disparity of the discs (signaling depth) and the zero disparity of the lined background (signaling no depth differences). Monocularly, the subjective contours are faint if existent at all. But binocularly, they jump right out. This implies that the subjective contours appear only after stereo fusion, which in turn implies an interaction among shape, figure–ground, and stereo processing. The mechanisms for these higher-level effects are not yet known, but in reflecting on these questions, it is pertinent that at higher processing levels—for example, V2, V4, and MT—most cells are binocular, they have larger receptive fields and hence a more global view, and they respond to more complex spatiotemporal patterns. Representations in these areas can be assumed to play a role in further reducing noise and disambiguation, perhaps via feedback connections to lower areas such as V1, or perhaps right on their own turf.

Stereopsis is a powerful depth cue, but, of course, it is only one among many other cues the visual system uses in perceiving depth. Indeed, as noted earlier, monocular depth perception is very nearly as good as the binocular variety. Moreover, in some conditions monocular depth cues, such as perspective, can override binocular depth signals. How do these cues mesh into a unified perception? One possibility is that the circuits computing these cues feed into a common representation of depth. It is instructive that in area MT, single neurons are tuned both for disparity and relative motion. Even more telling, cells

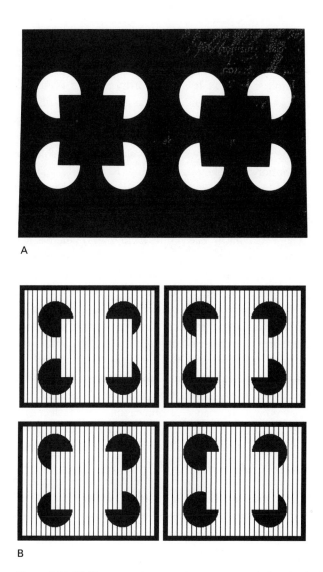

A

B

Figure 4.46 (A) Illusory contours can be seen monocularly in both the right and left diagrams; the left has concave edges, the right has convex edges. The pair of illusory polygons are fusable, though given the complexity of the stimulus, fusion may take a bit more time than usual. When the polygons fuse, what is seen is a sort of black Japanese bridge curving in depth toward the viewer. This is a very striking effect, the more so because nothing like that is seen in the unfused stimuli. (For divergent-eye technique, keep the page right side up; for the crossed-eye technique, turn the page upside down.) (B) Ramachandran's stero pairs of illusory squares are especially puzzling because the lines of the background are at zero disparity, yet when the topmost pair are fused, a striped square is seen well in front of the striped background; even more remarkably, in the bottommost pair, the striped square is behind the striped foreplane with the disks (vice versa using the crossed-eyed technique). Courtesy V. S. Ramachandran; based on Ramachandran 1986.)

in area MST receiving input from MT have direction selectivities that depend on the distance of the moving object from the plane of fixation (Roy and Wurtz 1990). This is consistent with these cells playing a role in both stereopsis and motion parallax. It is noteworthy that the override hierarchy of depth cues varies across conditions as well as across individuals.

Modules for stereopsis or motion or shape that take their task to completion in isolation of other tasks probably do not exist in the nervous system, and it may not be worthwhile to try to develop complete solutions to problems on the assumption that they are isolated. Real-world images typically contain information from assorted depth cues simultaneously, and when one cue channel is noisy or ambiguous or tricked, other cues may override or take up the slack. Concordant signals from several channels may lead to mutual enhancing as the channels confirm each other's judgment, whereas a discordant channel can be suppressed. There is a dramatic example of suppression in binocular rivalry. In this set-up, incompatible patterns are simultaneously presented to the right and left eyes (e.g., the right eye stimulus is a vertical bar pattern; the left eye stimulus, a horizontal bar pattern). The perception is not a conflation of the two, such as a checkerboard, but alternating perceptions of vertical and horizontal bars, with a periodicity of about 1 sec (Logothetis and Schall 1989).

That perception is interactive also bears upon how the circuits processing different sensory cues might fine-tune their performance with experience. On a given occasion, strong, concordant evidence in several circuits could be used to improve the performance of one circuit that produces a result inconsistent with the results of the other circuits. This would be an example of monitored, unsupervised learning, where the concordant circuits would provide internal teaching signals for the out-of-step circuit. Insofar as the internal teaching signal is an assessment of the output of a particular circuit, it is a local teaching signal, in contrast to that used in behavioral experiments where the animal is punished or rewarded for its decision. How much detail might be provided by an internal teacher ranges along two dimensions. First, the signal could be directed to a set of neurons, such as an entire column, or it could be directed even more locally, to an individual neuron. Second, the correction could be a gross "good/bad" signal, or it could specify the degree of correction needed.

Conceivably, these corrective modifications in the circuits should be made only when there is (1) a strong agreement between other circuits, (2) the odd man out is strongly, not just mildly, discrepant, and (3) the odd man out is not merely silent, but has a response that conflicts with its cohort circuits. Thus under some conditions the discrepancy might be ignored, under other conditions it might call for synapse modification, and these conditions might be differently specified at different periods in development. How could the system mark the satisfaction of the conditions calling for synapse modification?

Recently, synchronized firing of cells in distinct populations in the range of 30–60 Hz have been reported in visual cortex (Gray et al. 1989).[28] This is the sort of event that could mark satisfaction of the teaching conditions, and ipso facto, signal that changes should be made to the discordant channel to get its performance more in line with its informational mates. These synchronous bursts last only for a few hundred milliseconds and they are not ubiquitous but appear to be relatively rare. Why should we imagine they might relate to learning? The main hint is that high-frequency firings would be favorable conditions for inducing long-term potentiation (LTP) at synapses, as we shall see in the next chapter. Accordingly, the speculation is that synchronous bursts from several populations could signal the errant channel to modify its synaptic weights. (See also Granger and Lynch 1989). This is, to be sure, speculative, and there are many other possible roles for synchronous firing. One suggested by Crick and Koch (1990) is that it represents the binding of several features, such as color and shape, so that the subject may be visually aware of them as belonging to a single object. In their proposal also, oscillations might signal learning, not, as we are proposing, by letting the discordant circuit know it is out of step, but rather by strengthening the responses of the concordant circuits. Another possibility is that synchronously firing cells can have a much greater effect on their target cells than they would if they were firing independently. This may be a way for the brain to amplify the influence of a small population of neurons (Abeles 1982).[29]

10 HYPERACUITY: FROM MYSTERY TO MECHANISM

Hyperacuity involves the detection of intervals smaller than the resolving power of any single transducer. On the face of it, this seems a paradoxical property, for it suggests that one can squeeze even more information out of a signal than it contains. That would be a truly paradoxical state of affairs, but since hyperacuity is a psychophysically established fact, it cannot be impossible, so the description cannot be accurate for the nervous system. If not paradoxical, then it is nonetheless mysterious how the nervous system processes information such that hyperacute discrimination in certain perceptual domains is an everyday, routine phenomenon.

We have suggested that coarse coding is the key to solving the hyperacuity mystery. To clarify this claim and to demonstrate the generalizability of coarse coding to various dimensions, we consider three cases: color perception, spatial hyperacuity (x,y coordinates) and stereoptic hyperacuity (x,y,z coordinates). For the last case, a network aids in formulating hypotheses about the precise neural mechanism involved.

From Three Cones to 10,000 Hues by Coarse Coding

Color perception is perhaps the most phenomenologically dramatic example of how the cortex surpasses by several orders of magnitude the discriminative capacity of its individual transducers. Two brush-clearing points must be made first: (1) A red wagon may look red under a wide range of illuminations, including broad daylight, dusk, candle light, fluorescent light, and so forth, where the physical wavelengths actual impinging on the retina vary dramatically. This is known as color constancy. (2) Color perception depends on wavelength, but it is not identical to wavelength. Were color just wavelength,

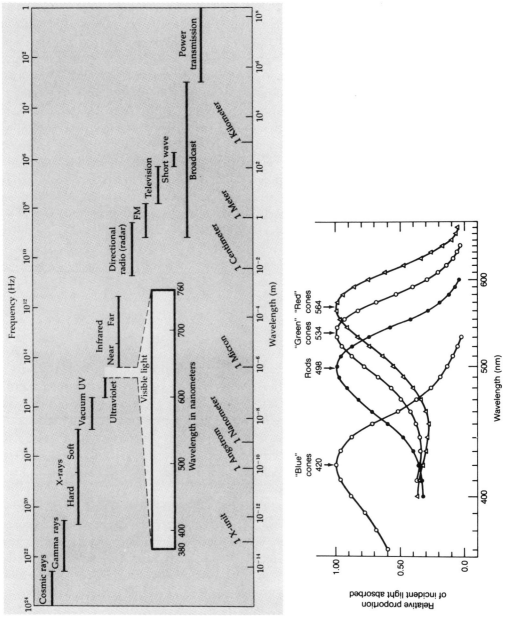

Figure 4.47 (A) The spectrum of electromagnetic (radiant) energy. (B) The relative absorption of various wavelengths of light by the

then the perceived color of a patch would vary solely as a function of the wavelength of the patch. It does not, however. The color perceived also depends on the wavelengths of light coming from other parts of the visual field. In other words, there are interactive effects. Notice, however, that perception begins in the retina where the photoreceptors respond only to the wavelength of the photon that they catch. Color perception, therefore, must emerge from processing at higher levels in the visual system.

The photoreceptors in human retina consist of rods and three classes of cones. Rods have a peak sensitivity to light at wavelengths of about 510 nm, but are believed not to be involved in color perception. The three cone types have peak sensitivity at 420, 530, and 560 nm, respectively (figure 4.47). These are commonly referred to as the "blue," "green," and "red" cones, respectively, though as David Hubel points out (1988),[30] the names, are really misnomers on several counts. First, monochromatic lights whose wavelengths are 420, 530, and 560 nm look not blue, green, and red, but violet, blue-green, and yellow-green, and second, if a cone of just one type were stimulated, the subject would see not blue, green, or red, but probably violet, green, or yellowish-red. Finally, the transducers have rather broad sensitivity curves, and they respond in varying degrees as the curve describes. Accordingly, light at 550 nm will evoke a response from both the green and the red cones. Light at 450 nm will evoke a response both from the rods and from the blue cones. The misnomers having been flagged, we forthwith follow the "blue," "green," and "red" labeling convention for cones.

The light falling on the retina has not only wavelength, but also intensity, as represented in the power spectrum of the stimulus (figure 4.48). If only one type of cone were present, it could not discriminate a stimulus with low intensity and highly favored wavelength from a stimulus with high intensity but less favored wavelength (see figure 4.15). By means of comparisons between the responses of the different cones types, the system can separate out wavelength. Skipping over much relevant detail, we now go to the heart of the matter. Any perceivable difference between two color stimuli corresponds to a distinct combination of responses of the activated cones (e.g., color A: .8, .2, .0; color B: .7, .5, .0, etc.). The power spectrum for each stimulus displays the various wavelengths of the light contained in the stimulus; for each power spectrum there will be a specific combination of cone responses. There are as many different discriminable hues as there are different response combinations that can be recognized by high-order cells.

This explanation may be easiest to conceptualize in terms of a state space, in which each class of cone is a dimension and responsivity to wavelength is a point along the axis (figure 4.49). The minimum distance between two points in the color space such that those two colors are discriminable by a subject is the just-noticeable difference (jnd), which is a measure of the lower bound below which variation in cone response differences in not significant. The distance in the state space between two jnd hues is a threshold, determined by the system's noise level. That is, below the threshold, the system cannot tell whether a response difference means something and hence is signal, or

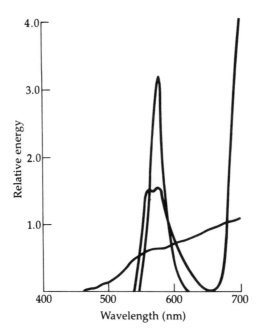

Figure 4.48 Power spectrum (relative energy as a function of wavelength) for three different physical light distributions, each of which looks yellow when seen at the same light level. (With permission from Hurvich [1981]. *Color Vision*. Sunderland, MA: Sinauer Associates.)

whether it is just slop within the neuron. If the jnd is measured as the Euclidean distance, using a sharp threshold, this is known as a line element model, but a probabilistically defined threshold as analyzed by signal detection theory may reflect more closely the decision process in the nervous system. In either case, the background assumption is that the three cone channels are independent. This assumption may have to be modified, since in the nervous system channels tend to carry overlapping information. Because the jn distance in color state space is small relative to the tuning curve of a cone, we have found it useful to consider color perception as an instance of hyperacuity.

The geometric representation also gives a sense of how vast is the trichromat's color space, and how relatively diminished will be the dichromat's color space. Notice too that perceptually similar colors are lodged in spatially neighboring areas.

Vernier-style Hyperacuity

In a two-dimensional plane, humans display hyperacuity in perceiving whether two rulers line up exactly or not. As a preliminary to the discussion of this achievement, it is useful to distinguish "resolution" from "accuracy" with respect to spatial judgments, that is, judgments of relative 2-D position. By "resolution" is meant the minimum spatial distance between two stimuli needed to distinguish them as two. Given the optics of the retina, if the two stimuli are so close together that only one transducer responds or if the responses of

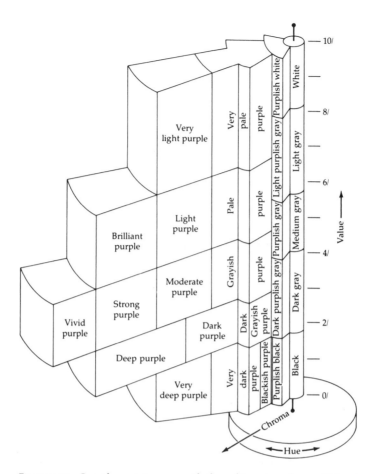

Figure 4.49 Consider a state space with three dimensions along which colors may vary: (1) chroma (degree of saturation, such as brilliant, nonvivid, soft, or moderate); (2) hue (green, blue, etc.); and (3) value (degree of lightness or darkness). The colors can be grouped so that each has a location in this space, and the shape filled by the colors can be made into a sphere. This scheme for organizing colors was developed by A. Munsell in A *Color Notation* (1905). The figure here depicts a segment sliced out from the Munsell sphere, showing the relations between the many purples, from that of an iris to the pale dusky mauve of the sky just after sunset. (With permission from Hurvich [1981]. *Color Vision*. Sunderland, MA: Sinauer Associates.)

neighboring transducers merge as one peak, then the system is beyond its resolving power. Accuracy in spatial location concerns how well the perceiver can locate the relative positions of 2-D shapes. Hyperacuity in spatial vision refers to an accuracy in judging relative position that exceeds the system's resolving power (figure 4.50). Whereas the resolution at the fovea in humans is about about 1 arc min, humans can detect positional discrepancies of as little as a few arc seconds.[31] Although this sounds rather paradoxical, as in the case of color perception, the bets are that the capacity depends on a coarse-coding strategy.

How does coarse coding yield hyperacuity? Suppose a stimulus is presented, say a sharp-edged bar, and consider the set of transducers responding to the end section of the bar. Each responds to the intensity at its location, where the

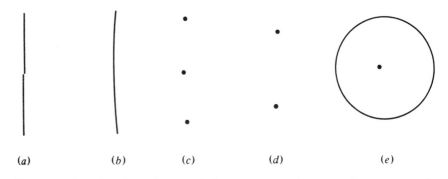

(a)   (b)   (c)   (d)   (e)

Figure 4.50 Examples where judgments of relative position can be made with a precision much finer than the separation of foveal receptors. The tasks are as follows: (a) aligning the two halves of a vernier; (b) adjusting the curvature of a line to 0; (c) aligning the three dots; (d) aligning two dots; (e) setting the dot to the center of the ring. A convenient measure of precision is given by the standard deviation of the settings, which would be under 5 sec of arc in all cases. In some cases it has been shown that these tasks can be performed nearly as well when the image is moving over the retina at a speed of 3 deg/sec^{-1}. (From Westheimer and McKee 1975.)

cross section displays the range of energy levels across the stimulus (figure 4.51). The first moment of the power spectrum (straight line dropped from the peak) can be computed from this. Comparisons require data on the first moment of two power spectra, so if another set of transducers responds to an adjacent bar, that population likewise contains information about its first moment. At some processing stage the two moments can be compared to determine relative position of the two bars. Exactly how and where this is performed is not known, but that the information is available in the population, though not in any single transducer, may be useful in guiding experimental hypotheses and lowering the baffle factor in vernier-style hyperacuity.

Hyperacuity in Depth Perception

Humans can discriminate miniscule differences in depth near the plane of fixation with an accuracy that is typically around 5 arc sec. This is, however, smaller by a factor of about 50 than the width of the narrowest cortical disparity tuning curves and a factor of 6 smaller than the width of a photoreceptor. Stereoacuity falls off rapidly away from the plane of fixation. The disparity discrimination curve in figure 4.52 plots the smallest discriminable change in disparity as a function of location of the stimulus pair relative to the plane of fixation (so-called pedestal disparity). It shows that close to the plane of fixation, a depth change between the stimulus pair of as little as 15 arc sec can be discerned, but if the stimulus pair are located further away, say 10 arc min aft, then the smallest discriminable change is about 50 arc sec, and so forth. Disparity increment threshold curves have been measured using a variety of stimuli, including line patterns (Westheimer 1979), random-dot stereograms (Schumer and Julesz 1984), and difference-of-Gaussians stimuli (Badcock and Schor 1985). The results are similar.

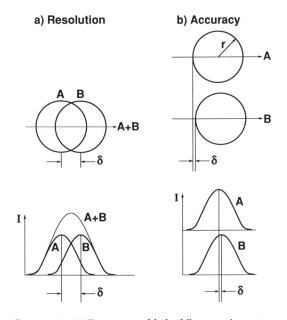

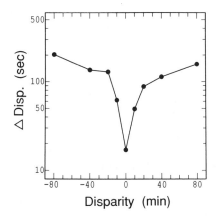

Figure 4.51 (a) Two spots of light falling on the retina cannot be resolved as two if their separation is much less than their radius, r. The cross-section of the intensity I across the image has one peak if ($\delta < r$), and hence the two spots cannot be resolved. (b) Two spots of light falling on the retina can be localized very accurately even when ($\delta << r$) if they are spatially separated. For this, it is possible to use the output from a population of photoreceptors accurately to measure the center of the distribution of light intensity for both spots. Estimates of the offset—vernier acuity—can therefore be much more accurate than the size of the spots. The resolution of the visual system in humans is approximately 35 arc sec; vernier acuity is 4 arc sec or even less in the best observers; the ability to judge differences in depth—stereo acuity—can be better than 2 arc sec. (Gerald Westheimer, personal communication.)

Figure 4.52 Psychophysical disparity discrimination curve. The smallest discriminable change in disparity, Δ Disp., plotted as a function of pedestal disparity. These data are used to constrain possible encodings of disparity in the model. (From Badcock and Schor 1985.)

227   Representing the World

Electrophysiological studies reveal that cells responding to stimuli at the plane of fixation ("tuned" cells) have a narrow tuning curve, and cells with receptive fields fore or aft of the plane of fixation have increasingly broad tuning curves proportional to the distance of the disparity peak from the plane of fixation (see figure 4.35). In trying to determine how the stereo system gets so much acuity out of the population of transducers, it is important to have a realistic estimate of the noise in each neuron. The signal/noise ratio reflects how much information is carried on average by a neuron, the average being relevant because a neuron's response to exactly the same stimulus varies a bit from trial to trial. For many neurons, it has been discovered that the variance of the noise is proportional to the magnitude of the response, and recordings showed this to hold in neurons in visual cortex of the monkey and the cat (Bradley et al. 1987). Given the nature of the neuronal tuning curves, the psychophysical data on sensitivity, and the estimate of noise in the channels, the question of how hyperacute information is extracted from a population can be approached.

One issue where modeling might lend a hand is this: given the assortment of disparity-sensitive cells found physiologically, what sort of mixture, and in what composition, would be adequate to the task of hyperacute depth perception? As we saw earlier, color vision manages with only three classes of cones, and it is possible that hyperacuity in depth might be achievable using just three classes of disparity-sensitive cells. The question for depth perception is thus a sort of extension of what has been asked and answered in color vision. A computer model might be more useful than back-of-envelope calculations in this regard, because it can efficiently and precisely test various samples to find out what the model requires to reproduce the human disparity sensitivity curve. Lehky and Sejnowski (1990) took this route. Their model enters the processing stream on the assumption that the correspondence problem has already been solved. Against that backdrop, it investigates the lower and upper bounds on the number and composition of tuning-curve types needed to give accurate depth perception. The human disparity sensitivity curve serves as the benchmark of performance.

They found that, unlike color perception, accurate depth perception requires more than three classes of neurons. The testbed was the bare minimum, namely three types of tuning curves: (1) near units maximally responsive at about 25 arc min in front of the plane of fixation, (2) far units maximally responsive 25 arc min aft the plane of fixation, and (3) units maximally sensitive at the plane of fixation. With only these three tuning curves, sensitivity was about 100 arc sec instead of the desired 5–10 arc sec. The shape of the disparity sensitivity curve was not the steep-sided crevice, but rather a lumpy curve (figure 4.53). Interestingly, just such a lumpy curve is observed in the spectral sensitivity curve for color. Step by step, additional classes of cells, with intermediate tuning curves, were added to the model, and performance was assessed. Performance improved as additional tuning curves were included, and at 17 tuning curves, the performance of the model was a respectable 10 arc sec. The shape of the benchmark curve is best matched when tuning curves are uniform-

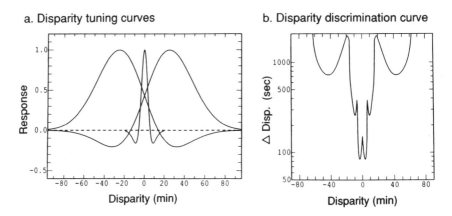

a. Disparity tuning curves

b. Disparity discrimination curve

Figure 4.53 (a) A population of units with 3 tuning curves for encoding disparity. These roughly match the average characteristics of near, far, and plane-of-fusion (tuned) cells described by Poggio (1984). Disparity discrimination with this limited population does not achieve the psychophysical curve in figure 4.52. (b) Psychophysical disparity discrimination curve of the Lehky-Sejnowski model produced by the 3 tuning curve population. The spiky appearance occurs because of insufficient overlap between tuning curves. Cf. figure 4.52. (From Lehky and Sejnowski 1990b.)

ly distributed over the range of disparities. Adding classes of units continued to improve depth-perception performance, and at 200, the model could detect differences in depth as small as 1 arc sec. This acuity is finer, however, than the ability of most humans (figure 4.54). On the basis of the model tests, it appears that the lower bound on independent classes of tuning curves is about 20 and the upper bound about 200. Why should the color system be so thrifty in cell types while depth vision is relatively unstinting? One possibility derives from genetic cost. Each type of pigment molecule must be genetically specified (Nathans et al. 1986), whereas a broad range of tuning curves may be turned out by varying gradation in biophysical and anatomical characteristics of a basic neuron prototype (Lehky and Sejnowski 1990b).

Analysis of the model revealed some surprises. First, the greatest contribution to depth-change discrimination close to the plane of fixation is made by units whose maximal response is to stimuli considerably farther from the plane of fixation. This seems odd at first, since one might expect that cells that maximally respond to the test stimuli would make the greatest contribution. The explanation for this seeming oddity is that discrimination of relative depth changes depends on the *changes* in firing rates of units. Consequently, the important variable is the slope of the tuning curve, not its width. Now the population of units in the model, based on a population sample of V1, divides between tuned, near cells, and far cells, roughly by thirds. Given this distribution, then for any point fore or aft the plane of fixation, many more broadly tuned than narrowly tuned units will have a response, and hence may contribute precision to the depth-change judgment. That this feature of the model holds true of the nervous system is a prediction that awaits experiment. A related psychophysical result and an analogous modeling result have been

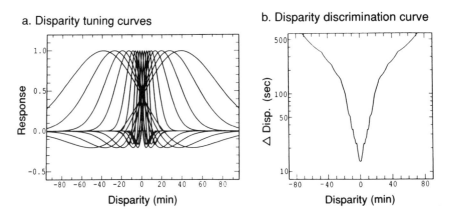

a. Disparity tuning curves

b. Disparity discrimination curve

Figure 4.54 (a) The smallest population (17 units) judged sufficient to give an output from the Lehky-Sejnowski model that matches the human disparity discrimination curve. Tuning curve width increased along with the peak of a cell's response from zero disparity. Thus the steepest portions of the near and far curves all fall near zero disparity. Since discriminability depends on tuning-curve slope, this organization produced highest discriminability at zero. This population gives a rough indication of the minimum size needed to encode disparity. (b) Disparity discrimination curve produced by the model. Cf. figures 4.52 and 4.53 (b). (From Lehky and Sejnowski 1990b.)

found by Thorpe and Pouget (1989, 1991) where the stimuli were oriented lines and the task was identification of a line as, for example, a $1°$ or $-1°$ line. As in the Lehky and Sejnowski model, Thorpe and Pouget showed that for fine discriminations, the critical factor in a unit's contribution to the network's performance was the *slope* of its tuning curve.

Psychophysical experiments show that subjects may see the continuation of a surface in depth even though those spatial points lie where no depth information exists. Imagine, for example, a sheet of cardboard leaning against the telephone, with part of the sheet's edge invisible against the background owing to odd lighting. This is the problem of interpolation through a blank space, and given the physiological and computational evidence available, the next question concerns what connectivity might account for these observed interpolations. Recall that the Lehky-Sejnowski model assumes that an earlier network has already found a plane of fixation. Now the model's task it to fill in small gaps and small blanks to generate a continuous boundary that passes through many depth planes.

The Lehky-Sejnowski model has lateral connections between pools of neurons maximally responsive to certain degrees of disparity (depth locations). Analysis indicates that the mutually excitatory, short-range, lateral connections between units with the same disparity tuning can admirably fill in and account for most of the psychophysical data with very natural, as opposed to ad hoc, mechanisms. Large depth discontinuities at a location will not be interpolated because the disparity tuning curves in between two locations receiving disparity information are not sufficiently broad to integrate inputs from the two pools. Thus, there will be insufficient overlap in response to excite the in-between cells, and the activity in the center pool will be confined to two separate subpopulations. This is exactly what is wanted, since the model ought not interpolate a boundary between two different objects. We do not, of course, want the visual system, or the model, to interpolate a boundary connecting two *distinct* sheets of paper in line on a tabletop. Whether the interpolation must be linear or whether curved interpolations are possible for the network has not yet been determined. Notice that the computation performing the interpolations is not feedforward, but recurrent. Note especially that this model uses *place coding* for location-in-space of the stimulus and *vector coding* for disparity at that particular location.

Vergence and Absolute Depth Judgments

Judgments about the relative depth of objects can be made efficiently given that the eyes have verged at a specific depth plane. Could vergence also play a role in judging *absolute* depth, i.e., in judging the distance between oneself as viewer and the viewed object? Absolute depth judgments are important in guiding the animal in reaching, grasping, throwing, and leaping. The psychophysical data indicate that even in the absence of monocular cues to egocentric depth, such as object size, humans are fairly accurate in reaching for objects in depth. Indeed, it appears that changing vergence angle is important for judging whether a small image is of a large object far away or of a small object nearby[32] (Cumming et al. 1991). How might the nervous system use vergence angle to judge egocentric depth?

Some neurons projecting to the visual cortex are tuned to vergence angle and, as we saw earlier, some neurons in cortex are tuned to the plane of fusion and to distances fore and aft the plane of fusion. Perhaps these two kinds of information can be combined to yield representations, though perhaps only coarse representations, of egocentric depth, where these representations can guide behavior. Pouget and Sejnowski (1990)[33] tested this possibility on a network whose input consisted of these two types of information: vergence angle, which is an absolute value, and disparity in the image, which is relative to the plane of fusion (figure 4.55). The input for the disparity units was drawn from the Lehky and Sejnowski model, and hence included a range of units with variously broad and narrow tuning curves. The net was trained by backpropagation to specify egocentric depth at the output units, and after training the output neurons displayed tuning curves of varying degrees of breadth. This demonstrates that indeed these two kinds of information—eye angle and disparity—can be combined to generate representation of egocentric depth. It is, moreover, a reminder that representations in one and the same cells can be used for different purposes, such as computing relative depth of objects viewed and absolute depth of an object from the viewer.

Analysis of the network revealed an interesting property. The hidden units had taken on the same type of disparity selectivity as the input disparity units were given, but they differed in that the amplitude of their responses was gated by vergence. In other words, they had acquired "gain fields," meaning

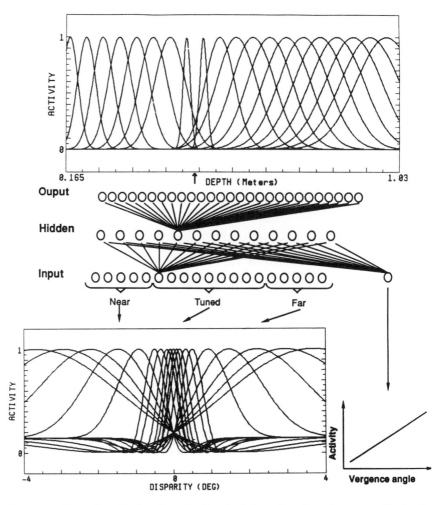

Figure 4.55 Network architecture for estimating depth from disparity and vergence. The input layer has one unit linearly coding eye vergence (bottom right) and a set of units coding disparity using a distributed representation (bottom left). The transformation between the input and the output is mediated by a set of hidden units. The output layer is trained to encode distance in a distributed manner (top). After training, the tuning curve for each output unit was a Gaussian function of depth centered on a value specific to each unit. The bandwidth of the curves increased with depth, except around the fixation point where the curves were narrower. These two types of bandwidth modulation produced depth estimates with relative accuracy similar to that found in humans. (Courtesy Alexandre Pouget.)

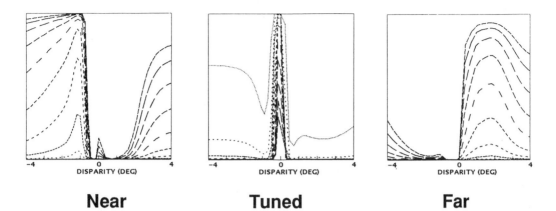

Near   **Tuned**   **Far**

Figure 4.56 Three hidden units showing changes in gain as a function of vergence. The hidden units get information from the input units about disparity and vergence, and analysis of their activation shows they are tuned neither to disparity nor to distance. What they represent is something between disparity and distance, though no name exists for an intermediate representation of that sort. At each of ten different vergences, the units show a change in gain (amplitude of response) though the response peak is always at the same disparity value. (Courtesy Alexandre Pouget.)

that the gain of a unit's response is dependent on eyeball angle (figure 4.56). The counterpart physiological experiment has been carried out in V1 by Trotter et al. (personal communication) and in lateral-inferoparietal by Gnadt (personal communication). In recording from cells in visual cortex, they found disparity-tuned cells whose gain changes as a function of changes in vergence, just as the model predicts. The discovery of units with gain field properties is interesting for the further reason that it coheres with a computationally related result found earlier by Zipser and Andersen (1988). Their net computes the 2-D location of an object in egocentric space on the basis of two kinds of input data: position of the stimulus on the retina, and position of the eyeballs on the head. In that model also, the hidden units were found to have gain fields, in the sense that the amplitude of the response was dependent on the position of the eyeballs. Recording from cells in parietal cortex area 7a of the macaque, Andersen et al. (1987) discovered that cells selective for spatial location likewise have gain fields. The rather striking presence of gain fields in networks performing these two problems in spatial representation suggests that the gain-field gambit may be rather widely employed when the nervous system needs to generate representations concerning location in objective space from subjective representations concerning location of a stimulus on the body and location of a movable body part.

11   VECTOR AVERAGING

The main focus of this chapter has been the nature of representations in sensory systems or, more correctly, in the visual system. For sensory representation in general and hyperacute representations in particular, the power and versatility of population coding—distributed representation—has been emphasized. Before leaving the chapter, we hasten to repeat that the nervous system is not restricted to a single style of coding, but in various places and for various purposes may prefer one or another strategy. Coding by *vector averaging*, to consider but one additional strategy on the shelf, is in evidence in several parts of the nervous system, most notably in the superior colliculus and the motor cortex.

To see the difference between vector-averaging and the population-coding strategy, recall that in color vision, the parameter of importance is wavelength, a one-dimensional variable, and that a hue corresponds to a three-element activity vector in cone-response space. Color representation is a three-element activity vector, and the three-element vector cannot be reduced to a single number. The three-element activity pattern is as simple as the representation gets. In the same vein, the depth-change detection model represents disparity, another one-dimensional parameter, in a high (possibly several-hundred)-dimensional unit activity-space. Again, the n-element activity vector is not reduced to a single number; it is as simple as representation of depth-change gets. In contrast, the "averaging" method reduces the dimensionality of a representation by summing the vector components to yield a single representation of direction in the relevant state space. This makes especially good sense when the output—for example, a motor decision—has to be unified rather than a conglomerate. We may hear a chord or see yellow, but the eyes cannot move to both $(3, 10)$ and to $(0, 0)$ at the same time.

One place where we see vector-averaging is the superior colliculus (SC), which is a many-layered structure, with a motor map on its bottom layer (see figure 3.8). As Sparks and his colleagues have discovered, this layer is mapped not absolutely, but relative to current eye position (Lee et al. 1988). It is a sort of "where-to-foveate-from-here" map for the eyeballs. To understand this, consider two conditions: (a) The fovea is currently at a particular position in eyeball space, say $(0°, 0°)$, eyes pointing straight ahead. The eyeballs will move to a new location in eyeball space, say $(12°, 8°)$, if a particular region of the SC is stimulated, or if we flash a light at $(12°, 8°)$. Now consider the second condition: (b) The eyeball's initial position is $(3°, 10°)$, and we stimulate *precisely the same* SC area as we did in (a). The final eyeball position will not be $(12°, 8°)$, but something else, say $(3°, 10°) + (12°, 8°)$, which is $(15°, 18°)$. The final position, therefore, is the vector sum of the current position of the eyeball plus the SC stimulation vector—in this instance, $(12°, 8°)$ (figure 4.57).

Essentially, therefore, the SC is vector averaging in order to specify the correct location to which the eyeballs are to move[34] (figure 4.58). Movement of the eyes can be in only one direction at a time, so it makes sense for the network to average the contributions of many vectors to produce a single value for direction (leaving magnitude aside). Under normal conditions, some thousands of neurons from a rather wide area in the SC contribute a component to the vector; the component is determined by the neuron's relative location in the map, weighted by its degree of activity. The final direction of movement and the resting place of the eyeballs depend on all the neurons in

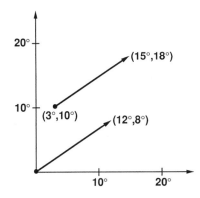

Figure 4.57 Vector averaging in the superior colliculus. The contribution of a cell to the movement of the eyeball depends on where the eyeball is when the cell is stimulated.

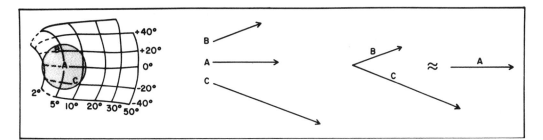

Figure 4.58 Population-averaging scheme of Sparks and coworkers (Lee et al. 1988). (Left) Diagram of the motor map of the left superior colliculus (SC). Isoamplitude lines (2° to 50°) run from the lateral edge to the medial aspect of the SC. Isodirection lines (−40° to +40°) run in the perpendicular direction. The stippled area represents the hypothetical extent of cells active before saccades to a target located 5° to the right of the fixation stimulus. (Middle) Neurons in the middle of the active population, A, represented as a motor vector, combine with vectors for other cells at B and C. (Right) These vectors are weighted by the activity of the population so that the neurons at points B and C yield the same movement as activity at the center of the active population, A. (From Lee, Rohrer and Sparks [1988]. Reprinted by permission from *Nature* 332: 357–360. Copyright © 1989 Macmillan Magazines Ltd.)

the group contributing activity to varying degrees. To test this hypothesis, lesion a small group of SC neurons, and measure the final position of the eyeball after foveation to where a light flashed. The position should deviate systematically by an amount reflecting the loss of the contribution of the lesioned neurons. This is precisely what is seen experimentally with a lidocaine lesion (figure 4.59).

Coding for movement by vector averaging appears to be used also in monkey motor cortex for controlling direction of movement of hand–arm in 3-D space. Georgopoulos et al. (1989) found individual neurons in motor cortex that respond before the arm movement, and their firing rate correlates with the actual direction of the hand–arm's subsequent movement; that is, the neurons fire maximally for their preferred direction in arm 3-space, and the firing rate declines with the cosine of the angle from that preferred direction.

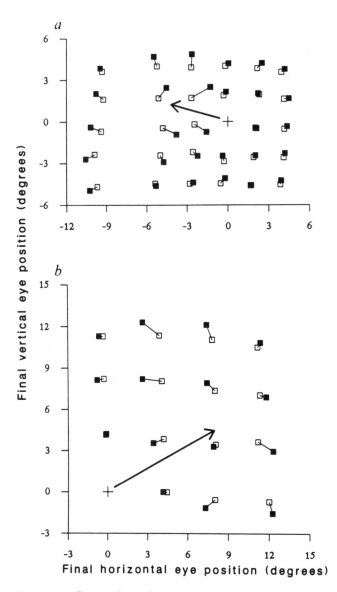

Figure 4.59 Effects on the amplitude and direction of visual saccades to a target when lidocaine is applied to a single region of the superior colliculus (SC) selectively to deactivate SC neurons. The axes represent the horizontal and vertical end points of visually-guided saccades. + indicates the location of the fixation target. Electrical stimulation of the SC drove the eyes to the location marked by the tip of the arrowhead. *Open squares* represent the average end points of visually guided saccadic eye movements to each target before deactivation; *filled squares*, the average end points of saccades to the same targets after deactivation. Lines connecting the open and filled squares represent the average error introduced by deactivation of part of the active population. (a) Results from an injection site in the left SC with an up and leftward "best saccade." (b) Results from an injection site in the left SC with an up and rightward "best saccade." (From Lee, Rohrer and Sparks [1988]. Reprinted by permission from *Nature* 332: 357–360. Copyright © 1989 Macmillan Magazines Ltd.)

Therefore when the monkey moves its arm in a particular direction, a large population of cells fire at varying rates depending on their preference for the direction in which the arm moves. Vector averaging is probably employed here to reduce dimensions of activity space and produce a command for movement in exactly one direction with a particular magnitude. Georgopoulos showed that recording the responses of several hundred neurons and computing the vector average does in fact accurately predict the direction of the arm movement that the animal makes. It remains an open question whether here, as in *Eigenmannia*, there is a population of local-coded neurons.

The averaging method would not have been suitable for the depth-change detection model because it would assign a single disparity for each pattern of activity. Depth-change detection requires a method that could assign multiple values to a single stimulus pattern. As we saw earlier, population coding also enables the model to interpolate across discontinuities, and it may be important also for coping with the screen-door problem. For these purposes, the higher dimensionality inherent in assigning meaning through an activity spectrum was more suitable than a single dimension. High-dimensional representations are also more suitable for multiplexing several parameters (depth, color, motion, etc.) in a single population (Lehky and Sejnowski 1990).

12 CONCLUDING REMARKS

Earlier we distinguished between occurrent representations and stored representations, the latter being in some sense stored for future use. In this chapter, the focus has been mainly on the nature of occurrent representations. The next addresses stored representations. One regret is that only vision figured prominently here. Research on the auditory system, especially in the barn owl and the bat, has revealed a tremendous amount, and the emerging story, quite apart from its intrinsic beauty, is important for a general theory of representing in nervous systems. This chapter has already exceeded its intended length, and however regretful, we must turn now to the next set of issues: how are representations learned, stored, and recovered for current use?

Selected Readings

Ashmore, J., and H. Sabil, guest eds. (1990). *Seminars in the Neurosciences*. Vol. 2, *Sensory Transduction*.

Bruce, V., and P. R. Green (1990). *Visual Perception*: Physiology, Psychology, and Ecology. *2nd* ed. Hove, U.K.: Erlbaum

Coren, S., and L. M. Ward (1989). *Sensation and Perception*. San Diego, CA: Harcourt, Brace, Javonovich.

DeValois, R. L., and K. K. DeValois (1988). *Spatial Vision*. Oxford: Oxford University Press.

Gallistel, C. R. (1990). *The Organization of Learning*. Cambridge, MA: MIT Press.

Gulick, W. L., G. A. Gesccheider, and R. D. Frisina. *Hearing: Physiological Acoustics, Neural Coding, and Psychoacoustics*. Oxford: Oxford University Press.

Heiligenberg, W. F. (1991). *Neural Nets in Electric Fish*. Cambridge, MA: MIT Press.

Hubel, D. H. (1988). *Eye, Brain, and Vision*. New York: Freeman.

Koenderink, J. J. (1990). *Solid Shape*. Cambridge, MA: MIT Press.

Marr, D. (1982). *Vision*. New York: Freeman.

Martin, K. A. C. (1988). From single cells to simple circuits in the cerebral cortex. *Quarterly Journal of Experimental Physiology* 73: 637–702.

Pentland, A. P., ed. (1986). *From Pixels to Predicates: Recent Advances in Computational and Robotic Vision*. Norwood, NJ: Ablex.

5 Plasticity: Cells, Circuits, Brains, and Behavior

I INTRODUCTION

Brains are continuously modifying and updating themselves. Virtually all of a brain's functions, including perception, motor control, thermoregulation, and reasoning, are modifiable by experience. The topography of the modifications is not haphazard, but orderly; the integration of the modifications appears not to be final and finished, but an ongoing process with a virtually interminable schedule. The constraints on modifications vary in an unknown but regular fashion with respect to brain functions, genetic endowment, and development, but also with age, gender, experiential history, and type of lesion. Behavioral observations indicate degrees of plasticity in an animal's repertoire: a malleable domain of fast-and-easy changes, a rather more durable domain of slower but perhaps deeper modifiability, and a more permanent but still deformable domain of "semi-constancies" that ballast a kind of unity-of-self through time.

In chapters 3 and 4, we explored the capacities and architecture of artificial neural networks, noting the power of associative nets to learn from examples. Modification of synapse-like weights according to an error-correcting algorithm gradually leads the network down a pathway to a point in weight space where errors are minimized, where the network responds more in tune with the reality it encounters. These models are a powerful inspiration to research on learning in real nervous systems, for in the last analysis the heart of the problem is to explain *global* changes in a brain's output, on the basis of orderly, *local* changes in individual cells. That is, we want to discover how neuronal plasticity—a local property—can result in learning—a global property. The basic puzzle is this: what causal interactions at the cellular level provide the bases for adaptive interactions between the organism and the external world?

Having seen how artificial networks can learn, we need now to turn to the physical mechanisms in nervous systems to determine whether these computational ideas might prove useful in discovering the structural bases and functional principles of plasticity in neural systems. The informationally relevant changes at the cellular level must somehow be orchestrated—and orchestrated even between cells not directly connected to one another—such that an overall coherent modification in system output is achieved. The local–global problem in memory is part of the more general problem of how to get device sophistication out of component simplicity. That is, a device as a whole may respond adaptively and intelligently, but its individual components are not themselves intelligent. This is the central mystery of machine intelligence, whether the machine is made of protoplasm or silicon or something different yet again. To reiterate a point of chapter 3, the importance to neuroscience of learning in artificial neural nets is that it demonstrates a number of ways in which the local–global feat and the stupid–intelligent feat can be performed.

Plasticity at the behavioral level has been studied intensively by experimental psychologists and neuropsychologists. What we know of the diversity, sensitivity, and character of learning capacities is owed to this work. While important gains have been made, the major questions spawned by the research are legion. A number of categories classifying ostensibly distinct plastic phenomena have been tendered as researchers investigate the diachronic properties of behavioral plasticity, the external conditions affecting learning and recall, the role of attention, awareness, age, lesions, and pharmacological agents.

The predominant categories invoked in the literature include (in no particular order) classical conditioning, operant conditioning, short-term memory, iconic memory, working memory, long-term memory, remote memory, procedural memory, motor memory, automatization, semantic memory, generic memory, episodic memory, contextual memory, priming, and habituation.[1] Specified in terms of prototypical cases and conditions that elicit a specific effect, these categories may overlap or compete, some may be orthogonal to others, and only a subset may refer to "memory" phenomena in the conventional sense of the word. Which is not to say that they are not *really* instances of memory, but only that in the early stages of research on plasticity, we rely on existing (and typically rough-hewn) categories. Then we bootstrap, as in any science, to more and more adequate categories. Premature definitions do nobody good, and hence we should damp the inclination to scold behavioral experimentalists for failing to have a tidier map of plastic capacities. Any fool can make a tidy map; the trick is to make an accurate one. With concurrent developments in neuroscience and psychology, the cognitive geography will yield to improved cartography.

Where is it most fruitful for neuroscientific research on plasticity to make contact with behavioral studies on learning? Selection of a research route determines a great deal about how illuminating and significant the results are, not to mention how efficiently and profitably the research proceeds. Ideally, one wants a well-studied behavioral phenomenon of an easily accessed preparation that is simple enough to analyze but complex enough to shed light on mammalian plasticity. Alas, at this stage, a wish-list beyond even the Fairy Godmother. The selection problem is, however, a constraint satisfaction problem, and several quite different but promising solutions can be reached.

Neuroscientific research on plasticity roughly divides into four main streams: (1) the neural mechanism for relatively simple kinds of plasticity, such as classical conditioning or habituation, either on invertebrates or on mammals, mainly rats and rabbits; (2) anatomical and physiological studies of temporal lobe structures, including the hippocampus, perirhinal structures, and amygdala, using human data where available, but relying mainly on the rat and monkey; (3) study of the development of the visual system, mainly in the cat and monkey, to understand how the organization of cells in the mature animal derives from the organization in the neonate; (4) the relation between the animal's genes and the development of its nervous system, mainly in *Drosophila*[2] and the nematode, *Caenorhabditis elegans*.[3] There are compelling and complementary reasons for opening up these four routes, though other avenues, such as taste aversion in birds and mammals,[4] song learning in birds,[5] imprinting in chicks,[6] working memory in prefrontal cortex of monkeys,[7] and odor learning in olfactory cortex[8] also broaden and balance the picture. Some advantages of studying the neural bases of classical conditioning are that the behavioral profile has been explored in great detail,[9] and conditioning can be produced not only in mammals, but in much smaller nervous systems, such as those of slugs[10] and worms.[11]

Since this can be only a chapter on plasticity, not an entire book, we found it necessary to select some topics at the expense of others. Although we shall refer to research on simple systems and on development, it is to the hippocampus and related structures that the bulk of the discussion is devoted. Our choice here was guided by three main considerations: (1) this research is on mammals, and (2) it illustrates the methodological principle of co-evolution of research on many structural levels and the way that links might be made between levels, and (3) there are two computational models based on data drawn from this domain that illustrate how the co-evolution of theory and computational models can be productive.

A constant background question for the "simple preparation/simple plasticity" research is this: will it generalize? Will it tell us anything about the kind of memory we see in ourselves? For example, how I remember where I put my glasses, or the words to "The Cremation of Sam McGee," or what a porcupine looks like? The hope, of course, is that it will. More specifically, cellular mechanisms mediating plasticity are probably highly conserved in evolution,[12] and the hope is that when new principles governing network interactions began to emerge, they exploited old mechanisms. Assuming so, discovery of the cellular mechanisms of simple learning in simple animals could provide a crucial foothold for research in mammalian plasticity.

On the other hand, if computer networks are any guide, representations of any significant degree of complexity are typically distributed across cells in a network, and the acquisition of stored representations consists in the pattern of weight changes across the population of cells. Thus understanding circuits and interactions is crucial. Knowing the cellular mechanisms whereby an individual cell changes its synaptic weights will not *ipso facto* divulge the cell's contribution to learning in the network, nor to the pattern of changes in the population, nor to the principles governing pattern formation and dissolution. Before this string of naysaying provokes pessimism, we hasten to foreshadow a point made in chapter 6: reflexes even in a simple animal such as the leech are the fruits of circuits. Because some circuit principles may be conserved and be-

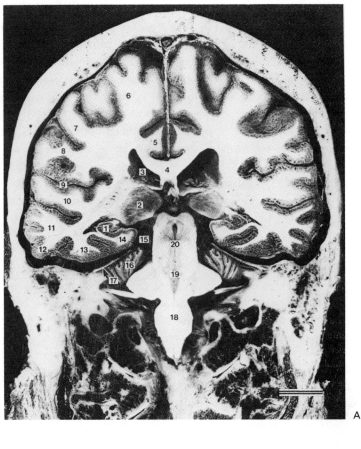

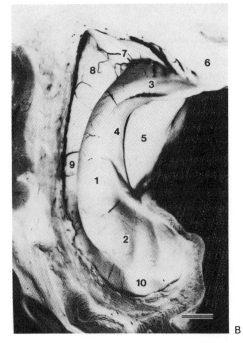

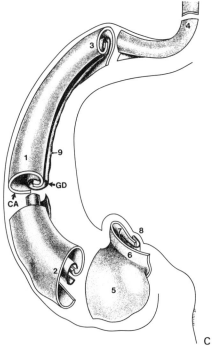

cause circuit innovations may be grafted on to the old principles, these simple circuits may be an important bridge between discoveries about cellular mechanisms of plasticity and research on learning in complex neural networks.

2 LEARNING AND THE HIPPOCAMPUS

The hippocampus is the darling of many who target mammalian learning. More correctly, the hippocampus and related temporal lobe structures, such as the entorhinal cortex, perirhinal cortex, parahippocampal gyrus, and fornix, have a kind of "favored structure" status (figure 5.1). The original basis for this interest lay in neuropsychology. In particular, curiosity was fueled by the discovery in the 1950s[13] that the patient H.M. who underwent bilateral resection of mesial temporal lobe structures for management of intractable epilepsy was left profoundly amnesic. In pioneering studies at McGill University, Milner (1973) and her colleagues showed that H.M. could not remember what had happened as recently as a few minutes or hours ago, even when the events were salient and important to him. More generally, H.M. had lost the ability to learn and retain new information (anterograde memory), though he could still remember many things that had happened before his surgery (retrograde memory). By contrast, H.M.'s short-term memory (about a minute) was within normal range.

In their studies of amnesic patients, Warrington and Weiskrantz (1974, 1978) made the extraordinary discovery that some tasks, such as completion of a picture seen earlier, could be learned at a normal rate, even though the patient was densely amnesic for recent events, and even when the patient denied awareness of having seen the very pictures he completed. When H.M. was tested, it was found that he too was able to learn some things—for example, a motor skill—though again, without awareness of his accomplishment or of his having encountered the task before. This work laid the basis for one of the most seminal hypotheses in memory research, namely, that there is a major division, honored by the nervous system, between memory for events and individuals that is reportable, and other kinds of plasticity, such as conditioning, skill acquisition, and recognition without explicit awareness (figure 5.2).

Figure 5.1 (A) Coronal section of a human brain showing the location of the hippocampus in relation to other structures. Main features: 1, hippocampus; 2, thalamus; 4, corpus callosum; 5, cingulate gyrus; 14, parahippocampal gyrus. (B) Intraventricular aspect of the human hippocampus. The temporal horn has been opened up, and obscuring tissue removed. 1, Hippocampal body; 2, head; 3, tail; 4, fimbria; 5, subiculum (parahippocampal gyrus); 6, splenium of the corpus callosum; 7, calcar avis; 8, collateral trigone; 9, collateral eminence; 10, uncal recess of the temporal horn. (C) General structure of the human hippocampus. The cornu ammonis (CA) and gyrus dentatus (GD) form two U-shaped interlocking laminae. 1, hippocampal body; 2, hippocampal head; 3, hippocampal tail; 4, terminal segment of the tail; 5, digitationes hippocampi; 6, vertical digitation; 7, cornu ammonis and gyrus dentatus in the medial surface of the uncus; 8, band of Giacomini; 9, Margo denticulatus. [Reprinted with permission from H. M. Duvernoy (1991). *The Human Hippocampus*. Bergman Verlag.]

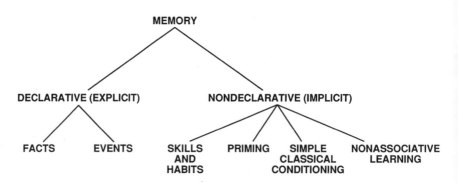

Figure 5.2 Classification of memory. Declarative (explicit) memory refers to conscious recollections of facts and events and depends on the integrity of medial temporal lobe cortex (see text). Nondeclarative (implicit) memory refers to a collection of abilities and is independent of the medial temporal lobe. Nonassociative learning includes habituation and sensitization. In the case of nondeclarative memory, experience alters behavior nonconsciously, without providing access to any memory content. (From Squire and Zola-Morgan, 1991.)

Because he was a surgical patient and because the surgery's side effects were so undesirable, H.M. is really a unique case. There are, however, other patients who resemble H.M. in certain respects; one such was discovered and studied by Antonio Damasio, Hanna Damasio, and their colleagues (Damasio et al. 1985). He came to their attention in the mid-1970s and has been intensively tested and observed for the past 15 years. The patient, Boswell, was infected with herpes simplex encephalitis, which caused bilateral lesions to the temporal lobes, as well as severe damage to orbitalfrontal cortex and the basal forebrain. Boswell's lesions to the temporal lobe were much more extensive than those of H.M. Boswell lost all of the temporal pole as well as neocortical fields in anterior compartments of the temporal lobe (figure 5.3).

What was the effect on his behavioral capacities? Boswell not only has a catastrophic impairment of anterograde memory, but his retrograde memory is devastated. His autobiographical memory, for example, is almost nonexistent, and he is as poor at cued recall as at free recall. For example, he remembers that he was married, though he cannot recognize recent photographs of his wife and recalls almost nothing of his life with her; he remembers that he has children and that he worked in advertising, but recalls no details of these parts of his life. He cannot order his prominent life events relative to each other—whether he worked in advertising before the children were born or after, whether he lived in a certain town before the Korean war or after, and so on. For many humdrum events in our lives, all of us can be hazy in recollection of relative time ordering; for Boswell, even important events in his autobiography, if remembered at all, are hazily sequenced.

Boswell resembles H.M. in the respect that his anterograde memory is seriously impaired. He has only a 40-sec memory provided he is not distracted, and has no memory for events outside that time width. He cannot remember that he was visited a few minutes ago, that he had tamales for lunch or even that he had lunch, that it was snowing this morning, and that he was surprised

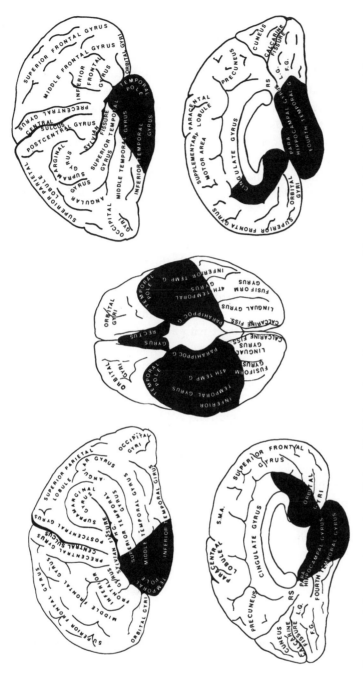

Figure 5.3 A diagram of patient Boswell's brain. The blackened areas show extensive areas of damage in both left and right temporal lobe cortices, and smaller lesions in both ventromedial frontal lobe cortices. Note that the temporal lobe lesions destroy not only the medial (internal) part of the lobe (which contains the hippocampal formation and the entorhinal cortex), but also the temporal pole, the lateral (external), and the inferior regions. It is because of the nonmedial temporal lobe damage that Boswell has such a remarkable retrograde memory loss, unlike patient H. M., whose damage is confined to the medial sector. (Courtesy Hanna Damasio.)

to see the snow only a few minutes earlier. To questions, he confabulates freely and easily, and he is described as alert, pleasant, and cooperative. Some knowledge is spared. As before the disease, he plays quite a good game of checkers, despite calling it "bingo," and he is affable to visitors. His casual speech sounds quite normal, he reads easy material quite well, he is socially conversant though not always appropriate, and he can use common objects such as a television, chair, toothbrush, etc. More about Boswell's profound deficits in recognizing, naming, and defining common natural objects such as a snail or a cat will be discussed below (section 10, Modules and Networks).

How much of the brain that Boswell and H.M. had lost was critical for storing information in long-term memory? Part of the answer emerged in studies by Larry Squire, David Amaral, and Stuart Zola-Morgan of a unique case in San Diego. The patient, R.B., had suffered an ischemic attack which selectively impaired his ability to learn and remember new information. His retrograde memory appeared to be normal. In this regard, he resembled H.M., although R.B.'s deficits were much milder. A wide range of behavioral tests was conducted to determine the nature and extent of R.B.'s amnesia. In addition to normal conditioning, R.B. also showed normal priming. The priming[14] test is as follows: present the subject with a list of words to read: "motel," "canary," etc. In a free recall test, or even a recognition test, amnesic patients fare far worse than controls. But in a test where they are asked to complete the word fragments on a list simply by *guessing*, amnesic patients reproduce the original list as well as controls. This, despite no conscious knowledge of having seen the words earlier (Warrington and Weiskrantz 1968).

Five years after the ischemic event, R.B. died of congestive heart failure. At this time, his brain was carefully sectioned and examined (Zola-Morgan et al. 1986). The lesion was discovered to have been bilateral and restricted to the hippocampus. Within the hippocampus, the lesion was mainly confined to a specific region, the CA1 field (figure 5.4). This case, especially in the context of other work on animal models of amnesia[15] as well as on human subjects,[16] narrowed down the short list of structures critical for learning new information and provided a clearer focus for anatomists and physiologists. High-resolution magnetic resonance imaging (MRI) brain scans have also been used recently to identify very precisely the location of lesions in humans on the same date at which their performance in memory tests is evaluated, rather than waiting until autopsy (Press et al. 1989, Squire et al. 1989).

In seeking a more exact specification of just what storage capacities were spared in amnesic patients, Squire and colleagues (Benzing and Squire 1989) found that patients who could no longer learn and recall new information could display other learning in addition to motor skills and priming. For example, they showed a roughly normal curve for learning to resolve random-dot stereograms[17] and the learned response persisted for at least seven days. (See figure 4.30 for a random-dot stereogram.) As in the other tests, the subjects had no recollection of having seen anything like the test-set before, but their improved performance belied the conscious judgment. Their brains had indeed learned to resolve random-dot stereograms quite efficiently (figure 5.5).

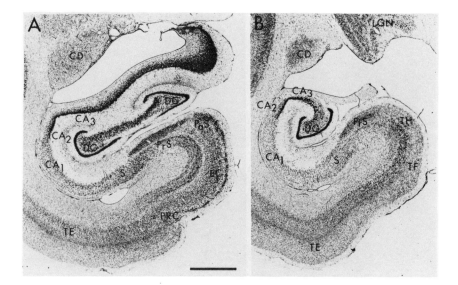

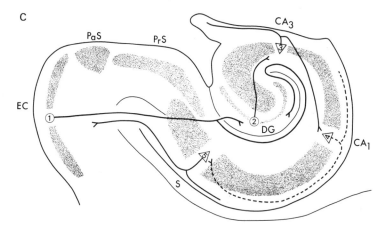

Figure 5.4 Coronal sections through rostral (A) and caudal (B) portions of Nissl-stained macaque monkey hippocampal formation. Calibration bar, 2 mm. CA1, CA2, CA3, hippocampal fields; DG, dentate gyrus; PaS, parasubiculum; PRC, perirhinal cortex; S, subiculum; TE, visual association isocortex; TF/TH, polymodal association cortex of parahippocampal gyrus; CD, caudate nucleus; LGN, lateral geniculate nucleus. (From Amaral 1987.) (C) Schematic drawing of the primate hippocampal formation. The numbers and the solid lines connecting them show the unidirectional flow of information (from entorhinal cortex [1], to DG [2], to CA3 [3], to CA1 [4], to the subiculum [5]). In case R. B., a lesion of the CA1 field (represented by cell 4 and the dashed lines) disrupted the sequence of information flow in the hippocampus. (From Zola-Morgan et al. 1986.)

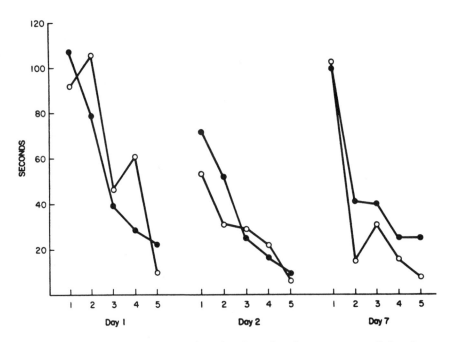

Figure 5.5 Mean response time per trial to identify random-dot stereograms. Filled circles, 9 amnesic patients; open circles, 9 control subjects. The standard errors of the mean were similar for the two groups, averaging 18.4 sec for the amnesic patients across the 15 data points (range, 3.9–28) and 13.8 sec for the control subjects (range, 1.3–25.7). (From Benzing and Squire 1989.)

Benzing and Squire also found "adaptation-level" effects, meaning that amnesic patients, like normal controls, showed that judgments about the weight of objects hefted were modified by previous encounters with the task.

Temporal lobe amnesia is a truly remarkable and terrifying neurological phenomenon. Because the structures implicated are relatively circumscribed, research aimed at discovering the neuronal plasticity relevant to memory for events and individuals has concentrated on primate hippocampus and related temporal lobe structures. A unique property of the hippocampus is its strategic location as a convergence region for information from nearly all high-order cortical areas, as well as from brain stem nuclei. Every sensory modality projects to the hippocampus (via entorhinal cortex), and most have reciprocal projections back (figure 5.6). In dramatic developments, the exploration of the connection between hippocampal structures and memory has advanced at all levels of brain organization from behavior to genes. With the intensive "to-ing and fro-ing" that is the hallmark of co-evolution in science, research has pushed forward at every level, from the study of the profiles of various kinds of amnesia, to exploring by lesion in animals the functional role of the hippocampal structures, to the pathways, cell types, and cellular organization of the hippocampus, to the identification of a modification in postsynaptic cells following simultaneous activation of presynaptic and postsynaptic cells, and most recently, to the isolation of the specific molecules that have a role in the modification and to the location of the modification. And finally, to the charac-

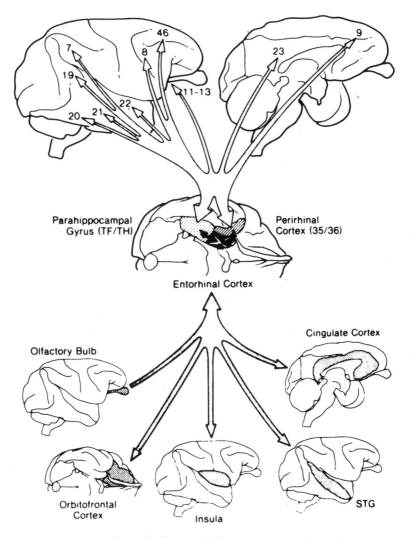

Figure 5.6 Summary of cortical afferent and efferent connections of entorhinal cortex, which is the major source of projections to the hippocampus. The major cortical input originates in the adjacent parahippocampal gyrus and in the perirhinal cortex. These regions in turn receive projections from several polysensory associational regions in the frontal, temporal, and parietal lobes. The entorhinal cortex also receives cortical inputs directly from other presumed polysensory regions and one unimodal input from the olfactory bulb. With the exception of the olfactory projection, these projections are reciprocal. The numbers refer to cortical areas identified by the Brodmann convention. STG, superior temporal gyrus. (From Squire and Zola-Morgan [1988]. Memory: brain systems and behavior. *Trends in Neurosciences* 11: 170–175.)

terization and cloning of the genes for the prominent proteins (Gasic and Heinemann 1991, Moriyoshi et al. 1991)

Although the main questions about what exactly the hippocampus does remain unanswered, this "long green limb" of research extending from behavior to receptor proteins and their genes is one of the burgeoning success stories in neuroscience. Because it is also a story where the wealth of neural detail makes realistic computer modeling seem almost ripe for the picking, it seems particularly germane in this context, though as we shall see, modeling a structure so removed from the periphery is problematic. In the next section, we shall dilate on the tale just summarized. For brevity's sake and because it is the fan-out point, we emphasize mainly the work on cellular modification, providing references for explication of the multitudinous details of behavioral, lesion, physiological, and anatomical findings.

3 DONALD HEBB AND SYNAPTIC PLASTICITY

If global learning depends on local changes in cells, how does a cell know, without the guiding hand of intelligence, when it should change and by how much, and just where? There are many possible ways a neuron could change to embody adaptations. For example, new dendrites might sprout, or there might be extension of existing branches, or existing synapses could change, or new synapses might be created. In the other direction, pruning could decrease the dendrites or bits of dendrites, and therewith decrease the number of synapses, or the synapses on remaining branches could be shut down altogether. These are all postsynaptic changes in the dendrites. There could also be changes in the axons; for example, there might be changes in the membrane (channels, etc.), or new branches might be formed, and genes might be induced to produce new neurochemicals or more of the old ones. Presynaptic changes could include changes in the number of vesicles released per spike and the number of transmitter molecules contained in each vesicle (figure 5.7). Finally, the whole cell might die, taking with it all the synapses it formerly supported. This broad range of structural modifiability can be conveniently condensed for this discussion by referring simply to synapses, since every modification either involves synaptic change directly or indirectly, or can be *reasonably* so represented. Connectivity is a neuron's *sine qua non*, and to change the population of synapses or the strength of a synapse is to change connectivity.

When and where should the decision to modify synapses be made? Basically, the choices are rather limited. Essentially, the decision to change can be made either globally or locally. If it is made globally, then the signal for change will be permissive, in effect saying, "You may modify yourself now," but not dictating exactly where or by how much or in what direction. On the other hand, if the decision for modification is to be specific to a synapse, then locality in space and locality in time are the two relevant variables. More exactly, if plasticity is going to depend on signals currently present at a synapse (i.e., present during a very small time window), then the modifications will be limited to structures close enough spatially to be causal players within the brief

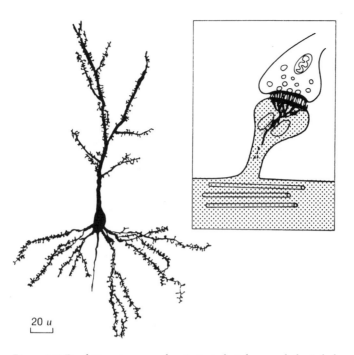

20 *u*

Figure 5.7 Dendritic spines may be strategic loci for morphological changes that subserve long-term memory. (Left) Drawing of a pyramidal neuron from the rat cortex, with a typically large number of dendritic spines. (Right) Schematic representation of a dendritic spine (shaded) with the characteristic filaments and sacs constituting the spine apparatus, and the postsynaptic density. The elongated tubes in the dendritic shaft are microtubules that participate in the formation of spines. Spines usually bear one excitatory synapse. (From Dudai 1989.)

time span. The next question, therefore, is this: assuming spatial contiguity is important, what *temporal* relations might signal a structural modification with the result that the weights change, and change in the appropriate direction (either stronger or weaker)?

These were the questions addressed by Donald Hebb in his 1949 book, *Organization of Behavior*.[18] The crux of his insight, slightly reconstructed, is this: coactivation of connected cells should result in a modification of weights so that the probability of the postsynaptic cell firing given the presynaptic cell fires, is increased. This makes eminently good sense, because it allows for associated world events to be represented by cell interaction. Taking a philosophical perspective, one might say that it is a general way, *consistent with mechanistic assumptions*, for the brain to get representations out of nonrepresenting events, and for transforming complex representations into more complex representations. It is a very general answer to "where does the knowledge come from?" that in its abstract formulation and mechanistic slant is akin to Darwin's answer to "where do species come from?" And like Darwin's insight, Hebb's insight provides only a framework to be fleshed out by experiments at the micro- and macrolevels. The nature of the mechanism for modifying synaptic weights is not specified by Hebb's proposal, and not until some hundred years after publication of *The Origin of Species* was the key mechanism for inheritance of characteristics unearthed. Of course, the general idea of Hebbian learning is nowhere near as broad and encompassing as Darwin's hypothesis, and as we shall see, there is already evidence for non-Hebbian modification of synapses in the course of learning.

Hebb's statement of his proposal for synaptic weight change says:

When an axon of a cell A is near enough to excite cell B or repeatedly or persistently takes part in firing it, some growth or metabolic change takes place in both cells such that A's efficiency, as one of the cells firing B, is increased. (1949, p. 62)

The simplest formal version of the Hebb rule for changing the strength of the weight w_{BA} between neuron A, with an average firing rate of V_A, projecting to neuron B, with an average firing rate V_B, is:

$$\Delta w_{BA} = \varepsilon V_B V_A \tag{1}$$

This states that the variables relevant to synaptic change are the co-occurring activity levels, and that increases in synaptic strength are proportional to the product of the presynaptic and postsynaptic values. The weight changes, note, are all positive, for the firing rates are all positive. The simple rule admits of many variations that still qualify as Hebbian. For example, the postsynaptic term, V_B, could be replaced with $(V_B - \bar{V}_B)$, where $\bar{V}_B$ is the average value of the postsynaptic activity. The average may be taken over a few seconds, or longer, perhaps several hours. This formulation may be preferred because it allows weight changes that can be positive or negative, and hence is more flexible than the simple Hebb rule. A further variation would be to make the postsynaptic term sensitive to the rate of change of the postsynaptic activity, $\dot{V}_B$ (Klopf 1982, Tesauro 1986).

What Hebb proposed is really a *principle* rather than an algorithm or a mechanism. A learning principle specifies only the general conditions under which plasticity should occur, such as temporal and spatial relationships between presynaptic and postsynaptic signals, but it may leave undetermined the exact nature of the pre and post conditions and the exact location of the plasticity. A learning algorithm supplies the abstract requirements of the mechanism, inasmuch as it must itemize and specify the conditions that must be satisfied in order that information gets stored. Notice that Hebb's learning principle could be realized by a variety of algorithms, each of which in turn could be implemented in a variety of physical mechanisms. Thus, Hebbian synapses can be featured in conditioning algorithms (Klopf 1987), associative nets (Kohonen 1984, Gluck and Thompson 1987), error-correcting nets (Anderson and Mozer 1981, Hopfield 1984), and developmental models (Linsker 1986 and 1988; Miller et al. 1989).

When a synapse is described as "anti-Hebbian," this usually means that there is a decrease in coupling strength owing to the same set of temporal conditions hitherto specified for synapse strengthening (figure 5.8). Thus in this sense, "anti-Hebbian" is still Hebbian, rather in the way that an antiparticle is still a particle, and unlike anti-intellectuals who are in no sense intellectuals. Likewise, "pseudo-Hebbian" refers to the condition where synaptic modifica-

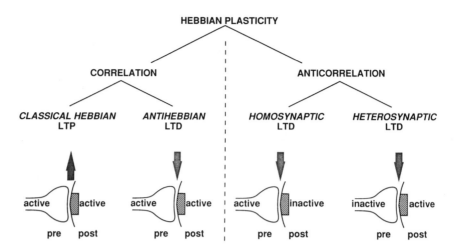

Figure 5.8 Tree diagram of the various forms of Hebbian changes of the synapse. Upward arrows represent increases in synaptic efficacy; downward arrows represent decreases. LTP, long-term potentiation; LTD, long-term depression.

tion depends only on depolarization of the postsynaptic cell and does not require an action potential in that cell (Kelso et al., 1986). For example, in the second formulation above, it is left unspecified whether firing of the post-synaptic cell is necessary or whether merely depolarization or perhaps even hyperpolarization by some critical amount is sufficient. Note, however, that whether the postsynaptic cell is only depolarized or whether it succeeds in generating an action potential, the change in synaptic efficacy is still, broadly speaking, Hebbian, even as punctuated equilibrium is still evolution (Gould and Lewontin 1979).

If, relative to the arena of presynaptic and postsynaptic structures, any modification whatever in synaptic weight gets described as Hebbian, then useful distinctions between significantly different kinds of modifications are obscured. Practical reasons, therefore, urge us to be a little more precise about what properties are conventionally considered essential to Hebbian plasticity: (1) the plasticity is specific to the *synapse* where the pre and post activity is, and (2) the plasticity depends conjointly on *both* the presynaptic and the post-synaptic cells, not on one or the other separately, and (3) it depends exclusively on those cells, not on the activity of additional cells.

On the basis of these criteria, some synaptic modifications have been found that are not Hebbian (figure 5.9). With respect to the first condition, Edelman (1987) has hypothesized a long-term modification that is a property of the whole cell in the sense that synaptic efficacy is modified at every terminal of the presynaptic cell. There is some evidence that this sort of change does in fact occur in cells in the rat hippocampus (Bonhoeffer et al. 1989). Because the modification is enjoyed by the whole cell and is not confined to the specific synapse where conjoint presynaptic and postsynaptic activity occurred, the modification is not Hebbian, strictly speaking. With respect to the second criterion, Kandel and his colleagues (1987) have found a synaptic modification in *Aplysia* where the conjoint activity is between the presynaptic neurons and

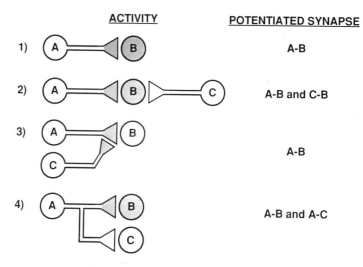

ACTIVITY   **POTENTIATED SYNAPSE**

1)   A-B

2)   A-B and C-B

3)   A-B

4)   A-B and A-C

Figure 5.9 Conditions for induction of plasticity and site of expression of plasticity may vary. Although there are many conceivable variations, so far there is evidence for a few, each of which requires concurrent activity in two elements. Shaded elements are active during induction. The sites of potentiation are indicated to the right. (1) Traditional Hebbian synapse, in which conjoint activity in A and B leads to a potentiated A–B synapse. (2) The same conditions for induction lead also to potentiation of another synapse (C–B) from an unstimulated cell, C. This is heterosynaptic potentiation. In (3), the condition for induction involves the activity in neurons A and C, and even though activity in B is not required, the A–B synapse may be potentiated nonetheless. In (4) concurrent activity in A and B is needed to trigger plasticity at the A–B synapse, but once triggered, then synapses between A and other neurons, e.g., A–C, are also strengthened.

its connecting *interneuron*, and this turns out to be sufficient for a presynaptic modification (figure 5.9). Such a modification thereby results in a larger effect transmitted to the postsynaptic cell. In this instance, the conjoint activity of the pre- and *post*synaptic cells is neither necessary nor sufficient for synaptic modification. As we shall soon discuss, Llinás and his colleagues (1990) have found a modification that appears to be independent of activity in the presynaptic cell. These criteria are, of course, semantic conventions, but they reflect real differences in phenomena that, at the current stage at least, are usefully tagged with a separate name.

4 MEMORIES ARE MADE OF THIS: MECHANISMS OF NEURONAL PLASTICITY

Why is it difficult to find cellular changes that are identifiable as learning dependent? Because minimally it must be shown that the changes are directly owed to effects of experience, not to some other property of the milieu or to an intrinsic developmental flowering of the cell, and it must be shown that the changes in behavior are dependent on cellular modifications. As well, it must be shown that there is modification in the cell's responses to the test stimulus, and that the modification lasts beyond the duration of the learning phase.

Evidently, single-cell recordings, extracellular or preferably intracellular, are needed to determine whether these circumstances obtain. This can be exceptionally tricky for a number of reasons. For example, the prime postsynaptic site will obviously be on dendrites, and dendrites, tiny as they are, present ferocious obstacles to intracellular recording (but see Taube and Schwartzkroin 1988). Controlling the cell's input, voltage, and diachronic biography is generally a supremely pernickety art. Care must be taken to exclude changes that might be occurring in other parts of the circuit such as a network of inhibitory interneurons.

Long-Term Potentiation (LTP)

In 1973 Tim Bliss and Terje Lømo, studying the rabbit hippocampus, discovered a property of dentate granule cells that had the earmarks of a learning effect. They had stimulated the primary afferents of the cells with a high-frequency volley of pulses, and tested the responses of postsynaptic cells to a low-frequency pulse before and after the experimental manipulation (figure 5.10). In comparing the cells' responses before and after the high-frequency volley, Bliss and Lømo discovered that the postsynaptic excitability was potentiated after the volley; that is, depolarization to a mild input exceeded the level seen prior to the volley. The potentiation lasted for as long as they could keep the preparation intact. Certainly for hours, sometimes for days or weeks, the cell displayed a potentiated depolarization, indicating that something in the chain involving presynaptic cell and postsynaptic cell had undergone a modification (see also Douglas and Goddard 1975). Subsequent studies revealed that LTP has *input specificity*; that is, the potentiation is confined to the synapse active during the tetanic stimulus. Inactive synapses on the same cell will not be potentiated. This effect came to be known as "long-term potentiation," or LTP.[19] Because the cells were hippocampal, and because of H.M.'s profile, about ten years after Bliss and Lømo's initial discovery, LTP became a celebrated neuronal player.

Before following the LTP ball of yarn further, we must pause and turn to the anatomists to reveal the wiring patterns, cell morphology, and (by means of electron and confocal microscopy) the synaptic distribution in the hippocampus. This will provide a clearer understanding of the research thrust and give the physiological findings a trellis on which to climb. (In honor of Kant, one might say that physiology without anatomy is blind, and anatomy without physiology is empty.) So provisioned, we can begin to speculate on computational resources of the hippocampus. Hunches about these resources drew upon the matrixlike connections made visible by Golgi staining, and later by horseradish peroxidase (HRP) staining (McNaughton and Morris 1987; Rolls 1989). Figures 5.4 and 5.10 make clear the basic pattern of connections in the hippocampus. Note that pyramidal cells in CA3 are excitatory and recurrent. The pattern of inputs and outputs of the CA3 region of the hippocampus has the watermark of a recurrent net (see chapter 3). In breathtakingly difficult anatomical studies on rats, Amaral et al. (1990) calculated that the mossy

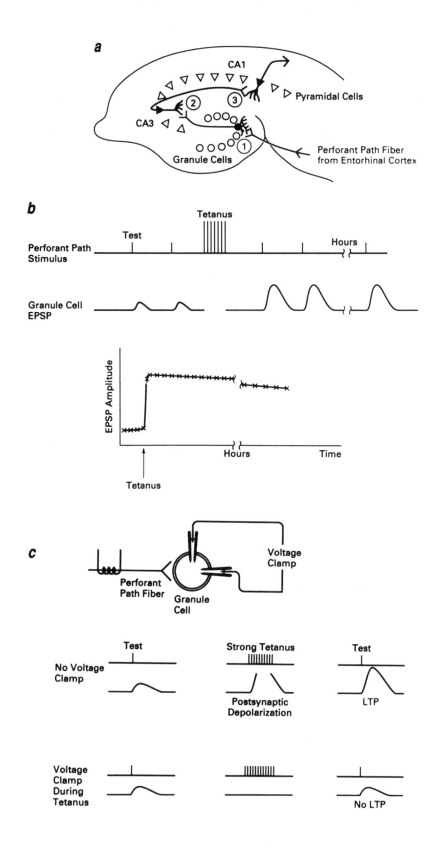

fiber projection to the CA3 field is both spatially and numerically surprisingly limited. Collectively the CA3 pyramidal cells get about 33×10^4 contacts from the mossy fibers; a single granule cell probably makes contact with only about 14 pyramidal cells, however, and each pyramidal is innervated by only about 46 granule cells, the upper reaches of the dendritic tree receiving the heaviest contact. The recurrent collaterals on a CA3 pyramidal cell from other CA3 pyramidals number about 6000, or about 1.8% of the CA3 cell population, located on the dendritic tree spaced between the mossy and perforant inputs[20] (figure 5.11).

Four key questions had to be asked at this point: (1) Does LTP have anything to do with learning as seen at the behavioral level? (2) What precisely are the loci of change? (3) What is the nature of the structural changes that result in LTP? (4) What are the principles whereby changes in individual cells yield changes in circuitry that can be interpreted as the animal having learned some specific thing; i.e., how do you get coherence in a cell population out of individual cell modification? The behavioral question (1) was not easy to answer, because the LTP Bliss and Lømo had seen was experimentally induced by stimulating afferent fibers with a 100-Hz volley for about 1 sec, not by recording while the animal was learning some task. Moreover, it was not known from just what cells one should record as the animal learned a particular task, even were the immense technical difficulties of recording from awake and behaving animals overcome. Negative results, for example, might merely mean you were not recording from the cells involved in the task.[21] The fourth question puts us squarely back in the local–global conundrum, and hypotheses from computer modeling will have to be pulled in to help weave the cellular data into a coherent story.

Researchers wishing to address the question of mechanism found, as had Bliss and Lømo, that it was experimentally far more convenient to work on a slice of hippocampal tissue kept alive in a nutrient bath than to study the cells in the whole animal. The in vitro preparation thus became the preferred set-up as various physiological and pharmacological studies were undertaken. To address the behavioral question, however, the whole animal must be studied. To do this, Richard Morris and his colleagues in Edinburgh designed a series of experiments that would ground a plausible hypothesis about the relation between LTP as seen in the experimental condition and learning as seen in the awake, behaving rat. Their results, though not conclusive, do lend positive evidence to the macrolevel significance of microlevel LTP. The results have

Figure 5.10 Long-term potentiation (LTP) in the hippocampus. (a) Schematic drawing of a hippocampal slice. Fibers from the entorhinal cortex enter the hippocampus via the perforant path and synapse on dendrites of granule cell neurons (1). These in turn synapse on pyramidal cell neurons in the CA3 region of the hippocampus (2). The CA3 pyramidal cells synapse on other pyramidal cell neurons in the CA1 region (3). (b) LTP of the perforant path to granule cell neuron synapse (excitatory postsynaptic potential [EPSP]). (c) When the postsynaptic cell is voltage-clamped to prevent depolarization during the tetanus, even a strong tetanic stimulus does not produce LTP. This implies that LTP is essentially Hebbian. (From Levitan and Kaczmarek [1991]. *The Neuron: Cell and Molecular Biology*. Oxford University Press.)

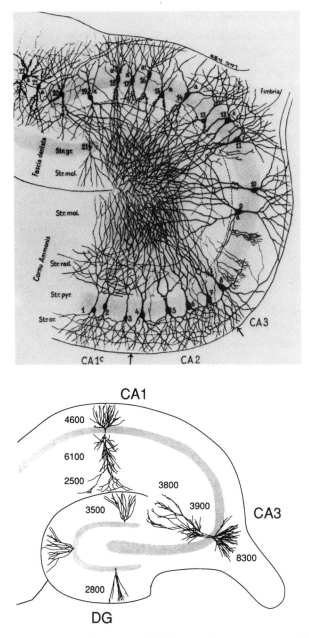

Figure 5.11 (A) Illustration of Golgi-stained neurons in mouse hippocampus. Large cells of polymorphic region of dentate gyrus (cells 21 and 22 "mossy cells") and pyramidal cells of the CA3 region (cells 8 and 10–19) have specialized spines on their proximal dendrites, which are the primary termination of mossy fibers from the dentate gyrus. Interneuron of basket type is pictured as cell 9. Str. mol., stratum moleculare; str. rad., stratum radiatum; str. pyr., stratum of pyramidal cell bodies; str. or., stratum oriens. (From Lorento de Nó, 1934.) (B) Diagram of the rat hippocampus with computer-generated drawings of reconstructed dentate granule cells and hippocampal pyramidal cells. In the dentate gyrus (DG) three cells are drawn. The total dendrite length of each neuron was measured for 48 granule cells. The average total dendritic length for cells in the suprapyramidal blade (3500 μm) is significantly larger than for cells in the infra-pyramidal blade (2800 μm). For the CA3 and CA1 cells, the dendritic lengths indicated are the

two parts, and both depend on the prior discovery of a substance called AP5 (also known as APV)[22] that blocks induction of LTP in slice preparations.[23] Given its selective effect on induction of LTP, its reversibility and its lack of toxic effects, AP5 became an enormously useful tool for manipulating conditions to test whether LTP and hippocampus-dependent learning are related.

First, Morris et al. showed that induction of LTP by tetanic stimulation in vivo was blocked by AP5, and the degree of blocking was dose-dependent. This was a crucial first step since the pharmacological profiles of in vitro and in vivo preparations do not always match, and there was no guarantee that AP5 would have the same effect in both conditions. Having achieved a success here, Morris then turned to the behavioral test. If AP5 reaches the hippocampus of the brain of a behaving rat would it have any effect on learning? For the experiment, he chose the well-known water-maze task, wherein a rat put into a vat of milky water must learn where the submerged platform is, assuming, quite safely in fact, that the rat would rather stand than swim. Learning the platform whereabouts, and spatial learning in general, is believed to require an intact hippocampus.[24]

What Morris discovered was that learning the water-maze task is indeed retarded by application of AP5, and moreover, that the degree of retardation is dose dependent. Not only that, but the AP5 *learning* curve at the behavioral level and the AP5 *blocking* curve at the cellular level are suggestively congruent (figure 5.12). The two parts of the Morris laboratory's results thus lend some support, jointly and severally, to the hypothesis that LTP is a cellular phenomenon that has something to do with learning in the natural state. The missing piece is this: LTP has not been seen in vivo as a result of *natural stimulation*, without the aid of tetanic stimulation from the experimenter. So the question is open: did the perfused AP5 block the in vitro style LTP in the animal, or was learning inhibited for some other reason? Although the first alternative is reasonable, it is well to bear in mind that the answer is not known for sure. (For criticism, see Keith and Rudy 1990.)

In the meanwhile, developments at the molecular level on the question of the locus and nature of the changes were proceeding apace, and various pieces are now beginning to interlock. As remarked earlier, the goal of research is to zero in on the loci and the nature of the changes; if we know *where*, then we might be able to figure *how*. To answer those questions, it is necessary to know, *inter alia*, about the transmitters, the receptors, and the details of cell behavior in a range of conditions. A great deal of this has now been uncovered, especially in slice preparations. Glutamate is the "first violin" of the neurotransmitters released by the hippocampal afferents. It is an excitatory neurotransmitter for most pyramidal neurons, and it binds to three different

averages for four CA3 neurons and eight CA1 neurons. In the population of CA3 neurons, about 8300 μm of dendrite were located in the stratum oriens, 3900 μm in stratum radiatum and approximately 3800 μm in stratum lacunosum-moleculare. For the population of CA1 cells, approximately 4600 μm of dendrite were located in the stratum oriens, 6100 μm in stratum radiatum and 2500 μm in stratum lacunosum-moleculare. (From Amaral et al. 1990.)

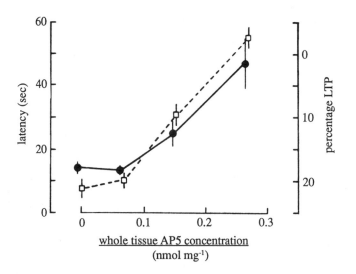

Figure 5.12 Plot showing the escape latency (the time it takes the rat to find the platform) and strength of LTP as a function of AP5 concentration in the hippocampus. Latency data are in open boxes, and plotted on the left axis; percentage of LTP 40 min after tetanus are the filled circles, plotted on the right axis. Whole-tissue AP5 concentration was measured at sacrifice; the measure includes the amount not only in neurons but in blood vessels, and so forth. To measure the amount in the neuronal extracellular space, Morris refined the analysis and discovered that the effective concentration was lower by a factor of about 30 than the whole-tissue concentration (not shown). The congruence between latency and AP5 concentration illustrated in this figure was unchanged by the analysis. (From Morris et al. 1990.)

types of receptors on the postsynaptic cell. The two glutamate receptor are run-of-the-mill ligand-gated ion channels, meaning the transmitter binds by virtue of fitting into the slots and juts of the receptor molecules. These are the kainate (or K) and quisqualate (or Q) receptors. The names derive from specific agonists (activating agents) concocted in the laboratory, not the brain. (These two types are now believed to be the same receptor, often labeled simply as the AMPA receptor, the name derived from the experimental agonist.) Other neurotransmitters, playing second fiddle in a modulating role, include glycine and norepinephrine, and biology being what it is, there may be others not yet detected.

The third receptor in the story (figure 5.13) turns out to be the critical piece for plasticity. Unlike the K−Q receptors, this receptor is both ligand gated and voltage sensitive. The NMDA receptor, so named because it is activated by the concocted glutamate analog, N-methyl-D-aspartate, turns out to be critical for LTP in the CA1 region. The NMDA receptor is a protein that has binding sites for both glutamate and glycine, but, in addition, it has a channel that opens to extracellular ions only when the cell is depolarized from its resting level by roughly 30 mV or more. Reflecting the dual ligand-binding/voltage-sensitive factors, the NMDA receptor is often referred to as the NMDA receptor-ionophore complex. Its kinetics are complex. So long as the cell is not depolarized by the critical amount, magnesium ions (Mg^{2+}) are attracted to the negativity of the cell's interior and sit astride the NMDA pore, barring

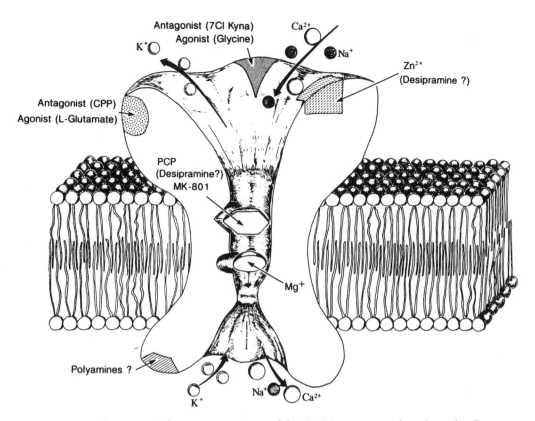

Figure 5.13 Schematic representation of the NMDA receptor ion channel complex illustrating sites for binding of glutamate, glycine, zinc, and magnesium, and also where certain pharmacological agents are believed to bind. PCP, phencyclidine; CPP, 3-(2-carboxy-piperazin-4-yl)propyl-1-phosphonic acid, an analog of AP5. (From Wong and Kemp 1991. Reproduced with permission, from *Annual Review of Pharmacology and Toxicology*, Vol. 31, © 1991 by Annual Reviews, Inc.)

other ions. When both glutamate and glycine are bound to their proper sites, and the cell is sufficiently depolarized, then Mg^{2+} ions tend to drift out of the pore and Na^+ and Ca^{2+} ions can enter the cell.

The temporal properties of the NMDA receptor are also unusual. Once the NMDA channel opens, it stays open for about 100–200 msec, this duration being determined by the "off rate" for glutamate, meaning how long it takes for the glutamate to move off the receptor protein (see figure 5.21). In the world of synaptic events, where ligand-binding glutamate channels typically open for only about 5 or 10 msec, 100–200 msec is a surprisingly long time. Perhaps this is a time constant that the system exploits in some manner related to efficiency of learning, or to coordination of events in the learning context, and thus plays a special role in associative memory.[25]

When events have moved along to the point where the NMDA pore opens, Ca^{2+} appears to be the next character in the modification story, and the problem is to determine the role of Ca^{2+} in cell modification. Bear in mind that the *cause* of LTP, or more correctly, the set of conditions necessary and sufficient

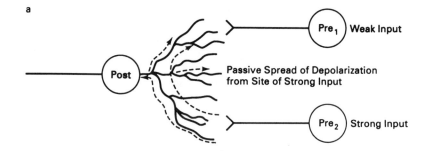

a

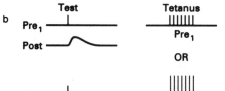

Passive Spread of Depolarization
from Site of Strong Input

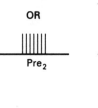

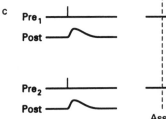

b

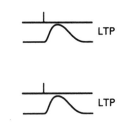

c

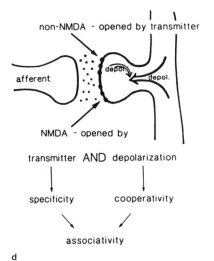

d

for inducing LTP, is one thing; the *effect*, that is, the structural changes subserving long-lasting postsynaptic potentiation, is another. Nothing in the described kinetics demonstrates that the long-lasting modification for *maintenance* of LTP is postsynaptic, but only that *induction* of LTP in certain cells, namely CA1 hippocampal cells, requires the postsynaptic NMDA receptor–ionophore complex. So far as we have gone in the story, the matter of location of the structural changes subserving LTP maintenance is still open.

It is remarkable that the search for Hebbian dynamics at the cellular level uncovered a component at the molecular level that is Hebbian—in effect, a Hebbian protein. That is, by requiring both receptor-site binding *and* previous depolarization of the cell, the NMDA receptor can act as a kind of conjunction detector. The way it works is this: the $K-Q$ receptors at a given synapse, S_1, cannot by themselves depolarize the membrane sufficiently to activate fully the NMDA receptor at that synapse, so the depolarization has to come by electrotonic spread from a different highly activated synapse, S_2, located elsewhere—for example, on a neighboring spine. When both S_1 and S_2 are activated, then depolarization at S_1 is sufficient for the NMDA channel to open, and then the pore admits Ca^{2+} to kick off the process leading to synapse modification that strengthens the synaptic connection between S_1 and the presynaptic cell (Kelso et al. 1986).[26] This is how LTP can be an associative phenomenon and how it subserves Hebbian learning. And this is why NMDA may be described as a Hebbian mechanism (figure 5.14).

As noted, AP5 blocks LTP in CA1 pyramidal cells, and the molecular studies reveal that in particular AP5 is an antagonist for glutamate and blocks by competition with glutamate for a specific receptor site on the NMDA receptor. Phencyclidine (PCP), the potent drug whose street name is angel dust, also exerts its effects at the NMDA receptor. In contrast to APV, however, it does so by blocking the pore. Accordingly, the linkage between NMDA and LTP, and between LTP and learning, and (by transitivity of "links"), between NMDA and learning, suggest that research is closing in on a cellular element that has an important role in one form of learning. Not, as some might have hoped in their unfettered fantasies, *the* cellular mechanism for learning, but a phenomenon whose conditions, profile, and consequences are decidedly worth tracking down.

Since one can find the LTP–NMDA–learning triad very heady stuff, there is a temptation to ignore the warts and to overestimate what has actually been

Figure 5.14 Associative long-term potentiation. (a) Diagram depicting the spatial relationships between a strong and a weak synaptic input. (b) Stimulation of the strong input produces LTP, but stimulation of the weak input alone does not. (c) When the strong and weak inputs are paired, the depolarization produced by the strong inputs spreads to the site of the weak input, and contributes to the induction of LTP. (From Levitan and Kaczmarek 1991.) (d) Schematic representation of the mechanism for input specificity and cooperativity. NMDA and non-NMDA receptor channels are located in each single spine, not necessarily separated as indicated here. The depolarization sufficient to open the NMDA channel is produced partly by non-NMDA channels in the spine itself as well as by the heterosynaptic spread of current from other active synapses. (From Wigström and Gustaffsson 1988.)

demonstrated. To counterbalance uncritical enthusiasm, we wish to summarize several cautionary considerations: (1) in vivo, AP5 may block learning by blocking certain normal cell functions, and hence blocking LTP may be a secondary, not a primary effect. If so, then the interpretation of the Morris experiments relating the failure of AP5 rats to learn the water-maze task to LTP suppression may be incorrect. (2) LTP has not yet been observed in the hippocampus of the whole brain except by stimulating the afferent fibers with a high-frequency volley. *No one has yet seen LTP simply by recording from post-synaptic cells during learning, where nature is left to provide the high-frequency volley.* Why is this a concern? First, note that the experimental stimulus is tetanic; i.e., a *set* of fibers is *synchronously* blasted for some part of a second with high-frequency impulses, and probably this sort of input does not exactly correspond, either in intensity or synchrony, to the stimuli the cells get in the intact animal. How close might it be?

LTP and Cell Populations

To begin to answer this question, we must now turn to populations of cells. The plan is to determine whether and when there is synchrony of activation, and how such effects might be related to LTP. In vivo recordings of field

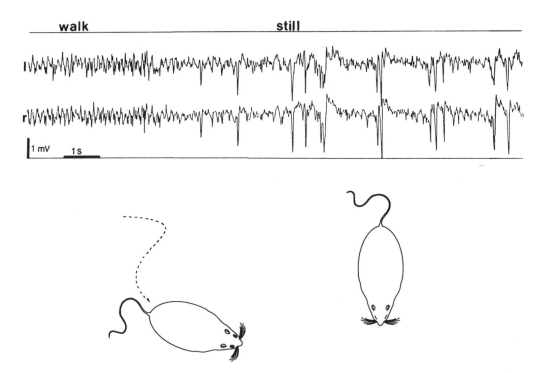

Figure 5.15 EEG recording from the striatum radiatum of the left (l) and right (r) CA1 regions of the hippocampus during the transition from walking (left) to being still (right). Note the regular theta waves during walking and large, monophasic, sharp waves during immobility. Note also that the sharp waves are synchronous bilaterally. (Adapted from Buzsáki 1989.)

potentials gives a profile of the activity of populations of cells. The cellular basis of the population wave forms is the synchrony in *synaptic* potentials, not, as one might have intuitively guessed, synchrony in action potentials. In the CA1 region of the hippocampus, two quite different population effects have been observed (Buzsáki 1989) (figure 5.15). One characteristic pattern, theta waves, is recorded when the rat is engaged in exploratory behavior, such as sniffing, rearing, and walking about, and, importantly, also during REM sleep (presumably dreaming). Theta rhythm is regular, about 4–8 Hz, and the waves are low amplitude. On the other hand, when the rat pauses in his explorations and is sitting quietly, drinking, eating, face-washing, or grooming, sharp waves are recorded. They occur most frequently during deep sleep (also known as slow-wave sleep). They occur irregularly, between about .02 and 3 per second, and their amplitude is much higher than that of theta waves (Buzsáki 1983, 1986). In figure 5.15, note especially the bilateral synchrony of both sharp waves and theta waves. Figure 5.16 also displays the impressive synchrony of sharp waves recorded from 16 different sites across a distance of 3.2 mm.

As Buzsáki points out,[27] if an activity is the au naturelle counterpart of the tetanic stimulus for LTP, it can be predicted to have features concordant with the experimental LTP stimulus: (1) the electrical activity should be relatively strong, preferably with a bursting pattern; and (2) it should involve coactivation of a number of cells. A third feature is behavioral: (3) these conditions should be satisfied when salient (memorable) events have recently occurred, such as a stimulus that is rewarded or punished. Inasmuch as sharp waves are strong relative to theta waves, involve synchrony of activations across a number of cells, and occur during a "quiet" phase following exploratory behavior, sharp waves are not implausible candidates for the natural counterpart of the experimental conditions leading to LTP[28] (Buzsáki 1989, Buzsáki and Gage 1991).

In examining this possibility, it has been found that the experimental tetanic stimulus that produces LTP in a cell also produces enhanced sharp waves as tested in vivo (Buzsáki 1984). Importantly, the enhancement lasted for several days and was seen both in sharp waves produced in response to a test stimulus and in spontaneous levels of sharp wave activity. This suggests that a sequel of LTP is increased synchrony in cellular responses (Buzsáki et al. 1987). Second, Buzsáki found that by experimentally producing sharp waves in the CA3 region in vitro, the population bursts of CA1 cells were potentiated. This synchrony of synaptic potentials he believes to be a result of the partially synchronized bursting of CA3 pyramidal cells contacting the CA1 dendrites via the Schaffer collaterals. And we know from the experimental conditions that just these conditions produce LTP at a synapse. Third, using pharmacological techniques, Horvath et al. (1988) found evidence that NMDA receptors are involved in the generation of the theta rhythm. These data are intriguing even though no one has yet seen in vivo the sharp wave–LTP pair that would be the intact counterpart of the experimental high-frequency volley–LTP pair.

What do we have so far? An experimentally induced potentiation (LTP), a possible behavioral correlate (spatial learning for reward), and a reasonable

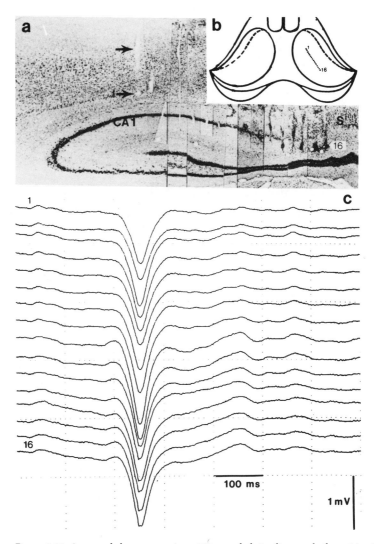

Figure 5.16 Averaged sharp waves ($n = 50$) recorded simultaneously from 16 microelectrodes along the longitudinal axis of the CA1 region of the hippocampus (a and b) as seen in (c). (a) Photomontage of the electrode tracks. (b) Dorsal view of the hippocampal formation. Dots 1–16 indicate positions of the microelectrodes. Spaces between the electrodes is 200 μm. Note simultaneous occurrence of sharp waves over a distance of 3.2 mm. (From Buzsáki 1989.)

candidate for a physiological condition (sharp waves emerging from synchrony of CA1 synaptic potentials) that might be the antecedent of a natural form of LTP. How do these elements arrange themselves into a coherent hypothesis to explain learning behavior?

Buzsáki (1989), drawing not only on the above considerations, but also on a broad range of anatomical and physiological data, presents a two-stage learning theory that knits together the behavioral, functional, population, and cellular properties of the hippocampus. It is predictive and implicational, in both the upward and downward directions. *Very* crudely speaking, the two-step routine is this: (1) *theta rhythm*: explore and experience (on line); (2) *sharp waves*: rest and consolidate (off line). More specifically, in stage (1) the fast-firing granule cells converge on the CA3 pyramidals, and produce weak and transient heterosynaptic potentiation. During this phase, the pyramidals are also receiving rhythmic inhibition originating from the septum. The pattern of potentiation in CA3 cells is a function of the pattern of input from cortical structures, and creates a temporary store of information. Because CA3 pyramidal output is silenced during this phase, CA1 cells are not activated by the CA3 pyramidal cells.

Once exploratory behavior has ceased, the CA3 cells are released from septal inhibition and they then discharge in bursts, the most recently and hence most strongly excited ones first. The extensive pattern of recurrent collaterals connecting a cell to itself and to other pyramidals in the region means the network self-organizes into complex patterns of activity. Excitation is spread to less active (earlier stimulated) cells by recurrent collaterals, which then also discharge (figure 5.17). The bursts from the CA3 pyramidals in effect "teach" the CA1 cells, the most recent "events" being the first and most strongly signaled. The CA1 cells in consequence undergo long-term modification, thereby establishing a strengthened connection that represents a correlation, for example, between the desired platform in the milky vat and a certain spatial location in the vat. A more permanent trace may also be left on some CA3 cells, as well as some cells in entorhinal cortex by way of feedback from CA1. This is the Buzsáki hypothesis (figure 5.18).

The order of events in cartoon description is this: (1) The rat moves about the maze. (2) Information about the rat's perceptions reaches the entorhinal cortex. (3) The activation vectors representing selected aspects of the information then reach the dentate granule cells. (4) Activation vectors from the granule cells code memorable representations across a subset of CA3 pyramidal cells where the information is temporarily held. Rhythmic inhibition of pyramidal through the septum ensures that only strongly stimulated cells respond to granule cell activity. (5) As soon as there is a pause in the stream of input vectors, the CA3 cells are disinhibited and discharge, potentiating the CA1 cells in such fashion as to code memorable correlations for a rather longer time.

Whether this sequence is correct to a first approximation is not yet established, and obviously the cartoon story is highly schematic. Nor do we have a precise idea how representations are coded, nor what exactly is coded. Notwithstanding all these soft spots, the hypothesis makes considerable sense as

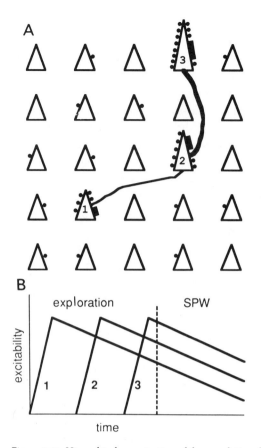

Figure 5.17 Hierarchical organization of the population sharp-wave burst depends on the recent history of the CA3 neuronal network. (A) The sizes of the pyramidal cells (triangles) represent their recent potentiation. Cells 1, 2, and 3 have been weakly potentiated by the mossy fiber terminals (black rectangles) as a result of successive activations during exploration. Two recurrent collaterals are shown (curved lines). (B) Graph illustrating the decaying potentiation of cells 1, 2, and 3. The population burst is initiated by the most potentiated cell, 3 (dashed line), and the excitation spreads progressively to the somewhat less potentiated neurons (2, 1, and unlabeled cells). A large portion of the neurons will eventually be recruited by polysynaptic reverberation. The recurrent converging excitation (black dots) will be maximum on cell 3, followed by cells 2 and 1, and sufficiently strong to induce LTP in these cells. SPW, sharp waves. (From Buzsáki 1989.)

an early venture. It is well rooted in data from cellular, circuit, and area levels, and it renders coherent some otherwise puzzling data. Importantly, it opens up a range of testable subhypotheses and predictions. One direct prediction, for example, is that the retention of a task will be significantly better if followed by a sleep episode than if followed by continuing intense activity, since sharp waves are especially manifest during deep sleep.

A caveat is in order. Nontrivial controversy prevails about whether theta waves exist in primates. Part of the problem derives from the fact that the condition of choice for eliciting theta waves is exploratory behavior, and recording from monkeys under such conditions is very difficult. Scalp recordings in humans do reveal waves in the 4–7 Hz range, but it is doubtful that these

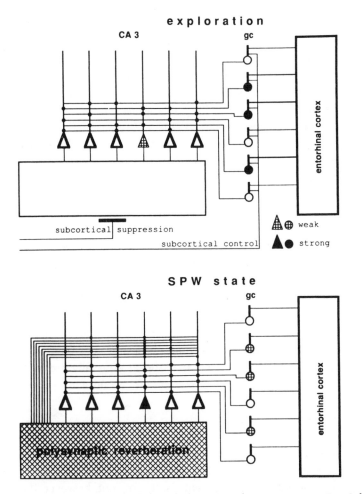

Figure 5.18 Two-stage hypothesis for hippocampal memory storage. (Top) Information transfer from entorhinal to CA3 during the exploratory (mobile) stage. Entorhinal inputs activates a subset of granule cells of the dentate gyrus which then fire at a higher frequency. (Bottom) After the termination of exploration (quiet stage), subcortical inhibition on CA3 cells decreases, allowing the CA3 cells to fire, beginning with the "initiator," shown here as a filled triangle. The initiator cell is the neuron potentiated last during the exploratory state, and hence its synapses are more strongly potentiated. SPW, sharp waves; gc, granule cells of the dentate gyrus. (From Buszáki and Gage [1991]. In *Memory Mechanisms: A Tribute to G. V. Goddard.* Ed. by Abraham, Corballis and White. Hillsdale, N.J.: L. Erlbaum Associates, Inc.)

arise from the hippocampus and hence doubtful that they are functionally equivalent to the theta seen in rat hippocampus. There are two possibilities: (1) Theta waves, or something comparable, exist in primates, but differences in anatomy mask them; newer techniques may yet uncover comparable wave forms, or (2) theta waves do not exist in primates, and the rat results are not generalizable—even with qualifications—to primates. Because the basic wiring believed responsible for theta waves in rat hippocampus is relevantly similar to the wiring seen in human hippocampus, it would be rather surprising if theta waves were absent rather than so-far-undemonstrated in the primate. Nevertheless, it is well to note that the issue is not yet settled, and biological results are all too often counterintuitive.

Sharp waves have been seen in humans (Freemon and Walter 1970), though an interesting difficulty in identifying them is that they may be difficult to differentiate from interictal (between seizure) spikes typically seen in the EEG of epileptic subjects. This also raises the question of the relation between sharp waves and interictal spike activity in epileptics and why the pyriform structure, hippocampus, amygdala, and other temporal lobe structures appear to be epilepsy prone (Traub and Wong 1982, Buzsáki et al. 1989).

Even as we write this section, new developments are expanding the knowledge and the puzzles concerning the scope and conditions for LTP. We briefly discuss two developments that appear especially provocative. The first concerns Ca^{2+} spikes in dendrites, and the second, a form of non-Hebbian LTP.

Beyond Vanilla LTP

The discussion so far has tacitly assumed that dendritic membrane is essentially passive, in contrast to the membrane on the axons which is known active and capable of action potentials. It turns out, however, that some neurons—pyramidal cells in the hippocampus, for example—have dendritic membrane containing voltage-dependent Ca^{2+} channels (figure 5.19). This means that when the depolarization in the dendrite reaches a certain threshold, these channels open, permitting Ca^{2+} to flood into the cell. As a result, the Ca^{2+} concentration can rapidly rise, causing further depolarization and the opening of yet other voltage-dependent Ca^{2+} channels in neighboring stretches of the dendritic membrane.[29] Under such conditions, a spike is produced in the dendrite. The current resulting from dendritic spikes can be more significant than passively spread synaptic current in depolarizing the membrane at the cell body because the passively spread current attenuates.

Why is spiking in the dendrites important? To begin with, the discovery calls for a revision in the classical view of dendritic function as consisting of simple signal integration, with passive conduction of current to the cell body.[30] Furthermore, the existence of such nonlinearities has important computational implications; namely, dendrites are semi-independent processing units that can "make decisions," suggesting that under some circumstances the "unit" of processing may really be the dendritic branch (of which there are some 10–100 per neuron), not, as the conventional wisdom has it, strictly the

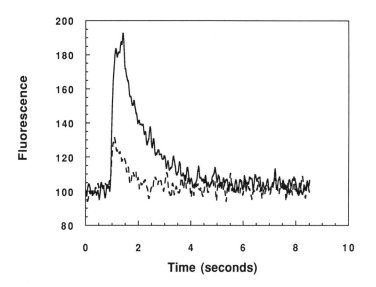

Figure 5.19 Changes in the Ca^{2+} concentration in the soma and apical dendrite of a CA1 pyramidal neuron in response to a depolarizing current pulse. A pyramidal cell in a rat hippocampal slice was filled with fluo-3, a fluorescent dye that is sensitive to the Ca^{2+} concentration within the cell. When the cell is depolarized to a level that activated voltage-dependent Ca^{2+} channels, Ca^{2+} flows into the cell. By monitoring the intensity of fluorescence under a confocal microscope, the change in Ca^{2+} concentration, signifying an activation of these channels, can then be recorded. The graph shows the Ca^{2+} concentration changing within a cubic micrometer volume within the soma (solid line) and at a second location 320 μm along the apical dendrite (dotted line) in response to a depolarizing current pulse to the cell body, administered intracellularly. Fluorescence in percent normalized to average fluorescence before stimulation. (Courtesy Richard Adams.)

whole neuron. Additionally, these Ca^{2+} currents may be activated not by run-of-the-mill levels of synaptic activity, but only by special conditions, such as the synchronized convergence of bursting activity seen in the hippocampus during sharp waves and in neocortex during certain stages of sleep (Hobson 1988).

The second new development pertains, as noted, to a non-Hebbian mode of long-lasting modification in synaptic strength. In a set of surprising results, Llinás and colleagues (Alonso et al. 1990) describe a potentiation phenomenon that looks like "vanilla" LTP so far as enhanced depolarization to a test stimulus is concerned, but is elicited by rather different conditions. They studied cells in layer II in slices of entorhinal cortex of the guinea pig.[31] The choice of entorhinal cortex was motivated by the fact that stellate neurons from this layer of entorhinal cortex provide the afferent drive into the hippocampus along the "perforant path."

In the very same cells—stellate cells in layer 2 of the entorhinal cortex—they found two flavors of LTP, one Hebbian and one not. The Hebbian effect was achieved in the classical way, namely high-frequency tetanus delivered to the presynaptic fibers. The non-Hebbian effect was achieved by injecting a 5-Hz oscillating current into the *postsynaptic* cell itself, for about 20 sec. Within 30

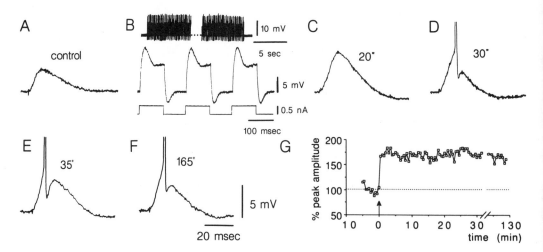

Figure 5.20 Time course of LTP of EPSPs induced by postsynaptic rhythmic membrane depolarization of a stellate cell in the entorhinal cortex. (A) Control EPSP, before rhythmic depolarization. The traces in C–F were recorded at the times indicated after rhythmic depolarization of the cell. (B) Characteristics of the postsynaptic stimulation. (C) The cell's potentiated response to a test stimulus 20 sec after the rhythmic depolarization. (D–F) The cell's response after 30 sec, 35 min, and 165 min, respectively. (G) Normalized peak EPSP amplitudes during the potentiation as a function of time. Arrow indicates the time of postsynaptic stimulation. (From Alonso et al. 1990.)

sec of onset of the stimulation, the cell developed a potentiated response, and the potentiation was vintage LTP stuff. Why 5-Hz current? Because theta rhythm is 4–8 Hz, and the experimental stimulation roughly simulates the input a stellate cell might receive as the animal explores its whereabouts. Why is that interesting? Because, as we consider below, it might tell us something about the processes that select what in the stream of experiences is to be remembered.

Notice that in the Llinás experiments, depolarizing postsynaptic current *only* was sufficient to produce LTP, *provided the current was oscillating*, not steady (figure 5.20). So produced, this second flavor of LTP, call it chocolate LTP, departs from the Hebbian prototype of LTP. First, no high-frequency presynaptic input is required in order that a mild presynaptic impulse following the intervention is potentiated. In other words, the Hebbian requirement of conjoint pre- and postsynaptic activity is not satisfied. Second, all the synapses of the cell receiving the oscillating current are affected, whereas in vanilla LTP,[32] just those synapses in direct communication with the presynaptic cell are modified.

Llinás also found that both vanilla and chocolate LTP are blockable by AP5, establishing therefore that NMDA receptors are involved in both kinds. He found two additional AP5 effects: (1) AP5 applied *after* induction of chocolate LTP wipes out the potentiation so long as the AP5 is present, and (2) applied *before* the oscillating current AP5 lowers the cell's EPSP to a test stimulus. The first results means that the role of the NMDA receptor in chocolate LTP is critical for *maintenance* as well as induction of the LTP. The results also show that the entire response after potentiation is owed to NMDA effects. The second result means that there is an NMDA component in the story even before the oscillating current is applied. This is puzzling since NMDA receptors are normally inactive until the cell is depolarized from its resting state by a critical amount. That NMDA plays a role in advance of potentiation is probably owed to the presence of extracellular glutamate, which may in turn be an index of high levels of activity generally in the cell's immediate neighborhood. It is also noteworthy that attempts to induce chocolate LTP in CA1 have so far been unsuccessful (Malenka et al. 1989).

But why should NMDA have a role apart from vanilla LTP if its primary function is as a coincidence detector? Chocolate LTP seems to lack precisely the feature that makes vanilla LTP interesting, namely, *specificity* of potentiated synapses. Why would one and the same cell have both a Hebbian and a non-Hebbian component, both mediated by NMDA receptors? The answer suggested by Llinás and colleagues is that non-Hebbian LTP may be involved in states relevant to learning, such as attention. If Buzsáki's hypothesis is on the right track, learning is typically carried on not during theta rhythm but during sharp-wave periods. Consistent with this hypothesis, therefore, chocolate LTP might involve some process, such as attention, that plays a role in memory but is not itself equivalent to the storing of information. In addressing the role of the chocolate LTP, Llinás and colleagues note first that the stellate cells are *intrinsically oscillatory* (Blake et al. 1988). They propose that the rhythmic depolarizations experimentally induced do two things: (1) unblock the NMDA pore, as in the standard case, assuming some background availability of glutamate, and (2) lock into the intrinsic frequency of the cell. This constructive resonance enables comparatively larger increases in Ca^{2+} concentration inside the cell, and consequently depolarization can spread quite far down the dendrite membrane, perhaps causing neighboring NMDA pores to unblock. An NMDA cascade means that there is a selective increase in the NMDA-mediated component of the cell's EPSP.

This non-Hebbian sort of effect at the cellular level is consistent with an attentional function. Imagine, for example, that during exploration of the milky water maze, the animal needs to pay attention to what it is about if it is to remember where the platform is located. Consequently some attention-related projections to the entorhinal cortex, perhaps via the thalamus or the cingulate gyrus, may release glutamate to confined regions, such as columns, that are responsive to the kinds of sensory information to be attended to. When a subset of neurons potentiated in this manner does receive input from sensory pathways, their potentiated responses will result in a strong signal relayed to the granule cells and thence to the CA3 region of the hippocampus for temporary storage. Thus there is some specificity in what inputs are "highlighted" as a result of chocolate LTP, while the vanilla LTP achieves a greater specificity in strengthened connections. Such is one conceivable scenario. To be sure, it is flagrantly sketchy, and doubtless there are many other equally plausible stories. What can be said for it is that it sets the stage for pulling together psychological data and physiological data, thereby catalyzing experimental plans.

One lesson from the Llinás research is that NMDA receptors should not, simply on the basis of the vanilla LTP experimentation, be assumed always to indicate that Hebbian plasticity is being served. More generally, the presence of NMDA receptors appears to have a role in activity-dependent development,[33] and they may also be indirectly related to learning in complex ways. Not only that, but NMDA may have a role in processes essentially unrelated to learning. NMDA receptors are found in many parts of the brain, and their special temporal and voltage-sensitive properties may be important for a range of functions other than associative memory. For example, Grillner (1981) showed that NMDA added to the bath of the spinal cord of the lamprey resulted in a pattern of motor activity like that seen in swimming, and later work implicated NMDA receptors in a variety of rhythmic motor behavior in a variety of species. (See also chapter 6, section 6, Modeling the Neuron.) In cat LGN some cells have a rather long response latency and are called "lagged cells." Heggelund and Hartveit (1990) found that these cells had NMDA receptors, but appear to lack K–Q receptors, whereas nonlagged cells (fast response latency) were weakly affected by NMDA blockers, and most of their response seemed to be from non-NMDA receptors, perhaps K–Q receptors. Whereas activation of the AMPA receptors results in a strong and fast depolarization, activation of the NMDA receptor results in a relatively weak, but more sustained depolarization (figure 5.21A). This profile for the NMDA channel opening may help explain the long latency of the lagged cells. (But perhaps not; see Kwon et al. 1991.) Additionally, and rather unexpectedly, Miller et al. (1989) found that in visual cortical area V1 the standard response of a cell to a visual stimulus depends on the NMDA receptor (see also Fox et al. 1989).

Recall that the NMDA receptor is voltage dependent, and near the resting potential, the conductance of the receptor is small when glutamate binds to it. When the postsynaptic membrane is depolarized, the conductance increases. Figure 5.21 shows the relationship between the conductance and the voltage, and the time course of the conductance changes.

LTP at the Molecular Level

Calcium is important in inducing vanilla LTP, and it probably plays an important role also in chocolate LTP. What, more precisely, is of the role of Ca^{2+} in these effects? Where is the locus of long-lasting modification and how is LTP maintained? These questions bring us to the forefront of the molecular research into LTP. As a background fact, note that at the resting level, the cell keeps Ca^{2+} concentration at a very low level—about 200 nanomolar. Consequently, even a little Ca^{2+} entering the cell causes a significant change in concentration. One of the first biochemical steps leading to LTP following Ca^{2+} entry into the postsynaptic terminal is the binding of Ca^{2+} to the protein calmodulin (figures 5.22, 5.23). Notice that calmodulin has slots for four Ca^{2+} ions. By virtue of the binding of Ca^{2+}, calmodulin undergoes a conformational change

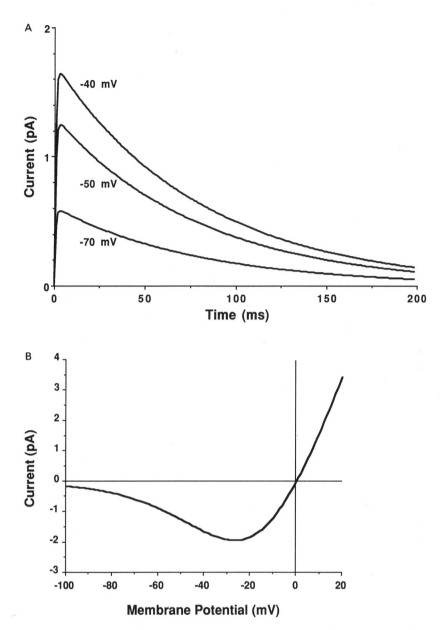

Figure 5.21 Voltage dependence and simulations of estimated NMDA-receptor currents in the spine of a hippocampal pyramidal neuron in response to a brief stimulus. (A) Time course of the NMDA-receptor current for three voltage clamped levels. The conductance change of the receptor was assumed to be 0.2 ns, and the external concentration of Mg^{2+} was 1 mM. Based on synaptic currents in hippocampal slices and single-channel recordings from cultured hippocampal neurons (Jahr and Stevens 1990a,b). See Zador et al. (1990) for model of NMDA-receptor dynamics in a dendritic spine. (B) Peak NMDA-receptor current plotted as a function of clamped membrane potential. The reversal potential is at 0 mV. The flow of ions through the channel is partially blocked at hyperpolarized potentials by Mg^{2+} in the extracellular medium.

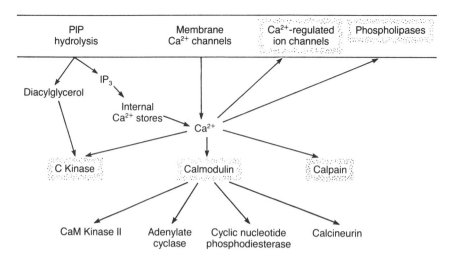

Figure 5.22 Immediate targets of Ca^{2+} in neurons. The $[Ca^{2+}]_i$ rises in the cytoplasm when Ca^{2+} flows through the membrane channels, or when it is released from intracellular stores in response to inositol triphosphate (IP_3). Membrane proteins that are directly regulated by the increase in $[Ca^{2+}]_i$ include several Ca^{2+}-regulated ion channels, phospholipase C, and A2. Cytoplasmic proteins regulated by Ca^{2+} include the C kinase and calpain, a protease. (For calmodulin, see figure 5.23). (From Kennedy [1989]. Regulation of neuronal function by calcium. *Trends in Neurosciences* 12: 417–420.)

enabling the calcium–calmodulin complex to bind other proteins, called protein kinases, which lead to phosphorylation of yet other proteins. Although there is evidence for the involvement of protein kinase C, the exact nature of the step beyond the formation of the calcium–calmodulin complex is not fully known; here the answers peter out. Before leaving this matter, however, we note a computer model that has been useful in answering one important question about the early steps in the causal sequence.

Consider a synapse on a dendritic spine. How much does the Ca^{2+} concentration change when the NMDA pore admits Ca^{2+}? The surprising answer is that the concentration even during intense activity increases by only a factor of ten or less relative to the resting state. (The NMDA receptor is not perfectly closed at the resting level, because a given Mg^{2+} ion may drift out and before another drifts in there can be some inward leakage of Ca^{2+} in the presence of glutamate and glycine.) But LTP will not be produced if the presynaptic fibers are stimulated at a low rate, say 5 Hz. At 100 Hz, however, LTP is robust. So there is a stimulation threshold below which no potentiation happens, and above which, the rather dramatic potentiation is produced. The small increase in Ca^{2+} concentration is therefore puzzling, for the blast needed to get LTP seems to imply that a flood of Ca^{2+} is required. The mystery then is how the cell gets so much bang for its buck, to put it in the military–industrial vulgate.

Zador et al. (1990) simulated the cellular conditions on a computer to try to discover the relation between levels of Ca^{2+} concentration and induction of LTP. On the basis of anatomical and physiological data, they assumed the relevant synaptic and intracellular events were taking place at a dendritic

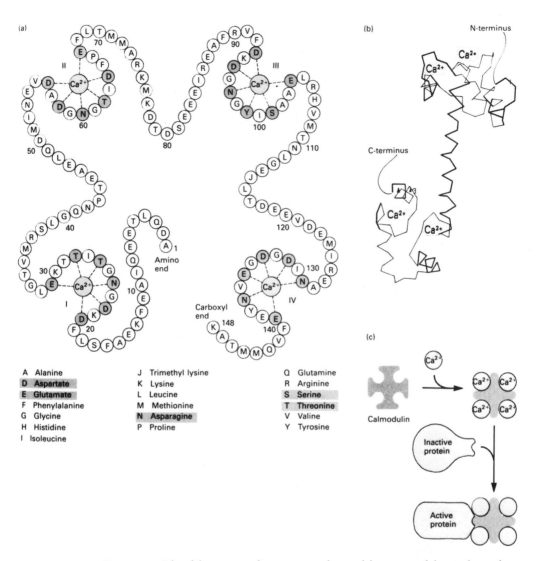

Figure 5.23 Calmodulin is a cytoplasmic protein that modulates most of the regulatory functions of the Ca^{2+} ions. (a) The chain has four domains, each binding one Ca^{2+} ion. (b) Drawing of the protein backbone. (c) On binding Ca^{2+}, calmodulin undergoes a major conformational change that allows it to bind other proteins, modifying their enzymatic activity. (From *Molecular Biology* by J. Darnell, H. Lodish, and D. Baltimore. Copyright © 1986 by Scientific American Books, Inc. Reprinted by permission of W. H. Freeman and Company.)

spine, as opposed to a length of dendritic shaft. Among experimental parameters incorporated were the measured voltage dependence of NMDA receptors (see figure 5.21), the Ca^{2+} concentration both inside and outside the cell both before and after tetanic stimulation, the estimated rate constants for the enzymes, the time course of the synaptic responses, and equations for diffusion of Ca^{2+} within the postsynaptic spine. It was already known that calmodulin has four sites for Ca^{2+}, all of which must be filled before it is active. At low levels of Ca^{2+} concentration, some of the calmodulin will have some of their slots filled, but few will have all four slots filled. If the concentration is doubled, there is suddenly enough Ca^{2+} to fill out the remaining slots of quite a few calmodulin molecules, thereby creating an abrupt change in the population of active calmodulin. In this manner, a small change in the level of Ca^{2+} will produce a large change in the level of "active" calmodulin. That is, it will increase as the fourth power of the Ca^{2+} concentration. This feature was also demonstrated in the simulation.

The second part of the answer emerged in the simulation. Because a spine head is extremely tiny—about 1 μm in diameter—it is rather like a miniature chemical retort, and hence a relatively minute change in the *number* of Ca^{2+} ions in the spine's intracellular space can mean a dramatic change in *concentration* in that local region. Thus in such a spine, one could raise the Ca^{2+} concentration by a factor of ten with only about 10^3 ions. This bit of biological cunning means that the very size of the spine retort and its narrow neck contributes to the amplification of the Ca^{2+} signal. Spines, it appears, may be ideally designed to be miniature chemical reactors, for they are economical of biochemicals and also of time, since sequences of reactions can proceed much faster in a small space. The virtue of the Zador model is that it makes this idea much more quantitative and plausible. Calcium-sensitive dyes make a direct test of this model possible (Müller and Connor, 1991).

Whether the long-term changes underlying LTP are presynaptic, postsynaptic, or both has not yet been determined. Recent experiments do point toward *presynaptic* modifications (Bekkers and Stevens 1990; Malinow and Tsien 1990) for maintenance of LTP. One intriguing hypothesis, explored by Read Montague (Montague et al. 1991), is that the signal to the presynaptic terminal is carried by nitric oxide (NO). NO is generated and released postsynaptically and diffuses to the presynaptic terminal within a millisecond or two of release. More research is needed to determine whether this is in fact the means whereby the presynaptic modification is signaled. There are several possible presynaptic mechanisms and at least as many postsynaptic mechanisms, and which of the various possibilities are realized in the nervous system is being worked out experimentally (figures 5.24, 5.25).

Extrasynaptic and Non-NMDA LTP

Two further complications must be mentioned to round out the story of LTP as we know it so far. First, Bliss and Lømo (1973) noticed that in addition to the potentiation at the synapse, the *threshold* is lowered for producing a spike

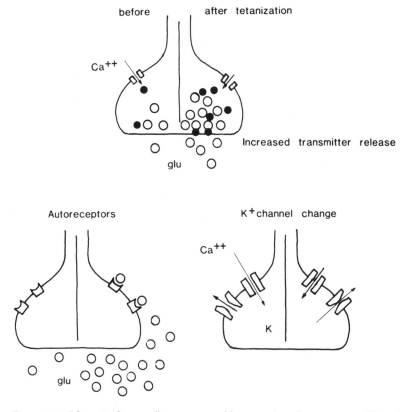

Figure 5.24 Schematic diagram illustrating possible presynaptic changes responsible for LTP. In all drawings with a vertical midline in the cell, the left side shows the control, and the right side the changed situation. Open circles represent glutamate or aspartate, and filled circles Ca^{2+}. Presynaptic changes may involve increased transmitter release because of increased Ca^{2+} influx (top). Autoreceptors may alter the release over time, and long-lasting changes could be due to biochemical changes activated by calcium. Alteration of K^+ channels seems a realistic candidate mechanism (bottom). (From Andersen 1987.)

when the signal enters at the potentiated synapse. In recording from inside the dendrites in CA1 pyramidal cells, Schwartzkroin and colleagues (Taube and Schwartzkroin 1988) verified this observation. The interpretation is that a component of vanilla LTP is owed to a change somewhere in the cell in addition to the change in synaptic weight but causally dependent on the potentiation of the synapse. Thus a further distinction must be drawn between *synaptic LTP* and *extrasynaptic LTP*, or what is called by Taube and Schwartzkroin (1988) "EPSP-spike potentiating LTP." In keeping with our "flavor taxonomy" as mnemonically more friendly than acronyms, we refer to this potentiation as strawberry ripple, since it is vanilla plus. Although the mechanism for this flavor of LTP is not known, there are voltage-sensitive Ca^{2+} channels (other

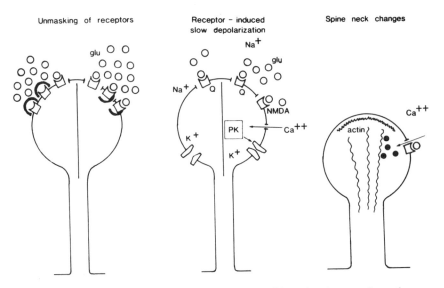

Figure 5.25 Postsynaptic changes responsible for LTP could involve the unmasking of receptors, an NMDA receptor-induced alteration in spine membrane, or morphological changes of the spine. (From Andersen 1987.)

than the NMDA channels) located on the dendritic shafts (Regehr et al. 1989). Computational modeling (Wathey et al., in press) has shown how specific changes in these channels could account for extrasynaptic LTP. If the changes permit more current to enter the cell, then more current will arrive at the axon hillock, thereby creating the extrasynaptic LTP effect when a signal enters the potentiated synapse (figure 5.26).

Second, several groups[34] have found that pyramidal cells in the CA3 region of hippocampus, which have different connectivity patterns from the CA1 pyramidals, display an LTP that may be synaptic as usual, but unusually, appears to depend on a voltage-sensitive receptor other than the NMDA receptor–ionophore complex. More exactly, the CA3 pyramidals have three main lines of excitatory input: the mossy fibers from the hippocampal granule cells, the perforant path fibers from the entorhinal cortex, and the recurrent collaterals from the hippocampi in both hemispheres. On the mossy fiber connections in particular, LTP is not blockable by AP5, a dead giveaway that the LTP etiologic profile here is different in some respect or other, justifying the label "non-NMDA LTP." The contrasting connectivity of the CA1 and CA3 regions suggests that they may be quite different computationally and hence functionally. As we shall see in the next section, the recurrent collaterals of CA3 pyramidals and their two very distinct lines of input invite comparison to recurrent nets. Consequently, a style of LTP suited to the unique wiring of the CA3 region would not be surprising.

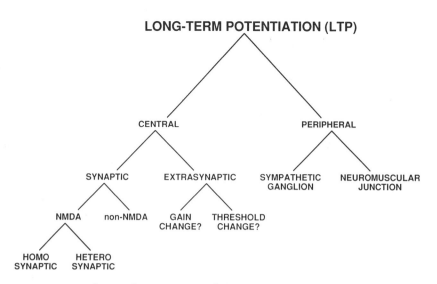

LONG-TERM POTENTIATION (LTP)

CENTRAL — PERIPHERAL

SYNAPTIC — EXTRASYNAPTIC

SYMPATHETIC GANGLION — NEUROMUSCULAR JUNCTION

NMDA — non-NMDA

GAIN CHANGE? — THRESHOLD CHANGE?

HOMO SYNAPTIC — HETERO SYNAPTIC

Figure 5.26 Tree diagram showing varieties of LTP.

Are these synapses—the ones involved in non-NMDA LTP—Hebbian? Some evidence argues positively, other evidence negatively. Jaffe and Johnson (1990) have found that pairing presynaptic activity with postsynaptic depolarization was necessary and sufficient for LTP at that synapse. On the other hand, Zalutsky and Nicoll (1990) presented evidence that activity in the postsynaptic neurons was not necessary. This issue has not yet been resolved; experiments for answering this question are extremely difficult and results may be difficult to interpret. For example, it would be easy to mistake stimulation of a polysynaptic pathway for stimulation of a monosynaptic pathway, and conditions between laboratories might vary in subtle ways.

5 CELLS AND CIRCUITS

It is time to come up for air. The molecular discoveries outlined above have taken us deep into the lower strata of nervous system organization and the ore mined has been tantalizingly rich. The impulse to linger and moil for more is hard to resist. But now we need to ask: what does it all mean, so far as understanding how an animal learns such things as the location of the platform in the milky-water maze? How does that *specific* information get represented in the hippocampus? If in a network, then what does the network look like and what computational principles describe it? If some region of the hippocampus has a content-addressable memory, how does the specific neural organization of the hippocampal structures lend itself to that function? If the representation is not permanently stored in hippocampal structures, what exactly gets into long-long-term store and where? By what mechanisms is *whatever is* stored transferred to *wherever* it is stored? How does it get "destored" in the hippocampus? Thick and fast, and still they come. The answers, alas, are far harder to pry loose.

The question about the role of the hippocampus in long-term storage is still puzzling. Is the hippocampus needed for a very brief interval, such as 1–5 sec, or is it perhaps longer, on the order of minutes or days, or perhaps longer still? To shed some light on this crucial matter, one needs to have a more exact accounting of how much time before a lesion to the hippocampus a stimulus must be presented in order that it be remembered in the long term. Put another way, is there a time, after a single experience, where damage to the hippocampus will not affect recall of the experienced event, and before which recall is impaired? In a recent large experiment, Zola-Morgan and Squire (1991) have provided crucial data and moved much closer to the answer.

Monkeys were trained on an object association task, where random pairs of junk objects were presented, but only one of the pair was associated with a food reward. The task was to remember which object was associated with food. Animals were presented with objects in groups of 20, and the groups were presented at varying times before the animals were lesioned: at 16, 12, 8, 4, and 2 weeks before lesions. The lesions were bilateral, and encompassed the almost-total ablation of the hippocampus, dentate gyrus, and entorhinal cortex, as well as bilateral damage to the parahippocampal cortex. The results were striking: on the objects learned 2 or 4 weeks before lesion, the animals performed about at chance, implying that hippocampal structures were not intact long enough after the stimulus presentation. By contrast, at 8 and 12 weeks, the animals performed as well as normal control animals (figure 5.27). In short, in the case of the lesioned animals, the remote past was remembered better than the recent past. This gives a lower bound, in terms of weeks, for how long this sort of event needs a hippocampus in order to be remembered in the long term, and when, so to speak, the storage of the event becomes independent of the hippocampal structures. Moreover, for the 2–12-week interval, the memory scores of the lesioned animals improved monotonically.

For those exploring LTP and those modeling hippocampal function, these time limits are intriguing, to say the least. As Zola-Morgan and Squire (1991) point out, the learning–surgery intervals show that the hippocampus is needed not only during the time when the animal experiences and learns, but also during consolidation. They suggest that the hippocampus may be doing at least two things: (1) binding the information from assorted cortical areas during the experience/learning phase, and (2) consolidating the information in a non-hippocampal location, probably neocortex, so that a record exists independently of the hippocampus. What exactly does the hippocampus do during the approximately 60 days it takes to "cure" an event engram? If short-term momory (STM) structures feed into the hippocampus, this raises anew questions of hippocampal function: is the hippocampus just a temporary holding tank, or are the representations in some sense prepared by the hippocampus for long-term keeping, perhaps by fixing spatiotemporal tags, docking "irrelevant" details, or integrating a representation into a contextual matrix? Or is it possible that the hippocampus serves as a temporary link between various areas of neocortex, and in that sense is not holding and "curing" the information at all, but only routing it?

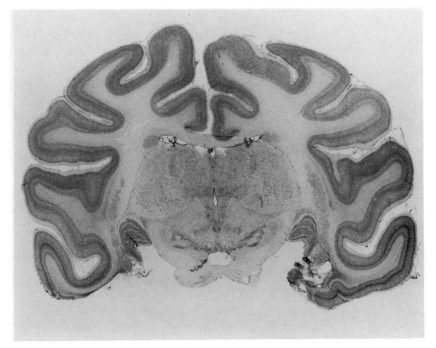

A

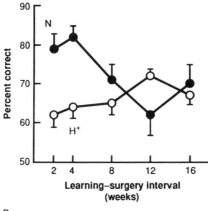

B

Figure 5.27 (A) A thionin-stained coronal brain section midway through the LGN from one monkey in the operated group. This animal sustained nearly total bilateral ablation of the hippocampal formation, including the dentate gyrus, subicular complex, and entorhinal cortex. Also, nearly all of the parahippocampal cortex was damaged bilaterally. Some additional damage extends into visual association cortex (TE), presumably as a result of an infarction during surgery. (B) Mean retention of 100 object discrimination problems learned approximately 2, 4, 8, 12, and 16 weeks before surgery. Open circles, lesioned animals ($n = 11$); filled circles, intact animals ($n = 7$). (From Zola-Morgan and Squire [1990]. The primate hippocampal formation: evidence for a time-limited role in memory storage. *Science* 250: 288–289. © AAAS.)

It is just as well to avoid the comfortable metaphors of filing cabinets, piggy banks, or digital computer memory for LTM, implying as they do an immutable and noninteractive *modus vivendi*. As introspection reveals only too well, long-term representations are not absolutely unchanging or inert. Integrative operations, periodic retrieval, re-exposure to the event, age of representation, affect level, relevance to environmental niche, neurological and psychiatric pathology, and other factors go into determining the vividness or fuzziness of events in LTM. Sometimes several separated but related events become conflated, and occasionally the imagination inserts a fiction. While rehearsal keeps working memory representations "hot," failure to recall periodically events stored in LTM may result in "cooling" or obliteration. Forgetting seems an ongoing process endemic to LTM, and it appears to have it own schedule (Squire 1989).

Reflecting on the elementary wiring properties seen in the hippocampus and the matrixlike face of its input-output architecture, Marr (1971) proposed that the hippocampus was essentially a short-term associative memory store, that is, a kind of staging area where raw associations could be directly stored before being transferred to long-term memory in the neocortex. Representations stored in the neocortex, he conjectured, were stripped of many irrelevant raw details but retained relevant categorial information. Marr's paper was published before the discovery of LTP and before many details of hippocampal circuitry had been determined. His model, consequently, was very general. The model was remarkable nonetheless, not least because it was a pioneering attempt to characterize the operation of a brain structure in computational terms, but also because of its clever use of computational ideas such as orthogonal coding, Hebbian synapses, and inhibitory normalization.[35]

Rolls (1989) discerned a resemblance between hippocampal anatomy and the associative nets of Hopfield and Kohonen. He suggested that the CA3 region is a recurrent net, where the mossy fibers provide a coarsely specified imput, the more dense and direct perforant input determines the finer discriminations, and the collaterals allow both for upgrading noisy patterns and completing partial patterns. According to his proposal, the CA3 region is a structure for recognition memory. Associating the spatial location of an object, such as a platform in a milky-water maze or a nut behind the yellow pail, would be achieved by orderly weight modification in the tri-input/pyramidal cell matrix. The CA1 region, as recipient of CA3 signals, Rolls sees as a matrix for competitive learning, where the function is to perform further classification on what it gets from a set of CA3 pyramidals (via the Schaffer collaterals), yielding a more general, or as he says "economical," classification of world events (figure 5.28). Since Rolls does not give a specific example of what that would mean, or of the contrast between CA1 and CA3 representations, it is not clear what sort of representation further classification by the CA1s produces, or why, given its Rollsian function, CA1 learning should be competitive. (See also McNaughten and Morris 1987.)

Rolls' hypothesis is a valiant attempt to make computational sense of the hippocampal anatomy. Although it initiates the modeling enterprise and prob-

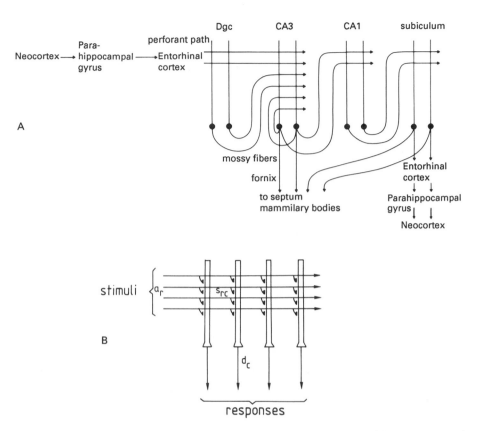

Figure 5.28 (A) Schematic representation of the connections of the hippocampus, showing also that the cerebral cortex is connected to the hippocampus via the parahippocampal gyrus and entorhinal cortex, and that the hippocampus projects back to the cortex via the subiculum, entorhinal cortex, and parahippocampal gyrus. (B) Matrix for competitive learning in which the input stimuli are presented along the rows of the input axons (a_r), which make modifiable synapses (s_{rc}) with the dendrites of the output neurons, which form the columns (d_c) of the matrix. A net with this architecture is rather like the neural architecture of feedforward Schaffer collaterals from CA3 to CA1 pyramidal cells. (From Rolls 1989.)

ably orients us in the right general direction, it remains at a very abstract level of explanation. Not to detract from its usefulness, the stern characterization says the Rolls hypothesis takes the matrix architecture of Hopfield nets and the matrixlike anatomy of the hippocampus, and arranges a shot-gun marriage, naming presumed CA3 recognition memory as issue. Seriously, however, what is missing from the account is the differential physiology of hippocampal cells and what, given the anatomy, could be its significance in learning new things. To flesh out the skeletal story, we need to know more exactly what is going on in CA3 cells in terms of producing a representation, and also about the nature of that representation. What, more precisely, does the output of the CA3 cells represent?

The legendary soft underbelly, with which Rolls, like everybody else, must come to terms, is that no one has the slightest idea how to specify concretely either the inputs or the outputs of the hippocampus. That is, what the input messages *represent*. What is the hippocampus being told, and what is it saying? In contrast to at least some areas of the visual system where the synaptic distance between the transducer and the cortical neuron is short, and the relation between a stimulus and a cellular response can be quite specific, the inputs to the hippocampus are already highly processed and the information they hold is obscure. They come, via the entorhinal cortex and the fornix, from widely distributed areas of the cortex, including frontal cortex, whose representations are themselves a dark mystery. Fibers originating in brain stem nuclei, notably the locus coeruleus and the raphe, also project into the hippocampal feeder stations. The entorhinal cortex has a vast catchment, and nontrivial signal integration appears to take place there before signals are sent from there to the hippocampus. But we do not know what integration is accomplished nor what the entorhinal output signals mean, and preliminary lesion data indicate that the entorhinal cortex may be as much a "recognition memory" as is the hippocampus (Zola-Morgan et al. 1989).

In fact, virtually every structure in the brain has a matrixlike architecture, so what precisely should we conclude from that? Perhaps that all such structures are engaged in recognition memory? Fine, but then what is the hippocampus *in particular* up to? Further, the hippocampus backprojects massively to the entorhinal cortex, and from there back to many areas of the brain. This connectivity is a trait typical of brain pathway design, but also one that deepens the difficulty of how to say something meaningful about what the hippocampus represents, about what, precisely, it is doing. The opacity of the inputs present a problem for network level computer models that we do well not to underestimate. At the same time, it should not frighten us off the project altogether.

Suppose we put the question of signal semantics on the back burner for the moment, and consider other strategies. In order better to incorporate the physiological data into a computational model, it might be useful first to have a model of the signal processing of a single cell, say a CA3 or a CA1 pyramidal cell. Once the computational profile of various cell types is charted, a network of such cells can be constructed according to the dictates of the known anatomy. A computer model, as realistic as data and computer power will allow, can then be run and analyzed. If we assume that the model is going to be essentially in the learning and memory business, then two questions loom large for the modeler: what shall the inputs be, and does the network learn by error correction via feedback, or is it unsupervised?

As a first pass on the second question, it may be noted that the circuitry so far visible in the hippocampus contains no pathways that are obviously feedback (excitatory), save the recurrent collaterals in CA3. Two possibilities present themselves: either feedback comes from within the hippocampus via obscure connections, or the feedback is external and comes into the hippocampus with the rest of the feedforward inputs. To develop this possibility, consider that since some projections of the perforant path neurons go directly to CA3 and CA1, while others have synaptic connections in the dentate which then project to CA3 and also directly to CA1, then one of the pair could act as an internal teaching signal or monitor (figure 5.29).

The first alternative invites us to re-examine the anatomy and physiology to determine whether we missed feedback connections. As observed by Rolls, the recurrent collaterals of the CA3 region can function as self-correcting feedback. But is that enough feedback information? What will prevent the network from "self-correcting" itself into self-satisfied error? Part of the answer here will depend on what the hippocampus is doing—just storing already processed information, or classifying and processing to ready representations for recall. So another part of the answer will depend on what the input is to the pyramidal cell via perforant (direct) pathways and via the mossy fiber pathway. With this step, we seem, alas, to have caught up with our tail. This is frustrating, since we had hoped that a realistic computational model would cast some light on these very questions.

Nevertheless, until the envisaged modeling proceeds a bit further, we simply do not know how the land lies. Science inevitably resorts to the seemingly impossible but oft successful art of bootstrapping. From the vantage point of ignorance, it is virtually impossible to guess just where that bootstrapping will lead, or what problems and solutions will be encountered at a distant and invisible height. This is, we confess, to sound a semi-cheerful note, but though the research problem does look truly awesome, it nevertheless is worth a run. We do admit, for the sake of argument, that the situation could turn out to be flatly impossible. The brain, as Mark Churchland once wondered, might be more complicated than it is smart. On the other hand, it is agreed by all hands, even the semi-dour, that it is much too early in the game to cry "Uncle."[36]

Having agreed to shelve signal semantics for now, let us also shelve the higher-order functional questions and focus on understanding cell interactions in hippocampal circuits. Discoveries at this level may provide insight into the capacities and limitations of the circuit, which in conjunction with physiological, pharmacological, and behavioral data, will be a basis for considering from a new slant the generation of sharp waves in CA1 fields and the Buzsáki two-stage learning hypothesis. Realistic modeling in this domain is just beginning, and Roger Traub and his colleagues are exploring models of a CA3 region as it behaves in slice (Traub et al. 1987a, b, 1989; Traub and Dingledine 1990). The Traub models of slice data have distinctive cell populations corresponding to excitatory pyramidal cells (9000), and two kinds of inhibitory cells (450 of each). They incorporate a great many biophysical and physiological properties of cells, such as fast and slow GABA receptors (inhibitory synapses), channel types, and time constants, as well as the details of synaptic distribution, and patterns of connectivity between the cardinal cell types (pyramidal cells, mossy fibers, inhibitory cells).

One question asked of the model concerned the generation of in vitro synchronized bursts, presumably corresponding, albeit approximately, to the sharp waves seen in vivo (Traub and Dingledine 1990). The model showed that if excitatory synapses between pyramidal cells are removed, the population activity becomes "disorganized"; that is, no rhythmic oscillations are pre-

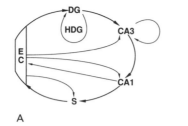

A

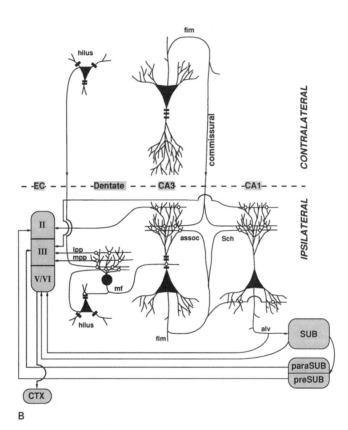

B

Figure 5.29 Hippocampal circuits. (Top) Schematic diagram of the major pathways between the entorhinal cortex (EC) and the hippocampus. The simple tri-synaptic pathway (heavy arrows making an oval) goes through the dentate gyrus (DG), areas CA3, CA1, the subiculum (S), and back to EC. This simple scheme has been supplemented by the discovery of direct projections from EC to CA3, CA1, and S and a direct projection from CA1 back to EC, shown here using lighter arrows. (Compare also figure 5.4.) (Bottom) This schematic redraws the top figure, adding anatomical detail and highlighting three main features: (i) commissural pathways that join the two hippocampi across the midline, (ii) layers II, III, and V/VI of the EC, and (iii) details of where fibers originate and terminate. Small open circles denote excitatory synapses; bars on the dendrites denote large spines. Neurons originate and terminate in distinct EC layers; layer II neurons project to the uppermost regions of the apical dendrites of the CA3 pyramidal cells, and some layer III neurons do the same for CA1 apical dendrites. Some axons from layers V/VI project to the neocortex (CTX). The perforant pathway from EC to DG terminates in different strata of the dendrites of the dentate granule cells, with the lateral performant path (lpp) termi- nating farther out on the dendrites than the medial perforant path (mpp). Hilar neurons receive imputs from the granule cells and form a feedback to granule cells on both sides of the midine.

sent. These results suggest that the recurrent connections of CA3 pyramidal cells are necessary for synchrony of the bursts. Traub and colleagues found that in the model synchronous bursts were preceded by a barrage of EPSPs, caused by granule cell action potentials. Experimentally it has been shown that CA3 cells spontaneously generate EPSPs when K^+ was added to the bath. This condition and the spontaneous EPSPs were simulated in the model. One aim here was to explore possible mechanisms for this effect and to consider a possible functional role, given the surrounding data concerning hippocampal function.

Are these simulation results useful? What do they tell us about large-scale properties? To begin with, they are useful because they address questions of the temporal and spatial relationships that underlie observed properties of hippocampal slices. The model helps clarify the role of spontaneous EPSPs and of recurrence in the CA3 pyramidal population, and to relate this to population properties such as sharp waves. In the model, spontaneous EPSPs in CA3 pyramidal cells were necessary to the initiation of the bursting phase, while recurrent collaterals were necessary for synchronization of the bursts.

Traub's modeling is very much on the bottom-up end of the business. This is both its virtue, since its realism enables serious physiological predictions, and also its weakness, since contact with behavioral data and hence with functional hypotheses may seem at first blush to be almost as remote as the physiological data on which the model rests. This property should not be draped in black, however. Reaching higher-level phenomena from the platform of Traub modeling together with the Buzsáki hypothesis may be rewarding, for the population rhythms are the link to behavioral phenomena on the level above and to physiological data on the level below.

6 DECREASING SYNAPTIC STRENGTH

Assuming that there is a mechanism, such as LTP, for strengthening connections between synapses, then to avoid saturation (meaning that all synapses end up at their maximum strength), some counterpart mechanisms probably exist to *decrease* synaptic strengths. In the absence of repetition, some connec-

Mossy fibers (mf) from the dentate granules cells in turn make contacts mostly on the proximal apical dendrites of CA3 pyramidal neurons. The associational (assoc) fibers feeding back onto the pyramidals are sandwiched between the mossy fibers and the perforant inputs. The CA3 pyramidal neurons project via the Schaffer collaterals (Sch) to the apical dendritic trees of CA1 neurons, but some fibers also project to the basal dendrites and some out of the hippo-campus to the fimbria fornix (fim). Axons from CA1 pyramidal neurons project via the alveus (alv) to the subiculum (SUB) and also back to the EC. Other cortical regions surrounding the SUB (the parasubiculum and the presubiculum) also carry information back to the EC. The EC receives inputs from the SUB and from CA1 via the alveus into layers V/VI, from the paraSUB into layer III, and from the preSUB into layer II. Major inhibitory systems that are missing from this diagram include feedforward and recurrent inhibitory interneurons, and specialized interneurons such as basket cells that make inhibitory synapses on the soma and proximal apical dendrites of pyramidal neurons. (Courtesy S. Chatterji and D. Amaral.)

tions may gradually decay over time, with the result that information is lost. Some such process might correlate with gradual forgetting on the psychological level. Weakening of the connections between synapses should not, however, automatically be identified with the psychological phenomenon of forgetting. Reduction in synaptic strength under specific presynaptic–postsynaptic conditions could well be an indispensable component of learning new information or, alternatively, a part of sloughing off the irrelevant.

Long-term depression (LTD), as the flip side of LTP, has been sought at the conventional LTP sites. Two broad classes have been postulated, and there is some evidence for both. The first class is *heterosynaptic LTD*, which means that the responsivity of the whole cell is downregulated, equivalent in its consequences to changing the gain of the cell. The second class is *homosynaptic LTD*, wherein responsivity is damped at the very synapse manipulated, leaving other (unmanipulated) synapses on the same cell undamped. In both cases, a postsynaptic structure hitherto potentiated loses that potentiation in exchange for a depressed response to the presynaptic stimulus (figure 5.30). Note that a

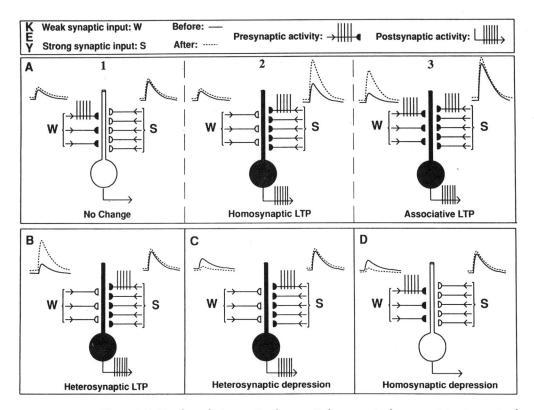

Figure 5.30 Use-dependent synaptic changes. Each neuron is shown receiving two sets of nonoverlapping synaptic inputs, one weak (W) and the other strong (S). The wave forms above each input illustrate schematically the excitatory postsynaptic potential produced by a single stimulation of that input before (solid curve) and after (broken curve) tetanic stimulation of one or both inputs. Filled elements indicate activity during the tetanic stimulation. (From Brown et al. 1990.)

depressed response is lower than a *de novo* response. Heterosynaptic LTD is conjectured to have a role in normalization, that is, in adjusting cells so that they are not saturated by LTP modifications. Homosynaptic LTD may be more selective, and thus may be speculated to have a role in culling out low-grade or "don't-care" information. The basic idea in either case is that whereas correlated responses produces LTP, *anticorrelation* should result in LTD (figure 5.31; see figure 5.8).[37]

Stanton and Sejnowski (1989), studying hippocampal cells in a slice preparation, produced what appears to be homosynaptic LTD in a CA1 pyramidal cell under the following conditions: LTP was first produced in the standard way, by high-frequency stimulation of the Schaffer pathway. In the next phase, current injected into the postsynaptic cell was manipulated so that it negatively correlated with presynaptic activation (figure 5.32). Accordingly, when the presynaptic cell was active, the postsynaptic cell was artificially hyperpolarized and hence not allowed to respond. Desmond and Levy (1983) got heterosynaptic LTD in the inverse condition: when the postsynaptic cell was depolarized, but the presynaptic cell was inactive. Thus, as a function of the nature of the anticorrelation, either the synapse or the whole cell's potentiation could be reversed. A repeat of the high-frequency stimulation could re-potentiate the cell. Recent data suggest that homosynaptic LTD is blockable by AP3, a sister to the drug AP5 that blocks NMDA-mediated LTP (Sejnowski et al. 1990, Stanton et al. 1991).

A possible correlate at the functional level for homosynaptic LTD would be a disruption in a previous connection between events A and B by a competing and overriding new connection between events C and B. For example, the first association of green and loud might be replaced by red and loud; a coincidental association might be replaced by a genuine association. Thus new coupling of the postsynaptic cell with some other cells might mean that the postsynaptic cell was in its after-hyperpolarizing phase when the old presynaptic cell was active, with divorce the inevitable sequel. This functional story, it should be clear, is rampant speculation.

All the cautions earlier flagged for LTP must be applied also to LTD, but with even greater emphasis. First, it is not known whether LTD can be induced in vivo by experimental stimulation. Second, even should LTD be produced experimentally in vivo, it is a further question whether anything comparable occurs under natural conditions, and even if it did, the behavioral correlate, if any, is a yet further unknown. The counterpart experiments for LTD of the original Bliss and Lømo experiments in the animal and for Morris' behavioral studies of LTP in the milky-water maze have not yet been done as this goes to press. Third, to compound the tenuousness, homosynaptic LTD is not as robust a phenomenon as is LTP. Some laboratories that routinely produce LTP have had difficulty in producing any homosynaptic LTD whatsoever. Conditions such as stimulation strengths and bath temperature vary between laboratories, and it is not yet known exactly what conditions are needed to elicit homosynaptic LTD, or even whether it might be judged an artifact once the eliciting conditions are understood.

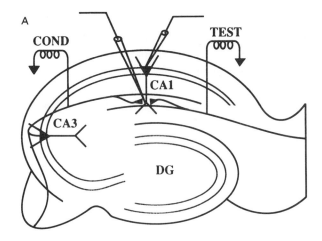

A

COND

TEST

CA1

CA3

DG

B

ASSOCIATIVE STIMULUS PARADIGMS

POSITIVELY CORRELATED - "IN PHASE"

TEST INPUT

CONDITIONING
INPUT

NEGATIVELY CORRELATED - "OUT OF PHASE"

TEST INPUT

CONDITIONING
INPUT

200 msec

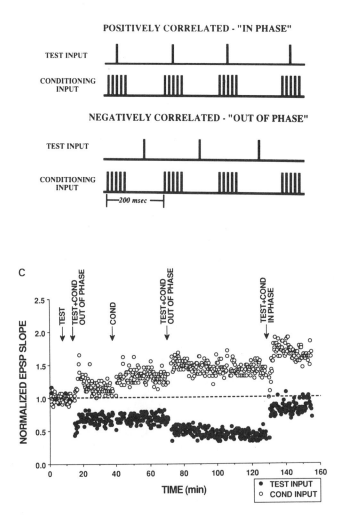

C

Studying homosynaptic LTP in visual cortex, Wolf Singer and his colleagues at Frankfurt found a rather subtle and intriguing set of conditions for producing homosynaptic LTD in cortical pyramidal cells in a slice preparation (Artola et al. 1990). As in the previous set-up (see figure 5.10), they could produce vanilla LTP in postsynaptic cells. They found they could induce either LTP or LTD in visual cortex by carefully adjusting the depolarizing current applied to the postsynaptic cell. Above a certain depolarizing threshold, the cell displayed LTP; below a rather lower threshold, no long-term modification of any kind was seen. But between the two bands was a narrow window where depolarizing current of the proper strength resulted in LTD. Moreover, the LTD threshold seems apt; if nothing is going on, then no change will occur, the voltage being below the threshold for LTD. This is a very refined customer indeed. Singer (1990) conjectures that the sign of the synaptic modification (LTP, or LTD, or no change) will depend upon the balance of depolarizing and hyperpolarizing currents at the synapse. On his analysis, LTD might have an associative function, but one of decreasing rather than increasing synaptic coupling representing associated events. Again, the usual cautions apply—can it be replicated in vivo? What is the behavioral significance?

In pondering these questions it is pertinent to consider that this threshold for LTD had been presaged on theoretical grounds by Sejnowski (1977) and Bienenstock et al. (1982) in their computer models of cortical development (figure 5.33). Additionally, as a general theoretical point it is known that more information can be stored in a network where synaptic modifications are in both the LTP and the LTD directions.[38]

Singer (1990) also raises the possibility that LTD, evinced within the narrow current window described above, explains certain puzzling results in the experimental manipulation of neural development. Prima facie, this is an appealing suggestion, because learning and development almost certainly share mechanisms and principles. Activity-dependent modification to cells, competition for space and activity, ion-induced modification to cell structure, and chemical induction of gene expression are manifest both in learning and in development. Indeed, prying the two apart may, from the point of view of Nature, be rather arbitrary. Obviously, development does not stop at birth, nor does learning begin at birth. In humans and many other mammals, the two overlap for a

Figure 5.31 (a) Schematic diagram of the in vitro hippocampal slice showing recording sites in the CA1 pyramidal cell body and dendritic layers. There are two separate stimulus sites: COND activates Schaffer collaterals, and TEST activates commissural afferents. (b) Conditioning input consisted of four trains of 100-Hz bursts. Each burst had five stimuli; interburst interval = 200 msec. Each train lasted 2 sec and had a total of 50 stimuli. Test input stimuli were four trains of shocks at 5-Hz frequency, each train lasting for 2 sec. When these inputs were *in phase*, the test single shocks were superimposed on the middle of each burst of the conditioning input as shown. When the test input was out of phase, the single shocks were placed symmetrically between the bursts. (c) Illustration of associative LTP and LTD using extracellular recordings from the dendritic layer in hippocampal field CA1. Each circle is the response to a single stimulation of the TEST (filled) or COND (open) pathways. (From Sejnowski, Chattarji and Stanton [1990]. Homosynaptic long-term depression in hippocampus and neocortex. *Seminars in the Neurosciences* 2: 355–363.)

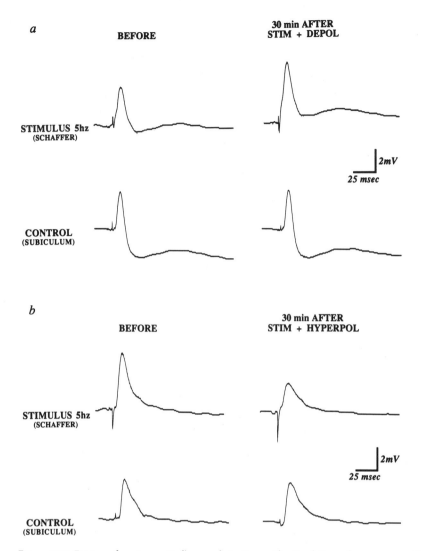

Figure 5.32 Pairing of postsynaptic hyperpolarization with stimulation of synapses on CA1 hippocampal pyramidal neurons produces LTD specific to the activated pathway, while pairing of postsynaptic depolarization with synaptic stimulation produces synapse-specific LTP. (a) (*LTP condition*) Intracellular evoked EPSPs are shown at stimulated (stimulus 5 Hz, Schaffer) and unstimulated (control, subiculum) pathway synapses before and 30 min after pairing depolarizing current injection with 5-Hz synaptic stimulation. The stimulated pathway exhibited associative LTP of the EPSP whereas the control, unstimulated input showed no change in synaptic strength. (b) (*LTD condition*) Intracellular EPSPs evoked at stimulated and control pathway synapses before and 30 min after pairing a 20-mV hyperpolarization at the cell soma with 5-Hz synaptic stimulation. The input (stimulus 5 Hz), activated during the hyperpolarization, showed associative LTD of synaptic evoked EPSPs, while synaptic strength of the silent input (control) was unaltered. (From Stanton and Sejnowski 1989.)

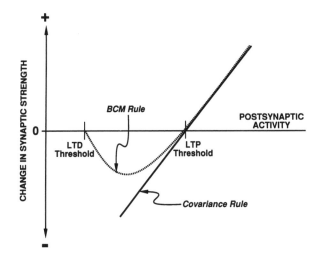

Figure 5.33 Drawing of change in synaptic strength as a function of postsynaptic activity for the Bienenstock, Cooper, and Munro (BCM) rule (dotted line) and the covariance rule (solid line). Both rules are variants of the Hebb rule and postulate a threshold above which there is LTP and below which there is LTD. In addition, the BCM rule has a threshold for LTD (Sejnowski et al. 1990).

significant percentage of the animals' lifetime, and there is no clear way to draw a line between when development tapers off and when learning in the fetus begins to take flesh (figure 5.34).

Weeding the irrelevant from our long-term recollections is one of the things we accomplish without effort and generally without conscious decisions, yet it must be one of the most sophisticated things the nervous system does. As anyone in housekeeping mode knows, pitching out everything in a cupboard is easy; saving the important things requires broad knowledge of the past as well as predictive intelligence. It cannot be left to the char. In Luria's horrifying documentary, "The Mind of the Mnemonist," we see a brain that cannot forget; that remembers all the humdrum details of every experience, down to the exact wording of a newspaper article read days ago, and every conversation heard in the office. S's brain is handicapped by a mountainous clutter of irrelevancies saved right along with the relevant information; he is paralyzed by an unceasing deluge of associations as he tries to make his way in the world. What are the principles by which a normal brain sorts and forgets—not always unerringly, but by contrast with S, remarkably efficiently? At the cellular level, what might be the mechanisms involved in forgetting? The answers are not known, and it would be premature to pin very much on LTD, either heterosynaptic or homosynaptic, as the cellular mechanism, for all the cautionary reasons cited.

7 BACK TO SYSTEMS AND BEHAVIOR

Neuropsychological data, derived from the cases of H.M. and R.B., indicate that ablation of the hippocampus does not seriously impair memory for events

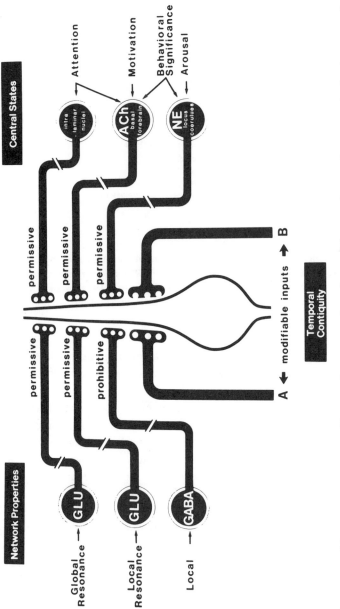

Figure 5.34 Schematic representation of factors influencing use-dependent modification of neuronal circuits in the developing visual cortex. The sign of the change in modifiable connections A and B depends on the temporal correlation of activity conveyed by the modifiable inputs. Whether a change occurs in response to this activity depends on the state of activation of additional synaptic inputs to the same neuron. These inputs constitute feedback loops originating within the same cortical column and the same cortical area and probably also remote cortical and subcortical structures. Additional gating inputs are derived from the more globally organized modulatory systems which originate in central core structures of the brain. (From Singer 1990.)

some considerable time before the lesion.[39] (See section 2, Learning and the Hippocampus.) The inference has been that the hippocampus itself cannot be the permanent store for information retrievable for some period after exposure. Rather, the hypothesis is that the hippocampus may in some suitable sense "teach" the cortex, where the cortex, perhaps a slower learner of less detailed, and more categorial, representations, gradually takes up and integrates salient aspects of the hippocampal representation. Receiving less emphasis is the observation that Boswell, R.B., and H.M., though their memory for postsurgical events is tragically abolished, nonetheless have some memory in the very short run. They can recall information for about a minute after its presentation, provided that distraction is minimized and uninterrupted rehearsal is permitted. By parity of reasoning, therefore, we should infer that the hippocampal structures are not the locus of the memory for very recent events; that is, remembering events for about 60 seconds does not depend on the hippocampus.

Having seen the concept of a unitary long-term memory (LTM) fragment into a theory postulating a collection of subsystems (see figure 5.2), it should be asked in turn whether short-term memory (STM) is a distinct system, or just the early segment of some subset of the LTM processes, and whether it too might be a collection of systems rather than a unitary function. "Short" is obviously a relative term (3 hours is short for labor but long for a burp), and hence a more precise metric is needed. What are the quantitative data on which the binning for "immediate," "short," and so forth is based? Unfortunately the complexity of the phenomenon makes for some confusion in the nomenclature, the more so as different time bands and different experimental conditions are used in different laboratories. Nevertheless, some fairly clear if surprising hypotheses have emerged from neuropsychology and experimental psychology. As computational models strive to achieve realistic simulation of the neurobiology, so also they must capitalize on the most current assessment of the plastic capacities if they are going to have a shot at modeling what the brain *actually* does, as opposed to modeling what, intuitively and introspectively, one *surmises* the brain does. In what follows, we shall focus on that sector of STM research that bears upon the role of hippocampal structures and illuminates the problem of what, at the systems level, is the empirical physiognomy of plasticity.

Studies of densely amnesic patients, as we saw earlier, showed a dissociation between memory for events within the last minute or so on the one hand, and LTM for experienced events on the other. Is a double dissociation ever seen? That is, can someone have poor STM for experienced events, but relatively normal LTM? Introspection steers us awry here, for it typically says no. The answer, in fact, is "yes." As a preliminary to the following discussion, we mention that a standard test for memory span consists in presenting a set of words and asking the subject to repeat the list. Normal controls have a span of about six or seven words. An STM deficit was discovered by Shallice and Warrington (1970) who studied a patient with a span of two words, though his long-term learning of words was normal. The STM deficit seemed to be con-

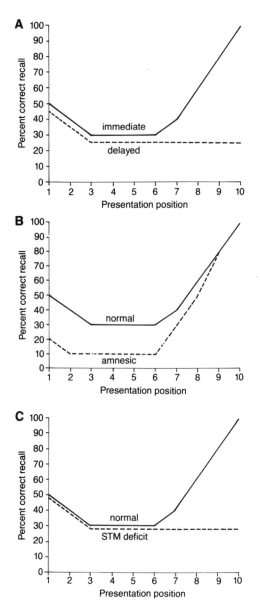

Figure 5.35 Performance of (A) normal subjects, (B) amnesic patients, and (C) patients suffering from a short-term memory deficit on a free-recall memory test. The solid line in (A) shows performance as a function of input position when recall is immediate. The last few items presented are very well recalled (the recency effect). The broken line shows performance when recall is delayed by a distracting task. Here the recency effect is abolished, suggesting that it depends on some temporary store. (B) In amnesic patients, the short-term recency effect is normal, but performance on other items is grossly impaired. (C) Typical performance from a patient with a specific deficit of short-term auditory memory; performance on earlier items is normal, but the recency effect is abolished. (From Baddeley [1988]. Cognitive psychology and human memory. *Trends in Neurosciences* 11: 176–181.)

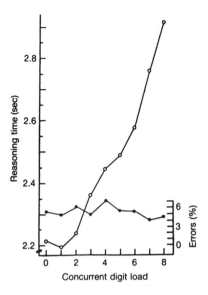

Figure 5.36 Effects on speed (open circles) and accuracy (filled circles) of reasoning of a concurrent immediate memory task. Subjects were required to verify sentences such as "A is not preceded by B–AB" at the same time as rehearsing strings of random numbers ranging in length from 0 to 8. While reasoning time does increase with load, errors do not. (From Baddeley 1988.)

fined to verbal material; nonverbal STM appeared normal. Baddeley and Hitch (1974) designed an experiment for normal controls to make the dissociation show up there too. A well-known memory phenomenon called the "recency effect" is typically seen in the span tests, among other places. The effect is that recall of the last few words presented is more accurate than recall of the middle range, and better even than the first item or two. Baddeley asked whether distraction at the end of the presentation of the word list would wipe out the recency effect. The answer, which most of us find somewhat counterintuitive, is that it does. That is, under the distraction conditions, earlier words are recalled better than the most recently presented words (figure 5.35). Patients with STM deficits likewise show no recency effect.

These data are interpreted to mean that there is a very short-term store, which Baddeley calls "working memory." "Short" here turns out to mean several seconds, as little as one or two, and conceivably as much as five or six. Events need not shuttle through working memory in order to be admitted into LTM, as the patients studied by Shallice and Warrington show. That is, these patients can recall much later a word that they could not recall immediately after the presentation of the word list. Presumably, however, they are aware of the stimulus at the time of presentation, even if only for a few hundred milliseconds. In probing the capacity of the working memory, Baddeley increased the load on it by giving normal subjects both a rehearsal task and a concurrent reasoning task. The reasoning times increase a little as the word list increased, but only by about a second or less, and errors in word recall did not go up significantly (figure 5.36). Using data from other tests involving concurrent tasks, Baddeley's research supports the idea that there are a number of working

Delayed Spatial Response

Visual Pattern Discrimination

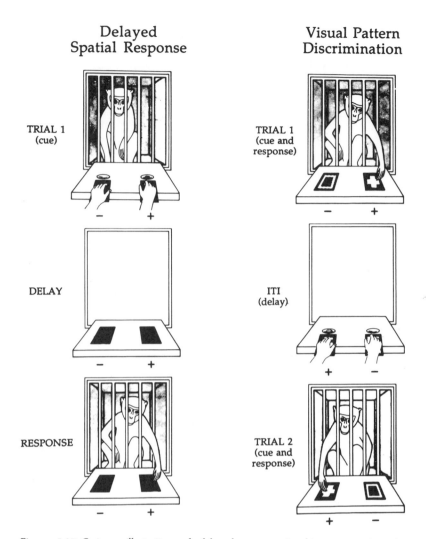

Figure 5.37 Cartoon illustration of delayed-response (working memory) and visual-discrimination (associative memory) tasks. In the delayed-response task, the monkey observes as the experimenter "hides" a food morsel in one of two food wells (top panel). The wells are then covered with identical plaques, the screen is lowered (middle panel), and, after a delay of several seconds, the screen is raised (bottom panel) and the monkey selects one of the wells. Note that at the time of the response, there is no cue in the test situation to guide the animal's choice: it must be guided by its memory of the baiting event, some seconds before. On the other hand, in conventional learning paradigms, illustrated by a visual discrimination problem, choice is elicited by external cues (trial 2) that have been consistently rewarded in the past (trial 1). Monkeys with prefrontal lesions are profoundly impaired on delayed-response tasks, but perform as well as unoperated controls on simple and conditional discrimination problems. The behavior can be reaching or a learned oculomotor response, such as moving eyes left or right. (From Goldman-Rakic 1990.)

memory "pods" (our word) standing in various relations to one another. One of these memory pods is mainly auditory, wherein items last about 1–2 sec, while another is visuospatial, another is primarily verbal, and possibly there are others. Presumably rehearsal, perhaps with the aid of visual or auditory images, keeps alive the processes that sustain working memory. This may explain why working memory for an event may seem introspectively to endure beyond a few brief seconds.

To make the links between behavior and anatomy and physiology, animal studies concerning memory at precise durations after the stimulus and relative to specific lesions are invaluable. Thus Goldman-Rakic (1987) has found that monkeys with lesions in the dorsolateral area of prefrontal cortex have a deficit in working memory that is specific to spatial relations and spares working memory for category of object. On the neurobiological side, she has recorded in intact animals from cells in that region that continue to fire throughout the delay between exposure to the stimulus and the cue to locate the task object (figure 5.37). When the task involves remembering the shape of an object rather than its location, these cells fail to show enhanced responses during the delay period.[40] (For a similar result in parietal cortex, see Gnadt and Andersen 1988.) Shape data are present in the stimulus, of course, but their irrelevance to the task means the dorsolateral cells need not "care" about them.[41] Apparently the cells found by Goldman-Rakic are holding task-relevant information until it can be used, although exactly what input drives them is not yet known. Once the information is no longer wanted, they return to a baseline state, prepatory to receiving and holding the next message. It appears that these experiments have uncovered a crucial fragment in the cellular basis for working memory. Notice too that it is a story about cells in *cortex*, not in the hippocampus (figure 5.38).

What possible mechanisms might serve working memory? One of the earliest suggestions was that activity initiated perceptually would continue to circulate in a recurrent network for the brief duration of the working memory period. While not without merit, this proposal has seemed unlikely for two main reasons. First, to be held in working memory for about 5 sec, a signal would have to circulate in the loop many times, on the order of 10^2–10^3 times, depending on loop size. That the signal can be precisely preserved over hundreds of synapses is somewhat improbable, biological systems being what they are. The second weakness in the proposal is that it typically assumes the signal is passed from one neuron to the next in the loop. The difficulty here is that single synapses are generally too weak by themselves to bring the post-synaptic neuron to threshold. If, on the other hand, each link consisted of a population of neurons, then given what is known physiologically, the circulation would have to be a statistical phenomenon, and no one quite knew how to model population circulation.

Investigating the population alternative of the "circulating signal" option, David Zipser (1991) has devised a simple recurrent network in which small groups of simple units (having only the sigmoid input–output relationships) can support a circulating STM. The model has two types of inputs. One is an

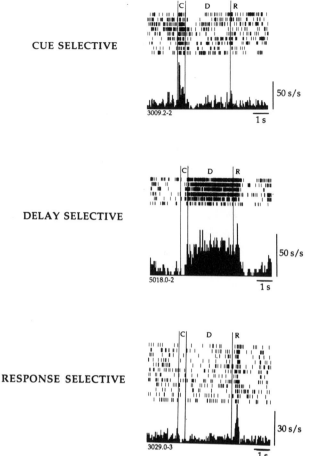

CUE SELECTIVE

DELAY SELECTIVE

RESPONSE SELECTIVE

Figure 5.38 Examples of three major types of neuronal processing exhibited by prefrontal neurons while a monkey performed the delayed response task. (Top) This cell exhibits a phasic response that is time locked to the presentation of a specific cue in the visual field. (Middle) This is an example of a neuron that is activated in the delay period when the to-be-remembered stimulus is no longer is view and the response has yet to be executed. The monkey is fixated during the delay, but the neuron responds directionally, i.e., it increased its rate of discharge only for specific cue locations. The tuning and "best direction" of the delay-period activity are highly similar to those of the cue-related activity for the cue-activated cells. It is presumed that these classes of cells are synaptically related. (Bottom) This cell has *presaccadic* activity, i.e., it discharges in a directionally specific manner after the fixation point disappears, but before the initiation of the required saccade. Such neurons presumably participate in the initiation of the oculomotor response. Possibly they are prefrontal neurons with direct connections to the deep layers of the superior colliculus. Other neurons (not shown) are also related to the response, but exhibit *postsaccadic* activity. The postsaccadic activity may serve as a signal from other centers to terminate the delay-period activity of synaptically linked prefrontal neurons. C, cue period; D, delay period; R, response period; 50 s/s, 50 spikes/sec. (From Goldman-Rakic 1990.)

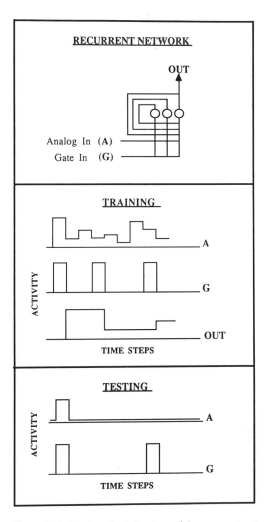

Figure 5.39 Input—output structure of the recurrent network model with diagrams of the training and testing paradigms. (From Zipser 1991.)

analog signal—for example, input representing visual stimuli. The second is a gating unit that is activated but only at regular intervals. When the gating unit is on, this is a command that the current analog signal be held until the gate opens again. The analog signal then enters a recurrent net, and recirculates until the gate next opens, whereupon the old signal is dumped out and a new one enters the recurrent nets to begin looping around (figure 5.39). This very simple arrangement serves to demonstrate how a population of units, configured in a recurrent net, is capable of holding a signal for a brief period. Whether this model is even roughly true to STM in real neural networks has not yet been shown, though it is at least consistent with the data from the Goldman-Rakic experiments. Misgivings might germinate because of several important model/reality differences: in Zipser's model a unit's output varies smoothly, and the units are densely interconnected. The output of real neurons,

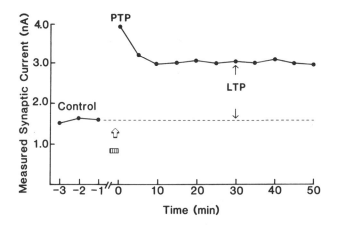

Figure 5.40 Mossy-fiber excitatory postsynaptic current (EPSC) amplitudes plotted over time, before and after the induction of LTP. Brief tetanic stimulation was applied at the time indicated (hatched bar and arrow). Note that the tetanic stimulation induces a posttetanic potentiation (PTP) that lasts a few minutes, superimposed on an LTP that lasts many minutes. (From Barrionuevo et al. 1986.)

by contrast, are action potentials that are not smoothly varying but discrete and that occur at distinct intervals rather than continuously. On the second matter, real neurons are more specifically and also more sparsely connected than in the model. These differences probably entail differences in network properties.[42]

The second possibility for a neuronal implementation of STM suggests a cellular mechanism with the same time course as the memory itself[43]—for example, a transient weight modification that lasts up to about 5 sec. Such modifications may be specific to synapses, or they could conceivably be a property of the whole cell, such as a shift in the firing threshold. No physiological evidence has yet confirmed this idea, so it lives by virtue of having escaped disconfirmation. One possibility is a phenomenon known as *post-tetanic potentiation*, or PTP (figure 5.40). This potentiation is a presynaptic effect, at least in those places it has been studied, and involves the release of larger amounts of transmitter from the presynaptic terminal following a high-frequency stimulus. PTP can be superimposed on an LTP effect. The potentiation of subsequent EPSPs is larger in PTP than in LTP, and decays in a matter of minutes. The brief duration has suggested that PTP may have a role in short-term or working memory. Because it is a presynaptic effect, however, all synapses the presynaptic cell talks to will be potentiated. This means less specificity than that seen in (vanilla) LTP. Throwing another log on the fires of speculation, one guess is that understanding oscillations, such as those studied by Llinás and his colleagues (Llinás 1988) or Gray et al. (1989),[44] may shed some light on mechanisms for transient weight change. It is possible, moreover, that biological systems exploit several mechanisms, and that transient synaptic modifications interact with recirculating activity to produce rather complex short-term effects.[45] (See table 5.1 for a list of known processes that modify synaptic efficacy at the neuromuscular junction.)

Table 5.1 Short-term processes that can affect synaptic efficacy

Presynaptic Factors	Magnitude[a] After One Impulse	Time Constant[b]
Components of increased transmitter release		
Facilitation		
First component	0.8	50 msec
Second component	0.12	300 msec
Augmentation	0.01[c]	7 sec
Potentiation (PTP)	0.01	20 sec to minutes[c]
Components of decreased transmitter release		
Depression		
Fast component	0–0.15[d]	5 sec
Slow component	0–0.001[d]	minutes[c]
Postsynaptic factors		
Desensitization of		
postsynaptic receptors	0–0.001[e]	5–20 sec

[a] Magnitude of the components of increased release is the fractional increase in release over the control level; a magnitude of 0.8 increases release by 80%. Magnitude of the components of decreased release is the fractional decrease of release below the control level; a magnitude of 0.15 decreases release by 15%. Magnitude for desensitization is the fractional decrease in end-plate potential amplitude resulting from a decreased number of functional postsynaptic receptors.
[b] Time constant is the time required to decay (or recover) to within 37% of the initial magnitude of release.
[c] Increases with the number of impulses.
[d] Depression is negligible under conditions of low quantal content and increases with increased extracellular calcium concentrations, which in turn increase quantal content.
[e] Not present under conditions of reduced transmitter release or normal physiological conditions. Can develop during extended high-frequency stimulation at increased levels of transmitter release.

(From K. L. Magleby, 1987)

8 BEING AND TIMING

Time is increasingly recognized as a factor that not only cannot be ignored, but must have pride of place in computational models. Time is especially relevant with respect to plasticity, since working or short-term memory is the nervous system's way of keeping a past signal in the present, and long-term memory is a way of making the more remote past available to the present. Although early parallel distributed processing (PDP) models simply left time out of consideration while other parameters were probed, realistic models such as Traub's (pp. 290–291) remind us of the importance of temporal relationships in circuits performing their function. Moreover, as suggested by the Llinás results where LTP in entorhinal cortex is elicited with oscillating current, coincidence of neural events may be critical for achieving certain functional results. Hints of this kind are also emerging from research elsewhere in the brain that show how certain cells have one or more intrinsic oscillating behaviors that can then entrain other cells in the projection basin.[46]

As noted in chapter 3, to get the relative timing of *current events* right, the nervous system probably exploits the biophysics of the system (Mead, 1987). Evolution has evidently stumbled upon solutions to space–time representation using, among other things, time constants for various neural activities, including oscillation frequencies, phase-locking oscillations, channel-open times, differential refractory periods, and bursting schedules, and the list could be extended. The cellular and circuitry architecture will then embody the design needed to make the times come out right for the particular brain and body in question, at least often enough for surviving in its niche, and mostly for a good deal more than merely scraping by. If the mechanism can also adapt to experience, then the temporal factors, Hebbian and otherwise, will be exploited in some ingenious fashion so that the timing comes out more accurately with experience. To repeat, timing accuracy for current events and for events that happen within a few seconds or minutes of the present will then be an architectural property of the system from top to bottom, not something added on to the basic anatomy and physiology of the network. Consequently such features as oscillation of cell types or populations probably cannot be written off as "mere implementation." Traub's model, it must be emphasized again, is pioneering in its exploration and incorporation of temporal parameters.

The strategy of letting time be its own representation (Mead 1987), extolled in chapter 3, has an important qualification, namely, that at best it applies only to "current events" or "current representations," where "current" means *roughly* "temporally close to now, on the order of a few seconds." Exploiting the time constants of nervous systems may be critical in how the nervous systems enable a bat to predict the trajectory of a moth so the bat may be at the right spot at the right time, but it appears to be an unsuitable strategy for representing events in one's own biography, for example. Consider these questions about temporal relations in one's life history: was your first kiss before or after receiving your driver's license? Did you have your first child before or after buying the color television set?[47] Most people know the answer to those questions very well, and, with reflection, other, less salient history can also be remembered with quite accurate temporal representation. It seems unlikely that biophysical properties such as channel-open times play the central role in representing time in autobiographical memory. More likely, some events have a date representation, and associated events can be remembered in that context.

Thus to remember the time period when a song—for example, "Polka Dot Bikin,"—was popular, one might start by specifying a large period (when I was in high school), then remembering a salient and dated event in that window (eighth grade when I got braces on my teeth), and from there one can relive in imagination events ordered relatively (the song was after eighth grade but before tenth grade when I got my license, and so on). In reconstructing relative temporal orderings, one's reliving appears to take the point of view of the original experience, involves associating other recollections, and may also involve recalling various events one did not necessarily set out to recall. It is more economical to store only a few absolute times and places, and to order other events and places only relatively.

Other temporal capacities may also require encoding time over various time scales. For example, birds can modify time spent searching for cryptic prey as a function of prey-capture intervals (on the order of a few seconds) averaged over time (minutes or hours) and taking into account the time left for foraging (time horizon) (Krebs and Kacelnik 1984). Moreover predators can time their hunting activities to coincide with circadian, tidal, and shorter-term activity rhythms of their prey (Daan and Aschoff 1982). There may be biochemical mechanisms such as hormonal cycles involved in such behavior.

9 DEVELOPMENT OF NERVOUS SYSTEMS

The most spectacular plasticity in the nervous system occurs during its development.[48] The learning which so fascinates and mystifies us when we contemplate acquisition of general and episodic knowledge, motor and cognitive skills, language and reading, pales by comparison with the electrifying conundrum that is development. Hundreds of different kinds of cells must be produced—Purkinje cells, motor neurons, amacrine cells, chandelier cells, etc.—with the morphology and physiology characteristic of their class (Reh 1991, Harris 1991) (figure 5.41). It is no good if a Purkinje cell behaves like a nonspiking amacrine cell, for example. Neurons must migrate from site of origin to the correct location, sometimes a distance of many centimeters—for example, to the correct layer in the cortical lamina or the correct vertebral site in the spinal cord (Shatz et al. 1991, Sur 1991); they must sprout suitable connections with the cells their type typically connect with, and fit themselves out with the appropriate receptor structures and neurotransmitters. And, as always in Nature, no Guiding Intelligence descends to cook it all up. Nor is the entire scenario written in the genes, spine by spine, synapse by synapse. There is not nearly enough DNA to code for it all.

A further remarkable fact about development is cell death.[49] In some structures, up to 75% of the founder cells die, and the prevailing hypotheses are that cell death may be programmed, as a genetic specification, or cell survival may be activity dependent. Although many factors may be involved in programmed cell death, the license-to-live that depends on level of activity in the context of trophic factors appears to be particularly important. Hebbian correlations can strengthen synapses, and in some manner this probably promotes the longevity of cells whose axons impinge, while other conditions may weaken synapses and in consequence may weaken also the cell whose process reached out. This activity-dependent developmental plasticity is modulated by the biochemical milieu of the local environment.

The research on development makes it sorely tempting to write as much again on that topic as we have already written on learning and memory. But, to echo our earlier lament, this is supposed to be only a chapter, not a book, on plasticity. Accordingly, this section must be trimmed with a harsh and heavy

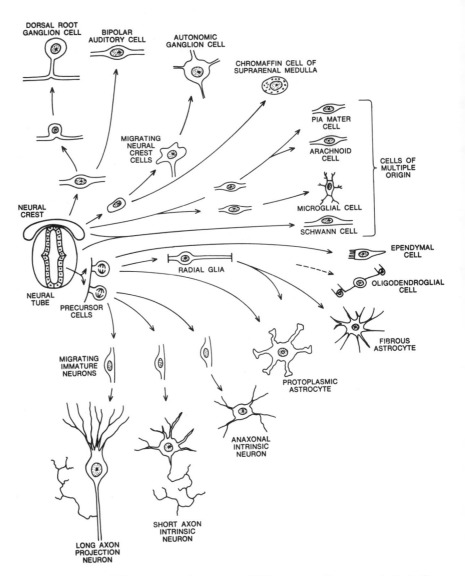

Figure 5.41 Origin, differentiation, and migration of different types of neurons and glia. In this figure, neurons of the peripheral nervous system are shown above, glial cells in the middle, and neurons of the central nervous system below. Note that precursor cells (in the ventricular zone) give rise directly to glial and neuronal lines before these cells migrate during development to their final positions and assume their final forms. (From Shepherd 1988; based on Rakic 1981.)

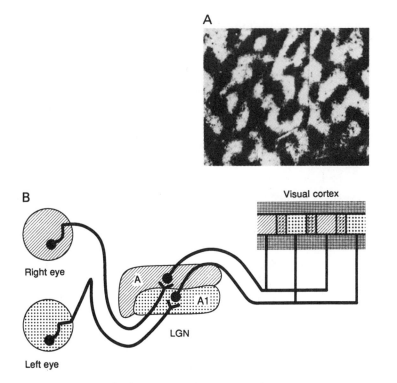

Figure 5.42 (A) Ocular dominance patches in layer 4 of the cat visual cortex. Photomontage was constructed from tangential sections taken through layer 4 of flattened cortex. Geniculostriate afferent terminals representing the ipsilateral eye were labelled and the populations appear white. (From Anderson et al. 1988.) (B) Schematic of the visual system after development of ocular dominance patches. The left LGN and visual cortex are pictured. Retinal ganglion cells from the two eyes project to separate laminae of the LGN, as shown, and LGN neurons in turn project to separate patches or stripes within layer 4 of cortex. (From Miller, Keller and Stryker [1989]. Ocular dominance column development: analysis and simulation. *Science* 245: 605–615. © AAAS.)

hand. Rather than compose a whirlwind summary, we have elected to describe a case study that will perhaps give a glimpse of the sort of understanding that can emerge from the interaction of neurobiological and computational experiments. The phenomena selected in this case study is the development of a striking organization in layer 4 of mammalian visual cortex called *ocular dominance patches* or *columns*. (See chapter 4.) This refers to a clustering of cells in layer 4 of visual cortex sharing a response-preference for input from either the left eye or the right eye. Layer 4 cells tend to be driven exclusively by one eye or the other, with about the same cortical space devoted to each eye. Upper layer cells, by contrast, may be activated by the right eye, the left eye, or by both with varying degrees of eye preference. With anatomical labeling of cells achieved by injecting a radioactive amino acid in one eye, the ocular dominance clustering shows up as wobbly bands wending across layer 4 (figure 5.42A). This case is apt for our purposes, because quite a lot of the anatomy and physiology of the relevant cells are known, and because here too the questions revolve around how global properties emerge out of local interactions.

Cells owe their ocularity to the pattern of nonoverlapping connections from right eye cells and left eye cells segregated in different layers of the LGN (figure 5.42B). In the very early developmental stages, however, neither the layers of the LGN nor layer 4 of visual cortex exhibit the segregation into monocularly driven cells. Rather, the axons from the right and left eyes are distributed randomly (LeVay et al. 1978). As the animal develops, axons segregate according to eye of origin into monocularly innervated patches—the ocular dominance patches (Hubel et al. 1977, Shatz and Stryker 1978). At the cellular level what happens is that the axons from the two eyes prune back branches to some areas, and extend and proliferate branches into other areas, eventually segregating themselves to distinct ocular dominance patches (Sretavan and Shatz 1986). What determines how the axons from right and left eye prune and proliferate during development such that at the end of the critical period they are segregated into monocularly innervated patches?

A major clue is that the normal cortical organization can be perturbed during a critical period (approximately $3\frac{1}{2}$ to 6 weeks of age in the kitten, and in monkeys it is largely prenatal) by monocular deprivation, that is, by shutting one eye. The result of monocular deprivation is that the nondeprived eye activates a larger cortical region, and the region of cortex activated by the deprived eye is shrunk (LeVay and Stryker 1979). On the other hand, closing both eyes during the same period has no abnormal effect (Wiesel and Hubel 1965).

The monocular deprivation results suggest that development of the characteristic patterns of ocular dominance patches in layer 4 of visual cortex of the mature animal involves an activity-dependent competition between the LGN axons originating in the right and left eyes. When the left eye is deprived, LGN axons originating from the right eye will be more active and end up with greater representation. Guillery (1972) refined the monocular deprivation paradigm by making a small lesion in the open eye to deprive the axons within only a small patch of otherwise active axons. He discovered that the usual effects of monocular deprivation were seen everywhere except for the area representing the axons from the lesioned, undeprived eye (and the corresponding region of the closed eye), where ocular dominance patches of a more normal size were found. Guillery's results indicate that the competition is quite local.

To explore further the hypothesis that synapse-dependent activity is the critical factor, Stryker and colleagues (Stryker and Harris 1986; Stryker 1986) designed experiments in which they pharmacologically blocked all impulse activity, from retina to cortex, for both right and left eyes in kittens. Unlike the condition where both eyes are closed during the critical period, the silencing condition disrupted ocular dominance segregation of layer 4 cells, which could be driven by either eye (the cells were binocular). This result suggests that the segregation seen when both eyes are closed is probably owed to spontaneous activity in the axons, of which there is quite a lot in the immature animal. Moreover, it is a clear demonstration of the necessity of neuronal activity for the segregation of monocularly driven cells.

The next question bears on what *temporal* relations among activity from right and left eyes are required to produce ocular dominance. To sort this out, Stryker and Strickland (1984) began by asking whether differences in the timing of left and right eye signals, and hence the timing of synaptic activity of cells in layer 4 of the cortex, would have an effect on ocular dominance organization. For this experiment, the activity in both left and right retina and LGN axons was pharmacologically silenced. Next, the optic nerve from the left and right eye of the kittens was artificially stimulated. In one group, the stimulation from left and right optic nerves was synchronous; in the other, it was asynchronous. If the two nerves were activated *synchronously*, the layer 4 cells failed to segregate into ocular dominance columns; if they were *asynchronously* activated, all cells showed ocularity.

To see that this makes sense, consider a layer 4 cortical cell with synapses from axons projecting from both right and left eye. When the left eye axons are stimulated but not the right, the "left synapses" are strengthened, the right are relatively weaker, and vice versa. Hence the cortical cells become increasing tied to input from one or the other eye, and thus become increasingly monocular. If, on the other hand, both left and right axons are synchronously activated, "left synapses" and "right synapses" will be equally strengthened, and the cell will remain binocular. The asynchronous case corresponds to the normal developmental conditions because the light falls on slightly different retinal locations, and hence a given layer 4 cortical cell may be driven only by the "left" axons and a nearby neighbor may be driven only by the "right" axons. It is also consistent with the development of ocular dominance columns in the fetal monkey. Spontaneous activity in unstimulated eyes would typically be asynchronous in left and right optic nerves, and hence would satisfy the asynchrony requirement. Additionally, Reiter and Stryker (1988) showed that involvement of the postsynaptic cells (cortical cells in layer 4) was necessary. When they silenced only the activity of the cortical cells, leaving the LGN axons intact, monocular eye closure had very different results from the standard case: in the silenced region of cortex, LGN axons from the closed eye dominated over those from the open eye. (For a review, see Shatz 1990.)

This range of results suggests that a Hebbian mechanism might be responsible for the selective strengthening of synapses and hence for the emergence of ocularity. One possibility is that synapses are strengthened in the way that pre- and postsynaptic cells interact in LTP, perhaps requiring NMDA. In fact, however, there are many possible mechanisms, including exposure of synapses, stabilization of synapses, trophic factors that are taken up in an activity-dependent way by presynaptic cells or perhaps by glial cells that then modify presynaptic cells, and so forth. What, in the nervous system, is the mechanism? Are there perhaps several mechanisms? Another question is this: Which of the parameters (arbor widths, intracortical spread of a given cell's effect, the width of correlations of activity between neighboring points in the retina) are key for the emergence of ocular dominance organization and for the scale of the column?

Miller and Stryker (1990) constructed a realistic computer model simulating development of kitten visual cortex to address these questions. They incorporated the basic pathways seen in the newborn kitten from cells in the lateral geniculate nucleus (LGN) to cortical cells in layer 4, the axonal arborization profile in cortex of the input LGN cells, as well as lateral connections between cortical cells along with their sign (excitatory or inhibitory) and, given their sign, their prototypical fan-out. The critical issue concerns intercellular activity—what changes and how, as a function of activity, and how the activity must be timed.

It turns out that the key factors for the emergence of ocular dominance organization are connectivity, activity correlations between eye represented, and interactions that depend only on the distance between neurons. Although Miller had conjectured this earlier using analytical techniques alone, the results of the simulation confirmed the analytical characterization. In addition, it permitted exploration of the monocular deprivation effects. Before discussing the model in more detail, it may be useful to flag one of its instructive features, namely, that despite the richness of the empirical constraints, and despite the model's successfully mimicking a wide range of experimental results on the emergence of ocularity, the model shows up as neutral on the question of whether the mechanism for synapse strengthening resembles the mechanism mediating LTP in CA1 cells, or involves an activity-dependent uptake of trophic factor by presynaptic cells, or both, or something else yet again. Given the model's realism, this is informative. For the model in effect identifies which biological parameters are critical for the development of ocular dominance columns and have to be pinned down mechanistically, and which are indifferent to the exact nature of the mechanism, so long as *some* mechanism does the job. The model therefore indicates what biological properties are not germane to the level of questions concerning correlation-based, activity-dependent development of cortical organization. The model thus guides researchers in deciding what experiments will be useful in helping explain development of cortical organization.

The mathematical aspect of the model derives from four biological parameters, summarized in figure 5.43: (1) the patterns of initial connectivity of the geniculocortical afferents onto cortical cells (the "arbor function"); (2) the patterns of activity in the afferents (four "correlation" functions for the four possible combinations between left and right sides—left–left, right–right, right–left, left–right); (3) lateral influences within the cortex in virtue of which synapses on one cell can influence the competition occurring on nearby cells ("cortical interaction function"); and (4) conservation of the total synaptic strength supported by a given input or output cell.[50] A network model should be a good tool for analyzing the relative contribution and significance of each of these four main factors under varying conditions, including monocular and binocular deprivation, and silencing. All of these parameters can be experimentally measured, and some values are already known. Hence the model can be constrained, tested, and used to make predictions. (See also Miller et al. 1989.)

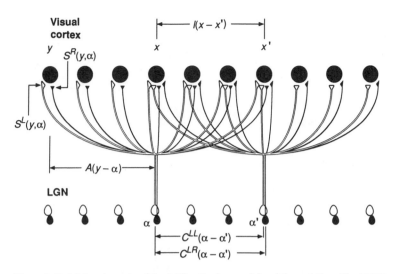

Figure 5.43 Major elements of the Miller-Stryker model and the notation. The LGN is modeled as consisting of two layers, one serving each eye. Each layer is two-dimensional (only one dimension is illustrated here). Greek letters α, α' label geniculate positions. The cortex is modeled as a single two-dimensional layer with position labeled by the roman letters x, x', y. In the figure, x and x' are taken to be the cortical positions retinotopically corresponding to α and α', respectively. Geniculate cells project synapses to a range of cortical cells, centered about the retinotopically corresponding cortical position. The anatomical strength of the projection (the number of synapses) from the geniculate cell of either eye at α to the cortical cell at position y is proportional to the arbor function $A(y - \alpha)$. This function depends on the distance between y and the point x that corresponds retinotopically to α. The physiological strength of the projection (the effectiveness of the geniculate cell's activity in driving the cortical cell) is given by the total synaptic strength, $S^L(y,\alpha)$ for the left eye or $S^R(y,\alpha)$ for the right eye. S^L and S^R change during development in the model, while the arbor function A is held fixed; the assumption is made that anatomical changes occur late in development, after a pattern of synaptic strengths is established. Geniculate inputs are locally correlated in their firing. The correlation of a left-eye afferent at α with a left-eye afferent at α' is given by $C^{LL}(\alpha - \alpha')$, while the correlation with the right-eye afferent at α' is given by $C^{LR}(\alpha - \alpha')$. There is an influence across cortex, by which activation at the point x' influences growth of synapses at point x. The sign and strength of this influence is given by the intracortical interaction function $I(x - x')$. (From Miller et al. 1989.)

The architecture was specified by two sets of equations based on the four parameters outlined, one equation specifying the dynamical response of the cortical neurons to a pattern of geniculate inputs, and the second equation specifying the synaptic update rule. The simulation contained units representing single neurons, an array of 25 × 25 units in each layer of the LGN and another 25 × 25 array representing layer 4, making a total of 1875 units. Each LGN unit arborized to contact a 7 × 7 square of cortical units. Thus there was a total of 61,250 synapses in the model. Although this is relatively small by the standards of mammalian cortex, it was sufficiently large to display a number of properties of cortical architecture that emerge during development. The inputs to the simulation were given by the correlation functions representing LGN activity, both within an eye and between eyes. The dynamics occurred on two time scales: (fast) the response of the cortical neurons to a visual input pattern

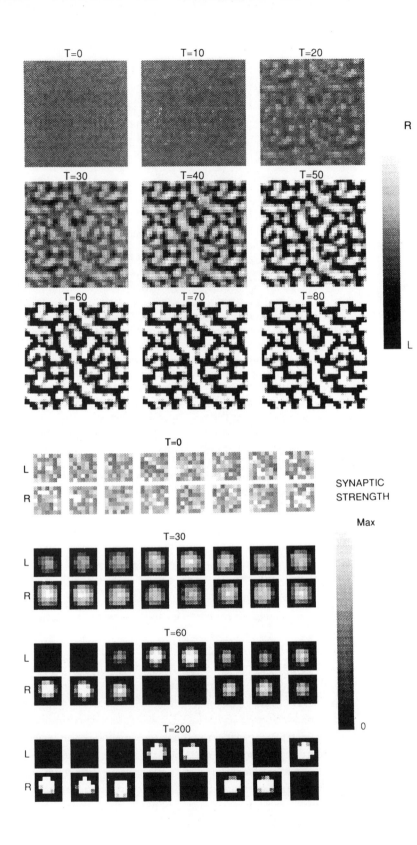

originating in the geniculate, and (slow) weight modification according to a Hebb rule, based on averaging over many input patterns. At start-up, the synaptic strengths between cells (representing physiological strength) are randomly set; that is, the total synaptic strength from cell α to cell γ is a random number (uniformly distributed between 0.8 and 1.2) multiplied by the arbor function from α to γ. This corresponds to giving each individual synapse a random weight between 0.8 and 1.2, with the arbor function specifying the number of synapses. Given this starting point, the simulated kitten cortex was then allowed to "develop." The question is, Given only these constraints, how does the simulated cortex self-organize?

Analyzing the results after various time steps, Miller and Stryker found that the organization of the simulated developing cortex captured a number of the important properties seen in experimental conditions. For example, ocular dominance patches had formed in "cortex," the simulated cortical cells, like real cortical cells, had refined their receptive fields and acquired ocularity, and axonal arbors sorted themselves into complementary dominance stripes. That is, left-eye LGN cells hooked up with left monocular cortical cells, next to stripes of right-eye LGN cells hooked up with right monocular cells, and so on (figure 5.44). Why are these useful results? Because they show, time step by time step, the emergence of a complex macroproperty from basically very simple local interactions. Whereas one might guess at such a mechanism on the basis of neurobiological data, it is a major step forward to show in simulation that these effects really could be produced by this handful of constraints. As we all know, this does not prove that actual cortical populations really do organize in the fashion of the simulation. Nevertheless, knowing that they *can* is reassuring, and the computer simulation grounds a plethora of testable predictions.

Miller, Keller, and Stryker (1989) found that correlation among nearest neighbors in the retinal input was sufficient to give a periodic pattern of columns, and that positive correlations over a somewhat larger radius was sufficient to produce a monocular cortical layer 4. They were also able to reproduce many of the abnormal patterns associated with both monocular deprivation and with alternating deprivation. These are benchmark tests showing that the model performs as it ought to in matching known observations.

Figure 5.44 Ocular dominance patterns in the Miller-Stryker developmental model of visual cortex. (Top) A 40 × 40 grid of model neurons in visual cortex is shown at nine stages. Each pixel represents a single cortical cell, and the gray level (key on right) shows the ocularity of the cell. (Bottom) Development of receptive fields of 8 cortical cells at four time steps. Each vertical L-R pair of large squares shows the synaptic strengths of the 7 × 7 left eye inputs and 7 × 7 right eye inputs onto a single cortical cell. The cells shown here are the 8 leftmost cells in the bottom row of the array in the upper figure. Synapses from the inputs start off ($T = 0$) with random values of their weights. During the first stage, the weights in the central region of the 7 × 7 array increase, but on the periphery they decrease ($T = 30$). In the next stage ($T = 60$), the units acquire ocularity. Finally ($T = 200$), adjacent groups of cells tend to become dominated by the same eye, so that ocular dominance patches become more sharply defined. (From Miller and Stryker 1990.)

Having created a model whose developmental profile relevantly resembles that of the kitten cortex, Miller et al. were then in a position to take the next step and ask questions of the model concerning the emergent macrofeatures, where such questions are difficult if not impossible experimentally. One question is, How does changing the sizes of the input and output arbors affect the scale of the patches? The answer out of model manipulations is that the primary parameter in determining the size of the patch is size of the cortical interaction function, that is, the distance over which a single cell will influence its neighbors with excitatory interactions. This implies that it is the cortex that sets the scale, while the LGN afferents conform. For all one knew in advance, the answer could have gone the other way: the LGN sets the scale and the cortex conforms. The further step is mathematically to analyze the simulation. Miller et al. found that in the limit, where the weights are small, the equations for the network are approximately linear and can be analyzed with Fourier transforms. The mathematical explorations showed several important things: (1) the size of the cortical interaction function sets the limits on the size of the ocular dominance patch, and (2) the actual size of the patch is determined by the fastest growing wavelength of ocular dominance oscillations (Fourier component) within the arbor diameter. Such results, it may be suggested, are worth a million simulations, but notice too that simulations are often necessary to identify what is worth trying to explore by mathematical means.

How does all this relate to Singer's window for LTD? The developmental result Singer mentions is actually owed to Reiter and Stryker (1988). Although rather complicated, it can be summarized as follows: consider monocularly deprived kittens where a GABA-A receptor agonist is applied to the cortex to prevent the cortical neurons from depolarizing normally (Reiter and Stryker 1988). The connections from the closed eye may not be significantly affected, since they are not stimulated anyhow. The connections that will be most affected are those from the open eye. This experiment tests the role of pre- and postsynaptic coactivation in turf wars. The result is that the turf expansion of open-eye cortical cells is prevented. Paradoxically, the open-eye cortical cells suffer a turf reduction, and the closed eye occupies a larger than normal region of cortex. Consider now that this situation may satisfy the conditions for LTD. That is, the presynaptic cells are active (i.e., the LGN afferents from the open eye), but the postsynaptic cells (cortical layer 4 cells) cannot respond normally. Hence not only is the activity level of the cortical neurons driven by the open eye down, it is subnormal, thus permitting the closed-eye neurons to expand their turf, while the open-eye neurons retreat to smaller regions. Reiter and Stryker's observation is at the level of the network. To see how the details of Singer's observations concerning LTD could fit into this framework, models such as that of Miller et al. could be used to explore the various possibilities.[51]

10 MODULES AND NETWORKS

Although the topics of computation, representation, and plasticity have been separated into three chapters, they are, of course, intimately connected. Their separation reflects only the practical necessity of saying one thing at a time. Boiled down to bare essentials, the general framework is this: *representations* are activation vectors, *learning* involves changing synaptic weights, and *computation* is a matter of vector–vector transformations through weights and squashing functions. Emphatically, this is only the sketch of a conceptual framework, stark and spare. The fleshing-out involves more—more by many orders of magnitude. To show how the framework looks with a little flesh on its bones, we have introduced several computational models, drawing where appropriate on the relevant psychophysics and neuroscience. These models have, however, been trained up to perform a single task, such as binocular depth perception or determining the shape of an object from its shading profile. The brain, however, is the very opposite of a one-trick pony. Nervous systems perform a stunning range of tasks simultaneously, and with such prevailing coherence as to suggest to the spiritually inclined the presence of a smart soul that orchestrates the unity. Souls there probably are not, but what is the organizational secret?

Although the answer is still over the horizon, some general observations that help get a bearing on the question are possible. First, nervous systems, unlike Fusion-Net, for example, are vast networks of networks, with various regions specializing for various tasks. This is evident in sensory systems, such as the visual system, the olfactory system, and so on, but it seems also true of functions more highly cognitive, such as speech production, speech comprehension, planning, and conforming to social conventions. On the other hand, reciprocal connections make it obvious that nervous systems are intensely recurrent in style, and a counterbalance to the specialization seen physiologically is the massive convergence endemic to neuroanatomy. Some pathways seem specialized for certain tasks, such as perception of motion, yet a single area, such as MT, cannot be fingered as *the center* for motion perception, at least for the reason that other areas also have neurons that selectively respond to motion and where lesions result in deficits in motion perception. To be *the center* for a capacity would presumably mean that so long as an area has input, then its normal functioning is *necessary and sufficient* for the exercise of the capacity. This is a very strong requirement indeed, and it is unlikely to be satisfied except in the simplest behaviors of the simplest animals, given the interactive nature of nervous systems and the distributed nature of representation. Thus specialization, to the degree that it exists, does not imply discrete localization.[52]

Memory storage in nervous systems appears entirely unlike memory storage in a digital computer, at least because modifications seem to be made to the very same structures that do the information processing. How can nervous systems achieve the consistency they do in perception, cognition, and sensorimotor control if the very processing architecture is itself changing? The puzzle is now a little more in focus: there is divergence but also convergence, specialization without dedicated localization, coherence and unity without anything analogous to a choir conductor. One thing this suggests is that nervous systems may be modularized, but in a distinctly biological and interconnected style of modularity. What can be learned about this style from data at the behavioral level as well as at the levels of the single cell, the circuit, the area, and the system?

Can we not just define "module" and then decide on available data whether nervous systems are modularized? Since dictionary definitions of "module" are tied to such things as "independently operated vehicle in a space ship," or "unit in a series of standardized units for use together," the dictionary is not very useful for the real questions we want answered. Our questions concern the nature of specialization, convergence, divergence, and coherence in nervous tissue. To get close to specifying at least roughly what is meant by "modularity" in the neurobiological context, we begin by noting that there are, inevitably, several different hypotheses about what makes a module. The sense of "module" current in neurology (Gazzaniga 1985, Caramazza 1988) and experimental psychology (Chomsky 1980, Fodor 1983) takes behavioral phenomena as the baseline, and postulates structurally separate modules from there, using, for example, lesion data showing double dissociation of a pair of tasks. In its psychological elaboration, the idea draws on a computer-based sense of modules, meaning "a component that is informationally impervious to lateral and top-down influences (also known as 'informationally encapsulated'), that goes through its processing paces obligatorily, without option or deviation, normally without modification or plasticity, and independently of what other modules are up to." (See also Minsky 1985.)

In neuroanatomy and neurophysiology, the sense of "module" is more closely tied to cells—their connectivity, their physiology, and their response profiles. Mainly on anatomical data regarding the connectivity patterns of cells, Szentagothai (1975) suggested that the cerebral cortex was a kind of "... mosaic of columnar units of remarkably similar internal structure and surprisingly little variation in diameter (200–300 microns)." About the same time, Mountcastle (1978) postulated "mini-columns" as the basic modular units of cortex. Drawing on physiological as well as anatomical evidence, he hypothesized that a mini-column "... is a vertically oriented cord of cells formed by the migration of neurons ... it contains about 110 cells ... (and) ... occupies a gently curving, nearly vertical cylinder of cortical space with a diameter of about 30 microns." Szentagothai's constructs came to be referred to as "macro-columns" to forestall confusion with Mountcastle's constructs. On the basis of evolutionary and connectivity considerations, Stevens (1989) also postulates a type of cortical module.[53] One important issue concerns whether modules postulated on behavioral criteria have any relation to modules postulated on neurobiological criteria; for example, if, as Fodor suggests, the lexicon[54] in language use is a module, with what neurobiological modules, if any, might it correlate? The more fundamental question, however, is whether macro-columns, mini-columns, or functional modules are empirically sound constructs, useful for organizing research and explaining nervous system phenomena at various levels.

One particular matter engages our attention in this section, and it concerns what light can be shed on neurobiological modularity from the perspective of lesion studies in human subjects. The wider issue of lesion studies in general is very important, but much too large to be discussed properly here (H. Damasio and A. Damasio 1989, Grobstein 1990). The debate concerning modularity in cortical columns is likewise important and captivating, but apologetically, we leave it also for other authors. (For a critique of this sort of modularity, see Swindale 1990 and LeVay and Nelson 1991.) Our rather narrow choice is motivated by the singular role of human data from neuropsychology[55] and what precisely loss of highly confined capacities tells us about modularity in brain organization. Considerations of space bid us narrow our focus even more, and confine the human case studies to those involving recognition deficits, for here is the major threshing ground for the lesion/modularity issues at hand. In keeping with our background prejudices, we shall bring the conceptual framework of networks to bear on various cases, in an effort to render them a little more comprehensible.

As a final preliminary, be warned that even within the small class chosen for discussion, there is considerable variation in lesion location and size, as well as in patients' capacities, histories, and ages. Lesions in human brains are, as it were, nature's unwelcome experiments. Because the exact repeatability and precise controls demanded of laboratory experiments are beyond the bounds of what is ethical, the neuropsychologist's main tool is observation of what nature presents—the behavioral profile as displayed in various standardized tests, the site of the lesion as seen in scans or at autopsy, and comparison with other patients. To the neuropsychologist's advantage, however, is the fact that human subjects, unlike rats and monkeys, may be guided by verbal instructions, and that they can provide singularly illuminating testimonies of what precisely is spared and what is not, and of what they are aware and what not.

Patients with bilateral lesions in the occipital–temporal border region often suffer facial agnosia (prosopagnosia), meaning that they are unable to recognize faces that before the brain damage were familiar to them. Thus they may not be able to recognize visually members of their family, their close friends, famous faces, or even their own face in a photograph. Nor are they able to identify individuals repeatedly encountered after the damage, such as their doctors and nurses (A. Damasio et al. 1990). They typically are also unable to identify as individuals various other things, such as their own dog, car, or house, though they may taxonomize them correctly. For example, such a patient may not recognize his dog, Daisy, even though he knows that the thing in front of him is a dog. One important fact here is that although visual recognition of individuals by face may be impaired, recognition of an individual, as the unique individual he is, may be achieved quite normally when gait or posture is observed, or when a different sensory modality is cued, as, for example, by hearing the wife's speaking voice or Daisy's familiar yapping.

There seem to be two general possibilities regarding the patient's representation of individuals such as Daisy. Either there are distinct "Daisy representations" for each modality (McCarthy and Warrington 1988), or there is a single composite representation of Daisy, accessible by means of a kind of reconstruction through different sensory channels (A. Damasio et al. 1990). The second may be rather more economical of hardware, and within the context of neural nets it is fairly easy to envisage output vectors from different sensory networks feeding into a common multimodal network to activate neurons whose values collectively represent Daisy. This need not imply an axonal convergence in one small place, but is consistent with distributed representation. In other words, the convergence is *informational* rather than spatial. Thus a lesion midway in the visual processing stream might prevent identification of Daisy's face by looking at her, but if the auditory pathway is intact, the Daisy representation can be accessed by the auditory route. Thus, on Antonio Damasio's interpretation of the data, it is not so much that the facial representation of Daisy is lesioned, as that visual access to the Daisy representation, abstractly characterized, is lesioned. In other words, at some processing level, there is a set of neurons that collectively display a unique activation vector when Daisy's bark is heard, or when someone says, "Daisy chased the ducks yesterday." Before the lesion, that unique pattern of activation could also have been elicited when Daisy's face appeared. Indeed, it could have been activated when a cocker spaniel very like Daisy had been installed in Daisy's basket as a practical joke.

In principle, vector completion allows for filling in of relevant visual information even when the input vector is basically auditory. Thus once the Daisy representation is accessed, a normal subject may be able to go on and describe Daisy's visual properties in loving detail. Depending on the location and extent of the lesion, a patient may also be able to describe some of Daisy's visual properties. Assuming the net is recurrent, the possibility of access to assorted visual aspects of the representation from an auditory cue is readily understandable. In the clinic, however, patients with very extensive damage, such as Boswell, are not able to specify visually observable characteristics even if the proper name of someone well-known, such as President Kennedy, is provided.

The second and related group of data concerns a rather puzzling deficit profile observed in several patients (Warrington and McCarthy 1987, A. Damasio et al. 1989[56]). These patients have assorted lesions in temporal cortex and may have defects in recognizing visually the category to which some objects belong, and hence fail to recognize visually a pig as a pig, or a tree as a tree. On the other hand, they score very well on such things as scissors and pens. For example, patient P.S.D. (A. Damasio et al. 1989) had poor recognition of natural objects, scoring only about 30% correct. Shown a picture of a snail, he replied that it was some kind of animal, but he really had no idea what it was. He was nevertheless quite able to define the word "snail" very accurately when asked to do so. By contrast, he was much more accurate in recognizing manmade objects, such as hammers and screwdrivers, telephones and automobiles (73–100%). The exceptions to this class were musical instruments, such as a violin or flute, where his score fell to less than 30% for visual recognition. He was, however, fast and highly accurate in *sound* recognition of musical instruments.

Boswell's deficits are more severe. He cannot recognize a camel from a photograph. In addition, his definitions for animals are poor; for example, when given the word "camel," he fudges around in generalities ("a little animal, only about a foot tall and one foot long; kind of a squarish-round shape, kind of furrish, and looks kind of like a puppy dog"). By contrast, his definitions for some semantic categories, especially those whose instances are devoid of visual aspects, can be very good. For example, he says that a "desire" is "a great wish for something," and he defines the economy as "the financial situation." More generally, superordinate categories tend typically to be spared ("animal," "plant," "building") when subordinate categories are impaired ("snail," "daffodil," "woodshed"), and if these more specific categorial capacities are impaired, recognition of individuals tends to be impaired as well.

Antonio Damasio's hypothesis for these cases extends the interpretation for the first data cluster; namely, recognition deficits imply impaired access to an abstract, as opposed to modality-specific, representation. The feedback projections normally in place from abstract to modality-specific representations are disrupted by lesions, and hence the patient cannot say much if anything about what the animal looks like. In the first sort of case, the representation was of a unique individual; in the second, of a rather specific subcategory of things whose most salient properties are usually discerned visually. Damasio's hypothesis is that the second range of deficits can be understood on the same principle as the first, but the location of the lesion means that different behavior is seen. Crudely, there are networks interacting with networks interacting with networks. To a first approximation, recognition defects may be described in terms of a network organization that involves both information convergence and feedback, and relative degree of categorial specificity (A. Damasio 1990).

Roughly speaking, there is a correlation between degree of *generality* of still-viable categories and location of lesion in the temporal lobe (A. Damasio et al. 1990). Patients whose lesions are more anterior in the temporal lobe are more likely to have lost highly specific taxonomy. That is, with a lesion in the right temporal pole, a patient may be able to describe something in a photograph as a animal, as a dog, and maybe even as a German shepherd, but not as his own dog Ferguson, nor as the publicly renowned television German shepherd, Rin Tin Tin. A more posterior lesion involving inferotemporal cortices means the probable loss of subcategories of dog but the retention of the capacity to distinguish dogs from cats from birds (Figure 5.45). With a more posterior lesion yet again, recognition may be limited merely to "animal." Doing the same anterior-to-posterior track on the left temporal lobe shows the loss first of proper names, followed by loss of highly specific common nouns, followed by loss of more encompassing common nouns (figure 5.46). This remarkable mapping of what Damasio calls a "categorial hierarchy" onto front-to-back regions of the temporal lobe suggests a recurrent net hierarchy whose anatomical apex is the entorhinal cortex, the source of input for the perforant path into the hippocampus, and a major zone of convergence for areas from all over the cortex.

The resources of the conceptual framework can be marshalled to encompass the data and to make the Damasio approach a little more familiar and systematic. This also provides the occasion for reconsidering the matter of

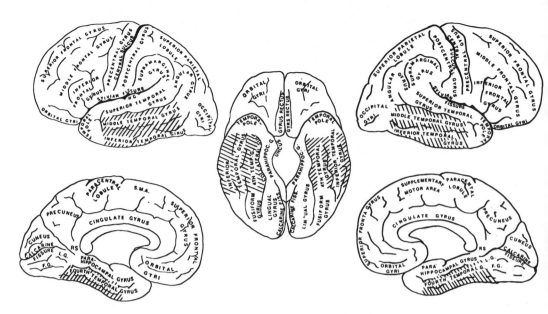

Figure 5.45 The cross-hatched areas represent the human inferotemporal (IT) regions. This is an area limited by the superior temporal sulcus (laterally) and the collateral sulcus (medially). It includes the middle, inferior, and fourth temporal gyri. Bilateral damage to this area in humans cause defects of recognition and naming of entities belonging to certain conceptual categories. (Courtesy Hanna Damasio.)

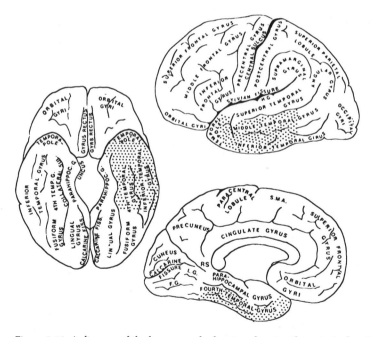

Figure 5.46 A diagram of the human cerebral cortex showing the extent of cortices related to lexical retrieval operations (stippled area). They include the *left* temporal pole and the middle (second), inferior (third), and fourth temporal gyri. Lesions in these areas have now been associated with a defect in retrieval of common nouns and proper nouns. (Courtesy Hanna Damasio.)

modularity.[57] First, that subordinate categories are more vulnerable than superordinate categories is a predictable consequence of hierarchical partitioning of activation space. Recall that activation space is partitioned by the weights, and when weights are destroyed it is obviously the fine-grained or more esoteric partitions that go first. This is because the more general partitions are relevant to many different input vectors. That is, "animal" will be the output for a very wide range of input vectors, whereas "bumblebee" requires a highly specific input vector. Moreover, incomplete input vectors will complete accordingly to the most general partitions for the simple reason that only a few elements are required relative to what is required for a highly specific partition such as bumblebee. Thus P.S.D. can usually recognize that something is an animal; he just cannot tell whether it is a bee or a pig or a moose. Recognition of unique individuals will be the same, only more so. That is, a wider range of vectors will activate the representation "dog" than will activate "collie dog" than will activate "Lassie." (See A. Damasio and H. Damasio, in press.)

What might be the basis of a dissociation between recognition of natural objects and musical instruments on the one hand, and manmade objects on the other? Does this imply, for example, that there is a module for "man-made" things and another module for "musical instruments"? First, it is important to note that the deficit is *statistical*, not absolute. P.S.D., for example, can in fact recognize a piano and an elephant, but not most animals or most musical instruments. Antonio Damasio (1990) suggests that a number of factors are probably relevant to the dissociation profiles observed. For starters, if someone has frequently had a motor interaction with an object—for example, a spoon or a piano—then motor patterns characteristic for interaction with that object may be a clue when the object is visually presented; that is, a motor system vector may be input to the relevant network. Since few of us interact frequently with a goat or a bee, no well-defined motor vector can provide a clue in these cases, though it might for a beekeeper or a goat herder.

Second, if an object has particular value to the patient, either strongly positive or strongly negative, its visual presentation may generate feelings, thus providing an affect input vector to the relevant network. This might be enough to enable the patient to identify a snake or a skunk, though not a saxophone or a palm tree. There are undoubtedly a variety of other factors at work as well (A. Damasio et al. 1990a, b). Damasio also suggests that the right temporal lobe executes highly complex configural analysis, and hence lesions here impair the patient's capacity to distinguish cats from bears, dogs from pigs. The left temporal lobe appears to be more specialized for linguistic functions and other tasks involving fine motor control, such as playing the violin or drawing or carving. Hence the loss of recognition of manmade objects may be expected following lesions in this region.

Modularity may be *consistent* with these data, but it is by no means *implied* by the data. On the contrary, the fact that nets can be trained up to categorize many different incoming vectors, and that they do this by partitioning activation space—for example, into "rock" or "mine" space—suggests that before acquiescing in a modularity hypothesis, the framework of neural nets should be considered as a more perspicuous way to accommodate the data. Thus rather than postulate a damaged "musical instrument module," one might instead hypothesize damage to neurons that typically represent a chunk of the incoming vector for a higher-up network, a chunk that happens to be important for coding musical instruments specifically.

To see how powerful may be the semblance of modularity, in both standard and lesioned conditions, consider NETtalk, which quite accurately maps graphemes onto phonemes, even for the irregular cases. An analysis of the activation of vectors, which clusters vectors according to their Euclidean distance from each other, shows a partitioning of activation space that is hierarchical, in the sense that it has one broad division, separating vowels and consonants. Within each of these categories there are further subdivisions, for example, the stopped sounds, "p" and "b," are grouped together, and "v" and "f" are grouped together. Suppose, through simulated anoxia, some of the units crucial for the coding of vowels are selectively lesioned. How will this present at the behavioral level? Well, the lesioned network will score poorly in vowel recognition, but still perform close to normally at consonant recognition. Now because the net is fully connected, the units coding primarily for vowels are in fact scattered throughout the hidden layer; their clustering is *functional not physical.* Imagine, however, that as a result of some unsupervised training regimen in an architecture with lateral interactions, there happens also to be some rough physical clustering of those units. Then a "stroke" in one location could well produce the selective loss of vowel pronunciation. (For an example relevant to dyslexia, see Hinton and Shallice 1991.)

The point is, no physical modularity worth its salt exists in NETtalk. One large net does a whole bevy of recognition jobs. The net is plastic, it learns to categorize, and the activation space is naturally partitioned in the course of training. Lesions of the kind described mean only that when an input vector in fact represents a vowel, then the activation normally produced in the vowel side of the main partition does not exist. So the net cannot give its normal output. What may give the appearance of modularity is the specificity of the deficit at the output level, but in NETtalk, this is known to be appearance only, not substance. On the other hand, we saw in the Hinton net (chapter 3) that was trained to recognize sounds, that modulelike mini-nets, in the "gang-of-experts" mold, could emerge as a result of the training organization. The partial separation of mini-nets meant that error correction could be a speedier undertaking.

In the context of the caution that modularity is not implied by deficit selectivity, consider two other case studies. A patient studied by Anderson et al. (1989) was unable to read letters or words, but could easily read single and multi-digit *numbers.* This carried over from reading into writing. That is, she could not write letters or words, but could write single and multi-digit numbers. This is an especially interesting dissociation because conditions and age of learning, motor control, and so forth were much the same for both classes of symbols, and, one might reason, if one abstract network was servicing letters as well as numbers, there should be comparable deficits. Not so. Partitions on activation spaces, and selective damage to vectors coding for words would produce exactly this result even were there no modularity but just a network capable of handling diverse categorizations. Consider also two patients studied by Caramazza and Hillis (1991), one of whom (S.J.D.) who was able to read but showed writing deficits, the other of whom (H.W.) could write well but showed reading deficits. In both cases, the impairment with respect to *verbs* was worse than the impairment with respect to *nouns*. When a homonym such as "walk" can be used as a noun or a verb, H.W. can *read* it better in its noun context, "Bill shoveled the walk," than in its verb context, "Do you walk with a limp?" (He writes both well.) S.J.D. can *write* "walk" better in the noun context than in the verb context (he can *read* both well). Here again, though the data are consistent with modularity, they by no means entail modularity.[58]

Maybe the vector/activation space is a modularity story after all, but in network disguise? Can we not think of a partition in activation space as a module? Not if we mean by "module" what is usually meant in this context, namely individual component, physically distinct and informationally encapsulated to a high degree. Assuming this psychological/functional sense of "module," the vector/activation space approach interprets the neurological data in a way fundamentally different from the interpretation given by the modularity approach. The two approaches license very different inferences and inspire different experiments. Notice in particular that the *statistical* profile of recognition deficits looks problematic on the modularity hypothesis, whereas it sits naturally with the vector/activation space hypothesis. Patient variability is predicted on the vector/activation space hypothesis, since as a function of experience and education, different nets may partition the activation space in somewhat different ways. Further to this point, the categorial partitioning actually achieved by a network, and as limned through the lens of neuro-psychological deficits, need not map onto the familiar taxonomy in common parlance. Additionally, substantial recovery of categorial recognition is sometimes seen when damage is not too extensive. For example, a recovering patient may be unable to do arithmetic calculations when the number "2" is involved, but the deficit is restricted to examples containing the number "2." After a time, the deficit disappears, and the patient can calculate quite normally. Recovery of function in such cases may be more plausibly understood along the lines of minor retraining of the remaining units of a net than as destruction of the "2" module and subsequent establishment of a new "2" module. To repeat the obvious, none of these arguments *rule out* the possibility of modularity; they imply merely that modularity is not the only, and may not be the best, hypothesis to square with deficit selectivity.

Might modularity not be the favored hypothesis on other grounds—specialization of function, for example? As remarked earlier, there is specialization in nervous systems. In standard conditions, visual pathways do not carry information about smell, for example.[59] But specialization does not imply modularity, as partitioning of activation spaces clearly demonstrates. Moreover, despite specialization seen at the behavioral level, there is significant interconnectedness at the neuronal level. Even within ostensibly segregated visual pathways, such as the parvo and the magno pathways (chapter 4), there appears to be crosstalk (Schiller and Logothetis 1990).[60] For example, Dobkins and Albright (1991) have found a subtle interaction between color information and motion information in cells in visual area MT as described below.[61] These cells are not selectively tuned to colored stimuli, but rather are tuned to moving stimuli in preferred directions.

Consider an experimental set-up for apparent motion, such that a dot appears transiently at one location, followed by the appearance of two dots, one to the first dot's right, one to its left. Psychophysically, it has been shown that when the stimuli are colored dots isoluminant with the background and with each other, the direction of the apparent motion is a function of which of the second dots is the same color as the first (Green 1989). What are the motion-sensitive cells in MT doing? Suppose a certain MT cell normally responds vigorously to motion from left to right. In the experimental situation, will it detect left-right apparent motion if all it has to go on is color? The answer, surprisingly, turns out to be yes. If the stimuli for left-right motion are *red dot followed by red dot*, it responds. If the stimuli for left-right motion are *red followed by green*, while the stimuli for right-left motion are *red followed by red*, the cell does not respond, thus fitting with the psychophysical data that predict the perception of motion will be from right to left (figure 5.47). It appears, therefore, that the cell's detection of the motion is facilitated by color, even though the cell shows no selective response to color. In other words, the cell seems to make use of color information even though it is not tuned to respond selectively to color as such.

The Dobkins and Albright results concern talking across submodalities. What about cross-talk *between* modalities, or via feedback routes, between higher and lower processing levels? Data are beginning to show just such effects. For example, John Maunsell and his colleagues (in press) have recorded effects of somatosensory information on the responses of neurons in visual area V4 of monkey visual cortex. The task for the monkey is match-to-sample, where the sample may be presented tactually and the monkey has to find the visual pattern that best matches the sample. The palm of the monkey's hand is stimulated with a tactile grating, where the lines of the grating are oriented in a specific direction. The tuning curves of a population of neurons in visual area V4 are established, and neurons preferring bars of light oriented in specific directions are identified. The monkey is then trained to pick the visual grating whose orientation matches the tactile grating he feels with his hand.

Maunsell and colleagues discovered neurons in V4 whose responses to their preferred visual stimulus could be modulated by the prior presentation of the *tactile* stimulus (figure 5.48). For example, a cell that before training responded vigorously to a vertical bar of light might respond little if at all to the vertical light stimulus after the tactile stimulus was presented, possibly but not necessarily as a function of a match with the tactile stimulus. Conversely, a cell that before training did not respond significantly to a horizontal bar of light might respond quite vigorously to such a stimulus, again in some relation—match or possibly mismatch—to the orientation of the tactile stimulus. Thus in the

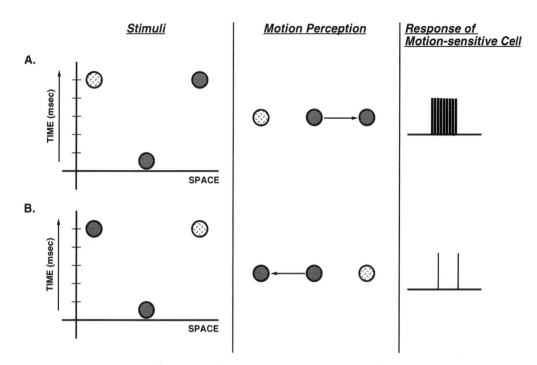

Figure 5.47 Apparent motion of a colored circle, isoluminant with the background, and hence detectable by color only. (A) Red light at the center location flashes on and off, followed by a red light flashing on to the right, and a green light flashing on to the left. What one sees (middle panel) is the red light move to the right (apparent motion), not to the left where the green light appears. Schematic recording (right panel) from a cell in MT that is selective for right-going motion showing that the cell is responsive in this condition. (B) Control experiment: when apparent motion is in the direction opposite to what the cell prefers, it does not respond. (Based on Dobkins and Albright 1990, 1991a,b.)

context of the task, the range of visual stimuli that drive a visual cell is altered by somatosensory information. This may be consistent with modularity, but it is more plausibly interpreted within the general framework of recurrent networks, vectors, and the partitioning of activation spaces.

What about the large-scale divisions postulated early in this chapter—for example, between declarative and procedural memory, or between episodic and semantic memory? Might these divisions be eroded and fuzzed by the same kinds of considerations that eroded the hypothesis that there are distinct modules for nouns and verbs, for manmade and natural objects? Or might these major divisions be rather more robust, perhaps like the modularity seen in the electric fish (Heiligenberg 1986) or perhaps a little like the Hinton mini-nets that emerge from neural networks in the course of training? Consistency, not to mention curiosity, demands such reevaluation. In exactly what sense are these really different memory *systems*? Might the data be better understood in terms of interacting recurrent networks, Damasio hierarchies, specificity of vectors, and emergent mini-net experts?[62] These are large questions. They require reexamination of the vast data base, and hence require far

Stimulus

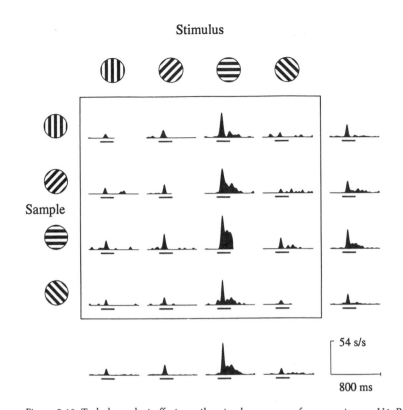

Figure 5.48 Task-dependent effects on the visual responses of neurons in area V4. Responses from an isolated V4 neuron were collected during 192 trials of a tactile-visual, orientation, match-to-sample task. The box encloses plots for combinations of sample and test stimulus orientations. Each column represents responses to a particular test stimulus, sorted into rows according to the orientation the animal was searching for at the time the stimulus appeared. Each plot is the average of 24 repetitions; the bars below each plot show the period (200 msec) during which the stimulus was on. Plots on the principal diagonal are responses to *matching conditions*. Each of these 4 plots is truncated at the time when the animal released its grasp. Plots below and to the right of the box show the column and row averages. The vertical axis of each plot is probability of firing in spikes/sec. Responses shown here were strongest during trials in which the animal was searching for the horizontal. The strongest overall response occurred when the horizontal grating appeared during a trial in which the animal was looking for a horizontal. This neuron had a conventional orientation preference for horizontal stimuli. (From Maunsell et al., in press.)

more discussion than is possible here. Having opened the door a crack, we quickly shut it again, stowing the reevaluation for another occasion.

Selected Readings

Abraham, W. C., M. C. Corballis, and K. G. White, eds. (1991). *Memory Mechanisms: A Tribute to G. V. Goddard*. Hillsdale, NJ: Erlbaum.

Baudry, M. and J. L. Davis, eds. (1991). *Long-Term Potentiation: A Debate of Current Issues*. Cambridge, MA: MIT Press.

Damasio, H., and A. Damasio (1989). *Lesion Analysis in Neuropsychology*. Oxford: Oxford University Press.

Diamond, A., ed. (1990). *The Development and Neural Bases of Higher Cognitive Functions. Annals of the New York Academy of Sciences*.

Dudai, Y. (1989). *The Neurobiology of Memory: Concepts, Findings, and Trends*. New York: Oxford University Press.

Gabriel, M., and J. Moor (1990). *Learning and Computational Neuroscience: Foundations of Adaptive Networks*. Cambridge, MA: MIT Press.

Gustafsson, B., and H. Wigstrom, guest eds. *Seminars in the Neurosciences*, vol. 2, October 1990.

Hall, Z. W. (1991). *Molecular Neurobiology*. Sunderland, MA: Sinauer.

Huttenlocher, P. R. (1990). Morphometric study of human cerebral cortex development. *Neuropsychologia* 28: 517–527.

Johnson-Laird, P. (1988). *The Computer and the Mind*. Cambridge, MA: Harvard University Press. (Part III. Learning, Memory, and Action).

Kanerva, P. (1988). *Sparse Distributed Memory*. Cambridge, MA: MIT Press.

McCarthy, R. A., and E. K. Warrington (1990). *Cognitive Neuropsychology*. New York: Academic Press.

Posner, M., ed. (1990). *Foundations of Cognitive Science*. Cambridge, MA: MIT Press.

Rubin, D. C., ed. (1986). *Autobiographical Memory*. Cambridge: Cambridge University Press.

Schacter, D. L. (1989). Memory. In Posner (1990), 683–726.

Shaw, G. L., J. L. McGaugh, and S. P. R. Rose (1990). *Neurobiology of Memory and Learning*. Singapore: World Scientific.

Sutherland, S. (1989). *The International Dictionary of Psychology*. New York: Continuum.

Traub, R. D., and R. Miles (1991). *Neuronal Networks of the Hippocampus*. Cambridge: Cambridge University Press.

Watkins, J. C., and G. L. Collingridge, eds. (1989). *The NMDA Receptor*. Oxford: Oxford University Press.

Wolpaw, J. R., J. T. Schmidt, T. M. Vaughan, eds. (1991). *Activity-Driven CNS changes in Learning and Development*. Vol. 627, *Annals of the New York Academy of Sciences*.

6 Sensorimotor Integration

1 INTRODUCTION

How does the brain control the immense array of muscle cells so that the whole body moves in the right way? This problem is probably the most basic one a nervous system evolved to solve.[1] If an animal is to survive, its brain must use its sensory information to guide its body movements, so that it can succeed in what Paul Maclean has dubbed the four Fs: fleeing, feeding, fighting, and reproducing. There are, of course, many different possible ways of executing any one of the four Fs, and an animal's repertoire is constrained both by its physical equipment (size and number of legs, exoskeleton or endoskeleton, muscles, fins, ink sprayer, poison fangs, wings, quills, etc.) and also by the computational and representational sophistication its brain can bring to bear on the problem. A spider that can build a robust web in a suitable place, detect the presence of a snared fly, paralyze it, and wrap it up for later delectation is displaying truly exquisite sensorimotor control—more extraordinary than, say, that of a slug withdrawing from a touch, though perhaps less fancy than humans conversing or building a suspension bridge across a canyon.

One's own motor repertoire includes many actions that are effortless, such as talking or maneuvering a car through traffic, and it is natural to assume that the sensorimotor problem is relatively trivial—but effort expended and attention demanded are poor indices of the underlying computational complexity. A visual system might encode the presence of a hanging peach, but how should those signals from the retina be transformed so that the hand can stretch out and grasp the fruit? A bat's auditory system might detect echo delay, but how does the motor system know how to move the body through the air to arrive exactly where the moth is? Between the sensory receptors detecting signals and the motor neurons innervating the muscles are interneurons, sometimes billions of interneurons. Most of the answer to the problem of sensorimotor control resides in how these interneurons connect up to form circuits, and how these circuits are hooked up to produce behavior suited to the perceived situation. The computational potential of a circuit with even a few score neurons is formidable. When the number of intervening neurons

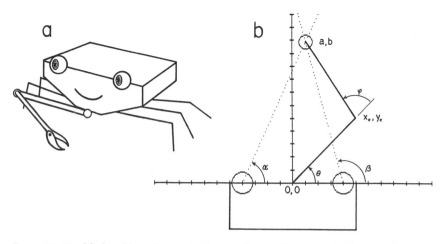

Figure 6.1 Simplified problem of sensorimotor coordination for an arm. (a) Cartoon of a computer "crab." (b) The "crab" has rotatable eyes and an extendable arm. As the eyes triangulate a target by assuming angles (α, β), the arm joints must assume angles (θ, φ) such that the tip of the "forearm" makes contact with the target. (From P. M. Churchland 1986.)

reaches a few million or many billion, the questions become more difficult to answer by many orders of magnitude.

The fundamental nature of the problem of coordinating sensory and motor representations can be understood in a simple context, and the superabundant complexities may be added incrementally from there. This is like facing the problem of fluid dynamics for *honey* by first looking at the fluid dynamics of a vastly simpler fluid, say, *liquid argon*.[2] Bearing this in mind, consider first a cartoon device, Roger the Crab (figure 6.1). Roger is a computer simulation, with a pair of rotatable "eyes" for detecting the presence of external stimuli and a single-jointed, extendable arm for making contact with what his eyes see in his impoverished 2-D space. Roger's sole task in his limited life is to detect stimuli and contact them with the tip of his hand. Roger's "visual" space is characterizable as a state space (see chapter 3) in which the position of the target is represented by the two eye-rotation angles, α and β.[3] Note that for any position of the target in external space, there is a corresponding position of the target in Roger's "visual" state space. Thus Roger's visual vector, such as (65, 105), represents the position of the apple in the world, since there is a systematic relation between where the apple is in the world, as described in external coordinates, and "where" in visual space it is, as specified by a pair of eye–angle coordinates.

Just as Roger has a 2-D "visual" space in which the position of the target is represented, so he has a 2-D motor space in which his arm position can be represented. But, and this is crucial to understanding the problem of sensory-motor coordination in its most general aspect, *these two state spaces are very different* (figure 6.2). Roger's motor state space is shaped by his motor equipment, not by his sensory equipment. The position of his limb in state space is given by the two angles by which it deviates from a standard position. Thus,

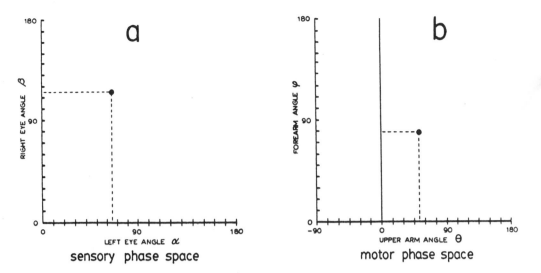

Figure 6.2 The respective configurations of the "crab's" sensory (a) and motor (b) systems can each be represented by an appropriate point in a corresponding state space. The "crab" needs a way to find the correct point in motor space given the point in sensory space. (From P. M. Churchland 1986.)

let the zero position of the upper arm be flush with the horizontal axis. Then a position of 45° on the upper arm axis will represent an upper-arm position of 45° off the horizontal (figure 6.3). Correlatively, let the zero position of the forearm be its position when extended straight out from the upper arm, wherever the upper arm happens to be positioned. Accordingly, a position of 78.5° on the forearm axis represents the forearm as rotated 78.5° counterclockwise from the line extending out from the upper arm, whatever the position of the upper arm. Notice, therefore, that we can give the overall position of Roger's arm in motor state space in terms of the two angles (45°, 78.5°). We can specify the position of the target, therefore, by specifying the arm position where the tip of the forearm touches the apple.

How does Roger's "brain" know, given the representation in visual state space, where in motor space the arm should be? Obviously if the motor system takes the visual coordinates (55, 85) and directly translates them into motor state space, then the arm will end up at (55, 85) in motor state space, nowhere near the target. The point is, if the target is at (55, 85) in visual space, then it is at (62, 12) in motor space. What Roger needs, therefore, is a mechanism that will give him systematically correct transformations in motor space of visual space coordinates. We can get a sense of what this transformation requires if we let the visual space be mapped out on a rubber sheet, and then define some set of points as representing a particular position in that space. Lay the visual state space grid on the motor state space grid, and deform it until the representation fits point for proper point on motor state space (figure 6.4). This deforming tactic yields a global transformation of state-space coordinates. Though rendered in cartoon simplicity and guided by the cartoonist's knowing hand, this situation characterizes the nub of the problem of sensorimotor coor-

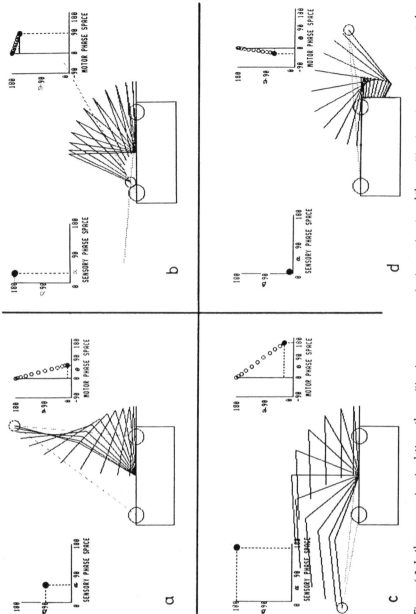

Figure 6.3 In these computer simulations, the position in sensory space is given as input, and the position in motor space is computed as output. The arm configuration is then directed along a straight line in *motor space*, from its folded resting position (0, 180), toward its target position, but in real space the trajectory is a curve. See upper right inset in each example for the movement in motor space that puts the arm in contact with the target. (From P. M. Churchland 1986.)

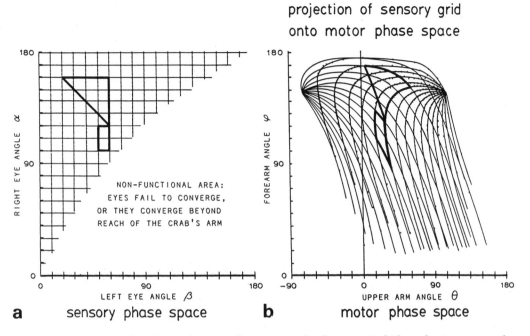

projection of sensory grid
onto motor phase space

a sensory phase space

RIGHT EYE ANGLE α

180

90

0

NON-FUNCTIONAL AREA:
EYES FAIL TO CONVERGE,
OR THEY CONVERGE BEYOND
REACH OF THE CRAB'S ARM

0   90   180

LEFT EYE ANGLE β

b motor phase space

FOREARM ANGLE φ

180

90

0

-90   0   90   180

UPPER ARM ANGLE θ

Figure 6.4 The coordinate transformation, graphically represented. The grid in (a) represents the set of points in sensory space that correspond to a triangulated object within the reach of the "crab's" arm. For each such point in (a), its corresponding position in motor space is entered in (b). The entire set of corresponding points in (b) displays the global transformation of state-space coordinates effected by the "crab's" coordinating function. The heavily scored triangle and rectangle illustrate corresponding position in each space and indicate how one is deformed relative to the other. (From P. M. Churchland 1986.)

dination and what, to a first approximation, is the general nature of its solution (figures 6.5, 6.6).

In starkest form, the problem can be specified as a problem in vector–vector transformation; a problem in bringing different state spaces into some sort of register via the auspices of a suitable matrix. The solution concerns using the stuff and substance—the geometry, if you prefer—of the device to achieve successful transformations from one state space to another. One way, a dead simple way, is to follow this recipe: position the sensory and the motor rubber grids relative to each other, then deform one or both so that the transforming matrix consists merely of a line dropped from a representation in sensory space will contact the correct "go-to" position in motor space. The deformation produces two state spaces that are physically and literally in register. Does the nervous system exploit this means? Perhaps in limited locations and then only approximately, and then only in certain species. Using physical registration of state spaces is a very special case; it is the frictionless plane, the gravitation-free zone, the two-body solution that does not really exist. It is a metaphor for whatever physical parameters really go into making a matrix through which a vector can be pushed to yield the vector for the appropriate state space. As a metaphor and an idealization, however, it orients us in the right direction. (For

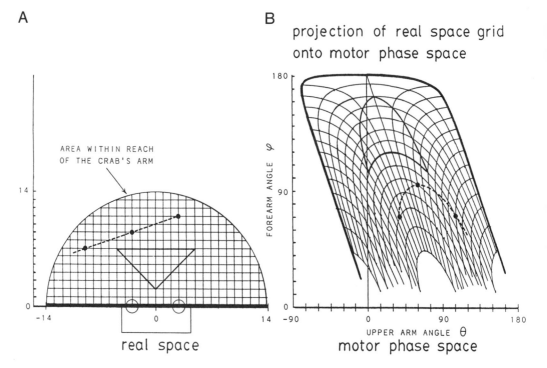

A

AREA WITHIN REACH
OF THE CRAB'S ARM

14

0

−14   0   14

real space

B

projection of real space grid
onto motor phase space

180

FOREARM ANGLE φ

90

0

−90   0   90   180

UPPER ARM ANGLE θ

motor phase space

Figure 6.5 The coordinate transformation between real space and motor space, graphically represented. The semicircular grid in (a) represents the set of points in *real* space within reach of the "crab's" arm. The deformed grid in (b) displays the corresponding points in motor state space. The large triangle is for orientation, and the three rectilinear points represent an object moving at uniform velocity in front of the crab. (Courtesy P. M. Churchland.)

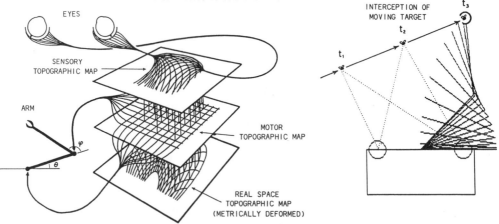

COORDINATE TRANSFORMATION BY CONTIGUOUS TOPOGRAPHIC MAPS

EYES

SENSORY
TOPOGRAPHIC MAP

ARM

φ

θ

MOTOR
TOPOGRAPHIC MAP

REAL SPACE
TOPOGRAPHIC MAP
(METRICALLY DEFORMED)

INTERCEPTION OF
MOVING TARGET

t_3

t_2

t_1

Figure 6.6 A metrically deformed topographic map of real space is here added to the robot crab's "brain" as a bottom layer, to which vertical connections extend from the upper layers. This layer provides the "crab" with an internal representation of the position of objects in real space. Given two sequential points in real space, a look-ahead feature built into the third layer can project a colinear third point. A signal from this point in the bottom map, conducted back up to the motor map, will position the arm to catch a moving object on the fly. (Courtesy P. M. Churchland.)

an earlier discussion of this idea in connection with the superior colliculus, see chapter 3, section 4.)

To begin to "realize" the cartoon, we need to introduce features of real nervous systems. Ratcheting up the complexity only slightly, we see that the visual vector would have to have many more than two components, and hence the visual state space would have to have many more than two dimensions— millions of photoreceptors might be needed, for example. Similarly of course for motor state space, which must deal with real limbs that have inertia, real joints that have friction, and a real world that reacts back on the arm. Two-dimensional state spaces serve well enough to establish the principle, but obviously the state spaces of neuronal activation vectors are gigantic. Up another notch, we add the fact that there will be a different vector specified at each synaptic level, so "visual state space and motor state space" is far too compact, and would have to be replaced by the relevant characterization, whatever that is, for each synaptic level. For another notch or three, add feedback connections and short-term memory. Other functions besides detecting eyeball angle and manipulating joint angle must be added also. Typically the nervous system has so much business to cope with, including multiple sensory modalities, multiple movable body parts, growth and development, limited cranial capacity, digestion, respiration, nutrient and oxygen supply, and so forth, that physical registration of the direct sort enjoyed by Roger is simply not feasible. (See chapter 3.)

Nevertheless, Roger's "brain" is conceptually useful in conveying the abstract nature of the solution to the problem of sensorimotor coordination; namely, exploit the geometry and physics of the system to make a physical matrix of connections to perform the coordinate transformations. To a first approximation, state spaces in nervous systems are only abstractly, not literally, in register. Transformations of vectors are accomplished through matrices of synaptic weights, which in turn are modifiable through learning and development. What makes the transformation from one activation vector to another is the living matrix of weights, whatever mechanisms the neurons use to establish and update them. Notice too that Roger's arrangement is basically a look-up table; more specifically, a grandmothered look-up table, for there is a neuron for every representable point in the 2-D space. The task could, however, be accomplished more economically by a simple feedforward net, wherein the representations would be distributed rather than punctate.

The notch in our next ratchet hoists the whole problem/solution pair to new heights of functional potential and computational craft. It is the stage where we embrace *time*—the rate at which variables change. This picks up threads left dangling in chapters 3 and 4, where we introduced the critical importance of timing in understanding a task-demand and in determining how the nervous system might perform the task (Eckmiller 1989). In the context of sensorimotor coordination, the matter of time is absolutely unignorable if we are to have a prayer of making progress. Thus the dominant feature of the landscape at this elevation is a dynamical system, meaning its inputs and internal states are varying with time; it is basically engaged in spatiotemporal vector coding and time-dependent matrix transformations.[4] Consistent with earlier hedges, we repeat that this is not the end of the climb, but only a ledge from which we hope to hoist ourselves to the next elevation whose topography can be but dimly perceived.

The basic strategy for addressing how sensorimotor integration is accomplished has been to study either very simple organisms with accessible nervous systems, such as the leech or the sea hare, or relatively small, relatively self-contained subsystems of the whole mammalian or avian CNS. Subsystems are more manageable than a whole mammalian CNS because in the principal circuit, only a few synapses intervene between transducer and effector. Hence the difficult matter of cortical contribution, though it cannot be ignored entirely, can be sidelined temporarily while the principal organization is explored.

In what follows we shall look at three cases where anatomical and physiological studies of circuits are co-evolving with computer models of the circuit. The first focuses on a simple reflex in the leech, that resourceful and resilient denizen of freshwater lakes (and, yes, that attaches to swimmers and sucks blood) (figure 6.7). The second is a network in mammals, the vestibulo-ocular reflex (VOR), that helps stabilize the visual image when the head is moving by making compensatory eye movements in the opposite direction. But for the action of the VOR, head movement would cause the image to slide on the retina, and hence perception would be smeary. The third example involves rhythmic behaviors generated by the spinal cord. It must be acknowledged that none of these studies involves sensorimotor control of a type that might immediately make contact with our favorite motor skills; the leech, because it is such a distant relative, and the VOR, because, well, the output is just eye movements, and eye muscles after all do not do anything other than move the eyes—they don't play the violin or whistle Bach's inventions. Most people don't even know that they have a VOR.

Nevertheless, experimental science has to be practical and opportunistic; it has to start where it can get started. Simplicity of the system, ease of experimentation, and availability of the organism count in favor of leeches, the VOR, and the spinal cord. The VOR is an excellent place to try to winnow out the

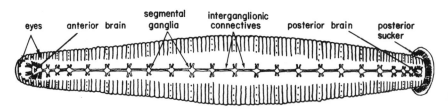

Figure 6.7 Central nervous system of the leech. There is a chain of 21 segmental ganglia topped with a head ganglion (anterior brain) and capped with a tail ganglion (posterior brain). The nerve cord lies along the ventral midline. The ganglia are linked to each other by bundles of axons (the connectives) and innervate the body walls by pairs of nerves (cut away in figure for clarity). (From Weisblat and Kristan, 1985.)

basic computational principles of mammalian sensorimotor control: (1) the fundamental circuit is relatively simple, so the input and output can be identified and controlled, (2) the complicating factor of load on muscles is absent, and (3) there is a limited range of movements of which the system is capable. The spinal cord also has special experimental virtues. In the lamprey, the cord can be isolated from the rest of the brain, and hence provides an experimentally accessible central pattern generator in which to explore the fundamental principles of how fish swim, insects fly, and land animals walk. Unlike the VOR, which is largely reactive, the spinal cord can continuously maintain complex patterns of activity. The leech is a very important animal in neurobiology for a number of very practical reasons, but especially because it has comparatively few neurons, about 10^4, and many neurons are sufficiently stereotyped in morphology, connectivity, development, and so on that they can be given identifying labels—for example, "P," "T," and "N," and identified as such from leech to leech (figures 6.8, 6.9) Such stereotypy is most helpful when replicating results. An additional reason for choosing the leech is that recording from behaving, nonanesthetized leeches is straightforward.

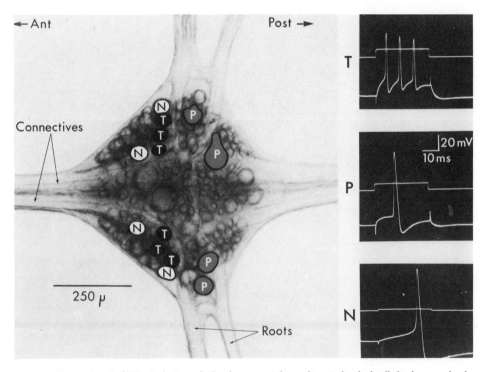

Figure 6.8 (Left) Ventral view of a leech segmental ganglion. Individual cells bodies are clearly visible. The pairs of sensory cells responding to touch (T), pressure (P), and noxious mechanical stimulation of the skin (N) are labeled. (Right) Each type of cell has a distinct electrical response when current is injected. Current injected through the microelectrode is shown in the top trace in each pair of traces, and a simultaneous recording of the membrane potential is shown below. Each cell is characterized not only by its anatomical location but as well by its distinctive action potential. (From Nicholls and Baylor 1968.)

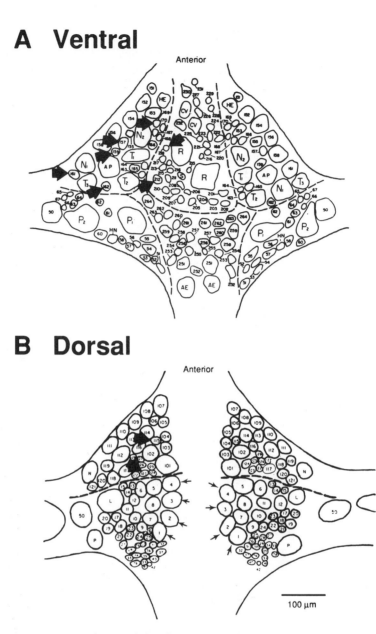

Figure 6.9 Ventral (A), and dorsal (B), aspects of a leech segmental ganglion. Locations of identified local bending interneurons are indicated by heavy arrows. Light arrows point to motor neurons for the longitudinal muscles. These neurons come in bilateral pairs, except for cell 218. Such small interneurons are relatively difficult to impale with microelectrodes. (From Lockery and Kristan, 1990b.)

The local bending reflex is the behavior of the leech on which we focus now. It is a very simple escape behavior wherein potential harm is recognized and avoidance action taken. Basically the leech withdraws from an irritating stimulus by making a kind of large kink in the length of it hoselike body. Many important computational issues arise in the domain of sensorimotor integration producing escape behaviors, and the leech's simplicity may make it easier to discern basic computational principles embodied in the system.

The computational model for the local bending reflex in the leech, shortly to be introduced, was worked out primarily by Shawn Lockery when he was a graduate student at University of California, San Diego and then a postdoctoral fellow at the Salk Institute (Lockery and Kristan 1990a, b). It is based on several decades of anatomical and physiological studies of the leech nervous system by Stephen Kuffler, John Nicholls, Denis Baylor, Gunther Stent, and William Kristan, and their colleagues.[5] It illustrates in a concrete example many of the general issues concerning representations and integration that were raised earlier. Moreover, it is a nice example of how constructing a model in parallel with physiological investigation sharpens the neurobiological research and makes it more comprehensive.

The neural circuits and motor repertoires of the leech are very different from those of mammals, and this raises queries about the generalizability of the results from leech neurobiology. The leech nervous system must have evolved over many millions of years to a specialization uniquely suited to specific leech tasks and to the leech's environment. Circuits found in the leech might therefore be expected to be highly idiosyncratic and to have evolved rather eccentric computational solutions. In that event, the discoveries about how the leech nervous system represents and computes might not generalize to other invertebrates, let alone to vertebrates. Thus, for example, the computational strategies evolved by mammalian cerebral cortex might not be remotely related to those governing leech bending, where no cortex is in sight.

So why should anyone pursue research on the leech? Whether leech neurobiology can shed light on or at least provide clues to the computational principles of mammalian nervous systems remains to be seen, but the accessibility of the invertebrate nervous systems makes investigating them worth the investment. In and of itself, the leech's computational organization is interesting, since its sensorimotor control, lowly as it may seem to adroit humans, is beyond the capabilities of current robotics. From this early stage in the engineering of robots, it is astonishing that as tiny a nervous system as that of the leech can be as sophisticated, flexible, and successful as it is. Even were its computational principles to fail to generalize to mammals, it is important to know how so much is done by so little. In any case, the pay-off is not likely to be an all-or-nothing matter. Some properties of computational strategies might be highly conserved and hence will have wide applicability, while others may emerge with evolution of special brain structures, such as the hippocampus or the cerebellum.

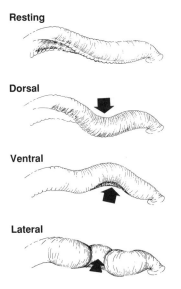

Resting

Dorsal

Ventral

Lateral

Figure 6.10 Local bending behaviors in the leech. The posterior half of the animal is shown in the resting state and following dorsal, ventral, and lateral mechanical stimulation (arrows). (From Lockery and Kristan 1990a.)

What does a leech do when it bends? In response to a mechanical stimulus, such as a pin poke, the leech withdraws from the site of contact (figure 6.10). It can bend to either side, as well as up or down, depending on where the poke is, and the strength of the bending is loosely related to the intensity of the stimulus. The muscular interaction whereby this reflex behavior is accomplished is elementary: contraction of the longitudinal muscles beneath the stimulus and relaxation of longitudinal muscles on the opposite side of the body (Kristan 1982). Moreover, the direction of the kink is dependent on the site of stimulation—stimulation of the top, bottom, or sides of the leech produce the appropriately oriented response, despite the fact the same muscles may be used in different responses.

What are the neural mechanisms of leech bending? The anatomy of the circuits contributing to the bending reflexes is well known. The leech is a segmented animal, and within each segment a ganglion of neurons coordinates behaviors. There are 21 mid-body ganglia, as well as head and tail "brains," in scare quotes because they are really more like agglomerations of ganglia than the highly structured brains typical of mammals. Although the ganglia do have connections with each other, each ganglion is basically responsible for the behavior of its own segment. The major sensory input for the local bending reflex arises from four pressure-sensitive mechanoreceptors, called P (for pressure) cells (Nicholls and Baylor 1968), each with an area of sensitivity (the receptive field) that is confined to a single quadrant of the body wall. The muscles are activated by a set of motor neurons: each quadrant is innervated by excitatory and inhibitory motor neurons, making eight types of motor neurons in all.

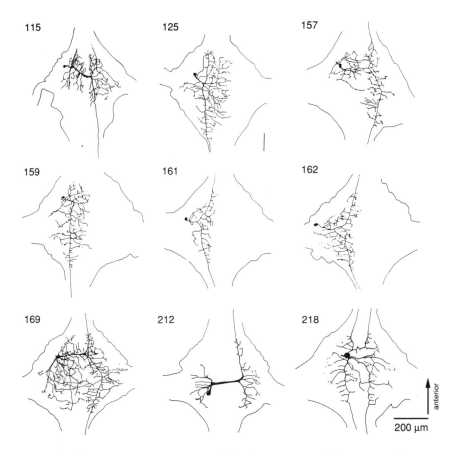

115 125 157

159 161 162

169 212 218

anterior

200 μm

Figure 6.11 Local bending interneurons in the leech. Drawings made from neurons that were impaled and filled with a fluorescent dye. Each of these cells has a distinct morphology and pattern of projections within and out of the ganglion. (From Lockery and Kristan 1990b.)

These sensory and motor neurons are not directly connected with each other, so the reflex is not monosynaptic, in contrast to the basic circuit underlying the familiar knee-jerk response in humans (figure 6.12). Rather, in the leech interposed between the sensory and motor neurons are a number of interneurons that mediate the interactions between sensory and motor neurons. Sensory stimulation produces a pattern of excitation among the interneurons that in turn project to the pool of eight motor neuron types. However humble the leech, this reflex is not a simple cause–effect relay. The reflex has a rather more complicated profile and a nontrivial range of variability. It involves extensive divergent and convergent connections, reminiscent of vertebrate circuits, and it uses these to compute the location of the stimulus and generate the appropriate response.

Nine types of bending interneurons have been identified that mediate the dorsal version of the leech's bending reflex—that is, withdrawal from a dorsal stimulus by contraction of dorsal muscles and relaxation of ventral muscles (figure 6.11) (Lockery and Kristan 1990b). These nine types are a subset of the local bending interneurons that contribute to dorsal bending by receiving

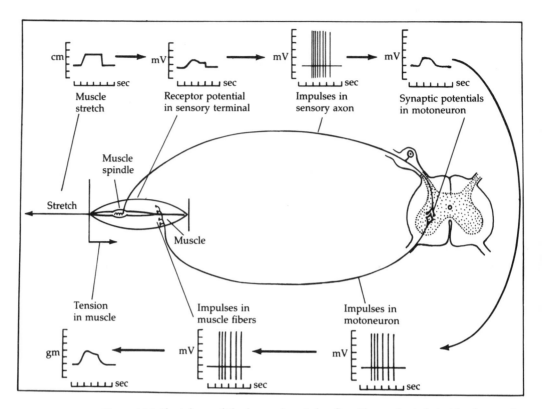

Figure 6.12 Physiology of the human knee-jerk reflex. The mechanical stretch of a muscle results in its contraction through a one-neuron arc in the spinal cord. Stretch of the muscle spindle is transduced into a receptor potential that is then converted into a train of impulses in the sensory axon. These nerve fibers make excitatory synapses on motor neurons in the spinal cord. The graded depolarization in the motor neuron then produces a train of action potentials. The axon of the motor neuron innervates the muscle fiber at an endplate, or neuromuscular junction. The resulting depolarization of the muscles leads to a contraction of the muscle fibers. The motor neuron receives many other synapses from other neurons in the spinal cord and descending fibers from the brain (not shown), so its response to the stretch receptors can be modulated by other influences. (With permission from Kuffler, Nicholls and Martin [1984]. *From Neuron to Brain*. Sunderland, MA: Sinauer Associates.)

excitatory input from the P cells and in turn exciting the dorsal excitatory motor neurons. There are no functional connections between the interneurons. In a series of experiments, the P cells, the dorsal bending interneurons, and the motor neurons were impaled with microelectrodes to record synaptic potentials and also to stimulate the reflex. It had been expected that specific interneurons would be identified that contributed selectively to the movements produced by dorsal, ventral, or lateral pokes. That is, the simple conception of this reflex would so predict. In contrast, it was found that most interneurons received substantial input from three or four P cells. This finding indicates that the local bending network forms a distributed representation of the sensory input, and that the input–output mapping is achieved by a vector transformation in a high-dimensional space rather than as a simple "push–splash" phenomenon in a low-dimensional space.[6]

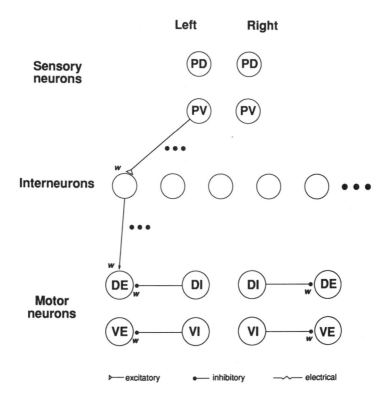

Figure 6.13 Local bending circuit in the leech: LeechNet I. The main input to the reflex is provided by the dorsal and ventral P cells (PD and PV). Control of the local bending is provided by motor neurons whose field of innervations is restricted to single quadrants of the body; the dorsal and ventral quadrants are innervated by both excitatory (DE and VE) and inhibitory (DI and VI) motor neurons. The inhibitory motor neurons also inhibit the excitatory motor neurons with the pattern shown. There are no direct connections between the sensory and the motor neurons; their interaction is mediated by a layer of interneurons. In this first model each neuron was modeled by a sigmoid unit and each connection had a weight. The input activity was propagated to the output units in two steps. (Courtesy of S. Lockery.)

Computer Models of Network for Dorsal Bending

The first computer simulation model, referred to here as "LeechNet I," was extremely simple (Lockery et al. 1989). It was confined to simulating a single ganglion from the array of 21 mid-body ganglia. In terms of cells, that meant the model had four input units, eight output units, and 18 interneurons, configured to represent the circuit that could execute the bending behavior seen in the leech. The four most important motor neuron-to-motor neuron connections were also included (figure 6.13). The model was trained by a supervised learning algorithm to reproduce the observed input–output relationship, that is, those input–output functions observed when stimulating any single neuron or pair of input neurons. Kristan and Lockery had made numerous intracellular recordings from the motor neurons (output units) during local bending behavior, and the model was trained to reproduce the amplitude of synaptic potentials seen in these recordings. At the end of the training period, the model reproduced exactly the observed input–output data.

Question: does the solution to the sensorimotor control problem found by the network resemble the physiological solution of the actual circuit? This can be discovered by comparing the properties of the hidden units of the network with those of the interneurons in the leech ganglion. The right way to do this comparison is not by testing one interneuron against one hidden unit in a given trained-up net. The trouble with such a strategy is that training by backpropagation means net-to-net variability in the weights. Consequently a single trained-up network used as the comparison would be artifactual, for each training session produces a slightly different pattern of weights for the same input–output profile.

To get a meaningful comparison, therefore, it was necessary to train up a set of distinct LeechNet models—18 in this case—and test response patterns of model units and neurobiological units. This was followed by a statistical analysis to determine whether the match between the biological data and the network data was better than chance. Questions on the list include: how many of the interneurons receive multiple sensory inputs? How many functional connections did each hidden unit have with the eight output units? What combinations of excitatory and inhibitory neurons are found? It was note-worthy that many computer units resembled certain identified dorsal bending interneurons in several respects. For example, over 95% received multiple sensory input and 88% had connections to seven or eight output units. The statistics revealed that getting matches this close merely by chance was van-ishingly small.

Although the first-generation LeechNet displayed good agreement with the input–output patterns of activity, some important parameters were missing. Most prominently, for example, the dynamics of the network, such as the time of synaptic delay, the overall reaction time of the neuronal component of the reflex, the duration of the contraction, and the overall coordination of the response with the stimulus, are entirely omitted. Second, in the real leech ganglion there are additional connections between various motor neurons, connections made by electrical synapses and inhibitory synapses, that do not fit with the feedforward scheme used in the model. Accordingly, for a model to be faithful not only to the input–output function as a whole, but also to intervening processes and their dynamics, it was necessary to develop a more sophisticated model that provided for these additional parameters. Thus LeechNet II was created (Lockery et al. 1990).

A number of improvements were introduced for LeechNet II (figure 6.14). First, the units were given some temporal integration by introducing a mem-brane time constant. Second, the delay at chemical synapses was explicitly included by dedicating a single unit to each synapse. Third, electrical coupling and additional inhibitory synapses were included among the motor neurons, necessitating a generalization of backpropagation to recurrent nets. This intro-duced additional parameters, namely many time constants for neurons and synapses, and coupling strengths between motor neurons. Fortunately, most

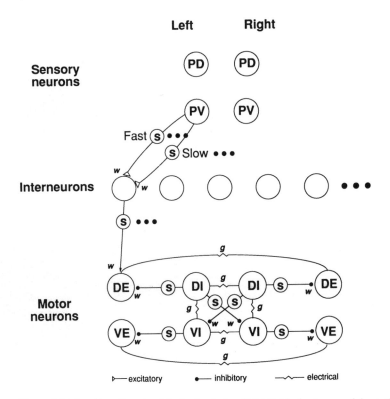

Figure 6.14 Local bending circuit in the leech: LeechNet II. The basic groundplan is the same as in LeechNet I (figure 6.13), but the model now includes chemical synapses with temporal delays, electrical synapses between the motoneurons, and an electrical time constant for each unit. The chemical synapses were modeled by two compartments called s-units, one with a fast time constant and the other with a slow time constant, chosen to match the temporal dynamics observed in these synapses. (From Lockery et al. 1990.)

of these parameters can be experimentally measured, and wherever possible, such measurements were incorporated into the model as constraints.

After training on the desired spatiotemporal pattern (size and shape of motor synaptic potentials), the interneurons of the actual leech and the hidden units of LeechNet II turned out to be quite similar in their mixtures of fast and slow responses (figure 6.15). In a comparison of actual and model response data, it is evident that the model reproduces crucial aspects of the temporal domain; it must be emphasized that some of these features are a result of network training, not of hand-setting or programming in the parameters. Additionally, that the activation of the units was distributed in both LeechNet I and II attests to the fact that the simpler LeechNet I had yielded some valid results despite its dearth of dynamics. This constancy across static and dynamic models suggests, consequently, that the property of having distributed representations is a robust feature of model networks.

The comparability between leech and model engenders confidence that backpropagation can be used as a high-fidelity design tool in building networks that can then be studied. In an inverse way, the leech research has a

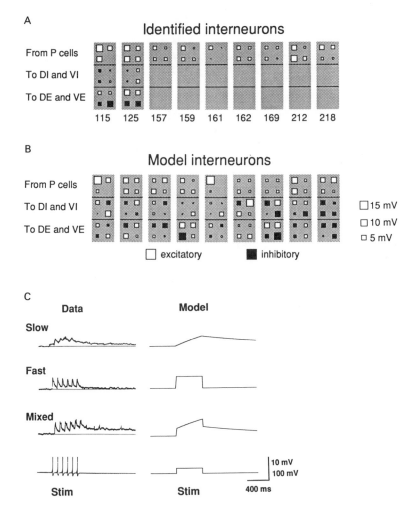

Figure 6.15 Comparison between the pattern of input and output connection strengths from identified leech interneurons (A) and model interneurons (B). Within each gray column, the upper box shows input connections from sensory neurons, the middle box shows output connections to inhibitory motoneurons (DI and VI), and the bottom box shows output connections to excitatory motor neurons (DE and VE). Box area is proportional to the amplitude of the connection determined from intracellular recording of interneurons and motor neurons. Small white boxes are excitatory connections, and small black boxes are inhibitory connections. Blank gray boxes in interneurons 157–218 denote connections whose strengths have not yet been determined. Note that most interneurons in both the leech and the model receive inputs from three or four sensory neurons. (C) The response profiles for 3 types of interneurons to stimuli (bottom trace) are shown in actual (data) and simulated (model) recordings. Some neurons respond slowly, some rapidly, and others show responses that are a mixture of these two. The synaptic potentials were recorded in response to a pulse of current in a P cell, which approximates a step change in the P cell firing frequency. The average synaptic potentials in the motoneurons were modeled by continuous variables. (From Lockery et al. 1990.)

special value in computational neuroscience. Because so much is known about the physiological details of the leech nervous system, close comparisons can be drawn, and the leech can thus be used as a kind of assay of the algorithms used to train model neural networks. If model networks should fail to match real leech networks in the relevant respects, then the algorithm for training them up cannot be relied upon. If, as in the case of LeechNet II, there is a satisfying match, this does not imply that the algorithm has definitely been validated as generally applicable, but only that it has *not* been *invalidated*. Even that much, however, marks progress and provides a foothold for further exploration.

An additional task of the model was to explain a rather paradoxical experimental finding; namely, all but one of the known interneurons have input connections that activate them during *ventral* local bending. Relative to one's naive expectations, they produce the "wrong" patterns of motor outputs, in the sense that their output in isolation tends to make the motor neurons produce bending *to* the stimulus rather than away from it. It is difficult to believe that these interneurons, which in the experimental conditions are working against the observed reflexes, are actually contributing to the solution of the local bending problem. When the model was carefully analyzed, it was discovered that there are some hidden units whose responses are similarly paradoxical. It is interesting in and of itself that there should be this match between model and actual networks, where the model network was not designed to have that property, but rather developed it during the course of training. What is even more interesting is that the model can be investigated to try to and answer why such neurons figure in the architecture, and what their role is. Why would Nature outfit the ganglion with interneurons that apparently frustrate the reflex?

One possibility is that each motor neuron contributes not just to local dorsal bending but to other behaviors such as ventral bending, shortening, stepping, and swimming. Perhaps the connections that seem paradoxical for local bending make sense in the context of these other behaviors. This proposal is currently being tested by Kristan and Wittenberg (personal communication) for the shortening behavior. The likelihood of multifunction interneurons is advanced by the discovery that one of the local bending interneurons, cell 115, turns out to be part of the central pattern generator (CPG) for swimming (Friesen 1985).

The recorded activity of the interneurons suggests vector-to-vector transformations, but a simpler hypothesis to explain away the ostensible oddity is this: certain interneurons, so far undetected, are actually responsible for the simple interaction, and act independently of the distributed computational circuit that has been identified. In other words, could it be that, in addition to the interneurons already found and studied, other interneurons with more selective patterns of activation might also exist in the ganglion and be essential to the reflex? After all, many of the interneurons are very small and difficult to identify and only a fraction of the total have already been studied. Until all of the neurons that contribute to the circuit have been found, this possibility cannot be definitely ruled out.

What the model showed was that the reflex is performed perfectly well without an additional set of more selective interneurons. The similarity between model and actual interneurons proves that the class of multiplexed interneurons already found *are sufficient* to compute the location of any stimulus, and to associate each stimulus with one of several motor patterns. Such a demonstration would have been next to impossible before neurobiologists could use a learning algorithm to configure a model. The LeechNet models require adjusting hundreds of parameters, too many for pencil-and-paper models or even the hand-wired network models of the past.

Having constructed the model, we can now do experiments on it that might be very difficult if not impossible on the animal. Computer experiments can be dreamed up and completed within an afternoon, but it might take a year to do a comparable experiment on the living leech. One important question concerns the locus of synaptic plasticity during a change in behavior. For example, repetition of an innocuous sensory stimulus leads to a decrement in the amplitude of the response, called habituation. Assuming that a large set of interneurons participate in the response, a great many synapses could be involved in the modification of the response to the stimulus. An efficient tactic might be to first determine the loci of plasticity in the model, a relatively easy job, and then check out the findings, at least partially, against the living leech—a Herculean job.

Lockery found this to be an illuminating tactic. A model which previously had been trained to reproduce all of the bending reflexes was retrained to produce a decremented dorsal bending reflex. After retraining, the magnitude of the response was half the original response. The synaptic changes that brought about this behavior change were distributed over all of the synapses (figure 6.16). Moreover, the distribution of changes in synaptic weights had a roughly normal distribution around 0 with a standard deviation of 1 millivolt (mV). About half of these changes are too small to be detectable in the leech under standard experimental conditions. Notice, however, that this is a worst-case condition, inasmuch as the training algorithm tends to distribute changes as widely as possible. This side of the worst case, however, more may be detectable, but even as a worst case, 50% detectability is not so bad. (The optimist says, "Half were detectable!")

Furthermore, as the number of interneurons in the model increased from 10 to 40, the average change in synaptic strength became smaller, for the same magnitude in behavioral effect. The prediction based on the model network would be that when the network habituates, there will be only a small effect on each interneuron, but larger effects will be found on output cells. This raises the possibility that under normal physiological conditions it may be very difficult to find detectable changes at the microscopic level, even though there are large changes in behavior. If this principle were to hold in general, then for vertebrates, with thousands of interneurons in small networks, the sizes of the changes may be equivalent to the fluctuation observed in the variation of quantal packets of transmitter released. Such an arrangement makes some sense if the interneurons are being used for several other behaviors—you

Difference in simulated peak synaptic potentials

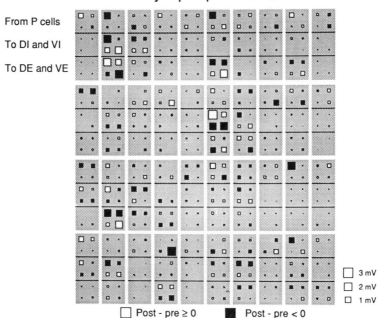

From P cells

To DI and VI

To DE and VE

3 mV
2 mV
1 mV

Post - pre ≥ 0   Post - pre < 0

Figure 6.16 Changes observed in the peak synaptic potentials following habituation of the bending reflexes to one half of their original amplitudes. The layout of the connection strengths for the 40 interneurons is the same as that in figure 6.15 except that the small boxes represent potential differences, and the sign of the change is indicated by white (post > pre) or black (post < pre). Note that most of the changes were small and distributed over most of the interneurons. Even the largest changes are less than 3 mV. (Courtesy Shawn Lockery).

don't want to disrupt all their output relationships even though some changes take place for modifying one behavior. Locating the sites of plasticity underlying normal learning will be much more difficult, however.

It is intriguing that both live and model networks display individual differences in the temporal integration properties of neurons, and this suggests yet another set of experiments designed to determine whether this property of the system has a behavioral role. Perhaps, for example, the system is designed to alter its response as the duration or intensity of the stimulus changes. Testing the model with longer-duration stimuli produced responses that were different from the trained responses to short-duration stimuli. This showed that the model is flexible in the temporal domain. Perhaps the real network is too. Given the model's prediction, there is a rationale for performing the physiology experiment.

The leech has a relatively simple nervous system with correspondingly simple behaviors. Even so, some of the same general problems arise—and arise in more extreme form—in studying the nature of sensorimotor transformations in other animals, including primates. Moreover, the data are inevitably drawn from a limited sample of all the neurons involved in the behavior, where we cannot tell how representative these data are. This is a standing problem in neuroscience. Optimistically, however, the known leech neurobiology is an assay for the modeling algorithm, precisely because the wealth of data on leech neurobiology makes comparisons with model neural nets a feasible strategy. The most basic lesson from LeechNet I and II is that neural circuits could be constructed for performing the desired behavior, with components whose properties are consistent with the limited data available. The model is an existence proof, therefore, that the task can be accomplished with resources that are known to be present in the biological system.

The model has also led to a series of questions that require further investigation. For example, if the same interneurons involved in the bending reflex are also involved in other behaviors, such as crawling, then what is their role in these other behaviors? The bending reflex has been studied in isolation as a convenience, but it is only one element of a wider range of behavior that exploits the same machinery as does the bending reflex. We know that there are projections to the pool of interneurons involved in the bending reflex from neurons in neighboring ganglia and perhaps also from head and tail "brains." The organization of head and tail "brains" must take into account the types of representations used at the abdominal ganglia. The models currently under development for distributed representations may help generate some hypotheses regarding the constraints imposed on these higher levels of organization, which are very likely to be different from the constraints of a system based on feature detectors and command neurons (Altman and Kien 1987a,b).

This example illustrates the level at which commonality might be found between invertebrate and vertebrate circuits. The details of the bending reflex in the leech are highly specialized, but the way that groups of neurons cooperate together to accomplish a set of tasks might be quite similar to the organization of neural populations in vertebrates, as we shall see in the next section.

The co-evolutionary benefits at the experimental level are therefore evident, but the interaction between the models and the living leech is also useful in prying loose the traditional conception of the reflex behavior as a cluster of three separate reflexes (dorsal, ventral, and lateral local bending), to conceiving of it in terms of a single *computational* device that performs a vector–vector mapping operation. This shift corresponds to the difference discussed earlier between sheerly mechanical and computational frameworks for understanding a device.

The reorientation in perspective may instill new ways of looking at old problems, and open up some quite new problems. For example, Lockery began to ask after the physiological value of each dimension of the vectors, initially so he could have exact data to feed the learning algorithm its input and feed the teacher the correct output. This is a project that would not have been well motivated in the old framework. Quite apart from the matter of data for the learning algorithm, this enterprise inspired a much more quantitative approach to neural circuit analysis than had been hitherto pursued. The experimental research on leech bending became both more exact, in the sense of determining exact value for input and output units, and more complete, inasmuch as it now made sense to measure as many connection strengths between neurons as possible to verify the predictions of the learning algorithm. Moreover, within the context of a single computational device, important questions emerged about the role of a bending behavior in other behaviors such as swimming, and about the computational differences that explain the orchestration of different body movements defining different behaviors.

3   COMPUTATION AND THE VESTIBULO-OCULAR REFLEX

The vestibulo-ocular reflex is commonly known by its acronym, the VOR. The function of the VOR is to stabilize the image of the world on the surface of the retina when the head is moving. The stimulus for the VOR is head acceleration, which is detected by the vestibular organ located in the middle ear (figure 6.17). The vestibular organ contains three semicircular canals oriented roughly at right angles to each other, each filled with endolymph. This fluid moves during head acceleration, bending the protruding hair cells, causing either a depolarization or a hyperpolarization in the hair cell, depending on the direction bent (figure 6.18).

The VOR circuit achieves its image-stabilizing effect by causing eye movements that compensate almost exactly for the head movement by rotating the eye in the opposite direction. This enables visual tracking with minimum perceptual smear. Notice that image stabilization is no mean feat since the head velocity and direction must be continuously calculated, and the messages must be transmitted to the motor neurons of the eye muscles (figure 6.19). The amount the muscles contract must be exactly calculated so that the head movement is quite precisely, and not merely roughly, countervailed. It is, in fact, a highly exacting instance of sensorimotor control. Moreover, the VOR must be very fast if it is to be useful. Indeed, the compensating eye movements begin about *14 msec* after the onset of the head movement, but can begin as soon as 6

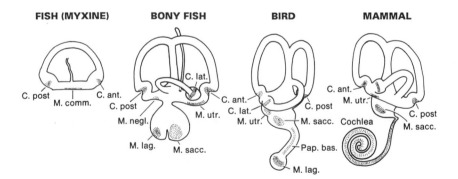

Figure 6.17 Evolution of the vestibular apparatus in vertebrates. Various parts of the labyrinth are specialized for sensing circular acceleration such as the anterior crista (C. ant.), the lateral crista (C. lat.), and the posterior crista (C. post). Other parts are specialized for sensing linear acceleration and gravity, such as the macula utriculi (M. utr.) and the macula sacculi (M. sacc.). The papilla basilaris (Pap. bas.) in birds and the cochlea in mammals are specialized for sensing sound vibrations. (From Wersall and Bagger-Sjoback 1974.)

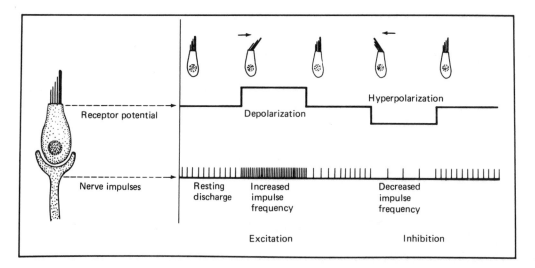

Figure 6.18 Directional selectivity of the vestibular hair cell. The receptor potential in the hair cell is depolarized when the stereocilia at its apical end is bent toward the large kinocilium (to the right) and is hyperpolarized in the opposite direction. The synapse on the basilar face of the hair cell is a "drip" synapse that responds to changes in the receptor potential and stimulates spike discharges in the postsynaptic afferent nerve. The mechanical motion of the tip of the hair cell is converted into modulation of the train of action potentials in the vestibular nerve fiber. (From Kelly 1985b.)

msec if the head velocity is high. This is also a network that can recalibrate itself in response to transducer realignment, as, for example, when reversing prisms or size-altering lenses are worn on the eyes. In a mild way this can be noticed when one's lens prescription changes. VOR compensation is not, therefore "hardwired'" in the narrow sense of the word—namely unmodifiable, inflexible, and fixed absolutely by the genes. Of which, more later.

For a demonstration of the VOR at work, you can produce the following contrast between perception in the absence of the VOR (smooth pursuit) and with the assistance of the VOR. (1) Keep the head steady, move one hand rapidly back and forth in front of your eyes, trying to track the movement as best you can. (This is smooth pursuit.) You will have a smeary, ill-defined perception of a hand. (2) Now reverse the conditions: keep the hand steady, and move the head back and forth. Though the speed is about the same in the two cases, the perception of the hand is much crisper in the second, where the head moves. This is because in the second condition, the VOR uses head acceleration information from the vestibular organ to make compensatory eye movements. So long as the slip across the retina is less than a few degrees per second, the image will not appear smeared. (See table 6.1 for a summary of gaze control systems.)

Without this reflex, recognizing objects would be a lost cause whenever one's head was anything but still. For animals detecting or chasing prey, defending against attack, or wooing a mate, keeping the head still in order to see is not a serious option. This is clearly evident during locomotion, when the

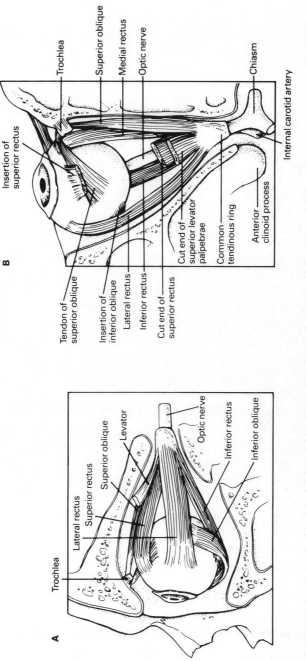

Figure 6.19 (A) Cutaway drawing of the eye in its orbit and the three pairs of eye muscles that control its movement. Lateral view of the lateral rectus, superior and inferior rectus, and superior and inferior oblique muscles (medial rectus, note shown, is on the other side of the eyeball). (B) Cutaway view showing the inferior rectus on the medial surface of the orbit, and the origins and insertions of the muscles. The optic nerve follows the eyeball as it gyrates in its gimbal. The optic nerves from both eyes join at the chiasm. (From Gouras 1985b.)

Table 6.1 Summary of primate gaze control systems

Hold gaze	Fixed target	Vestibular-ocular reflex (VOR). A system that uses knowledge of accommodation and vergence state together with head accelerations to stabilize the gaze vector.
	Moving target	Vergence. A binocular system for locking both foveas over the same three-dimensional target.
		Pursuit. A system for tracking moving objects by generating smooth-velocity control signals.
Change gaze	Saccades. High-speed, precomputed movements that rapidly change gaze over small to very large visual angles.	

From Ballard (1991). Animate vision. *Artificial Intelligence* 48: 57–86.

body and head are bobbing. If the outfielder has to stop to see where the fly ball is going, he will not have a prayer of making the catch; if a coyote has to stop to visually track the rabbit, he will forgo the meal. Had we wheels instead of legs, and smooth instead of uneven traveling surfaces, there would be less bouncing of the image; as it is, the head moves a great deal in walking, running, crawling, and swimming. An additional ploy used by the nervous system during locomotion is to stabilize the head to some degree while the body moves. For an owl or hawk targeting a mouse from the air, or a panther racing after a wildebeest, or even a skier negotiating moguls—the head is much steadier than the body as the neck muscles try to compensate for body movement. It is by no means perfectly steady, however, and residual head movement is picked up in the semicircular canals and compensated for by the VOR, thus keeping perception crisp. By using both the VOR and head stabilization, the nervous system is very efficient in delivering clean images to higher visual centers for more detailed analysis.

The circuitry that controls eye movements compensatory for head movements is one of the best understood parts of the mammalian brain. The oculomotor system extends over many brain-stem nuclei and numerous connecting pathways. To a considerable extent it has been possible to follow all the relevant signals from sensory transduction in the semicircular canals to the pathways in the brain-stem, to the oculomotor muscles that control eye movements (figure 6.20). Adaptation and learning occur as the oculomotor system interacts with the world, and this plasticity can be studied at all levels of investigation from molecules to behavior. Learning is much more difficult to study in other mammalian systems because of greater anatomical complexity and less complete knowledge of the representations used in the nervous system. For example, although we know a lot about mechanisms for synaptic plasticity in the hippocampus, we know very little about how neurons in the hippocampus represent information about the world or about the behavioral significance of activity in hippocampal neurons. (See chapter 5.)

The basic VOR circuit consists of detection by transducers, projection to the vestibular nucleus in the brain stem, and projection from there to cranial nerve nuclei, where motor neurons originate that project to the eyes muscles (figures

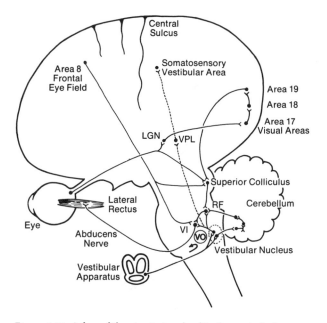

Figure 6.20 A few of the circuits involved in the control of eye movements. For simplicity, the control of only one muscle, the lateral rectus, is shown. This muscle is innervated by motoneurons in the abducens nucleus, via the 6th cranial nerve (VI), the abducens nerve. The shortest vestibulo-ocular loop (VO) from the vestibular apparatus to the lateral rectus has two synapses, one in the vestibular nucleus and one in the abducens nucleus. Nuclei in the reticular formation (RF) receive converging inputs from the superior colliculus, the vestibular nucleus, and the cerebellum. The superior colliculus carries signals that are important for saccadic eye movements and receives direct inputs from retinal ganglion cells. The frontal eye fields also have a role in generating saccadic eye movements and project to brain-stem nuclei. The retina also projects to the lateral geniculate nucleus (LGN) in the thalamus, and from there to visual cortex. Projections from extrastriate cortical areas project to the oculomotor centers in the brain stem to provide information about visual targets. Motion signals in visual cortex are used to track moving targets by information that is sent to the cerebellum via pontine nuclei (not shown) in the brain stem. (From Shepherd 1988a, p. 301.)

6.20, 6.21). Thus in the shortest pathway between transducers and muscles, there is just a three-link chain, which makes it an approachable circuit to study. Under normal conditions, the VOR works as a feedforward network. This is referred to as an "open-loop" circuit because it does not depend upon feedback from the muscles or visual system to compute the final output. ("Open loop" here really means "non-loop," and perhaps "straight-through" describes the situation more accurately.) Head velocity can exceed 300°/sec, and visual feedback reporting slip on the retina is relatively slow getting back to the oculomotor system (about 85 msec), so a feedback controller system for reaching a final position by gradual error reduction would be unacceptably slow.

If we assume that neurons projecting to the vestibular nuclei in the brainstem carry signals specifying head velocity, and that motor neurons carry signals specifying muscular contraction to produce an eye velocity, then the computational action, so to speak, is located between these two at the several

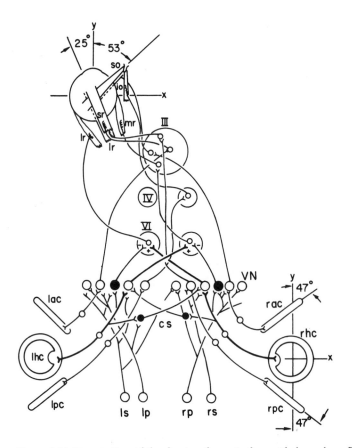

Figure 6.21 Organization of the direct pathway in the vestibulo-ocular reflex. The vestibular inputs from the three vestibular canals (right and left posterior canals, rpc and lpc; right and left horizontal canals, rhc and lhc; and right and left anterior canals, rac and lac) synapse on neurons in the vestibular nucleus (VN), which also receives lateralized inputs from pursuit and saccadic signals (rp, lp; rs, ls). The VN have projections to motor nuclei across the midline. The motor neurons in turn project to the eye muscles (lateral rectus, lr; superior rectus, sr; medial rectus, mr; inferior rectus, ir; superior oblique, so; inferior oblique, io). (From Anastasio and Robinson 1989.)

vestibular nuclei, lumped together for convenience as "VN." VN is actually an area of convergence, receiving not only vestibular signals, but also signals from smooth-pursuit neurons and saccadic-burst neurons. Single-unit recordings from cells in VN (Miles et al. 1980) revealed that neurons might respond either to VOR stimuli or to pursuit stimuli, perhaps equally, perhaps not, and generally with opposite signs. Some anomalous neurons fire more quickly for a vestibular eye movement in one direction and a pursuit movement in the opposite.[7] Despite many attempts to map specific functions onto specific neuron groups, it now seems evident that the VN neurons code in a distributed rather than a local fashion, and that they can serve in several different roles, performing either VOR computation, or saccade or pursuit computation.

The computational problem for the VN centers on what transformation should be applied to the input vector carrying the three kinds of information so as to solve the problem of how the eyes should move. Consequently, in designing a computer network, the array of VN neurons would constitute the hidden (middle) layer, where the input vector would represent head velocity as well as saccadic eye and pursuit velocity; the output layer would represent the solution, namely, eye velocity suited to the particular head velocity. Following this plan, Anastasio and Robinson (1989) designed model networks of varying populations to explore how a network constrained by the anatomy in the VOR pathways could accomplish the needed transformations. They used backpropagation to train up the network; retinal slip played the role of external teacher. To maximize biological realism, they permitted weight change at the input–hidden layer, but not at the hidden–output layer, assuming that in the real VOR, the connections between VN neurons and motor neurons are probably not plastic.

The beauty of using a learning algorithm such as backpropagation rather than setting the weights by hand[8] was that it allowed the network to discover an architecture that was efficient, accurate, and suited to neuronlike components (figure 6.22). Comparisons could then be made between the properties of hidden units and properties of actual neurons to determine whether the model was approximating the real thing. Contrariwise, setting the weights by hand typically smuggles in assorted engineering background assumptions about how the task must be performed. Backpropagation evolves up a network so it can tell us how the task is performed in the model, innocent of engineering prejudices, and hence how it could be performed in a real neural network (tables 6.2, 6.3, 6.4). Combining input signals from various sources, for example, seems decidedly queer from an engineering point of view. For convolved into a salad, the signals are hard to analyze. Engineers, consequently, tend to shun the idea as unworkable. But, of course, this is Nature, not Texas Instruments, and multitudinous advantages of vector-coding (distributed representing) accrue to an organization found by backpropagation—and apparently also by evolution. (See chapter 5.)

Earlier models segregated the VN neural pathways according to whether they carried specifically saccade-movement information, or pursuit commands, or VOR commands (Robinson 1981). Moreover, these models were decidedly black-boxy, in the sense that although they managed to approximate the general input–output character of the system, they were insensitive to the neural processing that solved the problem of what the output should be, given the input. Since there are many possible ways of rigging a system to conform to an input–output profile, it is desirable to have a means for narrowing down the search space by replacing the black boxes with units that, to a first approximation, are like neurons.

What do the Anastasio and Robinson models teach us? First, the analysis of hidden units revealed a range of responses, from purely pursuit or purely VOR to various combinations of VOR–pursuit responses in between. This organization thus resembles what is seen in real VN neurons, and consequently helps explain the heretofore-confusing nature of the data on VN neuron responses. Pursuit and VOR are complementary, and distribution of representation and multiplicity of function turn out to be an efficient and accurate way for neurons

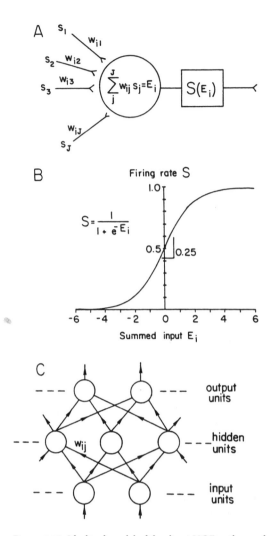

Figure 6.22 Idealized model of the direct VOR pathway shown in figure 6.21. (A) The output of each processing unit is a function of the weighted sums of all its inputs. (B) The nonlinear output function is a sigmoid with value of 0.5 at zero input. The function is approximately linear around zero input. (C) Feedforward architecture with the input units representing the vestibular inputs, the hidden units like the neurons in the vestibular nucleus, and the output units identified with the motoneurons driving the eye muscles. (From Anastasio and Robinson 1989).

Table 6.2 Vestibular input/output table

	Input		Output	
	lhc	rhc	lr	mr
Head still	0.50	0.50	0.50	0.50
Head left	0.60	0.40	0.40	0.60
Head right	0.40	0.60	0.60	0.40

From Anastasio and Robinson (1989).

Key: lhc, rhc: left, right horizontal canals; lr, mr: lateral, medial rectus muscles.

Table 6.3 Final weights of simple VOR model

To		h1	h2		lr	mr
From	lhc	1.63	− 2.64	h1	− 1.71	1.84
	rhc	− 1.21	2.25	h2	2.08	− 2.23

From Anastasio and Robinson (1989).

Table 6.4 Hidden and output unit responses for simple VOR model

Input		Hidden		Output	
lhc	rhc	h1	h2	lr	mr
0.50	0.50	0.55	0.45	0.50	0.50
0.60	0.40	0.62	0.33	0.41	0.60
0.40	0.60	0.48	0.57	0.59	0.40

From Anastasio and Robinson (1989).

to solve the various eye-movement problems (figure 6.23). Second, by running the simulations many times, Anastasio and Robinson found that there is no unique solution in such learning networks to the question of who should represent what. Hidden units may have different profiles from one simulation to the next. This is not especially mysterious. It is a consequence of using more units than are absolutely necessary , thus entailing that the mapping from input vector to output vector is underdetermined.

Third, Anastasio and Robinson discovered that simply in the course of training, units organize themselves to mimic the neural organization whereby each VN neuron excites one motor neuron and inhibits another, thus orchestrating the push—pull routines of the reciprocal eye muscles. As they remark, the model networks, like their bone fide counterparts, discover Sherrington's law of reciprocal innervation. They note that in nervous systems a single neuron generally is not both excitatory and inhibitory so an inter-neuron with fixed weight is interposed, and such an interneuron is implied in the model networks, though the details of weight-setting and so forth have not been worked out. Fourth, it is noteworthy that even a very austere model, with merely two units at each of the three levels, can in fact solve the VOR

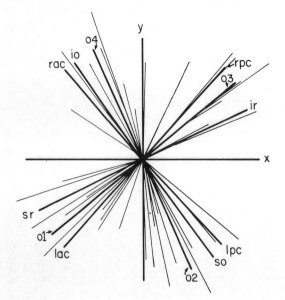

Figure 6.23 Distribution of the rotation axes preferred by hidden units (thin lines) and output units (thick lines labeled o1, o2, o3, and o4, where "o" means "output") of the Anastasio–Robinson VOR model. The axes of the muscle insertions (io, so, sr, ir) and vestibular canals (rac, lac, rpc, lpc) are also indicated by thick lines (see figure 6.21 for abbreviations). This shows that although there is a weak tendency for the hidden units to have preferred axes clustered around the sensory and motor axes, the variance is high. A similar variance is also seen in recordings from cat vestibular neurons. (From Anastasio and Robinson 1989.)

problem adequately. When additional units are added in order to imitate the greater population of neurons seen in the real VN, the network load balances and the information is broadly distributed across the whole population of units. This arrangement gives the network fault tolerance, so that if some units "die," the remaining units could fill in by small changes in the weights distributed through the population. The possibility raised by this finding is that systems as critical to perception as the VOR may augment the essential population of functionally critical cells by extra cells as a safety measure.

The role of backpropagation in training up the network deserves additional comment, lest it be misunderstood. Notice that "backprop" is used not because anyone thinks a real nervous system gets wired up in that way. Of course, it does not. Rather, backprop is used to get the network into a weight space where it functions accurately and with a behavioral profile that is comparable to its real counterpart. That is, it should perform well where the real network does, it should be fooled where the real network is, and it should falter, and falter over the same obstacles and with the same sequelae, as the real network. Backprop enables the network to find an error minimum, and it is not unreasonable to assume that evolution, over many trials and with countless errors, stumbled into much the same error minimum. Having a trained-up network in hand, the researcher can then study it, and more particularly, can study properties of the network that would be awesomely difficult or downright impossible to study in a real network. By why use backprop rather than just an exhaustive search of all possible weight-settings? In network with 100 variable weights, and a supercomputer to try out all the possibilities, it would take approximately 10^{30} centuries to examine all possible combinations of weights.[9] Backprop is a lot faster. Moreover, analyzing the response properties of tens or hundreds of hidden units is standard fare for research on computer nets. It is Sysiphean, to put it mildly, in real neural nets. And, of course, one does not stop there. With data from the computer net, one can generate predictions and experiments that are testable in varying degrees on real nets. Although the training rule per se is nonbiological, it picks out sites of plasticity and suggests local learning rules that might produce the same results. A singularly valuable spin-off of modeling are the clues regarding local rules for synapse modification. We shall consider this in detail below.

The early nets of Anastasio and Robinson were trained on steady-state data—input velocities and output velocities—but nothing about *changing* velocities. More recently, however, Anastasio (1991, in press) has developed a model with dynamical properties, including storage of vestibular velocity signals via mutually inhibitory, commissural feedback loops. His modeling question concerned the circuit explanation for experimental results showing that if one of the vestibular organs were ablated, then several distinct recovery adjustments in the VOR are seen, and each has its typical time course. The location and nature of the cellular changes has not yet been discovered experimentally, so Anastasio's plan was to see what choices the model made, and then determine whether changes in the real circuit were similar. Notice that once the semicircular canals on one side, say the left, are lesioned, the system reacts as though there is continual head movement to the right. Consequently the VOR makes compensatory eye movements (spontaneous nystagmus) to the left.[10] The three basic observations about nervous systems' recovery from vestibular lesions are these: (1) The spontaneous nystagmus disappears in a few days. (2) Initially, there is a reduction in gain of the VOR, but this inches back up and is normal at about a week and a half after the lesion. (3) The neurons in the VN normally exhibit "velocity storage," meaning that they hold information about the last head movement for about 20 sec after the onset of the head movement, although the head velocity afferents themselves turn off much earlier. After vestibular lesions, velocity storage is essentially never recovered. These observations, together with the known connectivity and physiology, constituted the additional constraints for Anastasio's dynamical model. What plausible circuit properties could explain the experimental observations?

For this exploration, Anastasio used a recurrent net with lateral interactions and nonlinear units (figure 6.24). This net had been pretrained to produce the VOR, complete with velocity storage. To simulate compensation, the left "canal" was lesioned (i.e., the left input was removed) and the net was retrained. A net in which the only modifiable weights were on the hidden units was adequate at the behavioral level, but it did not correspond at the cellular level to the experimental observations. In particular, although the VOR gain as a

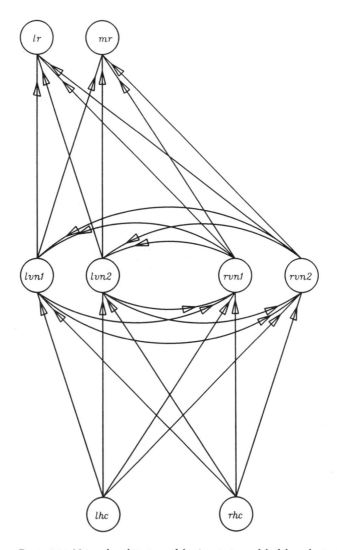

Figure 6.24 Network architecture of the Anastasio model of the velocity integrator of the VOR. Inputs from the left and right horizontal canals (lhc, rhc) project to a group of hidden units representing neurons in the left and right vestibular nuclei (lvn, rvn). These hidden units have reciprocal interconnections and also project to two output units that represent the motor neurons innervating a pair of eye muscles (lr, lateral rectus; mr, medial rectus). (From Anastasio, in press.)

whole largely recovers, the gain of the VN neurons remains low. This was not true of the model, where VN units largely recovered their normal gain. Second, although in real brains spontaneous nystagmus decreases, there is a persistent imbalance in VN neuron activity bilaterally, inasmuch as VN neurons on the lesioned side have reduced activity, but the activity of VN neurons on the unlesioned side is increased relative to normal conditions. This was not true of the model. The conclusion about the model was that either certain parameters were missing, or weight modification should be permitted between the VN units and the output units (standing for the motor neurons). Anastasio followed up the second alternative.

Anastasio discovered that the new model did indeed match the experimental results so long as the output weights were modifiable. And the time course of recovery of the three VOR properties was also preserved, in the sense that disappearance of spontaneous nystagmus came in early (after about two passes), recovery of VOR gain came in next (after about 200 passes), and velocity storage virtually never recovers. Moreover, the explanation of the failure of the real system to recover velocity storage could also be drawn out of the nature of the behavior of the model VN units in the compensated state.

The disappearance of spontaneous nystagmus could be accomplished by adjusting the thresholds on the motor neurons as well as the VN neurons, and hence nystagmus has the shortest time course recovery. Gain compensation is more difficult. The model makes those adjustments by modifying the input from the unaffected canal, since, of course, there exists no input from the ablated canal. This adjustment is more difficult because increasing the input from the intact canal causes an increase in the imbalance between the two vestibular nuclei and effectively contributes to the spontaneous nystagmus which is supposed to be decreasing. The connections between the hidden and the motor units can also increase their efficacy, but here again, this compensation is delicate because the compensatory actions can affect the rebalancing of the rest of the system.

Finally, why does velocity storage not recover? A possible reason emerges from the model. Because the thresholds on the output units are modifiable, changing the thresholds on the hidden units is not so critical. Overall, therefore, the easiest thing for the network to do is to leave silent the lesion-side units participating in the commissural loop, since they are already strongly inhibited from the opposite side anyhow. In effect then, the network chooses to eliminate velocity storage rather than perserverate in misinformation that would frustrate the other compensatory adjustments. Even though preliminary physiological data have not so far shown modification at the motor neuron synapses, the prediction from the Anastasio model is that this is what the real system does.

Plasticity in the VOR

A system built on the open-loop principle rather than the feedback principle must be recalibrated should the physical properties of the system change. In

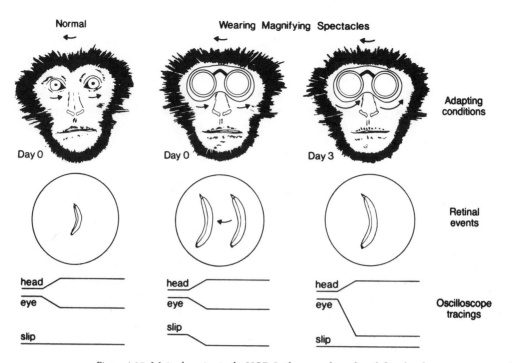

Figure 6.25 Motor learning in the VOR. In the normal monkey (left), a head turn causes an equal and opposite eye rotation. The oscilloscope tracings at the bottom show that the eye moves in just the correct way to compensate for the head movements, and the image of the banana on the retina remains stationary. On the first day wearing magnifying spectacles (middle), the magnification causes slip to occur, as shown in the oscilloscope tracings, and the banana slips across the retina. The VOR is now too small to compensate and keep the image crisp. On the third day wearing the goggles (right), the gain of the VOR had increased until it was just large enough to cancel the slip of the image. The compensatory eye movements are now twice what they were before the goggles were put on the monkey. In the oscilloscope records the slip trace is once again flat. (From Lisberger [1988b]. The neural basis for motor learning in the vestibulo-ocular reflex in monkeys. *Trends in Neurosciences* 11: 147–152.)

the case of the VOR, there are changes in the mechanical properties of the eye during development, slow changes in the optical properties of the eye such as changing magnification, especially as the head and eyeballs grow, and fast changes made after donning distorting lenses. To make matters more difficult, the VOR and the pursuit system share architecture, as noted above. Yet the VOR is a feedforward, open-loop system while pursuit is a negative-feedback, closed-loop system; the VOR has a latency of about 14 msec, while the pursuit system has a latency of about 100 msec. How can the neurons modify themselves to accommodate the VOR without gumming up smooth pursuit? What is the signal for recalibration, and where does the system modify itself in response to the signal?

The persistence of smeary images (retinal slip) despite compensating head turns during a VOR task tells the system to recalibrate. In response to the persistent signal of retinal motion, there is a gradual increase or decrease in the amplitude of the VOR until the eye movement comes once again to

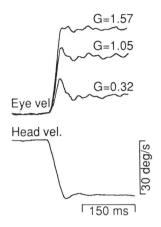

Figure 6.26 Measurements of the VOR under different conditions of gain. The head of a monkey is moved from rest to a velocity of 30°/sec. After a latency of around 14 msec, the eyes begin to counterrotate to compensate. Under normal conditions (G = 1.05) the gain is close to that needed to reduce the slip of the image on the retina to a few degrees/sec. The measurement at the top (G = 1.57) was made several days after the monkey was fitted with goggles that magnified the image on the retina; the measurement on the bottom (G = 0.32) was made after several days of wearing minifying goggles. In each condition, the VOR gain adapted to reduce the slip of the image on the retina. (From Lisberger, S. [1988b]. The neural basis for motor learning in the vestibulo-ocular reflex in monkeys. *Trends in Neurosciences* 11: 147−152.)

compensate precisely for retinal slip. Accordingly, persistent image slip leads to changes in the gain of the reflex such that slip is reduced. Gain change is learning, and that it takes place can easily be demonstrated by putting on an animal goggles that magnify or miniaturize the image of the world on the retina (figure 6.25). The result is that objects appear to move either at twice or at half their normal speed during head turns. Under the new viewing conditions, a normal VOR is too small or too large, and with each head turn there remains motion of the image on the retina. Over a period of hours, the system adjusts, and by a day or so, the eye movements are once again correct (figure 6.26).

A model network incorporating known pathways, connections, and physiology of the VOR and smooth pursuit has yielded some useful and surprising results (Lisberger and Sejnowski, 1992). Most surprisingly, the model explains a physiological discovery concerning the location of learning that had been shelved because it seemed odd and did not fit very well with the received neurophysiological wisdom. Most usefully, revealing the location of modification in the model allowed exploration of the nature of the modification, which meant that the local learning rule used by the model system could be reconstructed. Crudely, knowing *where* in the model was an essential first step in figuring out *how* in the model. Then, knowing where and how in the model engenders hypotheses concerning where and how in the real network. Thus predictions concerning the learning rule used in VOR modification in real neural networks can now be tested. To tell this story for full value, we need preliminary discussion about the neurobiology involved.

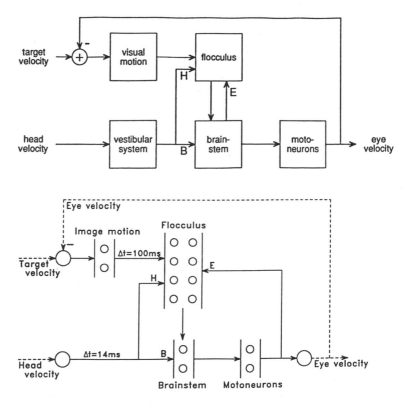

Figure 6.27 (Top) Diagram of the basic oculomotor circuits used for the VOR and smooth pursuit. The vestibular system senses head velocity and provides inputs to neurons in the brain stem (B) and the cerebellar flocculus (H). The output neurons of the flocculus make inhibitory synapses on neurons in the brain stem. The output of the brain stem projects directly to motor neurons, which drive the eye muscles, and also project back to the flocculus (E). This positive feedback loop has an "efference copy" of the motor commands. The flocculus also receives visual information from the retina, delayed for 100 msec by the visual processing in the retina and visual cortex. The image velocity, which is the difference between the target velocity and the eye velocity, is used in a negative feedback loop to maintain smooth tracking of moving targets. (Bottom) Diagram of the architecture for a dynamical network model of the system. The model incorporates model neurons that have integration time constants and time delays. The arrows indicate connections between the populations of units, indicated by small circles, in each cluster. The broken line between the eye velocity and the summing junction with the target velocity indicates a linkage between the output of the model and the input. (Courtesy of S. Lisberger.)

The basic VOR circuit addressed by the Anastasio and Robinson model needs be filled out somewhat to accommodate the additional features involved in VOR modification (figure 6.27, top). The main additions involve the flocculus of the cerebellum wherein three important inputs converge: image motion (via visual cortex), head movement (via the vestibular afferents), and a copy of the VOR's command to the motor neurons (efference copy). The sole output from the flocculus occurs in the form of Purkinje cell action potentials. These are inhibitory and they affect brain-stem nuclei that compute motor neuron activity. This enlarged circuit diagram makes explicit the problem of integrating the VOR and the smooth pursuit systems. The important fact to keep uppermost in mind is that the same motor neurons activate the muscles of the eyeball, whether the task is smooth pursuit or VOR, and the same neural nets in the brain stem compute input vectors from VOR, smooth pursuit, and saccades.

A walk through the circuit will acquaint us with what is a most artful design. Suppose one is scuba diving and tracking an octopus. The circuitry has to cope with three main tracking conditions: VOR tracking, eyes-only tracking (pursuit), and head-only tracking. Imagine first that the octopus is stationary and one's head is moving. Then a head velocity signal is detected, the equal and opposite eye movement is computed, and the motor neurons specify the corresponding eye movement. This happens within 14 msec, and this is the VOR at work. Second, suppose the head is stationary but the octopus is moving. The visual motion pathway detects movement on the retina, and sends a visual motion signal to the visual cortex and thence to the cerebellum which computes a command for an eye movement in the same direction as the object movement (and hence in the direction opposite to the retinal movement). This is smooth pursuit (figure 6.28). Notice that since no vestibular signal is detected (the head is not moving), there is no contribution by the VOR to the motor neurons in smooth pursuit.

In the third and very common condition, which we call "head-only tracking," imagine that both the head and the octopus are moving. For good tracking, the eyes must be kept stationary in the head while the head alone moves. This feat is known as VOR suppression, reflecting the fact that the reflex to make the compensating eye movement in response to detected head movement must not be allowed to exert itself. Achieving good tracking in this condition is obviously a bit more complicated than in the other two conditions. The basic steps are as follows. (1) Because the head moves, 14 msec after the stimulus onset the eyeball moves in response to the standard VOR command, though, as it happens, in the wrong direction given how the target is actually moving. (2) Image motion is detected in the visual motion pathways, and a corresponding pursuit signal is generated. (3) By the time the pursuit signal reaches the motor neurons at about 100 msec, the eye position will have already changed at the behest of the VOR, the swift VOR response having moved the eyes off-target. (This leaves aside saccades, which have a latency of about 200 msec.) There is, therefore, a delay in the feedback, and this delay needs to be incorporated into the model.[11]

On engineering as well as purely aesthetic criteria, the circuitry controlling eye movement is an exquisite bit of design on the part of evolution, and it is a telling illustration of how a very difficult set of tasks can be accomplished by a network. Like the Anastasio (1991) model and in contrast to the Anastasio and Robinson (1989) model of the VOR, the Lisberger–Sejnowski model is dynamical, and it incorporates floccular processing because it needs to accommodate feedback with temporally appropriate features. Dynamical (time-dependent) properties are critical, and especially so when shared networks must cope with different tracking conditions and different time constants, and must operate on time-averaged inputs. In the Lisberger–Sejnowski model, individual processing units have intrinsic time scales for integration of information that

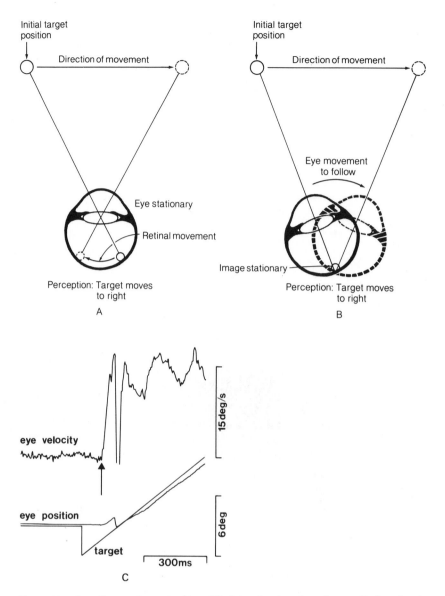

Figure 6.28 Smooth pursuit eye tracking. (A) A moving target produces retinal motion in a stationary eye. (B) The image of the target can be stabilized if the eye moves to follow the target. (Reprinted with permission from Coren and Ward 1989.) (C) Eye recordings from monkey responding to a step ramp target. The eye position and target position are shown below. The eye position signal was differentiated to produce the eye velocity signal above. The target jumped 3° to the right and immediately began moving to the left with a constant velocity of 15°/sec. After a delay of about 100 msec (arrow), the eyes began moving to the left to track the target. The fast jump in eye velocity is a corrective saccade. The steady-state tracking is accurate to within 3°/sec and shows an oscillation at around 6 Hz that is characteristic of negative feedback systems. (From Lisberger et al. 1987. Reproduced, with permission, from the *Annual Review of Neuroscience*, Vol. 10, © 1987 by Annual Reviews, Inc.)

are roughly analogous to the membrane time constant to real neurons (that is, the time it takes for the membrane potential to build up to steady state or to decay, which varies across neuron types). Input into a neuron will not lead to an instantaneous change in the firing rate, but rather will gradually approach a new level of firing. Additionally, the Lisberger–Sejnowski models allow for the 100-msec time delays in the feedback loop and the 14-msec latency in the VOR line. Perhaps the most striking contrast to Anastasio and Robinson (1989) is the presence of recurrent loops to the input layer and between the flocculus and the brain stem, due to visual feedback, for this means the system has dynamical properties relevantly like those of the real network.

Having squared away the preliminary presentation of the circuit, we next address modification of the VOR in response to miniaturizing lenses which halve the size of the target, entailing that the visual images are halved in size so that a head turn will cause images to move at half their normal speed, and the amplitude of the VOR will have to decrease by half in order to maintain stability of the image. (*Mutatis mutandis* for magnifying lenses.) This looks particularly fussy since the miniaturizing lenses will not affect pursuit velocity (once the system has locked on to it), so that part of the operation should not be altered. Thus we are back at the VOR condition, tracking a stationary object while the head moves, but now with miniaturizing goggles requiring recalibration of a basically feedforward system. (See figure 6.25.)

The question of the primary locus of synaptic modification has been vexed because the data have seemed to point in contrary directions. Ito (1972, 1977) reported experimental evidence in support of a theory first proposed by Brindley (1964) and developed by Marr (1969) and Albus (1971). This theory argued that the primary learning locus in the cerebellum was between the parallel fibers and the Purkinje cells. This made quite a lot of sense, and theoretically, such a change could explain VOR learning. A point in Ito's favor was that without the flocculus, there is no learning. Second, Ito found that very early in the learning the outputs from the flocculus do change in the appropriate direction for motor learning. Together, these two observations strongly supported the idea that the flocculus was the primary locus of learning. Ito conjectured that the likely site was the vestibular–flocculus connection, on a Purkinje cell.

When Miles and colleagues (1980) tried to confirm this very reasonable conjecture, they repeatedly found, to their great puzzlement, that there were indeed changes at the vestibular–flocculus connection, but the changes after learning was completed were *in the wrong direction* from those Ito claimed to cause the altered VOR. Lisberger (1988a,b), following this mystery up some years later, replicated the Miles results and, in addition, discovered that latency data implicated not the vestibular–flocculus connection, but the vestibular–brain stem connection as the primary locus of learning, where the modifiable neurons are a subset of brainstem neurons receiving direct input from the flocculus. Was it possible that the Ito hypothesis had misidentified the primary locus of learning?

On the basis of the data they and others had collected, Miles and Lisberger suggested a new hypothesis (see figure 6.27, top). According to the new conjecture, the necessity of a functioning flocculus for the occurrence of learning and the puzzling change at the vestibular–flocculus site make sense all right, but very different sense. The Miles–Lisberger (1981) hypothesis has four major elements:[12] (1) It is known that the VOR undergoes learning only when there is *persistent retinal slip*. By hypothesis, it is the flocculus that provides this signal to the brain stem (vestibular nucleus, or VN) using signals from the feedback visual motion neurons. The VN, however, is the primary locus of learning. Thus a functioning flocculus is necessary not because it is the locus of learning but because it announces when learning is needed. (2) The site of motor learning should receive *convergent* vestibular and visual inputs if adaption is to be achieved. Indeed, the VN does receive both direct vestibular inputs as well as indirect visual inputs from the Purkinje cells (PCs). (3) The PCs have altered output after learning not because they are the site of learning, but because the VN, which is the primary site of learning, sends copies of its modified motor messages to the flocculus on the positive feedback pathway. The reduced flocculus output from the PCs reflects the change in efference copy. (4) The vestibular–floccular change occurs in response to the reduction of the efference-copy signal owing to modification of the VN. The point here is that the vestibular inputs to the flocculus, which before learning exactly matched and hence offset the efference-copy signals, are now consistently larger than the reduced efference-copy signals. If their gain is not turned down, they will excite the PCs of the flocculus which will inhibit the brain-stem cells which will turn off eye movement and thereby foul up the VOR (Lisberger 1988a,b).

The Miles–Lisberger hypothesis is compelling and it does explain the available data in a satisfying way. Still, it had not been settled experimentally that the vestibular–brain stem connection was the site of learning and that the Miles anomaly was secondary regulation of vestibular–efference mismatches in the flocculus. One way to test how much sense the hypothesis makes is to see how a dynamical model network, conforming to the known neurobiology, handles learning—to see where in the model the learning occurs, what kind of changes take place, and what learning rules govern modifications.

Lisberger and Sejnowski constructed a recurrent network containing all the major players and pathways (figure 6.27, bottom). Target velocity and head velocity represented the input, and eye velocity was both the output and the recurrent input to the target velocity vector. First the network was trained by generalized backpropagation of error to perform accurate tracking in the three tracking conditions outlined above: VOR, smooth pursuit, and head-only tracking. In additional to the familiar feedforward signals, the model included two types of feedback: (1) Visual feedback of image velocity, defined as target velocity minus eye velocity. This provides the negative feedback signals to allow eye velocity to adjust so that the eye tracks the target. (2) A copy of the motor signal, the efference-copy information, goes from the brain stem to the cerebellum. During target acquisition this signal builds up and maintains a positive feedback memory so that as the slip velocity goes to zero, the eye will continue to track at the appropriate velocity. Both positive and negative feedback are necessary for stable tracking. Stable VOR is achieved by adjusting feedforward inputs to the cerebellum to cancel the positive feedback efference copy (figure 6.29).

Given that the network model contained the relevant anatomical constraints and model neurons that mimicked actual recording from each of the locations modeled, the next step was to see how the model adjusted itself to miniaturizing goggles. Accordingly, the visual input was altered to reflect the miniaturizing goggles effect, and the network was allowed to recalibrate itself. That is, changes were permitted at all synapses, and the network was free to decide which synapses out of the population it would change in order to get stable

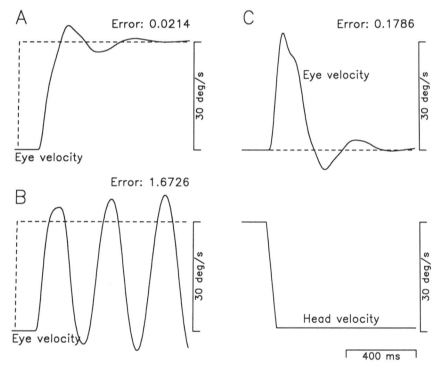

Figure 6.29 Performance of the model during tracking of a target moving with constant speed. (A) Tracking performance of model with a visual delay of 100 msec (solid line) in response to a target that started moving at 30°/sec (dashed line). (B) Tracking performance of a model in which the weights on the efference-copy feedback connections (E in figure 6.27) were set to zero. The instability in the tracking was caused by negative feedback and the 100-msec delay. (C) Performance of the model under conditions for VOR cancellation, when target and head were moved exactly together. Accurate tracking in this case required the model to suppress the VOR that would normally occur with head movement (lower right trace). Because of the difference in the latencies of the vestibular and visual systems, the early part of the response, caused by the faster VOR, was not suppressed for the first 100 msec. These models were trained with recurrent backpropagation to minimize the error with their targets (dashed lines). The value of the final error for the last 700 msec of the trajectory is shown above each trace. (From Lisberger and Sejnowski, 1992.)

VOR in the goggles condition. In the model, the flocculus output during VOR in the standard condition is relatively small, but during recalibration its output was much larger, just as in the real system. This increase reflects the imbalance between the feedforward and feedback signals. Once recalibration is achieved and the VOR is stable at a reduced gain, the flocculus output declines to about the level before the goggles manipulation (figure 6.30). Again, this matches the experimental data. Additionally, in the model the motor neurons had reduced amplitude for a given head velocity signal, as they should, and consequently the eye velocity was decreased appropriately. The model network had no trouble adjusting to the miniaturizing input, and its pursuit system remained accurate after the VOR modification. *Where did the learning occur in the model network?*

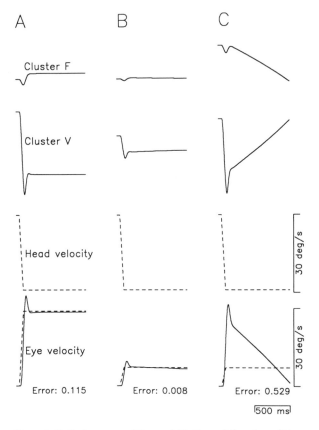

Figure 6.30 Performance of the model in three different conditions, comparing the eye velocity and the outputs from representative units in the flocculus (cluster F) and brain stem (cluster V) when the head is moved at 30°/sec. (A) Normal VOR before miniaturizing goggles and hence before motor learning reduces the amplitude of the VOR. (B) For motor learning, connections at B and H in figure 6.27 were permitted to modify. After exposure to miniaturizing goggle input, the model successfully learned to produce a VOR with a gain of 0.25 without altering performance of smooth pursuit. (C) For motor learning, only connections at H were permitted to modify. After miniaturizing goggle input, the model was unable to achieve a good steady-state solution. Note the contrast in error between conditions (B) and (C). (Courtesy of Lisberger and Sejnowski.)

Analysis of the model revealed exactly the pattern of modifications predicted on the Miles–Lisberger hypothesis, and, as we shall soon explain, the data turned out also to be consistent with Ito's data. First, the primary locus of modification was the nucleus in the brain stem—the VN neurons, whose gain decreased suitably. Second, there were only very tiny modifications to the synapses at the floccular–VN interface. Third, there was a considerable modification at the vestibular–flocculus synapse; at first, the synaptic weights increased (in the Ito direction), but they quickly reversed direction and, after learning, had significantly decreased (in the Miles direction), thus bringing about a match of vestibular input and efference copy (figure 6.31).

What should be concluded from this? After all, the model was just a computer model, and why should its dynamics be relevant to questions about real brains? The basic answer is this: the model is interesting because the network, given that it was trained by backpropagation and hence slid down an error gradient, found the best solution relative to the substantial anatomical and physiological constraints within which it worked. Note, moreover, that the network could have made synaptic changes at any one of nine different synapses. But in fact the synaptic modifications necessary to the behavioral change are limited to exactly *two* locations: vestibular–brain stem (lowered gain), and vestibular–flocculus (lowered gain) (see figure 6.27). It is, therefore,

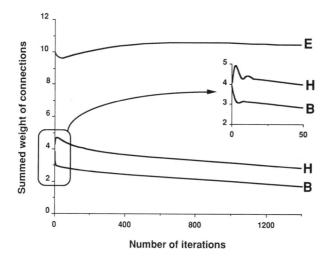

Figure 6.31 Time course of the weight changes during learning to produce a reduced amplitude in the VOR model. Each value was obtained by summing the absolute values of all the weights in a given set of connections after each iteration of the model. Only connections for the projections in figure 6.27 labeled B, H, E, and the output of the flocculus were modifiable. The inset shows the changes in the weights that occurred during the first 50 iterations. The connection strengths between the vestibular inputs and the flocculus, H, increased for the first five iterations but then reversed direction. The final change was in a direction that actually contributed an increase of the VOR amplitude because the output of the flocculus was constrained to be inhibitory, as it is for all outputs from the real cerebellum. The decrease in the weights in the brain-stem pathway, B, accounted for the decrease in the VOR gain. (Courtesy of Lisberger and Sejnowski.)

highly unlikely that the physiological data and the network data happen through mere luck to coincide, especially because the model is highly constrained in its anatomy and physiology. The circuit mimicked in the model is well studied, and all the major players are represented, if not in the same numbers, then at least with comparable properties.

In other words, given the richness of the biological constraints, the model has probably found not just *an* answer, but the uniquely *correct* answer. At the very least, the model data suggest that following up the Miles–Lisberger hypothesis by experimental research is not a waste of time. Because the relevant experiments are very time intensive, this is useful knowledge. Additionally, the model suggests that the inconsistency between the Ito data and the Miles data is only apparent—that Miles and Ito were looking at different time-slices in the modification in the vestibulofloccular connections.

An additional question that can be asked of the model is this: how well could it succeed in modifying its VOR if one or the other of the two sites of plasticity found so far were not allowed to change? Could the model succeed if, for example, the vestibular–brain stem neurons were not allowed to change, and only the vestibular–floccular neurons are plastic? And vice versa. The answer is that under no conditions can the model satisfy all the dynamical constraints if learning in the flocculus is prevented. There was, however, one condition in which good performance was achieved without learning in the brain stem but only in the flocculus. In this condition the flocculus received its usual complement of tonic inputs from the vestibular apparatus, but in addition, it was given phasic input; in other words, one of the inputs was sustained excitation, the other a brief pulse (the derivative with respect to the sustained signal). In this condition, the gain of the VOR was modified by opposite effects: the weights of the phasic inputs were increased, and the weights of the tonic inputs decreased. Notice, therefore, that there are two ways in which the ostensible conflicting Ito and Miles results might be reconciled: the experiments might have tapped into different phases of learning in the same population of neurons, as suggested above, or they might have consulted different subpopulations. The fact is, there are both phasic and tonic inputs from the vestibular apparatus to the flocculus, and how these various inputs are arrayed on Purkinje cells is just not known. They might, for example, segregate to distinct cells, or they might converge on the same cells, but even then they might segregate themselves according to favored locations on the Purkinje cell.[13]

In reaching a neurobiologically significant conclusion concerning sites of plasticity, constraints on the dynamical properties of the network were essential. In other words, without the dynamics, the changes could have been made in many combinations of locations, each equally successfully in stabilizing the steady-state VOR considered in isolation from other behaviors. Given the dynamical constraints, the good choices for modification locations are narrowed down to a small number of possibilities, thus making it likely that the network's choice is essentially the same as that of the nervous system.

The more general point, however, is this. As we saw in chapter 5, the crux of the mystery in nervous system learning is how you get an appropriate global effect out of local changes scattered hither and yon. Now backpropagation ensures that the trained-up network has the right global profile and yet has that profile by virtue of weight modification decisions, all of which could be made locally. Backpropagation is geared not to a fragment of a network, but to the global network; it can encompass training not only of the VOR but also of smooth pursuit, and it has within its scope not merely the synapses a single location, but all synapses in the system. It is as though eons of evolutionary trial and error are telescoped into a manageable time-bite. With a trained-up net in the trap, Lisberger and Sejnowski can predict what the local rules at the modification sites are—first in the model net, and then, guided by these results, in the real nets. The relevant physiological experiments are now underway in Lisberger's laboratory. Thus the ever-elusive global properties of the brain can be made discernible in the co-evolution of modeling and experimenting.

Notice too that if one did know the local rules, but *only* the local rules, then chances are that the global picture will remain obscure and the mystery of what is going on and how the network functions will be lifted only by a hem-width. It is precisely the global analysis that permits the interpretation of the local changes so that an explanation of how the system works is available (figure 6.32). The methodological lesson from the model is this: if, in trying to explain a phenomenon such as plasticity in the VOR, one looks at a single

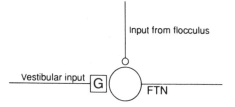

Vestibular input	Floccular input	Effect on G
Above resting	Above resting	Decrease
Above resting	Below resting	Increase
Below resting	Above resting	Increase
Below resting	Below resting	Decrease

Figure 6.32 A local learning rule that would produce the same changes in the brain stem as those predicted by the backpropagation model. A single neuron in the vestibular nucleus is illustrated. The variable weight G between the vestibular input and the floccular target neuron (FTN) should be modified contingently, as indicated in the table at the bottom. For example, if the vestibular inputs are above their resting levels at the same time that the floccular inputs from the Purkinje cell are also above its resting level, then the strength of G should decrease. This could be accomplished by an anti-Hebbian mechanism at G. (From Lisberger 1988a.)

location and finds a change, one may be inclined to interpret that as *the* change that correlates with the learning seen in behavior. But the interpretation may well be misleadingly narrow. The VOR, for example, is not a separate, isolated system, but rather is integrated with other oculomotor behaviors. Consequently, a change to one behavior unavoidably alters others, and the recalibration process involves making adjustment to adjustments, and hence involves modification in a number of locations. In discovering explanations for behaviors, correlations between neuronal responses and behavior is not enough. Additionally, one has to see how one piece fits into the wider system, and how making a change in one place affects global behaviors. The Lisberger–Sejnowski model is helpful in this regard, but it still leaves out important things. It is known, for example, that the oculomotor system can perform predictive tracking, in the sense that not only can it *follow* a target, but it can also *anticipate* where the target is heading.[14] This predictive function requires additional circuitry including more cortical contributions.

From the perspective of understanding the oculomotor system, backpropagation is a tool to create a kind of wind tunnel of the nervous system, wherein experiments relevant to the natural state can be made, and variables otherwise beyond control may be brought under control. To be sure, some wind tunnels are better than others, and some may unwittingly "cheat" at just the places where answers need to be extracted not manufactured. So each model network must be carefully thought out relative to the psychophysics and neurobiology available, and also relative to what one wants to find out. The rule of thumb, which is frankly discretionary, is this: invest as much realism in the model as is necessary to discover answers to the questions posed. For example, in the VOR net, only two units were used to handle the visual input. Given the purpose of studying the oculomotor part of the system, this was a convenient simplification when there was only one target. The next modeling step is to make the visual input more realistic by adding a front-end net to simulate the motion-sensitive cells in visual area MT. This will mean that instead of a single moving stimulus, several moving stimuli can be presented. Then the visual net and the VOR net jointly make a decision about which stimulus to track, a highly nonlinear step.

When the LeechNets and the various VOR model nets are compared, several dimensions of similarity stand out. To begin with, there is an important similarity between the representations used by the hidden units: (1) in both cases the representations are distributed, (2) they are not dedicated to a single kind of signal but carry more than one kind, and (3) sets of neurons act in concert to produce vector inputs or vector outputs. These observed effects are robust, so it is reasonable to predict that they will be seen in other places, such as higher processing centers, the visual system, and so forth. To amplify, quite often representations are best understood in terms of vectors rather than individual dedicated cells. A methodological consequence is that analyzing the system cell by cell to determine coding and computation may provide clues, but it will fall short of the full story.

To perform actions such as skinning a rabbit or climbing a tree, two hands are especially critical, though head position, eye movement, leg position, and the posture of the whole body is by no means incidental. Successfully to perform the action, the hands must move in coordinated fashion through space and in a suitable sequence through time (figure 6.33). It is important, therefore, to appreciate that behavior involves not simply vectors pushed through matrices, but *sequences of vectors* in the right order and at the right moments (Eckmiller 1989). Moreover, matrices are not immutable, but reconfigure through time, some mechanisms at one rate, others at their own very different rates. Notice too that the virtues of distributed representations discussed in chapter 3 apply equally to sensory and to motor representations within this dynamical framework. Assuming those earlier arguments had merit, we can expect therefore that motor representations are likely to be vector coded rather than local coded (Altman and Kien 1989).

As a reprise of the question asked in chapters 4 and 5, we ask again, how is time represented in the system? Indeed, is it represented, strictly speaking, or is it not so much represented as just part and parcel of the physical properties of the network? Let us stalk these questions starting from the known ground of simple network models. In many respects ultrasimple simulations such as NETtalk are unrealistic neurobiologically. Unlike neurons, the model units are homogeneous, morphologically and physiologically; unlike neural connectivity, every unit connects to every other unit on the next level. The most telling difference, interlaced with these, is the matter of time. In real neural systems, almost everything is time critical. One consideration is that processing must be fast if the animal is to survive, and another is that certain processes must be coordinated in time. Although a nervous system is spatially extended and many synapses may intervene between transducer and motor neuron, nevertheless, neural events must be timed to occur so that the percep-

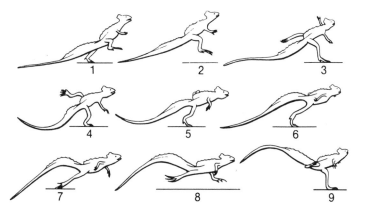

Figure 6.33 Running of the basilisk lizard. Note the changes in position of the whole body from frame to frame. (From Gray 1968.)

Sensorimotor Integration

tual world and one's interaction with it is smooth, integrated, and coherent. Time management is not just grafted on to a complex nervous system, like a sidekick. Temporally tuned dynamics will have to be a fundamental property, exploiting the basic thing a nervous system has to exploit in solving the problem, namely *temporal schedules of cellular events* (Feldman et al. 1990).

How do nervous systems solve the time-management problem? Although the detailed answer is not yet known, it is evident that the intrinsic morphological and physiological properties of neurons are the very stuff of time management (Llinás 1988, Getting 1989). Neurons are temporally tuned to deliver signals in certain time courses, and the connectivity ensures that there is a packaging of events in time slots so that, crudely speaking, the represented world—the world of perception and action—is coherent and unified. A weak analogy, but a helpful one nonetheless, can be drawn with putting a clock into a program of a conventional computer. Suppose the task is computer animation, and we want to generate a computer graphics display of the Little Mermaid swimming. We want the swimming to resemble, in its time course, the rhythmic back and forth movements a little fish's tail might actually make—slow enough so that it can be seen, but fast enough so that it can be seen as cartoon swimming.

Events in the computer happen on the order of nanoseconds, and even millisecond tail swishes will be too fast. How do you get the computer to slow down the display? Well you can't slow down electrical events, but you can package them into smaller and larger bundles. The answer, therefore, is that you give the relevant components in the program some intrinsic temporal properties, so that instead of yielding the next step as soon as possible, it cycles for a specified number of times before going to the next step. The programmer writes in how many time the component must tap its finger, so to speak, before taking the next step. For a very slow movement, he puts in a request for many finger taps; for a faster movement, he puts in fewer.

Obviously matters are very different in real nervous systems. Nevertheless, the analogy does makes contact with the overarching strategy that temporally tunes the dynamics of the system by orchestrating intrinsic properties of the components. Something along these lines appears to have evolved in nervous systems. An intrinsic bursting pattern, for example, could be a way for the nervous system to tap its finger; lengthening the AHP is a way to extend the intertap interval, in-phase oscillations of action potentials are a way to wrap together several messages so that they arrive together at their destination. To get the timing right, cells have to coordinate their various schedules with those of others; whether EPSPs are slow or fast will make a difference to how a signal is processed, and hence to what a signal means, and hence to the brain's representation of the world.

When neuroscientists lament that modelers are doomed to miss what is computationally and representationally special about nervous systems if they ignore the intrinsic properties of cells, it is this they are talking about. Consequently, incorporating dynamics, and doing it so as to reflect the worn-in, survival-hardened strategies of nervous systems, are devoutly to be desired.

Lest the utility of simplified model-structures be undervalued, we hasten to add that here, as elsewhere in science, they are a start. And it is much more sensible to start with simplicity and augment to complexity, than to stir in every detail in hopes that the basic principles will display themselves by floating to the top.

How then can we draw on the principles of the vector–matrix theory of coding and processing in a context where the dynamics are dyed in the wool, not superimposed on the woven fabric? Where should the wedge be placed so that we can get into the problem efficiently? Rhythmic behavior and the circuits that generate rhythms may be one such wedge. Exploration of these circuits may provide fundamental ideas for addressing the problem of timing in its more general aspect, and a selection of these circuits together with companion computational models are the focus of the next section.

Generating Repeatable Patterns: All God's Critters Got Rhythm

Many actions displayed by organisms are rhythmic: walking, swimming, chewing, flying, breathing, pumping blood, sleeping, migrating, hibernating, and so on. The time constants vary from a millisecond in bursting neurons to 17 years for the reproductive cycle of the cicadas. Getting the rhythm of behavior right depends on getting the timing of cellular events right, and unless the rhythm is right the organism's capacities are compromised. It may stumble and hence fail to escape or it may stay over winter and die. Moreover, some rhythmic behaviors are modifiable, not locked in. A walking gait suited to a smooth surface can be modified for uneven surfaces, hills, ice, mud, and water—waist deep, ankle deep, and in between. Three-legged dogs manage surprisingly well, as do one-legged humans supported by a crutch or one-legged birds that manage by hopping. Heartbeat and breathing vary as a function of physiological demand, Canada geese can give up the northern spring migration and stay in the south, one can swim using a host of different strokes. The stimulus-guided modifiability indicates that the domain is still characterized by computation and information processing, not merely wind-up-doll connectivity.

Why is so much behavior rhythmic? What does rhythmicity buy an organism and its brain? The answer here may be blatantly obvious, but as a counterbalance to a popular tendency to wax maudlin on the Rhythms of the Universe and our alleged Oneness with them, perhaps the answer is worth stating nonetheless. The basic point is that organisms do not have infinite resources, so they have to rely on getting partway, then doing the same thing again to get further. One cannot, for example, indefinitely suck in a long string of spaghetti. Eventually your breath runs out and you have to start again. If the sucking was successful for the first length, sucking in the same way again is likely appropriate. So for pumping blood, walking, swimming, digesting, and so on. Doing the same thing again to get along a bit further is undoubtedly a principle Evolution could not fail to seize upon very early in the game. Moreover, from an experimental point of view, repeating patterns are handy because the pattern of motor output remains relatively constant from cycle to cycle, and so experimental replication is ready to hand.

Oscillating Circuits in the Spinal Cord

The spinal cord is a long stretch of neural tissue with repeating segments that emerges from the brain stem and is protected by the vertebral column (figure 6.34). Leaving aside much detail, the basic structure of each segment consists of (1) the dorsal roots, (nerves carrying peripheral sensory information into the dorsal horn of the cord), (2) the ventral roots (nerves carrying motor information from the cord's ventral horn to the skeletal muscle cells), (3) local circuits relevant to sensorimotor integration of the segment, and (4) long circuits connecting other segments, and (5) projections to and from the brain and the brain stem (figure 6.35). In the cat, if the spinal cord is disconnected from the brain or even the brain stem, then so long as the cat's weight is supported by a sling, the cat can make typical walking movements. The capacity for birds (chickens and least) to flap their wings and locomote for a brief period after separation of brain and body has been known for centuries.

Mott and Sherrington (1895) had suggested that rhythmic activity such as locomotion or swimming or flapping might be understood as repeated instances of a reflex such as the flexion reflex, whereby a foot stepping on a sharp stimulus is abruptly raised and the other foot lowered to maintain balance. The idea was that alternating afferents trigger alternating stepping. While this seemed a promising avenue, T. Graham Brown (1911) discovered that if he lesioned both the cord and the dorsal roots, alternating muscle contractions could continue once initiated. (Rhythmic locomotion behavior can also be seen in deep anesthesia.) Because the mechanism, whatever it is, can continue to function without afferent input from the proprioceptors, it came to be known as a *central pattern generator* (CPG). Notwithstanding these results, it remained an open question whether the alternating contractions in the spinalized, deafferented animal were relevantly similar to the complex activity seen in locomotion in the intact animal. The CPG concept came to be defined in terms of the spinalized deafferented, preparation in which a neural circuit is capable of a repeated, stereotyped output in the absence of a repeated input. Thus a prevailing question was whether CPGs so defined function in the intact animal, or whether something more integrative and complex underlies normal rhythmic behavior (figure 6.36).

From his studies of reflex behavior, Brown (1911) speculated that the stepping or scratching rhythm depended on alternating excitation and inhibition of motor neurons in the right and left sides of the cord. He conjectured that there was a basic circuit in individual cord segments by which opposite sides were alternately turned off and on, and that this circuitry formed the substructure on which more complicated operations might be superimposed. For example, segmental circuitry would be augmented by intersegmental connections to coordinate front and back legs. He reasoned that the left and right halves of the cord would have matching circuits, and that paired inhibitory neurons would

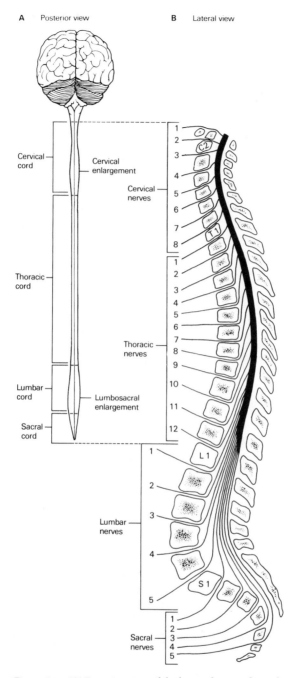

Figure 6.34 (A) Posterior view of the human brain and spinal cord. (B) Lateral view of the spinal cord, showing the spinal roots as they emerge between distinct vertebrae. The adult spinal cord does not run the whole length of the vertebral column but terminates at about the level of the L1 vertebra. The dorsal and ventral roots must therefore take a long course before exiting from the vertebral column. (From Kelly 1985b.)

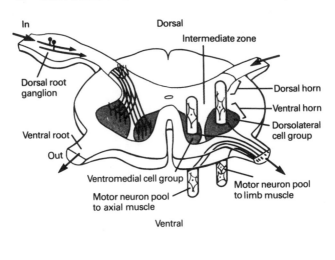

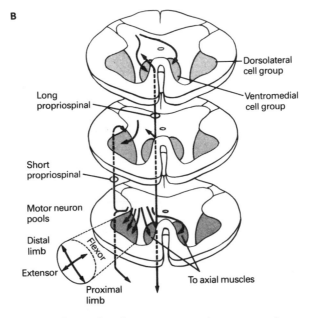

Figure 6.35 The spinal cord contains intra- and intersegmental connections. (A) Input—output organization of spinal segments and interconnections between segments. (B) Direction of impulse traffic in interneurons and propriospinal neurons. (From Ghez 1985.)

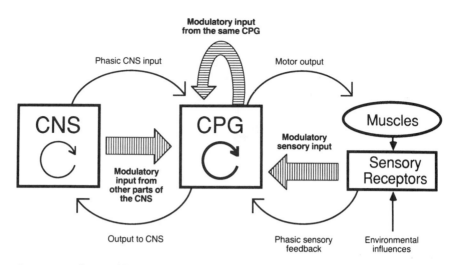

**Modulatory input
from the same CPG**

Phasic CNS input

Motor output

CNS

Muscles

CPG

**Modulatory
sensory input**

**Modulatory
input from
other parts of
the CNS**

Sensory
Receptors

Output to CNS

Phasic sensory
feedback

Environmental
influences

Figure 6.36 The possible sources of modulatory input to a central pattern generator (CPG) include all levels of motor control. Other parts of the CNS provide both conventional phasic inputs and slow modulatory inputs (left). These inputs include descending activating elements, hormonal influences, and inputs from other CPGs. The CPG can contain neurons that evoke modulatory effects on other CPG components (middle). Sensory inputs provide not only conventional feedback acting on a cycle-by-cycle basis, but also slow modulatory effects that alter CPG function over many cycles (right). (From Katz and Harris-Warrick [1990]. Actions of identified neuromodulatory neurons in a simple motor system. *Trends in Neurosciences* 13: 367–373.)

cross the cord to turn off the complementary circuit as the excited side became fatigued. Each side was believed to contain a center with a set of motor neurons to govern extensor muscles, and another set to govern flexors. The basic idea was that the flexor of one side and the extensors of the other would be phase locked, while the flexors of both sides, or the extensors of both sides, would be phase opposed. Brown called this the "half-center organization." In subsequent physiological research, Lundberg and co-workers (Jankowska et al. 1967a,b) outlined a feasible circuit diagram for Brown's half-center circuit, describing motor neurons, proprioceptive afferents, and interneurons and their connections (figure 6.37).

In studying deafferented cats whose spinal cord was disconnected from the brain, Shik et al. (1966) discovered that electrical stimulation of the midbrain could produce stepping in the cat. Grillner (1981) discovered that rhythmic output from motoneurons could be obtained pharmacologically by perfusing L-dopa (a dopamine precursor) into the cord, and hence locomotion could be induced without afferent input.[15] These two results thus confirmed Brown's conjecture concerning the sensory independence of sustained locomotion. That is, whereas some reflex behaviors such as the VOR are essentially input driven, rhythmic behaviors such as locomotion may be *input initiated* but are maintainable without continuous afferent control. As research on this question advanced, however, it became increasingly evident that afferent input is not at all inconsequential to the rhythmic behavior in locomotion (Bässler 1986, Pearson 1987).

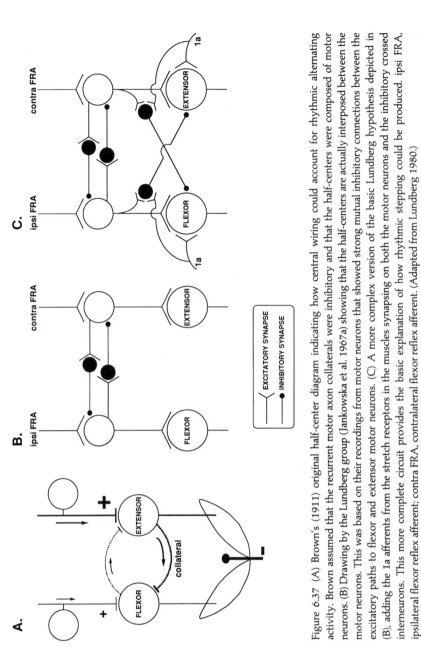

Figure 6.37 (A) Brown's (1911) original half-center diagram indicating how central wiring could account for rhythmic alternating activity. Brown assumed that the recurrent motor axon collaterals were inhibitory and that the half-centers were composed of motor neurons. (B) Drawing by the Lundberg group (Jankowska et al. 1967a) showing that the half-centers are actually interposed between the motor neurons. This was based on their recordings from motor neurons that showed strong mutual inhibitory connections between the excitatory paths to flexor and extensor motor neurons. (C) A more complex version of the basic Lundberg hypothesis depicted in (B), adding the 1a afferents from the stretch receptors in the muscles synapsing on both the motor neurons and the inhibitory crossed interneurons. This more complete circuit provides the basic explanation of how rhythmic stepping could be produced. ipsi FRA, ipsilateral flexor reflex afferent; contra FRA, contralateral flexor reflex afferent. (Adapted from Lundberg 1980.)

When analyzed more closely, motor neuron activity in the spinalized animal turned out to be somewhat similar but clearly *not* identical to that seen in the intact animal during locomotion, inasmuch as many of the timing subtleties and intensity variations are absent. Additionally, as is well known, the rhythmic stepping pattern can be modified by input from the periphery to produce changes in locomoting modes: cantering, galloping, swimming, scratching. More generally, it has slowly emerged that peripheral inputs are critically important to genuine locomotion of the intact animal even if not to motor neurons bursting during fictive locomotion in the deafferented animal (Bässler and Wenger 1983, Pearson and Wolf 1986). In light of an array of results along these lines, the concept of the CPG, as a largely encapsulated motor *module* (see chapter 5) that can link up in assorted ways with other CPG modules to produce different behaviors, has looked less applicable than it had earlier (Lundberg 1980, Pearson 1987). For this reason, the expression "central *rhythm generator*" (CRG), implying merely the *necessity* and not the *sufficiency* of a spinal cord circuit, was preferred by some researchers as more appropriate to the reality of rhythmic behavior in the intact animal (Arbib 1990) (figure 6.38).

The Brown–Lundberg half-center circuit appears to be correct, at least to a first approximation, and at least for the studied cases, including the tadpole, the lamprey (a simple aquatic vertebrate), and probably also the cat. To be sure, it is an idealization, in the sense that in normal conditions, segmental circuitry will get input from the brain stem and from the sensory neurons in the muscles, tendons, and skin. The role of these afferents is not specified in the hypothesis. It should also be noted that though the spinal cord may be somewhat more

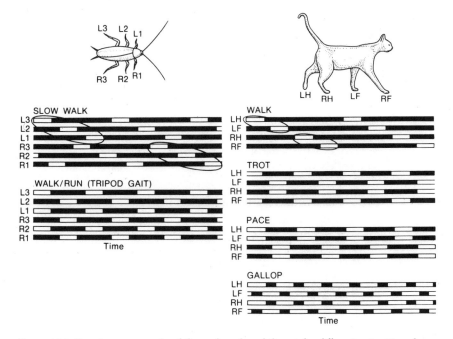

Figure 6.38 Stepping movements of the cockroach and the cat for different gaits. Open bars, foot lifted; closed bars, foot planted. (From Shepherd 1988; adapted from Pearson 1976.)

accessible than the brain, it too is exceedingly complex—more like a kind of brain in its own right than a mere conduit for signals to and from higher centers. To put it more bluntly, the cord too is in the representing and computing business. Because of the cord's complexity, identifying the interneurons postulated by the half-center hypothesis has been tricky and troublesome, especially in mammals, where the task is still not complete.

The pharmacology of mammalian cord has also turned out to be complex and interesting; for example, not only will perfused L-dopa initiate walking in the spinalized cat, so also will acetylcholine agonists. Perfused NMDA will initiate rhythmic swimming in the lamprey and the neonatal rat (Cazalet et al. 1990), but so far, not in the mature cat. Serotonin in the lamprey cord alters the bursting pattern of the motor neurons; in cats, it induces first a depolarization, followed by a long-lasting hyperpolarization (Zhang 1991). Even as the complicated and puzzling details come in, however, the Brown–Lundberg canonical half-center oscillator survives as the idealized and approximate circuit of coupled oscillators around which most research on spinal cord rhythmicity is organized.

Given our earlier emphasis on the role of intrinsic cellular properties in time management, a fundamental question is how much of the basic rhythmicity can be accounted for simply in terms of connectivity between model units endowed with relatively crude response repertoires, and what is added to the basic rhythm by the more complicated biophysical properties such as NMDA channel-open times. As a matter of strategy, it will be useful first to model the connectivity to see how far that takes us, and then to add biophysical details in subsequent models. In what follows, we shall discuss first a recent network in the canonical form: it has excitatory and inhibitory connections, and units whose activation level is put through a squashing function, but it omits biophysical data concerning the basis for the physiological properties. The second model incorporates more details, with about 30 parameters per neuron.

5 THE SEGMENTAL SWIMMING OSCILLATOR

The lamprey swims forward or backward as a wave of muscular activity travels down its length (figure 6.39). It has been a convenient animal to study because its spinal cord can be dissected out and kept alive in a nutrient bath, thus permitting more convenient investigation of spinal cord behavior and its mechanisms. Neurons in the cord can be excited by putting glutamate[16] in the bath, crudely mimicking by pharmacological intervention the physiological excitation from the brain stem, other spinal neurons, and the sensory stretch receptors.

James Buchanan and colleagues (Grillner et al. 1988, Buchanan 1990) constructed a network model of the half-center circuit, where the synapses were excitatory or inhibitory according to observations from intracellular recordings (figure 6.40). The model consists of three classes of units representing three classes of neurons that show oscillations in phase with locomotion. Each model unit stands for a pool of neurons, and the whole net consists of just six

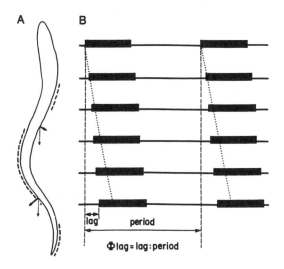

Figure 6.39 Characteristics of actual swimming behavior in lamprey. (A) Body outline at one particular instance during swimming. Dashed lines denote regions of active muscle contraction; arrows indicate forces being exerted against the water, with the caudally directed vector (dotted) propelling the animal forward. (B) Schematic diagram indicating bursts of EMG activity in six segments in the rostral part of the body. There is a caudally directed electromyographical wave of contraction, resulting in a phase lag between consecutive segments. (From Grillner et al. 1991. Reproduced, with permission, from the *Annual Review of Neuroscience*, Vol. 10, © 1991 by Annual Review, Inc.)

units. Activation levels of units represent the average firing rate of neurons in the pool. The connectivity is patterned on the basic connectivity seen between the three classes of neurons in the half-center circuit in the spinal cord of the lamprey (figure 6.37). At the beginning of the simulation, the model is quiescent; with gradual input of tonic excitation, the network spontaneously begins to generate a rhythmic output (figure 6.41).

Though this network has a bare minimum of parameters, it very easily falls into oscillating mode. This is not *per se* a remarkable result since it is actually rather easy to get oscillations from neural circuits. A more stringent requirement is that the phase relationships of the units in the model accord with the data from the three classes of neurons simulated (figure 6.42). The net passes this test adequately, and the next test is whether the network can mimic the adjustments in rhythmic pattern seen in the lamprey spinal cord. To discover this, model conditions are varied to simulate changing conditions for the spinal cord.

First, the amount of tonic excitation can be varied. In the cord-in-the-bath preparation, this is done by adding glutamate to the bathing solution, which will depolarize neurons having glutamate receptors. In the model, this is achieved by increasing the values of the excitatory drive to the network. The model behaves much as the isolated cord does, in that excitatory drive provokes increases of frequency and amplitude of the oscillations. Unilateral excitation of a crossed commissural (CC) neuron, to simulate ipsilateral brain-stem stimulation, resulted in the appropriate model effect, namely a slowing of cycle

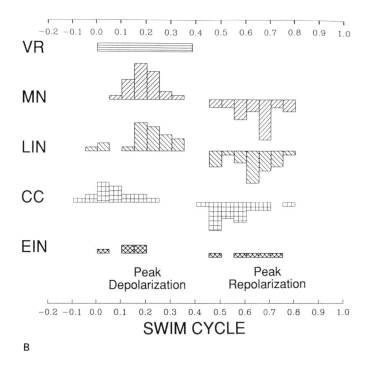

Figure 6.40 (A) Principal circuit of the spinal cord oscillator, similar to the Lundberg model. LIN, inhibitory lateral interneuron; EIN, excitatory interneuron; CC, inhibitory commissural interneurons; MN, motor neuron. (B) Time histograms based on intracellular recordings show the pattern of alternation between the sides of the spinal cord and the specific onset and peaks times for various cell types. Notice that the CC interneurons tend to peak earlier than the other cell types. VR, ventral root. (Courtesy of James Buchanan.)

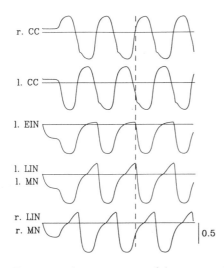

Figure 6.41 Activity patterns of the various cells types in the Buchanan model. After a short delay, oscillations begin in the cells and then continue unchanged for at least thousands of cycles. As in the lamprey, there is an alternation between cell activity on opposite sides of this network (left and right). Additionally, as in the lamprey, the CC interneurons are about 20% phase advanced with respect to the other cell types. LINs and MNs have the same inputs in the model and are thus shown together. Recurrent EINs are omitted for clarity. Abbreviations as in figure 6.40. (Courtesy of James Buchanan.)

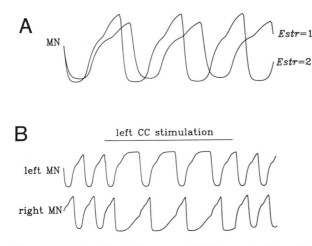

Figure 6.42 Tests of the Buchanan model. (A) Increasing the excitatory input to all cells of the Buchanan model by increasing a scaling factor, *Estr*, from 1 to 2, resulted in increased frequency and amplitude of the oscillations. This is similar to the effects of increasing the concentration of an excitatory amino acid bathing the isolated lamprey spinal cord. (B) Increasing the excitatory drive to a single cell, the left CC interneuron, mimics the effect of stimulating a single reticulo-spinal cell in the lamprey that is known to excite CC interneurons. The cycle frequency decreases, the ipsilateral burst activity increases, and the contralateral burst activity decreases. (Courtesy of James Buchanan.)

rate with increased burst activity in units on the same side, and a co-equal period of heightened inhibition of the contralateral units.

One of the most important architectural properties of the lamprey spinal cord is this: the bursting output of one segment bears a *constant phase lag* to the bursting output of the segment in front (figure 6.41). The phase lag between segmental activity is equal to about 1% of cycle time, and this is maintained regardless of swimming frequency. This is a critical feature because without constant phase lag there can be no coherent muscle movement such as to produce the coordinated wave of muscle contractions that yields swimming. Instead, there would be just a mess. For a crude analogy to bring this home, consider a chorus line in which each can-can dancer is kicking her legs so that a wave appears to pass down the line. When the music speeds up, each dancer must adjust her kicking frequency if the wave is to remain coherent. If, regardless of the beat, the dancer in the middle begins to raise her leg with an absolute time lag relative to her neighbor (always 2 sec), the wave will disintegrate. If, however, she begins to raise her leg whenever her neighbor is, say, $\frac{1}{8}$ through *her* kicking cycle, then the wave is coherent at every speed. Constant phase lag between segments ensures coordination of the muscle wave traveling the length of the cord. Notice too that the phase lag ought not to be zero. If it is, then instead of a traveling wave down the cord, the whole cord will act at once, producing a big C and then its mirror image. This might be an acceptable way for a tiny worm to swim, but whole-body thrashing entails moving a lot of water and it is far more efficient for the lamprey to avail itself of a travelling wave. But then it needs to ensure constant phase lag between the bursts of the segments.

Does constant phase lag come about simply as a result of the time delay, owing, for example, to conduction velocity and synaptic delay? The answer is no, for what remains constant is the *percentage* of cycle time, not the absolute duration of the delay. In other words, the intersegmental delay scales with cycle time and must therefore be a consequence of network interaction. This too is seen in Buchanan's model. The exact nature of the mechanism for maintaining constant phase lag in the lamprey spinal cord is not known, but some idea about this might be generated by discovering how constant phase lag is maintained in the model.

To explore the possibilities, Buchanan tried connecting pairs of cells in one segment to pairs of cells in another segment. While many of the possible combinations could produce stable coupling over a wide range of synaptic weights—for example, the excitatory interneurons (EIN) of one segment to the lateral interneurons of (LIN) of another segment—other combinations were usually not stable (figure 6.43). The coupling using single pairs of cells was deficient in several respects: (1) there was no phase constancy over a range of cycle frequencies; (2) the coupling could not tolerate differences in frequency of the two oscillators; and (3) several cycles were required before steady-state coupling was achieved. Clearly, the lamprey must be able to establish proper phase relations within a single cycle, and it should be able to cope with inherent frequency differences among segmental oscillators.

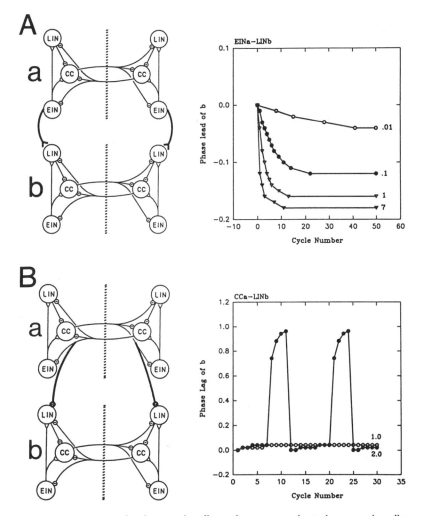

Figure 6.43 Two examples showing the effects of connecting identical segmental oscillators in the lamprey model by a single connection. (A) The EINs of the upper segment's network, *a*, are connected to the LINs of the lower segment's network, *b*. This coupling produces a stable phase lead of network *b*. The rate at which the steady state is achieved and the size of the steady-state phase difference are dependent on the strength of the coupling connection as shown in graph to the right. (B) This intersegment connection yields stable coupling over only a narrow range of synaptic weights. The CCs of *a* are connected to the LIN of *b*. At low weights a slight phase lag of *b* is maintained, but at higher weights there is a constant drift of the two networks (graph at right). (Courtesy of James Buchanan.)

Buchanan then tried coupling two or more sets of cells between two segments. An example of one such scheme (figure 6.44) demonstrates that multiple interconnections improve the coupling on all three counts. The prediction, therefore, is that intersegmental coupling will involve at least two pairs of cells and that these cells may be part of the oscillator itself. The model thus serves to narrow down the probable configurations and suggest experiments.

The model allowed Buchanan to try out many coupling configurations and to find a few that were successful. Those that worked are testable against the real system because they make a range of specific predictions; for example, both the cycle rate and amplitude of membrane potential oscillations should increase with increases in the amount of excitatory amino acids; if LIN cells are

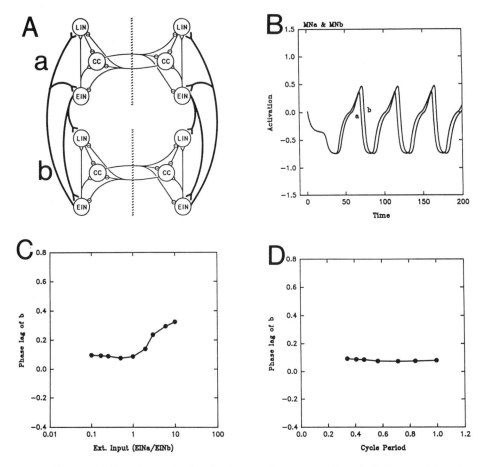

Figure 6.44 Example of multiple cell pair connections between two identical segmental oscillators in the lamprey model. (A) In this scheme, there is symmetrical coupling of EINs between the two networks. In addition, EINs are connected to LINs, with the synaptic weight of oscillator b to a favored by 10:1. (B) Graph shows that the scheme has the advantage of producing steady-state phase coupling within a single cycle. (C) A model with these intersegmental connections is also able to maintain stable coupling in spite of large differences in the excitatory drive to the two oscillators. (D) A constant phase lag is maintained over a range of oscillator cycle periods. (Courtesy of James Buchanan.)

repeatedly stimulated, the network should speed up, but if CCs are repeatedly stimulated, it should slow down. In addition to these specific predictions, some general observations with experimental implications can be made: (1) intersegmental coupling of a particular cell class may be similar in synaptic strength, and hence oscillators along the cord need not display a gradient of coupling strengths to achieve proper phase relationships; (2) head-to-tail propagation of swimming activity can be accomplished with either descending or ascending connections; (3) switching from forward to backward swimming can be accomplished by changing either the excitability or the coupling strengths of specific cell classes, but such changes in other cell classes will not be efficacious.

It is known that local oscillators are distributed along the cord because rhythmic bursting can be generated by as few as two segments, and they may be any two adjacent segments. The oscillators are nonlinear, "limit cycle" oscillators, in the sense that they have a baseline pattern to which they return after perturbations, such as afferent input. The intersegmental connections are, as figure 6.35 reveals, a means whereby the oscillator in one segment can be coupled to oscillators in other segments. Coupled oscillators can have very interesting and very complex properties, because the oscillation of a component O_1 after coupling to another oscillator O_2 is a function of O_1's intrinsic oscillation *and* the effect of O_2's rhythm on it, which in turn will be affected by O_1. A mathematical understanding of how an emergent oscillation of the coupled oscillator is related to the intrinsic oscillation of the components and the coupling effects might therefore be helpful in understanding how the spinal cord allows the lamprey to swim by virtue of a travelling wave, and how it may swim at varying speeds.

The mathematical analysis (Kopell and Ermentrout 1989, Williams et al. 1990) takes the lamprey spinal cord to be a chain of oscillators, and it abstracts away from the particulars of the mechanics of its oscillator properties and from baseline frequency of particular oscillators (figure 6.45). That something is a nonlinear oscillator and that it has some intrinsic frequency are the only relevant properties. Therefore the analysis applies whether the oscillator is a single bursting cell, a circuit, or something else altogether. In the case at hand, the central question is how coupling enables segments to change each other's bursting frequency, for we know that sensory inputs, for example, may speed up the swimming rhythm in the lamprey.

The ground-floor mathematical assumption of the Kopell and Ermentrout analysis is that the effects of neighboring oscillators on each other is additive.

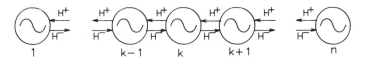

Figure 6.45 Lamprey spinal cord activity modeled as a chain of oscillators. Each segment of the spinal cord is a nonlinear oscillator symbolized by a circle occupied by a sine wave. The chain of oscillators is coupled by ascending (H^+) and descending (H^-) frequency increases (H_A and H_D in text, respectively). (From Williams et al. 1990.)

As an opening bid this is acceptable, for so long as the couplings are relatively weak rather than dominating, the speeding up or slowing down exhibited by the coupled oscillators is small relative to the intrinsic contribution. By adopting this assumption, we get a first-order approximation whose validity can then be checked by measurements of some actual coupled oscillators, such as those seen in the spinal cord of the lamprey. The intrinsic frequency is assumed on plausible biological grounds to be the same for all oscillators in a given cord. A change in frequency to an oscillator may be caused by downward effects, H_D, from the neighbor above, and by upward effects, H_A, from its lower neighbor. The change in frequency of a given oscillator as a result of neighboring interactions will depend on the phase differences between the neighboring segments, where ϕ_k is the phase lag, defined as the phase of the sending oscillator $k + 1$ minus the phase of the receiving oscillator k. (See Williams and Sigvardt, in press.) Where ω is the *intrinsic* frequency of an oscillator, and Ω is the *resultant* frequency of a given oscillator in the chain, the set of equations for a chain of n coupled oscillators, all cycling at the same frequency, is:

$$\Omega = \omega + H_A(\phi_1)$$

$$\Omega = \omega + H_A(\phi_k) + H_D(-\phi_{k-1}) \quad 1 < k < n$$

$$\Omega = \omega + H_D(-\phi_{n-1})$$

The mathematical analysis can now be brought to bear on whether a system described by these equations has a solution, whether the solution is stable to small perturbations (small random variations of the parameters on the model), and whether results of experimental manipulations of the biological system can be predicted from the analysis.

The mathematical analysis provides three general conditions under which the set of equations has a stable solution with nonzero uniform phase lags between segments. (1): There is a range of intersegmental phase lags over which H_A has only a positive slope, and H_D has only a negative slope. Phase lags within this range are such that changes from descending couplings will come at the point so as to catch the cycle on the upswing (front side), and those from ascending coupling will catch the cycle on the back side. This prevents instability through random variations in phase lag or intrinsic frequency. (2) Both functions pass through zero, which means that the couplings can both increase or decrease the frequency. (3) The ascending and descending coupling functions are assumed to be asymmetric for right and left sides of the animal so that one or the other coupling function dominates. Figure 6.46 shows that for each slope there is a place where the change in phase lag equals zero, regardless of the change in frequency of the oscillator. This is at the zero-crossing. The right–left asymmetry means that the value of H_D at H_A's zero-crossing is not equal to the value of H_A at H_D's zero-crossing. Were it not for this asymmetry, the phase lags could be different on either side of a "phase boundary," meaning that the head and the tail could end up swimming in different directions.

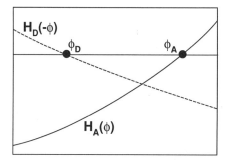

Figure 6.46 Example of a pair of descending, H_D ($-\phi$), and ascending, H_A (φ), coupling functions as a function of phase ϕ. The zero crossing of these two functions are shown at ϕ_D and ϕ_A, respectively. These coupling functions satisfy the criteria for a stable solution. (From Williams et al. 1990.)

What use is this analysis to us? Apart from allowing us to explain the general character of intersegmental coupling, it provides insight into the puzzling phenomenon of constant phase lag in the cord. The main point concerns the zero-crossings of the two coupling functions. Because this value does not change with changing level of activation, phase lag can be independent of swimming frequency. In other words, by finding the zero-crossing points, we find the points where frequency can be changed without altering the value of the phase lag. There will be two such points—one for ascending and one for descending waves. Williams (in press) has shown that this is precisely what happens in the Buchanan model. Because the system wants only one constant phase lag, it is well to pick the zero-crossing of one coupling function to be dominant. Experimental results indicate that evolution selected the ascending coupling to be dominant in the lamprey.

The Kopell et al. analysis also predicts that the longer the length of chain, the wider the range of frequencies over which it can be entrained. These predictions have been tested experimentally on lamprey spinal cords with varying numbers of coupled segments. As predicted, the frequency range was wider for pieces of spinal cord with 50 segments than for those with 25 segments.

The analysis of Kopell et al. has revealed very general answers to several dynamical questions. The strength of their analysis is that it applies to many different cases, such as the simplified model of Buchanan as well as the more realistic model described below. Does it apply to biological structures such as the spinal cord? That depends on whether its assumptions are true of the biological structures. Unfortunately, the extreme complexity of the nervous system means that it is difficult to establish that they are true. For a particular real lamprey cord, experimental values for Ω can be measured, but because of the cord's complexity, the intrinsic frequency ω of an uncoupled oscillator cannot be measured. The problem is, it has not been possible to get a single segment to oscillate all on its own, and the notion of intrinsic frequency is a bit like the notion of a frictionless plane. Moreover, because the cells carrying intersegmental coupling signals have not yet been identified, the ascending and descending coupling functions, H_A and H_D, have not been measured. On the other hand, one may use the model with its tentative assumptions to generate testable predictions. Should the predictions be falsified by neurobiological experiment, then the finger of suspicion points to the assumptions of the analysis. Should the predictions be borne out, then the analysis has been useful because something will have been learned about the nervous system. In that event, the assumptions will survive to live another day, though to be sure, simply escaping falsification on one test is not enough to establish their truth.

The Buchanan model shows how several segments whose connectivity is styled on the half-center circuit can yield rhythmic output, and the Williams et al. analysis reveals some general properties of a long chain of coupled oscillators. With this much in hand, we can address the next set of questions: how is rhythmic output from the motor neurons controlled such that the animal can swim at varying speeds and change speeds quickly, especially in response to sensory input? How do the biophysical properties of cells in the half-center circuit contribute to rhythmicity and to changes in frequency? What exactly is the mechanism that sustains constant phase lag and what mechanism turns the half-circuit off and on?

As we saw in Buchanan's model, a crude way to achieve frequency modulation is to regulate the amount of external excitation, which is the analog of squirting glutamate on the isolated cord in the bath. While this expedient does modulate frequency in the isolated preparation, simple dose-dependent glutamate excitation is unlikely to be the whole story of frequency control and frequency modulation in actual motor neurons. Why?

First, input to the half-center circuit comes peripherally from receptors in the skin, muscles, and tendons, and centrally from brain-stem neurons or from neurons in neighboring spinal segments. These different kinds of input may count more or less, depending on conditions, so they are unlikely merely to summate. More probably, distinct mechanisms will gate these inputs to achieve differential control.

Second, locomotion initiated by stimulation of the brain stem alternately produces EPSPs *and* (with a slight delay) IPSPs in motor neurons (Shefchyk and Jordan 1985). Stimulation of peripheral afferents produces only EPSPs. This is important because by changing properties at synapses, the operation of a network may be dramatically changed—for example, by shifting from a canter to a gallop, from swimming in a cruising fashion to burrowing or attacking (Marder et al. 1987, Getting 1989).[17]

Third, in pharmacological manipulations, it has been discovered that adding NMDA plus serotonin to the bath yields *slow* rhythmicity; when norepinephrine is added to that concoction a *high-frequency* rhythm is induced (Harrison 1990). There also appear to be two subtypes of glutamate receptors on neurons in the lamprey half-center circuit—NMDA receptors, and AMPA (kainate/quisqualate) receptors. According to Grillner's results (Wallen and Grillner 1987), the subtypes are selectively prominent in the cells' activities depending on whether the frequencies are high or low.[18] These biophysical observations suggest that the business is recondite. The nervous system may have various mechanisms sensitive to specific ranges of frequencies from low to high, various gating and timing mechanisms, as well as cellular properties that allow for the functional rewiring of the circuit in the presence of certain neurotransmitters. As we discuss below, these observations motivate including biophysical details such as channel properties in a computer model as a means of getting a bit closer to answering questions concerning amplitude and frequency control.

6 MODELING THE NEURON

The preliminary task is to model the whole neuron, albeit with simplifications. The granddaddy in this domain is the mathematical analysis of the action potential in the squid giant axon developed by Hodgkin and Huxley in 1952. Abstracting away from its physical composition, they treated the axon as a length of electrical cable, with electromotive force resulting from uneven distribution of ions across the membrane, and with resistance and capacitance displayed by sections of membrane. Some properties, such as ionic conductances, could change through time, and the rate constants for opening and closing ion channels were established experimentally. The rough schedule for an action potential is as follows: first, suppose external stimulation produces a depolarization of the membrane to above its threshold (about -60 mV). This is followed by an abrupt influx of Na^+ changing the membrane potential to about $+30$ mV, at which time the Na^+ channels begin to shut down and the voltage-dependent K^+ channel opens, repolarizing the cell (figure 6.47). Based on the empirical observations of the interactions of ionic conductances, membrane potential, and the time courses for various events, Hodgkin and Huxley described a differential equation that would predict the behavior of an axon when stimulated (box 6.1). It was accurate to within 10% of observed values.

The first genuinely quantitative model in neuroscience, the Hodgkin and Huxley equation, was a milestone achievement. Not only was it highly accurate in the standard condition, but when nonstandard values were substituted for the variables, it could describe the behavior of the axon in a range of experimental conditions, and it could explain refractory periods and the threshold for the action potential. Since the advent of the model, the Hodgkin and Huxley approach has been widely applied to the axons of neurons in many different species and in many different conditions. Variation in the values of the rate constants across different species and under different conditions can be plugged into the equations, and the model is adequate to an impressively wide variety of axon sizes and spike speeds. Only two channel types were included in the Hodgkin and Huxley model: the fast Na^+ channel, and the delayed rectifier K^+ channel. Although, in general, axon membranes contain just these two channel types, in dendrites and somas, by contrast, many more channel types have been discovered, with a great diversity of voltage dependences and ionic specificities. Combined in assorted configurations on neurons with distinct dendritic morphology, these channels permit the very same

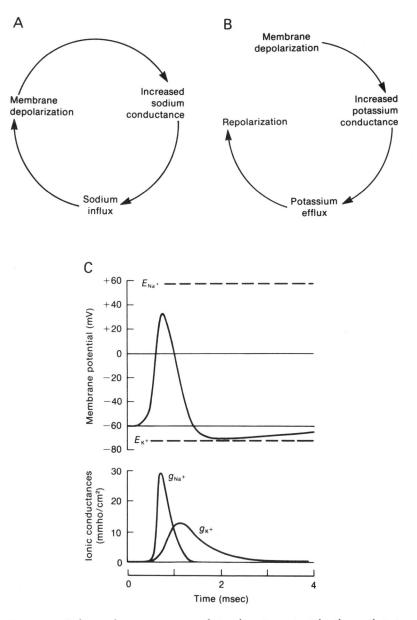

Figure 6.47 Sodium and potassium currents during the action potential in the squid giant axon. (A) Depolarization of the membrane potential leads to an increase in the conductance of the sodium channel, which further depolarizes the membrane owing to the efflux of sodium (positive feedback). The regenerative increase in the sodium current is terminated by inactivation of the sodium conductance and repolarizing effects of the potassium efflux. (B) Membrane depolarization also increase the potassium conductance, which leads to repolarization due to efflux of potassium. The potassium conductance increase is self limiting (negative feedback). (C) Theoretical solution of Hodgkin-Huxley equations for changes in membrane potential (upper) and Na^+ and K^+ conductances (lower) as a function of time. The equilibrium potentials for sodium (E_{Na^+}) and potassium (E_{K^+}) are indicated by dashed lines. (From *Introduction to Nervous Systems.* By T. H. Bullock et al. Copyright © 1977 by Scientific American Books, Inc. Reprinted by permission of W. H. Freeman and Company.)

stimuli on different neurons to produce a stupendous range of distinct "all-told" responses at the soma. Conduction-relevant variations in morphology together with choices in channel type and channel location mean that the responses of neurons can be breathtakingly complex.

There are only a few instances where a neuron's complement of channels has been characterized in sufficient detail to enable a model of the *whole neuron* that is as realistic and as successful as the Hodgkin and Huxley model of the *axon*. The exceptions include the bullfrog sympathetic ganglion cell, modeled by Koch, Adams, and colleagues (Yamada et al. 1989). The soma in this type of neuron has a spherical geometry that is easy to voltage clamp, a major advantage in determining the neuron's channel vitae. Controlling the voltage across the Na^+ and K^+ channels was essential to Hodgkin and Huxley's success with the squid axon, but such control is not technically possible in densely branching dendritic arbors. The problem is that dendrites are generally too tiny for recording and voltage clamping, so the measurements have to be taken at the soma. But if the current attenuates along a branch, a sharp signal to a synapse somewhere in the dendritic tree may be both a weaker signal and a smeared signal by the time it reaches the soma, thus frustrating precise biophysical measurements.

A second reason why detailed modeling of the whole neuron is very difficult is that at the level of the channels, each cell is unique. A third and related reason concerns completeness: it is virtually impossible to collect all the data for all the channels of one individual cell. The preferred solution, therefore, is to sample from a large population of ostensibly similar cells, and average over the variability. Fourth, the number of parameters per channel that must be experimentally determined is generally about ten, and a "typical" neuron has about ten types of channel. As noted above, the assorted channel types vary in density and distribution throughout the distinctive morphology of a given class of neuron. At a minimum, therefore, several hundreds of parameters need to be specified. In practice, one tries to measure the most important ones and to fill in the rest with "reasonable" values, a dodge affectionately known as the SSL (some small lies) constraint.[19]

Does the SSL constraint not undermine the whole enterprise? Obviously the biophysical phenomena are less yielding than one might wish. Nonetheless, a great deal can be accomplished even within the limitations, daunting and strenuous though the modeling project may be. Assuming the Hodgkin and Huxley equation is a reliable precedent, the aftercrop of modeling results may reward the effort manyfold. In collecting additional data, for example, it can be helpful to have a good, even if not an exact, model, because a good model makes explicit the *consequences* of what is already known and permits the experimenter to home in on those parameters most critical for determining the cell's overall behavior. In addition, having created a realistic model of the neuron, it then becomes possible to replace simplified units in a network model by more realistic units. The properties exhibited by the more realistic network can then be explored, and compared with those of its more streamlined precursor.

Until recently, biophysical data tended to simply pile up, paper upon paper, in fascinating isolation and without benefit of the quantitative integration that a model can supply. This came to pass partly because the experimental techniques for gathering the biophysical data antedated the computational power needed to simulate a neuron. The computer power required for these simulations is enormous, and as recently as ten years ago, such power was simply not available. One of the most remarkable developments in the last decade has been the pace of progress in computer technology. The power of computers continues to increase exponentially with time, and at this stage computer power is not generally an impediment to constructing a quantitative model.

Computer models of neurons in the central nervous system are now being developed, but not surprisingly they are much more schematic and tentative than Hodgkin and Huxley's rigorous biophysical models of the squid axon. Roger Traub, for example, has developed a model of hippocampal CA3 neurons (Traub et al., in press); Lytton and Sejnowski (1991) have modeled bursting neurons in the neocortex (figure 6.48); Purkinje cells in the cerebellum have been modeled by Segev (in press), and Bush and Sejnowski (1991) (figures 6.49, 6.50). We discuss briefly now one cellular model.

Christof Koch and colleagues (Bernander et al. in press) are using computer models of single cortical pyramidal neurons to address a puzzle concerning the electrical properties of neurons as measured in vivo and the same properties of the same neurons, but studied in vitro. It has been troubling that the best in vivo measurements of the input resistance have been about 5–10 times lower than the same measurements made in slices. A common conjecture has been that these differences are owed to differences in recording methods. Analyzing their computer models, Koch and colleagues have uncovered another and rather plausible explanation. If correct, this alternative idea will bear upon our understanding of what and how the single cell is computing. A major difference between the two preparations, namely the presence of ongoing spontaneous activity at a rate of a few spikes per second per cell seen in vivo but not in slice, changes the average membrane resistance, according to the model. Assuming a typical pyramidal cell has about 5000 synapses, and that incoming axons fire spontaneously about once per second, then the cell sustains on average 5000 excitatory and inhibitory conductance changes per second, or about 5/msec. These conductance changes have two effects: (1) they cause a background depolarization of about 10 mV,[20] and (2) all the small synaptic conductance changes effectively decrease the input resistance approximately five to tenfold. The models thus suggest that the effects of normal spontaneous activity may be functionally relevant to the internal signal traffic within the dendrites of the cell, for the membrane resistance directly affects the impact that distant synapses have on whether a spike is initiated at the axon hillock. These models point to direct experimental tests.

Aiming for the maximum realism given available data, a group led by Anders Lansner in collaboration with Sten Grillner have developed a model for neurons in the lamprey spinal cord that exhibit intrinsic oscillatory properties in the presence of NMDA.[21] When these neurons are isolated by blocking connectivity to their neighbors, they do not produce rhythmic output. When NMDA is added to the bath, however, they do. The goal of the Lansner–Grillner neuron model is to show how this particular behavior can be accounted for by interactions between a variety of channels found in these neurons.

NMDA receptors were earlier discussed in the context of plasticity, where we noted that their remarkable properties appeared to make them suitable for mediating associative memory: (1) they are both ligand binding and voltage dependent, (2) they open to admit both Na^+ and Ca^{2+}, and (3) they have a relatively long open-time—about 100–200 msec. These unusual properties, together with the result that NMDA added to the bath induces rhythmic firing in the lamprey cord, provokes the biophysical exploration of spinal neurons with NMDA receptors in order to understand whether NMDA receptors might have a special role in the timing of rhythmic behavior. Although a great deal is still unknown and some results are controversial, Grillner and colleagues claim several biophysical results that implicate the NMDA receptor. One of the more interesting claims is that under specific pharmacological conditions that inculpate the NMDA receptor, the axon membrane of certain cells, namely motor neurons and CC cells, show low-frequency, pacemaker potentials with brief plateaus (Wallen and Grillner 1987).

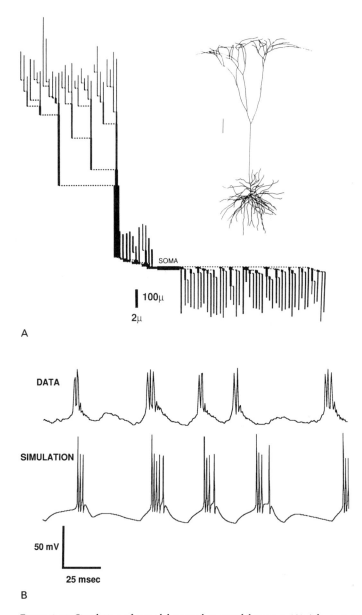

Figure 6.48 Simulation of a model cortical pyramidal neuron. (A) A layer 5 neuron was injected with an intracellular dye, and a 3-D model of the dendritic tree was reconstructed by digital computer (a 2-D projection is shown on the right, taken from Bush and Douglas, 1991). The result is a linked list of dendritic segments, drawn schematically on the left. The apical dendrites are displayed above the central segment that represents the soma, and the basilar dendrites are displayed to the right of the soma. The length and width of each segment are to scale, and the dotted lines indicate attachment points. These segments are then used to simulate the flow of currents in a compartmental model of the neuron. Each compartment has associated with it a set of electrical parameters, including longitudinal resistance, membrane resistance, and capacitance. In addition, 11 active membrane channels were simulated, including a fast and a persistent sodium channel, three types of calcium channels, and six types of potassium channels. The parameters for these channels were taken from voltage-clamp studies from a variety of sources (Lytton and Sejnowski 1991). (B) An intracellular recording from the pyramidal neuron reconstructed in (A) is shown in the top trace (from Bush and Douglas 1991). The neuron produced

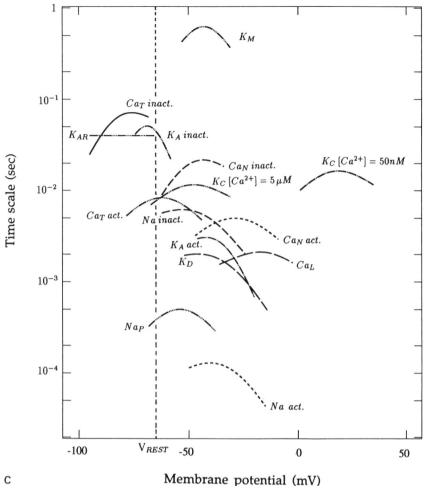

c

Membrane potential (mV)

repetitive, high-frequency bursts of action potentials. The bottom trace shows a simulation of the model pyramidal neuron in response to simulated excitatory synaptic input. The CABLE simulator written by Michael Hines was used to perform the simulations. (The digitized neuron was kindly provided by Rodney Douglas; from Lytton and Sejnowski, 1991.) (C) Activation and inactivation ranges of 10 voltage-dependent ion channels. Each channel is characterized by a time scale and voltage range for activation (and inactivation for some, as labeled). An activation curve's length along the horizontal axis represents the rough range of voltages over which a channel goes from being closed (left side) to open with a high probability (right side). The rate at which a channel opens (or closes) is not instantaneous and the time constant for opening is voltage dependent, as indicated on the vertical axis. The time scales range from seconds to fractions of a millisecond for different types of channels. For example, the fast, voltage-sensitive Na$^+$ channel involved in spiking begins to activate around -50 mV with a time constant around 0.1 ms, and the slowest K$^+$ channel, the M-current, activates with a time constant of nearly 1 sec. The inactivation curves span the range of voltages at which the channel begins to inactivate (left side) and is closed with high probability (right side). The time scale for inactivation is given on the vertical axis. Abbreviations: Na, inactivating sodium current; Na$_P$, persistent sodium current; Ca$_T$, low-threshold calcium current; Ca$_N$, high-threshold, inactivating calcium current; Ca$_L$, high-threshold, noninactivating calcium current; K$_D$, delayed rectifying potassium current; K$_A$, potassium A-current; K$_M$, potassium M-current; K$_{AR}$, anomolously rectifying potassium current; K$_C$, calcium-activated potassium current, shown at two calcium concentrations. (Courtesy Anthony Bell. Based on channel kinetics in Lytton and Sejnowski 1991.)

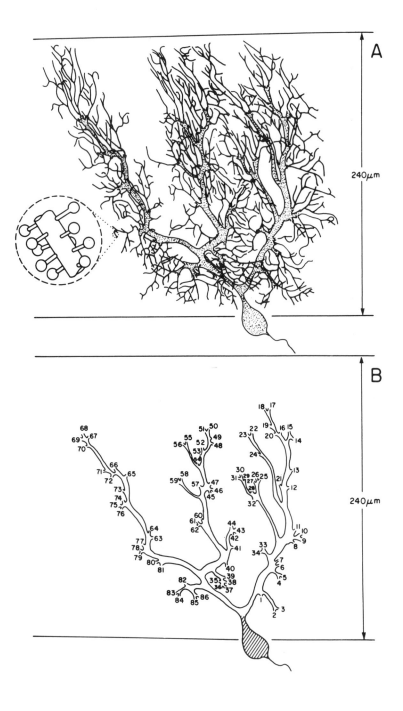

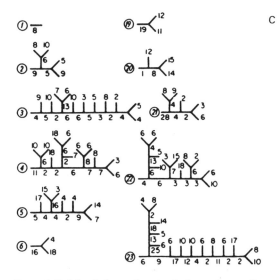

Figure 6.49 Morphology of rat cerebellar Purkinje cell. (A) Soma and proximal (smooth) dendrites are stippled. Spiny dendrites are drawn as lines. (B) Smooth dendritic tree only. Spiny dendritic tree attachments are numbered. The soma (hatched) contains potassium and sodium conductances, smooth dendrites contain fast calcium and potassium conductances, and spiny dendrites contain slow calcium and potassium conductances. (C) Branching pattern of a few spiny branchlets taken from (B). (Reprinted with permission from Shelton 1985.)

A key role in this model is played by Ca^{2+}, which (chapter 5) is generally kept at a very low concentration inside neurons. The plateau pattern appears to result from the following script: (1) NMDA receptors, when activated, allow Ca^{2+} as well as Na^+ to enter the cell, and since the NMDA channel is voltage dependent, the more depolarized the neuron, the larger the conductance of the NMDA channel. (2) When the concentration of Ca^{2+} rises sufficiently a *Ca^{2+}-dependent K^+ channel* opens, and the outward shift of K^+ counteracts the depolarization induced by the NMDA receptor. (3) There is a brief period where the plateau is manifest as the balance between these two currents, but sliding toward repolarization. (4) Once the voltage has slipped to a certain point, and the NMDA pore closes thus ending its contribution to depolarization, the repolarization rate speeds up. (5) The Ca^{2+} inside the neuron is either sequestered or pumped out so that the concentration of Ca^{2+} eventually falls below the level that activated the Ca^{2+}-dependent K^+ channel. (6) Thus the hyperpolarization by K^+ outflow terminates, the cell depolarizes, and another cycle begins, as shown in figure 6.51. Under more normal circumstances, a burst of Hodgkin–Huxley-like spikes can appear at the peaks of the plateau potentials, but these are not essential to the plateau oscillations since the latter go on merrily even when the spikes are blocked.

The timing of these events, the duration of the plateau, and the rate of recovery during the hyperpolarizing phase depend on the rate constants for these channels and on the speed with which Ca^{2+} is handled intracellularly. Unfortunately, few of these parameters have been experimentally pinned

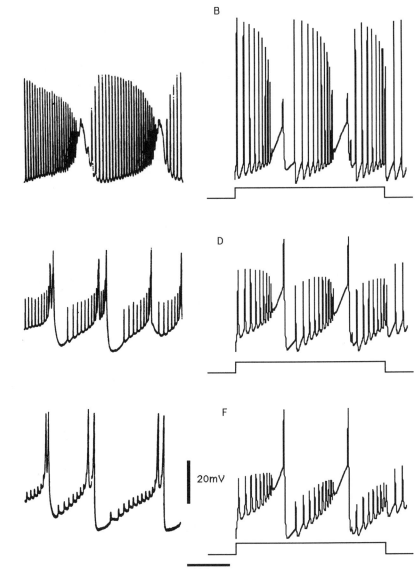

Figure 6.50 Comparison between experimental recordings (left column) and model simulations (right column) of a Purkinje cell in the soma (top row), proximal dendrite (middle row), and distal dendrite (bottom row). For the electrical recordings, constant depolarizing current was injected into the soma of a turtle cerebellar Purkinje cell (Hounsgaard and Midtgaard 1988); for the simulations, brief pulses of current were injected into the soma. (A) Recording from the soma. Somatic sodium spikes ride on a slow depolarization due to plateau currents. When sodium spikes are voltage inactivated, the membrane potential reaches the threshold of the dendritic calcium spike conductance. The resulting calcium spike is repolarized by potassium conductances, which resets the sodium spiking. (B) Model responses from soma. The model used the Purkinje cell morphology reconstructed by Shelton (1985) and had 1089 compartments. Seven ionic currents were included: the fast and persistent sodium channels, three types of potassium conductances, and two types of calcium conductances. (C) Recording from a proximal dendrite. (D) Model responses from soma, proximal, and distal dendrites. (E) Recordings from a distal dendrite. The small size of the sodium spikes and relatively large calcium spikes reflect their

down in the spinal cord. Borrowing generously from experiments in other areas of the brain and even from other species, one may come up with respectable SSL (some small lies) constraints so that the ensuing model roughly mimics the qualitative features observed in the experimental recordings.

Having modeled the single neuron to the indicated degree of realism, the next step was to replace the simple units in the Buchanan model with simulated neurons, preserving connectivity in the original network. This more realistic model, developed by Grillner, Wallen, and Brodin (1991), is therefore quite highly detailed, at the biophysical and neuronal levels and also in terms of basic connectivity. That this network model exhibits fictive swimming with the same general characteristics observed in the simpler Buchanan model is not too surprising. After all, parameters in both the Buchanan model and its biophysically embellished version were adjusted (or, in the modeling argot, "tweaked") until the models resembled the relevant experimental data. What is new about the more detailed model, however, is that the frequency of oscillations and the responses to physiologically realistic input differ in ways that can ultimately be experimentally tested. One might expect, for example, that the Grillner model would be more robust to variation in the strengths of the connections. The reason is that the rhythms in the Grillner model do not depend solely on the connectivity, as they do in the Buchanan model. Rather, the connectivity can serve the role of entraining neurons that will themselves oscillate intrinsically under suitable conditions. The interplay between these two influences—the intrinsic properties on one hand and the network properties on the other—provides the spinal cord with considerable computational subtlety as influences from the brain stem and afferent feedback selectively modulate the biophysical properties of the neurons.

To study the significance of stretch receptor input to the cord, the Grillner model added stretch receptors with properties based on physiological data. The model shows that stretch receptor stimuli will entrain the network, making it oscillate at a slower or a faster rhythm, relative to the "resting" rhythm displayed in the absence of stretch receptor input. In examining the role of the brain stem in rhythmic behavior, the simulation indicated that the motor pattern was more stable when the brain-stem neurons received feedback from the spinal cord than when they did not.[22] One advantage of having the model is that it becomes possible to make predictions for effects that would be difficult to isolate experimentally, such as the degree to which Ca^{2+}-activated current terminates the burst and regulates the frequency, and the role of inhibition from connections with other neurons. There may be species differences in the

respective sites of generation relative to the recording site. (F) Model responses from a distal dendrite. The model replicates all the essential features of Purkinje cell behavior. The duration of the stimulus is shown beneath each trace for the simulated Purkinje cell. Note that the firing continued after the stimulus was turned off due to the continued activation of plateau currents; this behavior has been observed in real Purkinje cell recordings. The CABLE simulator written by Michael Hines was used to perform the simulations. (Recordings from Hounsgaard and Midtgaard 1988; simulations from Bush and Sejnowski, 1991.)

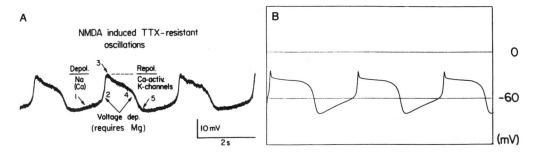

Figure 6.51 NMDA receptor-induced membrane potential oscillations in lamprey neurons. (A) Experimental recordings in the presence of tetrodotoxin (TTX). 1. The NMDA receptor allows Na^+ and Ca^{2+} ions to enter during the depolarizing phase. 2. Rapid depolarization occurs when the voltage is high enough to prevent Mg^{2+} from blocking the NMDA receptor channel. 3. The Ca^{2+} that enters the cell activates a Ca^{2+}-dependent K^+ channel, which leads to repolarization and a plateau. 4. The subsequent closing of the NMDA channels causes further repolarization. 5. As the intracellular concentration of Ca^{2+} in the cell decreases, the Ca^{2+}-dependent K^+ channel closes and another depolarizing phase begins. (B) Model simulations of the pacemaker-like membrane potential oscillations induced by NMDA. The model has a single compartment and includes four channels in addition to the NMDA receptor: a fast Na^+ channel, two K^+ channels, and a voltage-sensitive Ca^{2+} channel. The qualitative features of the experimental recordings in (A) are reproduced in (B). (From Grillner et al. 1991.)

prominence of one factor or another that could give rise to conflicting experimental interpretations. Experimentally, these differences might seem striking, though they could correspond only to very small changes in some parameters in the model.

The inevitable cautions notwithstanding, this work on CPG illustrates how links between levels of organization can be made. The Buchanan model provides some insight into how the basic rhythm of cord segments is achieved, and the Koppell analysis addresses the issue of intersegmental influence, thus linking behavior to the circuit and the chain of circuits. The Grillner model illustrates how the intrinsic properties of cells could, but not necessarily do, underpin the rhythmic repertoire, thus linking the circuit to cellular and molecular processes. By building on the Buchanan framework, the Grillner model thus facilitates an explanatory continuity from behavior to circuits to cells and molecules. Interesting predictions about what one should find in the actual nervous system can, moreover, be made. One issue concerns change of mode, for example, in the lamprey from swimming forward to swimming backward. On the basis of the model, it might be predicted that this could involve a change in the strength of certain synapses, such as lateral interneurons to CC interneurons, since the Buchanan model demonstrates that this connection promotes a phase advance of the more caudal segments. This set of interconnected models illustrates also the fruitfulness of co-evolution. Just as cellular data on its own is not enough because the interactive effects seen in circuits must be addressed, so also network connectivity on its own is not enough, because the cellular properties need to be understood in the context of their home circuit in order properly to explain the myriad subtleties and complexities observed in real behavior.[23]

7 CONCLUDING REMARKS

Isolation of a circuit, provisionally assumed in the discussion for reasons of simplicity, rarely occurs under natural conditions. The leech, for example, is constantly moving, and hence bending away from an intense stimulus would typically occur in the context of the other undulating movements such as are involved in crawling or swimming. Like many other animals, the leech does not respond stereotypically and inflexibly to a sensory stimulus registered by its transducers. Behavior will vary depending on the inner context, including, for example, the motivational state of the animal. Just as the lowly leech reflex can be modified by context, so also can the VOR, even though it too might seem at first blush to be hidebound and cognitively insensitive. In fact, it has been shown that when humans rotate their heads in the dark, the gain of the reflex can be increased merely by instructing the subject to "imagine fixating on a light," while the gain can be decreased when subjects do mental arithmetic while rotating their heads (Barr et al. 1976).

In addition, careful measurements of VOR gain-shifting as a function of the depth of the plane of fixation show that the gain of the VOR changes *before* vergence movements occur. This indicates that the VOR gets the input for this gain change directly from visual-cum-cognitive level processes rather than through an efference copy, since no relevant copy yet exists. If this seems a surprisingly high-level influence on a mere stereotypical reflex, then it is our conception of reflexes that needs modification.[24] Reflexes in living nervous systems are not like the unchangeable and mechanical behavior of a toy bird tipping repeatedly into a container of water. Even the knee-jerk response, ostensibly as hidebound as any, can be affected by clenching the teeth or fantasizing erotic encounters.

Selected Readings

Anastasio, T. J. (in press). Distributed processing in vestibulo-ocular and other oculomotor subsystems in monkey and cats. In *Visual Structures and Integrated Functions*, ed. M. A. Arbib and J.-P. Ewert. New York: Springer-Verlag.

Beer, R. D. (1990). *Intelligence as Adaptive Behavior*. San Diego, CA: Academic Press.

Cronin, J. (1987). *Mathematical Aspects of Hodgkin-Huxley Neural Theory*. Cambridge: Cambridge University Press.

Getting, P. A. (1989). Emerging principles governing the operation of neural networks. *Annual Review of Neuroscience* 12: 185–204.

Grillner, S., and M. Konishi, guest eds. (1991). *Current Opinion in Neurobiology*. Vol. 1, no. 4, *Neural Control*.

Hall, Z. W. (1991). *Molecular Neurobiology*. Sunderland, MA: Sinauer.

Heiligenberg, W. F. (1991). *Neural Nets in Electric Fish*. Cambridge, MA: MIT Press.

Marder, E., guest ed. (1989). *Seminars in the Neurosciences.* Vol 1, no. 1. *Modulation of Neural Networks Underlying Behavior.*

McKenna, T., J. Davis, and S. Zornetzer (1992). *Single Neuron Computation.* Cambridge, MA: Academic Press.

Miller, K. D., guest ed. (in press). *Seminars in the Neurosciences.* Vol. 4, no. 1. *Use of Models in the Neurosciences.*

7 Concluding and Beyond

The principles of organization of neural systems arose from the combination of the performance requirements for survival and the physics of neural elements.
John Lazzaro and Carver Mead (1989a)

Computer models of the kind we have discussed are helpful in fathoming the principles whereby the brain performs its manifold tasks. These models are, however, only a first step. Within the basic framework they share, almost everything remains to be done, and on all sides major puzzles loom—puzzles concerning, for example, the nature of net-to-net interactions,[1] specialization and integration, dynamics and time, and the role of neuronal synchronization. Moreover, extant models generally have not addressed a range of critically important factors such as attention and arousal,[2] the role of emotions such as fear, hope, and joy,[3] the role of moods, desires, expectations, long- and short-range plans, and so on. There is an implicit tendency to consider some of these factors as fluff on the basic cognitive hardpan. From the point of view of the brain, however, the separation between the cognitive and the noncognitive may be nothing like what is suggested by the metaphor. Motives, moods, and appetites may be part and parcel of information processing to a degree hitherto unsuspected. Like the well-entrenched distinction in medieval physics between the sublunary realm and the superlunary realm, the cognitive/noncognitive distinction may embody more misdirection than truth. In reminding ourselves of how much farther we have to go, we do well also to recall a point made in chapter 1, namely that if the modeling projects are to progress, there is still an enormous amount that must be learned by experiments: in anatomy, physiology, neuropsychology, developmental neurobiology, and developmental psychology.

Pushing at the bounds of the simulation paradigm are ambitions to go beyond *simulation* of a neural circuit to construction of a *synthetic* neural circuit—for example, in a chip. Applying this to a specific instance, we are referring to the difference between constructing a device that can respond to *real*, as opposed to *simulated*, light; that performs the same computational tasks performed in the retina by the network of amacrine, bipolar, and horizontal cells; and whose output is comparable to that of ganglion cells leaving the retina. The contrast we have in mind between a simulated retina and a *synthetic* retina is roughly this: in a simulated retina the input will be numerical values corresponding to properties of light such as wavelength and intensity, and the output will be numerical values corresponding to information carried by the ganglion cells. In a synthetic retina, the input is real light, and the output consists of electrical signals carrying much the same information as that carried by the ganglion cells, carried not in spike trains but in current pulses. Following this line, the constructive problem concerns how to go from simulating in a computer to making synthetic retinas, nuclei, spinal cords, cortices—in short, how to make synthetic brains (Beer 1990).

Why should the long-range project of understanding how the brain works engender such constructive ambitions? At bottom, we discern four interrelated reasons. First, in testing the strengths and weaknesses of a model, seeing how it interacts with the actual world may be more revealing, more stringent, and less susceptible to the modeler's wishful thinking than relying solely on simulated interactions. Real time, for example, is an unforgiving constraint. So is real space. A small simulation may in fact be rather misleading, since it may not accurately predict how well a large-scale simulation will work, let alone how a real-world robot will work. On the other side of the coin, a simulation may make the task even harder if the modeler relies on common sense about how difficult the processing must be, when in fact there exists a rather quick and easy real-world gimmick.[4] Additionally, seeing how a device works in real time may be a source of insights that would be missed by watching a slow simulation. That is, it appears to be a psychological fact about humans that being able to see and manipulate in real time often provokes ideas and hypotheses.[5]

Second, with regard to input and output, a modeler can either simulate the world, or use the world. For certain purposes and in the absence of suitable technology, it may be most convenient to simulate the world by entering strings of numbers as input to and output from the model net. In the long haul, however, this is second best, for several reasons. Simulating the world may turn out to be at least as difficult as simulating the brain. The point is, if the input to the transducers and the output from the effectors are to be highly accurate, it may be more efficient to let the world itself interact with synthetic but causally interactive components, thus letting a chip generate the representations in the way a real retina or a real spinal cord would. Simulations can often seem successful because on the basis of highly simplified assumptions, a network effect can be achieved.

Third, we often do not know precisely what parameters in the world are relevant.[6] A simulation of the world embodies assumptions about what in the teeming richness in the world is likely to be relevant to an organism. The fact is, however, that such assumptions may well miss parameters that an organism's brain represents and uses, and, on the other hand, they may include many parameters the organism neither uses nor needs. Simulation assumptions may seem obvious if we introspect in our own case, but notoriously, introspection is only a sometime guide even in one's own case, let alone for bats, owls, electric fish, sloths, and so on. Although there may be uniquely technological advantages to building interactive sensory–motor systems, since robots are likely to be useful in industry, the rationale we are tendering is essentially theoretical. As we illustrate below, interfacing with the real world can entail simplification of a device's mechanisms for sensorimotor control, as well as greater accuracy in capturing the variety and subtlety of real-world properties, including temporal and spatial properties, relational properties, rates of change of properties, and so forth.

Finally, models eventually need to encompass not merely a single level of organization, but several levels. Consider again the many levels of brain organization, ranging from the whole brain, down through circuits, to neurons, to molecules. To explain how the brain works, we need explanatory links between the levels, so that, for example, we can understand a system in terms of its component circuits, and understand circuits in terms of their component and interacting neurons, and neurons in terms of their intrinsic and interacting properties. To put it rather crudely, causation is both a more exacting taskmaster and a more bountiful source of parameters than arrays of 0s and 1s that the modeler pretends stand for real-world interactions.[7]

An explanation of higher-level phenomena in terms of lower-level phenomena is usually referred to as a *reduction*, though not in the pejorative sense that implies that the higher levels are unreal, explanatorily dismissable, or somehow empirically dubious. A model of a single level that simulates the input and components of that level might be illuminating in many respects, but it will have a decidedly cartoon character. This is because the numerical values representing certain macroproperties may gloss over a range of causally relevant microfactors of the macroproperty that are discriminated and responded to in real nervous tissue at the next level down. To continue the earlier example, a simulation might represent light in terms of numerical values for wavelength and intensity, but such a representation will be insensitive to other features of light, such as that it is quantized, that it is polarized, and that light levels in the environment may range over about eight orders of magnitude. These factors may be causally significant for the level of the single cell, and through evolutionary pressures have had their effect on the design of specific cell types and their patterns of connectivity.

On the output end, the contrast between simulating performance of a function and performance of the function by a synthetic brain might be put this way: how real nervous systems interact with the world cannot be adequately described where numbers stand for macroproperties. Consider a modeler who specifies a certain value as corresponding to the arm reaching out to a specific point in 3-D space, as we did for the "crab" in chapter 6. This helps marshall some of the initial conceptual resources, and to that extent is a useful beginning. In fact, of course, the brain must be so organized to cope with the physics of moving, in real time, an object with a certain mass, accelerating and decelerating appropriately, where the object is made of bones of certain lengths, several joints, as well as many tendons and many muscles attached to the bones in a particular configuration, where energy is consumed in performing the action, and so on and on. The physics of the world the body inhabits, the physics of the body the brain inhabits, and, indeed, the physics of the nervous system itself have shaped the evolution, and hence the computational style, of nervous systems.

To achieve a model that does justice to the reality of a range of levels, we shall need to be faithful to the reality of the world the brain is in, and to the components of all the relevant levels. This undoubtedly means we shall need to edge closer to constructing an artificial device, rather than making do with a simulation. As a first analysis, for example, it might be useful to characterize the visual perception of size constancy as involving "unconscious inference,"[8] but as we seek to incorporate neurobiological realism into the model of visual perception, such an idea will likely be replaced by computational hypotheses about vector–vector transformations in networks, the role of back projections from higher to lower visual areas,[9] and winner-take-all decisions at the level of neural interactions. Similarly, in linguistics it may be useful as a first pass to characterize a speaker's knowledge of semantics in terms of a list stored in memory.[10] If, however, we want to take the further step and ask how speech production and comprehension are really done, given a more neurobiologically realistic construal of memory, then the semantics-as-list is a caricature that must be replaced by something closer to the truth. And having a more neurobiologically realistic characterization of semantic memory may well result in new ways of looking at old data, and in new hypotheses that would not have seemed at home in the old framework. Thus it seems to us that the existence of levels of organization in the brain, together with aim of explanatory unity, means that the construction of synthetic brains is bound to be prominent in the next stage of brain modeling.

There are many ways to go about addressing the constructive problem; to give a sample of what is afoot, we shall briefly introduce just three: (1) Carver Mead's strategy of building artificial neural structures, such as retinas and cochleas, using silicon-based CMOS VLSI (complementary metal oxide semiconductor, very large-scale integration) technology; (2) Dana Ballard's method of integrating perception with motor control, thus constructing a sensory–motor device which perceives, responds, learns to perceive more adaptively, and learns to behave more successfully. (3) Rodney Brooks' method which consists in following evolution's footsteps by first making simple mobots (mobile robots) that get around in the world using limited reflex repertoires. In contrast to conventional AI approaches to robotics, Brooks' mobots have no capacity for symbol manipulation nor for extensive perceptual scene analysis.

Mead and Analog VLSI

Mead's approach is to make analog integrated circuits (silicon chips) with transducers that convert real-world signals into electrical representations, and with a design that mimics closely the real anatomy and physiology of the nervous tissue under consideration.[11] Neural systems and analog integrated circuits may appear to be two disjoint disciplines, but as Lazzaro and Mead (1989b) remark:

The physics of computation in silicon technology and in neural technology are remarkably similar. Both media offer a rich palette of primitives in which to build a structure; both pack a large number of imperfect computational elements into a small space; both are ultimately limited not by the density of devices, but by the density of interconnects. (p. 52)

Mead and his colleagues (Mead 1989, Lazzaro and Mead 1989a,b) have built a synthetic cochlea—brain stem nucleus to ground localization of a sound-emitting object in space by using only sound cues. They have also built a synthetic retina,[12] but in this discussion we have chosen to focus on the auditory chip. To give this research its proper backdrop, it is essential first to have a brief lesson in barn owl neurobiology.[13] Barn owls are very accurate in detecting the whereabouts of prey even in the dark of night, relying solely on sound emitted from the prey, such as rustles in the leaves. The owls use interaural amplitude differences to detect location in elevation, and interaural delay to detect an object's location in the horizontal plane. "Interaural delay" refers to the difference in arrival time of a signal at the two ears, and the extent of the delay varies as a function of location of the emitter relative to the ears. For example, if a mouse on the owl's left rustles the leaves, the rustle will be heard slightly earlier by the left ear than by the right, because the sound has to travel a bit farther to reach the right ear. How does the nervous system use interaural delay time to tell where the mouse is located in the horizontal plane?

In the barn owl, the nucleus laminaris receives input from both cochleas, and is spatially organized in a very cunning way (figure 7.1). Left and right ear signals with a given interaural delay will arrive at some particular neuron in the nucleus laminaris at the same time, owing to the placing of cells along the collaterals of the axons from the cochlear nucleus. Which neuron in the array gets the left and right ear signals simultaneously depends on its position along what is in effect an axonal delay line, and hence on the duration of the interaural delay (Konishi et al. 1988, Carr and Konishi 1988, 1990) (figure 7.2). The interpretation of these data is that the position of a cell in the nucleus laminaris encodes interaural time difference.[14] On the basis of other data, it appears that this information is integrated at subsequent nuclei with information about location in the vertical plane, thus enabling the owl to intercept the prey with great accuracy[15] (figure 7.3).

The chips constructed by Mead and his colleagues are meant to reproduce this very clever organization for auditory localization of objects in the horizontal plane in the barn owl. The chip has 220,000 transistors, and its architecture mirrors the targeted part of the nervous system of the barn owl. There are structures that play the role of the eardrums, and structures that function analogously to the basilar membranes of the cochleas. The chip includes synthetic pathways to a synthetic nucleus laminaris whose anatomical and physiological organization mimics the real thing, at least to the extent that data are available (figure 7.4). At this stage, the Mead synthetic nervous system reaches only as far as the nucleus laminaris, and further development will entail building the next stage, namely a synthetic inferior colliculus, with both of its

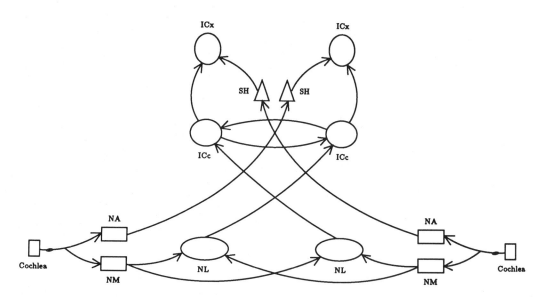

Figure 7.1 Schematic drawing of the auditory pathway of the barn owl. The pathway begins at the cochlea, the sound transducer. The cochlea projects to the nucleus angularis (NA), which begins the amplitude-coding pathway, and to the nucleus magnocellularis (NM), which begins the time-coding pathway. The NA projects contralaterally to the shell (SH) of the central nucleus of the inferior colliculus, which projects to the external nucleus (ICx) of the inferior colliculus. In the ICx there is a complete map of auditory space. The NM projects bilaterally to the nucleus laminaris (NL), which projects contralaterally to the central nucleus (ICc) of the inferior colliculus. Fibers connect the ipsilateral and contralateral sides of the ICc, returning information to the original side. The ICc then projects to the ICx. (From Lazzaro and Mead 1989a,b; based on Takahashi and Konishi 1988.)

functionally distinct regions, the central nucleus and the external nucleus. Although the auditory chip has no adaptive capacity, Mead's group is tackling the problem of creating adaptive circuits and they have begun by making a chip with Hebbian modifiability. Ideally, the analog VLSI strategy will lead to a synthetic auditory cortex, which can be helpful in understanding exactly what the cortex gets as input, what computations it performs, and how it interacts with other regions of the brain. In the meanwhile, however, even the existing chips have been valuable as a way of exploring interactions and emergent effects. For example, the delay-line organization copied in the chip circuitry does in fact serve marvelously well for coding interaural delay of cochlear signals as spatial position of the nucleus laminaris cells, just as the physiology indicated it should. Note that Mead's approach to the construction problem is particularly relevant to the microcircuit and macrocircuit levels.

Ballard and Active Perception

Dana Ballard and his colleagues (Whitehead and Ballard 1991; Ballard 1991) are addressing the construction problem at the systems level. In contrast to the conventional assumption that prior to initiating an action, a robot must first perform an extensive analysis and categorization of sensory input, they

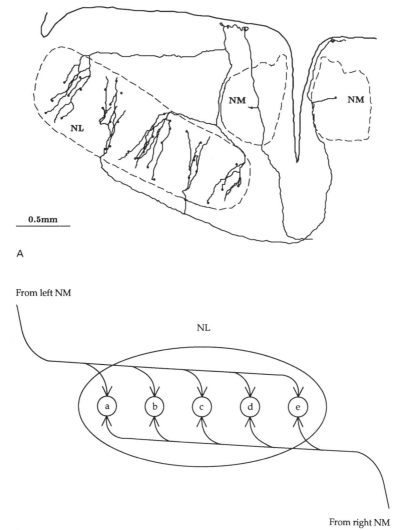

A

B

Figure 7.2 (A) Innervation of the nucleus laminaris in the barn owl. Axons from the ipsi- and contralateral nucleus magnocellularis (NM) enter, respectively, the dorsal and ventral surfaces of the nucleus laminaris (NL). Each axon runs along the respective surface until it comes to the isofrequency band which it is to innervate. Within this band, the axon sends two or three collaterals into the NL, each then dividing into several branches. These fibers, which may be as long as 1 mm, run along a relatively straight course toward the opposite surface. (From Carr and Konishi 1988, Konishi et al. 1988.) (B) Interaural time differences can be measured and encoded in the NL as follows: the NM fibers encode timing information in the temporal patterning of their action potentials. The NL neurons (circles labeled a–e) act as coincidence detectors, firing maximally when signals from two sources arrive simultaneously. The pattern of innervation of the NM fibers in the NL creates left–right asymmetries in transmission delays: when the binaural disparities in acoustic signals exactly compensate for the asymmetry of a particular neuron, this neuron fires maximally. The position in the array thus encodes interaural time differences. (From Lazzaro and Mead 1989a,b.)

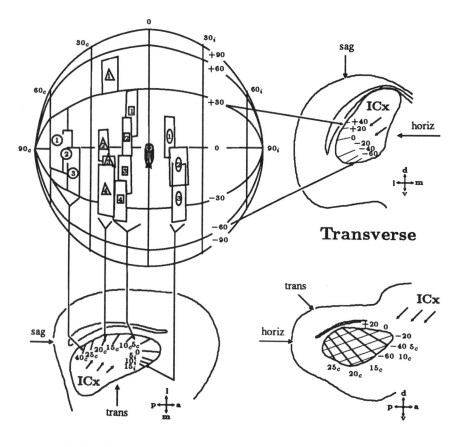

Transverse

Horizontal

Sagittal

Figure 7.3 Neural map of auditory space in the barn owl. Auditory space is depicted as an imaginary globe surrounding the owl. Projected onto the globe are the receptive field best areas of 14 neurons. The best area, a zone of maximal response within a receptive field, remains unaffected by variations in sound intensity and quality. The numbers surrounded by the same symbols (circles, rectangles, triangles, ellipses) represent neurons from the same electrode penetration; the numbers themselves denote the order in which the neurons were encountered. Below and also to the right of the globe are illustrations of three histological sections through the inferior colliculus; arrows point to the external nucleus, the ICx. The *iso-azimuth* contours are shown as thick lines in the horizontal and sagittal sections; *iso-elevation* contours are represented by thin lines in the transverse and sagittal sections. a, anterior; c, contralateral; d, dorsal; i, ipsilateral; m, medial; p, posterior; v, ventral. (From Lazzaro and Mead 1989a,b; based on Knudsen and Konishi 1978.)

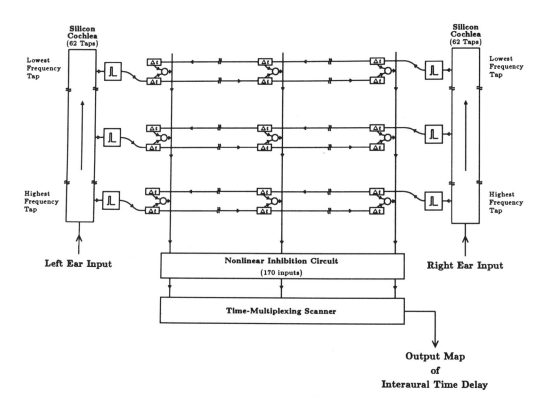

Figure 7.4 Floor plan of the silicon model of the time-coding pathway of the barn owl. Sounds for the left ear and right ear enter the respective silicon cochlea at the lower left and lower right of the figure. Silicon inner hair cells tap each silicon cochlea at 62 equally spaced locations; each silicon inner hair cell connects directly to a silicon spiral ganglion cell. The square box marked with a pulse represents both the silicon inner hair cell and silicon spiral ganglion. Each silicon spiral ganglion cell generates action potentials: these signals travel down silicon axons. The rows of small rectangular boxes, marked with Δt, represent the silicon axons. 170 silicon nucleus laminaris (NL) cells, represented by small circles, lie between each pair of antiparallel silicon axons. Each silicon NL cell connects directly to both axons, and responds maximally when action potentials present in both axons reach that particular neuron at the same time. In this way, interaural time differences map into a neural place-code. Each vertical wire that spans the array combines the response of all silicon NL neurons that correspond to a specific interaural time difference. These 170 vertical wires form a temporally smoothed map of interaural time difference, and they respond to a wide range of input sound frequencies. The nonlinear inhibition circuit near the bottom of the figure increases the selectivity of this map. The time-multiplexing scanner transforms this map into a signal suitable for display on an oscilloscope. (From Lazzaro and Mead 1989a,b.)

combine three ideas motivated by ethology and evolutionary biology: (1) an animal need not characterize and categorize everything in its perceptual domain, but only what is relevant to its tasks and survival (such perceptions are known as *indexical representations*; Agre and Chapman 1987), (2) task-relevant perception involves learning, minimally in the form of reinforcement of the perception–action pair when the action provoked by the indexical representation is successful;[16] (3) implementing the first two ideas leads to systems that actively control their environment. For example, a moving eye is more efficient in gathering information than is a stationary eye, assuming the organism has control over the eye movements. Motion parallax, detected by moving the head in its various degrees of freedom or by moving the whole body, provides powerful cues about the relative depth of an object. As we saw earlier, vergence "walks" in depth also provide cues as to depth of the stimulus, and hence where the stone should be thrown or where the leopard is hiding.[17] Animate vision, meaning visual systems with gaze control mechanisms that position the sensor in response to physical stimuli, are computationally far simpler than visual systems designed on the "fixed camera" plan (table 7.1).

Constructing a robot along these lines has also led to interesting discoveries concerning attention and the matter of learning what to attend to. For example, it turned out that the integration of sensorimotor systems with decision systems based on reinforcement learning gives rise to internal states that are perceptually ambiguous. The difficulty is that the decision system does not have access to the world itself, but only to the robot's representation of the world, and as we saw, its representations are limited to what it takes to be relevant to the task. In itself, this distinction between the external world and the animal's representation of the external world is insightful,[18] because reinforcement learning models typically make the highly unrealistic assumption of a perfect match between the two. To overcome the problems of ambiguity, the robot learns to detect which representations in its current perception are ambiguous. It then suppresses those representations while maintaining and using

Table 7.1 Comparison of the computational features of fixed camera vision and animate vision

Fixed Camera Vision	Animate Vision
Local constraints that relate physical parameters to photometric parameters are underdetermined.	Local constraints are sufficient.
Minimalist constraints such as smoothness used to regularize the solution.	Maximalist constraints such as specific behavioral assumptions used to obtain solution
Algorithm requires parallel iterations over the retinally indexed array.	Algorithm is local and has a constant time solution.
Frame of reference is camera-centered (egocentric).	Frame of reference is fixation point centered (exocentric).

From Ballard (1991). Animate vision. *Artificial Intelligence* 48: 57–86.

the unambiguous representations. Accordingly, it needs to learn not only suitably to control its behavior, but also to what it should pay attention. For this, being able to move around a lot gives the robot the latitude it needs to light on those world properties that *are* relevant and unambiguous, and hence to learn what it may safely ignore.

Brooks and Mobots

Rodney Brooks' slice into the real-world problem was to invert the time-worn rule in robotics that says, "Simplify the problem and make the robot sufficiently intelligent to succeed flawlessly in that toy world." Instead, he decided to simplify the robot, and see how it could manage to cope with problems in their unvarnished and undiluted state (Brooks 1989). His reasoning is rather like this: complex nervous systems evolved from simpler nervous systems with very crude sensory apparatus and very crude equipment for analyzing input data, "deciding" what to do, and making the body move. Why not find out how basically simple nervous systems do so well in the real world by finding out what basic principles get a simple robot by in the real world? To answer this question, Brooks and colleagues have built artificial insects with six legs as well as various robots equipped with wheels, heat sensors, laser-eyed vision, and mechanical "gripper" arms (figure 7.5). The mobots' innards are just simple finite state machines, with no recursive programs, no symbolic processing, and no central processor. Their repertoires consist of simple, blendable reflexes such as "track prey," "back off," and "avoid stuff," which are called up as a function of sensory input. The synthetic insect may not be able to distinguish a table from a cup, but it manages to avoid both and continue tracking the warm thing. The mobot can exhibit new, emergent behaviors as the outcome of blending component reflex behaviors, and a ranking allows resolutions between incompatible behaviors summoned by the sensory input (figure 7.6).

Although the details of the processing components in Brooks' mobots are nothing like the neurons and circuits of real insects, some features at the systems level are nevertheless relevant to computational neuroscience.[19] First, at the behavioral level, these very stupid machines look surprisingly smart and perform surprisingly well, relative to their supremely simple innards and to the conventional wisdom about how sophisticated a robot's internal representations must be. Moreover, as Altman and Kien (1989) point out, there are many systems-level similarities between their model of behavior choice in real insects and Brooks' models, particularly with respect to the property of decentralized, distributed control (Altman and Kien 1987a,b).

Some of the complexity we intuitively ascribe to internal cognitive states may actually be a matter of complexity in the world with which a relatively simple organization has evolved to mesh. Consider, for example, a honey bee's world, and consider that it contains not only flowers, the sun, and so forth, but also other bees as well as bee-enemies. Bee behavior in interacting with other bees may seem amazingly sophisticated, in, for example, swarming, hauling dead bees out of the hive, signaling the general whereabouts of nectar, and

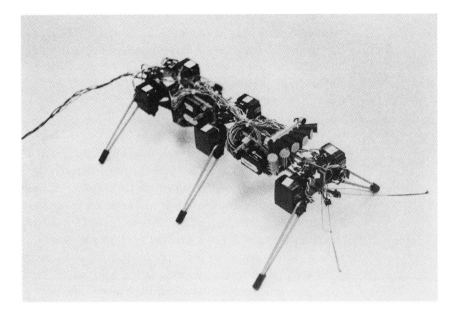

Figure 7.5 Genghis, the six-legged robot, is about 35 cm long, has a leg span of 25 cm, and weighs approximately 1 kg. Each leg is rigid and is attached at a shoulder joint with two degrees of rotational freedom, driven by two orthogonally mounted servo motors. An error signal has been tapped from the internal servo circuitry to provide crude force measurements on each axis, when the leg is not in motion around that axis. Other sensors are two front whiskers, two four-bit inclinometers (pitch and roll), and six forward-looking, passive, pyroelectric infrared sensors. The sensors have approximately 6° angular resolution and are arranged over a 45° span. There are four onboard 8-bit microprocessors linked by a 62.5 Kbaud token ring. The total memory usage of the robot is about 1 Kbyte of RAM and 10 Kbytes of EPROM. Three silver–zinc batteries fit between the legs to make the robot totally self-contained. (From Brooks 1989.)

attacking honey thieves. So much so that it is easy to forget that the bee's nervous system probably gets by without an exhaustive and intensive scene analysis and categorization. Apparently bees will remove anything from the hive, including other live bees, as long as they have oleic acid on them; dead bees exude oleic acid. Hence bees probably get by with "heave out oleic acid things," "attack non-bees," and other relatively simple, blendable, ranked, sensorimotor patterns. They do not need to know that a bear is a bear, let alone that a black bear is different from a grizzly and different from a human.[20] They simply need to drive off hive invaders. Could it be that to understand higher cognitive functions such as language production and comprehension, we can profit from sneaking up on the problem from a relevant but simpler case? Could it be that run-of-the-mill decision making and problem solving are rather less like theorem proving and rather more like constraint satisfaction?

The second point of relevance for computational neuroscience is that Brooks' mobots may be used as a kind of testbed for network hypotheses, where the simple innards Brooks uses can be pulled out and replaced by network innards that are more neurobiologically plausible. Some attempts of

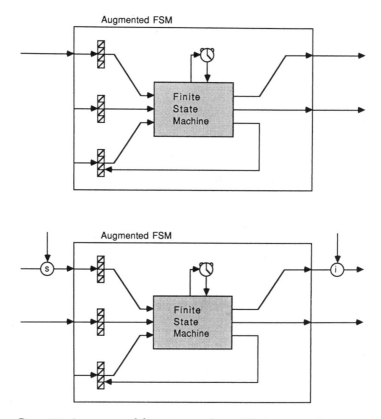

Figure 7.6 An augmented finite state machine (AFSM) consists of registers, alarm clocks, a combinatorial network, and a regular finite state machine. Input messages are delivered to registers, and messages can be generated on output wires. AFSMs are wired together in networks of message-passing wires. As new wires are added to a network, they can be connected to existing registers, they can inhibit existing outputs (i), and they can suppress existing inputs (s). Layers of these AFSMs can be augmented by adding new machines and connecting them into the existing network as shown. (From Brooks 1989.)

this kind are now underway (Chiel and Beer 1989). Because Brooks and colleagues have solved many of the technical problems of rigging the mechanics and the electronics for robot movement, modelers aiming for greater neurobiological realism in the innards can take advantage of the engineering successes and see how their networks fare in making the robot perform in the real world.

AFTERWORD

In these seven chapters, we have dwelt upon the deep and difficult problems facing brain research. Obstacles notwithstanding, the tenacity and creativity of researchers undoubtedly will produce discoveries that explain at least the general go of the thing. As with any scientific discovery about how something works, the possibility of intervening and changing what nature delivers will arise, and in some measure has arisen already. In step with the deep and difficult *theoretical* questions, are deep and difficult *ethical* questions concerning what to do with the knowledge. We can expect to ponder matters of human agency and responsibility, what justice requires in dealing with antisocial behavior, whether and how to intervene in the nervous systems nature supplies, what is appropriate in neural transplants both synthetic and real—just for starters.

Neuroscience *per se* cannot tell us what *ought* to be done, but only how things *are* in the brain. Even so, it may teach us a great deal about reasoning and decision making, superstitious proclivities and irrationality; about the neural basis for caring, for empathy and for representing social reality; about how humans learn and modify normative canons.[21] The ethical questions arising on the heels of neuroscientific knowledge are thus more convoluted and ticklish than elsewhere in science, because they concern manipulating efficiently and directly the very thing that makes us what we are—the very thing that reasons about scientific and ethical issues, that adapts and contributes to the cultural environment it responds to, that discovers the knowledge and makes the manipulations. We shall, all of us, need to keep our wits about us.

Appendix
Anatomical and Physiological Techniques

Nervous systems are dynamic, and physiological observations at each structural level can be arranged in a hierarchy of time scales. These scales range from microseconds in the case of opening of single ionic channels, to days or weeks for biophysical and biochemical events underlying memory, such as long-term potentiation (McNaughton and Morris 1987, Brown et al. 1989). A large battery of techniques has been developed to try to address physiological events and processes occurring at different time scales, and by understanding what kind of observations a given technique permits, we can begin to piece together hypotheses concerning the nature of information processing in a given structure, and how that structure contributes to the ongoing business of the brain.

A useful way to get an overview of the assorted techniques is to graph them with respect to temporal and spatial resolution. This permits us to spot areas where there do not yet exist techniques to get access to levels of organization at those spatiotemporal resolutions, and to compare their strengths and weaknesses (figure A.1). For example, it is apparent that we lack detailed information about processing in cortical layers and columns over a wide range of time scales, from milliseconds to hours. There is also a pressing need for experimental techniques designed to address the dendritic and synaptic levels of investigation in cerebral cortex. In this appendix we survey some of the primary techniques that neuroscientists use in systems neuroscience. This survey is selective and emphasizes techniques that are especially relevant to the examples covered in this book.

1 PERMANENT LESIONS

Human Studies

Sometimes the brain is damaged—for example, as a result of stroke, gunshot wound, tumors, and various illnesses. Neurological assessments of the deficits and residual capacities of brain-damaged patients is an important source of information about specialization of function. When behavioral observations

The appendix is based largely on section 2 of Sejnowski and Churchland (1989).

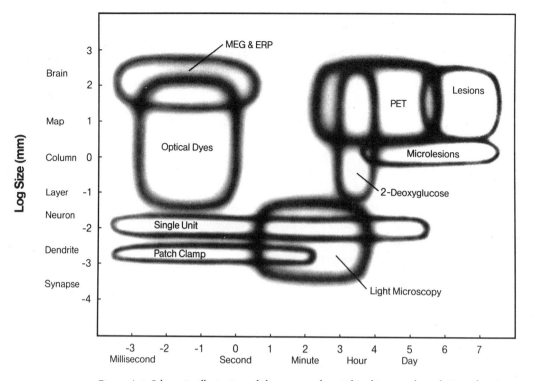

Figure A.1 Schematic illustration of the ranges of spatial and temporal resolution of various experimental techniques for studying the functions of the brain. The vertical axis represents the spatial extent of the technique, with the boundaries indicating the largest and smallest sizes of the region from which the technique can provide useful information. Thus, single-unit recordings can only provide information from a small region of space, typically $10–50$ μm on a side. The horizontal axis represents the minimum and maximum time interval over which information can be collected with the technique. Thus, action potentials from a single neuron can be recorded with millisecond accuracy over many hours. Patch recording allows the ionic currents through single ionic channels to be recorded. Optical dyes have been used with cellular resolution in tissue culture, where it is possible to obtain a clear view of single cells. However, recordings from the central nervous system are limited in resolution by the optical properties of nervous tissue and only about 0.1 mm resolution has been achieved. MEG (magneto-encephelography) and ERP (event-related potential) record the average electrical and magnetic activity over large brain regions and are limited to events that take place over about 1 sec. The temporal resolution of PET (positron emission tomography) depends on the lifetime of the isotope being used, which ranges from minutes to an hour. It may be possible to achieve a temporal resolution of seconds with O^{15} to study fast changes in blood flow using temporal binning of the gamma ray events (equivalent to the poststimulus time histogram for action potentials). The 2-deoxyglucose technique has a time resolution of about 45 min, and a spatial resolution of 0.1 mm with large pieces of tissue and 1 μm with small pieces. Lesions allow the interruption of function to be studied immediately following ablation of the tissue and for a long period of time following the ablation. Microlesion techniques make possible much more precise and selective interruptions of particular regions of the brain. Confocal microscopy, a promising technique for the study of nervous tissue, is a recent improvement of the light microscope for use with 3-D specimens. All of the boundaries shown here show rough regions of the spatiotemporal plane where these techniques have been used and are not meant to indicate fundamental limitations. (From Churchland and Sejnowski [1988]. Perspectives in cognitive neuroscience. *Science* 242: 741–745 © AAAS.)

are correlated with a determination of the site of the lesion(s)—for example, at autopsy or by MRI or PET scans (see below)—hypotheses can be generated concerning the brain areas that are particularly critical for certain functions. On this basis, left hemisphere lesions have been strongly implicated in language deficits, even in most left-handed humans; bilateral lesions of the medial temporal lobe typically result in anterograde amnesia (Milner 1966, Squire et al. 1989a); and lesions of the posterior parietal cortex have been implicated in loss of capacity to attend to the opposite side of the body and the opposite hemispace (Mesulam 1985). Some lesions produce surprisingly specific perceptual and linguistic deficits (Damasio 1985, McCarthy and Warrington 1988).

Although data from clinical neurology have traditionally been very important, and continue to be so, they do have well-known limitations. For example, the size and exact location of lesions are difficult to determine and vary considerably from patient to patient with the same behavioral profiles. Another factor relevant in using clinical data is that patients may display some recovery of function varying over time and depending on such things as patient age and gender. Additionally, the data are often difficult to interpret since a lesion may result in loss of function not because it interferes with the specific information-processing task of a given structure, but because it interrupts fibers of passage to and from areas crucial for the function in question, or some biochemical system that has a widespread influence. Moreover, a lesion may affect a number of functionally distinct areas, and may affect other areas through secondary degeneration. Further interpretive complications derive from other premorbid neurological and psychiatric factors, such as epilepsy, schizophrenia, and so forth. Finally, it is often difficult to find animal models for experimentation that are comparable to human cases. Despite these difficulties, important findings have been made which help to generate hypotheses concerning functional specialization of structures such as the hippocampus (e.g., Squire et al. 1989a).

Special mention should perhaps be given in this context to the split-brain studies, since these cases involved a fairly precise surgical intervention where any significant sparing of callosal fibers can now be detected by MRI. The disconnection effects discovered in split-brain patients (Sperry and Gazzaniga 1967) demonstrated the fragmentation of experience and awareness, and confirmed the lateralization of certain functions, particularly speech production and spatioconstructive tasks, in some patients. Even in these studies, however, there are interpretive complications since all the subjects were epileptic, and there were nontrivial differences in surgical technique and in the completeness of the commissural sections. Nonetheless, studies on split-brain patients can provide a unique source of information about the global organization of processing in the brain for perceptual and cognitive phenomena such as color constancy (Land et al. 1983) and mental imagery (Kosslyn et al. 1985).

Animal Models

Because humans cannot be the subjects of experimental lesions and recordings, it is essential to approach many questions concerning the human brain indirectly, via animal models. For example, the discovery in human patients that lesions to the hippocampus and related structures result in anterograde amnesia, but selectively spare learning of certain skills and priming, sparked the search for an animal model fitting essentially the same profile (Schacter 1989). Studies on monkeys (Zola-Morgan and Squire 1984) have revealed important similarities to the human cases, and these studies, in conjunction with anatomical, pharmacological, and physiological research on the hippocampus and related structures in a variety of animals (turtles, rats, and rabbits), permit a convergence on questions regarding the principles of declarative long-term memory. They also suggest new hypotheses about human memory which can be tested behaviorally. (Animal studies have also been crucial in research on the neurobiological basis for sleep and dreaming; Hobson 1985.)

Virtually everything we know about the micro-organization of nervous systems has derived from work on animal brains, and such research is absolutely indispensable if we are to have any hope of understanding the human brain. Of course, there are limitations, inasmuch as there are nontrivial differences between the brains of different species, and we cannot blithely generalize from cat and monkey brains to a human brain. Even the problem of identifying homologous structures in different species can be vexing (Campbell and Hodos 1970). Nevertheless, it may be that fundamental principles can be discovered in animal models, and that knowing these will provide the scaffolding for answering questions concerning those aspects of the human brain that make it unique.

2 REVERSIBLE LESIONS AND MICROLESIONS

Some of the shortcomings of the lesion technique are being overcome by recent technical advances that make more selective intervention possible. For example, kainic acid and ibotenic acid are neurotoxic substances that destroy neuronal cell bodies, but not fibers of passage. Additionally, the size and placement of the lesion can be carefully controlled by adjusting the amount and location of the injection. This new lesion method has been used to localize specific deficits in motion processing in MT, an extrastriate visual area in cerebral cortex (Newsome et al. 1985, Newsome and Pare 1986, Siegel and Andersen 1986).

Permanent lesions are often difficult to interpret for the reasons given above. Temporary lesions can also be made—for example, by locally cooling a region of the brain or applying local anesthetics such as lidocaine—and measurements made of the changes in the behavior of the animal or in the responses of neurons in other areas of the brain. Thus, it is possible to separate short-term changes specific to the lesion from general or long-term alterations.

Pharmacological agents are available that can selectively interfere with particular neurons or pathways. For example, 6-hydroxydopamine administered to newborn rat pups selectively destroys all the neurons in the brain that use catecholamines (such as dopamine and norepinephrine) as neurotransmitters. Even more specific lesions are possible by taking advantage of pharmacological agents that block specific synapses. The substance 4-amino-phosphono-butyric acid (APB) has been used to selectively block a class of glutamate receptors at synapses between photoreceptors and the on-center bipolar cells in the vertebrate retina (Schiller 1982, Horton and Sherk 1984). When administered to the vitreous humor, this drug reversibly blocks the entire on-center pathway to the visual system and allows the contribution of the off-center pathway to be assessed in isolation. This is very useful since it allows us to test hypotheses about the interaction of the on-center and off-center pathways, for example, in relation to the origin of orientation selectivity of cells in visual cortex. Another important pharmacological agent used to investigate functional properties is amino-phosphonovaleric acid (APV), which selectively blocks N-methyl D-aspartic acid (NMDA) receptors. This is fortunate because NMDA receptors are involved in the generation of long-term potentiation in the hippocampus, which is a change in the strengths of certain synapses when they are stimulated at a high rate (McNaughton and Morris 1987, Brown et al. 1988).

One of the most important inhibitory neurotransmitters in the brain is γ-aminobutyric acid (GABA). It can be applied exogenously in cerebral cortex and other areas to hyperpolarize certain neurons and thereby silence the generation of action potentials. This technique effectively lesions the cells from the local networks, and the lesion is reversible. It has been used to show that neurons in layer 6 of striate cortex contribute to the end-stop inhibition observed in the upper layers of the cortex (Boltz and Gilbert 1986). It is also possibly to chronically apply GABA and look for long-term effect of the activity of neurons on the effectiveness of synapses. For example, if the eye of a kitten is sutured shut during its developmental critical period, the geniculate afferents from the closed eye normally diminish in strength, with the result that afterward when both eyes are open, cortical neurons respond only to stimulation to the eye that had not been sutured closed. Reiter and Stryker (1988) have reported that when the visual cortex of a kitten is chronically silenced pharmacologically and the lid suture protocol is repeated, the responses from the closed eye are preserved, while the responses from the open eye are abolished, reversing the normal finding. As we discuss in chapter 5, these experiments show that neuronal activity plays an important role in the development of the normal cortical organization.

As evidence about the composition of the brain at the molecular levels accumulates, more selective and more powerful techniques will become available for dissecting out specific neural circuits and assessing their functional significance. In particular, monoclonal antibodies, which bind specifically to particular molecules, genetic cloning techniques, which can be used to identify particular genes, and retroviruses, which can be used to insert particular genes into cells, may soon make it possible to target specific classes of cells and subclasses of synapses (Kandel 1983). Already, many neurotransmitter receptors have been identified and their amino acid sequences determined by cloning their genes. Clearly, these new techniques cannot by themselves provide a deeper understanding of the function of the brain. But they can provide the answers to more detailed questions than was previously possible, though the questions must themselves evolve to exploit the potential of the techniques.

3 IMAGING TECHNIQUES

Sherrington (1940) has described his imaginary vision of what the nervous system might look like if only the electrical activity in the brain could be seen: "Millions of flashing shuttles weave a dissolving pattern, though never an abiding one; a shifting harmony of subpatterns." With the advent of imaging techniques in the last decade, his "enchanted loom" fantasy for large-scale visualization of the nervous system is becoming a reality, though by devices and with results that would have amazed Sherrington. Techniques for producing images of physiological activity depend on the introduction of tracers and dyes that are sensitive to physiological variables. Imaging also relies on computer power to handle the enormous flow of information, which is typically several orders of magnitude more than that collected with traditional techniques such as single-unit recording (see below). Some imaging techniques are noninvasive and can be safely used on a routine basis for studying normal processing in humans.

The first noninvasive mapping of brain structure was made possible by tomographic techniques that reconstructed a 2-D cross-section through the brain from a series of measurements on 1-D rays. The x-ray computed tomographic method (CT) uses differences in x-ray opacity of tissue as revealed on the reconstructed images to differentiate between major structures, and to determine whether nervous tissue contains abnormalities. CT has a spatial resolution of about 1 mm in the plane of section, which is good enough to distinguish brain regions such as the hippocampus from the amygdala. More recently, magnetic resonance imaging (MRI) has been developed and the most common maps are of hydrogen density. MRI maps (figure A.2) have a much higher spatial resolution (about 0.1 mm in the plane of section, good enough to distinguish the line of Gennari, layer 4 of striate cortex), a better signal-to-noise ratio, and involve no conditions harmful to the subject, thus permitting studies of normal brain. The principle of MRI depends on placing the tissue in strong magnetic fields and inducing and measuring changes in the magnetic orientation of the nuclei of atoms which make up tissue. Patients are merely required to lie still in a magnetic field for about 15 min. These two techniques are very useful for localizing lesions, tumors, and developmental abnormalities, but are thus far limited in not being able to assess functional damage that leaves the brain structures intact. So far they have provided only static images of brain anatomy, not dynamic information about brain activity. They can, however, be used in conjunction with techniques for measuring dynamic changes in brain activity; these techniques are summarized below.

In addition to mapping hydrogen, it is also possible to map other chemical elements in the brain using MRI, especially elements such as sodium and phosphorus whose concentrations vary with the functional state of the brain. However, the concentration of sodium, phosphorus, and other chemical ele-

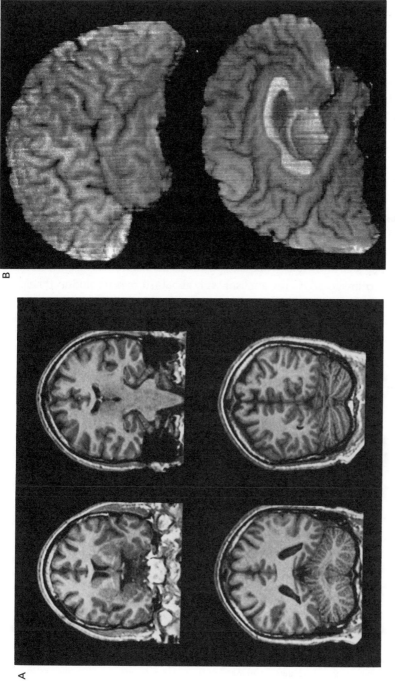

Figure A.2 (a) Four coronal sections of the human brain visualized with magnetic resonance imaging (MRI). Note the perfect separation of gray matter (cerebral cortex, basal ganglia and thalamus) from white matter. (Courtesy Hanna Damasio.) (b) Three-dimensional brain reconstruction obtained in a living human. The reconstruction is based on the manipulation of raw data from MRI using a multistep program (BRAINVOX, developed by Hanna Damasio and Randall Frank, University of Iowa). The technique permits the visualization of all major sulci and gyri, the rotation of the reconstructed volumes in space, the slicing of the 3-D volume in any desired plane of cut, and 2-D to 3-D conversion of data points. (Courtesy Hanna Damasio.)

ments in living tissue is much less than that of hydrogen, and hence the signal-to-noise ratio and the resolution with which a chemical element can be mapped using MRI is also much less. Strategies for increasing the sensitivity of MRI are, however, being explored, and functional MRI spectroscopy with millimeter resolution is on the horizon.

The link between electrical activity and metabolism is exploited in the 2-deoxyglucose (2-DG) technique (Sokoloff 1984) in which a radioactively labeled sugar analog is injected into the blood and is selectively absorbed by neurons that have elevated levels of metabolic activity. In animals it is possible to section brain tissue and expose the brain tissue to x-ray film, thereby producing an image of local glucose metabolism with about 0.1 mm resolution. Figure A.3 is an image of responses in monkey visual cortex produced after presentation of a visual stimulus (Tootell et al. 1982) consisting of a flickering bull's-eye pattern. This is the first image to portray the remarkable correspondence between features in the world and activity patterns in a topographically mapped area of cortex. In humans, positron emission tomography (PET) can be used to image 2-DG metabolism with about 10 mm resolution (Phelps and Mazziotta 1985).

One of the disadvantages of the 2-DG technique is that the activity must be averaged over 45 min, which is a very long time when we consider that a

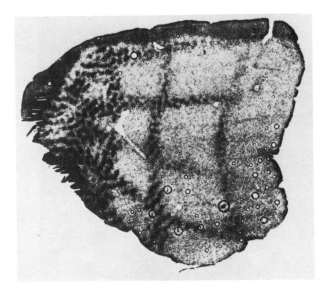

Figure A.3 Pattern of activity in layer 4 of primary visual cortex of a monkey visualized using the 2-deoxyglucose technique. About half of the total surface area of V1 in one hemisphere can be seen in this flattened map. The visual stimulus, presented to only one eye, was a flickering target centered on the fovea consisting of eight radial lines and five concentric circles equally spaced on a logarithmic scale. This bull's-eye pattern was flickered because most neurons in visual cortex respond best at the onset or offset of the stimulus. The pattern of elevated brain activity is shown in this autoradiogram by the dark regions. The stripes on the dark lines are interruptions from the ocular dominance columns of the unstimulated eye. (From Tootell et al. 1982.)

visual recognition task can be performed in under 500 msec. The time required to process the brain tissue and to expose it to x-ray film can be many months. Too much brain activity will saturate the response over large brain regions, obscuring any real differences between them. Moreover, it is not possible to match the experiment with a control run in the same animal since the animal must be sacrificed to produce an image on film, and humans are limited to a single PET scan in one session. Because of variability between individuals, and even the same human in different sessions, averages over many subjects must be obtained. There is the additional complication of an uncertain link between glucose metabolism and electrical activity. The presumption is that they are tightly coupled in the neuropil, but while this is reasonable, it is not known for sure in all brain areas. Nonetheless, comparisons between the 2-DG mapping and conventional electrical recordings provide a more comprehensive view of global processing (Jones et al. 1987) and have revealed important data about topographical organization of neuronal properties within brain areas and projections between regions.

Regional blood flow can be used to monitor variable metabolic demands due to electrical activity (Ingvar and Schwartz 1974, Roland 1984a, Raichle 1986). Blood flow is measured by following the clearance of a bolus of xenon-133 injected into the carotid artery monitored with external radiation detectors. A related method is to measure the changes in blood volume with PET following the injection of oxygen-15–labeled water into the blood. One great advantage of these methods is that several different conditions can be studied in a single session since the clearance times and half-lives are only several minutes. These techniques have been used to study voluntary motor activity (Fox et al. 1985) and selective attention to somatosensory stimuli (Roland 1984b). Typically the results are averaged, usually over ten individuals, to obtain results. The current spatial resolution of PET scanning is around 10 mm, and the ultimate resolution, limited by the range of positrons, is estimated to be 2–3 mm. However, using an averaging technique that is applicable to point sources it has been possible to map the visual field in the primary visual cortex of humans with a resolution of 1 mm (Fox et al. 1987). Locating the anatomical region corresponding to the region of activation is generally done by mapping the PET scan onto an idealized brain. Unfortunately, however, there are considerable individual differences between brain landmarks, and even within an individual there are asymmetries between left and right hemispheres that are ignored in the idealized brain. Given these individual differences, the error in location can be as much as 2 cm, a huge magnitude for the micro realm of nervous systems. Some researchers (Damasio) are setting up new PET facilities where an individual's own MRI scan is used as the anatomical template on which to map that very individual's PET scan. This presumably will lend greater accuracy to localization procedures.

PET recording offers significant opportunity to investigate the localization of higher functions, including language abilities in man. For example, cognitive tasks such as reading single words have been studied using a subtractive technique to localize individual mental operations (Petersen et al. 1988, Squire

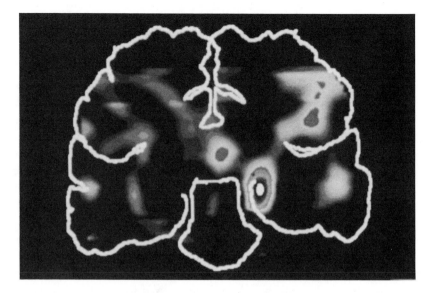

Figure A.4 A 2 mm-thick coronal section showing increased blood flow relative to baseline during a memory task using positron emission tomography (PET). The area of activation is in the right medial temporal lobe in the region occupied by the hippocampus and the right parahippocampal gyrus. (See figure 5.1A for the corresponding anatomy.) In this region, the "bull's-eye" is to be interpreted as a contour map: the center is the area of greatest relative increase in blood flow (about 6%). In order from the innermost torus to the outermost torus are presented relative increases of 5%, 4%, 3%, 2% and 0. Subjects were presented with a list of 10 words to study (MOTEL, ABSENT, INCOME, etc.). After about 3 minutes the scan was begun. During the scan, the subjects were given the first three letters of a word and asked to complete the stem. In condition A, the fragments given the subject for completion were the same as the first three letters of words drawn from the list (e.g., MOT, ABS) and subjects were told to complete the stem to form a list word. This, therefore, was a condition of cued recall. In condition B, the fragments were unrelated to the list words (e.g., DES, BOT), and subjects were asked to use the fragments to form the first word that came to mind. By contrast, this was not a cued recall task but a generation task. The highlighted areas in the PET scan represent the difference in blood flow between the recall and the generate conditions; specifically, the scan shows an increase in blood flow in the hippocampal regions during recall (condition A) relative to generation (condition B). (From Squire et al., in press.)

et al., in press) (figure A.4). There are, however, a number of confounding variables that have to be carefully separated, such as subvocal motor activity that often accompanies mental activity and the probability that *decreases* in activity might be as significant as increases.

A promising approach for use on animals is the optical recording of electrical and ionic changes in the brain by direct observation. New optical dyes have been developed for noninvasive monitoring of changes in the membrane potential of neurons (Salzberg et al. 1983, Grinvald et al. 1986). This technique has been used to visualize the ocular dominance and orientation columns in visual cortex (Blasdel and Salama 1986) (figure A.5). It also appears that small changes in the absorption of red light in visual cortex can be recorded, and that these changes are correlated with electrical responses of neurons even in the absence of dye (Grinvald et al. 1986; Frostig et al. 1990; Ts'o et al. 1990).

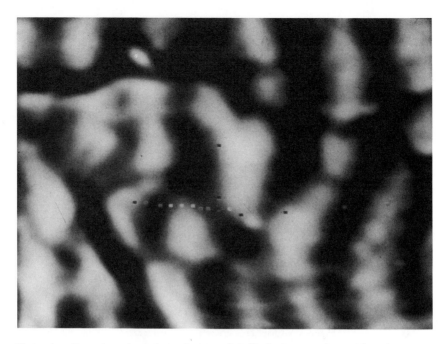

Figure A.5 Computer-enhanced visualization of ocular dominance columns of monkey striate cortex revealed using optical recordings. A voltage-sensitive dye was applied to the cortex. One eye was closed, and the open eye was visually stimulated. Elevated activity among the neurons in alternating bands on the cortex (around 0.3 mm wide) represent ocular dominance columns. Electrode penetrations were made into cortex tangential to layer 4, and the responses of single neurons were recorded (dots). The eye dominance recorded physiologically was consistent with the optical recording. (From Blasdel and Salama 1986.)

Ion-sensitive fluorescent dyes, such as the calcium-sensitive dye Fura-2, have also been developed that can monitor the change in intracellular ion concentration (Tsien and Poenie 1986, Connor et al. 1987; Adams et al. 1991). These optical techniques could be used with confocal microscopy to produce three-dimensional images of physiological activity in vivo (Boyde 1985).

Lest the beauty and remarkable achievements of these new imaging techniques inspire uncritical enthusiasm, it should be emphasized that these techniques introduce potential artifacts as well as many new problems of interpretation, and it may be some time before they can be used routinely and with confidence. Also, none of the imaging techniques is as yet nearly as flexible or has as good spatial and temporal resolution in vivo as recording from single neurons with microelectrodes. Despite such problems, the hope endures that we may someday obtain global views of processing in the nervous system under conditions that are close to normal.

4 GROSS ELECTRICAL AND MAGNETIC RECORDING

The earliest electrical recordings from the scalps of humans were obtained in 1929 by Hans Berger, who recorded the microvolt changes in potential with a string galvanometer. Significant differences in the electrical activity could easi-

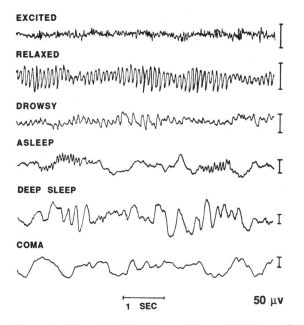

EXCITED

RELAXED

DROWSY

ASLEEP

DEEP SLEEP

COMA

1 SEC   50 μv

Figure A.6 Characteristic electroencephalogram (EEG) traces during variations in states of consciousness. (From Penfield and Jasper 1954.)

ly be seen depending on whether the subject was awake, in deep sleep, or dreaming (Penfield and Jasper 1954) (figure A.6). The electroencephalogram (EEG) has also been useful in determining the general regions of the brain specialized for certain modalities, and thus in locating auditory cortex, somato-sensory cortex, and so forth. A major advantage of the technique is that it is not invasive, and it can be used on alert, behaving, normal humans.

Although the EEG has been helpful in diagnosing diseases of the brain, it has been less useful in uncovering brain mechanisms than was initially hoped. One serious difficulty in relating waveforms to underlying processing activities of neurons is that the EEG recording is a composite signal from volume conduction in many different parts of the brain, and it is far from clear what a signal means in terms of how individual neurons in the relevant networks are behaving. In animals, depth electrodes can be inserted and used to sort out the locations of the strong sources, but in humans this technique can be used only under special conditions where there is clear clinical justification. But even under the most favorable circumstances, the localization of EEG sources is difficult and problematic.

The event-related potential (ERP) can be extracted from the EEG recordings by signal-averaging scalp potentials that are time-locked to a particular sensory stimulus or motor event (figure A.7) (for a review, see Hillyard and Picton 1987). For example, the experimenter might present a subject with a visual stimulus, take an EEG recording on each of ten trials, and then average these traces. Significant progress has been made in relating specific components of the ERP trace to different aspects of sensory perception. For example, reliable

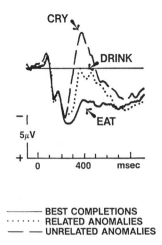

THE PIZZA WAS TOO HOT TO

BEST COMPLETIONS
······ RELATED ANOMALIES
— — UNRELATED ANOMALIES

Figure A.7 Results of experiment using the event-related potential (ERP) to study language processing in humans. Ten subjects were presented with 160 different seven-word sentences, one word presented every 700 msec via a slide projector. All subjects were presented with the same first six words (for example, "The pizza was too hot to," but for the final word saw one of three different words (in this example, either "cry" or "drink" or "eat"). Recording electrodes were placed on the scalp at the midline in the parietal zone. The figure shows the grand average ERPs to the most expected sentence completions (e.g., "eat"), anomalous completions (e.g., "cry"), and anomalous completions related to the most expected word (e.g., "drink"). The grand average for the final word is achieved by averaging waveforms across sentences (80 expected completions, 40 anomalous completions, and 40 anomalous but related completions) and across subjects. The N400 waveform is largest when the final word presented is an unrelated anomaly, as in "The pizza was too hot to cry," and flattest when the final word is fitting, as in "The pizza was too hot to eat." (Courtesy Marta Kutas and Cyma Van Petten).

patterns in waveform are produced in the first 50 msec after the stimulus has been presented, and these vary in reliable ways as a function of whether or not the stimulus was sufficiently long or intense to be consciously experienced. Other waveforms occurring later appear to reflect higher-level information processing. At about 300 msec after the stimulus, a large positive waveform (P300) is produced if the stimulus was surprising or unpredicted by the subject (Donchin et al. 1983), and this has been replicated in monkeys (Paller et al. 1989). The discovery of a large negative waveform (N400) in conditions where a subject is presented with a semantic incongruity (Kutas and Van Petten 1988) suggests that this technique can be used to study certain aspects of language processing. Other characteristics of the waveforms have been useful in arbitrating hypotheses about language processing and in addressing questions concerning the temporal sequence of language-processing events (Van Petten and Kutas 1987). Unfortunately, some of the components of the ERP are probably not unitary but have several sources of different magnitudes under different experimental conditions. For example, P300 appears to have both cortical and subcortical sources.

The currents in neurons give rise to magnetic as well as electric fields. These magnetic fields are not affected by volume conduction, as is the EEG, so current sources are more easily localized than are the electric fields, and can be measured with sensitive superconducting magnetometers (Williamson and Kaufman 1987). One strategy therefore, is to try to correlate magnetic field properties with aspects of information processing. However, it is not possible to reconstruct the internal current sources from the magnetoencephalogram (MEG) without making additional assumptions about the spatial distribution of the sources. Nonetheless, it has been possible to map parts of the visual cortex in humans, and to show that primary auditory cortex is tonotopically mapped with a logarithmic frequency scale. The MEG technique is still very new and its potential has not been fully explored. In particular, arrays of magnetic sensors will soon be available which will speed up the process of producing magnetic brain maps.

5 SINGLE-UNIT RECORDING

Most of our knowledge of the response properties of single neurons has been derived from the method of single-unit recording. In this technique a microelectrode with a sharp tip is inserted into the brain and used to record local extracellular potentials. Intracellular potentials can also be recorded using extremely fine glass micropipettes; however, stable intracellular recordings in vivo are possible for only a few minutes compared with several hours for extracellular recordings. One major advantage of recording from single units is high spatial and temporal resolution, and many groundbreaking results have been achieved using the technique. For example, we have learned much about the architecture of visual cortex in animals following the pioneering work of Hubel and Wiesel (1962). The discoveries concerning topographically mapped areas of cortex all depended on using single-unit recordings.

More recently, it has become possible to study the changes in single-unit responses in the visual cortex of awake behaving animals to directed visual attention (Moran and Desimone 1985) and task-dependent variables, such as whether the animal is searching for a specific visual pattern to match a presented tactile pattern (Maunsell and Newsome 1987, Hanny et al. 1988). However, the higher in the visual hierarchy one looks, the more difficult it is to find the adequate visual stimulus for a neuron, though there are tantalizing reports of neurons selective for hands and faces (Barlow 1985, Perrett et al. 1987) and of neurons in the hippocampus selective for spatial location of the animal (O'Keefe and Nadel 1978). However, in the higher visual areas and in association cortex it is not at all clear that the stimuli chosen are the appropriate ones to use, or even how the responses should be interpreted. For example, it may be that cells that were thought selective for faces may in fact also respond to more abstract stimuli, such as a particular class of fractal shapes (Mandelbrot 1983, Pentland, 1984, Miyashita and Chang 1988). Furthermore, there is always the worry that we are missing an important population of neurons because of low yield and selective sampling. (See also chapters 3 and 4.)

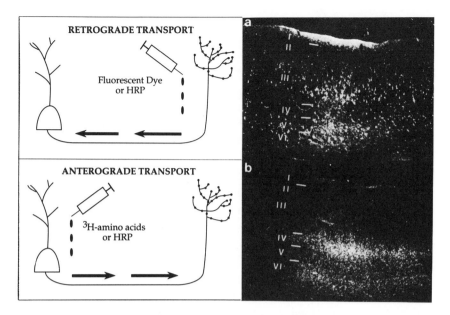

Figure A.8 Anatomical methods for tracing long-range axonal projections in the retrograde (backward) and anterograde (forward) directions. (a) Horseradish peroxidase (HRP) was injected into regions of cerebral cortex where it was taken up by the axon terminals and transported retrogradely to the cell bodies. Labeled neurons are shown in layers III and V. This is the typical pattern found in a feedback projection (see figure 2.3). (b) Radioactively labeled amino acids were injected into a cortical area, taken up by local cells, and transported anterogradely to another cortical area where the axonal terminal arborizations can be visualized with autoradiography. Dust-like silver grains are particularly dense in layers IV and VI. This is the typical pattern found in a feedforward projection (see figure 2.3). (From Goldman-Rakic 1990.)

Many response properties of single neurons are highly correlated with properties of sensory stimuli and movements, but the responses of relatively few cells have been correlated with what an organism perceives. For example, many neurons in the primate visual system respond differentially to the wavelength of light. However, our perception of color depends more on the reflectance properties of surfaces, so that the perception of color is roughly constant under varying illumination. Only a small subset of neurons in visual cortex respond in a way that is similar to the perceptual report of color (Zeki 1983). If most neurons in visual cortex respond to the spectral composition of a scene, why do we not have perceptual awareness of this information? For that matter, most neurons in V1 have an ocular preference, and some cells respond only to one eye, but when a spot of light is randomly shone into the one of the eyes, an observer cannot report which eye was stimulated despite all the information contained in single-unit responses. In general, the higher a neuron in a sensory system, the more likely that its response can be related to the animal's perceptual responses. For example, some neurons in V2 but not in V1 respond to illusory contours, such as Kanizsa figures (von der Heydt et al. 1984). A further problem is that responses correlated with behavior may not be causally necessary and sufficient for that behavior. For example, there is a massive change in the firing rate of hippocampal neurons in a rabbit during conditioning of an eye-blink response, but lesioning the hippocampus after training does not affect the acquired response and rabbits without a hippocampus show normal conditioning (Berger and Thompson 1978).

Properties of networks of neurons cannot be simply inferred on the basis of the properties of small samples of cells, yet determining network properties is probably essential for understanding perceptual mechanisms. Therefore, to understand the principles of spatiotemporal coding in networks of neurons, much more work has to be done to discover what is happening in a larger population of cells. Methods for obtaining simultaneous multi-unit recordings are being developed, and it is already evident that network properties to which we are blind when restricted to single-unit methods become accessible when behavior of a larger population is observed, such as synchronous firing (Reitboeck 1983, Gerstein et al. 1983, Llinás 1985, Gray et al. 1989). Desirable though these methods are, the technical problems in developing them are immense. Optical techniques for recording cellular responses (see above) may also prove useful in addressing population properties, but they have not yet achieved single-unit resolution in cortical structures in vivo.

6   ANATOMICAL TRACT TRACING

The earliest method devised for tracing the origins of axons projecting to a structure was to destroy the structure. This would destroy the axon terminals, and the projecting cell bodies throughout the nervous system would undergo chromatolysis, a reaction in which the Nissl bodies disappear. When the tissue is stained with a Nissl stain, such as cresyl violet, the cell bodies look pale but keep a dark blue edge. One problem with this method is that fibers of passage are also destroyed. This retrograde tracing technique has since been supplanted by other methods that rely on injecting substances into the area rather destroying it. One of the most important technique is based on the retrograde transport of horseradish peroxidase (HRP) (figure A.8). HRP is absorbed by the local nerve terminals and travels up the axons toward the cell body at a rate of about 200 mm a day. Following sacrifice and perfusion a few days later, the tissue is sliced in 50-μm sections and reacted with a substrate, such as diaminobenzidine. HRP is an enzyme that reacts with the substrate to produce a massive amount of pigment, easily localized in cell bodies, often filling the dendrites.

Axons can also be traced in the anterograde direction, toward their terminals. The earliest techniques depended on the selective staining of disintegrating axons and surrounding myelin following axotomy, a process called Wallerian degeneration. Axoplasmic transport can also be used to trace axonal pathways in the anterograde direction using radioactively labeled amino acids. Amino acids such as proline are absorbed by the cell bodies, where they are incorporated into proteins that are shipped down the axons to replenish turnover at the terminals. Following fixation and sectioning, the tissue is exposed to a photographic emulsion, which is sensitive to the decay of the radioactive label, typically tritium. Months later the sections are developed photographically and the silver grains visualized with light microscopy using dark-field illumination (figure A.8). In some cases, the radioactively labeled amino acids spill out of the terminals at the end of their first journey, to be taken up once again by local neurons, some of which may project to another area. In this manner it is possible to label pathways transneuronally. This method has been used to great advantage in labeling ocular dominance columns in primary visual cortex following the injection of tritiated proline into one eye (Hubel et al. 1977).

Heimer and RoBards (1981) provide more details about these tract-tracing techniques and many others methods. Nauta and Feirtag (1986) have an accessible account of the many fiber tracts that have been traced with these techniques.

Notes

CHAPTER 1

1 For a more complete account, see Selverston and Moulins (1987).

2 Howard Hughes conference on Neuroscience and Philosophy, Spring 1989, Coral Gables, Florida.

3 Actually, matters are a bit more complicated. For a fuller discussion of this issue, see P. M. Churchland (1975).

4 William Baxt has developed a net for diagnosis of coronary occlusion in patients presenting with acute anterior chest pain (Baxt 1990).

5 These levels have been postulated within a single brain. However, as Horace Barlow has suggested (personal communication), the levels diagram might be more accurate if it recognized the interaction *between* brains and added a step to the topmost level. The argument for the extension is that the interaction between brains is a major factor in what an individual brain can and does do. Natural selection is one form of interaction between brains that gives rise to the general capacities and predispositions of the brain of a given species. Additionally, given the predispositions an individual has at birth, interactions between conspecific brains as well as between contraspecific brains have much to do with the particular capacities, skills, knowledge, and representations an individual brain acquires. For example, the particular language a human learns may empower or limit him, both in how he interacts with other humans, how he solves certain kinds of problems, and how he thinks about things even when not explicitly conversing. A dog's interactions with its human owner can have a profound effect on the animal's temperament, and perhaps vice versa; seals growing up in an environment with killer whales and those without killer whales are likely to have a differently configured "predator space." Although we agree with Barlow that the social level is very important, it has not been the main focus of this book.

6 See, for example, Jack et al. (1975), Rall (1977, 1989), Perkel and Mulloney (1978), Segev et al. (1989), and Yamada et al. (1989).

CHAPTER 2

1 The original conception of levels of analysis can be found in Marr and Poggio (1976, 1977). While Marr (1982) emphasized the importance of the computational level, the notion of a hierarchy of levels grew out of earlier work by Reichardt and Poggio (1976) on the visual control of orientation in the fly. In a sense, the current view on the interaction between levels is not so much a departure from the earlier views as a return to the practice previously established by Reichardt, Poggio, and even by Marr himself, who published a series of papers on neural

network models of the cerebellar cortex and cerebral cortex (see, for example, Marr 1969, 1970). The emphasis on the computational level has nonetheless had an important influence on the problems and issues that concern the current generation of neural and connectionist models (Sejnowski et al. 1988).

2 Crick (1979); Churchland and Sejnowski (1988); Shepherd (1988).

3 Rockland and Pandya (1979); Maunsell and Van Essen (1983).

4 For data that undermine the idea that there is a neat processing hierarchy, see especially Malpeli (1983); Malpeli et al. (1986); Mignard and Malpeli (1991).

5 For a small sample of other reaction time experiments, see also Cooper and Shepard (1973), Posner (1978), Eriksen and St. James (1986), Rosenbaum et al. (1987), Treisman (1988).

6 Fetz and Cheney (1980), T'so et al. (1986).

7 For discussion of the computational significance and implications of the expanded foveal representation in visual cortex, see Schwartz 1984.

8 Allman 1982, Hubel and Livingstone 1987, Livingstone and Hubel 1987, Felleman and van Essen 1991.

9 For a review, see Guy and Conti (1990).

10 Crudely, the point is this: information is lost in the threshold-rule conversion of analog values to a discrete value. In a network of input-scanty neurons, the intermediate discrete decisions waste a good deal of the information carried by the intermediate analog signals, and a bigger network is needed to make up for this lost analog information by augmenting the number of intermediate discrete decisions. A *vast number of input-scanty* neurons will be needed to do the equivalent processing job of a *modest number of input-profuse* neurons. Depending on the processing job, the savings in wire and components could be enormous; the fancier the logic of the processing, the greater the savings (Abu-Mostafa 1989a).

11 That is, located well beyond the first cell's receptive field.

CHAPTER 3

1 Those who prefer to skip the philosophical discussion should go directly to section 2.

2 Specifically, what we wish to defuse is the gripe that until exact definitions of computation and computer are formulated, computational neuroscience is a mere pretender that must stop dead in its tracks. In the absence of precisely specified necessary and sufficient conditions, it might be argued, we do not know what we mean, and hence we do not know what we are talking about. But this reasoning is fallacious. Like any science, computational neuroscience begins with primitive ideas and crude results, and it can use its discoveries to revise and redefine its basic concepts, where the revised concepts can serve as a platform for the next research foray. To recognize this sort of co-evolution of theory and experiment is not to sully precision, for precision based on a genuine basis of evidence and theoretical coherence is greatly to be prized. But it is to resist phony precision, precision that cobbles together a contrived definition before the science can begin to decide between this definition and dozens of alternatives. It is to embrace what philosophers and historians of science have slowly come to realize: that the science essentially leads, rather than follows, definitions. (Daniel Dennett wittily dubs the eagerness to forge definitions in advance of adequate data as the "heartbreak of premature definition.") And it is to embrace what many cognitive psychologists and linguists suspect: that typically we learn concepts, including rather abstract concepts, by being presented with good examples of the type. We then expand the range of application as a function of further experience and pragmatics. (See Lakoff 1987, P. M. Churchland 1989.)

3 The one mapping that is generally not considered a function is a 1 : many mapping.

4 An alternative is to include time as one of the axes so that the state evolves along a state-time trajectory, in analogy with space-time trajectories in physics.

5 See also Jordan (1986).

6 For further discussion, see Cummins and Schwarz (1991).

7 Even the notion of "disease," which may seem to be a natural kind, does have an interest relative component. For a remarkable paper in the history of medicine, "The disease of masturbation: values and the concept of disease," see Tristram Englehardt (1974).

8 Determining which function a network computes and what its states represent are by no means straightforward tasks. We shall see in more detail in sections 5–7 how some of the difficulties are brought to heel. One worry to allay here is that there can be unresolvable ambiguities for the simple reason that the computational hypothesis is always underdetermined by the evidence. In other words, for any given computational hypothesis, others are also possible (though sometimes just *barely* possible) relative to the *same* body of evidence. For example, one typically assumes that the line connecting two data points is continuous with earlier segments of the line, but that is an *assumption*, not a hidebound necessity. The underdetermination is not, we submit, cause for despair. At least, it is no more problematic than is the assignment of functions to other structures in biological systems, such as hearts and kidneys. Underdeterminacy of hypotheses by the evidence is a rather philosophical consideration, in the lighthearted sense that it is a "don't-worry-now" problem. Ultimately it needs to be addressed because it is puzzling and nontrivial, but in fact most research proceeds perfectly well without paralyzing reflection on this problem.

9 For discussion on this point, see Millikan (1984) and Mitchell (1989).

10 If certain neurons are connected by pathways to transducers for light, and if they respond selectively to events in the visual field, there is a presumption in favor of supposing their job is to process visual information about the outside world. Even if a strangely gifted mathematician could find a completely different function which equally accommodated the neuronal data, say a function that computes the high and low tides in MacFarhlane Cove on the west side of Queen Charlotte Island, this is merely a coincidental, a sheerly fortuitous concurrence, like someone happening to have freckles on her back that can be read as the Tenth Commandment.

11 This game is played on a 3 × 3 board, by two players who alternately mark an "X" or "O" in one of the nine cells. The first person to place three marks in a straight line or diagonal across the board wins the game.

12 One may, of course, use a look-up table for the opening moves.

13 An ornithopter is an airplane that·flaps its wings.

14 In fact, in the 1960s, Steinbuch (1961) was working on this problem.

15 See also Kanerva (1988).

16 See also Amari (1972), Hummel and Zucker (1983), and Cohen and Grossberg (1983).

17 These analogies are useful for thinking but should not be taken literally.

18 The bias is defined as the negative of the threshold, $b_i = -\theta_i$.

19 See also Durbin and Willshaw (1987), Sejnowski (1987), and Peterson (1990).

20 The mathematical proof of convergence, however, assumes an extremely slow cooling schedule—too slow to be practical. In practice, faster cooling schedules are used to produce good solutions, though not necessarily the optimal solution.

21 There is an interesting comparison between how a Boltzmann machine settles into a global configuration and how instructions are executed in a digital computer. At each clock cycle or time step in a digital computer, the inputs set the initial conditions for current flow at the gates

of the digital circuit, but the physical process of reaching a digital answer is an analog settling process that depends on electrical currents and charging capacitors.

22 If it were left up to us, we would not call just any result of application of these procedures "learning." The reason is that we prefer not to prejudge the issue of whether the training exhibited by a given net in fact resembles the paradigm cases of learning by animals. As we shall see, some of the changes produced in nets are rather more akin to neural development or to classical conditioning or to reflex modification than to learning such things as that the chimney is on fire, or how to tie one's shoes, or learning social graces. Our choice was either to coin a new word in the teeth of well-established convention, or to follow the convention and post a caveat. The latter alternative seemed more sensible than a quixotic plan to retrain the linguistic habits of a whole generation of neural net researchers. Thus the caveat: using a learning procedure to train up a net does not guarantee that the net really does "learn" in the paradigm sense of the word.

23 A practical example of unsupervised, monitored learning can be found in the bootstrap algorithm of Hinton and Nowlan (1990). This algorithm is based on a real-world application, namely noise reduction in transmission lines (Widrow and Stearns 1985). The point is to use information already received along the transmission line to improve the accuracy of future transmissions. Moreover, the adaptive algorithm continually readjusts the filtering as the characteristics of the noise change with time. Most high-speed modems for transmitting digital information contain such adaptive algorithms.

24 Principal component analysis, or PCA, has a different name in nearly every discipline: in communication theory it is known as the Karhunen-Lòeve transform, in psychology it is factor analysis, in statistics it is the Hoteling transform, applied mathematicians called it singular value decomposition, electrical engineers use it to create matched filters. The common element to all of these approaches is the method of least squares.

25 When there are no hidden units, the network settles to a fixed state in one step; the Boltzmann learning rule then reduces to the perceptron learning rule (Rosenblatt 1961).

26 Major contributions to the development of these networks include von der Malsburg (1973); Fukushima (1975), Grossberg (1976), von der Malsburg and Willshaw (1981), Kohonen (1984), Oja (1982), Rumelhart and Zipser (1985), and Sanger (1989).

27 Other iterative schemes have been devised, such as linear programming, that converge much faster on some problems, such as this one. Gradient descent has the virtue of being local—a parameter can be updated without global knowledge of all the other parameters.

28 Gradient descent is not the only procedure for reducing error. If one has some knowledge of the shape of the error surface, one can take advantage of this knowledge in designing a suitable parameter-adjusting algorithm. For example, in some cases the error surface has a highly uneven shape, with steep walls for some parameters, gentle slopes for others. A method that took long steps along the valley and small steps on the steeper areas would be more efficient than one that took small steps everywhere without regard for whether it is in the valley or the slope. If the learning rate is too high (the steps are too large), gradient descent tends to oscillate back and forth along the valley walls, whereas other techniques such as line searches and conjugate gradient methods will sprint along the valley quite nicely.

29 This type of network is called a perceptron and was introduced by Rosenblatt (1961).

30 Actually rediscovered, though their paper had much greater impact than earlier work, which included Bryson and Ho (1969) in control theory, Werbos (1974) in nonlinear regression, and Le Cun (1985) and Parker (1985) in feedforward networks.

31 Also called the LMS rule (least mean square) and the Widrow-Hoff rule (Widrow and Hoff 1960) in adaptive signal processing and adaptive control (Widrow and Stearns 1985). The delta rule is also closely related to the perceptron learning rule (Rosenblatt 1961), applicable to feedforward networks with binary units and one layer of modifiable weights.

32 In the general case this is called the credit assignment problem. If something goes right or wrong at the output level, how is credit and blame assigned to internal degrees of freedom? Backpropagation is one way to assign blame to weights inside the network for errors occurring on the outside.

33 Methods for speeding up backpropagation have become a cottage industry because in practical applications time is money. For a sample of these methods see p. 124 of Hertz et al. (1991) and Battiti (1992).

34 The same feedforward network architecture, with suitably preprocessed inputs and more hidden units, can be applied to a wide variety of practical problems, including the prediction of protein structure (Qian and Sejnowski 1988), backgammon (Tesauro and Sejnowski 1989), and automobile navigation (Pomerleau 1991).

35 Pineda (1987a,b), Williams and Zipser (1989).

36 See Elman (1989, 1990) and P. M. Churchland (1989).

37 Semiconductor companies sometimes reverse engineer a chip from a rival company (this happened recently to the popular 80386 microprocessor from Intel). Engineers trying to mimic the chip design of a competitor must avoid patent infringement, and they hence do the reverse engineering by restricting themselves to input—output data but no access to the chip's insides. In particular, the "clean room" restriction for reverse engineering means that even if stolen chip specifications somehow found their way into the company's hands, those in the clean room would have no access to them. This "clean room" reverse engineering task would appear to be as daunting as the Zygon challenge.

38 Broomhead and Lowe 1988, Moody 1989, T. Poggio and Girosi 1990.

39 See Gould and Lewontin (1979).

40 See also Tank (1989) and Zipser and Rumelhart (1990). As Rick Grush has pointed out, strictly speaking the comparison of regions requires co-dimensionality.

41 See Sejnowski (1986).

CHAPTER 4

1 See, for example, Nagel (1974), Vendler (1984), Taylor (1985), Swinburne (1986), Sharp (1990).

2 Bullock et al. (1977); Shepherd (1988).

3 For up-to-date review articles on transducers, see Ashmore and Saibil (1990).

4 For a review paper on maturation of spatial vision, see Blakemore (1990a).

5 Pasternak and Leinen (1986).

6 Stryker et al. (1991) have recently reported evidence for asymmetries in projections from the LGN into layer 4 of cat visual cortex. For experiments concerning the relations between LGN cells and the responses of cells in visual cortex, see Malpeli (1983), Malpeli et al., (1986), Weyand et al. (1986), Schwark et al. (1986), Mignard and Malpeli (1991).

7 For a discussion of a possible computational role of end-stopped cells, see Dobbins, Zucker, and Cynader (1987).

8 Matters are proving to be more complicated than they appeared at first. For example, although V4 was thought to be the major "color" area in monkey, Cowey and his colleagues at Oxford have shown that this cannot be correct (Heywood et al., in press).

9 Jeffress (1948).

10 Knudsen and Konishi (1978), Carr and Konishi (1988).

11 Command neurons were originally described in crayfish, where stimulation of one or a small number of neurons elicited specific behaviors. During animal-initiated behavior, however, each neuron in the group only makes a minor contribution to the total motor output, so that no single neuron is necessary to generate the behavior (Larimer, 1988).

12 It should be said that Hubel and Wiesel themselves were quite cautious on this issue.

13 For further discussion of this issue, see Tesauro and Janssens (1988), Judd (1988), and Baum (1989). See also the earlier discussion of scaling in chapter 3.

14 A law is supposed to be general, and the wheels come off this law when temperature or density is very high. Hence it is the "ideal" gas law.

15 For a very readable account of these phenomena, see Hubel (1988).

16 P. M. Churchland (1986).

17 This network does not address the global problem of how local estimates of shape from shading could be combined with other cues for shape, such as bounding contours.

18 Although the Lehky-Sejnowski network is nonlinear, its "simple-cell" filters are approximately linear. The suggests that a linear analysis could extract the bulk of the information, and Pentland (1989a) has now shown this.

19 Wheatstone actually built the first stereoscope in 1838 using mirrors. Brewster's design is called a "lenticular" stereoscope and became the more common design in Victorian drawing rooms (Gregory 1970).

20 Size constancy refers to the visual perception of an object's size that corrects for viewing distance. Thus if the image of a person is small but the image is seen at a considerable distance from the viewer, the object looks its normal size, whereas if the location of the object is seen to be at close range, the object seems dwarfed—for exactly the same image.

21 Poggio and Fischer (1977); Poggio and Talbot (1981).

22 Barlow et al. (1967), Pettigrew et al. (1968), LeVay and Voigt (1988).

23 The analogous problem in the auditory system appears to be a bit more tractable. Stereophonic perception—the fusion of two slightly different sound signals in the two ears—is also a matching problem that involves frequency-dependent filtering characteristics of the pinnae, and differences in temporal delays and amplitude. A great deal of progress has been made in discovering how this matching problem is solved in the barn owl (Konishi, 1991).

24 For an clear account, see Frisby (1980).

25 In the literature, what we are calling "the screen-door problem" is known as "the transparency problem." There is a problem only when the foreground object is not in fact perfectly transparent, as a clean plate of glass, but has fusable data points, such as a grid, bits of mud, and so forth. Since the problem arises precisely in the imperfectly transparent case, we found it easier to code under the screen-door label. Fusion-Net actually solves certain instances of the screen-door problem straightforwardly and without any extra tweaking or training.

26 For a model of interpolation using a distributed representation of disparity see the section on hyperacuity in depth perception.

27 The problem of unsupervised learning of disparity was first formulated by Hinton who developed a model that was also capable of discovering disparity (Hinton and Becker 1990). It differed from the Schraudolph and Sejnowski model in that it exploited monitored or predictive learning.

28 See also Llinás and Grace (1989). E. Fetz in conversation has mentioned that such oscillations are easy to find in somatosensory, motor, and premotor cortex of the monkey.

29 Evidence for synchronous firing exists in other parts of the brain, most notably the somatosensory system (G. Poggio 1964), auditory cortex (Abeles 1982), and frontoparietal systems (Bouyer et al. 1981).

30 p. 163.

31 For a general overview, see Westheimer (1991).

32 In addition to horizontal disparity of the kind hitherto discussed, there is also some vertical disparity. When a book page, for example, is vertical at a given plane of depth, its right vertical edge will be farther away from the left eye than from the right, and vice versa for the left vertical edge. Consequently, the brain fuses as the same edge two images with slightly different heights. The farther away an object, the smaller the amount of vertical disparity. It can be shown mathematically that egocentric position of the object can be derived from vertical and horizontal disparity. (Mayhew and Longuet-Higgins 1982). It appears, however, that the brain may calculate egocentric distance without making much, if any, use of vertical disparity information.

33 For a more detailed discussion, see Lehky, Pouget, and Sejnowski (in press).

34 For a review, see McIlwain (1991), and note that he uses the expression "population averaging" where we use "vector averaging."

CHAPTER 5

1 See Tulving (1983), Squire (1987), Sutherland (1989).

2 Dudai (1989).

3 Stent (1981); White et al. (1986).

4 Garcia and Koelling (1966).

5 Nottebohm et al. (1981).

6 Horn (1986); Mason and Rose (1987).

7 Goldman-Rakic (1988). See also section 7, Back to Systems and Behavior.

8 Lynch et al. (1989a,b).

9 MacIntosh (1983).

10 Kandel et al. (1987).

11 Gelperin (1975), Gelperin et al. (1985). A fifth category might also be mentioned here, namely reorganization following a lesion (Merzenich et al. 1990, Pons et al. 1991).

12 Northcutt (1981); Menzel (1983); Alkon (1984); Hawkins and Kandel (1984); Hille (1984), (1987).

13 Scoville and Milner (1957).

14 Warrington and Weiskrantz first identified priming.

15 Zola-Morgan and Squire (1984, 1985, 1986); Zola-Morgan, et al. (1989).

16 For a review, see Squire and Zola-Morgan (1988).

17 See chapter 4, section 8, Stereo Vision.

18 See also Konorski (1948).

19 The expression "long-term potentiation" was first coined by Graham Goddard in 1979.

20 In their paper, "Neurons, numbers and the hippocampal network," Amaral et al. have made crucial calculations of many other computationally relevant properties: dendritic spine density on the CA1 and CA3 pyramidal cells (about 1 spine/μm), and hence larger pyramdals have about 12,000 spines. A CA1 pyramidal cell receives input from about 5500 CA3 cells, or about 1.8% of the population.

21 For more discussion of this problem, see Morris (1989).

22 This discovery was made by Collingridge et al. (1983). APV is 2-amino-5-phosphonopentanoic acid.

23 For a hypothesis to explain how APV selectively blocks the NMDA receptor, see Collingridge and Bliss (1987).

24 For lesion and cellular data concerning spatial sensitivity of the hippocampus, see O'Keefe (1976), McNaughton (1988), and Quirk et al. (1990), and for functions other than spatial mapping in spatially sensitive cells, see Eichenbaum et al. (1987).

25 For a discussion of the various possible roles of NMDA receptors, see N. Dale (1989).

26 This cooperativity between S_1 and S_2 was discovered by McNaughten et al. (1978) before the discovery of the NMDA receptor.

27 Buzsáki (1989), p. 558.

28 For further discussion about the origin of theta rhythm and its relation to inhibitory interneurons, see Stewart and Fox (1990).

29 Ca^{2+} spiking in dendrites was originally discovered by Llinás and Hess (1976) Llinás and Sugimori (1980) in Purkinje cells of the cerebellum. Regehr and Tank (1990) discovered Ca^{2+} spiking in the dendrites of hippocampal cells.

30 For a review, see Llinás and Walton (1989).

31 They also studied LTP in the isolated brain of the guinea pig, stimulating the piriform cortex with a burst that mimics the theta rhythm (See also Larson et al. 1986). For brevity, we confined our discussion to their slice preparation.

32 That is, the kind of LTP studied by Bliss and Lømo (1973), and Kelso et al. (1986).

33 For a recent review, see Cline (1991).

34 Harris and Cotman (1986) and Jaffe and Johnson (1990).

35 For discussion of Marr's paper, see Willshaw and Buckingham 1990, Willshaw 1991, and McNaughten 1991.

36 Or "Pax!" for the English, but meaning, "I give up!"

37 For an excellent and up-to-date discussion of LTP and LTD, see Siegelbaum and Kandel (1991).

38 See also Clothiaux et al. (1991), Willshaw and Dayan (1990), and Hancock et al. (1991).

39 See also the discussion in Brown (1990).

40 For a recent report on enhanced metabolic activity in the diencephalon during working memory tasks, see Friedman et al. (1990).

41 See also Miyashita and Chang (1988) and Fuster (1990).

42 For an interesting and different model, see Dehaene and Changeux (1989).

43 See Zucker (1989).

44 See also Eckhorn et al. (1988) and, for a short review, see Bressler (1990).

45 For a modeling of the Gray et al. data, see Baldi and Meir (1990).

46 Steriade et al. (1986), Marder et al. (1987), Barna and Erdi (1988); Llinás (1988), McCormick (1989), Pöppel (1989).

47 See the papers in the collection edited by Rubin (1986).

48 Cynader and Shaw (1985); Purves (1988); Cline (1991); Harris and Holt (1990); Lam and Shatz (1991).

49 Oppenheim (1985).

50 Miller, Keller, and Stryker (1989), pp. 605−606.

51 Kleinschmidt et al. (1987), Clark et al. (1988).

52 For some intriguing historical observations on brain specialization, see Harrington (1985).

53 See also Douglas et al. 1989 on the canonical microcircuit for neocortex.

54 The lexicon is essentially all the words in the speaker's vocabulary, together with their meanings.

55 This leaves aside also data from experimental psychology on normal subjects.

56 See also Warrington (1981); Warrington and McCarthy 1983; Caramazza (1988); Semenza and Zettin (1989); Caramazza and Hillis (1990).

57 We owe these ideas to Paul Churchland.

58 For a discussion of the problems in interpretation of single cases, see Bates et al. (1991).

59 Experimental rerouting of pathways in early development can induce the sensory afferents of one modality to project to central targets of a different modality. See Frost and Metin (1985), Neville (1990), and Sur et al. (1990).

60 It might be insisted that even if the network hypothesis to explain the lesions is approaching the issue correctly, still the behavioral dissociation means there are at least "virtual modules." Is any good done by introducing this notion? Perhaps, but it is not obvious. Ultimately, it is a pragmatic and semantic issue whether someone can profitably invoke "virtual modules" when a single network is trained up to a hierarchy of categorizations. Doing so may, however, promote more confusion than insight. In the same way, one could call a wagon a bicycle, adding that it merely has four wheels instead of two, a pulling handle instead of handlebars, and that one pushes one's feet on the ground instead of pedaling. But apart from these details, a wagon is basically a bicycle.

61 See also Charles and Logothetis (1989).

62 This possibility was raised by Antonio Damasio (personal communication), and is currently being explored by him.

CHAPTER 6

1 Beer (1990), Gallistel (1990).

2 This analogy was drawn from a remark made by John Hopfield during a lecture at the University of California, San Diego in 1990.

3 This is not really a visual space, but a space for eyeball position. Simplicity is the goal here, however, so for sheerly didactic purposes, it is useful to represent visual location in this unrealistic manner.

4 A static system, by contrast, is one whose functions are time independent.

5 Nicholls and Baylor (1968), Ort et al. (1974), Granzow et al. (1985).

6 This sort of organization has been found in other species. For example, cricket head-cleaning behavior (Hensler 1988) involves distributed control of motor neurons. See also Larimer (1988) and Murchison and Larimer (1990).

7 Fuchs and Kimm (1975), Lisberger and Miles (1980).

8 For example, Pellionisz (1985).

9 This calculation was pointed out by Steve Lisberger.

10 A cell-killing infection or warm water in the semicircular canals on one side will also produce this effect, though less severely than ablation.

11 The head-only tracking condition requires the suppression of VOR-induced eye movements. In this condition, therefore, the interaction of VOR commands and pursuit commands eventually settles into a "no command" situation and the eyes remain fixed. A computer model trying to do head-only tracking but limited to feedforward VOR and feedback pursuit pathways turns out to be unstable. Shortly after getting started, the network oscillates wildly and hence does not settle into good tracking. This is because the VOR pulls the eyeballs one direction, the pursuit system pulls them another, the image motion signal increases, and the system cannot converge on zero eye movement. What prevents oscillatory pathology in real networks? How is VOR suppression achieved? There is a positive feedback loop from the VN to neurons in the flocculus to let the flocculus know the magnitude of the signal sent to the motor neurons. In the normal VOR condition, this positive signal is exactly cancelled by the negative signal from H (image motion signal) because image motion and eye motion cancel and hence the Purkinje cell (PC) has no output. In the eyes-only tracking condition, the PC drives the brain-stem neurons, but the vestibular input does not because the head is stationary. In head-only tracking condition, signals from VOR and the image motion signal interact in the flocculus to compute a more exact motor neuron command than could be computed by either acting on its own. Consequently the feedback loop signal and the VOR signal damp each other down, and cancel each other out in about 100 msec. The final step is VOR suppression. As the amplitude of eye-movement commands decrease, the head-movement signal to the flocculus is proportionally larger than the efference copy that normally cancels it. The vestibular input is therefore allowed to excite the PC, whose output then inhibits the neurons of the brain stem, thereby preventing any residual eye movement commands. Thus VOR suppression is achieved.

12 We present basically the version updated in 1991, including some substantiating facts, rather than the more conjectural version Miles and Lisberger actually presented in 1981.

13 Indirect evidence from latency studies (Lisberger and Pavelko 1988) tips the balance slightly in favor of the first alternative but by no means rules out the second.

14 Paulin et al. (1989) have proposed a model of the cerebellum that has the properties of a predictive filter. Other brain areas that contribute to predictive pursuit include the frontal eye fields (MacEvoy et al. 1991) and parietal contex (Eckmiller 1987).

15 Jankowska et al. (1967a,b) had shown that L-dopa intravenously injected into spinalized cats had a profound effect when the muscles were stimulated, thus indicating a role for L-dopa in regulating neurons in the cord.

16 More correctly, an artificial form of glutamate not found in biological systems, D-glutamate, is used because exogenous glutamate (L-glutamate) tends to be taken up quickly by the transport system and thus cannot sustain activity.

17 This shift in functional wiring is also seen in the stomatogastric ganglion of the lobster (Selverston 1988, Harris-Warrick and Marder 1991).

18 In the electric fish, *Eigenmannia*, NMDA receptors mediate slow changes in signal frequency and non-NMDA receptors mediate fast changes in signal frequency (Heiligenberg 1991).

19 "SSL" contrasts with the OBL constraint (one big lie) that is often made with respect to units in simplified models, namely that activation of a unit is the weighted sum of the inputs (J. A. Movshon, personal communication).

20 Because the excitatory synapses outnumber the inhibitory synapses by roughly 5:1.

21 Brodin et al. (1991) Ekeberg et al., (in press).

22 On the question of burst termination, Grillner et al. (1991) found in simulation that the inhibitory interneurons (LIN) which become active mid-cycle had some effect on burst termination, but were not the only factor. As the additional factor, they hypothesized gradual lengthening of the after-hyperpolarization (AHP) following each action potential in a burst that leads to interruption of the burst, with the consequence that the contralateral CC interneurons would be disinhibited, while the ipsilateral CC interneurons would be inhibited. Simulations suggest that lengthening the AHP could play a role in burst termination and that reducing the AHP results in longer burst periods. On the other hand, when locomotion is induced in the cat, not by injecting depolarized current into the cell but by stimulation of the brain stem, AHPs are either very small or nonexistent, and burst termination proceeds quite nicely nonetheless (Brownstone et al., in press). The discrepancy between model and experiment is perhaps a reminder that a property's being derived from a computer model is not enough for neurobiological truth.

23 For a detailed model of swimming in *Tritonia*, see Getting (1989) and Kleinfeld and Sompolinsky (1989); for piriform cortex, see Wilson and Bower (1991) and Granger and Lynch (1989).

24 This is not a new idea. For reviews of corticofugal control of spinal reflexes see Lennard and Hermanson 1985; Sillar 1989.

CHAPTER 7

1 See Poggio et al. (1988).

2 For exceptions, see Metcalfe Eich (1985), Fukushima (1988), Whittlesea (1989), and Jennings and Keele (1991). On attention and the brain, see Neville and Lawson (1987a,b), Posner and Petersen (1990), Johnson (1990), and Hillyard et al. (in press).

3 For a discussion of this issue, see LeDoux (1990).

4 This is Paul Viola's observation, noting that R. Brooks calls the make-it-difficult syndrome "puzzilitis."

5 This is a point sometimes made by Carver Mead.

6 This point was suggested by Paul Viola.

7 For a discussion of the real-world problem of relating symbols in the system to objects in the world, see Harnad (in press).

8 See, for example, Helmholtz (1867), Gregory (1970), and Rock (1983).

9 See Mignard and Malpeli (1991).

10 See Fodor (1975) and Kintsch (1974).

11 See also Koch (1989).

12 Lazzaro and Mead (1989), Faggin and Mead (1990).

13 See Knudsen and Konishi (1978), Knudsen et al. (1987), and Carr and Konishi 1988.

14 This is place-coding, discussed earlier in chapter 4.

15 This is a truly truncated account. For a review, see Knudsen et al. (1987).

16 See Barto et al. (1990) and Sutton (1990).

17 For a discussion of neurobiological data concerning sensory control of movement to a target, see Cordo and Flanders (1989).

18 See J. J. von Üxküll (1921).

19 For earlier attempts along these lines, see Grey Walter (1953) and Braitenberg (1984).

20 See also Dennett (1987), especially chapter 7.

21 For a bit more discussion see P. S. Churchland (1991).

Glossary

Note: Terms in *italics* are defined in the glossary.

A1 See *primary auditory cortex*.

abeyant representation Stored knowledge, equivalent to *long-term memory*, as opposed to current representation, which is equivalent to *short-term memory*.

accuracy Minimum distance that can be perceived between the centers of two stimuli presented in nonoverlapping regions of a sensory space. Also termed acuity or *hyperacuity*. Not to be confused with *resolution*.

acetylcholine Common chemical in the nervous system acting as a *neurotransmitter* when binding to nicotinic *receptors* and as a *neuromodulator* when binding to muscarinic receptors.

action potential Spike or impulse. Output signal of an activated neuron. Brief, all-or-none, regenerative *depolarization* that propagates across an excitable membrane such as an *axon* or muscle fiber.

activation function Input-output function of a connectionist processing unit. Typically, it is a nonlinear, S-shaped sigmoid function, but it can also be a gaussian or some other function, depending on the computation needed for the network.

activation space Neural network term meaning a *state space* with the number of dimensions equal to the number of units in the network. Each point in state space is an *activation vector*. As the state of the network evolves in time, the activation vector sweeps out a trajectory.

after-hyperpolarization (AHP) Hyperpolarization of a neuronal membrane following an action potential or burst of action potentials. Often associated with a particular (I_{AHP}) potassium current.

agnosia Inability to recognize (visual) objects because of an inability to combine components of a visual image into a complete percept. Associated with damage to *inferotemporal cortex*. Agnosia can be very specific, e.g., *prosopagnosia*.

agonist Chemical that binds to a particular *neurotransmitter receptor* and causes the same effect as that transmitter. Thus *NMDA* is a *glutamate* agonist for one class of receptors.

AHP *After-hyperpolarization*.

algorithm Systematic procedure or recipe for carrying out a computation. An instantiation of a rule specifying a computable *function*.

amacrine cell Retinal interneuron receiving input from *bipolar cells* and projecting to *retinal ganglion cells*, other amacrine cells, and bipolar cell axons. Amacrine cells do not have a conventional *axon* and do not fire *action potentials*.

α-amino-3-hydroxy-5-methyl-4-isoxazole propionic acid (AMPA) *Agonist* binding to a subset of *glutamate receptors* (also known as kainate−quisqualate receptors) that are permeable to sodium and potassium ions, causing a brief *depolarization* called an *EPSP*.

2-amino-3-phosphonopropionic acid (AP3)   Glutamate *antagonist* for a subset of glutamate receptors that affect the internal milieu of a neuron, but do not directly alter membrane currents. Found to block homosynaptic *LTD*.

2-amino-5-phosphonovaleric acid (APV or AP5)   Selective *NMDA antagonist*. Infusions of APV block the induction of the NMDA-dependent form of *LTP*.

amnesia   Loss of all *declarative memory* for times before (retrograde) or after (anterograde) the amnesic episode. Associated with damage to *temporal lobe* or diencephalic structures such as the *mammillary bodies* and medial dorsal nucleus of the *thalamus*.

AMPA   *α-Amino-3-hydroxy-5-methyl-4-isoxazole propionic acid.*

AP3   *2-Amino-3-phosphonovaleric acid.*

APV or **AP5**   *2-Amino-5-phosphonovaleric acid.*

amygdala   Collection of nuclei deep in the *temporal lobe* reciprocally connected to *hypothalamus, hippocampus,* and *thalamus*. Part of *limbic system*, controlling emotional behavior and associated autonomic responses.

antagonist   Chemical that binds to the *receptor* of a particular *neurotransmitter* and prevents the neurotransmitter from activating the receptor. *APV* is an *NMDA* antagonist; atropine is an antagonist for muscarinic *acetylcholine receptors*.

anti-Hebbian synapse   *Synapse* that decreases in efficacy when the pre- and postsynaptic elements are active concurrently.

Aplysia   Marine mollusc widely used in neurophysiological studies of invertebrate synaptic modification underlying learning.

apparent motion   Phenomenon whereby spatially separated static stimuli flashed successively at appropriate interstimulus intervals appear to move between the sites of stimulation.

architecture   Structure of a neural network, generally referring to the numbers and types of processing units and their internal organization, such as layers and connections between layers.

association cortex   Areas of neocortex not involved in the processing of primary sensory and motor information. These areas combine sensory information from several modalities and produce motor plans. Once thought to form most of the neocortex in primates, but now believed to be a relatively small fraction.

associative network   One of the simplest types of neural networks, associating one *vector* with another. This is done by multiplying the input vector by a vector of *weights*, component by component, and then adding the products (computing the inner product of the vectors).

astrocyte   Star-shaped *glial cells* that remove debris, buffer extracellular potassium, and contain uptake mechanisms for various *neurotransmitters*. May prove to be an important adjunct for the memory function of neurons.

autonomic nervous system   Division of the nervous system innervating (efferent only) the viscera, skin, smooth muscle, and glands. Divided into the sympathetic and parasympathetic systems.

autoradiogram   Image obtained from placing radioactive material (e.g., neurons labeled with radioactive *neurotransmitter*) next to photographic emulsion.

axon   Principal output process of a neuron. Often branched, sometimes *myelinated*, conducts *action potentials* from the *soma* to the presynaptic terminal where the action potential is transformed into a chemical signal. Can carry information a long distance.

axon hillock   Initial segment. Beginning of *axon* process coming from the *soma*. Contains high density of sodium channels, thus is the site for *action potential* initiation.

backpropagation   Learning *algorithm* for adjusting *weights* in neural networks. The error for each unit (desired minus actual output) is calculated at the output of the network and recursively propagated backward into the network. This makes it possible to decide how to change the weights inside the network to improve its overall performance (*credit assignment problem*).

basal forebrain   Structures including the septum, nucleus basalis, and diagonal band of Broca. They send cholinergic and GABAergic fibers to the forebrain, probably important in memory and arousal systems.

basal ganglia   Forebrain nuclei including the caudate nucleus and putamen (these two make up the neostriatum), globus pallidus, *substantia nigra*, and subthalamic nuclei. Lesion data indicate that this system is involved in the generation of voluntary movement.

basket cell   Class of smooth, inhibitory interneurons making multiple synaptic contacts on the *soma* and proximal *dendrites* of its target. May affect timing of impulses as well as firing rate of the postsynaptic neuron.

binary threshold unit   Type of processing unit, originally studied by McCulloch and Pitts. The activity of such a unit is 1 if the sum of the activity of all units connected to the unit in question multiplied by the value of the connecting *weights* is greater than a certain *threshold*, and 0 otherwise. Used in a variety of networks, such as *perceptrons, Hopfield networks*, and *Boltzmann machines*.

binocular rivalry   Perceptual phenomenon that occurs when incompatible visual patterns (such as vertical and horizontal stripes) are presented one to each eye. These are perceived as alternating with a period of about 1/sec.

bipolar cell   Retinal interneuron connecting photoreceptor to *retinal ganglion cell*. Bipolar cells are divided into on- and off-center cells, being *depolarized* and *hyperpolarized*, respectively, by light activation of photoreceptors.

Boltzmann machine   *Optimization* network guaranteed to find the global *energy minimum* (best solution) to a constraint satisfaction problem. *Simulated annealing* allows the net to jump out of local minima. Has a learning algorithm for setting the values of weights for the hidden units.

brain stem   Base of the brain, made up of medulla, *pons*, and midbrain. Contains many motor and sensory nuclei (including taste and hearing) as well as many fiber tracts going both rostrally to the rest of the brain and caudally into the *spinal cord*.

CA1   *See hippocampus.*

CA3   *See hippocampus.*

calcium   Divalent cation maintained at a low concentration inside neurons and most cells. Used for intracellular signaling, such as release of transmitter from *presynaptic terminals* and induction of *long-term potentiation*. May be the most important ion in the universe.

calmodulin   A 17 KD molecular weight protein. When bound to four calcium ions, this protein reversibly binds to many key enzymes (e.g., *protein kinases*), altering their function. Thus calcium entering through *ion channels* or released internally can modulate many processes occurring inside the neuron.

caudal   Navigational aid meaning "toward the tail end of the organism."

cell death   Process occurring naturally during development whereby up to 75% of initial cells in a structure die. The cells that survive tend to be those that were most active, or were well connected, during their critical period. In some creatures, such as the *nematode*, neurons are genetically programmed to die.

center–surround   Type of contrast-sensitive *receptive field* displayed by *retinal ganglion cells* and *LGN* cells. Consists of circular center that generates an excitatory (on-center) or inhibitory (off-center) response to a light stimulus, surrounded by an annulus of the opposite polarity.

central nervous system (CNS)   Division of the nervous system including the brain, retina, and *spinal cord*.

central pattern generator (CPG)   Functional group of neurons generating intrinsic, coherent, oscillatory patterns. Controls muscles involved in executing well-defined, rhythmic behavior such as chewing or swimming.

central sulcus Cleft in cerebral cortex separating *frontal lobe* anteriorly from the *parietal lobe*, which lies caudal to it.

cerebellum Structure posterior to the pons on the *brain stem* consisting of cortex and deep nuclei. Has a role in the high-level control of motor activity. Lesions lead to characteristic motor deficits.

cerebrospinal fluid Clear liquid chemically similar to extracellular fluid. Found in the ventricles and subarachnoid space of the brain and covering the surface of the whole *CNS*. Has a homeostatic role as a mechanical and chemical buffer for the *CNS*.

chandelier cells Smooth, inhibitory interneurons in cortex making their synaptic contacts exclusively on the *axon hillocks* of their target neurons. Strategically positioned to affect the timing of impulses in the postsynaptic neuron.

chaotic behavior Pattern of activity that appears random (cannot be predicted) and is very sensitive to the initial conditions of the system generating the activity. Occurs in some networks that feed back activity to their own input units.

classical conditioning Learning consisting of acquiring responsiveness (conditioned response) to a stimulus that originally was ineffective (conditioned stimulus) by pairing it with a stimulus (unconditioned stimulus) that elicits an overt response (unconditioned response).

claustrum Thin vertical lamina of gray matter separated from putamen by external capsule. Has reciprocal connections with the cerebral cortex and contributes to *end-stopping* shown by cells in visual cortex. Its overall function remains a mystery, but it is well positioned to help synchronize neurons distributed in the many visual areas.

climbing fiber Cerebellar afferent originating in the inferior olive. A single *Purkinje cell* receives one climbing fiber which makes many synaptic contacts. A climbing fiber discharge causes a large, complex spike in the Purkinje cell.

closed loop Neural circuit operating with negative feedback. Important in homeostatic systems and motor systems, such as eye tracking. Feedback circuits are able to maintain a stable operating point.

CMOS *Complementary metal oxide semiconductor.*

CNQX Antagonist for the *AMPA* subtype of glutamate receptor.

CNS *Central nervous system.*

coarse-coding Term describing the selectivity to stimuli of units mediating a *distributed representation*. Coarse-coding means that the response selectivities of units overlap, because the units have broad *tuning curves*. This allows phenomena such as *hyperacuity*.

cochlea Organ of hearing in the *inner ear* consisting of a spiral structure containing three fluid-filled compartments. Fluid set into oscillation by sound waves causes movement of stereocilia (hairs) on *hair cells* which are the auditory neural transducers. Frequency response of hair cells is place coded on the cochlea, with high frequencies represented at the base of the spiral.

color constancy Phenomenon by which objects appear the same color despite wide changes in the spectral composition of the ambient lighting.

commissure Fibers joining functionally similar areas from each half of the brain across the midline. The *corpus callosum* is a central commissure, and the largest fiber tract in the brain.

compatibility function First step in solving the correspondence problem. For a binary (black/white) image the compatibility for a point on the image is 1 if the image location on the two *retinae* have the same value, and zero otherwise.

complementary metal oxide semiconductor (CMOS) Type of circuit used in *VLSI* utilizing both p- and n-channel transistors. Using both types of transistor means that CMOS circuits have low power dissipation, and high noise immunity and can be used to construct a nearly perfect switch. All the ICs in your PC are probably CMOS.

complex cell   Neuron of visual cortex displaying nonlinear response properties. *Receptive fields* are large and oriented, but the position of the stimulus within the receptive field is not critical. Many complex cells are motion sensitive.

computer   Physical system computing some *function* where the inputs and outputs are taken to represent the states of some other system by an external observer. This definition includes the digital electronic computer, but also covers slide rules and tic-tac-toe machines.

cone   Type of photoreceptor in the *retina* made up of three classes with peak wavelength sensitivities at about 430, 530, and 560 nm, termed blue (short-wavelength), green (middle-wavelength), and red (long-wavelength) systems, respectively. Found at high density in the *fovea*, responsible for color vision at high light levels (scotopic vision).

confocal microscopy   Type of light microscopy that allows focusing on a single image plane within a three-dimensional specimen. Greatly improves the resolution of fluorescently stained tissue.

conjugate gradient descent   Optimization technique for efficiently moving down valleys in an error surface. Uses gradient information but will not follow the gradient when there is a faster way to get to the bottom.

connectionism   Term introduced by Jerome Feldman for a style of computation that emphasizes the pattern of the connections in a networks of neuronlike elements. Usually uses semilinear *activation functions* connected by variable strength *weights*, but includes more complex units such as higher-order units and radial-basis function units.

content-addressable memory   Representations that are accessed not by presenting some filing system reference number but by presenting a partial or distorted form of the representation itself. The output is then the completed representation (pattern/vector completion). This task can be performed by a type of *associative network* with as many output units as input units.

corpus callosum   Largest fiber bundle in the brain. Consists of cortico-cortical axons crossing the midline, integrating the functions of the two cerebral hemispheres. Also allows neurons in the two hemispheres to synchronize their activity.

correspondence problem   Problem in *stereopsis* of knowing which features in one eye's image to match with which features in the other eye's image. Can be solved by the human visual system even for stimuli made up of identical, randomly positioned dots.

CPG   *Central pattern generator.*

credit assignment problem   A general problem with large, complex systems that arises when it is necessary to change internal parameters to reward good performance or penalize poor performance.

critical period   Phase of development during which the components of a brain area are organized, often under the influence of sensory experience (e.g., into *ocular dominance columns*). If this organization is prevented (e.g., by sensory deprivation) during the critical period, it will occur with difficulty or not at all later in life.

curve-fitting   Setting the parameters in a model to fit a set of data points, often by minimizing the squared error between the model and the data for the whole data set.

cytoskeleton   Network of protein fibrillar elements within a neuron that determines neuronal form and mediates the movement of organelles from one region of the neuron to another. Maintains shape, a form of long-term memory.

declarative memory   Memory for explicit experiences and facts, directly accessible to conscious recollection. This type of memory is lost in *amnesia*.

dendrite   Input process of a neuron, upon which *synapses* are made. Consists of a number of branching, tapering cables extending from the *soma*. Conduction of current from the synapse to the soma is often assumed to be passive, though *voltage-dependent* conductances are known to exist on dendrites in some neurons.

dentate granule cells   Cells arranged in a single layer in the *hippocampus* receiving input via the *perforant path* and projecting to the *CA3* field via the *mossy fibers*.

2-deoxyglucose (2-DG)   Analog of glucose taken up by active cells but not metabolized. Radioactively labeled 2-deoxyglucose reveals areas with a high glucose demand. (Brain areas that are highly active electrically are usually highly active metabolically.)

depolarize   Act of making the internal surface of a neuronal membrane more positive with respect to the external surface, usually by the entry into the cell of positively charged ions (sodium and calcium).

2-DG   *2-Deoxyglucose.*

dichromat   Person missing one of the three *cone* systems, usually red or green. Dichromats lose a whole dimension of color vision and cannot, for example, tell red from green. Monochromats have only one cone system and cannot see any color.

disparity   Mismatch in the relative spatial location of images of the same object on the *retinae* of the two eyes, due to the spatial separation of the eyes. Cells exist in visual cortex tuned to specific retinal disparities relative to the plane of fixation. These cells are thought to mediate *stereopsis*.

distributed representation   Representation of information as activity across a large number of units. This allows generalization to occur because of overlapping patterns of activity for related items and makes the information resistant to damage. Also known as *vector*-coding.

dopamine   Catecholamine *neuromodulator*. Dopaminergic neurons are found in the midbrain. Loss and malfunction of dopaminergic neurons are implicated in Parkinson's disease and schizophrenia, respectively.

dorsal   Navigational aid, meaning "toward the back."

dorsal root ganglion   Location of cell bodies of primary somatosensory afferent fibers. Found between vertebrae, adjacent to *spinal cord*.

Drosophila   Fruit fly. Mutations of a single gene can be easily studied due to *Drosophila*'s short generation interval.

EEG   *Electroencephalogram.*

efference copy   Signal from motor *axon* collaterals to an earlier point in the circuit controlling the motor behavior. Allows the network direct access to its own output.

electric fish   Fish generating electrical signals from electric organs (modified muscles) that can be used to stun prey. The electrical signals can also be monitored by some fish, and changes in the patterns of these signals can be used to locate objects in their environment. Common in fish where the water is made opaque by mud.

electroencephalogram (EEG)   Record of the summated electrical activity of large numbers of neurons using surface (often scalp) electrodes. Made up of summated synaptic potentials, not *action potentials*.

electrotonic conduction   Passive transfer of charge (ions) along a neural process (usually a *dendrite*). Velocity, temporal structure, and conservation of charge transferred depend on the membrane resistance and capacitance.

endolymph   Fluid filling the *vestibular organ* and cochlear duct. Chemical composition similar to intracellular fluid (high potassium, low sodium).

end-stopping   Property of hypercomplex cells and special simple cells in visual cortex, whereby the response to an appropriately oriented bar decreases if the bar extends out of the excitatory part of the *receptive field* into an inhibitory zone. This property makes hypercomplex cells good candidates for representing curvature.

energy landscape   *Activation space* or *weight space* of a network with an extra dimension ("height") added representing the energy of the whole network. For networks *relaxing* to the solution of an *optimization* problem, the minimum energy level (global *energy minimum*) represents the optimal solution to the problem. For other networks, can be thought of as an error surface, with the global minimum representing least error.

energy minimum   State that a system is in if changing the activity of any unit results in an increase in energy of the system. A local energy minimum is an attractor because all of the states around the minimum in the *energy landscape* will converge to the minimum upon *relaxation*. A global energy minimum is the lowest possible energy state of the system. For *optimization* networks such as *Hopfield networks* or *Boltzmann machines*, the global energy minimum is the optimal solution to the constraint satisfaction problem the network is configured to solve.

enkephalin   Endogenous opiate peptide *neuromodulator*, a chain of five amino acids. Thought to have many functions, including a primary role in analgesia.

entorhinal cortex   Five-layered cortex receiving input from neocortical sensory and *association areas* and projecting to the *hippocampus* via the *perforant path*. Receives input back from the hippocampus and has feedback projections back to the neocortex. The neurons in this area have complex response properties and can be polymodal.

epilepsy   Common neurological disease characterized by seizures resulting from large collections of neurons discharging in abnormal synchrony. Associated with specific pathologies in only 50% of cases. Often originates in temporal structures such as the hippocampus and inferior temporal cortex.

episodic memory   Division of *declarative memory* concerned with past events in a person's life. This system has a temporal structure—each event is stored associated with some particular time, as in an autobiography.

EPSP   *Excitatory postsynaptic potential.*

EPSP-spike potentiation (E-S potentiation)   Extrasynaptic *LTP*. An increase in the probability of *action potential* firing independent of any increase in *EPSP* size displayed by neurons given *LTP*-inducing *tetanic* stimuli. May be the result of a shift in the balance between excitation and inhibition, but may also be due to changes in the conductance of nonsynaptic, *voltage-dependent ion channels on dendrites.*

ERP   *Event-related potential.*

E-S potentiation   *EPSP-spike potentiation.*

event-related potential (ERP)   Change in potential recorded from many neurons in response to a sensory stimulus. Typically lasts for several hundred milliseconds and consists of a number of positive and negative waves. The potentials are generally recorded on the scalp, and it is very difficult to localize the internal sources of these waves.

excitatory postsynaptic potential (EPSP)   Transient, graded *depolarization* of a postsynaptic cell in response to the release of an excitatory *neurotransmitter* by an activated presynaptic terminal.

exclusive or (XOR)   Binary *function* taking two inputs, each of which can be 1 or 0, and producing an output of 0 if neither or both of the inputs are 1, and 1 if only one of the inputs is 1.

extrastriate visual cortex   Large region of visual cortex outside of the primary visual cortex, area *V1*. Has many (over 24) subdivisions, including: *V2*, a belt of cortex around *V1* that receives input from *V1*; *V3*, an area that receives input from *V2*, and projects in separate pathways to *V4* and *MT*; *V4*, a visual area at the junction of temporal, occipital, and parietal cortices where neurons are responsive to the wavelength and orientation of stimuli; *MT*, in the medial temporal region (also called area V5) which has neurons with *receptive fields* that are large and characterized by motion selectivity; and *MST*, a visual area in medial superior temporal lobe where cells respond preferentially to rotation and expansion/contraction of images.

feature detector   Unit in a network that responds to a particular systemacity in its input, such as an edge (continuous boundary). Unsupervised nets can structure themselves via *weight* changes to represent these features without an external *teacher*.

field potential   Extracellular recording of electrical activity from a population of cells. Cellular basis is generally synchronized *synaptic* currents, not *action potentials*.

finite-state automata   Devices taking sequences of input *vectors* and producing sequences of output vectors. Their state transitions may depend on an internal, finite memory. They can be modeled by recurrent networks.

floccular target neurons (FTN)   Neurons in the *vestibular nuclei* receiving monosynaptic input from floccular *Purkinje cells*. These *neurons* are thought to be a possible site of the plasticity shown by the *VOR*.

flocculus   Flocculonodular lobe of *cerebellum*. Receives primary and secondary vestibular afferents as well as diverse visual input. Projects to *vestibular nuclei*, controlling eye movements and balance of the whole body.

fornix   Fiber bundle connecting the hippocampal area to areas such as the *mammillary bodies*, septum, and contralateral *hippocampus*.

fovea   Small, central area of *retina* ($1°−2°$ in diameter) containing highest density of *cone* photoreceptors to provide high spatial *resolution*. Intervening neural layers are spread to the side to allow light maximum access to the photoreceptors.

frontal lobe   Area of *neocortex* involved in planning, movement, and the generation of speech.

FTN   *Floccular target neurons.*

function   A mapping between the elements of one set (the domain) and the elements of another (the range). A computable function can be specified in terms of some *algorithm* (rule). A noncomputable function is a mapping for which no rule can be provided, e.g., randomly associated elements.

GABA γ-aminobutyric acid. Common inhibitory amino acid *neurotransmitter* in the brain. Binds to GABA-A *receptors*, directly opening chloride-permeable *ion channels*, and GABA-B receptors, opening potassium-permeable ion channels via a *second-messenger* system.

gain field   Modulation of response of a neuron in the visual system by eye position or eye vergence. Found in some neurons in parietal cortex, and likely to be found in neurons at earlier stages of visual processing.

ganglion   Discrete collection of nerve cells, often a nodular mass defined by connective tissue.

gap junction   Physical connection between cells at an electrical *synapse*. Hexagonal connections made from membrane proteins that are bidirectionally permeable to the flow of ions.

Gestalt   Global organization that emerges from multiple interactions between features in an image. Central concept of Gestalt theory of perception.

glial cells   A variety of small cells thought not to generate active electrical signals as neurons do. Function in a supporting role for neurons through buffering the extracellular fluid, scavenging debris, and providing physical structure and *myelin* which sheaths axons. See also *astrocyte*.

glutamate   Excitatory amino acid *neurotransmitter*. Causes opening of *ion channels* permeable to sodium, potassium, and sometimes calcium. Principal excitatory transmitter in cortex.

glycine   Inhibitory amino acid *neurotransmitter* associated with an *ionic channel* permeable to chloride ions. Thought to be important inhibitory transmitter in *spinal cord*. Normal physiological levels of glycine potentiate the response of the *NMDA receptor* to *glutamate*.

Golgi staining   Technique developed in 1873 by Camillo Golgi for impregnating a small, random sample of neurons in a piece of tissue with silver deposit. The stain spreads through the entire dendritic tree and fills some of the *axon*. The staining of axons is more complete in neonatal tissue, which is less myelinated.

gradient descent   Procedure for reducing error while training a neural network based on taking the derivative of the error with respect to each parameter, then changing the parameters such that the net moves down the error gradient to an error minimum.

grandmother cell   Extreme place/local coding theory of neuronal representation. Proposes that a single cell in a particular place with very specific stimulus requirements (e.g., grandmother) is responsible for representing a specific feature in a visual scene.

habituation   Decrease in the behavioral response to a repeatedly presented stimulus. Shown to be due to a decrease in the synaptic efficacy between sensory and *motor neurons* in *Aplysia*.

hair cell   Sensory cell located in *vestibular organ* and cochlea. When stereocilia (hairs) projecting from the cell are displaced by the movement of surrounding *endolymph*, the cell is *depolarized* or *hyperpolarized* depending on the direction of displacement.

hardwired   Term describing neural connectivity, meaning that all connections are specified by the genes, thus essentially fixed and unmodifiable.

Hebbian synapse   Synapse that changes its efficacy according to Hebb's rule: the strength increases when both pre- and postsynaptic elements are active. The synapse may decrease in strength if there is presynaptic activity without concurrent postsynaptic activation.

hidden units   Units in a neural network equivalent to biological *interneurons*, i.e., not input or output units.

higher-order network   Neural network using an *update rule* that defines the output of a unit as the *weighted* product of the inputs, pushed through some *nonlinear function*. Ordinary (first-order) nets specify the output as the weighted sum of inputs.

hippocampus   Located in medial *temporal lobe*, forming a semicircle around the *thalamus*. Receives input from and projects back to *association cortex*. Has role in consolidation of episodic memory. Site of extensive investigation into *LTP*. Composed of a number of distinct regions: *CA3* contains *pyramidal cells* that receive input from *dentate granule cells* and some *perforant path* input. CA3 pyramids send *axons* coursing orthogonally across other CA3 pyramidal apical *dendrites*, also collaterals to *CA1* and into the *fornix*. CA1 *pyramidal cells* receive input from *CA3* pyramids via the *Schaffer collaterals* and project out of hippocampus into subiculum and *entorhinal cortex*.

Hopfield network   *Associative network* that *relaxes* to the solution of an *optimization* problem. Consists of a number of *binary threshold units* with symmetrical *weights* between them. Randomly selected units are flipped on or off if such a change decreases the energy of the system, repeated until the system reaches a local *energy minimum*. Such a network can implement *content-addressable memory*.

horizontal cell   Retinal interneuron receiving input from and providing feedback to photoreceptors. These cells do not fire *action potentials*; indeed their *axons* may be electrically isolated from their *somata*. Some horizontal cells have electrical synaptic couplings between them.

horopter   Curved surface wrapping around the visual field and defined as the set of points from which light falls on the same *retinal* location in the two eyes. Near the fovea these points are in the plane of fixation of the subject.

horseradish peroxidase (HRP)   Method of staining cells by intracellular injection or by extracellular injection and terminal uptake of HRP an enzyme that catalyzes a reaction. The HRP reaction product fills the entire dendritic tree and the entire length of *axons*, so is used for morphological studies and tracing of fiber tracts.

HRP   *Horseradish peroxidase.*

hyperacuity   Perceptual detection of intervals smaller than the resolving power of any single transducer. In visual perception, can be spatial, *stereoscopic*, or chromatic.

hyperpolarize   The act of making the internal surface of a neuronal membrane more negative with respect to the outside, usually by the exit from the cell of positively charged ions (potassium).

hypothalamus   Structure located below *thalamus* regulating *autonomic*, endocrine, and visceral integration.

iconic memory   Very brief (< 1 sec) memory of the preceding visual image, susceptible to masking by subsequent stimuli. May be due to a transient physical change in the sensory transduction system.

indexical representation   Perceptual representation characterizing only what is relevant to the tasks the subject must perform, rather than categorizing everything in the perceptual domain.

inferior colliculus   Midbrain nucleus receiving auditory input, contains a tonotopic map and, in the barn owl, a map of auditory space. Correspondingly, it projects to *A1* via the medial geniculate nucleus and to the *superior colliculus*.

inferior olive   Nucleus in the medulla of the *brain stem* sending *climbing fibers* into the *cerebellum*. Cells here fire at low, irregular rates and probably have a role in motor adaptation.

inferotemporal cortex   Area in anterior *temporal lobe*, concerned with visual processing, specifically the visual recognition of objects. Neurons from this area are reported responding specifically to complex objects such as hands.

inhibitory postsynaptic potential (IPSP)   Generally a transient, graded *hyperpolarization* of a postsynaptic cell in response to the release of a *neurotransmitter* by an activated presynaptic terminal. Inhibition does not *always* reduce the probability that the neuron will reach threshold.

inner ear   Structures in temporal bone including the *vestibular organ* and the organ of hearing, the *cochlea*.

input specificity   Property of *LTP* meaning that the potentiation is confined to the *synapse* active during the tetanic stimulus inducing LTP.

interaural delay   Difference in the arrival time of a sound at the two ears. Delay interval varies as a function of the location of the source. Used by many creatures to detect the location of objects in the horizontal plane.

interictal spike   Intermittent, large-amplitude, negative *EEG* wave recorded between seizures during *epileptic* episodes. Thought to be due to a calcium current-mediated *depolarization* in *cortical pyramidal cells*.

interneuron   Intrinsic neuron that neither conveys sensory information from the periphery nor sends motor signals to effectors. More generally, interneurons do not project out of their own local brain area. Many interneurons are inhibitory.

invariance   Phenomenon displayed by the visual system whereby the image of an object is recognized as the same object regardless of changes in size, rotation, and velocity. Also called size, rotation, or velocity constancy. Invariant recognition of objects reduces the memory required to store the representations of the objects.

in vitro   In the test tube. Living preparation of tissue outside the body, such as *tissue culture* or a *slice preparation*.

in vivo   In the living body. Experimental preparation using a whole animal.

ion channel   Water-filled pore in a cell's membrane that allows ions to flow in and out of the cell (ionic current) according to chemical concentration and electrical gradients. The flow is gated by voltage or chemical binding to associated receptors. The ionic conductance is a measure of the ease of flow.

ion pump   Integral membrane ATPase enzyme (protein) that uses energy to move ions across neuronal membranes against their concentration gradients. Often exchanges pairs of ions, e.g., potassium in and sodium out of the cell.

IPSP   *Inhibitory postsynaptic potential.*

jnd   *Just-noticeable difference.*

just-noticeable difference (jnd)   Difference threshold. Minimum difference between two stimuli that can be detected. The jnd increases in proportion to the magnitude of the reference stimulus.

lagged cells Neurons with long response latency located in the *LGN* possessing *NMDA* receptors but appearing to lack *AMPA* receptors. Postulated that the slow kinetics of the NMDA *receptor/ion channel* complex is responsible for the long response latency.

lateral Navigational aid meaning "away from the midline." This term is used relative to a particular landmark. Thus, each nucleus has a lateral portion, such as the *lateral geniculate nucleus*.

lateral geniculate nucleus (LGN) A nucleus of the *thalamus*, it receives input from the *retina* and projects primarily to layer 4 of *primary visual cortex*. Often referred to as a relay nucleus, its function is largely unknown, possibly having some role in visual attention, or more generally in regulating the flow of information into primary visual cortex.

lateral inhibition Phenomenon exhibited by many perceptual systems that increases the signal strength (activity) of a unit at a point, relative to the background, by inhibiting surrounding units. This mechanism reduces the salience of constant fields and enhances the salience of borders and point sources.

L-dopa Chemical precursor of the *neurotransmitter dopamine*. Provides nonpermanent alleviation of symptoms of Parkinson's disease.

LGN *Lateral geniculate nucleus.*

lidocaine Local anesthetic that prevents *action potentials* in neurons by blocking voltage-sensitive Na^+ channels. Can be used as a reversible lesion: when it wears off, the response should return to normal.

ligand Substrate bound by a *receptor* such as *neurotransmitter* or *neuromodulator*.

limbic system Term designating C-shaped structures bordering *corpus callosum*, including the cingulate gyrus, orbitofrontal cortex, *hippocampus*, and *amygdala*. Devoted to motivation, emotion, and memory. Strongly connected with the *hypothalamus* to control the interaction between emotion and visceral function via the *autonomic system*.

limit cycle State that a system giving a periodic output (e.g., an oscillator) is in if it returns to producing the baseline output pattern after perturbation.

linear function *Function* where the relationship between the elements of one domain and the elements of another (the range) can be described by a straight line. Thus the output of a linear function to a combination of inputs is just the sum of the outputs to each input presented separately.

linearly separable function *Function* in which the input space can be segregated with a straight line. *XOR* is not linearly separable because a straight line cannot be used to separate the inputs that give 1 from the inputs that give 0. Networks must have *hidden units* to solve nonlinearly separable functions. In high-dimensional spaces, the separating surface of a semilinear unit is a hyperplane.

local bending reflex Localized movement of a leech's body away from a mechanical stimulus.

locus coeruleus Nucleus in *brain stem* filled with *norepinephrine*-containing cells projecting widely to almost the whole *CNS*. Has vital role in controlling the stages of sleep/wakefulness.

long-term depression (LTD) Decrease in the efficacy of a *synapse*. Found in the cerebellum when the presynaptic parallel fiber input and a Purkinje cell are simultaneously stimulated. Found in the hippocampus when the presynaptic input is stimulated and the postsynaptic cell is *hyperpolarized* or the postsynaptic cell is *depolarized* without presynaptic activation. Also found in neocortex.

long-term memory Long-lasting, potentially permanent store of information about past experiences. Thought to be due to physical, *plastic* changes in the structure of the brain.

long-term potentiation (LTP) Persistent increase in synaptic strength (lasting hours to days) following a brief, high-frequency stimulation of synaptic inputs. First described in the hippocampus, but found in many brain areas. May be a mechanism for storing long-term memories.

Can be homosynaptic (change restricted to stimulated synapse) or heterosynaptic (other synapses on postsynaptic cell changed).

look-up table Very simple computational principle based on precalculating the answers to a problem and storing them in an organized way such that they can be speedily accessed.

LTD *Long-term depression.*

LTP *Long-term potentiation.*

M1 *See primary motor cortex.*

Mach bands Brightness illusion occurring at a high contrast edge, whereby a thin, very dark band appears on the dark side of the edge and a thin, very light band appears on the light side of the edge. Can be explained by the phenomenon of *lateral inhibition*.

magnetic resonance imaging (MRI) Method for mapping the spatial distribution of atomic nuclei such as hydrogen and phosphorus, based on the precession of nuclear spin in a strong magnetic field. The fine structure in the frequency spectrum of the resonances can be used for studying the chemical environment of these atomic species.

magneto-encephalography (MEG) Dynamic recording of the magnetic field generated by relatively large brain areas. Picks up information that is in a sense complementary (perpendicular) to that recorded by an *EEG*, and has the advantage that magnetic fields are not as heavily filtered by the skull.

magnocellular layers Layers 1 and 2 of the primate *LGN* containing large cells sensitive to motion and gross structure of the stimulus.

mammillary bodies Pair of nuclei located in the posterior *hypothalamus*, connected to the *hippocampus* via the *fornix*. Has a putative role in memory.

mean-field approximation Term from condensed-matter physics referring to the replacement of the detailed, fluctuating behavior of units in a system with their mean activity for purposes of a simpler analysis.

mechanoreceptor End-organ of a sensory neuron that transduces mechanical stimuli (pressure) into a *depolarization* called a generator potential.

medial Navigational aid meaning "a position toward the midplane." This term is used relative to some landmark. Thus, each nucleus can have a medial portion, such as the medial geniculate nucleus.

MEG *Magneto-encephalography.*

membrane time constant Reciprocal of the rate at which a neuron's membrane passively charges or discharges. Defined as the product of the membrane's specific resistance and capacitance.

middle ear Air-filled space between outer and *inner ears* containing bones that conduct vibrations of the eardrum into the fluid-filled cochlea.

mini-nets Extending *vector quantization* from single units to whole networks, such that networks compete with each other to respond to sets of input *vectors*. Each mini-net becomes an expert on one type of input, and a separate "referee net" determines which mini-net should provide the output to any particular input pattern.

mitochondria Intracellular organelles that supply energy for neurons and other cells by producing ATP. Found in high densities in areas with a high energy demand, such as *somata* and *synaptic* terminals.

mobot Mobile robot with small set of behavioral reflexes, responding with little sensory processing to real-world stimuli on a priority basis. Alternative to conventional robotics strategy of simplifying the robot's environment in which relatively complex tasks must be performed.

monoamine Class of chemicals including the catecholamines *dopamine*, epinephrine (adrenaline), and *norepinephrine* (noradrenaline) and the indole *serotonin* acting as *neurotransmitters* in the *CNS* and also having *neuromodulatory* functions.

mossy fibers   Axonal projections from *dentate granule cells* to *CA3* cells in the hippocampus, displaying non-*NMDA*-dependent *LTP*. Also the name for fibers coming into the *cerebellum* and exciting granule cells that in turn activate *Purkinje cells*.

motion capture   Illusion that a stationary foreground object containing many spatial frequencies moves in the same direction as a moving large-field background containing low spatial frequencies.

motion parallax   Monocular cue to depth. Results from the fact that when an observer moves, the images of closer objects pass more rapidly over the *retina* than do those of more distant objects.

motor neuron   Motor output of nervous system. *Soma* located in brain or spinal cord sends *axon* to muscle fiber, ending on the muscle at *neuromuscular junction*.

MRI   *Magnetic resonance imaging.*

MST   *See extrastriate visual cortex.*

MT   *See extrastriate visual cortex.*

multiplexing   Representation of more than one dimension of information in one sensory channel or population of units. In computers this is done by time slicing—each channel gets its turn.

muscle spindle   Stretch receptor within a muscle containing sensory ending of a primary neuron coiled around a specialized muscle fiber (intrafusal fiber).

myelination   Wrapping of axons in layers of the lipid membrane of Schwann cells to provide electrical insulation. This means that the *action potential* has to be regenerated only at certain intervals along the axon (nodes of Ranvier), thus allowing faster transmission.

nearest neighbor   Method of representing similarity of examplars within a category. Exemplars with features in common are clustered together, around a central *prototype* in similarity space. Distance from the prototype defines the degree of similarity of an exemplar (similarity metric). A neural network is naturally configured for this method of representation.

Necker cube   2-D line drawing of a 3-D cube that can be seen alternately in two different 3-D configurations. The switch can be under conscious control, but both configurations cannot be seen simultaneously.

nematode   *Caenorhabditis elegans*, a nematode, or roundworm, with simple nervous system is used in genetic studies because it has a short generation time and is a self-fertilizing hermaphrodite, thus able to rapidly produce many identical copies of itself. Has been serially sectioned and the lineage of every cell determined. (Sidney Brenner)

neocortex   A six-layered, convoluted sheet of cells forming the outer surface of the cerebral hemispheres. Composed primarily of spiny, excitatory pyramidal cells and smooth inhibitory cells. A recent development in evolution, associated with higher mammals. Thought to be the locus of cognition and complex sensorimotor processing.

NETtalk   Artificial neural network trained by *backpropagation* to map letters onto phonemes (reading written text aloud).

neuromodulator   Chemical released from a presynaptic terminal that has a modulatory effect on the postsynaptic cell, such as changing the response of the cell to a *neurotransmitter* or producing a lasting change in the dynamics of a *voltage-dependent* conductance. Peptides and *monoamines* often act as neuromodulators. Typically activate intracellular *second-messenger* systems.

neuromuscular junction   Synapse between *motor neuron axon* terminal and muscle fiber membrane. Site of classic work to demonstrate the quantal nature of *neurotransmitter* release.

neuropil   Tangle of neuronal fibers (*axons and dendrites*) and their associated synaptic contacts. Usually the only locus of *synapses* in invertebrates.

neurotransmitter Chemical signal passed from one neuron to another at a *synapse*. Binds to *receptors* in the postsynaptic cell membrane, usually causing a conductance change.

NMDA *N-methyl-D-aspartate.*

N-methyl-D-aspartate (NMDA) Glutamate analog. Effective agonist for the NMDA *receptor*.

NMDA receptor Normally activated by the binding of presynaptically released *glutamate* and postsynaptic *depolarization* to open its associated *ion channel*. LTP at *Schaffer collateral synapses* in area CA1 of the hippocampus is dependent upon activation of NMDA receptors.

nociception Perception of painful/damaging stimuli.

norepinephrine Catecholamine *neuromodulator* localized in *locus coeruleus* cells. Has a variety of postsynaptic *receptors* and a consequent variety of effects on cells, primarily on *ion channels* permeable to potassium.

normalization Keeping the total activity in a system constant (e.g., by including feedforward inhibition) or the sum of *weights* in a system constant. In a network undergoing learning, this prevents one unit or weight from responding to too many input *vectors*.

nucleus laminaris Nucleus in brain stem of birds receiving auditory input from both ears, computing the *interaural time delay* between the signals from the two ears. This allows localization of the sound source in the horizontal plane. Equivalent to the medial superior olive in mammals.

occipital lobe Area of *neocortex* at back of brain involved in visual processing.

ocular dominance columns Alternating vertical columns of cells in *V1* within the center of which neurons respond only to stimulation in either the left or right eye. The neurons at the borders respond to binocular stimulation.

olfactory bulb Outgrowth of forebrain receiving all input from olfactory receptors, projects directly to olfactory cortex. Spatially segregates neuronal representations of different odors.

open loop Neural circuit operating without error feedback. Allows fast response from simple circuitry, but at the cost of insensitivity to performance.

operant conditioning Instrumental conditioning. Learning by association of an organism's own behavior with a subsequent reinforcing or punishing environmental event.

optic nerve Fiber tract carrying *axons* of *retinal ganglion cells* to many places in the brain, including the *LGN* and *superior colliculus*. The center of the optic nerve carries an artery into the eye to supply the *retina*.

optimization Finding the best solution to a problem bounded by a number of constraints (such as the *traveling salesman problem*). Solutions can be found by *relaxation* of a suitable network such as the *Boltzmann machine* to a global *energy minimum*.

orientation columns Vertical columns of cells in *V1* tuned to a stimulus bar of a particular orientation. Organized in patches of continuously varying orientation, punctuated by discontinuities and singularities.

outer product Method of multiplying two *vectors* to form a matrix. If the outer product of an input vector and the vector representing the activation of units in an *associative net* is taken, a *weight matrix* is created.

Panum's fusional area Region about 10–20 arc min behind and in front of the *horopter* where mildly disparate images can be fused by the visual system to yield perceptions of single objects.

parahippocampal gyrus Three-layered cortex surrounding *hippocampus*. Panic attacks have been linked to abnormalities In the right parahippocampal gyrus.

parallel distributed processing (PDP) Theory assuming that information processing takes place through excitatory and inhibitory interactions between a large number of simple processing units. Hypotheses and concepts are represented as the distributed activity of many units.

parietal lobe   Area of *neocortex* concerned with language, somatic sensation, visuospatial processing, and representation of space in general.

parvocellular layers   Layers 3, 4, 5, and 6 of the primate *LGN* containing small cells sensitive to the detailed spatial structure and wavelength of the stimulus.

patch recording and **patch clamp**   Low- noise technique for recording from single *ion channels* or single cells (whole-cell clamp) based on sucking a patch of membrane onto the end of the microelectrode to form a high-resistance (gigaohm) seal.

P cell   Pressure-sensitive *mechanoreceptor* of the leech projecting to *interneurons* involved in the *local bending reflex*.

PDP   *Parallel distributed processing.*

perceptron   Type of feedforward network using *binary threshold units* studied by Rosenblatt. Has one layer of modifiable weights between the input and output layers. The perceptron learning rule for the weights can be used to improve performance.

perforant path   Fibers projecting from *entorhinal cortex* into *hippocampus*. Mainly terminate in *dentate gyrus* but also go to *CA3* and *CA1*.

PET   *Positron emission tomography.*

phase lag   Fraction of a cycle delay between two systems oscillating at the same frequency. Measured in degrees or radians. Systems with no phase lag between them are phase locked.

pineal gland   Midline structure that receives inputs from the the sympathetic division of the *autonomic* nervous system. Releases melatonin, more during the night than during the day and more in the winter than in the summer. Despite links to circadian rhythms and mood shifts, the function of melatonin is unknown, so the pineal remains a mystery. It is unlikely, though, to be the seat of the soul as conjectured by Descartes.

piriform cortex   Largest olfactory cortical area, consisting of three layers. Receives input from *olfactory bulb*, projects to other areas of olfactory cortex, *neocortex*, and many subcortical structures.

plasticity   Changes in the nervous system that can occur as the result of experience or damage. Plasticity can occur as *synaptic* modification, growth of *axons/dendrites*, and changes in the densities and kinetics of *ion channels*.

plateau potential   Prolonged depolarized shift in the membrane potential of a neuron due to the activation of a conductance permeable to sodium or calcium ions.

pons   Ventral brain stem caudal to the midbrain. Contains pontine nuclei that relay information from the cerebral hemispheres to the cerebellum.

positron emission tomography (PET)   Imaging technique based on detection of radiation emitted by radioactive isotopes inhaled by subject. Blood flow (containing isotope) increases at sites of increased electrical activity, so a dynamic picture of neural processing is possible. Resolution limited to a few minutes and a few millimeters.

post-tetanic potentiation (PTP)   Short-lived increase in the efficacy of a *synapse* that has been subjected to sustained high-frequency stimulation. Thought to be due to loading of the presynaptic terminal with calcium.

power spectrum   Representation showing the amount of energy of a stimulus at each frequency. This representation can be produced by calculating the Fourier transform of the stimulus.

prefrontal cortex   *Association cortex* occupying most of the rostral *frontal lobe*. Lying far from primary sensory or motor areas, it is poorly understood. It has a role in planning voluntary movement. Some areas are known to have a role in guiding eye movements.

premotor cortex   Area 6 of *neocortex*. Closely connected to *prefrontal* and *parietal* cortices, projects to *primary motor cortex*. Involved in identifying targets in space, choosing actions, and programming movement.

presynaptic nerve terminal Synaptic bouton; specialized structure for releasing *neurotransmitter*.

primary auditory cortex (A1) Located in superior temporal gyrus, receives input from medial geniculate nucleus. Contains tonotopic frequency maps and is organized in columns in an analogous way to primary visual cortex, area *V1*.

primary motor cortex (M1) Area 4 of *neocortex*, precentral gyrus. Main output of the cortical motor system. Organized topographically into a distorted motor map of the whole body. Contains giant layer 5 pyramidal cells (Betz cells) that project via the pyramidal tract onto motor neurons in the *spinal cord*.

primary visual cortex (V1) Striate cortex (also called area 17). Region of *neocortex* at pole of *occipital lobe* receiving input from *LGN*. Contains cells responsive to (oriented) bars of light or spots of different wavelengths.

priming Short-term facilitation of performance by the prior presentation of particular stimuli (words, etc.). Can be subconscious, and spared in *amnesia*.

principal component analysis Mathematical method of analysis that finds the most important directions of variance in the data, in a linear fashion. Applicable to neural networks with linear *hidden units*, finding the subset of *vectors* that is the best linear approximation to the set of input vectors. Data containing higher-order statistical properties can be characterized by nonlinear hidden units.

principal curvatures Directions of maximum and minimum curvature along the surface of a curved object. These directions are always at right angles to each other and, together with the orientation of the axes, provide a complete description of the local curvature.

principal sulcus Fold in prefrontal cortex concerned with working memory used for strategic planning for higher cognitive and motor actions.

procedural memory Nondeclarative memory occurring as changes in the way existing cognitive or motor operations are carried out. Many brain areas could be involved. These forms of memory are spared in *amnesia*.

process In anatomy, any linear extension of a neuron, such as a *dendrite* or *axon*. Also called a neurite. In computer science, a program that runs on a computer.

processing unit Node in a network that receives converging information from other processing units and in turn sends outputs to other processing units. The transformations inside the node can be quite varied, ranging from a *binary threshold unit* to a *higher-order* unit and a *radial basis function*.

projective field Output equivalent of a *receptive field*. The projective field of a unit is the group of upstream units activated by the unit in question in response to a specific stimulus. Unfortunately, dynamical measurements of projective fields are currently limited to low-resolution *field potential* recordings in real neural networks.

prosopagnosia Type of *agnosia* in which the subject cannot recognize previously familiar faces. Reported to extend to recognition of individual animals, such as a pet cat, and unique cars. Associated with damage to a specific area in *extrastriate cortex* in which cells responding specifically to faces have been reported.

protein kinase Enzymes present in neurons activated by *second messengers*. When activated, the enzymes phosphorylate (add a charged phosphoryl group to) other proteins . within the cell, such as *ion channels*. Phosphorylation might cause the ion channel to stay open longer or close faster. The time course for these actions is generally much longer than primary events such as *EPSPs*.

prototype Average exemplar of a category, containing the common features that most members of the category possess. Storing the prototype, rather than lots of examples, in a representational system reduces memory demand and speeds recognition.

pseudo-Hebbian synapse   *Synapse* whose change in efficacy is dependent only on *depolarization* of the postsynaptic cell and does not require an *action potential* in that cell.

psychophysics   Branch of psychology based on treating a perceptual system (e.g., visual system) as a black box, giving the system a characterized input and observing the output (often a verbal response). These data are then used to infer principles of operation of the system.

PTP   *Post-tetanic potentiation.*

Purkinje cell   Output cell of cerebellar cortex. Large inhibitory neuron with extensive dendritic arbor confined to a single plane. May receive over 100,000 synapses from parallel fibers running perpendicular to arbor. Named after J. E. von Purkinje, a 19th-century physiologist.

pyramidal cells   Spiny, excitatory neurons with a pyramidal-shaped soma. They have a distinct apical *dendrite* and a locally branching *axon* collateral system, and often project out of their own local area.

quantal size   Size of the postsynaptic response (*EPSP*) to the release of a single quantum of *neurotransmitter*. Dependent on the number of transmitter molecules in one *vesicle* and the density and properties of *receptors* on the postsynaptic membrane.

radial basis function   *Processing unit* sensitive only to a limited range of input patterns. In three dimensions it carves out a sphere in the input space for each hidden unit. This allows part of an already trained network to be modified without affecting responses to other inputs, in an attempt to solve the *scaling problem.*

random-dot stereogram   Pair of images made up of random patterns of black and white dots. The images are identical except that in one image some set of dots has been displaced to the right or left by a few dot widths. When fused by the two eyes, the displaced dots appear to be at a different depth plane from the background.

raphe nuclei   Series of nuclei lying close to the midline of the *brain stem* containing neurons using *serotonin* and various peptides as neurotransmitters, often localized in the same cell. Projects to most of the *CNS* and regulates behavioral arousal and levels of mental awareness.

rapid eye movement (REM) sleep   Stage of sleep associated with profound loss of muscle tonus, desynchronized *EEG*, and broad sympathetic activation. Dreaming is thought to occur during REM sleep.

recency effect   Phenomenon whereby the last few items on a list to be remembered are recalled better than words from the middle of the list. Attributed to the fact that the last items are stored in *short-term memory.*

receptive field   Area in sensory space within which an adequate stimulus causes an excitatory response of the cell in question. Often surrounded by a sensory region, called the *nonclassical receptive* field, that can modulate the central response.

receptor   Integral synaptic membrane protein with one or more binding sites for *neurotransmitters*. Binding of the transmitter (ligand binding) induces a conformational change in the receptor that can cause a change in conductance of an associated *ion channel* or the activation of a *second messenger.*

recurrent network   Neural network incorporating feedback connections, allowing the network to handle temporally extended sequences of inputs. The feedback also allows recurrent networks to produce temporal sequences, including oscillations and *chaotic behavior.*

refractory period   Period after an *action potential* or burst of action potentials during which the *threshold* for firing spikes is infinite or at least increased. Results from inactivation of depolarizing currents such as that carried by sodium and residual activation of hyperpolarizing currents such as that carried by potassium.

relaxation   Process undergone by neural networks to reach an optimal solution to a problem bounded by a number of constraints (constraint satisfaction). Constraints are embodied in the network as the pattern and strength of connections (*weights*) between units. Relaxation involves convergence to a steady level of global network activity through repeated local interactions.

REM sleep   *Rapid eye movement sleep.*

resolution   Minimum distance between two stimuli in some sensory space that is needed to distinguish them as two separate stimuli. Not to be confused with *accuracy*.

resting membrane potential   Potential difference across a cell's membrane in the absence of synaptic input. Determined by the conductance of the resting membrane to each ion (primarily potassium) in the intra- and extracellular fluid.

retina   Sensory transducer of the visual system. Three layers of neurons at the back of the eye containing five basic cell types, including photoreceptors and *retinal ganglion cells*.

retinal ganglion cell   Projection cell of the *retina*. Receives indirect input from photoreceptors and projects out of the retina to many sites including the *LGN, superior colliculus*, nuclei in the accessory optic system, and hypothalamic structures.

retinal slip   Movement of the visual image across the *retina*. Serves as the input driving the *smooth-pursuit* eye movement system and also occurs when the gain of certain eye movements such as the *VOR* is not correct. Provides an error signal to the VOR system to correct its gain.

reverse engineering   Technique for investigating very complex physical systems based on taking the system apart to see how it works. Can be applied to computer chips and brains circuits.

rod   Type of photoreceptor in the *retina* with a low absolute *threshold* to light, but response adapts in normal daylight, where cones are most sensitive. Peak wavelength sensitivity around 510 nm, responsible for photopic (night) vision.

rostral   Navigational aid meaning "the end of the organism nearest the nose."

RT   Reaction time. Time elapsed between presentation of a stimulus and elicited response of a subject.

S1   Primary somatosensory cortex. Located in postcentral gyrus, receiving input from ventral posterior nucleus of *thalamus*. Contains distorted somatotopic representations of body surface.

saccade   High-speed ballistic eye movement used to direct the *fovea* to a target of interest in the visual field. Occurs on average three times a second.

scaling problem   General issue in complexity theory: how does the time taken to solve a problem increase with the size of the problem? In the context of networks, the issue is how long it takes to train a network as a function of the number of weights and amount of data.

Schaffer collaterals   Fibers projecting from *CA3* pyramidal cells to *CA1* cells. The *synapses* at the termination of these *axons* are the most studied site of *LTP* in the brain.

second messenger   Molecule such as cyclic AMP whose intracellular concentration is affected by the binding of a *neurotransmitter* or *neuromodulator*. The second messenger itself initiates a series of often diverse biochemical reactions ending in the physiological response.

segmentation problem   Separation of information in an input (e.g., a visual image) into separate batches for separate processing. Figure-ground segmentation refers to the separation of one coherent object in an image from the background, a task that requires a global analysis of the whole image to reach a solution. Motion segmentation refers to the separation of all components of an object that are moving together, though not necessarily with the same velocity.

semantic memory   Division of *declarative memory* concerned with knowledge of the world; organized information such as facts, vocabulary, and concepts. This reference memory has no temporal structure.

serotonin   5-Hydroxytryptamine. Indoleamine *neuromodulator* found in *raphe nuclei*. A variety of postsynaptic *receptors* have been identified, but the effects of serotonin are still unclear.

sharp waves   Irregular high-amplitude *field potentials* at 0.02–3 Hz recorded in the *hippocampus* of rats that are eating, grooming, resting, or in slow-wave sleep. Proposed as a natural stimulus that might induce *LTP*.

short-term memory System that retains information temporarily in a particular status while it is transformed into a more stable, long-term memory. Information in this form is immediately accessible to consciousness.

simple cell Class of neuron found in cortical area *V1* with linear response properties. *Receptive field* is made up of discrete excitatory and inhibitory subfields with a specific axis of orientation.

simulated annealing Optimization technique for finding a global *energy minimum*. Can be used with a network such as a *Boltzmann machine* to find solutions to *constraint satisfaction* problems. Based on allowing increases in energy of the network early on during *relaxation* to jump out of local *energy minima* into the global minimum. As the relaxation process progresses, the *temperature* is gradually lowered so that the system moves down to the bottom of the global minimum.

slice preparation Thin (<0.5 mm) slice of brain tissue kept alive in a chamber using oxygenation and perfusion with artificial cerebral spinal fluid. Cells at the edges of the slice are damaged, and cells in the middle of the slice last for only a few hours, unless steps are taken to provide conditions for long-term *tissue culture*.

slow-wave sleep Deep sleep. Stages of sleep characterized by progressively lower-frequency, higher-amplitude *EEG*, correlated with depth of sleep (high threshold of arousal). Parasympathetic activity predominates.

smooth pursuit Moving the eyes to track a moving object in order to keep the retinal image stabilized on the *fovea*.

soma Cell body of a neuron. Contains the nucleus and most of the metabolic machinery of the cell. Integration point for dendritic input and site of origin of *axon*. In invertebrates, the soma is displaced from the processes in the *neuropil*.

sparse representation A small subset of processing units, (typically $\log n$, of n available units in a network) are used to represent any given input *vector*. This means that there is less overlap between representations, allowing an *associative network* to store a greater number of representations.

spinal cord Caudal end of *CNS*. Consists of white matter (*axons*) surrounding a core of gray matter (cell bodies and *neuropil*), divided into dorsal (sensory) and ventral (motor) horns. Contains networks subserving simple and not-so-simple reflexes.

spine Small, thornlike structure located on *dendrite*. Spines have many sizes and shapes, but those on pyramidal neurons are usually composed of thin (0.1 μm) neck and head (approximately 1 μm in radius). Usually receive excitatory *synapses* only, but some have both excitatory and inhibitory synapses. Function unknown, possibly to isolate synaptic inputs or provide a small vessel for biochemical reactions.

spin glass Substance characterized by unpaired electrons with spin, either up or down, in mixtures of attractive and repulsive interactions. The properties of spin glasses are similar to associative Hopfield nets.

squashing function Smoothly varying *function*, such as a sigmoid, mapping the input that a unit receives onto output. Provides processing units with a particular type of *nonlinearity*.

state space Space of vectors that describes the state of the network. Typically means activation levels of processing units, but can also include internal state variables, such as previous history of inputs.

stellate cells Neurons with roughly spherical *somata* and radial *dendritic* arbors. Their *axonal* projections usually stay within their own local area.

stereopsis Term literally meaning "solid vision" but taken as referring just to binocular depth perception, which is 3-D perception arising from the *retinal disparity* of images in the two eyes.

stereoscope Device that presents a different image to each eye. If the images are identical except that elements of one scene are shifted slightly to the left or right with respect to the other, then the resulting *retinal disparity* produces *stereoscopic* vision of the scene.

stomatogastric ganglion Network of about 28 neurons in the spiny lobster controlling muscles that rhythmically grind teeth in the stomach of the lobster. Subject of intense investigation into the nature of *central pattern generators*.

substantia nigra Nucleus of *basal ganglia* in midbrain divided into two parts: pars reticulata and pars compacta. Cells of the compacta send dopaminergic fibers to the neostriatum. Loss of these cells is the principal pathology associated with Parkinson's disease.

superior colliculus Midbrain structure receiving projections from the visual, auditory, and somatosensory systems in register with neurons that drive saccadic eye movements. Responsible for orienting the subject to salient sensory stimuli. Homologous to the optic tectum in birds.

supervised learning A characteristic of some types of learning *algorithms* for setting *weights* in neural networks, meaning that the weight change in the network is influenced by an externally generated report on its performance—an error signal. Unsupervised nets can monitor their own performance through internal feedback.

sylvian fissure Prominent cleft separating *temporal lobe* from adjoining *parietal* and *frontal lobes*.

synapse Functional contact between two cells, consisting of a presynaptic terminal bouton separated by a narrow gap, called the synaptic cleft, from an area of postsynaptic membrane containing *receptors*. Electrical synapses are physical connections between cells, usually allowing bidirectional flow of ions. At a chemical synapse, a release of *neurotransmitter* from the presynaptic terminal carries a signal to the *receptors* on the postsynaptic membrane. Autoreceptors on the presynaptic terminal may be affected as well, and if the transmitter escapes from the synaptic cleft, it may influence other nearby *glial cells* and neurons.

tapped delay line Technique for dealing with a temporally structured input of limited complexity with a feedforward network. The temporal sequence of input events is pushed through the input units from one side to the other. Found in the nucleus laminaris in the barn owl, where it is used for computing horizontal delays in the arrival times between the two ears.

taste-aversion learning *Classical conditioning* paradigm in which a neutral food is paired with a noxious experience. The neutral food on its own is then avoided by the subject due to its association with the noxious experience. Also called the Garcia effect, or bait shyness in rats. The sensory modality used to identify the food varies among species.

teacher Element of a *supervised learning algorithm* that computes the error of the network, usually the difference between the desired and actual outputs. Can be supplied by an internal source, such as monitors in other parts of the brain, and need not be a literal teacher, outside the brain.

temperature Parameter used in *simulated annealing* to determine the probability of a unit making a state change that decreases the energy of the system. The temperature is gradually decreased during the *annealing* process, causing the system to settle to the bottom of the global *energy minimum*.

temporal lobe Area of cortex concerned with auditory processing, visual learning, *declarative memory*, and emotions.

tetanus Repeated high-frequency stimulation of a neuron or set of neurons. This stimulus is optimal for inducing *long-term potentiation* in the hippocampus.

texture gradient Pattern formed by a regularly textured surface extending away from the observer. Elements in the texture gradient that are far from the observer appear small relative to corresponding elements that are close.

thalamus "Gateway" to the *neocortex*. All sensory information bound for the cerebral cortex passes through the thalamus. May perform an attentional gating on the flow of information to cortex, as yet poorly understood.

thermoregulation   Homeostatic control of body temperature. Mediated by structures in the medulla of the *brain stem*.

theta wave   Low-amplitude *field potential* oscillating at 4–8 Hz recorded in *hippocampus* of some mammals, such as rats, that are engaged in exploratory behavior or *REM sleep*.

threshold   Amount of *depolarization* needed to activate a conductance or an *action potential*. For an *action potential*, it is the level of depolarization at which there is a net depolarizing ionic current, usually carried by sodium or calcium ions. For an artificial network, it is the amount of input a unit must receive before it produces any output.

tissue culture   Small amounts of neural tissue grown outside the nervous system from dissociated cells. Allows easy access for biochemical analysis and visualization of the neurons, but the development of the neurons may not be typical of neurons *in vivo*.

topographic map   Representation used by many sensory modalities in the nervous system meaning that the cortical surface (e.g., primary sensory cortex) contains an orderly spatial map of *receptive fields* (e.g., of the visual field or body surface). Probably serves to reduce wiring and delays by placing areas that need to communicate close together.

traveling salesman problem (TSP)   Difficult *optimization* problem involving finding the shortest route to take in visiting a set of points without visiting any point more than once.

truth table   *Look-up table* specifying all the outputs of a *function* as true or false (1 and 0) for all possible inputs. Used to completely characterize Boolean functions such as *XOR*.

TSP   *Traveling salesman problem.*

tuning curve   Description of the selectivity of a unit (neuron) to a dimension of the stimulus (e.g., orientation). Many neurons respond best to one particular orientation though they also also respond significantly to other orientations with broad tuning curves.

update rule   Instructions for determining the activity of a network on the next time step based on the activity of units at the current time and on the values of internal state variables. The new activity of a unit is usually some *function* (*activation function*) of the activity of units projecting to it multiplied by the *weights* of those connections. More sophisticated update rules include functions of past inputs (dendritic processing) and the recent history of output firing (accommodation).

V1   *See primary visual cortex.*

V2   *See extrastriate visual cortex.*

V3   *See extrastriate visual cortex.*

V4   *See extrastriate visual cortex.*

vector   Ordered set of numbers. *Functions* performing vector-to-vector mapping are used to model the evolution of the *state* of a network with time. In contrast, a scalar has just a single value.

vector averaging   Reducing the dimensionality of representing by summing the *vector* components to yield a single representation, often a direction, in the relevant *state space* (often a motor space).

vector quantization   Partitioning of the input space into groups of similar *vectors*, performed by unsupervised networks that stage a competition between units for input vectors. This results in each unit becoming a *feature detector*, responding to a set of vectors that share feature(s) in common.

ventral   Navigational aid meaning "toward the front, or belly."

vergence   Disjunctive movements of the eyes to foveate objects that are moving in depth. When the object moves closer, the eyes converge; when it moves away, they diverge.

very large-scale integration (VLSI)   The fabrication of a complex electronic circuit consisting of millions of components on a single piece of silicon. Exponential increase in the number of components over the last two decades was made possible by technical advances in lithography and improvements in the design methodology.

vesicle   Membranous sacks thought to contain *neurotransmitter* located inside presynaptic terminals. Fuse with presynaptic membrane upon entry of calcium into terminal. Following fixation of the tissue for electron microscopy, excitatory synaptic terminals usually contain round vesicles and inhibitory synapses have flattened vesicles, a very helpful histological artifact.

vestibular nuclei   Nuclei in the *brain stem* receiving input from the *vestibular organ*. Important in the dynamic control of posture, through projections to the *spinal cord*, and in controlling many eye movements, through projections to the oculomotor nuclei.

vestibular organ   Organ of balance located in the *inner ear* that detects acceleration based on the deflection of stereocilia of *hair cells* by moving *endolymph* fluid. The hair cells are located in three semicircular canals, which are at right angles to each other, covering the three spatial dimensions.

vestibulo-ocular reflex (VOR)   Short-latency movement of the eyes in the opposite direction to head movement. Stabilizes image on the retina.

VLSI   *Very large-scale integration.*

voltage dependent   Term usually referring to *ion channels* meaning that the conductance of the channel is a function of the voltage across the cell membrane.

voltage-sensitive dye   Molecule that changes its absorbance or wavelength of fluorescence depending on the voltage across the membrane to which it is bound.

VOR   *Vestibulo-ocular reflex.*

weight   Strength of connection between one unit and another in an artificial neural network. Often variable; tweaking weights is the most common method of network training. Has some of the properties of a biological *synapse*.

weight matrix   A matrix is an operator that maps a *vector* from one *state space* into another. A weight matrix is an array of numbers (*weights*) that is multiplied by an input vector to produce an output vector (vector–matrix transformation).

weight space   *State space* with each axis representing a *weight* in a network. If another axis is added representing the error of the network, an error surface is constructed. Learning usually proceeds by changing weights in directions that reduce the errors, that is, downhill in the error surface.

winner-take-all   The unit in a group responding most strongly to an input has its activation increased and that of the other units decreased. This process is the basis of *vector quantization*. Can be combined with a learning rule in competitive learning networks.

XOR   *Exclusive or.*

working memory   Term proposed by Baddeley and Hitch, referring to a memory buffer in which information is maintained while it is being processed. Now thought of as a collection of temporary capacities associated with different modalities.

zero-crossing   Point along a dimension at which the value is zero, changing from positive to negative or *vice versa*.

References

Abeles, M. (1982). *Local Cortical Circuits*. Berlin: Springer-Verlag.

Abeles, M. (1991). *Corticonics: Neural Circuits of the Cerebral Cortex*. Cambridge: Cambridge University Press.

Abraham, W. C., M. C. Corballis, and K. G. White, eds. (1991). *Memory Mechanisms: A Tribute to G. V. Goddard*. Hillsdale, NJ: Erlbaum.

Abu-Mostafa, Y. (1989a). Complexity in neural systems. Appendix D of Mead (1989), *Analog VLSI and Neural Systems*.

Abu-Mostafa, Y. (1989b). The Vapnik-Chervonenkis dimension: information versus complexity in learning. *Neural Computation* 1: 312–317.

Ackley, D. H., G. E. Hinton, and T. J. Sejnowski (1985). A learning algorithm for Boltzmann machines. *Cognitive Science* 9: 147–169.

Adams, S. R., A. T. Harootunian, Y. J. Buechler, S. S. Taylor, and R. Y. Tsien (1991). Fluorescence ratio imaging of cyclic AMP in single cells. *Nature* 349: 694–697.

Agre, P. E., and D. Chapman (1987). Pengi: an implementation of a theory of activity. In *Proceedings of the AAAI-87*, Los Altos, CA: Morgan Kaufmann. 268–272.

Albright, T. D. (in press). Color and the integration of motor signals. *Trends in Neurosciences*.

Albus, J. (1971). A theory of cerebellar function. *Mathematical Biosciences* 10: 25–61.

Alkon, D. L. (1984). Calcium-mediated reduction of ionic currents: a biophysical memory trace. *Science* 226: 1037–1045. Reprinted in Shaw et al. (1990), 502–510.

Allman, J. (1982). Reconstructing the evolution of the brain in primates through the use of comparative neurophysiological and neuroanatomical data. In *Primate Brain Evolution*, ed. E. Armstrong and D. Falk, 13–28. New York: Plenum.

Allman, J. (1990). The origin of the neocortex. *Seminars in the Neurosciences* 2: 257–262.

Allman, J., F. Miezin, and E. McGuinnes (1985). Stimulus-specific responses from beyond the classical receptive field: neurophysiological mechanisms for local–global comparisons in visual neurons. *Annual Review of Neuroscience* 8: 407–430.

Alonso, A., M. de Curtis, and R. R. Llinás (1990). Postsynaptic Hebbian and non-Hebbian long-term potentiation of synaptic efficacy in the entorhinal cortex in slices and in the isolated adult guinea pig brain. *Proceedings of the National Academy of Sciences USA* 87: 9280–9284.

Altman, J. S., and J. Kien (1987a). A model for decision making in the insect nervous system. In *Nervous Systems in Invertebrates*, ed. M. A. Ali, 621–643. New York: Plenum.

Altman, J. S., and J. Kien (1987b). Functional organization of the suboesophageal ganglion in insects and other arthropods. In *Arthropod Brain: Its Evolution, Development, Structure, and Function*, ed. A. P. Gupta, 265–301. New York: Wiley.

Altman, J. S., and J. Kien (1989). New models for motor control. *Neural Computation* 1: 173–183.

Amaral, D. G. (1987). Memory: anatomical organization of candidate brain regions. In *Handbook of Physiology: The Nervous System V*, Baltimore, MD: American Physiological Society 211–294.

Amaral, D. G., N. Ishizuka, and B. Claiborne (1990). Neurons, numbers, and the hippocampal network. In *Progress in Brain Research*, vol. 83, ed. J. Storm-Mathisen, J. Zimmer, and O. P. Otterson, 1–11. Amsterdam: Elsevier.

Amari, S. (1972). Characteristics of randomly connected threshold element networks and network systems. *Proceedings of the IEEE* 59: 35–47.

Amit, D. (1989). *Modeling Brain Function*. Cambridge: Cambridge University Press.

Anastasio, T. J. (1991). Neural network models of velocity storage in the horizontal vestibulo-ocular reflex. *Biological Cybernetics* 64: 187–196.

Anastasio, T. J. (in press). Distributed processing in vestibulo-ocular and other oculomotor subsystems in monkey and cats. In *Visual Structures and Integrated Functions*, ed. M. A. Arbib and J.-P. Ewert. New York: Springer-Verlag.

Anastasio, T. J., and D. A. Robinson (1989). Distributed parallel processing in the vestibulo-oculomotor system. *Neural Computation* 1: 230–241.

Andersen, P. O. (1987). Properties of hippocampal synapses of importance for integration and memory. In Edelman et al. (1987), 403–430.

Andersen, P. O. (1991). Parameters controlling the induction of long-term potentiation. In Abraham et al. (1991), 47–58.

Andersen, R., and V. B. Mountcastle (1983). The influence of the angle of gaze upon the excitability of light-sensitive neurons of the posterior parietal cortex. *Journal of Neuroscience* 3: 532–548.

Andersen, R., G. K. Essick, and R. M. Siegel (1985). Encoding of spatial location by posterior parietal neurons. *Science* 230: 450–458.

Andersen, R. A., R. M. Siegel, and G. K. Essick (1987). Neurons of area 7 activated by both visual stimuli and oculomotor behavior. *Experimental Brain Research* 67: 316–322.

Anderson, J. A., and M. C. Mozer (1981). Categorization and selective neurons. In *Parallel Models of Associative Memory*, ed. G. Hinton and J. Anderson, 213–236. Hillsdale, NJ: Erlbaum.

Anderson, J. A., J. W. Silverstein, S. A. Ritz, and R. S. Jones (1977). Distinctive features, categorical perception, and probability learning: some applications of a neural model. *Psychological Review* 84: 413–451.

Anderson, P. A., J. Olavarria, and R. C. van Sluyters (1988). The overall pattern of ocular dominance bands in cat visual cortex. *Journal of Neuroscience* 8: 2183–2200.

Angevine, J. B. Jr., and C. W. Cotman (1981). *Principles of Neuroanatomy*. Oxford: Oxford University Press.

Arbib, M. (1987). *Brains, Machines, and Mathematics*. Berlin: Springer-Verlag.

Arbib, M. (1989). *The Metaphorical Brain 2: Neural Networks and Beyond*. New York: Wiley-Interscience.

Arbib, M. A. (1990). Cooperative computation in brains and computers. In *Natural and Artificial Parallel Computation*, ed. M. A. Arbib and J. A. Robinson, 123–154. Cambridge, MA: MIT Press.

Arbib, M. A., and J. A. Robinson, eds. (1990). *Natural and Artificial Parallel Computation*. Cambridge, MA: MIT Press.

Artola, A., S. Brocher, and W. Singer (1990). Different voltage-dependent thresholds for inducing long-term depression and long-term potentiation in slices of rat visual cortex. *Nature* 347: 69–72.

Asanuma, H. (1973). Cerebral cortical control of movement. *Physiologist* 16: 143–166.

Ascher, P., and C. Stevens, guest eds. (1991). *Current Opinion in Neurobiology*, vol. 1.

Ashmore, J., and H. Saibil, guest eds. (1990). *Seminars in the Neurosciences*, vol. 2, no. 1: Sensory Transduction.

Atkinson, J., and O. J. Braddick (1990). The developmental course of cortical processing streams in the human infant. In Blakemore (1990b), 247–253.

Badcock, D. R., and C. M. Schor (1985). Depth-increment detection function for individual spatial channels. *Journal of the Optical Society of America* [A]2: 1211–1216.

Baddeley, A. D. (1988). Cognitive psychology and human memory. *Trends in Neurosciences* 11: 176–181.

Baddeley, A. D., and G. J. Hitch (1974). Working memory. In *Recent Advances in Learning and Motivation*, vol. 8, ed. G. H. Bower, 47–90. New York: Academic Press.

Bailey, C. H., and P. Gouras (1985). The retina and phototransduction. In Kandel and Schwartz (1985), 344–355.

Baldi, P., and R. Meir (1990). Computing with arrays of coupled oscillators: an application to preattentive texture discrimination. *Neural Computation* 2: 458–471.

Ballard, D. H. (1991). Animate vision. *Artificial Intelligence* 48: 57–86.

Ballard, D. H., G. E. Hinton, and T. J. Sejnowski (1983). Parallel visual computation. *Nature* 306: 21–26.

Barlow, H. B. (1972). Single units and sensation: a neuron doctrine for perceptual psychology? *Perception* 1: 371–394.

Barlow, H. B. (1985). The Twelfth Bartlett Memorial Lecture: The role of single neurons in the psychology of perception. *Quarterly Journal of Experimental Psychology* 37A: 121–145.

Barlow, H. B. (1990). The mechanical mind. *Annual Review of Neuroscience* 13: 15–24.

Barlow, H., C. Blakemore, and J. Pettigrew (1967). The neural mechanism of binocular depth discrimination. *Journal of Physiology (London)* 193: 327–342.

Barna, G., and P. Erdi (1988). "Normal" and "abnormal" dynamic behavior during synaptic transmission. In Cotterill (1988), 293–302.

Barr, C. C., L. W. Schulteis, and D. A. Robinson (1976). Voluntary non-visual control of the human vestibulo-ocular reflex. *Acta Otolaryngolica* 81: 365–375.

Barrionuevo, G., S. R. Kelso, D. Johnston, and T. H. Brown. (1986). *Journal of Neurophysiology* 55: 540–550.

Bässler, U. (1986). On the definition of central pattern generator and its sensory control. *Biological Cybernetics* 54: 65–69.

Bässler, U., and U. Wegner (1983). Motor output of the denervated thoracic ventral nerve cord in the stick insect *Carausius morosus. Journal of Experimental Biology* 105: 127–145.

Barto, A. G., R. S. Sutton, and P. S. Brouwer (1981). Associative search networks: a reinforcement learning associative memory. *Biological Cybernetics* 40, 201–211.

Barto, A. G., R. S. Sutton, and C. Watkins (1990). Sequential decision problems and neural networks. In Touretzky (1990), 686–693.

Bates, E. M. Apfelbaum, and L. Allard (1991). Statistical constraints on the use of single cases in neuropsychological research. *Brain and Language* 40: 295–329.

Battiti, R. (1992). First and second order methods for learning: between steepest descent and Newton's method. *Neural Computation*. 4.

Baudry, M., and J. L. Davis, eds. (1991). *Long-Term Potentiation: A Debate of Current Issues*. Cambridge MA: MIT Press.

Baum, E. B. (1989). A proposal for more powerful learning algorithms. *Neural Computation* 1: 201–207

Baxt, W. G. (1990). Use of an artificial neural network for data analysis in clinical decision-making: the diagnosis of acute coronary occlusion. *Neural Computation* 2: 480–489.

Becker, S., and G. E. Hinton (1989). *Spatial coherence as an internal teacher for a neural network*. Technical Report CRG-TR-89-7, University of Toronto.

Beer, R. D. (1990). *Intelligence as Adaptive Behavior*. San Diego, CA: Academic Press.

Bekkers, J. M., and C. F. Stevens (1990). Presynaptic mechanism for long-term potentiation in the hippocampus. *Nature* 346: 724–729.

Benzing, W. C., and L. R. Squire (1989). Preserved learning and memory in amnesia: intact adaptation-level effects and learning of stereoscopic depth. *Behavioral Neuroscience* 103: 538–547.

Berger, H. (1929). Über das Elektrenzephalogramm des Menschen. *Archiv für Psychiatrie und Nervenkrankheiten* 87: 527–570.

Berger, T. W., and R. F. Thompson (1978). Neuronal plasticity in the limbic system during classical conditioning of the rabbit nictitating membrane response. 1. The hippocampus. *Brain Research* 145: 323–346.

Berman, N. J., R. J. Douglas, K. A. C. Martin, and D. Whitteridge (1991). Mechanisms of inhibition in cat visual cortex. *Journal of Physiology* 440: 697–722.

Bernander, O., R. J. Douglas, K. A. C. Martin, and C. Koch (in press). Synaptic background activity determines spatio-temporal integration in single pyramidal cells. *Proceedings of the National Academy of Sciences USA*.

Bienenstock, E., L. Cooper, and P. Munro (1982). Theory for the development of neuron selectivity: orientation specificity and binocular interaction in visual cortex. *Journal of Neuroscience* 2: 32–48.

Black, I. B. (1991). *Information in the Brain: A Molecular Perspective*. Cambridge, MA: MIT Press.

Blake, J. F., M. W. Brown, and G. L. Collingridge (1988). CNQX blocks acidic amino acid induced depolarizations and synaptic components mediated by non-NDMA receptors in rat hippocampal slices. *Neuroscience Letters* 89: 182–186.

Blakemore, C. (1990a). Maturation of mechanisms for efficient spatial vision. In Blakemore 1990(b).

Blakemore, C., ed. (1990b). *Vision: Coding and Efficiency*. Cambridge: Cambridge University Press.

Blasdel, G. G., and G. Salama (1986). Voltage-sensitive dyes reveal a modular organization in monkey striate cortex. *Nature* 321: 579–585.

Bliss, T. V., and T. Lømo (1973). Long-lasting potentiation of synaptic transmission in the dentate area of the anaesthetized rabbit following stimulation of the perforant path. *Journal of Physiology (London)* 232: 331–356.

Bogen, J. E., and G. M. Bogen (1976). Wernicke's region—where is it? *Annals of the New York Academy of Sciences* 280: 834–843.

Boltz, J., and C. D. Gilbert (1986). Generation of end-inhibition in the visual cortex via inter-laminar connections. *Nature* 320: 362–365.

Bonhoeffer, T., V. Staiger, and A. Aertsen (1989). Synaptic plasticity in rat hippocampal cultures: local "Hebbian" conjunction of pre- and postsynaptic stimulation leads to distributed synaptic enhancement. *Proceedings of the National Academy of Sciences USA* 86: 8113–8117.

Bouyer, J. J., M. F. Montaron, and A. Rougeul (1981). Fast fronto-parietal rhythms during combined focused attentive behavior and immobility in cat: cortical and thalamic localizations. *Electroencephalography and Clinical Neurophysiology* 51: 244–252.

Boyde, A. (1985). Stereoscopic images in confocal (tandem scanning) microscopy. *Science* 230: 1270–1272.

Bradley, A., B. Skottum, I. Ohzawa, G. Sclar, and R. Freeman (1987). Visual orientation and spatial frequency discrimination: a comparison of single neurons and behavior. *Journal of Neurophysiology* 57: 755–772.

Braitenberg, V. (1984). *Vehicles.* Cambridge, MA: MIT Press.

Bressler, S. L. (1990). The gamma wave: a cortical information carrier? *Trends in Neurosciences* 13: 161–162.

Brindley, G. S. (1964). The use made by the cerebellum of the information that it receives from sense organs. *IBRO* Bulletin 3: 80.

Brodfeuhrer, P. D., and W. O. Friesen (1986). From stimulation to undulation: a neuronal pathway for the control of swimming in the leech. *Science* 234: 1002–1004.

Brodin, L., H. G. C. Traven, A. Lansner, P. Wallen, O. Ekeberg, and S. Grillner (1991). Computer simulations of N-methyl-D-aspartate (NMDA) receptor induced membrane properties in a neuron model. *Journal of Neurophysiology.* 66: 473–484.

Brooks, R. A. (1989). A robot that walks: emergent behaviors from a carefully evolved network. *Neural Computation* 1: 253–262.

Brooks, V. B. (1986). *The Neural Basis of Motor Control.* Oxford: Oxford University Press.

Broomhead, D. S., and D. Lowe (1988). Multivariable functional interpolation and adaptive networks. *Complex Systems* 2: 321–355.

Brown, M. W. (1990). Why does the cortex have a hippocampus? In Gabriel and Moore (1990), 233–282.

Brown, T. G. (1911).The intrinsic factors in the act of progression in the mammal. *Proceedings of the Royal Society Series B* 84: 308–319.

Brown, T. G. (1916). Die Reflexfunktion des Zentralnervensystems mit besonderer Berünck-sichtigung der rhythmischen Tätigkeiten beim Säugetier. Zweiter Teil. *Ergebnisse der Physiologie* 15: 480–490.

Brown, T. H., A. H. Ganong, E. W. Kariss, C. L. Keenan, and S. R. Kelso (1989). Long-term potentiation in two synaptic systems of the hippocampal brain slice. In Byrne and Berry (1989), 266–306.

Brown, T. H., A. H. Ganong, E. W. Kariss, and C. L. Keenan (1990). Hebbian synapses: bio-physical mechanisms and algorithms. *Annual Review of Neuroscience* 13: 475–511.

Brownstone, R. M., L. M. Jordan, D. J. Kriellaars, and B. R. Noga (1987). Evidence for a spinal mechanism regulating the afterhyperpolarization amplitude in lumbar motoneurons during fictive locomotion in the cat. *Society for Neuroscience Abstracts* 13: 244.15.

Brownstone, R. M., L. M. Jordan, D. J. Kriellaars, R. B. Noga, and S. J. Shefchyk (in press). On the regulation of repetitive firing in the lumbar motor neuron during fictive locomotion in the cat.

Bruce, V., and P. Green (1990). *Visual Perception: Physiology, Psychology, and Ecology*, 2nd ed. Hillsdale, NJ: Erlbaum.

Bryson, A., and Y.-C. Ho (1969). *Applied Optimal Control*. New York: Blaisdell.

Buchanan, J. T. (1990). Simulations of lamprey locomotion: emergent network properties and phase coupling. *Society for Neuroscience Abstracts* 16: 184.

Buchanan, J. T. (in press). Neural network simulations of coupled locomotor oscillators in the lamprey spinal cord.

Bullock, T. H., R. Orkand, and A. Grinnell (1977). *Introduction to Nervous Systems*. San Francisco: Freeman.

Bush, P., and R. J. Douglas (1991). Synchronization of bursting action potential discharge in a model network of neocortical neurons. *Neural Computation* 3: 19–30.

Bush, P., and T. J. Sejnowski (1991). Simulations of a reconstructed cerebellar Purkinje cell based on simplified channel kinetics. *Neural Computation* 3: 321–332.

Buzsáki, G. (1983). Situational conditional reflexes: physiological studies of the higher nervous activity of freely moving animals: P. S. Kupalov. *Pavlovian Journal of Biological Sciences* 18: 13–21.

Buzsáki, G. (1984). Feed-forward inhibition in the hippocampal formation. *Progress in Neurobiology* 22: 131–153.

Buzsáki, G. (1986). Hippocampal sharp waves: their origin and significance. *Brain Research* 398: 242–252.

Buzsáki, G. (1989). Two-stage model of memory trace formation: a role for "noisy" brain states. *Neuroscience* 31: 551–570.

Buzsáki, G., and E. Eidelberg (1982). Direct afferent excitation and long-term potentiation of hippocampal interneurons. *Journal of Neurophysiology* 48: 597–607.

Buzsáki, G., and F. H. Gage (1991). Long-term potentiation: does it happen in the normal brain? When and how? In Abraham et al. (1991), 79–104.

Buzsáki, G., L.-W. S. Leung, and C. H. Vanderwolf (1983). Cellular bases of hippocampal EEG in the behaving rat. *Brain Research Reviews* 6: 139–171.

Buzsáki, G., H. L. Haas, and E. G. Anderson (1987). Long-term potentiation induced by physiologically relevant stimulus patterns. *Brain Research* 435: 331–333.

Buzsáki, G., G. Ponomareff, F. Bayardo, R. Ruiz, and F. H. Gage (1989). Neuronal activity in the subcortically denervated hippocampus: a chronic model for epilepsy. *Neuroscience* 28: 527–38.

Byrne, J. H., and W. O. Berry, eds. (1989). *Neural Models of Plasticity*. New York: Academic Press.

Campbell, C. B. G., and W. Hodos (1970). The concept of homology and the evolution of the nervous system. *Brain, Behavior, and Evolution* 3: 353–367.

Caramazza, A. A. (1988). Some aspects of language processing revealed through the analysis of acquired aphasia: the lexical system. *Annual Review of Neuroscience* 11: 395–421.

Caramazza, A. A., and A. E. Hillis (1990). Where do semantic errors come from? *Cortex* 26: 95–122.

Caramazza, A. A., and A. E. Hillis (1991). Lexical organization of nouns and verbs in the brain. *Nature* 349: 788–790.

Carbonell, J. G., ed. (1989). *Artificial Intelligence* (special volume on Machine Learning), vol. 40, nos. 1–3.

Carpenter, G. A., and S. Grossberg (1987). A massively parallel architecture for a self-organizing neural pattern recognition machine. *Computer Vision, Graphics, and Image Processing* 37: 54–115.

Carr, C. E., and M. Konishi (1988). Axonal delay lines for time measurement in the owl's brainstem. *Proceedings of the National Academy of Sciences USA* 85: 8311–8315.

Carr, C. E., and M. Konishi (1990). A circuit for detection of interaural time differences in the brain stem of the barn owl. *Journal of Neuroscience* 10: 3227–3246.

Cazalet, J. R., P. Grillner, I. Menard, J. Cremieux, and F. Clarac (1990). Two types of motor rhythm induced by NMDA and amines in an in vitro spinal cord preparation of neonatal rat. *Neuroscience Letters* 111: 116–121.

Chamberlin, N. L., R. D. Traub, and R. Dingledine (1990). Role of RPSPs in initiation of spontaneous synchronized burst firing in rat hippocampal neurons bathed in high potassium. *Journal of Neurophysiology* 64: 1000–1008.

Changeux, J.-P. (1985). *Neuronal Man*. Oxford: Oxford University Press.

Chattarji, S., P. K. Stanton, and T. J. Sejnowski (1989). Commissural synapses, but not mossy fiber synapses, in hippocampal field CA3 exhibit associative long-term potentiation and depression. *Brain Research* 495: 145–150.

Chiel, H. J., and R. D. Beer (1989). A lesion study of a heterogeneous artificial neural network for hexapod locomotion. *IJCNN International Joint Conference on Neural Networks* 1: 407–414.

Chomsky, N. (1980). Precis of *Rules and Representations*. *Behavioral and Brain Sciences* 3: 1–15.

Churchland, P. M. (1975). Karl Popper's philosophy of science. *Canadian Journal of Philosophy* 5: 145–156.

Churchland, P. M. (1985). Reduction, qualia, and the direct introspection of brain states. *Journal of Philosophy* 82: 8–28.

Churchland, P. M. (1986). Some reductive strategies in cognitive neurobiology. *Mind* 95: 279–309.

Churchland, P. M. (1988). *Matter and Consciousness*, rev. ed. Cambridge, MA: MIT Press.

Churchland, P. M. (1989). *A Neurocomputational Perspective*. Cambridge, MA: MIT Press.

Churchland, P. M., and P. S. Churchland (1990a). Intertheoretic reduction: a neuroscientist's field guide. *Seminars in the Neurosciences* 2: 249–256.

Churchland, P. M., and P. S. Churchland (1990b). Could a machine think? *Scientific American* 262: 32–37.

Churchland, P. S. (1986) *Neurophilosophy: Toward a Unified Science of the Mind-Brain*. Cambridge, MA: MIT Press.

Churchland, P. S. (1991). Our brains, our selves: reflections on neuroethical questions. In *Bioscience and Society*, ed. D. Roy, B. E. Wynne, and R. W. Old. West Sussex: Wiley & Sons. 77–96.

Churchland, P. S., and T. J. Sejnowski (1988). Perspectives in cognitive neuroscience. *Science* 242: 741–745. Reprinted in Kelner and Koshland (1989), 364–372.

Churchland, P. M. (1992). A feed-forward network for fast stereo vision with a movable fusion plane. In *Android Epistemology: Proceedings of the 2nd International Workshop on Human and Machine Cognition*. ed. K. Ford and C. Glymour. Cambridge, MA: AAAI Press/MIT Press.

Clark, S. A., T. Allard, W. M. Jenkins, and M. M. Merzenich (1988). Receptive fields in the body-surface map in adult cortex defined by temporally correlated inputs. *Nature* 332: 444–445.

Cline, H. T. (1991). Activity-dependent plasticity in the visual systems of frogs and fish. *Trends in Neurosciences* 14: 104–111.

Clothiaux, E. E., M. F. Bear, and L. N. Cooper (1991). Synaptic plasticity in visual cortex: comparison of theory with experiment. *Journal of Neurophysiology* 66: 1785–98.

Cohen, M., and S. Grossberg (1983). Absolute stability of global pattern formation and parallel memory storage by competitive neural networks. *IEEE Transactions on Systems, Man, and Cybernetics* 13: 815–826.

Collingridge, G. L., and T. V. P. Bliss (1987). NMDA receptors—their role in long-term potentiation. *Trends in Neurosciences* 10: 288–293.

Collingridge, G. L., S. J. Kehl, and H. McClennan (1983). Excitatory amino acids in synaptic transmission in the Schaffer collateral-commissural pathway of the rat hippocampus. *Journal of Physiology (London)* 334: 33–46.

Connor, J. A., H. S. Tseng, and P. E. Hockberger (1987). Depolarization- and transmitter-induced changes in intracellular calcium of rat cerebellar granule cells in explant cultures. *Journal of Neuroscience* 7: 1384–1400

Connors, B. W., and M. J. Gutnick (1990). Intrinsic firing patterns of diverse neocortical neurons. *Trends in Neurosciences* 13: 98–99.

Constantine-Paton, M., and P. Ferrari-Eastman (1987). Pre- and postsynaptic correlates of interocular competition and segregation in the frog. *Journal of Comparative Neurology* 255: 178–195.

Constantine-Paton, M., H. Cline, and E. Debski (1990). Patterned activity, synaptic convergence and the NMDA receptor in developing visual pathways. *Annual Review of Neuroscience* 13: 129–154.

Cooper, L. A., and R. Shepard (1973). *Mental Images and Their Transformations*. Cambridge, MA: MIT Press

Cordo, P. J., and M. Flanders (1989). Sensory control of target acquisition. *Trends in Neurosciences* 12: 110–117.

Coren, S., and L. W. Ward (1989). Sensation and Perception. San Diego, CA: Harcourt Brace Jovanovich.

Cotterill, R. M. J., ed. (1988). *Computer Simulation in Brain Science*. Cambridge: Cambridge University Press.

Cottrell, G., P. Munro, and D. Zipser (1987). Learning internal representations from gray-scale images: an example of extensional programming. In *Ninth Annual Conference of the Cognitive Science Society*, 462–473. Hillsdale, NJ: Erlbaum.

Cowan, W. M., J. W. Fawcett, D. D. M. O'Leary, and B. B. Steinfeld (1984). Regressive events in neurogenesis. *Science* 225: 1258–1265.

Crick, F. H. C. (1979). Thinking about the brain. *Scientific American* 241: 219–232.

Crick, F. H. C., and C. Asanuma (1986). Certain aspects of the anatomy and physiology of the cerebral cortex. In Rumelhart et al. (1986), 219–232.

Crick, F. H. C. and C. Koch (1990). Towards a neurobiological theory of consciousness. *Seminars in the Neurosciences* 2: 263–275.

Cronin, J. (1987). *Mathematical Aspects of Hodgkin-Huxley Neural Theory*. Cambridge: Cambridge University Press.

Cumming, B. G., E. B. Johnson, and A. J. Parker (1991). Vertical disparities and perception of three-dimensional shape. *Nature* 349: 411–413.

Cummins, R., and G. Schwarz (1991). Connectionism, computationalism, and cognition. In *Connectionism and the Philosophy of Mind*, ed. T. Horgan and J. Tienson. Dordrecht The Netherlands: Kluwer Academic Publishers.

Cutting, J. E. (1986). *Perception with an Eye for Motion*. Cambridge, MA: MIT Press.

Cynader, M., and C. Shaw (1985). Mechanisms underlying developmental alterations of cortical ocular dominance. In Keller and Zee (1985), 53–61.

Daan, S., and J. Aschoff (1982). Circadian contributions to survival. In *Structure and Physiology of Vertebrate Circadian Rhythms*, ed. J. Aschoff, S. Daan, and G. A. Groos, New York: Springer-Verlag. 305–321.

Dale, N. (1989). The role of NMDA receptors in synaptic integration and the organization of complex neural patterns. In *The NMDA Receptor*, ed. J. C. Watkins and G. L. Collingridge, 93–108. Oxford: IRL Press.

Damasio, A. (1985). Disorders of complex visual processing: agnosias, achromotopsia, Baliant's syndrome, and related difficulties of orientation and construction. In *Principles of Behavioral Neurology*, ed. M. M. Mesulam, 259–288. Philadelphia: F. A. Davis.

Damasio, A. (1989). Time-locked multiregional retroactivation—a systems-level proposal for the neural substrates of recall and recognition. *Cognition* 33: 25–62.

Damasio, A. (1990). Category-related recognition defects as a clue to the neural substrates of knowledge. *Trends in Neurosciences* 13: 95–98.

Damasio, A., and H. Damasio (in press). Cortical systems underlying knowledge retrieval: evidence from human lesion studies.

Damasio, A., H. Damasio, and G. W. van Hoesen (1982). Prosopagnosia: anatomic basis and behavioral mechanisms. *Neurology* 32: 331–341.

Damasio, A., P. Eslinger, H. Damasio, G. W. Van Hoesen, and S. Cornell (1985). Multimodal amnesic syndrome following bilateral temporal and basal forebrain damage. *Archives of Neurology* 42: 252–259.

Damasio, A., H. Damasio, and D. Tranel (1989). Impairments of visual recognition as clues to the processes of memory. In *Signal and Sense: Local and Global Order in Perceptual Maps*, ed. G. Edelman, M. Cowan, and E. Gall, 451–473. New York: Wiley.

Damasio, A., H. Damasio, D. Tranel, and J. Brandt (1990a). The neural regionalization of knowledge access. In *Cold Spring Harbor Symposium on Quantitative Biology: The Brain*, vol. 55, ed. E. Kandel, T. Sejnowski, C. Stevens, and J. Watson. New York: Cold Spring Harbor Press.

Damasio, A., D. Tranel, and H. Damasio (1990b). Face agnosia and the neural substrates of memory. *Annual Review of Neuroscience* 13: 89–110.

Damasio, H., and A. Damasio (1989). *Lesion Analysis in Neuropsychology*. Oxford: Oxford University Press.

Damasio, H., and A. Damasio (1990). The neural basis of memory, language and behavioral guidance: advances with the lesion method in humans. *Seminars in the Neurosciences* 2: 277–286.

Darnell, J., H. Lodish, and D. Baltimore (1986). *Molecular Cell Biology*. New York: Scientific American Books.

DeFelipe, J., and E. G. Jones (1988). *Cajal on the Cerebral Cortex*. Oxford: Oxford University Press.

Dehaene, S., and J.-P. Changeux (1989). A simple model of prefrontal cortex function in delayed-response tasks. *Journal of Cognitive Neuroscience* 1: 244–261.

Dennett, D. (1987). *The Intentional Stance*. Cambridge, MA: MIT Press.

Desimone, R. (1991). Face-selective cells in the temporal cortex of monkeys. *Journal of Cognitive Neuroscience* 3: 1–24.

Desimone, R., and L. G. Ungerleider (1989). Neural mechanisms of visual processing in monkeys. In *Handbook of Neuropsychology*, vol. 2, ed. F. Boller and J. Grafman, 267–299. Amsterdam: Elsevier.

Desmond, N. L., and W. B. Levy (1983). Synaptic correlates of associative potentiation/depression: an ultrastructural study in the hippocampus. *Brain Research* 265: 21–30.

DeValois, R. L., and K. K. DeValois (1988). *Spatial Vision*. Oxford: Oxford University Press.

Dewdney, A. K. (1989). Computer recreations: a Tinkertoy computer that plays tic-tac-toe. *Scientific American* 261: 120–123.

DeYoe, E. A., and D. C. Van Essen (1987). Concurrent processing streams in monkey visual cortex. *Trends in Neurosciences* 11: 219–226.

Diamond, A., ed. (1990). The Development and Neural Bases of Higher Cognitive Functions. *Annals of the New York Academy of Sciences*. New York: New York Academy of Sciences.

Dobbins, A., S. W. Zucker, and M. S. Cynader (1987). Endstopped neurons in the visual cortex as a substrate for calculating curvature. *Nature* 329: 438–441.

Dobkins, K. R., and T. D. Albright (1990). Color facilitates motion correspondence in visual area MT. *Society for Neuroscience Abstracts* 16: 1220.

Dobkins, K. R., and T. D. Albright (in press). The use of color- and luminance-defined edges for motion correspondence. *Society for Neuroscience Abstracts*.

Dobkins, K. R., and T. D. Albright (1991). What happens if it changes color when it moves? *Investigative Opthamology and Visual Science* 32: 823.

Donchin, E., G. McCarthy, M. Kutas, and W. Ritter (1983). Event-related potentials in the study of consciousness. In *Consciousness and Self-Regulation*, ed. G. E. Schwartz and D. Shapiro, 81–121. New York: Plenum.

Douglas, R. J., and K. A. C. Martin (1990a). Neocortex. In Shepherd (1990), 389–438.

Douglas, R. J., and K. A. C. Martin (1990b). Control of neuronal output by inhibition at the axon initial segment. *Neural Computation* 2: 283–292.

Douglas, R. J., and K. A. C. Martin (1991). A functional microcircuit for cat visual cortex. *Journal of Physiology* 440: 735–769.

Douglas, R. J., K. A. C. Martin, and D. Whitteridge (1989). A canonical microcircuit for neocortex. *Neural Computation* 1: 480–488.

Douglas, R. J., K. A. C. Martin, and D. Whitteridge (1991). An intracellular analysis of the visual responses of neurons in cat visual cortex. *Journal of Physiology* 440: 659–696.

Douglas, R. M., and G. V. Goddard (1975). Long-term potentiation in the perforant path-granule cell synapse in the rat hippocampus. *Brain Research* 86: 205–215.

Dowling, J. E. (1987). *The Retina: An Approachable Part of the Brain*. Cambridge, MA: Harvard University Press.

Dudai, Y. (1989). *The Neurobiology of Memory: Concepts, Findings, and Trends*. New York: Oxford University Press.

Durbin, R., and D. Willshaw (1987). An analogue approach to the travelling salesman problem using an elastic net method. *Nature* 326: 689–691.

Durbin, R., C. Miall, and G. Mitchison (1989). *The Computing Neuron*. Reading, MA: Addison-Wesley.

Eccles, J. C. (1977). Part II of Popper and Eccles (1977).

Eccles, J. (1982). The human brain and the human person. In *Mind and Brain*, ed. J. Eccles, 81–98. Washington, DC: Paragon.

Eckhorn, R., R. Bauer, W. Jordan, M. Brosch, W. Kruse, M. Munk, and H. J. Reitboek (1988). Coherent oscillations: a mechanism of feature linking in visual cortex? *Biological Cybernetics* 60: 121–130.

Eckmiller, R. (1987). Neural control of pursuit eye movements. *Physiological Reviews* 67: 797–857

Eckmiller, R. (1989). Generation of movement trajectories in primates and robots. In *Neural Computing Architectures*, ed. I. Aleksander, 305–326. Cambridge, MA: The MIT Press.

Eckmiller, R. (1990). The design of intelligent robots as a federation of geometric machines. In Zornetzer et al. (1990), 109–138.

Edelman, G. M. (1987). *Neural Darwinism*. New York: Basic Books.

Edelman, G. M., W. E. Gall, and W. M. Cowan, eds. (1987). *Synaptic Function*. New York: Wiley.

Eichenbaum, H., M. Kuperstein, A. Fagan, and J. Nagode (1987). Cue-sampling and goal-approach correlates of hippocampal unit activity in rats performing an odor discrimination task. *Journal of Neuroscience* 7: 716–732.

Ekeberg, O., P. Wallen, A. Lansner, H. Traven, L. Brodin, and S. Grillner (in press). A computer based model for realistic simulations of neural networks. *Biological Cybernetics*.

Elman, J. L. (1989). *Representation and structure in connectionist systems*. CRL Technical Report. San Diego: Center for Research in Language, UCSD.

Elman, J. L. (1990). Finding structure in time. *Cognitive Science* 14: 179–211.

Elman, J. L. (1991). Incremental learning, or the importance of starting small. CRL Technical Report 9101. San Diego: Center for Research in Language, UCSD.

Elman, J., and D. Zipser (1988). Learning the hidden structure of speech. *Journal of the Acoustical Society of America* 83: 1615–1626.

Engelhardt, H. T., Jr. (1974). The disease of masturbation: values and the concept of disease. *Bulletin of the History of Medicine* 48: 234–248.

Eriksen, C. W., and J. D. St. James (1986). Visual attention within and around the field of focal attention: a zoom lens model. *Perception and Psychophysics* 40: 225–240.

Evarts, E. V. (1966). Pyramidal tract activity associated with a conditioned hand movement in the monkey. *Journal of Neurophysiology* 29: 1011–1027.

Evarts, E. V. (1981). Role of motor cortex in voluntary movements in primates. In *Handbook of Physiology, Section 1: The Nervous System. Vol. II: Motor Control*, ed. V. B. Brooks, 1083–1120. Bethesda, MD: American Physiological Society.

Faggin, F., and C. Mead (1990). VLSI implementation of neural networks. In Zornetzer et al. (1990), 275–292.

Fant, G. (1973). *Speech Sounds and Features*. Cambridge, MA: MIT Press.

Farah, M. J., P. A. McMullen, and M. M. Meyer (in press). Can recognition of living things be selectively impaired? *Neuropsychologia*.

Feldman, J. (1990). An essay concerning robotic understanding. *AI Magazine* 11: 12–13.

Feldman, J., and D. Ballard (1982). Connectionist models and their properties. *Cognitive Science* 6: 205–254.

Feldman, J., M. A. Fanty, N. H. Goddard, and K. J. Lynne (1990). Computing with structured connectionist networks. In Zornetzer et al. (1990), 434–454.

Feldman, J., J. C. Smith, H. H. Ellenberger, C. A. Connelly, G. Liu, J. J. Greer, A. D. Lindsay, and M. R. Otto (1990). Neurogenesis of respiratory rhythm and pattern: emerging concepts. *American Journal of Physiology* 259: R879–R886.

Felleman, D. J., and D. C. Van Essen (1991). Distributed hierarchical processing in the primate cerebral cortex. *Cerebral Cortex* 1: 1–47.

Ferrier, D. (1876). *The Functions of the Brain.* London: Smith, Elden.

Ferster, D., and C. Koch (1987). Neuronal connections underlying orientation selectivity in cat visual cortex. *Trends in Neurosciences* 10: 487–492.

Fetz, E., and P. Cheney (1980). Postspike facilitation of forelimb muscle activity by primate corticomotoneuronal cells. *Journal of Neurophysiology* 44: 751–772.

Fodor, J. A. (1974). *The Language of Thought.* New York: Crowell.

Fodor, J. A. (1983). *The Modularity of Mind.* Cambridge, MA: MIT Press.

Fox, K., H. Sato, and N. Daw (1989). The location and function of NMDA receptors in cats and kitten visual cortex. *Journal of Neuroscience* 9: 2243–2254.

Fox, K., H. Sato, and N. Daw (1990). The effect of varying stimulus intensity on NMDA-receptor activity in cat visual cortex. *Journal of Neurophysiology* 64: 1413–1428.

Fox, P. T., J. M. Fox, and M. E. Raichle (1985). The role of the cerebral cortex in the generation of voluntary saccades: a positron emission tomographic study. *Journal of Neurophysiology* 54: 348–369.

Fox, P. T., F. M. Miezin, J. A. Allman, D. C. van Essen, and M. E. Raichle (1987). Retinotoptic organization of human visual cortex mapped with positron emission tomography. *Journal of Neuroscience* 7: 913–922.

Fox, S. S. (1970). Evoked potential, coding, and behavior. In *The Neurosciences Second Study Program,* ed. F. O. Schmitt, 243–259. New York: Rockefeller University Press.

Freemon, F. R., and R. D. Walter (1970). Electrical activity of human limbic system during sleep. *Comparative Psychiatry* 11: 544–551.

Fregnac, Y., D. Shulz, S. Thorpe, and E. Bienenstock (1988). A cellular analogue of visual cortical plasticity. *Nature* 333: 367–370.

Friedman, H. R., J. D. Jana, and P. S. Goldman-Rakic (1990). Enhancement of metabolic activity in the diencephalon of monkeys performing working memory tasks: a 2-deoxyglucose study in behaving rhesus monkeys. *Journal of Cognitive Neuroscience* 2: 18–31.

Friesen, W. O. (1985). Neuronal control of leech swimming movements: interactions between cell 60 and previously described oscillator neurons. *Journal of Comparative Physiology* 156: 231-242.

Frisby, J. P. (1980). *Seeing: Illusion, Brain, and Mind.* Oxford: Oxford University Press.

Frost, D. O., and C. Metin (1985). Induction of functional retinal projections to the somatosensory cortex. *Nature* 317: 162–164.

Frostig, R. D., E. E. Lieke, D. Y. Ts'o, and A. Grinvald (1990). Cortical functional architecture and local coupling between neuronal activity and the microcirculation revealed by in vivo high-resolution optical imaging of intrinsic signals. *Proceedings of the National Academy of Sciences USA* 87: 6082–6086.

Fuchs, A. F., and J. Kimm (1975). Unit activity in vestibular nucleus of the alert monkey during horizontal angular acceleration and eye movement. *Journal of Neurophysiology* 38: 1140–1161.

Fukushima, K. (1975). Cognitron: a self-organizing multilayered neural network. *Biological Cybernetics* 20: 121–136.

Fukushima, K. (1988). A hierarchical neural network model for selective attention. In *Neural Computers*, ed. R. Eckmiller and C. v. d. Malsburg, 80–100. Berlin: Springer-Verlag.

Fuster, J. (1990). Inferotemporal units in selective visual attention and short-term memory. *Journal of Neurophysiology* 64: 681–697.

Gabriel, M., and J. Moore, eds. (1990). *Learning and Computational Neuroscience: Foundations of Adaptive Networks*. Cambridge, MA: MIT Press.

Gallistel, C. R. (1990). *The Organization of Learning*. Cambridge, MA: MIT Press.

Garcia, J., and R. A. Koelling (1966). Relation of cue to consequence in avoidance learning. *Psychonomic Science* 4: 123–124.

Gasic, G. P., and S. Heinemann (1991). Receptors coupled to ionic channels: the glutamate receptor family. *Current Opinion in Neurobiology* 1: 20–26.

Gazzaniga, M. S. (1985). *The Social Brain*. New York: Basic Books.

Gelperin, A. (1975). Rapid food-aversion learning by a terrestrial mollusc. *Science* 189: 567–570.

Gelperin, A., J.J. Hopfield, and D. W. Tank (1985). The logic of Limax learning. In *Model Neural Networks and Behavior*, ed. A. Selverston, 237–261. New York: Plenum.

Geman, S., and D. Geman (1984). Stochastic relaxation, Gibbs distributions, and the Bayesian restoration of images. *IEEE Transactions on Pattern Analysis and Machine Intelligence* 6: 721–741.

Georgopoulos, A. P., A. B. Schwartz, and R. E. Kettner (1986). Neuronal population coding of movement direction. *Science* 233: 1416–1419.

Georgopoulos, A. P., J. T. Lurito, M. Petrides, A. B. Schwartz, and J. T. Massey (1989). Mental rotation of the neuronal population vector. *Science* 243: 234–236.

Gershon, M. D., J. H. Schwartz, and E. R. Kandel (1985). Morphology of chemical synapses and patterns of interconnection. In Kandel and Schwartz (1985), 132–147.

Gerstein, G. L., and A. M. Aertsen (1985). Representation of cooperative firing activity among simultaneously recorded neurons. *Journal of Neurophysiology* 54: 1513–1528.

Gerstein, G. L., M. J. Bloom, I. E. Espinosa, S. Evanczuk, and M. R. Turner (1983). Design of a laboratory for multineuron studies. *IEEE Transactions on Systems, Man, and Cybernetics* SMC 13: 668–676.

Getting, P. A. (1989). Emerging principles governing the operation of neural networks. *Annual Review of Neuroscience* 12: 185–204.

Ghez, C. (1985). Introduction to motor systems. In Kandel and Schwartz (1985), 429–442.

Gibbon, J., and L. Allan (1984). *Timing and Time Perception*. New York: New York Academy of Sciences.

Gilbert, C. D., and T. N. Wiesel (1981). Laminar specialization and intracortical connections in cat primary visual cortex. In: *Organization of the Cerebral Cortex*. Ed. F. O. Schmitt, F. G. Worden, and F. Dennis. Cambridge MA: MIT Press.

Gilbert, C. D., and T. N. Wiesel (in press). Receptive field dynamics in adult primary visual cortex.

Giles, C. L., G. Z. Sun, H. H. Chen, Y. C. Lee, and D. Chen (1990). Higher order recurrent networks and grammatical inference. In Touretzky (1990), 380–387.

Gluck, M. A., and R. F. Thompson (1987). Modeling the neural substrates of associative learning and memory: a computational approach. *Psychological Review* 94: 176–191.

Gnadt, J., and R. A. Andersen (1988). Memory related motor planing activity in posterior parietal cortex of macaque. *Experimental Brain Research* 70: 216–220.

Goldman-Rakic, P. S. (1987). Circuitry of the pre-frontal cortex and the regulation of behavior by representational memory. In *Higher Cortical Function: Handbook of Physiology*, ed. F. Blum and V. Mountcastle, 373–417. Washington, DC: American Physiological Society.

Goldman-Rakic, P. S. (1988). Topography of cognition: parallel distributed networks in primate association cortex. *Annual Review of Neuroscience* 11: 137–156.

Goldman-Rakic, P. S. (1990). Parallel systems in the cerebral cortex: the topography of cognition. In Arbib and Robinson (1990), 155–176.

Goldman-Rakic, P. S., and L. D. Selemon (1986). Topography of corticostriatal projections in nonhuman primates and implications for functional parcellation of the neostriatum. In *Cerebral Cortex*, ed. E. G. Jones and A. Peters, 447–466. New York: Plenum.

Goldreich, D., R. J. Krauzlis, and S. G. Lisberger (in press). Effect of changing feedback delay on spontaneous priming in smooth pursuit eye movements of monkeys. *Journal of Neurophysiology*.

Gorman, R. P., and T. J. Sejnowski (1988a). Analysis of hidden units in a layered network trained to classify sonar targets. *Neural Networks* 1: 75–89.

Gorman, R. P., and T. J. Sejnowski (1988b). Learned classification of sonar targets using a massively parallel network. *IEEE Transactions on Acoustics, Speech, and Signal Processing* 36: 1135–1140.

Gould, S. J., and R. Lewontin (1979). The spandrels of San Marco and the Panglossian paradigm: a critique of the adaptationist programme. *Proceedings of the Royal Society of London B* 205: 581–598.

Gouras, P. (1985a). Color vision. In Kandel and Schwartz (1985), 384–395.

Gouras, P. (1985b). Oculomotor system. In Kandel and Schwartz (1985), 571–583.

Granger, R., and G. Lynch (1989). Rapid incremental learning of hierarchically organized stimuli by layer II sensory (olfactory) cortex. In Morris (1989), 309–328.

Granger, R., J. Ambros-Ingerson, P. S. Anton, J. Whitson, and G. Lynch (1990). Computational action and interaction of brain networks. In Zornetzer et al. (1990), 25–41.

Granzow, B., W. O. Friesen, and W. B. Kristan, Jr. (1985). Physiological and morphological analysis of synaptic transmission between leech motor neurons. *Journal of Neuroscience* 5: 2035–2050.

Gray, C. M., P. Konig, A. K. Engel, and W. Singer (1989). Oscillatory responses in cat visual cortex exhibit inter-columnar synchronization which reflects global stimulus properties. *Nature* 338: 334–337.

Gray, J. (1968). *Animal Locomotion*. New York: Norton.

Graybiel, A. M., and T. L. Hickey (1982). Chemospecificity of ontogenetic units in the striatum: demonstration by combining [^{3}H]thymidine neuronography and histochemical staining. *Proceedings of the National Academy of Sciences USA* 79: 198–202.

Green, M. (1989). Color correspondence in apparent motion. *Perception and Psychophysics* 45: 15–20.

Gregory, R. L. (1970). *The Intelligent Eye*. New York: McGraw-Hill.

Gregory, R., and J. P. Harris (1974). Illusory contours and stereo depth. *Perception and Psychophysics* 15: 411–416.

Grey, W. (1953). *The Living Brain*. New York: Norton.

Grillner, S. (1981). Control of locomotion in bipeds, tetrapods, and fish. In *Handbook of Physiology, Section 1: The Nervous System. Vol. II: Motor Control*, ed. V. B. Brooks, 1179–1236. Bethesda, MD: American Physiological Society.

Grillner, S., and M. Konishi, guest eds. (1991). *Current Opinion in Neurobiology*. Vol. 1, no. 4, *Neural Control*.

Grillner, S., and T. Matsushima (1991). The neural network underlying locomotion in lamprey—synaptic and cellular mechanisms. *Neuron* 7: 1–15.

Grillner, S., J. T. Buchanan, and A. Lansner (1988). Simulation of the segmental burst generating network for locomotion in lamprey. *Neuroscience Letters* 89: 31–35.

Grillner, S., P. Wallen, and L. Brodin (1991). Neuronal network generating locomotor behavior in lamprey: circuitry, transmitters, membrane properties, and simulation. *Annual Review of Neuroscience* 14: 169–199.

Grinvald, A. (1985). Real-time optical mapping of neuronal activity: from single growth cones to the intact mammalian brain. *Annual Review of Neuroscience* 8: 263–305.

Grinvald, A., E. Lieke, R. D. Frostig, C. D. Gilbert, and T. N. Wiesel (1986). Functional architecture of cortex revealed by optical imaging of intrinsic signals. *Nature* 324: 361–364.

Grobstein, P. (1988). On beyond neuronal specificity: problems in going from cells to networks and from networks to behavior. In *Advances in Neural and Behavioral Development*, vol. 3, ed. P. Shinkman. Norwood, NJ: Ablex

Grobstein, P. (1990). Strategies for analyzing complex organization in the nervous system: I. Lesions experiments. In Schwartz (1990), 19–37.

Grossberg, S. (1976). Adaptive pattern classification and universal recoding: I. Parallel development and coding of neural feature detectors. *Biological Cybernetics* 23: 121–134.

Groves, P. M., and G. V. Rebec (1988). *Introduction to Biological Psychology*, 3rd ed. Dubuque, IA: Brown.

Guillery, R. W. (1972). Binocular competition in the control of geniculate cell growth. *Journal of Comparative Neurology* 144: 117–130.

Gulick, W. L., G. A. Gescheider, and R. D. Frisina (1989). *Hearing: Physiological Acoustics, Neural Coding, and Psychoacoustics*. Oxford: Oxford University Press.

Gustafsson, B., and H. Wigstrom (1988). Physiological mechanisms underlying long-term potentiation. *Trends in Neurosciences* 11: 156–162.

Guy, H. R., and F. Conti (1990). Pursuing the structure and function of voltage-gated channels. *Trends in Neurosciences* 13: 201–206.

Hall, Z. W. (1991). *Molecular Neurobiology* Sunderland MA: Sinauer.

Hancock, P. J. B., L. S. Smith, and W. A. Phillips (1991). A biologically supported error-correcting learning rule. *Neural Computation* 3: 200–211.

Hanny, P. E., J. H. Maunsell, and P. H. Schiller (1988). State-dependent activity in monkey visual cortex: II. Visual and nonvisual factors in V4. *Experimental Brain Research* 69: 245–259.

Hanson, S. J., and C. R. Olson, eds. (1990). *Connectionist Modeling and Brain Function: The Developing Interface*. Cambridge, MA: MIT Press.

Harnad, S. (in press). Connecting object to symbol in modeling cognition. In *Connectionism in Context*, ed. A. Clark and R. Lutz. Berlin: Springer-Verlag.

Harries, H. R., and D. I. Perrett (1991). Visual processing of faces in the temporal cortex: physiological evidence for modular organization and possible anatomical correlates. *Journal of Cognitive Neuroscience* 3: 9–24.

Harrington, A. (1985). Nineteenth-century ideas on hemisphere differences and "duality of mind." *Behavioral and Brain Sciences* 8: 617–659.

Harris, E. W., and C. W. Cotman (1986). Long-term potentiation of guinea-pig mossy fiber responses is not blocked by N-methyl-D-aspartate antagonists. *Neuroscience Letters* 70: 132–137.

Harris, W. A. (1991). Neurogenesis and determination in the Xenopus retina. In Lam and Shatz (1991), 95–105.

Harris, W. A., and C. Holt (1990). Early events in the emrbyogenesis of the vertebrate visual system: cellular determination and pathfinding. *Annual Review of Neuroscience* 13: 155–170.

Harrison, P. H. (1990). Induction of locomotion in spinal tadpoles by excitatory amino acids and their antagonists. *Journal of Experimental Zoology* 254: 13–17.

Harris-Warrick, R. M., and E. Marder (1991). Modulation of neural networks for behavior. *Annual Review of Neuroscience* 14: 39–58.

Hartveit, E., and P. Heggelund (1990). Neurotransmitter receptors mediating excitatory input to cells in the cat lateral geniculate nucleus. I. Nonlagged cells. *Journal of Neurophysiology* 63: 1361–1372.

Haugeland, J. (1985). *Artificial Intelligence: The Very Idea*. Cambridge, MA: MIT Press.

Hawkins, R. D., and E. R. Kandel (1984). Steps toward a cell-biological alphabet for elementary forms of learning. In *Neurobiology of Learning and Memory*, ed. G. Lynch, J. L. McGaugh, and N. M. Weinberger, 385–404. New York: Guilford.

Hebb, D. O. (1949). *Organization of Behavior*. New York: Wiley.

Heggelund, P., and E. Hartveit (1990). Neurotransmitter receptors mediating excitatory input to cells in the cat lateral geniculate nucleus. I. Lagged cells. *Journal of Neurophysiology* 63: 1347–1360.

Heiligenberg, W. (1986). Jamming avoidance responses. In *Electroreception*, ed. T. H. Bullock and W. Heiligenberg, 613–649. New York: Wiley.

Heiligenberg, W. (1990). Electrosensory system in fish. *Synapse* 6: 196–206.

Heiligenberg, W. (1991). The neural basis of behavior: a neuroethological view. *Annual Review of Neuroscience* 14: 247–268.

Heiligenberg, W. (1991). *Neural Nets in Electric Fish*. Cambridge MA: MIT Press.

Heiligenberg, W., C. Baker, and J. Matsubara (1978). The jamming avoidance response revisited: the structure of a neuronal democracy. *Journal of Comparative Physiology* 127: 267–286.

Heimer, L., and M. J. RoBards (1981). *Neuroanatomical Tract-Tracing Methods*. New York: Plenum.

Heineman, S., J. Boulter, E. Deneris, J. Conolly, R. Duvoisin, R. Papke, and J. Patrick (1990). The brain nicotinic acetylcholine receptor gene family. *Progress in Brain Research* 86: 195–203.

Heit, G., M. E. Smith, and E. Halgren (1990). Neuronal activity in the human medial temporal lobe during recognition memory. *Brain* 113:1093–1112.

Helmholtz, H. von (1867). *Handbuch der physiologischen Optik*. Translated from the 3rd German edition as: Southall, J. P. S., ed. (1962). *Treatise on Physiological Optics*, vol. III. New York: Dover Publications.

Hensler, K. (1988). Intersegmental interneurons involved in the control of head movements in crickets. *Journal of Comparative Physiology* 162: 111–126.

Hertz, J., A. Krogh, and R. G. Palmer (1991). *Introduction to the Theory of Neural Computation.* Redwood City, CA: Addison-Wesley.

Heywood, C. A., A. Cowey, and F. Newcombe (in press). Chromatic discrimination in a cortically colour blind observer. *European Journal of Neuroscience.*

Hilbert, J., and S. Cohn-Vossen (1952). *Geometry and the Imagination.* New York: Chelsea.

Hille, B. (1984). *Ionic Channels in Excitable Membranes.* Sunderland, MA: Sinauer.

Hille, B. (1987). Evolutionary origins of voltage-gated channels and synaptic transmission. In Edelman et al. (1987), 163–176.

Hillyard, S., and T. W. Picton (1987). Electrophysiology of cognition. In *Handbook of Physiology, Section 1: Neurophysiology,* 519–584. New York: American Physiological Society.

Hillyard, S., G. Mangun, S. Luck, and H. Heinze (in press). Electrophysiology of visual attention. In *Machinery of Mind,* ed. E. R. John. Boston: Birkhauser.

Hinton, G. E. (1989). Connectionist learning procedures. *Artificial Intelligence* 40: 185–234.

Hinton, G. E., and S. Becker (1990). An unsupervised learning procedure that discovers surfaces in random-dot stereograms. In *Proceedings of the International Joint Conference on Neural Networks,* vol. 1, ed. L. A. Jeffress, 218–222. Hillsdale, NJ: Erlbaum

Hinton, G. E., and S. J. Nowlan (1990). The bootstrap Widrow-Hoff rule as a cluster-formation algorithm. *Neural Computation* 2: 355–362.

Hinton, G. E., and T. J. Sejnowski (1983). Optimal perceptual inference. *Proceedings of the IEEE Computer Science Conference on Computer Vision and Pattern Recognition,* 448–453. Silver Spring, MD: IEEE Computer Society Press.

Hinton, G. E., and T. Shallice (1991). Lesioning an attractor network: investigations of acquired dyslexia. *Psychological Review* 98: 74–95.

Hobson, J. A. (1985). The neurobiology and pathophysiology of sleep and dreaming. *Discussions in Neuroscience* 2: 9–50.

Hobson, J. A. (1988). *The Dreaming Brain.* New York: Basic Books.

Hodgkin, A. L., and A. F. Huxley (1952). A quantitative description of membrane current and its application to conduction and excitation in nerve. *Journal of Physiology (London)* 117: 500–544.

Hokfelt, T., D. Millhorn, K. Seroogy, Y. Tsuruo, S. Ceccatelli, B. Lindh, B. Meister, T. Melander, M. Schalling, and T. Bartfai (1987). Coexistence of peptides with classical neurotransmitters. *Experientia* 43: 768–780.

Hopfield, J. (1982). Neural networks and physical systems with emergent collective computational abilities. *Proceedings of the National Academy of Sciences USA* 79: 2554–2558.

Hopfield, J. (1984). Neurons with graded response have collective computational properties like those of two-state neurons. *Proceedings of the National Academy of Sciences USA* 81: 3088–3092.

Hopfield, J. (1991). Olfactory computation and object perception. *Proceedings of the National Academy of Sciences USA* 88: 6462–6466.

Hopfield, J., and D. Tank (1985). "Neural" computation of decisions in optimization problems. *Biological Cybernetics* 52: 141–152.

Horn, B. K. P., and M. J. Brooks (1989). *Shape from Shading.* Cambridge, MA: MIT Press.

Horn, G. (1986). Imprinting, learning, and memory. *Behavioral Neuroscience* 100: 825–832.

Hornik, K., M. Stinchcombe, and H. White (1989). Multilayer feedforward networks are universal approximators. *Neural Networks* 2: 359–368.

Horton, J. C., and H. Sherk (1984). Receptive field properties in the cat's lateral geniculate nucleus in the absence of on-center retinal input. *Journal of Neuroscience* 4: 374–380.

Horvath, Z., A. Kamondi, J. Czopf, T. V. P. Bliss, and G. Buzsáki (1988). NMDA receptors may be involved in generation of hippocampal rhythm. In *Synaptic Plasticity in the Hippocampus*, ed. H. L. Haas and G. Buzsáki, 45. Berlin: Springer-Verlag.

Hounsgaard, J., and J. Midtgaard (1988). Intrinsic determinants of firing pattern in Purkinje cells of the turtle cerebellum in vitro. *Journal of Physiology (London)* 402: 731–749.

Hubel, D. H. (1988). *Eye, Brain, and Vision.* New York: Freeman.

Hubel, D. H., and M. S. Livingstone (1987). Segregation of form, color, and stereopsis in primate area 18. *Journal of Neuroscience* 7: 3378–3415.

Hubel, D. H., and T. N. Wiesel (1959). Receptive fields of single neurones in the cat's striate cortex. *Journal of Physiology (London)* 148: 574–591.

Hubel, D. H., and T. N. Wiesel (1962). Receptive fields, binocular interaction and functional architecture in the cat's visual cortex. *Journal of Physiology (London)* 160: 106–154.

Hubel, D. H., and T. N. Wiesel (1963). Shape and arrangement of columns in cat's striate cortex. *Journal of Physiology* 165: 559–568.

Hubel, D. H., and T. N. Wiesel (1977). Ferrier Lecture. Functional architecture of macaque monkey visual cortex. *Proceedings of the Royal Society of London B* 198: 1–59.

Hubel, D. H., T. N. Wiesel, and S. LeVay (1977). Plasticity of ocular dominance columns in the monkey striate cortex. *Philosophical Transactions of the Royal Society (London) B* 278: 377–409.

Hummel, R. A., and S. W. Zucker (1983). On the foundations of relaxation labeling processes. *IEEE Transactions on Pattern Analysis and Machine Intelligence* 3: 267–287.

Hurlbert, A. C., and T. A. Poggio (1988). Synthesizing a color algorithm from examples. *Science* 239: 482–485. Reprinted in Kelner and Koshland (1989), 338–343.

Hurvich, L. M. (1981). *Color Vision.* Sunderland, MA: Sinauer.

Huttenlocher, P. R. (1990). Morphometric study of human cerebral cortex development. *Neuropsychologia* 28: 517–527.

Ingvar, D. H., and M. S. Schwartz (1974). Blood flow patterns induced in the dominant hemisphere by speech and reading. *Brain* 97: 273–288.

Ishizuka, N., J. Weber, and D. G. Amaral (1990). Organization of intrahippocampal projections originating from CA3 pyramidal cells in the rat. *Journal of Comparative Neurology* 295: 580–623.

Ito, M. (1972). Neural design of the cerebellar motor control system. *Brain Research* 40: 81–84.

Ito, M. (1977). Neural events in the cerebellar flocculus associated with an adaptive modification of the vestibulo-ocular reflex of the rabbit. In *Control of Brain Stem Neurons, Developments in Neuroscience 1*, ed. R. Baker and A. Berthoz, 391–398. Amsterdam: Elsevier.

Ito, M. (1987). Long-term depression as a memory process in the cerebellum. In Edelman et al. (1987), 431–446.

Ito, M. (1989). Long-term depression. *Annual Review of Neuroscience* 12: 85–102.

Jack, J. J. B., D. Noble, and R. W. Tsien (1975). *Electric Current Flow in Excitable Cells.* Oxford: Clarendon Press.

Jacobs, R. A., M. I. Jordan, S. J. Nowlan, and G. E. Hinton (1991). Adaptive mixtures of local experts. *Neural Computation* 3: 79–87.

Jaffe, D., and D. Johnson (1990). Induction of long-term potentiation at hippocampal mossy-fiber synapses follows a Hebbian rule. *Journal of Neurophysiology* 64: 948–960.

Jahnsen, H., and R. Llinás (1984). *Journal of Physiology (London)* 349: 227.

Jahr, C. E., and C. F. Stevens (1990a). A quantitative description of NMDA receptor-channel kinetic behavior. *Journal of Neuroscience* 10: 1830–1837.

Jahr, C. E., and C. F. Stevens (1990b). Voltage dependence of NMDA-activated macroscopic conductances predicted by single-channel kinetics. *Journal of Neuroscience* 10: 3178–3182.

Jan, Y. N., L. Y. Jan, and S. W. Kuffler (1978). A peptide as a possible transmitter in sympathetic ganglia of the frog. *Proceedings of the National Academy of Sciences USA* 76: 1501–1505.

Jankowska, E., M. G. M. Jukes, S. Lund, and A. Lundberg (1967a). The effects of DOPA on the spinal cord. 5. Reciprocal organization of pathways transmitting excitatory action to α motoneurones of flexors and extensors. *Acta Physiologica Scandinavica* 70: 337–341.

Jankowska, E., M. G. M. Jukes, S. Lund, and A. Lundberg (1967b). The effects of DOPA on the spinal cord. 6. Half-centre organization of interneurones transmitting effects from the flexor reflex afferents. *Acta Physiologica Scandinavica* 70: 389–402.

Jeannerod, M. (1985). *The Brain Machine*. Cambridge, MA: Harvard University Press.

Jeannerod, M. (1988). *The Neural and Behavioral Organization of Goal-Directed Movements*. Oxford: Clarendon Press.

Jeffress, L. A. (1948). A place theory of sound localization. *Journal of Comparative and Physiological Psychology* 41: 35–39.

Jennings, P. J., and S. W. Keele (1991). A computational model of attentional requirements in sequence learning. In Touretzky et al. (1991), 236–242.

Johnson, M. H. (1990). Cortical maturation and the development of visual attention in early infancy. *Journal of Cognitive Neuroscience* 2: 81–95.

Johnson-Laird, P. (1988) *The Computer and the Mind*. Cambridge, MA: Harvard University Press.

Jones, E. G., S. L. Juliano, and B. L. Whitsel (1987). A combined 2-deoxyglucose and neurophysiological study of primate somatosensory cortex. *Journal of Comparative Neurology* 263: 514–525.

Jordan, M. I. (1986). An introduction to linear algebra in parallel distributed processing. In *Parallel Distributed Processing*, vol.1, ed. J. McClelland, D. Rumelhart, and the PDP Research Group, 365–422. Cambridge, MA: MIT Press

Jordan, M. I. (1989). Serial order: a parallel distributed processing approach. In *Advances in Connectionist Theory*, ed. J. L. Elman and D. E. Rumelhart. Hillsdale, NJ: Erlbaum.

Jordan, M. I., and D. E. Rumelhart (1990). *Forward Models: Supervised Learning with a Distal Teacher*. Technical Report.

Judd, J. S. (1988). On complexity of loading shallow neural networks. *Journal of Complexity* 4: 177–192.

Judd, J. S. (1990). *Neural Network Design and the Complexity of Learning*. Cambridge, MA: MIT Press.

Julesz, B. (1971). *Foundations of Cyclopean Perception*. Chicago: University of Chicago Press.

Kaas, J. H., R. J. Nelson, M. Sur, C.-S. Lin, and M. M. Merzenich (1979). Multiple representations of the body within the primary somatosensory cortex of primates. *Science* 204: 521–523.

Kammen, D., and A. Yuille (1988). Spontaneous symmetry-breaking energy functions and the emergence of orientation selective cortical cells. *Biological Cybernetics* 59: 23–31.

Kandel, E. (1983). Neurobiology and molecular biology: the second encounter. In *Cold Spring Harbor Symposia on Quantitative Biology*, 891–908. Cold Spring Harbor, NY: Cold Spring Harbor Laboratory Press.

Kandel, E. R. (1985). Processing of form and movement in the visual system. In Kandel and Schwartz (1985), 366–383.

Kandel, E. R., and J. Schwartz, eds. (1985). *Principles of Neural Science*, 2nd ed. New York: Elsevier

Kandel, E. R., M. Klein, B. Hochner, M. Shuster, S. A. Siegelbaum, R. D. Hawkins, D. L. Glanzman, V. F. Castellucci, and T. W. Abrams (1987). Synaptic modulation and learning: new insights into synaptic transmission from the study of behavior. In Edelman et al. (1987), 471–518.

Kandel, E. R., J. Schwartz, and T. M. Jessell, eds. (1991). *Principles of Neural Science*, 3rd ed. New York: Elsevier.

Kanerva, P. (1988). *Sparse Distributed Memory*. Cambridge, MA: MIT Press.

Katz, P. S., and R. M. Harris-Warrick (1990). Actions of identified neuromodulatory neruons in a simple motor system. *Trends in Neurosciences* 13: 367–373.

Kauer, J. A., R. C. Malenka, and R. A. Nicoll (1988). A persistent postsynaptic modification mediates long-term potentiation in the hippocampus. *Neuron* 1: 911–917.

Keith, J. R., and J. W. Rudy (1990). Why NMDA-receptor-dependent long-term potentiation may not be a mechanism of learning and memory: reappraisal of the NMDA-blockade strategy. *Psychobiology* 18: 251–257.

Keller, E. L., and D. S. Zee, eds. (1985). *Adaptive Processes in Visual and Oculomotor Systems*. Oxford: Pergamon.

Kelly, J. P. (1985a). Anatomical basis of sensory perception and motor coordination. In Kandel and Schwartz (1985), 222–243.

Kelly, J. P. (1985b). Vestibular system. In Kandel and Schwartz (1985), 584–596.

Kelner, K., and D. E. Koshland, eds. (1989) *Molecules to Models: Advances in Neuroscience*. Washington, DC: American Association for the Advancement of Science.

Kelso, S. R., A. H. Ganong, and T. H. Brown (1986). Hebbian synapses in the hippocampus. *Proceedings of the National Academy of Sciences USA* 83: 5326–5330.

Kennedy, M. B. (1989). Regulation of neuronal function by calcium. *Trends in Neurosciences* 12: 417–420.

Kienker, P. K., T. J. Sejnowski, G. E. Hinton, and L. E. Schumacher (1986). Separating figure from ground with a parallel network. *Perception* 15: 197–216.

Kimia, B. B., A. Tannenbaum, and S. W. Zucker (1989). *Toward a computational theory of shape: an overview*. Technical Report TR-CIM-89-13, Computer Vision and Robotics Laboratory, McGill University.

King, A. J., and D. R. Moore (1991). Plasticity of auditory maps in the brain. *Trends in the Neurosciences* 14: 31–37.

Kintsch, W. (1974). *The Representation of Meaning in Memory*. Hillsdale, NJ: Erlbaum.

Kirkpatrick, S., C. D. Gelatt, and M. P. Vecchi (1983). Optimization by simulated annealing. *Science* 220: 671–680.

Kleinfeld, D., and H. Sompolinsky (1989). Associative network models for central pattern generators. In Koch and Segev (1989), 195–246.

Kleinschmidt, A., M. F. Bear, and W. Singer (1987). Blockade of "NMDA" receptors disrupts experience-dependent plasticity of kitten striate cortex. *Science* 238: 355–358.

Klopf, A. H. (1982). *The Hedonistic Neuron: A Theory of Memory, Learning, and Intelligence.* New York: Hemisphere.

Klopf, A. H. (1987). *A Neuronal Model of Classical Conditioning.* US Air Force, Wright Aeronautical Laboratories, Technical Report AFWAL-TR-87-1139.

Klopf, A. H. (1988). A neuronal model of classical conditioning. *Psychobiology* 16: 85–125.

Knudsen, E. I., and M. Konishi (1978). A neural map of auditory space in the owl. *Science* 200: 795–797.

Knudsen, E. I., S. du Lac, and S. D. Esterly (1987). Computational maps in the brain. *Annual Review of Neuroscience* 10: 41–65.

Koch, C. (1989). Seeing chips: analog VLSI circuits for computer vision. *Neural Computation* 1: 184–200.

Koch, C., and T. Poggio (1987). Biophysics of computation: neurons, synapses, and membranes. In Edelman et al. (1987), 637–697.

Koch, C., and I. Segev, eds. (1989). *Methods in Neuronal Modeling.* Cambridge, MA: MIT Press.

Koch, C., R. J. Douglas, and U. Wehmeier (1990). Visibility of synaptically induced conductance changes: theory and simulations of anatomically characterized cortical pyramidal cells. *Journal of Neuroscience* 10: 1728–1744.

Koenderink, J. J. (1990). *Solid Shape.* Cambridge, MA: MIT Press.

Kohonen, T. (1984). *Self-organization and Associative Memory.* New York: Springer-Verlag.

Kohonen, T. (1987). *Content-Addressable Memories*, 2nd ed. Berlin: Springer-Verlag.

Konishi, M. (1986). Centrally synthesized maps of sensory space. *Trends in Neurosciences* 9: 163–168.

Konishi, M. (1991). Deciphering the brain's codes. *Neural Computation* 3: 1–18.

Konishi, M., T. T. Takahashi, H. Wagner, W. E. Sullivan, and C. E. Carr (1988). Neurophysiological and anatomical substrates of sound localization in the owl. In *Auditory Function*, ed. G. M. Edelman, W. E. Gall, and W. M. Cowan, 721–745. New York: Wiley.

Konorski, J. (1948). *Conditioned Reflexes and Neuron Organization.* London: Cambridge University Press.

Kopell, N., and G. B. Ermentrout (1989). Coupled oscillators and the design of central pattern generators. *Mathematical Bioscience* 89: 14–23.

Kossel, A., T. Bonhoeffer, and J. Bolz (1990). Non-Hebbian synapses in rat visual cortex. *Neuroreport* 1: 115–118.

Kosslyn, S. M., J. D. Holtzman, M. S. Gazzaniga, and M. J. Farrah (1985). A computational analysis of mental imagery generation: evidence for functional dissociation in split brain patients. *Journal of Experimental Psychology: General* 114: 311–341.

Krebs, J. R., and A. Kacelnik (1984). Time horizons of foraging animals. In *Timing and Time Perception*, ed. J. Gibbon and L. Allan, 278–291. *Annals of the New York Academy of Sciences*, vol. 423.

Kristan, W. B., Jr. (1982). Sensory and motor neurons responsible for local bending responses in leeches. *Journal of Experimental Biology* 96: 161–180.

Kristan, W. B., Jr., G. S. Stent, and C. A. Ort (1974). Neuronal control of swimming in the medicinal leech. I. Dynamics of the swimming rhythm. *Journal of Comparative Physiology* 94: 97–119.

Kuffler, S. W. (1953). Discharge patterns and functional organization of mammalian retina. *Journal of Neurophysiology* 16: 37–68.

Kuffler, S. W. (1980). Slow synaptic responses in autonomic ganglia and the pursuit of a pepti-dergic transmitter. *Journal of Experimental Biology* 89: 257–286.

Kuffler, S. W., and T. J. Sejnowski (1983). Peptidergic and muscarinic excitation at amphibian sympathetic synapses. *Journal of Physiology* (*London*) 341: 257–278.

Kuffler, S. W., J. G. Nicholls, and A. R. Martin (1984). *From Neuron to Brain: A Cellular Approach to the Function of the Nervous System*, 2nd ed. Sunderland, MA: Sinauer.

Kutas, M., and C. Van Petten (1988). Event-related brain potential studies of language. In *Advances in Psychophysiology*, ed. P. Ackles, J. R. Jennings, and M. Coles. Greenwich, CT: JAI Press.

Kwon, Y. H., M. Esguerra, and M. Sur (1991). NMDA and non-NMDA receptors mediate visual responses of neurons in the cat's lateral geniculate nucleus. *Journal of Neuroscience* 66: 414–428.

Lakoff, G. (1987). *Women, Fire, and Dangerous Things: What Categories Reveal About the Mind*. Chicago: University of Chicago Press.

Lam, D. M.-K., and C. J. Shatz, eds. (1991). *Development of the Visual System*. Cambridge, MA: MIT Press.

Land, E. H., D. H. Hubel, M. S. Livingstone, S. H. Perry, and M. M. Burns (1983). Colour-generating interactions across the corpus callosum. *Nature* 303: 616–618.

Larimer, (1988). The command hypothesis: a new view using an old example. *Trends in Neuro-sciences* 11: 506–510.

Larson, J., and G. Lynch (1986). Induction of synaptic potentiation in hippocampus by patterned stimulation involves two events. *Science* 232: 985–988.

Larson, J., D. Wong, and G. Lynch (1986). Patterned stimulation at the theta frequency is optimal for induction of hippocampal long-term potentiation. *Brain Research* 368: 347–350.

Lazzaro, J., and C. Mead (1989a). A silicon model of auditory localization. *Neural Computation* 1: 47–57.

Lazzaro, J., and C. Mead (1989b). A silicon model of auditory localization. (Revised) In Zornetzer et al. (1990), 155–173.

Le Cun, Y. (1985). Une procedure d'apprentissage pour reseau a seuil assymetrique. In *Cognitiva 85: A la Frontiere de l'Intelligence Artificielle des Sciences de la Connaissance des Neurosciences*, 599–604. Paris: CESTA.

LeDoux, J. E. (1990). Information flow from sensation to emotion: plasticity in the neural compu-tation of stimulus value. In Gabriel and Moore (1990), 3–52.

LeDoux, J. E., L. Romanmski, and A. Xagoraris (1989). Indelibility of subcortical emotional memories. *Journal of Cognitive Neuroscience* 1: 238–243.

Lee, C., W. R. Rohrer, and D. L. Sparks (1988). Population coding of saccadic eye movements by neurons in the superior colliculus. *Nature* 332: 357–360.

Leen, T. K. (1991). Dynamics of learning in recurrent feature-discovery networks. In Lippmann et al. (1991), 70–76.

Lehky, S. R., and T. J. Sejnowski (1988). Network model of shape-from-shading: neural function arises from both receptive and projective fields. *Nature* 333: 452–454.

Lehky, S. R., and T. J. Sejnowski (1990a). Neural network model of visual cortex for determining surface curvature from images of shaded surfaces. *Proceedings of the Royal Society of London B* 240: 251–278

Lehky, S. R., and T. J. Sejnowski (1990b). Neural model of stereoacuity and depth interpolation based on a distributed representation of stereo disparity. *Journal of Neuroscience* 10: 2281–2299.

Lehky, S. R., A. Pouget, and T. J. Sejnowski (in press). Neural models of binocular depth perception. In *Cold Spring Harbor Symposium on Quantitative Biology: The Brain. Vol. 55*, ed. E. Kandel, T. Sejnowski, C. Stevens, and J. Watson. New York: Cold Spring Harbor Press.

Leibniz, G. W. (1714). *The Monadology*. Trans. in Ariew, R. and Garber, D. (1989). *G. W. Leibniz: Philosophical Essays*. Indianapolis: Hackett.

Lennard, P. R., and J. W. Hermanson (1985). Central reflex modulation during locomotion. *Trends in Neurosciences* 8: 483–486.

LeVay, S., and S. B. Nelson (1991). Columnar organization of the visual cortex. In *The Neural Basis of Visual Function*, ed. J. R. Cronly-Dillon. London: Macmillan.

LeVay, S., and M. P. Stryker (1979). The development of ocular dominance columns in the cat. In *Aspects of Developmental Neurobiology*, ed. J. A. Ferrendelli, 83–98. Bethesda, MD: Society for Neuroscience.

LeVay, S., and T. Voigt (1988). Ocular dominance and disparity coding in cat visual cortex. *Visual Neuroscience* 1: 395–414.

LeVay, S., M. P. Stryker, and C. J. Shatz (1978). Ocular dominance columns and their development in layer IV of the cat's visual cortex. *Journal of Comparative Neurology* 179: 223–244.

Levitan, I. B., and L. K. Kaczmarek (1991). *The Neuron: Cell and Molecular Biology*. Oxford: Oxford University Press.

Levy, W. B., and N. Desmond (1985). The rules of elemental synaptic plasticity. In *Synaptic Modification, Neuron Selectivity, and Nervous System Organization*, ed. W. B. Levy, J. A. Anderson, and S. Lehmkuhle, 105–121. Hillsdale, NJ: Erlbaum

Levy, W. B., and O. Steward (1983). Temporal contiguity requirements for long-term associative potentiation/depression in the hippocampus. *Neuroscience* 8: 791–797.

Linsker, R. (1986) From basic network principles to neural architecture (series). *Proceedings of the National Academy of Sciences USA* 83: 7508–7512, 8390–8394, 8779–8783.

Linsker, R. (1988). Self-organization in a perceptual network. *Computer* 21: 105–117

Linsker, R. (1990a). Perceptual neural organization: some approaches based on network models and information theory. *Annual Review of Neuroscience* 13: 257–282.

Linsker, R. (1990b). Self-organization in a perceptual system: how network models and information theory may shed light on neural organization. In Hanson and Olson (1990), 255–350.

Lippmann, R. (1989). Review of neural networks for speech recognition. *Neural Computation* 1: 1–38.

Lippmann , R. P., J. E., Moody, and D. S. Touretzky, eds. (1991). *Advances in Neural Information Processing Systems 3*. San Mateo, CA: Morgan Kaufmann.

Lisberger, S. G. (1984). The latency of pathways containing the site of motor learning in the monkey vestibulo-ocular reflex. *Science* 225: 74–76.

Lisberger, S. G. (1988a). The neural basis for learning of simple motor skills. *Science* 242: 728–735. Reprinted in Kelner and Koshland (1989), 205–218.

Lisberger, S. (1988b). The neural basis for motor learning in the vestibulo-ocular reflex in monkeys. *Trends in Neurosciences* 11: 147–152.

Lisberger, S. G., and F. A. Miles (1980). Role of primate medial vestibular nucleus in long-term adaptive plasticity of vestibulo-ocular reflex. *Journal of Neurophysiology* 43: 1725–1745.

Lisberger, S. G., and T. A. Pavelko (1988). Brain stem neurons in modified pathways for motor learning in the primate vestibulo-ocular reflex. *Science* 242: 771−773.

Lisberger, S. G., and T. J. Sejnowski (1992). *Computational analysis predicts the site of motor learning in the vestibulo-ocular reflex.* Technical Report INC-92.1, UCSD.

Lisberger, S. G., E. J. Morris, and L. Tychesen (1987). Visual motion processing and sensory-motor integration for smooth pursuit eye movements. *Annual Review of Neuroscience* 10: 97−130.

Livingstone, M. S., and D. H. Hubel (1987). Psychophysical evidence for separate channels for the perception of form, color, movement, and depth. *Journal of Neuroscience* 7: 3416−3468.

Llinás, R. R. (1985). Electronic transmission in the mammalian central nervous system. In *Gap Junctions*, ed. M. E. Bennett and D. C. Spray, 337−353. Cold Spring Harbor, NY: Cold Spring Harbor Laboratory.

Llinás, R. R. (1988). The intrinsic electrophysiological properties of mammalian neurons: insights into central nervous system function. *Science* 242: 1654−1664. Reprinted in Kelner and Koshland, 83−102.

Llinás, R. R., and A. A. Grace (1989). Intrinsic 40 Hz oscillatory properties of layer IV neurons in guinea pig cerebral cortex in vitro. *Society for Neuroscience Abstracts* 15: 660.

Llinás, R. R., and R. Hess (1976). Tetrodotoxin-resistant dendritic spikes in avian Purkinje cells. *Society for Neuroscience Abstracts* 2: 112.

Llinás, R., and H. Jahnsen (1982). Electrophysiology of mammalian thalamic neurones in vitro. *Nature* 297: 406−408.

Llinás, R., and M. Sugimori (1980). *Journal of Physiology (London)* 305: 171.

Llinás, R. R., M. Sugimori, and B. Cherskey (1989). Voltage-dependent calcium conductances in mammalian neurons. In *Calcium Channels: Structure and Function* (Annals of the New York Academy of Sciences Vol. 560), ed. D. W. Wray, R. I. Norman, and P. Hess, 103−111. New York: The New York Academy of Sciences.

Lockery, S. R., G. Wittenberg, W. B. Kristan, Jr., and G. Cottrell (1989). Function of identified interneurons in the leech elucidated using neural networks trained by back-propagation. *Nature* 340: 468−471.

Lockery, S. R., Y. Fang, and T. J. Sejnowski (1990). A dynamical neural network model of sensorimotor transformation in the leech. *Neural Computation* 2: 274−282.

Lockery, S. R., and W. B. Kristan, Jr. (1990a). Distributed processing of sensory information in the leech. I. Input-output relations of the local bending reflex. *Journal of Neuroscience* 10: 1811−1815.

Lockery, S. R., and W. B. Kristan, Jr. (1990b). Distributed processing of sensory information in the leech. II. Identification of interneurons contributing to the local bending reflex. *Journal of Neuroscience* 10: 1816−1829.

Logothetis, N., and E. R. Charles (1990). The minimum motion technique applied to determine isoluminance in psychophysical experiments with monkeys. *Vision Research* 30: 829−838.

Logothetis, N., and J. D. Schall (1989). Neural correlates of subjective visual perception. *Science* 245: 753−761.

Logothetis, N., P. H. Schiller, E. R. Charles, and A. C. Hurlbert (1990). Perceptual deficits and the activity of the color-opponent and broad-band pathways at isoluminance. *Science* 247: 214−217.

Lorento de Nó, R. (1934). Studies on the structure of the cerebral cortex. II. Continuation of the study of the ammonic system. *Journal of Psychology and Neurology* 46: 113−177.

Lund, J. (1987). Local circuit neurons of macaque monkey striate cortex. I. Neurons of laminae 4C and 5A. *Journal of Comparative Neurology* 257: 60–92.

Lundberg, A. (1980). Half-centres revisited. In *Advances In Physiological Sciences. Vol. 1: Regulatory Function of the CNS*, ed. J. Szentagothai, M. Palkovits, and J. Hamori (1980), 155–167. Budapest: Pergamon.

Luria, A. R. (1968). *The Mind of a Mnemonist: A Little Book About a Vast Memory*. New York: Basic Books. Trans. by L. Solotaroff, 1987. Cambridge, MA: Harvard University Press.

Lynch, G., R. Granger, M. Baudry, and J. Larson (1989a). Cortical encoding of memory: hypotheses derived from analysis and simulation of physiological learning rules in anatomical structures. In Nadel et al. (1988), 180–224.

Lynch, G., R. Granger, and J. Larson (1989b). Some possible functions of simple cortical networks suggested by computer modeling. In Byrne and Berry (1989), 329–362.

Lytton, W. W., and T. J. Sejnowski (1991). Simulations of cortical pyramidal neurons synchronized by inhibitory interneurons. *Journal of Neurophysiology* 66: 1059–1079.

MacAvoy, M. G., J. P. Gottlieb, and C. J. Bruce (1991). Smooth-pursuit eye movement representation in the primate frontal eye field. *Cerebral Cortex* 1: 95–102.

MacIntosh, N. J. (1983). *Conditioning and Associative Learning*. Oxford: Oxford University Press.

Magleby, K. (1987). Short-term changes in synaptic efficacy. In Edelman et al. (1987), 21–56.

Malenka, R. C., J. A. Kauer, D. J. Perkel, and R. A. Nicoll (1989). The impact of post-synaptic calcium on synaptic transmission—its role in long-term potentiation. *Trends in Neurosciences* 12: 444–450.

Malpeli, J. G. (1983). Activity of cells in area 17 of the cat in absence of input from layer A of lateral geniculate nucleus. *Journal of Neurophysiology* 49: 595–610.

Malpeli, J. G. , C. Lee, H. D. Schwark, and T. G. Weyand (1986). Cat area 17. I. Pattern of thalamic control of cortical layers. *Journal of Neurophysiology*. 56: 1062–1073.

Mandelbrot, B. (1983). *The Fractal Geometry of Nature*. San Francisco: Freeman.

Marder, E., guest ed. (1989). *Seminars in Neurosciences*. Vol. 1, no. 1. *Modulation of Neural Networks Underlying Behavior*.

Marder, E., S. L. Hooper, and J. S. Eisen (1987). Multiple neurotransmitters provide a mechanism for the production of multiple outputs from a single neuronal circuit. In Edelman et al. (1987), 305–327.

Marr, D. (1969). A theory of cerebellar cortex. *Journal of Physiology (London)* 202: 437–470. Reprinted in Vaina (1991), 11–46.

Marr, D. (1970). A theory for cerebral neocortex. *Proceedings of the Royal Society of London B* 176: 161–234. Reprinted in Vaina (1991), 129–203.

Marr, D. (1971). Simple memory: A theory for archicortex. *Philosophical Transactions of the Royal Society of London B*. 262: 23–81. Reprinted in Vaina (1991), 59–117.

Marr, D. (1982). *Vision*. New York: Freeman.

Marr, D., and T. Poggio (1976). Co-operative computation of stereo disparity. *Science* 194: 283–287. Reprinted in Vaina (1991) 239–244.

Marr, D., and T. Poggio (1977). From understanding computation to understanding neural circuitry. *Neuroscience Research Program Bulletin* 15: 470–488.

Martin, K. A. C. (1984). Neuronal circuits in cat striate cortex. In *Cerebral Cortex: Functional Properties of Cortical Cells*, vol. 2, ed. E. G. Jones and A. Peters, 241–284. New York: Plenum.

Martin, K. A. C. (1988). From single cells to simple circuits in the cerebral cortex. *Quarterly Journal of Experimental Physiology* 73: 637–702.

Mason, R. J., and S. P. R. Rose (1987). Lasting changes in spontaneous multi-unit activity in the chick brain following passive avoidance training. *Neuroscience* 21: 931–941.

Maunsell, J. H. R., and W. T. Newsome (1987). Visual processing in monkey extrastriate cortex. *Annual Review of Neuroscience* 10: 363–401.

Maunsell, J. H. R., and D. van Essen (1983). Connections of the middle temporal visual area (MT) and their relationship to a cortical hierarchy in the macaque monkey. *Journal of Neuroscience* 3: 2563–2586.

Maunsell, J. H. R., and D. C. van Essen (1987). The topographic organization of the middle temporal visual area in the macaque monkey: representational biases and relationship to callosal connections and myeloarchitectonic boundaries. *Journal of Comparative Neurology* 266: 535–555.

Maunsell, J. H. R., G. Sclar, T. A. Nealey, and D. D. DePriest (in press). Extraretinal representations in area V4 in the macaque monkey. *Visual Neuroscience*.

Mayhew, J. E. W., and H. C. Longeut-Higgins (1982). A computational model of binocular depth perception. *Nature* 297: 376–379.

McCarthy, J. (1959). Programs with common sense. In *Proceedings of the Symposium on Mechanization of Thought Processes*, National Physics Laboratory, 75–84. London: Her Majesty's Stationery Office. Reprinted in Semantic Information Processing, ed. M. Minsky (1968), 403–410. Cambridge, MA: MIT Press.

McCarthy, R. A., and E. K. Warrington (1988). Evidence for modality-specific meaning systems in the brain. *Nature* 334: 428–430.

McCarthy, R. A., and E. K. Warrington (1990). *Cognitive Neuropsychology*. San Diego, CA: Academic Press.

McClelland, J., and D. Rumelhart (1988). *Explorations in Parallel Distributed Processing*. Cambridge, MA: MIT Press.

McClelland, J., D. Rumelhart, and the PDP Research Group (1986). *Parallel Distributed Processing: Explorations in the Microstructure of Cognition, vol. 2.* Cambridge, MA: MIT Press.

McCormick, D. (1989). Cholinergic and noradrenergic modulation of thalamocortical processing. *Trends in Neurosciences* 12: 215–221.

McCulloch, W. S., and W. H. Pitts (1943). A logical calculus of ideas immanent in nervous activity. *Bulletin of Mathematical Biophysics* 5: 115–133.

McIlwain, J. T. (1991). Distributed spatial coding in the superior colliculus: a review. *Visual Neuroscience* 6: 3–13.

McKenna, T., J. Davis, and S. Zornetzer (1992). *Single Neuron Computation*. Cambridge, MA: Academic Press.

McNaughton, B. L. (1988). Neural mechanisms for spatial computation and information storage. In Nadel et al. (1988), 285–350.

McNaughton, B. L. (1991). Commentary on "Simple memory: a theory for archicortex," by D. Marr. In Vaina (1991), 118–120.

McNaughton, B. L., and R. G. M. Morris (1987). Hippocampal synaptic enhancement and information storage within a distributed memory system. *Trends in Neurosciences* 10: 408–415.

McNaughton, B. L., R. M. Douglas, and G. V. Goddard (1978). Synaptic enhancement in fascia dentata: cooperativity among coactive afferents. *Brain Research* 157: 277–293.

Mead, C. (1987). Silicon models of neural computation. *IEEE First International Conference on Neural Networks*, ed. M. Cuvdill and C. Butler, I-93–I-106.

Mead, C. (1989). *Analog VLSI and Neural Systems*. Reading, MA: Addison-Wesley.

Menzel, R. (1983). Neurobiology of learning and memory: the honeybee as a model system. *Naturwissenschaften* 70: 504–511. Reprinted in Shaw et al. (1990), 494–501.

Merzenich, M., and J. F. Brugge (1973). Representation of the cochlear partition on the superior temporal plane in the macaque monkey. *Brain Research* 50: 275–296.

Merzènich, M., and J. H. Kaas (1982). Reorganization of mammalian somatosensory cortex following peripheral nerve injury. *Trends in Neurosciences* 5: 434–436.

Merzenich, M., G. H. Recanzone, W. M. Jenkins, and R. J. Nudo (1990). How the brain functionally rewires itself. In Arbib and Robinson (1990), 177–210.

Mesulam, M. M. (1985). Attention, confusional states, and neglect. In *Principles of Behavioral Neurology*, ed. M. M. Mesulam, 125–168. Philadelphia: F. A. Davis.

Metcalfe Eich, J. (1985). Levels of processing, encoding specificity, elaboration, and CHARM. *Psychological Review* 92: 1–38.

Mignard, M., and J. G.Malpeli (1991). Paths of information flow through visual cortex. *Science* 251: 1249–1251.

Mikami, A., W. T. Newsome, and R. H. Wurtz (1986a). Motion selectivity in macaque visual cortex. I. Mechanisms of direction and speed selectivity in extrastriate area MT. *Journal of Neurophysiology* 55: 1308–1327.

Mikami, A., W. T. Newsome, and R. H. Wurtz (1986b). Motion selectivity in macaque visual cortex. II. Spatiotemporal range of directional interactions in MT and V1. *Journal of Neurophysiology* 55: 1328–1339.

Miles, F. A., and S. G. Lisberger (1981). Plasticity in the vestibulo-ocular reflex: a new hypothesis. *Annual Review of Neuroscience* 4: 273–299.

Miles, F. A., D. J. Braitman, and B. M. Dow (1980). Long-term adaptive changes in primate vestibulocular reflex. II. Electrophysiological observations on semicircular canal primary afferents. *Journal of Neurophysiology* 43: 1477–1493.

Miles, F. A., D. J. Braitman, and B. M. Dow (1980). Long-term adaptive changes in primate vestibuloocular reflex. IV. Electrophysiological observations in flocculus of adapted monkeys. *Journal of Neurophysiology* 43: 1477–1493.

Miller, K. D. (1990). Correlation-based models of neural development. In *Neuroscience and Connectionist Theory*, ed. M. A. Gluck and D. E. Rumelhart, 267–353. Hillsdale, NJ: Erlbaum.

Miller, K. D., guest ed. (in press). *Seminars in the Neurosciences*. Vol. 4, no. 1. *Use of Models in the Neurosciences*.

Miller, K. D., and M. P. Stryker (1990). Ocular dominance column formation: mechanisms and models. In Hanson and Olson (1990), 255–350.

Miller, K. D., B. Chapman, and M. P. Stryker (1989a). Responses of cells in cat visual cortex depend on NMDA receptors. *Proceedings of the National Academy of Science USA* 86: 5183–5187.

Miller, K. D., J. B. Keller, and M. P. Stryker (1989b). Ocular dominance column development: analysis and simulation. *Science* 245: 605–615.

Millikan, R. G. (1984). *Language, Thought, and Other Biological Categories*. Cambridge, MA: MIT Press

Milner, B. (1966). Amnesia following operations on the temporal lobes. In *Amnesia*, ed. C. W. M. Whitty and O. Zangwill, 109–133. London: Butterworth.

Milner, B. (1970). Memory and the medial temporal regions of the brain. In *Biology of Memory*, ed. K. H. Pribram and D. B. Broadbent, 29–50. New York: Academic Press.

Milner, B. (1973). Hemispheric specialization: scope and limits. In *The Neurosciences: Third Study Program*, ed. F. O. Schmitt and F. G. Worden, 75–89. Cambridge, MA: MIT Press.

Milner, B., Corkin, S., and H. L. Teuber (1968). Further analysis of the hippocampal amnesic syndrome: 14 years follow-up study of H.M. *Neuropsychologia* 6: 215–234.

Minsky, M. (1985). *The Society of Mind*. New York: Simon and Schuster.

Minsky, M., and S. Papert (1969). *Perceptrons*. Cambridge, MA: MIT Press.

Mishkin, M. (1982). A memory system in the monkey. *Philosophical Transactions of the Royal Society of London B* 298: 85–95.

Mishkin, M., L. G. Ungerleider, and K. A. Macko (1983). Object vision and spatial vision: two cortical pathways. *Trends in Neurosciences* 6: 414–417.

Mitchell, S. D. (1989). The causal background of functional explanation. *International Studies in the Philosophy of Science* 3: 213–229.

Miyashita, Y., and H. S. Chang (1988). Neuronal correlate of pictorial short-term memory in the primate temporal cortex. *Nature* 331: 68–70.

Montague, P. R., J. A. Gally, and G. M. Edelman (1991). Spatial signaling in the development and function of neural connections. *Cerebral Cortex* 1: 199–220.

Moody, J. (1989). Fast-learning in multi-resolution hierarchies. In Touretzky (1989), 29–39.

Moody, J., and C. J. Darken (1989). Fast learning in networks of locally-tuned processing units. *Neural Computation* 1: 281–294.

Moran, J., and R. Desimone (1985). Selective attention gates visual processing in the extrastriate cortex. *Science* 229: 782–784.

Moriyoshi, K., M. Masu, T. Ishii, R. Shigemoto, N. Mizuno, and S. Nakanishi (1991). Molecular cloning and characterization of the rat NMDA receptor. *Nature* 354: 31–37.

Morris, R. G. M., ed. (1989). *Parallel Distributed Processing: Implications for Psychology and Neuroscience*. Oxford: Oxford University Press.

Morris, R. G. M., P. Garrud, J. N. P. Rawlins, and J. O'Keefe (1982). Place navigation impaired in rats with hippocampal lesions. *Nature* 297: 681–683.

Morris, R. G. M., S. Davis, and S. P. Butcher (1990). Hippocampal synaptic plasticity and NMDA receptors: a role in information storage? *Philosophical Transactions of the Royal Society of London B* 329: 187–204.

Mott, F. W., and C. S. Sherrington (1895). Experiments upon the influence of sensory nerves upon movement and nutrition of the limbs: preliminary communication. *Proceedings of the Royal Society of London B* 57: 481–488.

Mountcastle, V. B. (1957). Modality and topographic properties of single neurons of cat somatic sensory cortex. *Journal of Neurophysiology* 20: 408–434.

Mountcastle, V. B. (1978). *The Mindful Brain: Part I*. Cambridge, MA: MIT Press.

Muller, D., M. Joly, and G. Lynch (1988). Contributions of quisqualate and NMDA receptors to the induction and expression of LTP. *Science* 242: 1694–1697.

Müller, W., and J. A. Connor (1991). Dendritic spines as individual neuronal compartments for synaptic Ca^{2+} responses. *Nature* 354: 73–75.

Mumford, D., S. M. Kosslyn, L. A. Hillger, and R. J. Herrnstein (1987). Discriminating figure from ground: the role of edge detection and region growing. *Proceedings of the National Academy of Science (USA)* 20: 7354–7358.

Munsell, A. H. (1905). *A Color Notation*. Boston: Ellis.

Munsell Color Company (1976). *Munsell Book of Color*. Baltimore, MD.: Munsell Color Co.

Murchison, D., and J. L. Larimer (1990). Dual motor output interneurons in the abdominal ganglia of the crayfish *Procambrus clarkii*: synaptic activation of motor outputs in both the swimmeret and abdominal positioning systems by single interneurons. *Journal of Experimental Biology* 150: 269–293.

Nadel, L., L. A. Cooper, P. Culicover, and R. H. Harnish, eds. (1988). *Neural Connections and Mental Computations*. Cambridge, MA: MIT Press.

Nagel, T. (1974). What is it like to be a bat? *Philosophical Review* 83: 435–450.

Nakayama, K., S. Shimojo, and V. S. Ramachandran (1990). Transparency: relation to depth, subjective contours, luminance, and neon color spreading. *Perception* 19: 497–513.

Nathans, J. (1987). Molecular biology of visual pigments. *Annual Review of Neuroscience* 10: 163–194.

Nathans, J. (1989). The genes for color vision. *Scientific American* 260: 42–49.

Nathans, J. , D. Thomas, and D. S. Hogness (1986). Molecular genetics of human color vision: the genes encoding blue, green, and red pigments. *Science* 212: 193–202.

Nauta, W. J. H., and M. Feirtag (1986). *Fundamental Neuroanatomy*. New York: Freeman.

Nelson, J. I., and B. J. Frost (1978). Orientation-selective inhibition from beyond the classic visual receptive field. *Brain Research* 139: 359–365.

Nelson, J. I., and B. J. Frost (1985). Intracortical facilitation among co-oriented, co-axially aligned simple cells in cat striate cortex. *Experimental Brain Research* 61: 54–61.

Neville, H. J. (1990). Intermodal competition and compensation in development: evidence from studies of the visual system in congenitally deaf adults. In Diamond (1990), 71–91.

Neville, H. J., and D. Lawson (1987a). Attention to central and peripheral visual space in a movement detection task: I. Normal hearing adults. *Brain Research* 405: 253–267.

Neville, H. J., and D. Lawson (1987b). Attention to central and peripheral visual space in a movement detection task: II. Congenitally deaf adults. *Brain Research* 405: 268–283.

Newsome, W. T., and E. B. Pare (1986). MT lesions impair visual discrimination of direction in a stochastic motion display. *Society of Neuroscience Abstracts* 12: 1183.

Newsome, W. T., R. H. Wurtz, M. R. Durtsteler, and A. Mikami (1985). Deficits in visual motion processing following ibotenic acid lesions of the middle temporal visual area of the macaque monkey. *Journal of Neuroscience* 5: 825–840.

Newsome, W. T., A. Mikami, and R. H. Wurtz (1986). Motion selectivity in macaque visual cortex. III. Psychophysics and physiology of apparent motion. *Journal of Neurophysiology* 55: 1340–1351.

Newsome, W. T., K. H. Britten, and J. A. Movshon (1989). Neuronal correlates of a perceptual decision. *Nature* 341: 52–54.

Nicholls, J. G., and D. A. Baylor (1968). Specific modalities and receptive fields of sensory neurons in the CNS of the leech. *Journal of Neurophysiology* 31: 740–756.

Nilsson, N. J. (1990). *The Mathematical Foundations of Learning Machines*. San Mateo, CA: Morgan Kaufmann.

Northcutt, R. G. (1981). Evolution of the telencephalon in nonmammals. *Annual Review of Neuroscience* 4: 301–350.

Nottebohm, F., S. Kasparian, and C. Pandazias (1981). Brain space for a learned task. *Brain Research* 213: 99–109.

Nowlan, S. J. (1990). *Competing Experts: An Experimental Investigation of Associative Mixture Models*. Technical Report CRG-TR-90-5, University of Toronto.

Oja, E. (1982). A simplified neuron model as a principal component analyzer. *Journal of Mathematical Biology* 15: 267–273.

Ojemann, G. A. (1988). Effect of cortical and subcortical stimulation on human language and verbal memory. In *Language, Communication, and the Brain*, ed. F. Plum, 101–115. New York: Raven Press.

Ojemann, G. A. (1990). Organization of language cortex derived from investigations during neurosurgery. *Seminars in the Neurosciences* 2: 297–306.

Ojemann, G. A. (1991). Cortical organization of language. *The Journal of Neuroscience* 11: 2281–2287.

O'Keefe, J. (1976). Place units in the hippocampus of the freely moving rat. *Experimental Neurology* 51: 78–109.

O'Keefe, J. (1988). Computations the hippocampus might perform. In Nadel et al. (1988), 225–284.

O'Keefe, J., and L. Nadel (1978). *The Hippocampus as a Cognitive Map*. Oxford: Clarendon Press.

Oppenheim, R. W. (1985). Naturally occurring cell death during neural development. *Trends in Neurosciences* 8: 487–493.

Ort, C. A., W. B. Kristan, Jr., and G. S. Stent (1974). Neuronal control of swimming in the medicinal leech. II. Identification and connections of motor neurones. *Journal of Comparative Physiology* 94: 121–154.

Paller, K. A., S. Zola-Morgan, L. R. Squire, and S. A. Hillyard (1989). P-3 like brain waves in normal monkeys and monkeys with medial temporal lesions. *Behavioral Neuroscience* 102: 714–725.

Parker, D. (1985). *Learning Logic*. Technical Report TR-47, Center for Computational Research in Economics and Management Science, Massachusetts Institute of Technology, Cambridge, MA.

Pasternak, T., and L. Leinen (1986). Pattern and motion vision in cats with selective loss of cortical directional selectivity. *Journal of Neuroscience* 6: 938–945.

Paulin, M. G., M. E. Nelson, and J. M. Bower (1989). Neural control of sensory acquisition: the vestibulo-ocular reflex. In Touretzky (1989), 410–418

Pearlmutter, B. (1989). Learning state space trajectories in recurrent neural networks. *Neural Computation* 1: 263–269.

Pearson, K. G. (1976). The control of walking. *Scientific American* 235: 72–86.

Pearson, K. G. (1987). Central pattern generation: a concept under scrutiny. In *Advances in Physiological Research*, eds. H. McLennan, J. R. Ledsome, C. H. S. McIntosh, and D. R. Jones, 167–185. New York: Plenum.

Pearson, K. G., and H. Wolf (1986). Comparison of motor patterns in the intact and deafferented flight system of the locust. 1. Electromyographic analysis. *Journal of Comparative Physiology* 160: 259–268.

Pellionisz, A. (1985). Tensorial aspects of the multidimensional approach to the vestibulo-oculomotor reflex and gaze. In *Adaptive Mechanisms in Gaze Control*, ed. A. Berthoz and G. Melvill Jones, 231–296. Amsterdam: Elsevier.

Penfield, W., and H. Jasper (1954). *Epilepsy and the Functional Anatomy of the Human Brain*. Boston: Little, Brown.

Penrose, R. (1989). *The Emperor's New Mind: On Computers, Minds, and the Laws of Physics*. New York: Oxford University Press.

Pentland, A. P. (1984). Local shading analysis. *IEEE Transactions on Pattern Analysis and Machine Intelligence* PAMI-6: 170–187.

Pentland, A. P. (1989a) Shape information from shading: a theory about human perception. *Spatial Vision* 4: 165–182.

Pentland, A. P. (1989b). Part segmentation for object recognition. *Neural Computation* 1: 82–91.

Perkel, D. H., and B. Mulloney (1978). Electrotonic properties of neurons: steady-state compartmental model. *Journal of Neurophysiology* 41: 627–639.

Perrett, D. I., A. J. Mistlin, and A. J. Chitty (1987). Visual neurons responsive to faces. *Trends in Neurosciences* 10: 358–364.

Petersen, S. E., P. T. Fox, M. I. Posner, M. A. Mintun, and M. E. Raichle (1988). Positron emission tomographic studues of the cortical anatomy of single word processing. *Nature* 331: 585–589.

Peterson, B. W., J. F. Baker, and J. C. Houk (1991). A model of adaptive control of vestibulooocular reflex based on properties of cross-axis adaptation. In *Activity-Driven CNS Changes in Learning and Development (Annals of the New York Academy of Sciences, Vol. 627)*, ed. J. R. Wolpaw, J. T. Smith, and T. M. Vaughan, 319–337. New York: The New York Academy of Sciences.

Peterson, C. (1990). Parallel distributed approaches to combinatorial optimization: benchmark studies on the traveling salesman problem. *Neural Computation* 2: 261–269.

Pettigrew, J. D. (1990). Is there a single, most-efficient algorithm for stereopsis? In Blakemore (1990), 283–290.

Pettigrew, J. D. , T. Nikara, and P. O. Bishop (1968). Binocular interaction on single units in cat striate cortex: simultaneous stimulation by single moving slit with receptive fields in correspondence. *Experimental Brain Research* 6: 391–410.

Phelps, M. E., and J. C. Mazziotta (1985). Positron emission tomographic studies of the cortical anatomy of single-word processing. *Nature* 331: 585–589.

Pineda, F. J. (1987a). Generalization of backpropagation to recurrent neural networks. *Physical Review Letters* 18: 2229–2232.

Pineda, F. J. (1987b). Generalization of backpropagation to recurrent and higher order networks. In *Proceedings of the IEEE Conference on Neural Information Processing Systems*, ed. D. Z. Anderson, 602–611.

Pineda, F. J. (1989). Recurrent backpropagation and the dynamical approach to adaptive neural computation. *Neural Computation* 1: 161–172.

Poggio, G. F. (1984). Processing of stereoscopic information in primate visual cortex. In *Dynamic Aspects of Neocortical Function*, ed. G. M. Edelman, W. E. Gall, and W. M. Cowan, 613–635. New York: Wiley.

Poggio, G. F., and B. Fischer (1977). Binocular interaction and depth sensitivity in striate and prestriate cortex of behaving rhesus monkey. *Journal of Neurophysiology* 40: 1392–1405.

Poggio, G. F., and W. Talbot (1981). Mechanisms of static and dynamic stereopsis in foveal cortex of the rhesus monkeys. *Journal of Physiology (London)* 315: 469–492.

Poggio, G. F., and L. J. Viernstein (1964). Time series analysis of impulse sequences of thalamic somatic sensory neurons. *Journal of Neurophysiology* 27: 517–545.

Poggio, T. (1990) A theory of how the brain works. *Cold Spring Harbor Symposium on Quantitative Biology: The Brain* 55, 88–9.

Poggio, T., and F. Girosi (1990). Regularization algorithms for learning that are equivalent to multilayer networks. *Science* 247: 978–982.

Poggio, T., E. B. Gamble, and J. J. Little (1988). Parallel integration of vision modules. *Science* 242: 436–440.

Pollen, D. A., J. R. Lee, and J. H. Taylor (1971). How does striate cortex begin reconstruction of the visual world? *Science* 173: 74–77.

Pollen, D. A., J. P. Gaska, and L. D. Jacobson (1988). Responses of simple and complex cells to compound sine-wave gratings. Vision *Research* 28: 25–39.

Pomerleau, D. A. (1991). Efficient training of artificial neural networks for autonomous navigation. *Neural Computation* 3: 88–97.

Pons, T. P., P. E. Garraghty, A. K. Ommaya, J. H. Kaas, E. Taub, and M. Mishkin. (1991). Massive cortical reorganization after sensory deafferentation in adult macaques. *Science* 252: 1857–60.

Pöppel, E. (1989). Taxonomy of the subjective: an evolutionary perspective. In *Neuropsychology of Visual Perception*, ed. J. W. Brown, Hillsdale, NJ: Erlbaum. 219–232

Popper, K. (1959). *The Logic of Scientific Discovery*. New York: Harper & Row.

Popper, K., and J. Eccles (1977). *The Self and Its Brain*. Berlin: Springer-Verlag.

Posner, M. I. (1978). *Chronometric Explorations of Mind*. Hillsdale, NJ: Erlbaum.

Posner, M. I., ed. (1989). *Foundations of Cognitive Science*. Cambridge, MA: MIT Press.

Posner, M. I., and S. E. Petersen (1990). The attention system of the human brain. *Annual Review of Neuroscience* 13: 25–42.

Posner, M. I., S. E. Petersen, P. T. Fox, and M. E. Raichle (1988). Localization of cognitive operations in the human brain. *Science* 240: 1627–1631.

Pouget, A., and T. J. Sejnowski (1990). Neural models of binocular depth perception. *Cold Spring Harbor Symposia on Quantitative Biology* 55: 765–777.

Pouget, A., and S. J. Thorpe (1991). Connectionist model of object identification. *Connection Science* 3: 127–142.

Press, G. A., D. G. Amaral, and L. R. Squire (1989). Hippocampal abnormalities in amnesic patients revealed by high-resolution magnetic resonance imaging. *Nature* 341: 54–57.

Purves, D. (1988). *Body and Brain: A Trophic Theory of Neural Connections*. Cambridge, MA: Harvard University Press.

Purves, D., and J. T. Voyvodic (1987). Imaging mammalian nerve cells and their connections over time in living animals. *Trends in Neurosciences* 10: 398–404.

Pylyshyn, Z. (1984). *Computation and Cognition*. Cambridge, MA: MIT Press.

Qian, N., and T. Sejnowski (1988). Predicting the secondary structure of globular proteins using neural network models. *Journal of Molecular Biology* 202: 865–884.

Qian, N., and T. Sejnowski (1989). Learning to solve random-dot stereograms of dense transparent surfaces with recurrent backpropagation. In Touretzky et al. (1989), 435–443.

Quirk, G. J., R. U. Muller, and J. L. Kubie (1990). The firing of hippocampal place cells in the dark depends on the rat's recent experience. *Journal of Neuroscience* 10: 2008–2017.

Raichle, M. E. (1986). Neuroimaging. *Trends in Neurosciences* 9: 525–529.

Rakic, P. (1981). Developmental events leading to laminar and areal organization of the neocortex. In *The Organization of the Cerebral Cortex*, ed. F. O. Schmitt, F. G. Worden, G. Adelman, and S. G. Dennis, et al., 7–28. Cambridge, MA: MIT Press.

Rakic, P. (1986). Mechanisms of ocular dominance segregation in the lateral geniculate nucleus: competitive elimination hypothesis. *Trends in Neurosciences* 9: 11–15.

Rakic, P., J.-P. Bourgeois, M. F. Eckenhoff, N. Zecevic, and P. S. Goldman-Rakic (1986). Concurrent overproduction of synapses in diverse regions of the primate cerebral cortex. *Science* 232: 232–235.

Rall, W. (1964). Theoretical significance of dendritic tree for input-output relation. In *Neural Theory and Modeling*, ed. R. F. Reiss, 73–97. Stanford, CA: Stanford University Press.

Rall, W. (1977). Core conductor theory and cable properties of neurons. In *Handbook of Physiology: The Nervous System, vol. 1*, ed. E. R. Kandel, J. M. Brookhardt, and V. B. Mountcastle, 39–98. Baltimore: Williams & Wilkins.

Rall, W. (1989). Cable theory for dendritic neurons. In Koch and Segev (1989), 9–62.

Rall, W., and I. Segev (1987). Functional possibilities for synapses on dendrites and dendritic spines. In Edelman et al. (1987), 605–636.

Ramachandran, V. S. (1986). Capture of stereopsis and apparent motion by illusory contours. *Perception and Psychophysics* 39: 361–373.

Ramachandran, V. S. (1988). Perceiving shape-from-shading. *Scientific American* 259: 76–83.

Ramachandran, V. S. (1990a). Interactions between motion, depth, color and form: the utilitarian theory of perception. In Blakemore (1990), 346–360.

Ramachandran, V. S. (1990b). Visual perception in people and machines. In *AI and the Eye*, ed. A. Blake and T. Troscianko, 21–77. New York: Wiley.

Ramachandran, V. S. (1991). Form, motion and binocular rivalry. *Science* 251: 950–951.

Ramachandran, V. S., V. M. Rao, and T. R. Vidyasagar (1973). The role of contours in stereopsis. *Nature* 242: 412–414.

Regehr, W. G., and D. W. Tank (1990). Postsynaptic NMDA receptor-mediated calcium accumulation in hippocampal CA1 pyramidal cell dendrites. *Nature* 345: 807–810.

Regehr, W. G., J. A. Connor, and D. W. Tank (1989). Optical imaging of calcium accumulation in hippocampal pyramidal cells during synaptic activation. *Nature* 341: 533–536.

Reh, T. A. (1991). Determination of cell fate during retinal histogenesis: intrinsic and extrinsic mechanisms. In Lam and Shatz (1991), 79–94.

Reichardt, W., and T. Poggio (1976). Visual control of orientation behavior in the fly. Part I. A quantitative analysis. *Quarterly Review of Biophysics* 9: 311–375.

Reitboeck, H. J. P. (1983). A 19-channel matrix drive with individually controllable fiber microelectrodes for neurophysiological applications. *IEEE Transactions on Systems, Man, and Cybernetics* SMC 13: 676–683.

Reiter, H. O., and M. P. Stryker (1988). Neural plasticity without postsynaptic action potentials: less-active inputs become dominant when visual cortical cells are pharmacologically inhibited. *Proceedings of the National Academy of Sciences USA* 85: 3623–3627

Requin, J., A. Riehle, and J. Seal (1988). Neuronal activity and information processing in motor control: from stages to continuous flow. *Biological Psychology* 26: 179–198.

Riehle, A., and J. Requin (1989). Monkey primary motor and premotor cortex: single-cell activity related to prior information about direction and extent of an intended movement. *Journal of Neurophysiology* 61: 534–548

Robinson, D. A. (1981). The use of control systems analysis in the neurobiology of eye movements. *Annual Review of Neuroscience* 4: 463–504.

Rock, I. (1983). *The Logic of Perception*. Cambridge, MA: MIT Press.

Rockland, K. S. (1985). A reticular pattern of intrinsic connections in primate visual areas V2 (area 18). *Journal of Comparative Neurology* 235: 467–478.

Rockland, K. S., and D. N. Pandya (1979). Laminar origins and terminations of cortical connections of the occipital lobe in the rhesus monkey. *Brain Research* 179: 3–20.

Roland, P. E. (1984a). Organization of motor control by the normal human brain. *Human Neurobiology* 2: 205–216.

Roland, P. E. (1984b). Somatotopic tuning of postcentral gyrus during focal attention in man. *Journal of Neurophysiology* 46: 744–754.

Rolls, E. T. (1989). Parallel distributed processing in the brain: implications of the functional architecture of neuronal networks in the hippocampus. In Morris (1989), 286–308.

Rosenbaum, D. A., V. Hindorff, and E. M. Munro (1987). Scheduling and programming of rapid finger sequences: tests and elaborations on the hierarchical editor model. *Journal of Experimental Psychology: Human Perception and Performance* 13: 193–203.

Rosenblatt, F. (1961). *Principles of Neurodynamics: Perceptrons and the Theory of Brain Mechanisms*. Washington, D.C.: Spartan Books.

Rowat, P. F., and A. I. Selverston (1991). Learning algorithms for oscillatory networks with gap junctions and membrane currents. *Network* 2: 17–41.

Roy, J.-P., and R. H. Wurtz (1990). The role of disparity-sensitive cortical neurons in signalling the direction of self-motion. *Nature* 348: 160–162.

Rubin, D. C., ed. (1986). *Autobiographical Memory*. Cambridge: Cambridge University Press.

Rubner, J., and P. Tavan (1989). A self-organizing network for principal-component analysis. *Europhysics Letters* 10: 693–698.

Rumelhart, D. and J. McClelland, eds. (1986). *Parallel Distributed Processing: Explorations in the Microstructure of Cognition, vol. 1*. Cambridge, MA: MIT Press.

Rumelhart, D. E., and D. Zipser (1985). Feature discovery by competitive learning. *Cognitive Science* 9: 75–112.

Rumelhart, D. E., G. E. Hinton, and R. J. Williams (1986). Learning internal representations by error propagation. In Rumelhart and McClelland (1986), 316–362.

Salzberg, B. M., A. L. Obaid, D. M. Senseman, and H. Gainer (1983). Optical recording of action potentials from vertebrate nerve terminals using potentiometric probes provides evidence for sodium and calcium components. *Nature* 306: 36–40.

Salzman, C. D., K. H. Britten, and W. T. Newsome (1990). Cortical microstimulation influences perceptual judgments of motion direction. *Nature* 346: 174–177.

Sanger, T. (1989). Optimal unsupervised learning in a single-layer linear feedforward neural network. *Neural Networks* 2: 459–473.

Schacter, D. L. (1987). Implicit memory: history and current status. *Journal of Experimental Psychology: Learning, Memory and Cognition* 13: 501–518.

Schacter, D. L. (1990). Memory. In Posner (1990), 683–726.

Schiller, P. H. (1982). The central connections of the retinal on and off pathways. *Nature* 297: 580−583.

Schiller, P. H. (1984). The superior colliculus and visual function. In *Handbook of Physiology, Section I: The Nervous System*, ed. I. Darian-Smith, vol. 3, 457−504. Bethesda, MD: American Physiological Society.

Schiller, P. H., and N. K. Logothetis (1990). Role of the color-opponent and broad-band channels in vision. *Visual Neuroscience* 5: 321−346.

Schiller, P. H., N. K. Logothetis, and E. R. Charles (1990). Functions of the color-opponent and broad-band channels of the visual system. *Nature* 343: 68−71.

Schmidt, R. F., ed. (1978). *Fundamentals of Neurophysiology*. Berlin: Springer-Verlag.

Schmidt, R. F. (1978). Synaptic transmission. In Schmidt, ed. (1978). 72−105.

Schraudolph, N. N., and T. J. Sejnowski (1992). Competitive anti-Hebbian learning of invariants. In *Advances in Neural Information Processing Systems*, ed. J. E. Moody, S. J. Hanson, and R. P. Lippmann, vol. 4, 1017−1024. San Mateo, CA: Morgan Kaufmann.

Schumer, R. A., and B. Julesz (1984). Binocular disparity modulation sensitivity to disparities offset from the plane of fixation. *Vision Research* 24: 533−542.

Schwark, H. D., J. G. Malpeli, T. G. Weyand, and C. Lee (1986). Cat area 17. II. Response properties of infragranular layer neurons in the absence of supragranular layer activity. *Journal of Neurophysiology* 56: 1074−1087

Schwartz, E. L. (1984). Anatomical and physiological correlates of visual computation from striate to infero-temporal cortex. *IEEE Transactions on Systems, Man, and Cybernetics SMC-14*: 257−271.

Schwartz, E., ed. (1990). *Computational Neuroscience*. Cambridge, MA: MIT Press.

Scoville, W. B., and B. Milner (1957). Loss of recent memory after bilateral hippocampal lesions. *Journal of Neurology, Neurosurgery, and Psychiatry* 20: 11−21.

Searle, J. (1980). Minds, brains, and programs. *Behavioral and Brain Sciences* 3: 417−457.

Searle, J. (1983). *Intentionality*. Cambridge: Cambridge University Press.

Searle, J. R. (1990). Is the brain's mind a computer program? *Scientific American* 262: 26−31.

Segev, I., J. W. Fleshman, and R. E. Burke (1989). Compartmental models of complex neurons. In Koch and Segev (1989), 63−98.

Segev, I., M. Rapp, Y. Manor, and Y. Yarom (in press). Analog and digital processing in single nerve cells: dendritic integration and axonal propagation. In *Single Neuron Computation*, ed. T. McKenna, J. Javis, and S. Zornetzer. New York: Academic Press.

Sejnowski, T. J. (1977). Storing covariance with nonlinearly interacting neurons. *Journal of Mathematical Biology* 4: 303−321.

Sejnowski, T. J. (1986). Open questions about computation in cerebral cortex. In McClelland, et al. (1986), 372−389.

Sejnowski, T. J. (1987). Computational models and the development of topographic projections. *Trends in Neurosciences* 8: 304−305.

Sejnowski, T. J., and P. S. Churchland (1989). Brain and cognition. In Posner (1989).

Sejnowski, T. J., and C. R. Rosenberg (1987). Parallel networks that learn to pronounce English text. *Complex Systems* 1: 145−168.

Sejnowski, T. J., and G. Tesauro (1989). The Hebb rule for synaptic plasticity: implementations and applications. In Byrne and Berry (1989), 94−103.

Sejnowski, T. J., and G. Tesauro (1990). Building network learning algorithms from Hebbian synapses. In *Brain Organization and Memory: Cells, Systems, and Circuits*, ed. J. L. McGaugh, N. M. Wienberger, and G. Lynch, 338–355. New York: Oxford University Press.

Sejnowski, T. J., C. Koch, and P. S. Churchland (1988). Computational neuroscience. *Science* 241: 1299–1306. Reprinted in Kelner and Koshland (1989).

Sejnowski, T. J., S. Chattarji, and P. K. Stanton (1990). Homosynaptic long-term depression in hippocampus and neocortex. *Seminars in the Neurosciences* 2: 355–363.

Selemon, L. D., and P. S. Goldman-Rakic (1988). Common cortical and subcortical target areas of the dorsolateral prefrontal and posterior parietal cortices in the rhesus monkey: a double label study of distributed neural networks. *Journal of Neuroscience* 8: 4049–4068.

Selverston, A. I. (1988). A consideration of invertebrate central pattern generators as computational data bases. *Neural Networks* 1: 109–117.

Selverston, A. I., ed. (1990). *Neural Computation: Short Course*. Washington, DC: Society for Neuroscience.

Selverston, A. I., and M. Moulins (1987). *The Crustacean Stomato-gastric System: A Model for the Study of Central Nervous Systems*. Berlin: Springer-Verlag.

Semenza, C., and M. Zettin (1989). Evidence from aphasia for the role of proper names as pure referring expressions. *Nature* 342: 678–679.

Sereno, M. (1988). The visual system. In *Organization of Neural Networks*, ed. I. W. Seelen, U. M. Leinhos, and G. Shaw, 167–184. Weinheim, Germany: VCH Verlagsgesellschaft.

Shallice, T. (1988). *From Neuropsychology to Mental Structure*. Cambridge: Cambridge University Press.

Shallice, T., and E. K. Warrington (1970). Independent functioning of the verbal memory stores: a neuropsychological study. *Quarterly Journal of Experimental Psychology* 22: 261–273.

Sharp, D. L., and L. E. Mays (1990). Signal transduction required for the generation of saccadic eye movements. *Annual Review of Neuroscience* 13: 309–336.

Sharp, R. A. (1990). *Making the Human Mind*. London: Routledge.

Shastri, L., and J. A. Feldman (1986). Neural nets, routines, and semantic networks. In *Advances in Cognitive Science I*, ed. N. E. Sharkey 158–203. New York: Halsted.

Shatz, C. J. (1990). Impulse activity and the patterning of connections during CNS development (review). *Neuron* 5: 745–756.

Shatz, C. J., A. Ghosh, S. K. McConnell, K. L. Allendoerfer, E. Friauf, and A. Antonini (1991). Subplate neurons and the development of neocortical connections. In Lam and Shatz (1991), 175–196.

Shaw, G. J., J. L. McGaugh, and S. P. R. Rose, eds. (1990). *Advanced Series in Neuroscience, vol. 2: Neurobiology of Learning and Memory*. (Reprint volume) Singapore: World Scientific.

Shefchyk, S. J., and L. M. Jordan (1985). Excitatory and inhibitory postsynaptic potential in a-motoneurons produced during fictive locomotion by stimulation of the mesencephalic locomotor region. *Journal of Neurophysiology* 53: 1345–1355.

Shelton, D. P. (1985). Membrane resistivity estimated for the Purkinje neuron by means of a passive computer model. *Neuroscience* 14: 111–131.

Shepherd, G. M. (1979). *The Synaptic Organization of the Brain*, 2nd ed. Oxford: Oxford University Press.

Shepherd, G. M. (1988a). *Neurobiology*, 2nd ed. Oxford: Oxford University Press.

Shepherd, G. M. (1988b). The basic circuit of cortical organization. In *Perspectives in Memory Research*, ed. M. S. Gazzaniga, 93–134. Cambridge, MA: MIT Press.

Shepherd, G. M., ed. (1990) *The Synaptic Organization of the Brain*, 3rd ed. Oxford: Oxford University Press.

Shepherd, G. M., R. K. Brayton, J. P. Miller, I. Segev, J. Rinzel, and W. Rall (1985). Signal enhancement in distal cortical dendrites by means of interactions between active dendritic spines. *Proceedings of the National Academy of Sciences* USA 82: 2192–2195

Sherrington, C. S. (1906). *The Integrative Action of the Nervous System*. New Haven: Yale University Press.

Sherrington, C. S. (1940). *Man and His Nature*. Cambridge: Cambridge University Press.

Shik, M. I., F. V. Severin, and G. N. Orlovskii (1966). Control of walking and running by means of electrical stimulation of the mid-brain. *Biofizika* 11: 659–666.

Siegel, R. M., and R. A. Andersen (1986). Perceptual deficits following ibotenic acid lesions of the middle temporal area (MT) in the behaving rhesus monkey. *Society for Neuroscience Abstracts* 12: 1183.

Siegelbaum, S. A., and E. R. Kandel (1991). Learning-related synaptic plasticity: LTP and LTD. *Current Opinion in Neurobiology* 1: 113–120.

Sigvardt, K. A., S. Grillner, P. Wallen, and P. A. M. Van Dongen (1985). Activation of NMDA-receptors elicits fictive locomotion and bistable membrane properties in the lamprey spinal cord. *Brain Research* 336: 390–395.

Sillar, K. T. (1989). Synaptic modulation of cutaneous pathways in the vertebrate spinal cord. *Seminars in the Neurosciences* 1: 45–54.

Singer, W. (1990). Search for coherence: a basic principle of cortical self-organization. *Concepts in Neuroscience* 1: 1–26.

Snyder, S. H. (1985). The molecular basis of communication between cells. *Scientific American* 257: 91–194. Also in *The Biology of the Brain: From Neurons to Networks*, ed. R. R. Llinás (1989), 20–33. New York: Freeman.

Sokoloff, L. (1984). *Metabolic Probes of Central Nervous System Activity in Experimental Animals and Man*. Sunderland, MA: Sinauer Associates.

Somogyi, P., J. D. B. Roberts, A. Gulyas, J. G. Richards, and A. L. De Blas (1989). GABA and the synaptic or nonsynaptic localization of benzodiazepine/GABA receptor/Cl-channel complex in visual cortex of cat. *Society for Neuroscience Abstracts* 15: 1397

Sparks, D. (1988). Neural cartography: sensory and motor maps in the superior colliculus. *Brain, Behavior, and Evolution* 31: 49–56.

Sperry, R. W., and M. Gazzaniga (1967). Language following surgical disconnection of the hemispheres. In *Brain Mechanisms Underlying Speech and Language*, ed. C. Millikan and F. Darley, 108–115. New York: Grune & Stratton

Squire, L. R. (1986). Mechanisms of memory. Science 232: 134–141. Reprinted in Kelner and Koshland (1989).

Squire, L. R. (1987). *Memory and Brain*. Oxford: Oxford University Press.

Squire, L. R. (1989). On the course of forgetting in very long-term memory. *Journal of Experimental Psychology: Learning, Memory, and Cognition* 15: 241–245.

Squire, L., editor-in-chief (1992). *Encyclopedia of Learning and Memory*. New York: Macmillian.

Squire, L. R., and S. Zola-Morgan (1988). Memory: brain systems and behavior. *Trends in Neurosciences* 11: 170–175.

Squire, L. R., and S. Zola-Morga (1991). The medial temporal lobe memory system. *Science* 253: 1380–1386.

Squire, L. R., A. P. Shimamura, and D. G. Amaral (1989a). Memory and the hippocampus. In Byrne and Berry (1989), 208–239.

Squire, L. R., D. G. Amaral, S. Zola-Morgan, M. Kritchevsky, and G. Press (1989b). Description of brain injury in the amnesic patient N. A. based on magnetic resonance imaging. *Experimental Neurology* 105: 23–35.

Squire, L. R., J. G. Ojemann, F. M. Miezin, S. E. Petersen, T. O. Videen, and M. E. Raichle (in press). A functional anatomical study of human memory. *Proceedings of the National Academy of Sciences USA.*

Sretavan, D. W., and C. J. Shatz (1986). Prental development of retinal ganglion cell axons: segregation into eye-specific layers. *Journal of Neuroscience* 6: 234–251.

Stanton, P. K., and T. J. Sejnowski (1989). Associative long-term depression in the hippocampus induced by Hebbian covariance. *Nature* 339: 215–218.

Stanton, P. K., S. Chattarji, and T. J. Sejnowski (1991). 2-Amino–3-phosphonopropionic acid, an inhibitor of glutamate-stimulated phosphoinositide turnover, blocks induction of homosynaptic long-term depression, but not potentiation, in rat hippocampus. *Neuroscience Letters* 127: 61–66.

Staubli, U., D. Fraser, R. Faraday, and G. Lynch (1987). Olfaction and the "data" memory system in rats. *Behavioral Neuroscience* 101: 757–765.

Steinbuch, K. (1961). Die Lernmatrix. *Kybernetik* 1: 36–45.

Stent, G. (1981). Strength and weakness of the genetic approach to the development of the nervous system. *Annual Review of Neuroscience* 4: 163–194.

Steriade, M., and M. Deschenes (1984). The thalamus as a neuronal oscillator. *Brain Research Review* 8: 1–63.

Steriade, M., L. Domich, and G. Oakson (1986). Reticularis thalami neurons revisited: activity changes during shifts in states of vigilance. *Journal of Neuroscience* 6: 68–81.

Steriade, M., L. Domich, G. Oakson, and M. Deschenes (1987). The deafferented reticular thalamic nucleus generates spindle rhythmicity. *Journal of Neurophysiology* 57: 260–273.

Sterling, P., W. M. Cowan, E. M. Shooter, C. F. Stevens, and R. F. Thompson (1983). Microcircuitry of the cat retina. *Annual Review of Neuroscience* 6: 149–185.

Stevens, C. F. (1989). How cortical interconnectedness varies with network size. *Neural Computation* 1: 473–479.

Stewart, M., and S. E. Fox (1990). Do septal neurons pace the hippocampal theta rhythm? *Trends in Neurosciences* 13: 163–169.

Stewart, W., J. Kauer, and G. Sheperd (1979). Functional organization of rat olfactory bulb analyzed by the 2-deoxyglucose method. *Journal of Comparative Neurology* 185: 715–734.

Stryker, M. P., and W. Harris (1986). Binocular impulse blockade prevents the formation of ocular dominance columns in cat visual cortex. *Journal of Neuroscience* 6: 2117–2133.

Stryker, M. P., and S. L. Strickland (1984). Physiological segregation of ocular dominance columns depends on the pattern of afferent electrical activity. *Investigative Ophthalmology and Visual Science (Suppl.)* 25: 278.

Suga, N., G. Edelman, W. Gall, and W. Cowan (1984). The extent to which biosonar information is represented in the bat auditory cortex. In *Dynamic Aspects of Neocortical Function*, ed. G. M. Edelman, W. E. Gall, and W. M. Cowan, 315–373. New York: Wiley.

Sugimori, M., and R. R. Llinás (1990). Real-time imaging of calcium influx in mammalian cerebellar Purkinje cells in vitro. *Proceedings of the National Academy of Sciences USA* 87: 5084–5088.

Sur, M. (1991). Sensory inputs and the specification of neocortex during development. In Lam and Shatz (1991), 217–228.

Sur, M., S. L. Pallas, and A. W. Roe (1990). Cross-modal plasticity in cortical development: differentiation and specification of sensory neocortex. *Trends in Neurosciences* 13: 227–233.

Sutherland, S. (1989). *The International Dictionary of Psychology*. New York: Continuum.

Sutton, R. S. (1990). Integrated architectures for learning, planning, and reacting based on approximating dynamic programming. In *Proceedings of the Seventh International Conference on Machine Learning*, 216–224. San Mateo, CA: Morgan Kaufmann.

Sutton, R. S., and A. G. Barto (1981). Toward a modern theory of adaptive networks: expectation and prediction. *Psychological Review* 88: 135–170.

Sutton, R. S., and A. G. Barto (1990). Time-derivative models of Pavlovian reinforcement. In Gabriel and Moore (1990), 497–537.

Swinburne, R. (1986). *The Evolution of the Soul*. Oxford: Oxford University Press.

Swindale, N. V. (1990). Is the cerebral cortex modular? *Trends in Neurosciences* 13: 487–492.

Swindale, N. V., J. Matsubara, and M. Cynader (1987). Surface organization of orientation and direction selectivity in cat area 18. *Journal of Neuroscience* 7: 1414–1427.

Szentagothai, J. (1975). The "module" concept in cerebral cortex architecture. *Brain Research* 95: 475–496.

Tank, D. W. (1989). What details of neural circuits matter? *Seminars in the Neurosciences* 1: 67–79.

Tank, D. W., and J. Hopfield (1987). Neural computation by time compression. *Proceedings of the National Academy of Sciences USA* 84: 1896–1900.

Tank, D. W., M. Sugimori, J. A. Connor, and R. R. Llinás (1988). Spatially resolved calcium dynamics of mammalian Purkinje cells in cerebellar slice. *Science* 242: 773–777.

Taube, J. S., and P. A. Schwartzkroin (1988). Mechanisms of long-term potentiation: EPSP/spike dissociation, intradendritic recordings, and glutamate sensitivity. *Journal of Neuroscience* 8: 1632–1644.

Taylor, C. (1985). *Human Agency and Language: Philosophical Papers*, 1. Cambridge: Cambridge University Press.

Tesauro, G. (1986). Simple neural models of classical conditioning. *Biological Cybernetics* 55: 187–200.

Tesauro, G., and B. Janssens (1988). Scaling relationships in back-propagation learning. *Complex Systems* 2: 39–44.

Tesauro, G., and T. J. Sejnowski (1989). A parallel network that learns to play backgammon. *Artificial Intelligence Journal* 39: 357–390.

Thompson, R. F. (1975). *Introduction to Physiological Psychology*. New York: Harper and Row.

Thorpe, S. J. (1989). Local vs. distributed coding. *Intellectica* 8: 3–40.

Thorpe, S. J. (1990). Spike arrival times: a highly efficient coding scheme for neural networks. In *Parallel Processing in Neural Systems and Computers*, ed. R. Eckmiller, G. Hartman, and G. Hauske, 91–94. Amsterdam: Elsevier.

Thorpe, S. J., and M. Imbert (1989). Biological constraints on connectionist models. In *Connectionism in Perspective*, ed. R. Pfeifer, Z. Schreler, and F. Fogelman-Soulie, 63–92. Amsterdam: Elsevier.

Thorpe, S. J., and A. Pouget (1989). Coding of orientation in the visual cortex: neural network modeling. In *Connectionism in Perspective*, ed. R. Pfeifer, Z. Schreler, and F. Fogelman-Soulie. Amsterdam: Elsevier.

Tootell, R. B. H., M. S. Silverman, E. Switkes, and R. L. De Valois (1982). Deoxyglucose analysis of retinotopic organization in primate striate cortex. *Science* 218: 902–904.

Touretzky, D. S. , ed. (1989). *Advances in Neural Information Processing Systems*, vol. 1. San Mateo, CA: Morgan Kaufmann.

Touretzky, D. S. , ed. (1990). *Advances in Neural Information Processing Systems*, vol. 2. San Mateo, CA: Morgan Kaufmann.

Touretzky, D. S., J. Hinton, and T. Sejnowski, eds. (1988). *Connectionist Models: Proceedings of the 1988 Summer School*. San Mateo, CA: Morgan Kaufmann.

Touretzky, D., J. L. Elman, T. J. Sejnowski, and G. E. Hinton, eds. (1991). *Connectionist Models: Proceedings of the 1990 Summer School*. San Mateo, CA: Morgan Kaufmann.

Traub, R. D., and R. Dingledine (1990). Model of synchronized epileptiform bursts induced by high potassium in CA3 region of rat hippocampal slice: role of spontaneous EPSPs in initiation. *Journal of Neurophysiology* 64: 1009–1018.

Traub, R. D., and R. Miles (1991). *Neuronal Networks of the Hippocampus*. Cambridge, UK: Cambridge University Press.

Traub, R. D., and R. K. S. Wong (1982). Cellular mechanism of neuronal synchronization in epilepsy. *Science* 216: 745–747.

Traub, R. D., R. Miles, and R. K. S. Wong (1987a). Models of synchronized hippocampal bursts in the presence of inhibition. I. Single population events. *Journal of Neurophysiology* 58: 739–751.

Traub, R. D., R. Miles, R., R. K. S. Wong, L. S. Schulman, and J. H. Schneiderman (1987b). Models of synchronized hippocampal bursts in the presence of inhibition. II. Ongoing spontaneous population events. *Journal of Neurophysiology* 58: 752–764.

Traub, R. D., R. Miles, and R. K. S. Wong (1989). Model of the origin of rhythmic population oscillations in the hippocampal slice. *Science* 243: 1319–1325.

Traub, R. D., R. K. S. Wong, R. Miles, and H. Michelson (in press). A model of a CA3 hippocampal pyramidal neuron incorporating voltage-clamp data on intrinsic conductances. *Journal of Neurophysiology*.

Treisman, A. (1988). Features and objects. The Fourteenth Bartlett Memorial Lecture. *Quarterly Journal of Experimental Psychology* 40A: 201–237.

Tsien, R. Y., and M. Poenie (1986). Fluorescence ratio imaging: a new window into intracellular ionic signaling. *Trends in Biochemical Sciences* 11: 450–455.

T'so, D. Y., C. D. Gilbert, and T. N. Wiesel (1986). Relationship between horizontal interactions and functional architecture in cat striate cortex as revealed by cross-correlation analysis. *Journal of Neuroscience* 6: 1160–1170.

Ts'o, D. Y., R. D. Frostig, E. E. Lieke, and A. Grinvald (1990). Functional organization of primate visual cortex revealed by high resolution optical imaging. *Science* 249: 417–420.

Tulving, E. (1983). *Elements of Episodic Memory*. Oxford: Clarendon Press.

Tulving, E. (1986). What kind of hypothesis is the distinction between episodic and semantic memory? *Journal of Experimental Psychology: Learning, Memory, and Cognition* 12: 307–311.

Turing, A. M. (1937). On computable numbers, with an application to the Entscheidungsproblem. *Proceedings of the London Mathematical Society* 42: 230–265.

Turing, A. M. (1950). Computing machinery and intelligence. *Mind* 59: 433–460.

Ungerleider, L. G., and R. Desimone (1986). Cortical projections of visual area MT in the macaque. *Journal of Comparative Neurology* 248: 190–222.

Ungerleider, L. G., and M. Mishkin (1982). Two cortical visual systems. In *Analysis of Visual Behavior*, ed. D. J. Ingle, M. A. Goodale, and R. J. W. Mansfield, 249–268. Cambridge, MA: MIT Press.

Vaina, L., ed. (1991). *From Retina to the Neocortex: Selected Papers of David Marr*. Boston: Birkhauser.

van der Loos, H., and T. A. Woolsey (1973). Somatosensory cortex: structural alternations following early injury to sense organs. *Science* 179: 395–398. Reprinted in Shaw et al. (1990), 226–228.

van Essen, D. C. (1979). Visual areas of the mammalian cerebral cortex. *Annual of Review of Neuroscience* 2: 227–263.

van Essen, D., and C. H. Anderson (1990). Information processing strategies and pathways in the primate retina and visual cortex. In Zornetzer et al. (1990), 43–72.

van Essen, D., and J. H. R. Maunsell (1980). Two-dimensional maps of the cerebral cortex. *Journal of Comparative Neurology* 191: 255–281.

van Essen, D., and J. H. R. Maunsell (1983). Hierarchical organization and functional streams in the visual cortex. *Trends in Neurosciences* 6: 370–375.

van Essen, D., D. Felleman, E. DeYoe, and J. Knierim (1991). Probing the primate visual cortex: pathways and perspectives. In *Advances in Understanding Visual Processes*, ed. A. Valberg and B. B. Lee. New York: Plenum.

van Petten, C., and M. Kutas (1987). Ambiguous words in context: an event-related potential analysis of the time course of meaning activation. *Journal of Memory and Language* 26: 188–208.

Vendler, Z. (1984). *The Matter of Minds*. Oxford: Clarendon Press.

Volman, S. F., and M. Konishi (1990). Comparative physiology of sound localization in four species of owls. *Brain, Behavior and Evolution* 36: 196–215.

von der Heydt, R., E. Peterhans, and G. Baumgartner (1984). Illusory contours and cortical neuron responses. *Science* 224: 1260–1262.

von der Malsburg, C. (1973). Self-organization of orientation sensitive cells in the striate cortex. *Kybernetik* 14: 85–100.

von der Malsburg, C. (1985). Neurvous structures with dynamical links. *Physical Chemistry* 89: 703–710.

von der Malsburg, C., and E. Bienenstock (1986). Statistical coding and short-term synaptic plasticity: a scheme for knowledge representation in the brain. In *Disordered Systems and Biological Organization*, ed. E. Bienenstock, F. Folgelman-Soulie, and W. Weisbuch, 247–272. Berlin: Springer-Verlag.

von der Malsburg, C., and D. Willshaw (1981). Co-operativity and brain organization. *Trends in Neurosciences* 4: 80–83.

von Neumann, J. (1951). The general and logical theory of automata. In *Cerebral Mechanisms in Behavior: The Hixon Symposium*, ed. L. A. Jeffress, 1–31. New York: Wiley. Reprinted in: *John von Neumann: Collected Works*, vol. 5, ed. A. H. Taub (1963), 288–318. New York: Pergamon.

von Neumann, J. (1952) *Lectures on Probabilistic Logics and the Synthesis of Reliable Organisms from Unreliable Components*. Pasadena, CA: California Institute of Technology.

Üxküll, J. J. (1972). *Unwelt and Innenwelt der Tiere*. Berlin: Springer-Verlag.

Waibel, A., T. Hanazawa, G. Hinton, K. Shikano, and K. Lang (1989). Phoneme recognition usng time-delay neural networks. *IEEE Transactions on Acoustics, Speech, and Signal Processing* 37: 328–339.

Wall, P. D., and S. B. McMahon (1986). The relationship of perceived pain to afferent nerve impulses. *Trends in Neurosciences* 9: 254–255.

Wallen, P., and S. Grillner (1987). N-Methyl-D-aspartate receptor-induced, inherent oscillatory activity in neurons active during ficitive locomotion in the lamprey. *Journal of Neuroscience* 7: 2745–2755.

Waltz, D. (1975). Understanding of line drawings of scences with shadows. In *The Psychology of Computer Vision*, ed. P. Winston, 19–91. New York: McGraw-Hill.

Warrington, E. K. (1982). The double dissociation of short- and long-term memory deficits. In *Human Memory and Amnesia*, ed. L. S. Cermak. Hillsdale, NJ: Erlbaum. 61–76.

Warrington, E. K., and R. A. McCarthy (1983). Category specific access dysphasia. *Brain* 106: 859–878.

Warrington, E. K., and R. A. McCarthy (1987). Categories of knowledge: further fractionations and an attempted integration. *Brain* 110: 1273–1296.

Warrington, E. K., and L. Weiskrantz (1968). A new method of testing long-term retention with special reference to amnesic patients. *Nature* 217: 972–974.

Warrington, E. K., and L. Weiskrantz (1974). The effect of prior learning on subsequent retention in amnesic patients. *Neuropsychologia* 6: 419–428.

Warrington, E. K., and L. Weiskrantz (1978). Further analysis of the prior learning effect in amnesic patients. *Neuropsychologia* 12: 169–177.

Wasserman, P. D., and R. M. Oetzel (1990). *NeuralSource: The Bibliographic Guide to Artificial Neural Networks*. New York: Van Nostrand Reinhold.

Wathey, J. C. (1990). Computer simulations of quantal events mediated by NMDA receptors. *Neuroscience Abstracts*.

Wathey, J. C., W. W. Lytton, J. M. Jester, and T. J. Sejnowski (in press). Computer simulations of ES potentiation in hippocampal CA1 pyramidal cells. *Journal of Neuroscience*.

Watkins, J. C., and G. L. Collingridge, eds. (1989). *The NMDA Receptor*. Oxford: Oxford University Press.

Werbos, P. (1974). Beyond regression: new tools for prediction and analysis in the behavioral sciences. PhD thesis, Harvard University.

Wershall, J., and D. Bagger-Sjoback (1974). Morphology of the vestibular sense organ. In *Handbook of Sensory Physiology, Vol. 6: Vestibular System, Part 1: Basic Mechanisms*, ed. H. H. Kornhuber, 123–170. New York: Springer-Verlag.

Westheimer, G. (1979). Spatial sense of the eye. *Investigative ophthalmology and Visual Science* 18: 893–912.

Westheimer, G. (1991). The grain of visual space. In *Cold Spring Harbor Symposium on Quantitative Biology: The Brain*, vol. 55, ed. E. Kandel, T. Sejnowski, C. Stevens, and J. Watson. New York: Cold Spring Harbor Press. 759–764.

Westheimer, G., and S. P. McKee (1975). High acuity with moving images. *Journal of the Optical Society of America* 65: 847.

Weyand, T. G., J. G. Malpeli, C. Lee, and H. D. Schwark (1986a). Cat area 17. III. Response properties and orientation anisotropies of corticotectal cells. *Journal of Neurophysiology* 56: 1088–1101.

Weyand, T. G., J. G. Malpeli, C. Lee, and H. D. Schwark (1986b). Cat area 17. IV. Two types of corticotectal cells defined by controlling geniculate inputs. *Journal of Neurophysiology* 56: 1102–1108.

White, E. L. (1989). *Cortical Circuits*. Boston: Birkhauser.

White, H. (1989). Learning in artifical networks: a statistical perspective. *Neural Computation* 1: 425–464.

White, J. G., E. Southgate, J. N. Thomson, and S. Brenner. (1986). The structure of the nervous system of the nematode *Caenorhabditis elegans*. *Philosophical Transactions of the Royal Society of London B* 314: 1–340.

Whitehead, S. D., and D. Ballard (1991). Connectionist designs on planning. In Touretzky et al. (1991), 357–370.

Whittlesea, B. W. A. (1989). Selective attention, variable processing, and distributed representation: preserving particular experiences of general structures. In Morris (1989), 76–101.

Widrow, B. (1962). Generalization and information storage in networks of adaline neurons. In *Self-Organizing Systems*, ed. M. Yovits, G. Jocabi, and G. Goldstein, 435–462. New York: Spartan Books.

Widrow, B., and M. Hoff (1960). Adaptive switching circuits. In *1960 IRE WESCON Convention Record*, vol. 4: 96–104. New York: IRE.

Widrow, B., and S. D. Stearns (1985). *Adaptive Signal Processing*. Englewood Cliffs, NJ: Prentice-Hall.

Wiesel, T. N., and D. H. Hubel (1963). Effects of visual deprivation on morphology and physiology of cells in the cat's lateral geniculate body. *Journal of Neurosphysiology* 26: 978–993.

Wiesel, T. N., and D. H. Hubel (1965). Comparison of the effects of unilateral and bilateral eye closure on cortical unit responses in kittens. *Journals of Neurophysiology* 28: 1029–1040.

Wigstrom, H., and B. Gustafsson (1988). Presynaptic and postsynaptic interactions in the control of hippocampal long-term potentiation. In *Long-Term Potentiation: From Biophysics to Behavior*, ed. P. W. Landfield and S. A. Deadwyler, 73–107. New York: Alan R. Liss.

Williams, R. J., and D. Zipser (1989). A learning algorithm for continually running fully recurrent neural networks. *Neural Computation* 1: 270–280.

Williams, T. J. (forthcoming). Models of central pattern generators as oscillators: mathematical analysis and simulations of the lamprey locomotor CPG. *Seminars in Neurosciences*.

Williams, T. L., and K. A. Sigvardt (in press). Modeling neural systems: interactions between mathematical analysis, simulation, and experimentation in the lamprey. In *Analysis and Modeling of Neural Systems*, ed. F. Eeckmann.

Williams, T. L., K. A. Sigvardt, N. Kopell, G. B. Ermentrout, and M. P. Remler (1990). Forcing of coupled non-linear oscillators: studies of intersegmental coordination in the lamprey locomotor central pattern generator. *Journal of Neurophysiology* 64: 862–871.

Williamson, S. J., and L. Kaufman (1987). Analysis of neuromagnetic signals. In *Handbook of Electroencephalography and Clinical Neurophysiology*, ed. A. Gevins and A. Remond. Amsterdam: Elsevier.

Willshaw, D. J. (1981). Holography, associative memory, and inductive generalization. In *Parallel Models of Associative Memory*, ed. G. E. Hinton and J. A. Anderson, 83–104. Hillsdale, NJ: Erlbaum.

Willshaw, D. J. (1989). Holography, associative memory, and inductive generalization. In *Parallel Models of Associative Memory (updated edition)*, ed. G. Hinton and J. Anderson, 103–124. Hillsdale, NJ: Erlbaum.

Willshaw, D. J. (1991). Commentary on "Simple memory: a theory of archicortex" by David Marr. In Vaina (1991), 118–121.

Willshaw, D. J., and J. T. Buckingham (1990). An assessment of Marr's theory of the hippocampus as a temporary memory store. *Philosophical Transactions of the Royal Society B* 329: 205–215.

Willshaw, D. J., and P. Dayan (1990). Optimal plasticity from matrix memories: what goes up must come down. *Neural Computation* 2: 85–93.

Willshaw, D. J., and C. von der Malsburg (1976). How patterned neural connections can be set up by self-organization. *Proceedings of the Royal Society of London B* 194: 431–445.

Wilson, M. A., and J. M. Bower (1991). A computer simulation of oscillatory behavior in primary visual cortex. *Neural Computation* 3: 498–509.

Witkovsky, P., and X. P. Shi (1990). Slow light and dark adaptation of horizontal cells in the Xenopus retina: a role for endogenous dopamine. *Visual Neuroscience* 5: 405–413.

Wong, E., and J. Kemp (1991). Sites for antagonism on the N-methyl-D-aspartate receptor channel complex. *Annual Review of Pharmacology and Toxicology* 31: 401–425.

Woolsey, T. A., and H. van der Loos (1970). The structural organization of layer IV in somatosensory region (SI) of mouse cerebral cortex. *Brain Research* 17: 205–242.

Yamada, W. M., C. Koch, and P. R. Adams (1989). Multiple channels and calcium dynamics. In Koch and Segev (1989), 97–134.

Yamaguchi, S., and R. T. Knight (1991). Anterior and posterior association cortex contributions to the somatosensory P300. *Journal of Neuroscience* 11: 2039–2054.

Zador, A., C. Koch, and T. H. Brown (1990). Biophysical model of a Hebbian synapse. *Proceedings of the National Academy of Sciences USA* 87: 6718–6722.

Zalutsky, R. A., and R. A. Nicoll (1990). Comparison of two forms of long-term potentiation in single hippocampal neurons. *Science* 248: 1619–1624.

Zeki, S. (1983). Colour coding in the cerebral cortex: the reaction of cells in monkey visual cortex to wavelengths and colours. *Neuroscience* 9: 741–765.

Zhang, L. (1991). Effects of 5-hydroxytryptamine on cat spinal motorneurons. *Canadian Journal of Physiology and Pharmacology* 60: 154–163.

Zipser, D. (1991). Recurrent network model of the neural mechanism of short-term active memory. *Neural Computation* 3: 178–192.

Zipser, D., and R. A. Andersen (1988). A back-propagation programmed network that simulates response patterns of a subset of posterior parietal neurons. *Nature* 331: 679–684.

Zipser, D., and D. E. Rumelhart (1990). The neurobiological significance of the new learning models. In Schwartz (1990), 192–200.

Zola-Morgan, S., and L. R. Squire (1984). Preserved learning in monkeys with medial-temporal lesions: sparing of motor and cognitive skills. *Journal of Neuroscience* 4: 1072–1085.

Zola-Morgan, S., and L. R. Squire (1985). Medial-temporal lesions in monkeys impair memory on a variety of tasks sensitive to human amnesia. *Behavioral Neuroscience* 9: 22–34.

Zola-Morgan, S., and L. R. Squire (1986). Memory impairment in monkeys following lesions to the hippocampus. *Behavioral Neuroscience* 10: 155–160.

Zola-Morgan, S., and L. R. Squire (1991). The primate hippocampal formation: evidence for a time-limited role in memory storage. *Science* 250: 288–289.

Zola-Morgan, S., L. R. Squire, and D. G. Amaral (1986). Human amnesia and the temporal lobe region: enduring memory impairment following a bilateral lesion limited to field CA1 of the hippocampus. *Journal of Neuroscience* 6: 2950–2967.

Zola-Morgan, S., L. R. Squire, D. G. Amaral, and W. Suzuki (1989). Lesions of perirhinal and parahippocampal cortex that spare the amygdala and hippocampal formation produce severe memory impairement. *Journal of Neuroscience* 9: 4355–4370.

Zornetzer, S. F., J. L. Davis, and C. Lau, eds. (1990). *An Introduction to Neural and Electronic Networks*. San Diego, CA: Academic Press.

Zucker, R. S. (1989). Short-term synaptic plasticity. *Annual Review of Neuroscience* 12: 13–31.

Index

Note: Italic *f* following page numbers indicates figures; *t* indicates tables.

Axons, tracing of, 442–443
Axoplasmic transport, 442–443

Backpropagation
  algorithm, 109–111
  of error, 112–113
  evolution of, 359
  generalizations of, 123
  for global network, 377
  as high-fidelity design tool, 347–349
  role of in training up network, 362–363,
    375–376
  for understanding oculomotor system, 378
Ballard, Dana
  active perception and, 418–423
  integration of perception and motor
    control, 416
Barn owl
  auditory object localization by, 417–418
  auditory pathway of, 418f
  innervation of nucleus laminaris in, 419f
  neural map of auditory space in, 420f
  silicon model of time-coding pathway of,
    421f
Basal ganglia, organization of, 35
Basket cells, 36f
  effects of on synapse, 52
Behavioral plasticity, 240
Behavior response, measurement of accuracy
    of, 24–25
Bending reflex. *See also* Local bending reflex
  Lockery's modeling of, 15
  model of in leech, 13
Berger, Hans, 437
Binary threshold rule, in Hopfield network, 90
Binary threshold units, 87
Binocular fusion, 208–209
Binocular perception, 189, 218
  depth, 147, 317
    development of, 145
Biological structure, function of, 69
Biophysical mechanisms, and computations
    they help perform, 45t
Blood flow monitoring, 436
Body
  physics of, 415–416
  surface maps of in nervous system, 32–34
Boltzmann distribution, 100
  at equilibrium, 101
Boltzmann machine, 91–92
  figure-ground constraint satisfaction by, 96
  fluctuating units of, 91–92
  network to solve segregation task in, 93
  nonlinear hidden units in, 100

pattern completion by, 102
  schematic diagram of, 101f
  supervised vs. unsupervised, 101
Bottom-up strategy, 4
  test of, 5
Boundary detection, binocular, 209
Brain. *See also specific areas of*
  computational principles of, 7–11
  continual modification of, 239
  contribution of to perception, 144–147
  coronal section of, 242–243f
  detecting functional damage to, 432
  energy consumption for computation in, 9
  experimental techniques for study of
    function of, 428f
  facts about, 48–59
  gross recordings of, 157–158
  highly parallel character of, 59
  inability of to forget, 295
  layers and columns of, 35–37
  magnetic resonance imaging sections of,
    433f
  mapping regions of specialization in,
    157–158
  maps of body surface in, 32–34
  materials of construction for computational
    strategies in, 9–10
  matrixlike architecture of structures of, 286
  molecular composition of, 431–432
  noninvasive mapping of structure of, 432
  oxygen and nutrient supply for, 9–10
  physiological levels of, 20
  plasticity of, 239–329
  possible research strategies for, 12f
  posterior view of, 383f
  processing of transducer signals by, 144–
    145
  protein and lipid supply of, 10
  reciprocal connections between areas of, 31
  representation in, 143, 157–163
  in sensorimotor integration, 331–411
  spatial limitation of, 9
  special-purpose systems of, 7
  specific connectivity in, 51
  structural components of, 1
  systems of, 29–31
  temporal factors in computational strategies
    of, 8–9
  topographic maps of, 31–34
  visually mapped areas of, 158–160
  weak cell-to-cell interactions in, 52
  wide projection of neurons over, 58f
Brain–brain stem connections, 382
Brain function study techniques, 428f